# The Almanac of World Military Power

# The Almanac of World Military Power

Fourth Edition

Colonel Trevor N. Dupuy, U.S. Army, Retired
Grace P. Hayes, Former Lieutenant, U.S. Navy
Colonel John A. C. Andrews, U.S. Air Force, Retired

Gay Hammerman, Coordinating Editor

Presidio Press • San Rafael, California

**Library of Congress Cataloging in Publication Data**

Dupuy, Trevor Nevitt, 1916–
    The almanac of world military power.

    Bibliography:  p.
    1.  Armed Forces.  2.  Armaments.  I.  Hayes,
Grace P., joint author.  II.  Andrews, John A. C.,
joint author.  III.  Hammerman, Gay M.  IV.  Title.
UA15.D9  1980   355′.033′0047   80-11844
ISBN 0-89141-070-8

Copublished by Presidio Press of San Rafael, California,
and Jane's Publishing Company of London, England


Endpapers reprinted with permission of
C. S. Hammond & Company

Composition by Publications Services of Marin

Printed in the United States of America

# CONTENTS

# Introduction:
# THE NATURE OF MILITARY POWER

What is military power? We define it as the capability of a nation to employ armed forces effectively in support of national objectives by exerting influence on the performance of other nations.*

Some would assert that military power is the only effective power in the world today. There is, for instance, the perhaps apocryphal story of Stalin's contemptuous dismissal of the power of the Pope: "How many divisions does he have?" Stalin pretended, at least, to recognize no power but that of naked military force. And it was unquestionably the apparent willingness of the United States to use such force, if necessary, which caused him to withdraw from Persian Azerbaijan in 1946, and to call off the Berlin Blockade in 1949.

Stalin's successors, however, have revealed that they understand, and respect, other kinds of power, including that indefinable and unquantifiable influence which the Pope can still exert, even without divisions. They have also demonstrated considerable respect for the power of ideas. Sometimes this has been shown by modifying aspects of their autocratic and dictatorial rule of their own country and its satellite neighbors. Sometimes, also, they have shown that respect quite negatively, by armed aggression, as in Hungary in 1956, and Czechoslovakia in 1968.

Soviet leaders have also demonstrated an awareness of the importance of economic power. Khruschev's famous threat to America: "We will bury you," made in 1956, shortly after he came to power, was a declaration of economic war combined with a promise to greatly increase Soviet economic power to match that of the United States. It is noteworthy, however, that either because he was impatient, or because he recognized that the promise was not achievable during his lifetime (if ever), he resorted to the more traditional Soviet concepts of power in 1962 by threatening the United States with Cuban-based nuclear blackmail. However, like Stalin before him, he backed down when he recognized that the United States was ready, if necessary, to employ superior nuclear and conventional power against the Soviet Union.

These three examples of power confrontation between the U.S. and USSR—Azerbaijan, Berlin, and Cuba— suggest that, no matter how persuasive and influential non-military forms of power may be, they cannot *in themselves,* and as a last resort of national policy, prevail against military power. Also, all three instances involved the use, or threatened use, of military forces actually in being.

There is, however, a very important difference between military power in being, and potential military power. Many relatively weak nations have been able to achieve their objectives, in peace and in war, despite the contrary objectives of more powerful neighbors, because the weaker nation could apply superior military strength readily available. Sparta earned a place in history by the careful cultivation of the maximum possible military strength from a small, sparsely populated area with scanty resources. Macedonia dominated the world briefly because the rulers of that otherwise undeveloped country created the most sophisticated military machine in the world for its time. A major factor in the rise of the Roman republic was the willingness of Rome's citizens to convert their resources into highly-organized military strength. The ability of Genghis Khan to implement a similar decision was the sole reason for the earthshaking conquests of the Mongols.

These historical examples must have been in the mind of a thoughtful American general, active a century ago, Winfield Scott Schofield, when he wrote: "Population and wealth do not constitute military strength. They are only the elements from which military strength may be developed in good time and by appropriate means. They are like the fat of the over-fed giant, which may be converted into muscle in due time by appropriate training. But it is too late for the giant to commence training after he has met his well-trained antagonist."*

In modern history, Japan in the first half of this century provides two classic case studies of the difference between actual and potential military power.

In 1904 Japan challenged Russia for dominance in northeast Asia. At that time the population of Russia was nearly 150 million, the population of Japan was 45 million; the total military strength of Japan was 280,000 troops (with 400,000 reserves); Russia had about 1,000,000 men in its active army (with perhaps double that number in reserves); the Japanese navy had 59 warships (not counting 85 torpedo boats); Russia's navy was almost twice as large.

*For a valuable theoretical discussion of military power, see Klaus Knorr, *Military Power and Potential* (Lexington, Mass.: D. C. Heath & Co., 1970).

*Annual Report, Secretary of War, 1887 (Washington, D.C.: GPO).

A pygmy was defying a giant. Furthermore, the record of the war demonstrates that, man-for-man, division-for-division, the Japanese on land had no discernible superiority in combat effectiveness. And, while their warships were slightly more modern, even there the man-for-man, ship-for-ship difference was not—in itself—enough to offset the tremendous Russian numerical superiority.

But most of this Russian military strength was not available to influence the outcome of a war fought in and near Manchuria. Even less relevant to such a war was the still greater disparity in manpower, economic, and industrial strength. Had Russia been willing, or able, to continue the fight, its potential power must inevitably have overwhelmed Japan. But Japanese military leaders were aware of the limitations of the 6,000-mile-long Trans-Siberian Railway, aware of the inability of Russia to unite its scattered fleets without overcoming a concentrated Japanese fleet stronger than any of them, and perhaps above all aware of internal social weaknesses in Russia. Thus they were confident that they could keep the war limited to their part of the world, that they could overwhelm in detail Russian piecemeal reinforcements, and that internal troubles would preclude determined Russian prosecution of the war. It was a close thing, but the Japanese calculations proved right.

A similar situation seemed to face Japan in 1941. The potential military strength of the United States was obviously far greater than anything Japan could possibly mobilize. The similarities of the 1904 and 1941 situations were remarkable, particularly in the exposure of a sizable naval force to a surprise pre-war attack, and in the existence of major internal divisions among the people of the larger and potentially more powerful opponent. And, as in 1904, the Japanese in 1941 had a substantial military superiority on land and sea in the part of the world they had selected as the theater of combat.

There were two major differences in these situations, however, which Japanese planners in 1941 did not sufficiently appreciate. The major internal divisions in the United States at that time were political, not social and socio-economic as they had been in Russia in 1904. The Japanese offensives in Manchuria in 1904 increased the divisive social pressures in Russia; the 1941 attacks on Pearl Harbor and Southeast Asia united the divergent political forces in America. Japanese planners also failed to recognize that geography and distance affect a land power differently from a naval power. The land masses of the Eastern Hemisphere effectively hobbled both the Russian army and the Russian navy by creating long and extremely limited and inflexible lines of communication both on land and on sea. The vast reaches of the Pacific Ocean were a barrier to American land and naval power (and air power, of course!) only so long as Japan could maintain sufficient force to interfere with American use of the sea as a broad and flexible line of communications.

On the other hand, as Alfred Thayer Mahan pointed out, although the seas afford greater strategic flexibility and versatility to a maritime power, the absolute limiting effects of geography on the employment of its power are greater than for a continental power. This was demonstrated in Britain's many wars against continental powers in Europe, and against this country in both the Revolution and the War of 1812. This was one of the limiting factors affecting the United States effort in Vietnam.

From these random examples from history it is possible to draw some conclusions about the interrelationship of actual and potential military power as components of national power. The following are generally accepted as the classic elements of national power:

1. Natural resources
2. Industrial capacity
3. Social-political structure
4. Military strength

Another formulation, presented in an official publication of the U.S. Air University at Maxwell Air Force Base, Alabama, lists the factors of national power as follows:

Geographic (including location, configuration, topography, and size)

Demographic (including rate of growth, age, and productivity)

Economic (including mineral, agricultural, energy, and water resources, and the production policies for employing these resources)

Organizational (including social and governmental structure and management skills and methods)

Psychosocial (relating to attitudes, values, and motivation)

Military (with consideration to national policy, military policies, forces in being, research and development, and education and training)

These two formulations of national power are really different ways of slicing the same loaf of bread—at least if "natural resources" in the first is assumed to include "geographic situation." In either formulation, military strength, or power, comprises only one of several elements, or factors. Yet in terms of absolute national power, the others are significant in an ultimate test only to the extent that they contribute to potential *military* power and, more precisely, to the extent that they can be converted or mobilized to become *actual* military power.

Military power can be considered to have twelve characteristics:

1. Size of the armed forces
2. Composition of the armed forces (in terms of balance or allocation of resources to the military services, and within services)
3. Quantity and performance of equipment or hardware
4. Logistical reach, or range
5. Availability of forces for effective employment
6. Capability of performing sustained, active operations
7. Mobilizable resources and productive capacity
8. National willingness to employ force
9. Leadership and doctrine
10. Communications and control
11. Military intelligence effectiveness
12. Manpower quality in terms of skill, training, physical stamina, morale

In his splendid study of *Military Power and Potential*, Dr. Klaus Knorr suggests that there are at least three different aspects of military power: (1) its exercise in war as by threat or by readiness, (2) its availability, and (3) its effectiveness.

He suggests that effectiveness is essentially a reflection of quality, and stresses the danger of accepting the power of sheer numbers, or even of superior industrial capability, by itself. This aspect of quality as a determinant of effective military power can raise disturbing questions in the minds of those who can recall how twice in this century Germany, overwhelmingly outmatched by the potential military power of its enemies, came alarmingly close to military victory.

There is a fourth aspect of military power, which Knorr recognizes, but which has been most aptly described by Dr. Henry Kissinger as its "usability." The concept of "usable" military power is quite a different thing from "actual" or "available" military power. Power can in fact be actual, it can be available, and yet still not conceivably, or credibly, or rationally usable in relation to certain national objectives. This idea of usable military power is to some extent a reflection of changed political attitudes in a post-colonial era world, but it is to an even greater extent a consequence of the existence of nuclear weapons with cataclysmic destructive power, weapons which are terribly important components of the military power of the nations that possess them. But the use of nuclear weapons is credible only in support of the most fundamental national objectives. Thus, a tremendous proportion of American power, vital in any confrontation between the U.S. and USSR, was simply not usable in Vietnam against either the Vietcong or North Vietnam.

A slightly different perspective of this concept of usable military power can be found in another recent historical example involving the United States. In January 1968, the North Korean navy attacked and seized on the high seas the American electronic intelligence vessel USS *Pueblo*. In earlier times a major power would have responded to such an insult by sending a naval task force to inflict a certain amount of punishment upon such a brash, small power. In fact, in 1871, the U.S. did respond in just such a fashion when earlier Koreans seized and destroyed an American vessel stranded off the Korean coast.

It should be noted that the United States was not reluctant to respond forcefully to much more blatant Korean lawlessness 97 years later because the United States was afraid of North Korea, or lacked the means to inflict the punishment. It is doubtful we were inhibited seriously by the possibility of some censure in the United Nations. We simply were unwilling to incur the risk, small though it might be, of precipitating a war that could become nuclear war with one of North Korea's neighbors—over an issue or an objective not worth such a risk, not vital to American national security.

This one example shows three new concepts affecting the employment of military power which have emerged as a result of the development of nuclear weapons. There is a higher "threshold" of response, inhibiting actions by a nuclear power which would have been taken as a matter of course by an insulted or damaged major nation in the pre-nuclear era. The raised threshold is a result (despite mixing of metaphors) of the "umbrella" of mutual nuclear deterrence, which permits smaller powers considerably more leeway in their dealings with greater powers than would have been possible in those earlier eras.

Finally, and most significant, there are limits on usable military power (conventional as well as nuclear) because of the existence of the threshold and the umbrella.

T. N. Dupuy
Colonel, U.S. Army, Retired

# PREFACE

Although the fundamental strategic geography of the world changes little in six years, shifts in the strategic situations of nations have been many since the third edition of the *Almanac of World Military Power* was published at the end of 1974. We need only mention the independence of what used to be Portugal's African possessions, the Vietnamese seizure of Cambodia, the dramatic peace developments in the Arab-Israeli confrontation, the extensive Cuban involvement in Africa, the striking growth of Eurocommunism, the devastating assault of terrorism in Italy, the government overthrow in Nicaragua, the revolution in Iran, and the Soviet invasion of Afghanistan.

Less obvious from the front pages of our newspapers, but at least equally significant for world military power, has been the steady Soviet buildup in weapons. The USSR now surpasses the United States, at least quantitatively, in most categories and has increased its lead in those—notably tanks and artillery—in which it has led in the past. In this fourth edition of the *Almanac,* we have tried to cover the changes, of which these are a sample, and to provide the most accurate current statistical data on potential power as well as inventories of weapons and forces.

We have chosen a somewhat different format for this edition, with the countries arranged alphabetically, and the surveys for each region grouped together at the beginning of the book. The regional surveys have been carefully reviewed and updated, and most have been extensively rewritten. The Middle East survey includes not only a summary of the 1978 peace initiatives in the Arab-Israeli confrontation, but also a special section describing and assessing the military lineups of the opposing sides.

As in previous editions, three sets of data are provided for each nation treated in the book: (1) power potential statistics; (2) summaries of the nation's defense structure, its politico-military policies, and its strategic problems; and (3) inventories of armed forces strength, organization, and equipment. The figures in most cases are the most recent ones available in late 1978.

Sources for this edition include the extremely helpful data and comments provided, at our request, by the defense ministries of many countries, either directly or through their attaches in Washington. Many points were cleared up in conversations with U.S. government officials. However, the bulk of the data has been taken from open, unclassified sources, including standard reference works, periodicals, and daily newspapers. A list of the chief sources used is at the end of this volume.

This fourth edition of the *Almanac* has benefited from the work of a number of specialists. The extensive new writeups on China and the Republic of China (Taiwan) were prepared by Col. Angus M. Fraser (USMC, Ret.), who also supplied the statistical estimates for those countries; Col. George K. Osborn III of the U.S. Military Academy faculty updated the entries on South and Southeast Asia; Capt. Richard Witherspoon of the U.S.M.A. faculty prepared the African entries; and Maj. C. Bryan Ross (USA, Ret.) prepared the Middle East entries, including a new and extensive treatment of the region. Our colleague Gay Hammerman updated the sections on North America, Western Europe, Eastern Europe, and the South and Southwest Pacific, and also coordinated research and writing on the volume. Lt. Col. John F. Sloan (USA, Ret.) and Paul Martell of the T. N. Dupuy Associates staff gave valuable assistance as consultants on the Eastern Europe regional survey and country entries, and Lt. Col. E. Joe Shimek II (USA, Ret.) contributed useful information on that region. Gordon S. Brown provided authoritative data on the Soviet navy and also carried out a final updating of all naval and power potential statistics except those of the two Chinas. All other work has been a joint effort of the coauthors, who jointly assume full responsibility for the contents of this book.

# I. REGIONAL SURVEYS

## MILITARY GEOGRAPHY

The North American continent, here understood to include the United States, Canada, Mexico, and the massive and largely unpopulated island of Greenland, has a total of about nine million square miles.

Northern North America has generally sparse to moderate population density, stable populations (a rate of natural increase of 0.9 percent yearly for Canada and 0.6 percent for the United States), high literacy, and high per capita income. Mexico shares with other Latin American countries to the south a high birth rate, relatively low literacy, and low per capita income. Mexico's rate of national population increase, 3.4 percent, is one of the highest in the world. At the present rate, the population would double in twenty years without the escape valve of emigration.

The political systems of all North American countries are considered stable, although Mexico's recent economic problems have threatened its stability, causing some observers to fear increased worker and student turbulence and a right-wing coup. Its rich new oil fields, which will make Mexico one of the top twelve oil exporters by 1982, should be both economically and politically stabilizing. Canada and the United States are both in reality democratic republics, with two of the most representative governments in the world. Canada, with dominion status in the British Commonwealth, nominally owes allegiance to the British crown. Mexico's government, republican and democratic in form, is characterized by a very strong executive branch; in practice, one party controls the government, and the president is chosen by a relatively small group of party leaders. The centrally placed United States is bound to each of its contiguous neighbors by a tradition of close, friendly relations stretching back at least forty to fifty years, and by mutual assistance defense treaties. The psychological ties with Canada are especially strong.

The continent is crossed by north-south mountain ranges, dividing it into an eastern coastal plain; an eastern mountain region comprising the Laurentian plateau and the Appalachian and Ozark mountains; the great central plains; and the rugged Cordilleran highlands, which comprise the Rockies and the Pacific coastal ranges, and which stretch from Alaska and northern Canada down through Mexico. Mexico falls almost entirely in this mountainous western region and has only very narrow coastal plains. The Great Lakes and St. Lawrence River form the most important inland waterway, extending across most of the eastern half of the continent between Canada and the United States.

## STRATEGIC SIGNIFICANCE

The area is dominated—although not controlled—politically, economically, and militarily by the United States. Eastern North America, including the eastern United States and southeastern Canada, is one of the four leading economic power regions of the world, along with Western Europe, Eastern Europe, and Japan. This power is derived from generally literate, technically skilled populations, wealth in a variety of natural resources, and highly developed methods of economic management. The area's great military strength, including the United States' nuclear-warhead ICBMs, is based on this economic power.

Military invasion from outside the continent has not occurred for more than 100 years.* The central fact of North American military geography for at least two centuries has been the isolation of this land mass, separated from other world powers by the world's two largest oceans. The new significant fact is the revolution in vulnerability that occurred with the development of thermonuclear weapons and ICBM delivery systems. Because the United States has no reliable defense against these weapons that are now in the hands of its chief adversary, the Soviet Union, and because it is within striking distance across the North Polar region, the United States and its North American allies are in constant danger of devastation. The Soviet Union, of course, faces the same threat. The danger of amphibious invasion remains as negligible as ever.

## REGIONAL ALLIANCES

The United States and Mexico are both members of the Organization of American States (see Central American and West Indies Regional Survey).

The United States and Canada are members of the North Atlantic Treaty Organization (see Western Europe Regional Survey.)

The United States has no formal bilateral treaties with either Mexico or Canada, but bilateral planning agencies

---

*The French involvement in Mexico in the 1860s' was the last such event; prior to that were British actions against the United States in 1814.

NORTH AMERICA

LAMBERT AZIMUTHAL EQUAL-AREA PROJECTION

SCALE OF MILES

SCALE OF KILOMETRES

Capitals of Countries.................☆
International Boundaries...............
Other Boundaries.....................
Canals.............................

Copyright by C.S. HAMMOND & Co., N.Y.

exist with both nations, permitting direct military planning for defense of the North American continent.

## RECENT INTRA- AND EXTRA-REGIONAL CONFLICTS

There have been no international armed conflicts or incidents involving the use of force in North America since 1917, nor have there been any internal conflicts, except in Mexico shortly after World War I. Both the United States and Canada, however, have been engaged in conflict or crisis operations outside the region. Following is a list of the most important of these actions since World War II:

| | |
|---|---|
| 1948–49 | Berlin Blockade (U.S.) |
| 1950–53 | Korean War (U.S. and Canada) |
| 1954–65 | Assistance to South Vietnam (U.S.) |
| 1955–65 | Formosa Straits crises (U.S.) |
| 1958 | Intervention in Lebanon (U.S) |
| 1961 | Bay of Pigs abortive invasion of Cuba (U.S.) |
| 1961–62 | Berlin Crisis (U.S. and Canada) |
| 1962 | Cuban Missile Crisis (U.S.) |
| 1965–73 | Indochina War (U.S.) |
| 1965 | Intervention in Dominican Republic (U.S.) |

# CENTRAL AMERICA AND ISLANDS OF THE WESTERN HEMISPHERE

## MILITARY GEOGRAPHY

This region includes two principal geographical groupings: the states of Central America and the islands of the West Indies. The first is made up of Belize, Costa Rica, El Salvador, Guatemala, Honduras, Nicaragua, and Panama on a long isthmus connecting North and South America. The West Indies is a collection of islands in the Caribbean Sea and the Gulf of Mexico, east of Central America. The major political entities of the West Indies are Cuba, the Dominican Republic, Haiti, Jamaica, Trinidad and Tobago, Puerto Rico, the British Caribbean Islands, the Netherlands Antilles, and the French possessions of Guadeloupe and Martinique. Also included in this selection are other islands of the Western Hemisphere.

## STRATEGIC SIGNIFICANCE

The Central American–West Indies area has strategic importance for the United States and for the northern republics of South America as well. The island chain dominates the Atlantic Ocean approaches to the Panama Canal, to the Gulf coasts of the United States and Mexico, and to the Caribbean coasts of Venezuela and Colombia. Under friendly or neutral governments these islands comprise a protective screen; in unfriendly hands they could become dangerously hostile bases. The states of Central America, to a lesser degree, cover the Pacific Ocean approaches to the Panama Canal and to the most vulnerable areas of North and South America, and could also provide potential bases for attack against these areas.

The most important single feature of the region is the Panama Canal. In the half century since it was opened it has stimulated regional and intercontinental commerce. It has been particularly valuable for the Pacific republics of South America. It has also made possible the rapid transfer of U.S. naval forces between the two oceans. While this feature has been less significant with the advent of air power and the growth of U.S. naval strength during and since World War II, it is still important, particularly for the defense of the region itself. Caribbean-basin oil is adding greatly to the strategic importance of a region that is also increasingly important in international banking and in both legal and illegal trade.

Mexico, Panama, and Venezuela are all important in the politics of oil and the politics of Panama Canal defense.

After several years of negotiation, in September 1977 the presidents of the United States and Panama signed treaties to guarantee permanent neutrality of the canal and to give control of the canal to Panama at the end of 1999. Despite strong and vocal opposition, the United States Senate ratified both treaties, in March and April 1978.

Responsible for the security of the canal area is the U.S. Southern Command (SOUTHCOM), which also is responsible for administering all U.S. forces and missions in Latin America. Headquarters of SOUTHCOM is in the Canal Zone.

In June 1972, after a conference on maritime problems held in Santo Domingo, the foreign ministers of fifteen Caribbean nations announced support for a 12-mile limit for territorial waters and patrimonial limits (sovereignty over natural resources but not navigational rights) at 200 miles from their coastlines. Other nations have followed the lead. The 200-mile limit for natural resources confirms the control of these countries over the rich, proven oil reserves off their shores.

## REGIONAL ALLIANCES

Because of the conventional grouping of Central and South America as Latin America, alliances involving both are discussed in this survey.

*Organization of American States (OAS).* Barbados, Costa Rica, Cuba, the Dominican Republic, El Salvador, Guatemala, Haiti, Honduras, Jamaica, Nicaragua, Panama, and Trinidad and Tobago are members, along with the United States, Mexico, and all countries of South America except Guyana. (Cuba, although officially a member, has been excluded from active participation since the 1962 Punta del Este conference.) Eight countries (Belgium, Canada, France, West Germany, Guyana, Israel, The Netherlands, and Spain) have observer status. The origins of the OAS go back to the First International Conference of American States in 1889–90, which led to the establishment of the Pan-American Union. Creation of the Inter-American Defense Board in 1942, and the signing

4

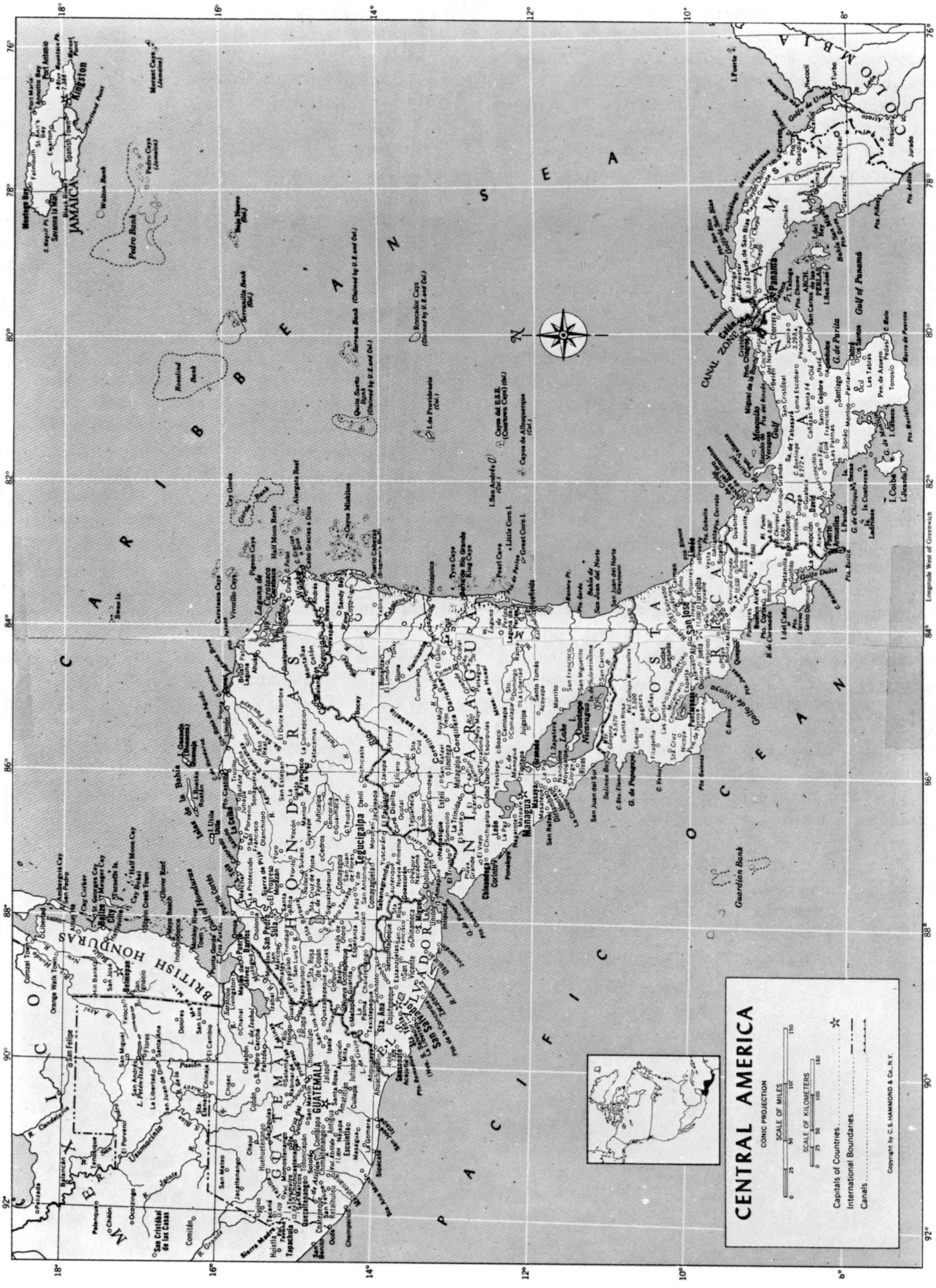

CARIBBEAN SEA

PACIFIC OCEAN

JAMAICA

BRITISH HONDURAS

GUATEMALA

HONDURAS

NICARAGUA

COSTA RICA

PANAMA

COLOMBIA

MEXICO

SALVADOR

CANAL ZONE

Kingston

Belize

Guatemala

Tegucigalpa

Managua

San José

San Salvador

Panamá

Longitude West of Greenwich

**CENTRAL AMERICA**

CONIC PROJECTION

SCALE OF MILES

SCALE OF KILOMETERS

Capitals of Countries..........
International Boundaries..........
Canals..........

Copyright by C. S. HAMMOND & Co., N.Y.

of the Treaty of Rio (Inter-American Treaty of Reciprocal Assistance) finally led in 1948 to the formalization of the regional organization as the Organization of American States within Article 51 of the United Nations Charter. The OAS Charter, drawn up and signed at Bogota in April 1948, recognizes the sovereignty of each member, calls for nonintervention in the affairs of other states and contains certain provisions to maintain peace and security.

*Inter-American Defense Board (IADB).* This defense organization was established in 1942 in response to concern among Western Hemisphere nations—and particularly the United States—regarding the need for coordination of defense against possible Axis attack. Now an organ of the OAS, the IADB prepares plans for hemispheric defense and operates the Inter-American Defense College to provide advanced study of hemispheric politico-military problems. Membership is identical with that of the OAS, except that Cuba was expelled at Punta del Este in 1962. Unlike NATO, the IADB maintains no joint forces.

*Organization of Central American States (ODECA)* and *Central American Defense Council (CONDECA).* ODECA was established in 1962 by Costa Rica, Nicaragua, Honduras, El Salvador, and Guatemala in an attempt to create a more localized OAS-type organization. CONDECA was created in the following year and concerns itself with matters of regional defense and collective security. Although CONDECA coordinates its planning with the IADB, and ODECA is informally involved with the OAS, neither organization is controlled by the OAS.

CONDECA has conducted a series of joint annual sea-surveillance exercises against the seaborne infiltration of guerrillas from Cuba. Similar counter-guerrilla land exercises have also been conducted. A permanent joint staff is headquartered in Guatemala.

*Latin American Solidarity Organization (OLAS).* Founded in Havana in 1966, this is a Cuban-based organization which seeks to unite various revolutionary groups throughout Latin America. Unsuccessful in raising overt revolution in Latin America, it has promoted agitation in many areas.

*Unitas.* To promote cooperation among the naval forces of the Western Hemisphere for its defense, each August or September since 1961 the United States Navy has conducted joint naval exercises with the navies of various South American countries.

The Treaty for the Prohibition of Nuclear Weapons in Latin America, approved by the UN General Assembly in 1967, has been ratified by twenty-two nations. It is overseen by the Agency for the Prohibition of Nuclear Weapons in Latin America, whose headquarters is in Mexico.

Several regional organizations have been formed in an attempt to foster free trade and common markets. The Central American Common Market (CACM), was created in 1960 with five members (Costa Rica, El Salvador, Guatemala, Honduras, Nicaragua). The Latin American Economic System (SELA), strongly backed by Cuba and specifically excluding the United States, was formed in 1975, to protect economic interests and present a united front internationally. Twenty-five nations of Latin America and the Caribbean signed the charter. The Caribbean Free Trade Association (CARIFTA) became operational in 1968, and was superseded by the Caribbean Community (CARICOM), based on a 1973 agreement providing for a Caribbean common market.

## RECENT INTRA- AND EXTRA-REGIONAL CONFLICTS

| | |
|---|---|
| 1964 | Anti-United States and anti-canal riots in Panama |
| 1965 | Dominican Republic civil war, United States and OAS intervention |
| 1967 | El Salvador-Honduras border dispute |
| 1968 | Military coup in Panama |
| 1969 | British invasion of secessionist Anguilla |
| 1969–76 | El Salvador-Honduras border conflict |
| 1969 | Surinam-Guyana border clash |
| 1970 | Disorder in Trinidad-Tobago |
| 1972 | Military coup in Honduras |
| 1972–79 | Guerrilla and civil warfare in Nicaragua |
| 1975 | Military coup in Honduras |
| 1978 | Military coup in Honduras |
| 1979 | Coup in Grenada |

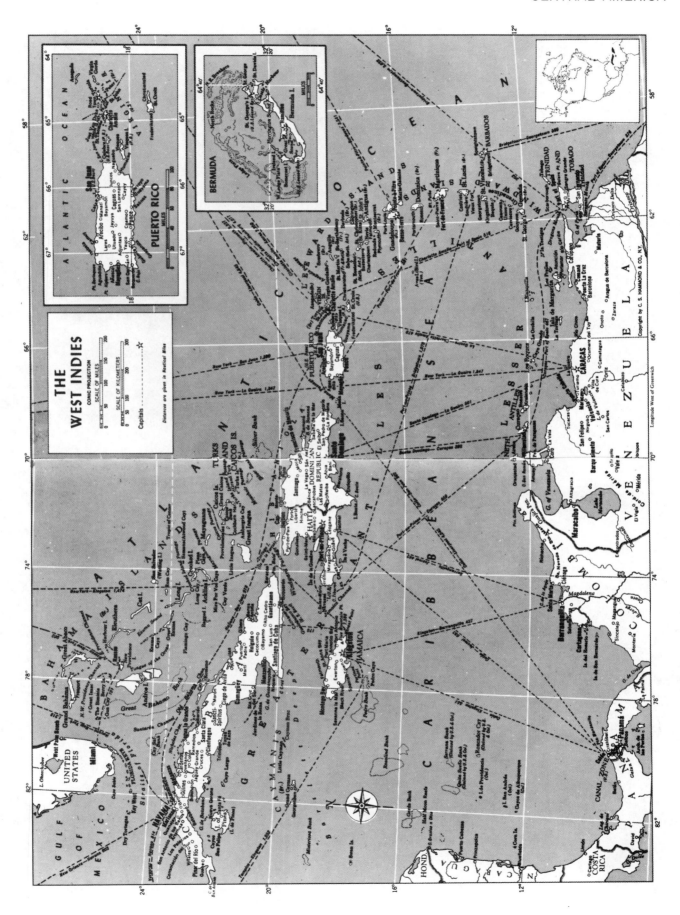

THE
WEST INDIES

CONIC PROJECTION

SCALE OF MILES

0    50    100    150    200

SCALE OF KILOMETERS

0    50    100    200    300

Capitals ★

Distances are given in Nautical Miles

PUERTO RICO

ATLANTIC OCEAN

BERMUDA

ATLANTIC OCEAN

CARIBBEAN SEA

GULF OF MEXICO

UNITED STATES

BAHAMA ISLANDS

CUBA

JAMAICA

HAITI

DOMINICAN REPUBLIC

PUERTO RICO

LEEWARD ISLANDS

LESSER ANTILLES

WINDWARD ISLANDS

VENEZUELA

COLOMBIA

CANAL ZONE

COSTA RICA

Copyright by C. S. HAMMOND & CO., N.Y.

Longitude West of Greenwich

# SOUTH AMERICA

## MILITARY GEOGRAPHY

South America comprises the nations of Argentina, Bolivia, Brazil, Chile, Colombia, Ecuador, Guyana, Paraguay, Peru, Uruguay, Venezuela, Surinam, and French Guiana. Several major geographical features create natural defense barriers for parts of the frontiers of most nations of the continent: the Pacific Ocean, the Atlantic Ocean, the Andes mountain chains, and the jungle areas of the Amazon River basin. There are few natural divisions protecting the various nations from neighbors to the north or south, although some protection is provided by the lack of roads and of ground transportation in relatively unpopulated border regions. This lack of natural frontiers has resulted in numerous border disputes since the breakup of the Spanish domain in the early nineteenth century. Many of these have yet to be settled to the satisfaction of all parties concerned.

Most South American countries share the common vulnerability of concentration of population, services, and industry in a single core region. Because of the difficulty of overland travel within the continent, however, the areas are mainly susceptible to air attack or internal insurgency.

Perhaps the greatest strategic significance of this continent is its wealth of natural resources, many relatively untapped: a variety of extensive mineral reserves, e.g., copper and nitrates in Chile; bauxite in Surinam; agricultural products such as Argentine beef and wheat; petroleum reserves in the northern part of the continent, especially Venezuela; and the vast, only partially explored, resources of Brazil. In addition, there is interdependence of the economies and transportation systems among the South American nations that in turn produces mutual concern with regard to strategic and political matters.

Almost without exception the nations of Latin America have been going through a period of serious social and political unrest resulting from severe economic problems and their exploitation by dissidents of various political factions. Inflation is rampant. Despite reform programs and increased industrialization, the gap between rich and poor remains, and a more equitable distribution of income and new solutions to old problems are imperative.

Although each nation maintains armed forces, in the event of an attack in force from outside the hemisphere, the continent would be dependent upon the United States for effective defense.

Economically, the South American nations are increasingly less dependent upon the U.S. market. Japan, Communist China, and the Soviet Union in particular are participating in trade and industrial development in many areas. When the U.S. government threatened cuts in aid to a number of Latin American nations because of human rights violations, further military aid was declined by six nations in 1977: Argentina, Brazil, Chile, Uruguay, Guatemala, and El Salvador.

## REGIONAL ALLIANCES

For the Organization of American States (OAS), the Inter-American Defense Board (IADB), the Organization of Latin American Solidarity (OLAS), UNITAS, and the Latin American Economic System (SELA), see the regional survey for Central America.

In December 1974, representatives of Argentina, Bolivia, Chile, Colombia, Ecuador, Panama, Peru, and Venezuela, meeting in Ayacucho, Peru, signed an agreement called the Declaration of Ayacucho, which was a commitment to political and economic solidarity. In addition, it pledged to devote resources to national development and to limit purchases of arms. In a separate military document it was agreed that armaments would be limited and the acquisition of offensive weapons would halt.

The Latin American Free Trade Association (LAFTA), presently with eleven members (Mexico, Brazil, and the Spanish-speaking countries of South America) came into existence as a result of the Treaty of Montevideo signed in 1960. The Andean Group, a subgroup of LAFTA, was established in 1969. Colombia, Ecuador, Peru, Bolivia, Chile, and Venezuela are members. In 1975 military leaders of the six nations agreed to recommend to their governments banning of nuclear, biological, chemical, toxic, and other special weapons. Chile resigned from the pact in 1976 in opposition to common external tariffs and the limits imposed on foreign investment.

## INTRA- AND EXTRA-REGIONAL CONFLICTS

| | |
|---|---|
| 1964 | Military coup in Bolivia |
| 1964 | Military coup in Brazil |
| 1966 | Military coup in Argentina |
| 1966 | Anti-military coup in Ecuador |
| 1967 | Cuban-sponsored insurgency in Bolivia |
| 1968 | Military coup in Peru |

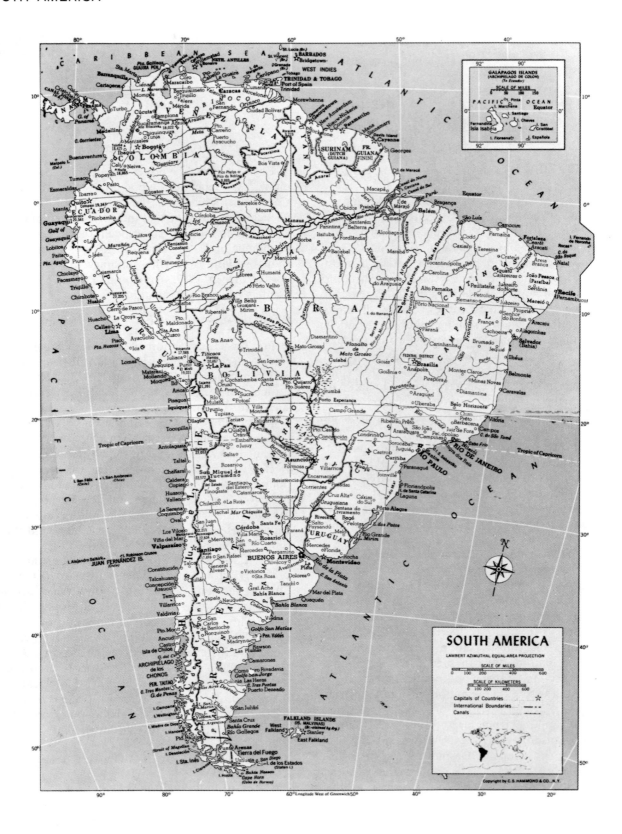

SOUTH AMERICA

LAMBERT AZIMUTHAL EQUAL-AREA PROJECTION

SCALE OF MILES
0    100    200    400    600

SCALE OF KILOMETERS
0  100 200    400    600

Capitals of Countries ☆
International Boundaries -·-·-
Canals

Copyright by C. S. HAMMOND & CO., N.Y.

| | | | |
|---|---|---|---|
| 1969 | Uprising by Indians and planters in Guyana | 1972 | Military coup in Ecuador |
| 1969 | Military coup in Bolivia | 1973 | Military coup in Chile |
| 1969 | Frontier clashes between Guyana and Surinam | 1975 | Coup in Peru |
| 1970 | Military coup in Argentina | 1976 | Military coup in Argentina |
| 1970 | Military coup in Bolivia | 1976 | Military coup in Ecuador |
| 1971 | Military junta replaces president in Argentina | 1978 | Military coup in Bolivia |
| 1971 | Military coup in Bolivia | 1979 | Military coups in Bolivia |

# WESTERN EUROPE

## MILITARY GEOGRAPHY

Western Europe is a mountainous peninsula from which project a number of other peninsulas, and adjacent to which are a number of large and populous islands. This peninsular-insular geography contributed to the development in early history of a number of isolated, self-contained societies, from which emerged the modern nations of Western Europe. The same geography also stimulated the maritime interest which eventually became a prime factor in Europe's world predominance for more than four centuries.

The tides of war have flowed across Europe generally along the routes most feasible for transport and trade: the rivers, the corridors between mountain ranges, and the coastal lowlands. Principal among these routes have been the Danube basin and the North European Plain.

## STRATEGIC SIGNIFICANCE

In addition to the influence of geography, a combination of climatological, demographic, and possibly cultural factors led to the preeminence of Western Europe in world affairs beginning late in the fifteenth century. This dominance has not entirely disappeared even as the loci of world power have shifted east and west in the mid-twentieth century. After the United States and Canada, Western Europe still has the most highly skilled and educated manpower in the world. It has the highest overall standard of living in the world outside North America, the greatest accumulation of economic and financial power outside the United States, and the greatest combined military potential aside from the United States and the Soviet Union.

## NORTH ATLANTIC TREATY ORGANIZATION

For centuries military rivalries among the nations of Western Europe—most notably between France and Germany—led to recurrent wars. Since World War II, such conflicts have dwindled or disappeared in the face of common political and economic problems and the hard destructive and geographical realities of modern war. During the years immediately following World War II, Soviet truculence posed a serious threat to the postwar recovery of the nations of Western Europe. American economic assistance through the Marshall Plan helped Western Europe avoid the economic chaos, internal turmoil, and revolution that indigenous and Russian Communists were primed to exploit. Full economic recovery in these nations was hampered by fears that Soviet Russia, whose armed strength had increased rather than decreased after the war, would take by invasion what its Communist agents had been unable to subvert from within. Although the United States still possessed a monopoly of nuclear weapons, most Western Europeans feared overt Soviet military aggression that could overrun the militarily impotent nations of Western Europe in less than a week. They recognized the weakness of their own defense efforts, and doubted that America would be able to react in time to prevent a sudden Soviet take-over.

This situation led to negotiations that resulted first in the Brussels Treaty of March 17, 1948, to establish the Western European Union (see below), and that culminated in the establishment of the North Atlantic Treaty Organization (NATO). The NATO treaty was signed April 4, 1949, in Washington, (effective August 24) by Belgium, Canada, Denmark, France, Iceland, Italy, Luxembourg, the Netherlands, Norway, Portugal, the United Kingdom, and the United States. Greece and Turkey joined later (February 1952), and West Germany became a member on May 5, 1955.

The members of NATO agreed to settle disputes by peaceful means, to develop their individual and collective capacity to resist armed aggression, to regard an attack on one as an attack on all, and to take necessary action to repel such an attack under Article 51 of the UN Charter.

The political basis for NATO was somewhat altered in the early 1970s by the development of the spirit of detente between East and West, the growing economic strength of the Western European countries (which made them less dependent on the United States), and political pressures to cut defense spending. The United States was under political pressure to reduce military forces in Europe. NATO was also affected by the tension between the Soviet Union and Communist China brought on by large Soviet forces on the Chinese border. Relations between the United States and other NATO nations were strained by the Arab-Israeli war of 1973, when all but Portugal and the Netherlands refused to assist in rushing aid to Israel. In June 1974 the NATO countries reached agreement on a

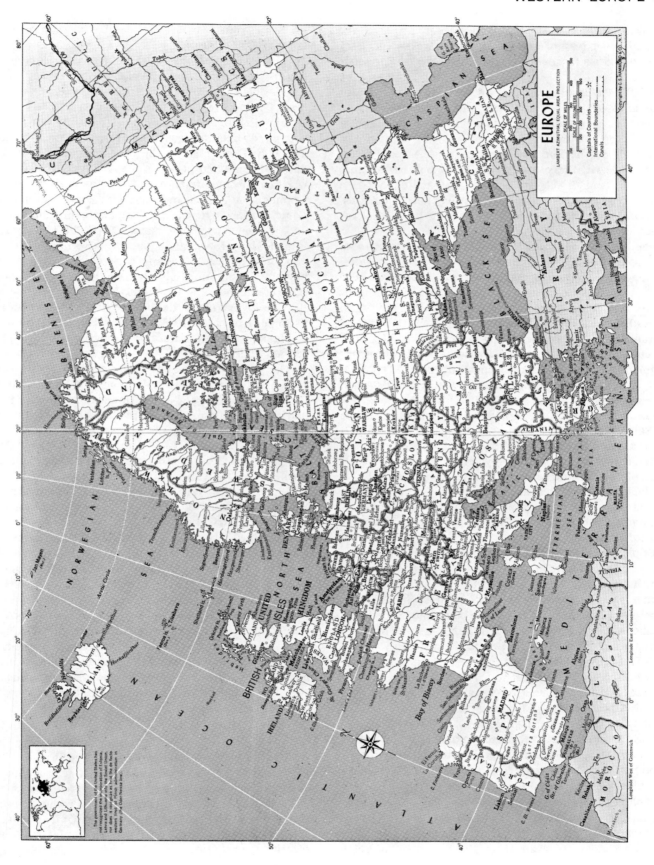

EUROPE

LAMBERT AZIMUTHAL EQUAL AREA PROJECTION

SCALE OF MILES

SCALE OF KILOMETERS

Capitals of Countries ............ ★
International Boundaries .......... ─────
Canals ........................... ─────

Copyright by C. S. HAMMOND & CO., N.Y.

new Declaration on Atlantic Relations that reaffirmed the original objectives of the treaty and restored much of the harmonious facade that had been cracked the previous October.

NATO defense areas are divided into three major commands—Europe, Atlantic, and Channel—with a number of subsidiary commands and a United States-Canada Regional Planning Group.

Until 1966 the Supreme Headquarters Allied Powers Europe (SHAPE) was located near Paris, but when France withdrew from the NATO Military Committee, SHAPE moved to a new location at Casteau, Belgium, near Mons. NATO headquarters moved from Paris to Brussels at the same time.

The Allied Command Europe (ACE) is charged with defense of Turkey, Iceland, Canada, the United States, and all continental European members except France. The Supreme Allied Commander, Europe (SACEUR), heads the ACE and also serves as commander in chief, U.S. Forces Europe (CINCUSFE). At present SACEUR is Gen. Alexander M. Haig of the United States; deputy SACEUR is Gen. Gerhard Schmuckle of Germany. ACE subsidiary commands are Allied Forces Central Europe (AFCENT), with headquarters at Brunssum, Netherlands; Allied Forces Northern Europe (AFNORTH) with headquarters at Kolsaas, Norway; and Allied Forces Southern Europe (AFSOUTH) with headquarters at Naples. There is also a small, air-supported ACE Mobile Force (AMF), combat-ready on short notice for deployment to points of strain, especially on the northern and southeastern flanks.

AFCENT comprises all land and air forces in the Central Europe sector (West Germany, Netherlands, Belgium, and Luxembourg). There are twenty-two divisions assigned by seven countries (forces of the four continental states plus U.S., British, and Canadian forces) and about 1,600 tactical aircraft in the command. About 350 of the aircraft are U.S. Air Force fighter-bombers. U.S. and German forces have Sergeant and Pershing SSMs at the corps and army level. There are Hawk and Nike SAM battalions in AFCENT. Within AFCENT are the Northern Army Group (NORTHAG) and the Central Army Group (CENTAG). NORTHAG is composed of all the British, Belgian, and Dutch divisions on the Continent, and four German divisions. These forces are supported by the Second Allied Tactical Air Force, composed of British, Belgian, Dutch, and German air units. CENTAG includes all U.S. ground forces, seven German divisions, and a Canadian battle group and is supported by the Fourth Allied Tactical Air Force (U.S., German, and Canadian units plus the U.S. Army Air Defense Command).

AFNORTH provides for the defense of Norway, Denmark, Schleswig-Holstein, and the Baltic approaches. It is composed of most of the Danish and Norwegian land, sea, and tactical air forces, one German division

(in Schleswig), two German combat air wings, and the German Baltic Fleet.

AFSOUTH defends Italy, Greece, and Turkey, safeguards communications in the Mediterranean, and is responsible for the Turkish territorial waters of the Black Sea. There have been fourteen Turkish divisions, nine Greek divisions, and seven Italian divisions in the command, plus the tactical air forces of these countries. The U.S. Sixth Fleet in the Mediterranean, while under national command in peacetime, is NATO-committed for wartime. Ground defense is divided between the Southern Command at Naples and the South Eastern Command at Izmir, Turkey. There is an overall air command at Naples and a single naval command (NAVSOUTH) under an Italian admiral, also at Naples. For several years, strained relations between Greece and Turkey, mainly over Cyprus, have raised questions about the military effectiveness of these commands. In the serious Cyprus crisis of mid-1974, the Greek government announced its decision to withdraw its forces from NATO. With Greek-Turkish relations near a breaking point, future collaboration under NATO seemed doubtful.

The Allied Command Atlantic (ACLANT) extends from the North Pole to the tropic of Cancer, and from the coastal waters of North America to those of Europe and North Africa. The Supreme Allied Commander, Atlantic, (SACLANT), has headquarters at Norfolk, Virginia. Under SACLANT are the Western Atlantic, Eastern Atlantic, and Iberian Atlantic Commands, the Striking Force Atlantic (the nucleus of which is the U.S. Second Fleet), the Submarine Command, and STANAVFORLANT (Standing Naval Force Atlantic—a multinational naval squadron).

The Allied Command Channel (ACCHAN) includes the English Channel and the southern portion of the North Sea. Naval forces are those of Britain, Belgium, and the Netherlands. ACCHAN is commanded by a British admiral with headquarters at Northwood, Middlesex.

NATO air defense is to be supported by the NADGE (NATO Air Defense Ground Environment) system. This is essentially a sophisticated, computerized system for tracking aircraft and correlating target information with locations of interceptor aircraft and missiles, using data supplied by numerous ground radar stations.

## OTHER ALLIANCES

*Western European Union (WEU).* The Brussels Treaty of March 17, 1948, established a fifty-year alliance for collaboration in economic, social, and cultural matters and for collective self-defense of Belgium, France, Luxembourg, the Netherlands, and the United Kingdom. The obvious principal objective was military—mutual security against feared Soviet Communist aggression. The military aspects were merged with NATO when that alliance was created one year later. When France rejected the proposed European Defense Community in 1954, the existence of the WEU provided a useful means of integrating West Germany into the Western Alliance, thus facilitating West Germany's rearmament, its eventual inclusion within NATO, and the end of the Allied occupation. This was accomplished when West Germany and Italy adhered to the Brussels Treaty on May 6, 1955. After the breakdown of negotiations for Britain's entry into the Common Market in 1963, the WEU provided a useful vehicle for continuing meetings between the six members of the Common Market and the United Kingdom to take stock of the political and economic situation in Europe.

*European Communities.* Pursuant to the Treaty of Rome of March 25, 1957, the European Economic Community (EEC) was established on January 1, 1958, by Belgium, France, West Germany, Italy, Luxembourg, and the Netherlands (the "Inner Six"). The objective was to move gradually toward integrating and strengthening the economies of the members, and ultimately to move toward political unity.

On July 1, 1967, the EEC, generally known as the Common Market, was merged with two other related organizations with the same membership: the European Coal and Steel Community, established on August 10, 1952, pursuant to the Treaty of Paris of April 18, 1951; and the European Atomic Energy Community (Euratom), which was established on January 1, 1958, pursuant to the Treaty of Rome of March 25, 1957.

In 1960, seven European nations—Austria, Denmark, Norway, Portugal, Sweden, Switzerland, and Great Britain—became associated in the European Free Trade Association (EFTA). Finland and Iceland subsequently joined. Two of the members, Great Britain and Denmark, together with Ireland, joined the EEC on January 1, 1973. The seven remaining members joined in signing a treaty at Brussels in July 1972, which effectively merged the two economic groups into a single trading bloc by establishing free trade through a gradual reduction of tariffs among the sixteen signatories.

While the purposes of these communities are primarily economic and secondarily political, their military implications are great, as they tend to weld the EEC increasingly into what is in effect the third most powerful economic entity in the world.

## INTERREGIONAL NEGOTIATIONS

*Helsinki Act.* Talks on security and cooperation in Europe—held among European nations (Warsaw Pact and NATO members, as well as the unaligned) plus the United States and Canada—culminated in 1975 in the final act of the Helsinki Conference. The act, usually referred to as the Helsinki Agreement, although it is not a legally binding agreement, recognized boundaries, pledged peaceful settlement of disputes, and pledged the governments to respect the individual rights and human freedoms of their citizens. (See Eastern Europe Regional Survey.)

*Mutual and Balanced Force Reductions.* Since November 1973 negotiations toward the reduction of forces in central Europe have been going on in Vienna. Called the Mutual and Balanced Force Reductions (MBFR) negotiations, the talks affect only the "reductions area," which includes East and West Germany, the Benelux countries, Poland, and Czechoslovakia. The so-called "direct participants" in the negotiations are the countries whose territory is involved, plus those countries that have troops stationed in the reductions area—the United States, the United Kingdom, and the Soviet Union. The other NATO and Warsaw Pact countries also participate.

Basically, the Eastern position is that there already exists rough numerical equality in central Europe. The Eastern delegates have proposed equal percentage decreases by both sides, in three phases. The Western side, on the other hand, estimates that, in addition to the East's obvious geographic advantage (much faster redeployment), it also has considerably more manpower and weapons. The West sees, in particular, a major imbalance in tanks. The West has proposed to move by phased reductions—first primarily of Soviet tanks and troops and U.S. nuclear warheads, aircraft, and missiles—to equality of forces at a lower level. At the lower level there would be a "common collective ceiling" for each side of about 700,000 ground forces, or about 900,000 total troops. The East in mid-1978 made a proposal that accepts the concept of the common collective ceiling and represents the first movement from the East in five years. However, the problem remains of verifying what Eastern force strengths actually exist, and no real progress can be made until it is solved.

## REGIONAL POLITICO-MILITARY TRENDS

*More U.S. Support for NATO.* U.S. budgets and statements have reflected increased efforts to help build up NATO strength. (See United States.)

*Eurocommunism.* At least temporarily the Communist parties of Western Europe have shown moderation and independence from Moscow in the past few years. In Italy, the Communist party has joined forces with centrists to combat both economic problems and the terrorist Red Brigades. In Spain, party leaders have denounced leftist terrorism, supported the new (1978) Constitution, and have been much embarrassed by the 1978 publication of a novel purporting to show that in the 1950s and 1960s they were Stalinists and Soviet agents. Western European Communists generally have denounced Soviet trials of dissidents. Communists have shifted tactics and joined in "popular front" movements in the past, and the trend must be viewed with caution. However, for the time being, Communist parties in Western Europe are not creating police problems or threats to internal stability, and it cannot be assumed that they will wish to topple moderate governments, or that they will follow any Moscow propaganda line.

*Terrorism,* primarily, but not entirely, by groups that identify themselves as leftist or revolutionary, and in some cases by ethnic separatist groups, has been strikingly common throughout Europe in the past five years. Most devastating to internal security have been the Red Brigades in Italy, followed by the Basque ETA group in Spain, and the Baader-Meinhof group in West Germany; most leaders of this last group are now dead or in prison. These groups, who have carried out political murders, maimings, kidnappings, and bombings of public facilities, have varied and unclear goals. The disruption and fear they cause is a danger to public confidence, invites governmental abrogation of individual rights in efforts to control the terrorists, and could lead to power seizures by authoritarian factions of opposed political views.

*Separatism, Autonomy, Devolution.* Throughout Western Europe, these movements continue to be strong. While the Northern Ireland violence diminished somewhat in 1977 and 1978, the United Kingdom has taken constitutional steps to make possible the devolution of some governmental power to Scotland and Wales. Basques and Catalans in Spain, and Bretons and Corsicans in France, have demanded autonomy or independence. In Belgium, demonstrations have led to violence, and a new Constitution has been written that would give much more autonomy to the Flemish-speaking and French-speaking populations. In some cases small but violent terrorist groups are among the supporters of autonomy, and they pose serious police problems. In most cases (but not necessarily those of the Northern Irish or Basques), it appears that the ethnic and language minorities would rally to the support of the state in case of outside aggression.

## RECENT INTRA- AND EXTRA-REGIONAL CONFLICTS

There have been no international armed conflicts in Western Europe since World War II. There have been several instances of internal hostilities, and several of the members have been engaged in conflict or crisis operations outside the region. There have also been several crises among Western European nations (individually, or as members of the Western Alliance) and members of the Communist bloc, the most serious being those involving the Western powers and the USSR in Berlin. A list of hostilities, or crises involving military operations in the last ten years, follows:

| | |
|---|---|
| 1968–71 | Intervention in Chad, at local request (France) |
| 1968–74 | Defense of overseas territories of Mozambique, Angola, and Portuguese Guinea (Portugal) |
| 1969 | U.K. intervention in Anguilla |
| 1970–date | Violence in Northern Ireland |
| 1974 | Military coup in Portugal, followed by moves toward independence and peace in Portuguese overseas territories |
| 1974 | Coup in Cyprus, followed by Turkish invasion |
| 1978 | French-Belgian rescue operation for Europeans in rebel-held province of Zaire |

# EASTERN EUROPE

## MILITARY GEOGRAPHY

Geographically, Eastern Europe includes all of Europe east of a line running generally along the Finnish-Soviet border, the Gulf of Finland, and the Baltic Sea, and from the southwest corner of the Baltic Sea to the northeast corner of the Adriatic. Politically it comprises all the European nations with Communist governments. The largest state geographically and the most important politically in Eastern Europe is the USSR, most of whose territory is actually in Asia. Since the USSR is not divisible, this survey includes both Eastern Europe and Soviet Asia.

Within this vast region, there are three major subregions, each with numerous distinct geographic areas. The subregions are the plains and rolling terrain of northeastern Europe, the Carpathian-Balkan mountain complex, and Soviet Asia.

The open terrain of northeastern Europe is characterized, in the Soviet portions, by short, hot, dry summers and bitterly cold winters; the temperatures are remarkably consistent from north to south, considering Soviet Russia's great extent. However, in the far south these extremes are ameliorated by the tempering effect of the Black Sea, and west of the Soviet Union, in East Germany and Poland, there is considerable rainfall in summer and less variation in temperature year round. In the center of the subregion, and throughout its northern extent, there are great swamps that can seriously interfere with military movement in summer but are easily traversed in winter. The spring thaws and fall rains make for mud seasons that have virtually halted armies in the past. There are many broad rivers, some of which create difficult obstacles to east-west movement. Extensive forests stretch through much of the region. The road net is relatively limited, compared to that of Western Europe.

The Carpathian-Balkan region is an essentially mountainous peninsula extending southward from the heart of Europe and cut by the generally broad and fertile Danube basin and a number of smaller river valleys. A good portion of the terrain is inhospitable, and some raw materials are in short supply, but this area is rapidly becoming industrialized. Despite its general ruggedness, two factors have made the subregion a traditional highway of war: the proximity of the Turkish straits area to the westernmost tip of Asia; and the traversability of the river valleys, which facilitate commerce and other east-west transit, not only across the straits, but between central Europe and the southern Soviet Union.

Soviet Asia includes practically every type of terrain except tropical: rocky and sandy deserts, steppes, tundra, lofty mountains, great expanses of forests, and a varied assortment of temperate farming areas. This tremendous region extends across the entire northern half of Asia; even without European Russia, of which it is an extension, it comprises the largest single political territory in the world.

## STRATEGIC SIGNIFICANCE

The first, and possibly most impressive, strategic consideration relating to this region is the fact that it includes the bulk of the Heartland area of Sir Halford J. Mackinder's geopolitical concept of political and spatial relationships. The combination of Mackinder's Heartland and his Eastern Europe in this region requires consideration of Mackinder's famous thesis: who rules Eastern Europe commands the Heartland; who rules the Heartland commands the World Island (Eastern Hemisphere); who rules the World Island commands the World. Whether or not one agrees with its validity, the idea cannot be ignored.

All except two of the countries of Eastern Europe are solidly within the Soviet orbit, and are members of the Soviet-dominated Warsaw Pact. The two exceptions are Yugoslavia and Albania. The extent of Soviet domination over the other six nations of the region varies from country to country. Romania has a limited but significant degree of independence in both internal and foreign matters. Hungary has considerable independence in economic matters. However, overall Soviet domination in Eastern Europe was dramatically reaffirmed by the 1968 invasion and occupation of Czechoslovakia. Furthermore, Soviet control is continually demonstrated by the lock-step voting of these countries in international bodies, and by the way Eastern European countries have recently done the Soviet Union's work in other regions, especially Africa. Soviet troops are stationed in East Germany, Hungary, Poland, and Czechoslovakia.

The Soviet-allied countries of Eastern Europe are a strategic protective belt, garrisoned by Soviet and other Warsaw Pact ground forces, within which the Soviet

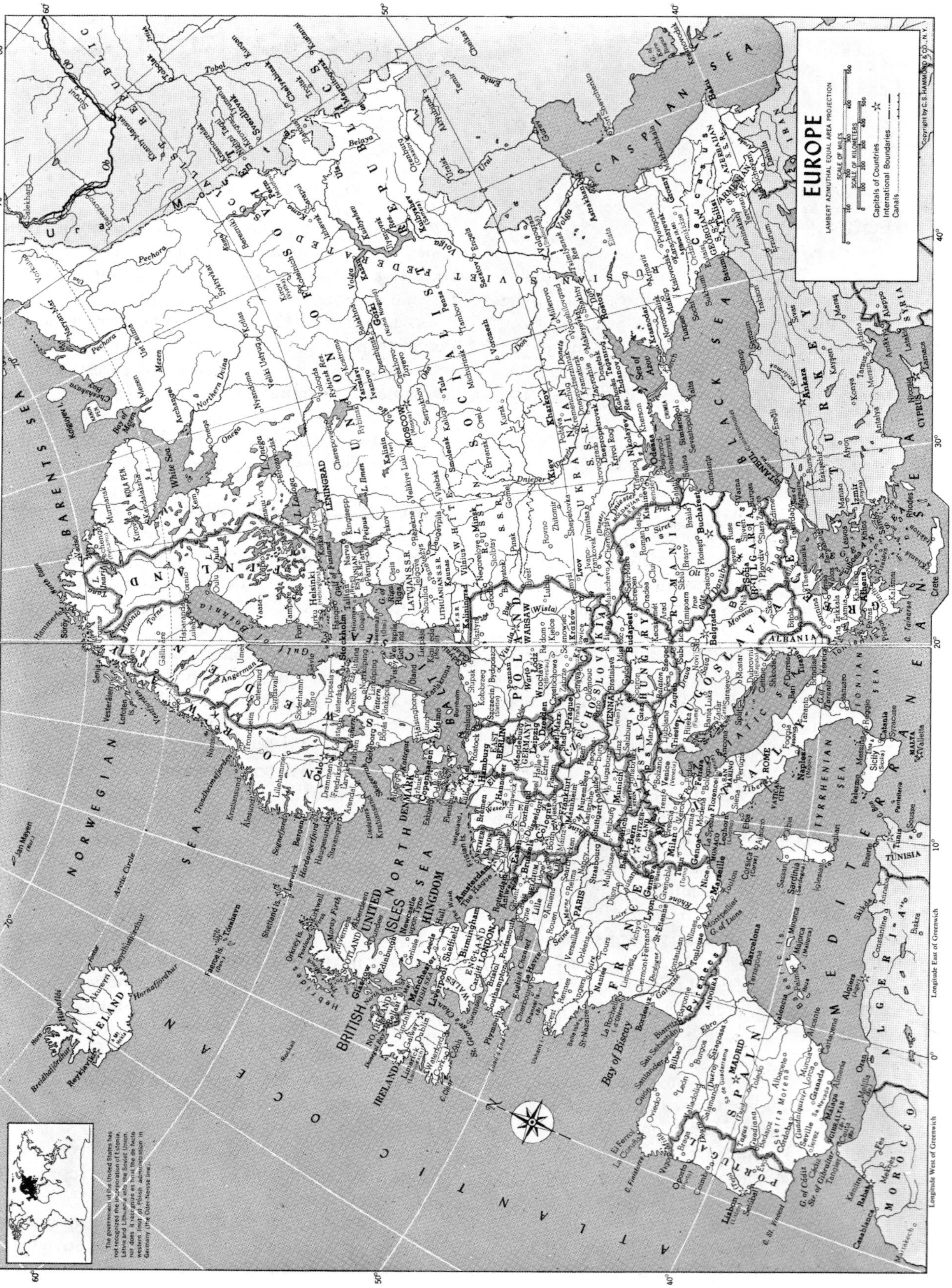

EUROPE

LAMBERT AZIMUTHAL EQUAL AREA PROJECTION

SCALE OF MILES

SCALE OF KILOMETERS

Capitals of Countries ........ ☆
International Boundaries ....... 
Canals ................

Copyright by C. S. HAMMOND & CO., N.Y.

advanced air defense system functions. This belt also encompasses some of the terrain's military obstacles noted previously, including the Carpathian Mountains, and the Elbe, Oder, and Vistula rivers. Moreover, politically, this belt helps to insulate the Soviet population from Western influence, and at the same time affords an advance base for penetration of Western Europe by Communist intelligence, subversion, and propaganda. It also provides an advance base that would be militarily useful in war. It projects the Soviet military frontier 750 miles westward and 400 miles southward from Russia's pre-World War II border. The Rhine would be the first serious natural obstacle in the path of Soviet armies attacking West Germany.

The Helsinki Agreement, the final act of the three-day Conference on Security and Cooperation in Europe, was signed August 1, 1975, by leaders of thirty-three Eastern and Western European countries and by the United States and Canada. The agreement pledges its signatories to respect each other's frontiers, to settle disputes peacefully, and not to intervene in each other's affairs. It also pledges them to respect human rights and fundamental freedoms. Although the agreement is not a treaty, and not legally binding, it provides official international recognition for several disputed Eastern European boundaries for the first time since World War II—notably those between Hungary and Romania, between Czechoslovakia and Poland, and between the USSR and other countries. It also recognizes the boundary between East and West Germany, and the existence of these two as separate states, ending for the foreseeable future the idea of a united Germany. Efforts by signatories and by individuals in Eastern Europe to monitor the adherence of Eastern European governments to the human rights provisions of the Helsinki Act have led to the harassment and arrest of such individuals and have contributed to a cooling of detente behavior by the Soviet government.

Negotiations toward Mutual and Balanced Force Reductions (MBFR) of Warsaw Pact and NATO forces in central Europe have been going on in Vienna since 1973. There appeared to be some progress in those talks in 1978. (See Western Europe Regional Survey.)

## REGIONAL ALLIANCES

*Warsaw Pact.* Also called the Warsaw Treaty Organization (WTO), this is an alliance of the Soviet Union and six of the other Communist states of Eastern Europe: East Germany, Poland, Czechoslovakia, Hungary, Romania, and Bulgaria. It was established as a twenty-year mutual-defense alliance in May 1955 in a conference called at Warsaw in response to the ratification (March 1955) of West Germany's admittance to NATO. The treaty provided for its own automatic renewal for ten additional years. Albania was one of the original pact members, but it has been excluded from all Warsaw Pact activities since 1962, when it aligned itself with Communist China in the Sino-Soviet dispute. Albania formally withdrew from the pact in September 1968, after the Soviet invasion of Czechoslovakia.

East Germany participated in the Warsaw conference of 1955, but was not officially admitted to the WTO until 1958. By then it had become obvious that Communist-bloc pressures would not reverse the rearmament of West Germany.

Under the terms of the Warsaw treaty, armed attack in Europe against a member of the pact obliges all other members to come to its assistance. The top political organ of the WTO is the Political Consultative Committee, which, according to a Soviet publication, meets periodically to discuss various problems connected with strengthening "the defensive capacities of the socialist countries." It has been noted by Western observers that these meetings never last longer than two days, and it seems likely that they merely rubber-stamp decisions already made. In a group of 1969 reforms (following the invasion of Czechoslovakia and probably designed partly for public relations outside the WTO and partly for morale building within it), a Committee of Defense Ministers of the WTO was established. The Joint High Command of the WTO armed forces was to be subordinated to this body. Continuing the emphasis on political matters, in 1967 the WTO members, meeting in Romania for the first time in ten years, established a Committee of Foreign Ministers and a Unified Secretariat.

The WTO Joint High Command consists of the commander in chief of the WTO Joint Armed Forces, who is always a Soviet marshal, and a Military Council. With headquarters in Moscow, the Military Council includes the chief of staff (also a Soviet officer) and permanent representatives from the armed forces of each WTO nation. Deputy commanders in chief come from the member states, and joint exercises and maneuvers are carried out regularly.

It must be stressed that this organization is for peacetime only. In case of war, the forces of the other pact countries would be operationally under the Soviet High Command. The entire air defense system for the pact is —even in peacetime—under the control of the commander of the Soviet Air Defense Force.

*Other Alliances.* The USSR has twenty-year bilateral treaties of friendship, cooperation, and mutual assistance, renewable on expiration, with each of the other members of the Warsaw Pact. These treaties broaden the terms of assistance in war to specify an attack by any state or combination of states, whether in Europe or not. There are similar bilateral treaties among the other members. Additionally, there are status-of-forces treaties with all Warsaw Pact countries where Soviet troops are stationed.

In 1949, with the other Eastern European countries under its domination, the USSR established the Council for Mutual Economic Assistance (COMECON, or CEMA). Albania left in 1961, and Mongolia joined in 1962. Cuba became the ninth member in 1972. It was originally stated to be a consultative, cooperative body to facilitate through joint action the economic development of all, but the USSR soon assumed dominance in all matters. By 1962 no national midrange (three-year or five-year) plan, annual fulfillment plan, or budget could be put into effect without USSR approval; items and quantities in international trade were virtually dictated, as were the categories of goods to be produced in each country.

## RECENT INTRA- AND EXTRA-REGIONAL CONFLICTS

There have been a few major conflicts or incidents within the Eastern European region involving the use or threatened use of armed forces since the Soviet Union's dominance over the region was sealed with the 1948 takeover of Czechoslovakia. There has also been direct involvement outside the region (the incident of Soviet missiles in Cuba), and there has been fighting along the border with China. No attempt is made here to assess the extent to which Soviet influence has been involved, directly or indirectly, in other incidents or conflicts outside the region. Many of these involvements are discussed in the appropriate regional surveys.

The major incidents are:

| | |
|---|---|
| 1948–49 | Berlin Blockade (USSR, U.K., France, U.S.) |
| 1953 | Uprising in East Germany, suppressed by Soviet troops |
| 1956 | Civil disturbance in Poland, resolved by political compromise |
| 1956 | Suppression of the Hungarian Revolution by Soviet troops |
| 1962 | Cuban Missile Crisis (USSR) |
| 1961–62 | Berlin Crisis (USSR, U.K., France, U.S.) |
| 1968 | Warsaw Pact (less Romania) occupation of Czechoslovakia |
| 1969 | Sino-Soviet border engagements along frontiers with Manchuria and Sinkiang (these were only the most publicized of many border incidents since 1961) |
| 1970 | Civil disturbances in northern Poland resulting in major changes in party and government leadership |

# MIDDLE EAST

## MILITARY GEOGRAPHY

The political and military realities of the second half of the twentieth century make it desirable to consider together the countries clustered about the shores of three major bodies of water that approach each other near the western extremity of Southwest Asia: the Mediterranean Sea, the Red Sea, and the Persian Gulf. These countries, collectively called the Middle East, include Egypt, Israel, Jordan, Lebanon, Syria, Iraq, Iran, Kuwait, Saudi Arabia, Oman, Yemen (Aden), Yemen (San'a), Bahrain, Qatar, and the United Arab Emirates.

## STRATEGIC SIGNIFICANCE

The military and strategic significance of the Middle East is the result of two major geographical factors: its location linking the three major continents of the Eastern Hemisphere, and its fabulously wealthy deposits of oil. The region is generally barren, consisting mostly of lightly inhabited deserts, with relatively dense population in those regions having sufficient water and arable land to support agriculture.

As the land bridge linking Africa, Asia, and Europe, the Middle East has been the scene of conflict between contending powers from the beginnings of recorded history. The Hyksos and the Egyptians clashed near Megiddo Pass in Palestine c. 1969 B.C.; the Assyrians, Persians, Alexander the Great, the Seleucids, the Ptolemies, and the Romans in turn established hegemony over the area, which became a frequent battleground in the wars of the later Romans and Byzantines against various Persian dynasties. The Moslems overran the region in the seventh century; Crusaders fought Saracens, colonized, and were in turn ejected. After the brief Mongol conquest of the thirteenth century, the Ottoman Turks established an empire that withstood Napoleon's onslaught, only to lose all except Anatolia through the combined pressure of British arms and Arab revolt in World War I. Meanwhile, the building of the Suez Canal (the short, rapid route to the Far East from Europe which became the lifeline of the British Empire), and the later discovery of oil in the Persian Gulf area, both ensured the continuing strategic and economic importance of the region.

The nationalization of the Suez Canal by Egypt in 1956 and its closure from 1967 to 1975, along with the gradual withdrawal of the British from their Indian Ocean enclaves in the early 1970s, contributed to the overall decline in importance of the canal link. Oil companies that formerly made substantial use of the canal have opted for the more economical choice of transporting oil around the Cape of Good Hope in supertankers, and additional pipelines have been opened, essentially bypassing the conventional canal route that had been used by smaller tankers. United States and European powers, including the Soviets, recognized that the vulnerability of the canal to closure by local conflict or political decision significantly weakened its importance for the strategic mobility of their fleets. It is no longer a dependable strategic waterway, but access to the canal would permit the Soviet fleet in the Black Sea or Mediterranean easy passage to and from the Indian Ocean and the Far East. The canal's role in regional commerce will probably increase.

Arab opposition to the existence of Israel has flared in four wars in which Israel has fought several other nations of the area. Between wars, opposition has been focused in terrorist groups based in the camps of displaced Palestinians in Lebanon and (formerly) Jordan. The conflict has resulted in the indirect involvement of the United States and the Soviet Union, on opposite sides. A major objective of international diplomacy continues to be the establishment of a political situation agreeable to both the Arab nations and Israel.

American support for Israel, fostered by widespread revulsion at Hitler's treatment of the Jews and the vehement urging of large numbers of Jewish citizens of the United States, is complicated by growing U.S. dependence on the Arab nations for a significant proportion of its oil needs. The Middle East has five-eighths of the non-Communist world's proven oil reserves. Because both the United States and the Soviet Union have much at stake in the Middle East, it is difficult for either to exert overt pressure on the governments of the oil-rich nations without risking confrontation with the other.

The Palestine Liberation Organization (PLO) was formed in 1964. Its basic operating principles are to oppose the existence of Israel as a Jewish state and to promote the establishment of a secular state in the territory historically

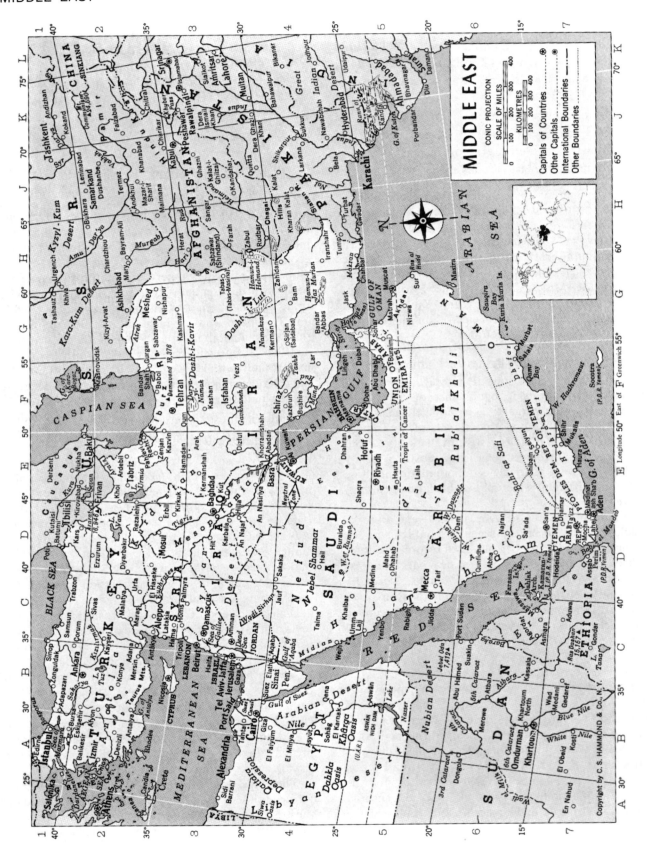

referred to as Palestine. The PLO contains several loosely allied factions, which subscribe to PLO opposition to Israel with varying degrees of intensity. The PLO divisions derive in large part from the fact that the factions receive their support from different Arab nations: Libya, Algeria, Iraq, Saudi Arabia, Egypt, and Syria. Al-Fatah is by far the largest of the PLO's groups. Its leader, Yassir Arafat, is also chairman of the PLO. Since 1974, the PLO has been recognized by the nations of the Arab League as spokesman for Palestinian interests.

The PLO has a recognized military wing, the Palestinian Liberation Army (PLA), consisting of two to three brigades. The PLA is not to be confused with Sa'iqa, which is a Syrian-sponsored, Syrian-controlled military force consisting of one large brigade. It is difficult to document the allegiances of the guerrillas operating against Israel from Lebanon. In large part they probably are members of al-Fatah. The Popular Front for the Liberation of Palestine and the Black June and Black September factions are probably not large in membership. They have gained prominence, however, through their conspicuous acts of terror in Israel and elsewhere in the world.

The combination of the withdrawal of the British from the Persian Gulf area, the entry of the Soviets into the eastern Mediterranean, the increase in the price of oil, with its effect on the economy of oil-producing states, widespread Arab antagonism to the Egyptian peace offensive, and the ever-present tension of the Palestinian question, has brought about several potentially dangerous politico-military situations in the area. The overthrow of the Shah and substitution in Iran of a poorly organized government has effectively destroyed that nation as a bulwark between the Soviet Union and the Persian Gulf area and even raises questions about the future of the nation itself. The Soviet entry into Afghanistan has introduced a new threat to Iran and Pakistan and to the countries on the Persian Gulf.

In a situation so potentially dangerous all major states of the region have made serious efforts to build up their weapons inventories. Saudi Arabia has strengthened itself with equipment from Britain, France, and the United States, as have Jordan, Kuwait, Oman, and the United Arab Emirates. Following the border incidents of early 1979, North Yemen also received military equipment from both the United States and the USSR. Egypt was formerly dependent on the Soviet Union for arms, but, since the peace initiative of President Sadat, has been building its forces at an accelerated pace with U.S.-supplied equipment. Israel has been receiving massive military aid from the U.S. since 1967; earlier it obtained important arms from France and Britain. It also has in its inventory Soviet materiel captured from the Arab states in the Middle East wars. The Soviet Union continues to supply equipment to Iraq, Syria, Libya, Algeria, and South

Yemen, and maintains military advisors in all these countries. Soviet equipment is also provided to the PLO.

Lebanon's armed forces almost completely disintegrated after its catastrophic civil war, and the outcome of the government's efforts to rebuild a new national force is not yet clear.

Western Europe, because of its heavy dependence on oil from the region, has become especially sensitive regarding its relationships with oil producers. In the decade of the 1970s all the major producing countries have acquired at least 51 percent ownership of the companies operating in their lands and thus have control of the rate of oil production. This has increased the effectiveness of the Organization of Petroleum Exporting Countries (OPEC) and its more limited Arab counterpart (OAPEC) in setting oil prices and production levels. There seems to be little doubt that in the event of another Arab-Israeli conflict, OAPEC would again, as in 1973, use its political leverage and enact oil supply cutbacks or selective embargoes. Among the world's foremost oil producers, Saudi Arabia's decision to use the oil weapon would be essential for an effective embargo. The potential for damage to the overall economic structure of the non-Communist world would be severe, and would place the Soviets at a disproportionate advantage inimical to the basically anti-Communist values of the Islamic Arabs.

Occasionally Israelis express confidence that eventually the Western world's heavy dependence upon Arab oil will slacken as alternative forms of energy are developed. Yet there are few authorities who agree to such optimism. Viable sources of energy are not seen as practicable until beyond the turn of the century; this is too long for the world to tolerate the difficult situation of the Arabs and Israelis in the eastern Mediterranean.

## THE PEACE INITIATIVES, 1977–78

Egyptian President Anwar Sadat's peace initiative of November 1977, in which he recognized Israel's right to exist in the region, and the Camp David agreements on guidelines for a settlement (September 1978), were the most promising steps toward peace since Israel's founding. At the U.S. presidential retreat, Camp David, in Maryland, under the sponsorship and close observation of President Carter, Prime Minister Menachem Begin and President Sadat reached agreement on a number of points and signed two documents incorporating them.

After difficult negotiations, and with vigorous U.S. pressure and support, a peace treaty between Egypt and Israel was signed in Washington on March 26, 1979. Closely paralleling the Camp David agreements, the treaty package included the following main provisions: (1) Israel was to carry out a phased withdrawal from the Sinai over a three-year period, with two-thirds of the territory, including the Sinai oilfields, to be evacuated within nine months of the treaty's ratification. (2) After this same nine-month period, Israel and Egypt were to establish normal diplomatic relations. (3) Israel would have free right of passage for its ships through the Suez Canal and the right to buy oil from the relinquished Sinai oilfields, and Egypt would end its economic boycott of Israel. (4) UN troops would be stationed in some border areas to monitor the carrying out of the agreements. (Within one month after ratification, negotiations on self-rule for the West Bank of the Jordan and the Gaza Strip would begin.)

The United States also promised to support Israel if Egypt violated the treaty (and offered a similar pledge to Egypt, which was not accepted), and promised to sell oil to Israel if Egypt failed to sell enough to supply that country's needs. The United States also promised, informally, to underwrite the costs of withdrawal, and to provide both Egypt and Israel with additional military materiel.

All Arab countries except Egypt denounced the agreements, and all broke relations with Egypt. OPEC immediately raised oil prices by 9 percent, beginning April 1.

## THE ARAB-ISRAELI MILITARY/STRATEGIC SITUATION

Efforts to bring peace to the Middle East were carried out against a background of military and strategic realities. If the peace should fail, these realities would shape any future conflict.

*Israel.* The Israelis know that for the next few years they are capable of coping with any likely Arab military threat. Israel's assessment of the 1973 war has led to some reorganization of commands and units, and to adoption and creation of new concepts and doctrine for employing weapons and allocating forces. Effort has been concentrated on reequipping and replenishing the Israel Defense Force and modifying, producing, and acquiring new equipment and materiel. The Israelis are certain that their military capabilities are greater now than in 1973, when the war started badly for them. The IDF has a high regard for the effectiveness of the Arab air defense forces that kept the IDF from providing close air support to ground troops in 1973 and inflicted relatively high losses to Israeli aircraft. The IDF has adopted a more balanced combined-arms doctrine. It will quite likely deploy more infantry and rely on fire from self-propelled artillery to protect its armor operations from Arab infantry equipped with individual antitank weapons. Intelligence has been upgraded to provide improved warning of impending hostilities based on evident Arab capabilities, and is relying less on estimates of Arab intentions.

The already rapid and efficient mobilization procedures have been further streamlined to insure sufficient forces to meet unexpected threats. Despite severe domestic economic burdens, Israel is maintaining a larger standing army.

There are ample supplies and materiel to carry out Israel's improvement program. Sophisticated equipment, including modern tanks, armored personnel carriers, self-propelled artillery, Hawk surface-to-air missiles (SAMs), the Lance battlefield support missile, the F-15 air superiority fighter, and Harpoon surface-to-surface missiles—all acquired from the United States—along with submarines from the United Kingdom, have made the IDF one of the world's best-equipped armies. Additionally, Israel's own defense industry can support much of this equipment and in many cases improve upon its standards. It produces, for instance, its own patrol boats (Dabur), guided missile patrol boats (Reshef), aircraft (Kfir, Arava), missiles (Shafrir AAM and Gabriel SSM), tanks (Chariot), and communications gear. Yet the Israel Defense Force is not trouble free. The country has a finite pool of manpower upon which its forces must draw. The burdens of maintaining even a peacetime force are staggering, and severely limit economic growth. Wartime mobilization nearly paralyzes the economy.

*Overview of the Arab Side.* The 1979 peace treaty removes from the Arab side its strongest military member. Unless the treaty fails, Syria would be the principal state confronting Israel in any future armed conflict, with Jordan, Iraq, Libya, and Saudi Arabia participating in various more limited ways. There are notable Arab strengths and weaknesses. By about 1975 the substantial losses of equipment in 1973 were replaced, and combat units now have their full complement of materiel. Equipment levels in almost all categories, except some in Egypt, probably exceed those of the 1973 period, and the equipment is generally more modern and improved.

Although total Arab inventories exceed the IDF's in most respects, Arab capabilities to operate and maintain equipment are not up to the level of Israel's. Arab soldiers appeared as well motivated as the Israelis and fought particularly well in the 1973 war. Leadership is good at the top levels, sometimes less so at the middle and lower levels. Coordination among units and responses to unexpected circumstances have not approached Israeli flexible efficiency. Arab naval forces do not have much capability against Israel's navy. And Israeli air forces have outperformed and outshot Arab air forces in the past because of superior pilots, aircraft, and weapons systems. On the other hand, Arab defenses, artillery, and antitank weaponry are plentiful and proved very effective in 1973. The Arab states have developed a keen awareness of the importance of cooperation, coordination, and surprise.

*Egypt.* Egypt has the largest and most powerful armed force in the Arab world. However, it has not expanded much since 1973, largely because of the rift with the Soviet Union in 1975, which ended that source of supply. The Egyptian inventory includes T-62 tanks and BMP armored personnel carriers as well as modern antitank and surface-to-air missiles. Egypt's air defense forces provide a formidable defensive umbrella over most important targets and have displayed a reasonable capability to provide cover for army maneuver elements. The air force has a limited ground attack capability and currently is formed around the MiG-21 as a point defense interceptor. Inability to obtain Soviet replacement parts has probably degraded the readiness of some elements of the Egyptian forces. However, alternate sources of supply have been found in the United States, the United Kingdom, France, China, and possibly Eastern Europe. The United States has supplied military transports (C-130) and F-5E fighters, and will supply more weaponry as a result of the 1979 peace treaty.

*Syria.* President Assad has consistently demanded that the Golan Heights be returned to Syrian sovereignty and that the Palestinian issues be dealt with expeditiously and completely, and he has strongly opposed Sadat's peace moves. Even if he wished to move toward a settlement with Israel, strong opposition forces within Syria would make it difficult. Before Assad's ascent to power, Syria's political situation was very volatile and characterized by frequent coups d'etat. He is heavily committed to Syria's stake in restoring Lebanon to stable conditions, albeit to the future interest of Syrian influence there. A significant number of Syrian combat brigades, some 30,000 troops, have been in Lebanon for about two years to provide a measure of stability and support to the central governing authority of Lebanon.

Syria's forces in Lebanon are poorly deployed to confront Israel, and their absence from the Golan front has weakened Syria in this key area so close to its capital, Damascus. Nevertheless, Syria intends to exercise strong control over the Palestinian armed presence in Lebanon. Syria and Israel will closely monitor the effectiveness of the United Nations Interim Force in Lebanon (UNIFIL) in limiting Palestinian infiltration back into Fatahland in southern Lebanon. Israel will probably continue to support the Christian militia forces in Lebanon. The chronic, bitter conflict among Lebanon's religious sects and militia, complicated by the involvement of Palestinian elements, offers little grounds for optimism. The killing of the son of former President Franjieh by the most powerful Christian militia sect (Phalange) in June 1978 dramatized the savagery of the disputes. Both Syria and Israel will have to act cautiously in order to avoid a long and bloody involvement.

Unlike Egypt, Syria has continued to receive large quantities of Soviet arms since 1973. Its units probably possess a higher percentage of more modern equipment than Egypt's, including many tanks, BMPs, and artillery. Syria has also dealt with Western Europe to acquire such items as antitank weapons. Syria's air defense network has expanded to protect important facilities. Mobile SA-6 systems can provide protective cover to maneuver elements. The Syrian air force, built around the MiG-21 and MiG-23, is not on a par with the Israeli air force.

*Jordan.* King Hussein, like President Assad, has considered Israel's responses to Sadat's initiatives insufficient to promise an overall settlement satisfactory to Arab interests. While his position is less hard-line, he has been disappointed in past efforts to deal with Israel. He feels restricted by the Arab League's decision at Rabat in 1974 to recognize the PLO as official representative of substantive Palestinian interests. He is unlikely to associate himself with the Sadat program unless there is a weakening elsewhere of Arab opposition to the Camp David agreements.

Jordan's small but competent forces are becoming better equipped. Hawk surface-to-air missiles and Vulcan firing batteries will significantly improve air defense. Mechanization of infantry units with APCs and the addition of self-propelled artillery weapons will improve Jordan's defensive posture against Israel and any Arab elements that might threaten Hussein's throne, including Palestinians and Iraqi or Syrian Baathists (Arab National Socialists). Although Hussein is unlikely to open a separate front against Israel in another war, he would probably again be drawn into supporting Syrian forces on the Golan. In recent years King Hussein and President Assad have enjoyed cordial personal relations, leading to limited military and political cooperation.

*Iran.* The Shah, a close friend of King Hussein, was interested in increasing the involvement of non-Arab but Moslem Iran with the Arab world, and especially with fostering trust and improving relations with the sheikdoms of the Arabian Peninsula and with Saudi Arabia. He loaned Egypt a billion dollars and Syria several millions after the 1973 war. In the Arab-Israeli wars, however, Iran was essentially neutral, giving some token medical support to Saudi Arabia in the 1973 war. This picture has changed with the coming to power of the Ayatollah Khomeini. In early 1979 Iran cut all ties with Israel, recognized the PLO, and vowed the liberation of Jerusalem. Formerly the chief oil supplier of Israel, Iran now gives that country none. In any future war, Iran would have very large quantities of modern weapons, some of which might be placed at the disposal of Arab combatants.

*Iraq.* Iraq could make a substantial military contribution to Arab operations against Israel. Iraqi forces have expanded significantly in recent years and have acquired large quantities of modern Soviet weapons. Iraq could probably send several divisions to reinforce Syrian forces on the Golan front, and deploy its air force to Syrian airstrips. Although Iraq competes with Syria for Baath party leadership, the Iraqis and Syrians would probably fight side by side in any future war against Israel.

*Libya.* Libya has more Soviet equipment than it can use, even if its forces were skilled enough (which they are not) to use it effectively for training or operations. The large stockpile is presumably a resource Kadhafi can use to increase his influence in Arab and African affairs. In case of war the most helpful thing Libya could do for the Arab cause would be to transfer its equipment to other Arab armies. However, the means to transport it quickly is not available, and Libyan stocks are not likely to be a major factor in a short war. They could considerably expedite the rebuilding of forces after a war, however, or help sustain a long, low-level war, in the unlikely event one developed.

*Saudi Arabia.* Since 1973 Saudi Arabia's preeminence in the Arab world has increased. While it lacks military forces to contribute significantly to a future conflict, it can broaden the Arab options by diplomatic and financial support, both regionally and worldwide. While it might well send token troops to the Golan or to Jordan, it would exert more influence by exercising its leading role in oil-production cutbacks or embargoes for political pressure.

The Saudis have a Moslem antipathy for communism, distrust the Soviet Union, and oppose Soviet aims in the Middle East. They are deeply committed to Arab unity and have avoided direct, forthright support of Sadat's peace initiatives to avoid a split with the "rejectionist" Arab states.

Saudi Arabia and the Gulf sheikhdoms have undertaken to subsidize development of an Arab Industrial Organization (AIO) which in large part will be devoted to increasing the production of military equipment, mainly in Egypt, because of that nation's ample manpower resources. The Saudis have provided substantial financial assistance to the governments of Egypt, Jordan, and Syria, and have made some grants for weapons purchases. Although it is not certain, they have probably also supported Syria's operations in Lebanon.

*Weapons.* Several new weapons systems would probably increase the scale and intensity of any future Arab-Israeli war. The Israelis have F-15 aircraft, which, along with their F-4s, have significant long-range combat capability with inflight refueling. The Iraqis and Libyans have Tu-22 Blinders, whose supersonic speed makes them less vulnerable to Israel's airborne air defenses and possibly capable of penetrating to the interior of Israel. The Arabs would probably attempt to deploy submarines or missile boats against Israel's Mediterranean and Red Sea supply routes, and Arab rockets and missiles could, as in 1973, be directed against centers of population and other targets within Israel.

There has been considerable speculation about Israel's capability of producing nuclear warheads and about the possible possession of chemical weapons by Egypt and Iraq. A CIA document released in early 1978 revealed CIA estimates that Israel has had atomic weapons since 1974. While both sides would probably prefer to limit any future war to conventional operations, both would like to keep options open and capabilities ambiguous so that in the event of impending overwhelming defeat or unexpected threat they could act decisively. In the meantime, mutual deterrence is undoubtedly an important factor.

*NATO and the USSR.* Until the conference and breakthrough at Camp David, there was an undercurrent of concern in the Western democracies over what was seen as Israel's lack of responsiveness to the initial Egyptian overtures in late 1977 toward a peace settlement. There was also a widespread feeling that the United States could do more to foster negotiations. Having felt the sting of higher oil prices and reduced oil imports as the result of OAPEC production cutbacks since 1974, Western European nations were particularly concerned about any repetition of these actions. They were also concerned about the threat to NATO cohesiveness that would appear if another conflict should raise again the problem that caused tension in NATO in 1973—that of refueling bases and overflight rights for U.S. transport planes en route to Israel.

The underlying major threat in the Middle East remains the possibility that U.S. and Soviet forces might be drawn into conflict with each other as a result of their support of opposite sides in the area. Continuation of the Arab-Israeli discord offers major advantages to the Soviet Union. Especially in times of crisis it is in a position to apply powerful leverage because of its strong standing with its arms clients, and the heavy dependence of NATO and Japan (U.S. allies) on Middle East oil. Other factors favorable to Russia are its own naval strength in the Mediterranean Sea and the Indian Ocean, and the sizable Soviet and Cuban presence in South Yemen and in nearby Africa. The Soviets appreciate the strength of their position. Before the October 1973 war, they explicitly encouraged the Arab oil producers to use oil as a political weapon and raise prices. This action confronted the industrialized world with its severest crisis since World War II.

## REGIONAL ALLIANCES

*The Arab League* was formed shortly before the end of World War II (March 22, 1945) by the governments of Egypt, Iraq, Jordan, Lebanon, Saudi Arabia, Syria, and

Yemen. The principal purpose was to prevent Palestine from becoming a separate and independent Jewish state. The league has since been joined by Algeria, Kuwait, Libya, Morocco, Sudan, Tunisia, South Yemen, Oman, Bahrain, Qatar, the United Arab Emirates, Djibouti, Somalia, and Mauritania. Cairo has been the headquarters for the secretary general of the league, and its official activities and pronouncements have been much influenced by the government of Egypt. In 1974, at the Rabat Conference, the league designated the PLO the official representative of the Palestinian people.

Because of the often divergent, and sometimes hostile, policies of the individual members of the league, it has been able to represent its members in only one area of policy and activity: opposition to Israel. Even in this matter, Morocco, Tunisia, and Jordan (covertly) have indicated belief that Israel's existence should be recognized diplomatically as well as practically, as Egypt's Sadat has already done. The possibility that the league would ever act unanimously in according recognition to Israel is remote. Ideological interests are too diverse for that. On the other hand, and in spite of ingrained animosities, rivalries, and competition, the league shows remarkable tolerance by holding together. The monetary rewards accruing to the oil producers, and the promise of some of that money to the poorer Arab states, provide the league with sufficient cohesiveness.

*The Central Treaty Organization of the Middle East* (CENTO) is a successor organization to the Middle East Treaty Organization (METO), which was established on November 21, 1955, in Baghdad—and hence was known as the Baghdad Pact. METO was created to discourage the possibility of Soviet aggression into Southwest Asia; its original members were Iran, Iraq, Turkey, Pakistan, and the United Kingdom. The United States, while not joining the pact, sent observers to its meetings, provided some financial and secretarial support, and participated in its deliberations.

METO was reorganized as the Central Treaty Organization on October 7, 1959, shortly after the withdrawal of Iraq, following its revolution in 1958. Otherwise the membership is the same. It has not been very active or influential.

*The Regional Cooperation for Development* (RCD) is an important outgrowth of the CENTO alliance and includes Iran, Turkey, and Pakistan. It functions primarily to improve economic, commercial, and communication ties for the Northern Tier countries. Its potential for growth into the political-military field is clearly evident.

*The Organization of Petroleum Exporting Countries* (OPEC) was formed in 1960 by Iran, Iraq, Kuwait, Saudi Arabia, and Venezuela and now includes Algeria, Ecuador, Gabon, Indonesia, Libya, Nigeria, Qatar, and Abu Dhabi of the United Arab Emirates.

## RECENT INTRA- AND EXTRA-REGIONAL CONFLICTS

| | |
|---|---|
| 1967 | Third Arab-Israeli war |
| 1967–present | Israeli raids on Lebanon, primarily against Palestinian guerrilla bases in refugee camps |
| 1967–present | Palestinian guerrilla action against Israel |
| 1968–70 | "War of Attrition" between Egypt and Israel along the Suez Canal |
| 1968 | Coup d'etat in Iraq |
| 1969 | Border clashes between Saudi Arabia and South Yemen |
| 1969 | Near civil war in Lebanon between the army and Palestinian guerrillas |
| 1969 | Coup d'etat in Syria |
| 1970 | Attempted coup in Iraq crushed |
| 1970 | Hostilities in Jordan between Jordanian forces and Palestinian Arab guerrillas |
| 1970 | Syrian invasion of Jordan repulsed |
| 1970 | Coup d'etat in Muscat and Oman; becomes Sultanate of Oman |
| 1970 | Coup d'etat in Syria |
| 1971 | Iran seizes Persian Gulf islands claimed by Arab Emirates |
| 1973 | Fourth Arab-Israeli war (October War) |
| 1974–75 | Iraqi army battles and suppresses Kurdish insurgency |
| 1975–76 | Oman's forces combat Dhofar rebellion with Iran's aid |
| 1975–present | Civil war in Lebanon |
| 1976–present | Syrian army intervenes in Lebanon; becomes nominally an element of Arab League peacekeeping force |
| 1977 | Libyan-Egyptian border clash |
| 1978 | Israel invades southern Lebanon, withdraws at UN request |
| 1978 | Coup d'etat in South Yemen |
| 1979 | Syrian-Israeli aerial clashes over Lebanon |
| 1979 | North Yemen—South Yemen border incident |

# AFRICA

## MILITARY GEOGRAPHY

Largely colonial before 1960, largely independent thereafter, Africa is characterized by rich natural resources, inadequate economic development, increasing overpopulation in relation to food production in many areas, widespread and disruptive tribal differences, and friction engendered by the antagonism of the Organization of African Unity and indigenous black nationalists against several countries in southern Africa controlled by white minorities. These conditions have resulted in internal tensions, disorders, military coups, civil wars, and overt and covert military support of insurgencies against the white-dominated regimes as well as against moderate governments maintaining close ties with former colonial rulers.

Vast—measuring 4,000 miles by 4,000 miles along its greatest dimensions—Africa is divided for this discussion into four disparate regions: North Africa, the Horn of Africa, Equatorial Africa, and southern Africa. Egypt and Libya, geographically a part of North Africa, are included in the discussion of the Middle East.

In North Africa civilization is mostly concentrated in a narrow coastal strip along the Mediterranean and Atlantic shores. Most of the littoral, as well as the interior, is desert in Egypt and Libya. In Tunisia, Algeria, and Morocco the coastal regions are relatively fertile and enjoy a typical Mediterranean climate, but farther inland there are mountains and deserts. In the eighth century this region served as a base for Arab penetration into Europe and, although separated from the rest of Africa by the formidable Sahara Desert, for expansion of Arab trade and Islamic religion and culture into sub-Saharan Africa. The countries of North Africa gained their independence after World War II. Significant oil discoveries provide them funds for future economic development.

The Horn of Africa consists of the Abyssinian massif, bisected by the Great Rift Valley containing the headwaters of the Blue Nile, and the surrounding arid coasts of the Red Sea, Gulf of Aden, and Indian Ocean. Historically, Christian Ethiopia, from its mountain fastness, has been able to defend itself successfully against waves of Moslem invaders and against all colonialists except Italy (1935–41). Recently it has been under renewed pressure from its own lowland Moslem population and the surrounding Moslem states. For half its external trade it

depends on a railroad which reaches the sea through Moslem Djibouti (formerly the French-ruled territory of Afars and Issas).

Equatorial Africa is the savannah and forest area between the southern borders of the Sahara and the temperate and arid areas of southern Africa. Both coasts are uninviting, with few natural harbors, and largely swampy terrain between the coast and the African escarpment, which begins 50 to 100 miles inland. Most river navigation stops at this point. Exceptions are the Senegal, Gambia, and Niger rivers, which are navigable 300 to 500 miles from the sea. Also, above the Congo rapids, 80 miles from the sea, there are over 7,000 miles of river transportation routes in use. The forbidding coastal features inhibited exploration and colonial penetration of the central African plateau for centuries, and still complicate the development of the interior and the exploitation of its vast mineral resources. The jungle-covered lowlands and Congo basin are bordered on the north and south by savannah plains.

The interior of southern Africa is also in large part guarded by the African escarpment. The savannah uplands of Angola, Zambia, Rhodesia, Malawi, and northern Mozambique give way to the southwest African deserts, the Kalahari desert of Botswana, and the lowland savannah of central and southern Mozambique. East-west railroads running through Angola and Mozambique serve the land-locked, mineral-rich interior states. South of this area to the Cape of Good Hope lies prosperous, developed, but racially divided, South Africa.

## STRATEGIC SIGNIFICANCE

Most of Africa, surrounded on all sides by water since the 100-mile Suez isthmus was cut by a canal a century ago, has always been isolated from the rest of the world. North Africa since prehistoric times has been closely tied to events in Southern Europe and the Middle East and has influenced and been influenced by their civilizations. However, Africa south of the Sahara was effectively isolated until the mid-nineteenth century except for coastal trading posts and an occasional explorer.

Africa has become an East-West area of contention. Former colonial powers try to maintain special military and economic relationships with their one-time colonies. The Soviet Union, Communist China, Cuba, and radical

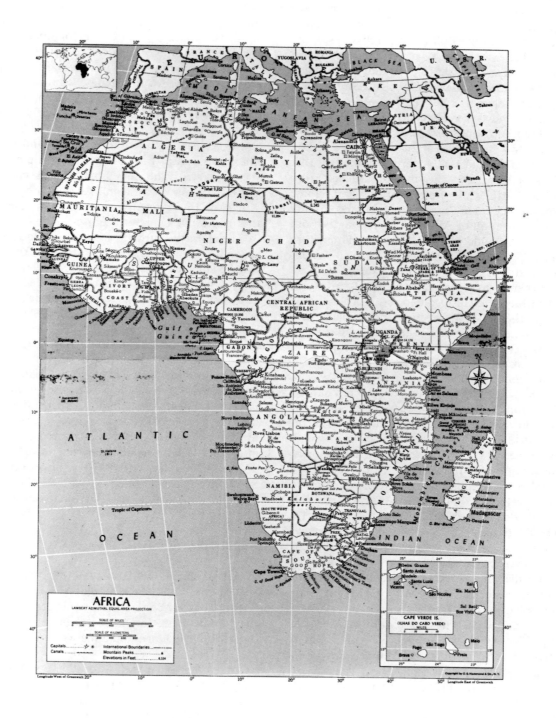

AFRICA
LAMBERT AZIMUTHAL EQUAL-AREA PROJECTION

SCALE OF MILES

SCALE OF KILOMETERS

Capitals............ ⋆    International Boundaries............
Canals.............      Mountain Peaks............ ▲
                        Elevations in Feet............ 4,534

CAPE VERDE IS.
(ILHAS DO CABO VERDE)
MILES

African states attempt political subversion, economic penetration, and military influence, while the United States tries to offset these moves through economic assistance and limited, selective military aid. The last quarter of the century began inauspiciously as military intervention from East and West—most notably Cuba and France—accelerated sharply. Political repercussions of the Arab-Israeli conflict extend into Africa as the Arab world has flexed its petroleum muscle to persuade many black African states to break with Israel. Similarly, conservative and radical Arab regimes compete for allies through support for like-minded governments or opportunistic promotion of domestic opposition groups.

Throughout newly independent black Africa friction and minor conflicts are constantly caused by the fact that boundary lines of the new nations are legacies from colonial Africa and do not follow tribal and ethnic divisions. The African nations, separately and jointly (through the Organization of African Unity), have set out on a course of nation building that puts national territory and unity ahead of ethnic ties. In general, African nations have exercised restraint in assisting or encouraging dissident ethnic elements in other states, even when ethnic loyalty might influence them to do so, both because they are vulnerable to the same kind of threat and because they are committed to the preeminence of the national concept.

North Africa's coastal strip was a route of conquest for Carthaginian, Roman, Vandal, and Arab armies in the distant past, and for Allies and Axis during World War II. Commerce in the Mediterranean has always been subject to interdiction from North Africa, and more than one invasion of Europe has been mounted from its shores, the latest being in 1943 and 1944. North Africa in turn has been equally vulnerable to invasion and colonial penetration from Europe and the Middle East. The Soviet Union has established a continuing naval presence in the Mediterranean, seeking to outflank NATO and to gain control of the world's richest oil reserves by winning the Arab region of North Africa and the Middle East. To some extent related to the growing Soviet presence is the fact that today North Africa is a base for the dissemination of Arab radical socialism to the rest of Africa, a phenomenon comparable to the historical southern movement of Islam along the sub–Saharan trade routes.

Northeast Africa—the Horn—is a bastion flanking the Red Sea and Gulf of Aden, overlooking the narrow waters between the two. The Strait of Bab el Mandeb provides a short sea passage between Arabia and Africa. The African Horn has been the scene recently of sub-Saharan Africa's largest modern war and most turbulent political realignments. The collapse of the Ethiopian empire proved fruitful for Soviet interests, although it cost the USSR its close relationship and naval base rights with Somalia. Along with Africa's largest country, Sudan, Ethiopia and Somalia find themselves at the crossroads of three great conflicts: East vs. West; Moslem, Arab North vs. black sub-Sahara; and radical vs. conservative.

Southern Africa guards the historic sea routes between east and west, which are of increased importance when the Suez Canal is closed. The white-dominated regimes of southern Africa are the target of liberation movements supported by most other African states (particularly the radical ones), the communist world, and many sympathizers in the West. Portuguese withdrawal from Mozambique and Angola brought a costly and continuing civil war to the latter, and, more significantly, removed crucial strategic white-ruled buffer zones protecting Rhodesia, South Africa, and Namibia. Soviet and Chinese-backed liberation groups now operate from states contiguous to these regimes. The new situation has caused a shift in Western policy away from South Africa, which itself is struggling to arrange transitions in Rhodesia and Namibia that will prove benign to future South African interests.

The countries through which runs the Sahelian climate-vegetation strip—the southern fringe of the Sahara Desert—have suffered several years of failed rains, culminating in 1973 in the worst drought of recorded African history. The countries most severely affected—Chad, Niger, Mauritania, Upper Volta, Mali, and Senegal—have been hampered in distributing famine-relief aid by generally primitive transportation and governmental administration. The famine brought serious damage to the nomadic life patterns of large segments of the population, a decrease in the measure of internal power held by the nomadic groups, increased unemployment and other urban problems as nomads were forced into the cities, coups d'etat triggered by dissatisfaction with governmental relief efforts, and intervention by outside powers in drought-weakened countries. Similar effects were also seen in Ethiopia. Severe drought continued through the Sahel; 1978 was an especially bad year, with worse conditions for Ethiopia than in 1973.

## REGIONAL ALLIANCES

*Arab League.* (See also Middle East Regional Survey.) The states of North Africa, plus Mauritania, Somalia, and Sudan, are members. The league is concerned mainly with the Middle East, but it has been involved in mediating disputes in the Horn and Sahel regions.

*The Maghreb.* (Arabic for the West) The Arabs and Berbers of Morocco, Algeria, Tunisia, and Libya have thought of their region as an entity from early times. This was reflected at the 1958 Tangier Conference, which resulted in establishing a short-lived secretariat of the Arab Maghreb. Achievement of the immediate goal of a consultative assembly and eventual federation was prevented by border disputes and Algerian radical nationalism, which was not in accord either with Moroccan conservative monarchism or Tunisian moderation. Subsequent consultations have had no tangible results, but have kept channels open for intergovernment communications and cooperation on regional matters of interest.

*Organization of African Unity (OAU)* was formed in 1963 through the efforts of the leaders of Nigeria, Ethiopia, and Guinea and was the culmination of earlier efforts to form a broad-based continental organization. All African countries are members except South Africa and Rhodesia. The charter prescribes noninterference in the internal affairs of states; observance of sovereignty and territorial integrity of members; peaceful settlement of disputes; condemnation of political assassination and subversive activities; nonalignment with power blocs; and emancipation of the white-ruled African territories. The latter goal has resulted in formation of the OAU Liberation Committee, which has a planning staff and budget. It recognizes and supports the various liberation movements directed against the white-dominated regimes. In January 1973, the committee issued a Declaration on African Liberation calling for an increased effort to remove the colonial and white minority regimes still in Africa. The committee has given strong backing to the diplomatic initiatives of the five front-line states (all of which are committee members) in the Rhodesian situation.

The OAU succeeded in arbitrating the Algerian-Moroccan border war of 1963 and in helping Tanzania replace with African troops the British troops that had quelled its 1964 army mutiny. However, it was ineffective in assisting the Congo (Kinshasa), which is now Zaire, during its rebellion in 1964–65, in resolving the Nigerian-Biafran civil war in 1969, or in reconciling various rival liberation movements. It has also been unable to settle the conflicts in Chad or Western Sahara. The OAU has been sharply divided over the issue of foreign intervention in Africa since the Angolan civil war. Following an allegedly Portuguese-inspired mercenary raid on Guinea, in December of 1970, the OAU Defense Commission was instructed to study the establishment of a common army. Nothing seems to have come of this.

*The Commonwealth* in Africa was to have been a community of common economic interests and mutual defense objectives. British assistance to the East African states in suppressing army mutinies in 1964, and a show of force against Somali insurgents in support of Kenya in 1965, underscored this policy. However, the ability of the Commonwealth's African states to force out South Africa, Tanzania's break with Britain over Rhodesia, and reaction to British equipment sales to South Africa, indicate declining British influence over its former territories. The

affiliation remains, however loose, as one of mutual interest based on historic ties, and has relevance to mutual defense in the absence of action by broader international organizations.

*Common Organization of Africa and Mauritius (OCAM)* was formed in 1965 as an outgrowth of earlier attempts at cooperation between French-speaking states, including the African and Malagasy Union and the Regional Council of France, Ivory Coast, Niger, and Dahomey (now Benin). Aside from political and economic motives, the prime factors were establishment of a common front to meet Ghana's subversive activities, Chinese Communist infiltration and subversion, and endemic chaos in the Congo (now Zaire). OCAM's influence has sharply declined; Congo and Zaire withdrew from membership in 1972, and Cameroon, Chad, and Madagascar withdrew in 1973. The future of the organization now appears to lie in economic cooperation rather than political or military action. Most OCAM members have bilateral defense treaties with France which ensure their immediate internal and external security when threatened beyond their means to cope, and so far these treaties have not been affected in the cases of the states that have withdrawn from OCAM. The nine current OCAM members are Benin, Central African Empire, Ivory Coast, Mauritius, Niger, Rwanda, Senegal, Togo, and Upper Volta.

France maintains close ties with most of the Francophone African nations. Heads of state meet regularly for joint talks, most recently at Paris in May 1978. The possibility of an inter-African strike force to meet military crises has been discussed at these meetings, and is apparently supported by the leaders of Ivory Coast, Senegal, Togo, and Gabon. Meanwhile, France has a total of 13,700 French troops stationed in Africa, including 2,000 on each of the tiny Indian Ocean islands of Reunion and Mayotte.

*West African Economic Community (CEAO)* was established in a treaty signed in June 1972 by seven West African states, all former French colonies. In April 1973, six of these countries—Ivory Coast, Mali, Mauritania, Niger, Senegal, and Upper Volta—agreed to ratify and implement the treaty by January 1, 1974. Benin signed the 1972 treaty but later chose observer status. The purpose of the group is the promotion of regional economic development. Most of the CEAO countries have recently suffered severely as a result of famine.

*The East African Community (EAC),* made up of Kenya, Uganda, and Tanzania, grew out of the British colonial East Africa High Commission and was established by treaty in 1967. The EAC countries formed a single trade unit and operated common rail, port, airline, and communications facilities. In 1976 and 1977 bitter commercial and ideological conflicts effectively ended the community.

*Conseil de l'Entente* is a political-economic regional grouping comprising Benin, Ivory Coast, Niger, Togo, and Upper Volta. The emphasis is on economic cooperation, and especially on a common fund used for capital development projects.

*Organization of Petroleum Exporting Countries (OPEC).* Four African countries—Algeria, Gabon, Libya, and Nigeria—are OPEC members. (See Middle East Regional Survey for discussion of this organization.)

*The Economic Community of West African States (ECOWAS)* was formed at the instigation of Nigeria and Togo in 1975. It has fifteen members and a basic purpose of promoting broad West African commercial development with a view toward full economic integration in a customs union within fifteen years.

*The Front-line States* is the term applied to the five countries—Angola, Botswana, Mozambique, Tanzania, and Zambia—that cooperate politically in opposing white rule in southern Africa. The front-line states border on Namibia (South-West Africa), South Africa, or Rhodesia.

## INTRA- AND EXTRA-REGIONAL CONFLICTS

| | |
|---|---|
| 1974 | Military coup in Niger |
| 1974 | Military coup deposed emperor in Ethiopia |
| 1975 | Collapse of the Ethiopian state into anarchy and rebellions; escalation of Eritrean secession struggle |
| 1975 | Military coup in Chad |
| 1975 | Attempted coup and later assassination of Madagascar head of state |
| 1975 | Bloodless military coup in Nigeria |
| 1975 | Angolan civil war (MPLA government established in 1976) |
| 1975 | Western Sahara war: Algerian-backed Polisario vs. Morocco and Mauritania (later supported by France) |
| 1975–present | Intensification of SWAPO guerrilla activity in Namibia |
| 1976–79 | Assassination of Nigerian head of state during aborted coup |
| 1976 | Intensification of guerrilla war in Rhodesia after failure of talks between white and black leaders |
| 1976 | Soweto riots in South Africa |
| 1976 | Israeli rescue of hijacked airline passengers in Uganda |
| 1976 | Breakup of East African Community, and commercial conflict among Kenya, Tanzania, and Uganda |
| 1976 | Failed coup attempt in Sudan |
| 1976 | Military coup in Burundi |
| 1977 | Presidential assassination in Congo |
| 1977 | Katangese invasion of Shaba, Zaire; Moroccan forces aid Zaire |
| 1977 | Libya-Egypt frontier hostilities |
| 1977–78 | Ogaden war: Somali invasion of Ethiopia crushed by Cuban and Ethiopian forces with Soviet aid |
| 1978–79 | Civil war in Chad. Increased French intervention in Chad to halt rebel advances |
| 1978 | Second Katangese invasion of Shaba, Zaire; French and Belgian forces aid Zaire |
| 1978 | Forced resignation of Ghanaian military head of state by army leaders |
| 1978 | Bloodless military coup in Mauritania |
| 1979 | Tanzanian invasion and civil war in Uganda |
| 1979 | Coup in Central African Empire (Republic) with French assistance |
| 1979 | Libyan abortive attempt to occupy Northern Chad |

# CENTRAL AND EAST ASIA

## MILITARY GEOGRAPHY

This region comprises Mongolia, the Koreas, Japan, and China. Soviet territories in East and Central Asia are excluded from this consideration; they are discussed in the Eastern Europe Regional Survey.

This region includes some of the most densely populated and some of the most sparsely populated areas in the world. Dense populations are to be found in the river valleys of China and on the islands of Japan. Sparse populations eke out an existence in the vast expanse of mountains north of the spine of the Himalayas, and in the broad deserts of the Gobi and Sinkiang.

The coastal and island regions have a monsoon climate quite similar to that found in South and Southeast Asia, although not so precisely patterned and predictable. Little of the monsoon moisture reaches the steppes and deserts of Central Asia, however, because of the intervening Himalayas to the south, and the mountains of China to the east.

## STRATEGIC SIGNIFICANCE

China's access to the open sea is blocked to the south by the rimland states of South and Southeast Asia. To the east this access to open sea is also impeded, even though not so rigidly blocked, by the island chain extending from the southern tip of the Kamchatka Peninsula to the southern tip of the Malay Peninsula.

China is not vulnerable from the lands to the south; there has never been a major successful overland invasion of East or Central Asia from that direction. However, China—like the rest of mainland East Asia—is vulnerable to invasion by seapowers controlling all or a significant portion of the chain of East Asian islands. This vulnerability is lessened by the great difficulty a maritime nation would have exerting military power inland through regions in which mountains and large rivers form serious military obstacles, and in which vast populations defy easy control.

To the north and west, however, there are fewer military obstacles and smaller populations. In these areas the tides of conquest have often shifted rapidly and widely. Usually these tides have reflected the extent to which the regime controlling eastern and central China could extend its power farther inland. In some instances, however, exceptionally powerful Central Asian regimes (most notably that

of Genghis Khan) have been able to seize the initiative from China in a positive manner, rather than merely as a reflection of Chinese weakness. Thus, until relatively modern times, the military history of East and Central Asia has been largely that of the fluctuations of power between China and evanescent, usually nomadic regimes of the lands to the north and west.

In the age of technology, however, the nomads of Central Asia suffered from insuperable disadvantages, and gradually succumbed to pressures of Russia from the north and west, and China from the south and east. More recently, the amazing technological progress of Japan, interrupted only briefly by defeat in World War II, has brought that island kingdom to a position of preeminent industrial power in the region. In addition, it has retained a potential military capability that was to some degree evidenced in the Russo-Japanese War, in the various pre-1941 Japanese invasions of China, and even in its ill-fated aggressions of World War II.

The role of nuclear weapons in the area is increasingly important. Japan, with its high concentration of industry and population, is extremely vulnerable. The People's Republic of China, poised between the two nuclear superpowers, protects itself by conciliating one and by deploying its modest nuclear resources against the other in a way that threatens to permit some measure of effective retaliation.

## REGIONAL ALLIANCES

There is no major regional alliance relative to this area. There are, however, a number of relevant bilateral alliances and mutual security pacts, and there is in effect one major international alliance as a result of United Nations declarations and actions regarding Korea. The major alliances are listed below:

*United Nations Support for the Republic of Korea.* This stems directly from the United Nations Declarations of June 1950. Active combat participants in the Korean War were Australia, Belgium, Canada, Colombia, Ethiopia, France, Greece, Luxembourg, Netherlands, New Zealand, Thailand, Turkey, Union of South Africa, United Kingdom, and the United States. Noncombatant participants were Denmark, India, Italy, Norway, and Sweden.

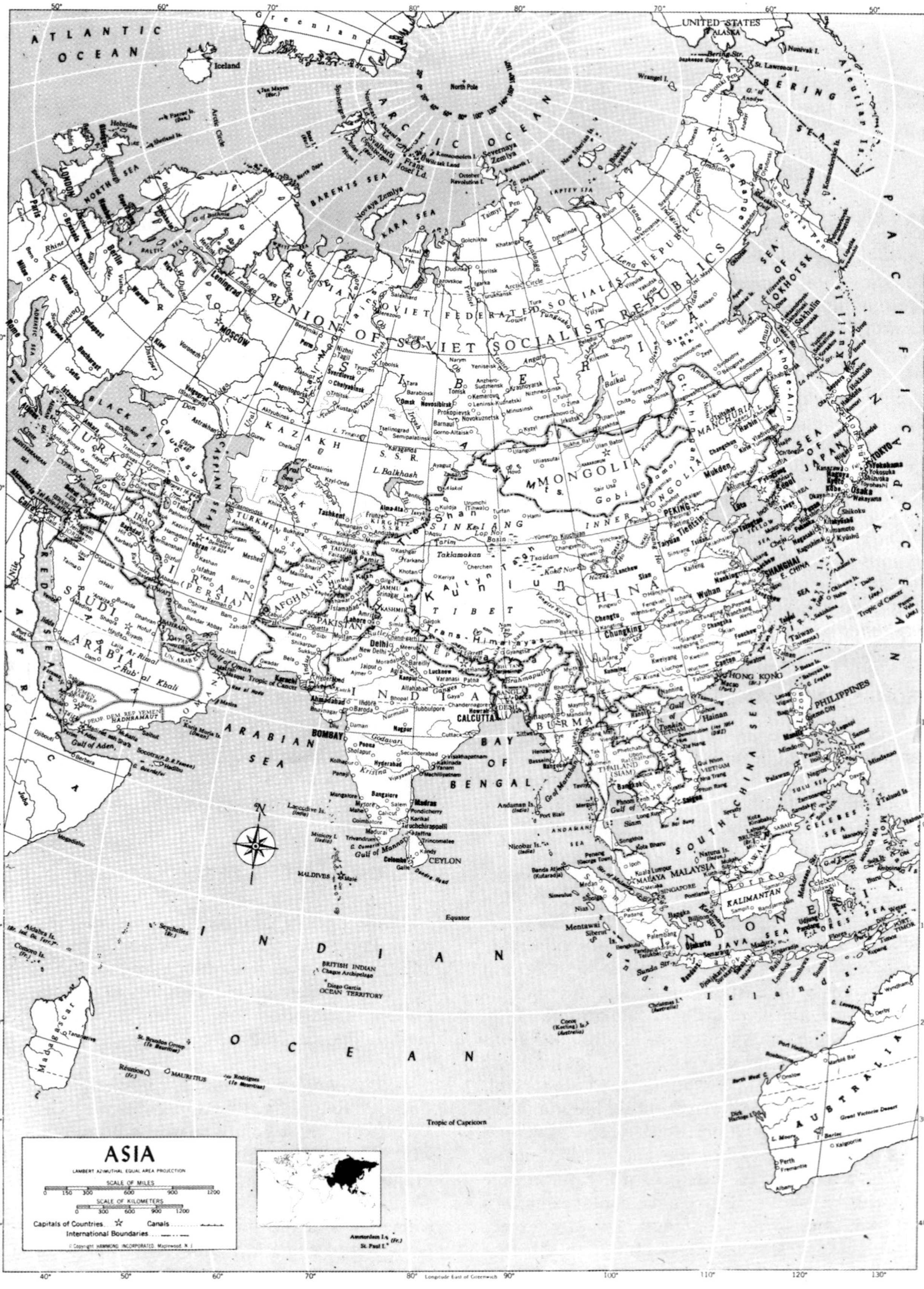

ATLANTIC OCEAN
ARCTIC OCEAN
North Pole
Greenland
Iceland
BARENTS SEA
KARA SEA
LAPTEV SEA
NORTH SEA
BALTIC SEA
BLACK SEA
CASPIAN SEA
UNITED STATES
ALASKA
Bering Str.
BERING SEA
Aleutian Is.
SEA OF OKHOTSK
SEA OF JAPAN
PACIFIC OCEAN
UNION OF SOVIET SOCIALIST REPUBLICS
RUSSIAN SOVIET FEDERATED SOCIALIST REPUBLICS
SIBERIA
MOSCOW
Leningrad
L. Baikal
KAZAKH S.S.R.
L. Balkhash
UZBEK
TURKMEN S.S.R.
KIRGHIZ S.S.R.
TADZHIK
TURKEY
IRAQ
IRAN (PERSIA)
SAUDI ARABIA
AFGHANISTAN
PAKISTAN
INDIA
MONGOLIA
INNER MONGOLIA
CHINA
TIBET
SINKIANG
Gobi
Kunlun
Tien Shan
Trans-Himalayas
Taklamakan
MANCHURIA
KOREA
JAPAN
TOKYO
PEKING
BURMA
THAILAND (SIAM)
VIETNAM
PHILIPPINES
HONG KONG
Hainan
Taiwan (Formosa)
CEYLON
MALDIVES
MALAYSIA
SINGAPORE
INDONESIA
KALIMANTAN
Borneo
BAY OF BENGAL
ARABIAN SEA
RED SEA
SOUTH CHINA SEA
CELEBES SEA
JAVA SEA
SULU SEA
INDIAN OCEAN
AFRICA
Madagascar
AUSTRALIA
Arctic Circle
Tropic of Cancer
Equator
Tropic of Capricorn
BRITISH INDIAN OCEAN TERRITORY
BOMBAY
CALCUTTA
Delhi
SHANGHAI
Longitude East of Greenwich
ASIA
LAMBERT AZIMUTHAL EQUAL AREA PROJECTION
SCALE OF MILES
0 150 300 600 900 1200
SCALE OF KILOMETERS
0 300 600 900 1200
Capitals of Countries
Canals
International Boundaries
© Copyright HAMMOND INCORPORATED, Maplewood, N.J.

*Sino-Mongolian Mutual Assistance Treaty* (May 1960)

*Sino-North Korean Mutual Assistance Treaty* (July 1961)

*United States bilateral Mutual Assistance Treaties* with: Republic of Korea (November 1954), Republic of China (March 1955), and Japan (January 1960).

*Soviet-Mongolian Mutual Assistance Treaty* (1936, 1946, 1966)

## RECENT INTRA- AND EXTRA-REGIONAL CONFLICTS

Two of the three most important wars since the end of World War II have taken place in this region: the Chinese civil war and the Korean War. One other important but brief conflict took place along the frontiers of the region between China and India in 1962. It is perhaps significant that the People's Republic of China (Communist China) was involved in all three of these wars. A list of all recent major hostilities, or crises involving military operations in the region follows:

| | |
|---|---|
| 1963–present | Intermittent border violence along Sino-Soviet frontiers, notably in 1969 |
| 1968 | Seizure of U.S.S. *Pueblo* by North Korean naval forces |
| 1969 | North Korea downs U.S. aircraft over Japan Sea |
| 1973 | Soviet Union intensifies intrusions into Japanese airspace; sends naval task force down Taiwan Strait |
| 1974 | January: People's Republic of China takes Paracel Islands from South Vietnam forces |
| 1974 | February: People's Republic of China takes position in Spratley Islands, also claimed by Republic of China and Republic of Vietnam |
| 1976 | North Korean troops kill two U.S. Army officers in demilitarized zone |
| 1979 | Chinese invasion to "punish" Vietnam |

# SOUTH AND SOUTHEAST ASIA

## MILITARY GEOGRAPHY

South and Southeast Asia comprise, in combination, the southern rimland of the vast Central Asian heartland. These are the regions of Asia most vulnerable to Western-based seapower, and thus they were affected particularly by the expansion of Europe in the sixteenth through the nineteenth centuries.

Both South and Southeast Asia are peninsular subcontinents. Separated from the rest of Asia, and from each other, by lofty mountain ranges, they have, for the most part, developed independently. Yet even before the advent of the Europeans there were important maritime contacts between these two regions, both military and economic. The preponderant influence came from the larger and more powerful society of the Indian subcontinent. It was in Southeast Asia that the earliest important meetings of Chinese and Indian cultures took place, because Chinese influence also had been exerted on Southeast Asia both by sea and overland from earliest historical times.

Also common to South and Southeast Asia is the climatological influence of the Indian Ocean and South China Sea, as reflected in the monsoon seasons. The alternating prevailing winds and wet and dry seasons caused by the monsoon climate have not only greatly affected agricultural and social development, but have also exercised a dominating influence on patterns of war, trade, and conquest, on land as well as on sea.

South Asia is considered here to include the following: Afghanistan, Bangladesh, Bhutan, India, Nepal, Pakistan, and Sri Lanka. Southeast Asia includes Brunei, Burma, Cambodia, Laos, Malaysia, Singapore, Thailand, and Vietnam. Indonesia and the Philippines, which are often considered Southeast Asian nations, are for geographical reasons included in the South and Southwest Pacific region. It is recognized, of course, that geopolitically Indonesia is linked closely with Southeast Asia, sharing with Malaysia and Singapore control of the Malacca and Singapore Straits, through which passes massive seaborne commerce, including 80 percent of Japan's oil.

## STRATEGIC SIGNIFICANCE

The nations of South and Southeast Asia and the towering mountain system that extends almost without break from the Caucasus nearly to the Gulf of Tonkin block access to the Indian Ocean from East and Central Asia. The mountain barrier continues southeastward into the Southwest Pacific through the geographic juxtaposition of the peninsulas of Southeast Asia and the Indonesian and Philippine archipelagos.

No nation or combination of South or Southeast Asian states ever has been strong enough to contemplate seriously a career of conquest north of the Himalayas. There have been, on the other hand, a number of instances in history when Central or East Asian empires have been strong enough to conduct extensive campaigns of conquest in these southern rimlands. Never, however, have these forays from the north had more than transitory success or provided the invaders with a permanent outlet to the Indian Ocean. Their failure to do so has been due primarily to the difficulties of supporting military operations or occupations or occupation forces across the Himalayas or over the jungled extensions of the mountain barrier in Southeast Asia. The entry of Soviet troops into Afghanistan at the end of 1979 posed a threat to the security of neighboring Iran and Pakistan and raised speculation as to the final objective of the Soviet Union in the area.

It is perhaps significant that the only nations that have ever dominated the Indian Ocean (Portugal and Great Britain) did so only after they had gained footholds for bases on, and achieved effective control of, the seacoasts of South and Southeast Asia and control of the straits connecting the Indian Ocean with the South China Sea and the Southwest Pacific Ocean. In this connection, the Soviet Union, in pursuing its expanded naval policy, routinely maintains naval units in the Indian Ocean, and Soviet naval vessels visit many ports in the area and westward to the Middle East. There are frequent reports of special basing arrangements or other accommodation by some of the nations in the area. There is rivalry in the Indian Ocean, and the United States Navy seeks to offset the Soviet presence by making improvements in the facilities on the island of Diego Garcia.

## ALLIANCES

United States efforts to establish a mutual security alliance for Southeast Asia were initiated during the 1954 Geneva Conference which confirmed the expulsion of France from its Indochina colonies. The pact creating a

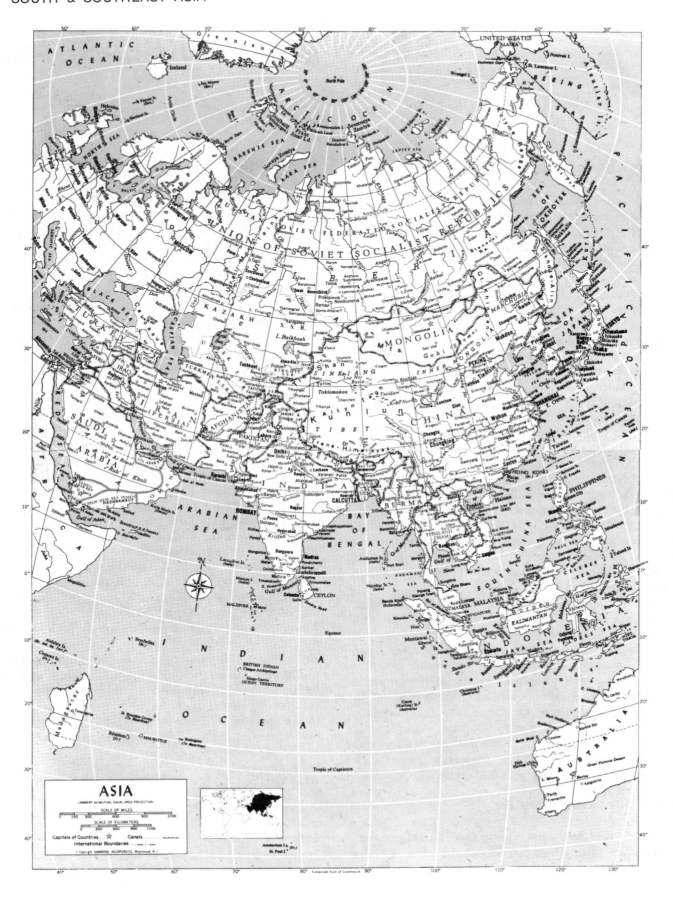

ASIA

LAMBERT AZIMUTHAL EQUAL AREA PROJECTION

SCALE OF MILES

SCALE OF KILOMETERS

Capitals of Countries........ ☆        Canals
International Boundaries

© Copyright HAMMOND INCORPORATED, Maplewood, N.J.

Southeast Asia Treaty Organization (SEATO) was signed on September 8, 1954, and came into effect on February 19, 1955; its purpose was to provide for collective defense and economic cooperation in Southeast Asia and to protect the weak nations of former French Indochina (South Vietnam, Cambodia, and Laos) from aggression. The signatory powers were Australia, France, New Zealand, Pakistan, the Philippines, Thailand, the United Kingdom, and the United States. Headquarters of SEATO was established in Bangkok. In some respects patterned after NATO, SEATO was relatively ineffective because of three major factors: lack of widespread support among Southeast Asian nations fearful of angering China and suspicious of each other; skilled exploitation of differences within SEATO and Southeast Asia by the Communist powers; and French (and later Pakistani) indifference and opposition. Nevertheless, the treaty provided some basis for the support and active combat involvement of the United States and most of the other signatory powers in response to North Vietnam's aggression against South Vietnam. In virtual desuetude, the organization was disbanded formally at the end of the Vietnam War, but the treaty remains in force, providing a limited military guarantee to Thailand.

Through a meeting of the Commonwealth countries concerned, and at the initiative of the United Kingdom, a Five-Power Defence Pact came into existence in November 1971, when Britain's Far East Command was dissolved. Members are the United Kingdom, Malaysia, Singapore, Australia, and New Zealand. Malaysia and Singapore furnish the bulk of the forces, while Australia and New Zealand contribute token, rotating forces in peacetime.

Five nations of the area—Indonesia, Malaysia, the Philippines, Singapore, and Thailand—are members of the Association of Southeast Asian Nations (ASEAN), a regional organization established in 1967 to promote economic, political, and social cooperation. There is comment, from time to time, concerning extension of ASEAN into mutual defense and security spheres, but this so far has come to naught.

## RECENT INTRA- AND EXTRA-REGIONAL CONFLICTS

| | |
|---|---|
| 1954–date | Naga insurgency in northeastern India |
| 1956–75 | Vietnam War |
| 1959–date | Malaysian Communist party presence and sporadic conflict astride Thai-Malaysian border |
| 1962–date | Dispute (without hostilities) between Malaysia and the Philippines over ownership of Sabah (N. Borneo) |
| 1963–66 | Sporadic hostilities between Indonesia and Malaysia |
| 1965–72 | Active U.S. combat involvement in Vietnam War |
| 1965 | India-Pakistan border hostilities in Rann of Kutch, later in Kashmir and Punjab |
| 1965–date | Growing insurgency in Thailand |
| 1970 | Coup in Cambodia |
| 1970–75 | Cambodian involvement in Vietnam War |
| 1971 | Unsuccessful revolt in Sri Lanka |
| 1971 | Internal violence in East Pakistan |
| 1971 | India-Pakistan war; East Pakistan declares independence as Republic of Bangladesh |
| 1973–74 | Coups in Thailand; overthrow of military leadership and following civilian regime |
| 1974 | People's Republic of China forces take over Paracel Islands, defeating South Vietnamese garrison |
| 1975 | North Vietnam defeats South Vietnam; initial steps toward unification. Khmer Rouge expel Lon Nol in Cambodia. Communist government in Laos |
| 1976–77 | Coups in Thailand; military regime in power |
| 1978 | Coup in Afghanistan ousts and kills President Daoud. Communist-controlled regime takes power; anti-Soviet Moselm rebels start unit war |
| 1978–79 | Unrest and civil war in Pakistan following coup; new pro-Soviet regime opposed generally by anticommunist Moslem population |
| 1978–79 | Vietnamese forces invade Cambodia, supporting rebels, and Khmer Rouge government is deposed |
| 1979 | China invades Vietnam and withdraws |
| 1979 | Soviet armed forces intervene in Afghanistan to support threatened pro-Soviet regime |

Wake Is. (U.S.)

MARSHALL IS.
Bikar
Taka
Mejit
Maloelap
Majuro
Mili
Jaluit
Ebon Atoll
Namorik
Kusaie
Pingelap
Mokil
Ponape
Bikini
Rongelap
Wotho
Kwajalein
Ailinglapalap
Lib I.

GILBERT IS.
Abaiang Tarawa
Kuria Abemama
Maiana
Nonouti Onotoa
Tabiteuea Arorae
Nanomana
Nukufetau Funafuti
Nanumea Niutao
Nui I.
Ocean I.
Nauru (Great Britain)

Rotuma
Conway Reef
Suva
Kandavu
Vanua Levu
Viti Levu FIJI

P O L Y N E S I A

Enewetok
Ujelang
Oroluk Is.
Namoluk Is.
Nomoi Is.
Pulusuk
Mokil

M I C R O N E S I A

C A R O L I N E   I S.

TERRITORY OF THE PACIFIC ISLANDS
(U.S. Trust Terr.)

MARIANA IS.
Asuncion
Pagan
Sapan
Guam (U.S.)
Rota
Tinian
Saipan

Truk
Hall Is.
Uiil
Pikelot
Gaferut
Faraulep
Fais
Ulithi
Yap
Ngulu
PALAU IS.
Koror
Babelthuap
Peleliu
Sonsorol
Merir

M E L A N E S I A

SANTA CRUZ IS.
Ndeni
Vanikoro Tikopia
Rennell I.
Torres Gr.
Banks Gr.

NEW HEBRIDES (Br.-Fr.)
Espiritu Santo
Malekula
Efate
Eromanga
Tana
Anatyum

LOYALTY IS.
Ouvéa
Lifou
Maré
NEW CALEDONIA (France)
Nouméa
I. of Pines
I. Walpole

Norfolk I. (Austr.)
Lord Howe I. (N.S. Wales)
Macquarie

BISMARCK ARCH.
Admiralty Is.
New Ireland
Lavongai
Rabaul
New Britain

SOLOMON IS.
Bougainville I.
Choiseul
Santa Isabel I.
New Georgia
Malaita
San Cristobal
Guadalcanal

Madang
Aitape
Wewak
NEW GUINEA
TERR. of NEW GUINEA
Lae
Salamaua
PAPUA
Port Moresby
D'Entrecasteaux Is.
Woodlark I.
Louisiade Arch.

WEST IRIAN
(Indonesia)
Sorong
Biak
Manokwari
Fakfak
Mapia Is.

C O R A L   S E A
(Australia)
2493

Halmahera
Ternate
Morotai I.
Talaud Is.
Sangihe Is.
Menado
Gorontalo
CELEBES
Makassar
Balikpapan
Kendari
Buton

Borneo
Pontianak
Tanahgrogot
Banjarmasin
Samarinda
Tarakan

PHILIPPINES
Manila
Quezon City
Luzon
Legaspi
Mindoro
Panay
Cebu
Negros
Samar
Leyte
Mindanao
Davao
Zamboanga
Jolo
SULU SEA
Palawan

BRUNEI
Kuching
SARAWAK
MALAYSIA
Kota Kinabalu
Sandakan
Sabah
Labuan

Batan Is.
Babuyan Is.
Aparri
Laoag
Lingayen
Subic
Cavite

HONG KONG (Br.)
Macao (Port.)
HAINAN
Haikow
Haiphong
HANOI
NORTH VIETNAM
Da Nang
Hué
SOUTH VIETNAM
Saigon
CAMBODIA
Phnom Penh

THAILAND
Bangkok
BURMA
Rangoon
Mandalay
Bassein

I N D O N E S I A

SUMATRA
Medan
Palembang
Padang
Bengkulu
Jakarta
JAVA
Bandung
Semarang
Surabaja
BALI
LOMBOK
SUMBAWA
FLORES
SUMBA
TIMOR

BANDA SEA
ARAFURA SEA

Darwin
NORTHERN
TERRITORY
Alice Springs
Tennant Creek
Daly Waters
Wyndham
Derby
Broome
Port Hedland

WESTERN
AUSTRALIA
Perth
Fremantle
Kalgoorlie
Geraldton
Carnarvon
Albany
Esperance

AUSTRALIA

SOUTH
AUSTRALIA
Adelaide
Port Augusta
Port Pirie
Port Lincoln
Ceduna

Great Australian Bight
1363

QUEENSLAND
Brisbane
Rockhampton
Townsville
Cairns
Mackay
Bundaberg
Maryborough
Gympie
Longreach
Charleville
Cloncurry
Normanton
Cooktown

NEW SOUTH WALES
Sydney
Newcastle
Canberra (Austr. Cap. Terr.)
Broken Hill
Bourke
Dubbo
Wagga Wagga
Albury
Bathurst
Armidale

VICTORIA
Melbourne
Geelong
Ballarat
Bendigo

Tasmania
Hobart
Launceston
Devonport
King I.

T A S M A N   S E A

NEW ZEALAND
NORTH I.
Auckland
Wellington
Napier
New Plymouth
Whangarei
Thames
Palmerston N.

SOUTH I.
Christchurch
Dunedin
Invercargill
Greymouth
Nelson
Westport
Timaru

Stewart I.
Bounty Is. (N.Z.)

I N D I A N   O C E A N

ANDAMAN Is. (India)
Nicobar Is. (India)
Bay of Bengal

Christmas I. (Australia)
Cocos Is. (Australia)

SINGAPORE
Kuala Lumpur
Malaya

S O U T H   C H I N A   S E A

CELEBES SEA

Copyright HAMMOND INCORPORATED, Maplewood, N.J.

# SOUTH AND SOUTHWEST PACIFIC

## MILITARY GEOGRAPHY

This region comprises the collections of archipelagos and great islands often known as Australasia. The principal nations of these archipelagos are Australia, New Zealand, Indonesia, and the Philippines. To the north and east are a number of minor island groups with little military significance of their own, except as they provide bases from which larger powers can project military force across the reaches of the Pacific Ocean.

## STRATEGIC SIGNIFICANCE

The Australasian archipelagos possess considerable natural wealth. Since these resources have been only partially developed, and since the populations are weak —either in numbers, or in technological development, or both—the region is vulnerable to penetration by more powerful nations. Efforts to accomplish such penetration have marked the history of the region for centuries.

In the past, efforts to penetrate Australasia have been made only by powers with substantial maritime strength. The apparent ability of communism to offset maritime weakness to some extent by means of ideological subversion suggests that Indonesia and the Philippines, at least, are more vulnerable to Communist penetration than might have been expected in earlier, prenuclear eras when naked force could be exerted by nations possessing it without danger of precipitating conflicts elsewhere on the globe. Nevertheless, successful Indonesian resistance to Chinese Communist subversion in 1965, put down by a military coup, took place in a general climate of benevolent oversight by U.S. Navy forces. Below the massive nuclear level, effective seapower is probably still the key to stability in the region. The growth of Soviet naval strength worldwide may be significant for this region.

## ALLIANCES

There are two overlapping regional alliances which affect this region: The Southeast Asia Collective Defense Treaty (or Manila Pact, or SEATO) of September 1954, now no longer backed by a SEATO organization (see South and Southeast Asia Regional Survey), and the Australia, New Zealand, United States (ANZUS) Council Treaty, of August 1952, which had for its objective the preservation of peace in the Pacific.

The United States has a Mutual Defense Treaty with the Philippines, and in addition has bilateral mutual assistance agreements with the Philippines, Australia, and New Zealand.

## RECENT INTRA- AND EXTRA-REGIONAL CONFLICTS

The same kind of disorders and hostilities that have plagued South and Southeast Asia have also affected Indonesia and (to a lesser extent) the Philippines. A list of recent hostilities or crises involving the employment of armed forces is given below:

| | |
|---|---|
| 1963–66 | Sporadic Indonesian guerrilla attacks against Malaysia |
| 1965 | Military coup d'etat in Indonesia; massacre of Communists and sympathizers |
| 1968–present | Moslem insurrection in Mindanao, Philippine Republic |
| 1972–present | Communist-inspired insurgency in northern Philippines |
| 1975–76 | Civil war in East Timor, leading to incorporation by Indonesia |

# II. COUNTRIES

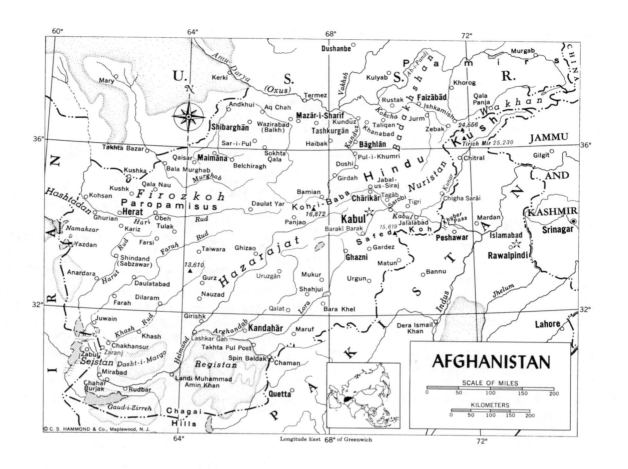

# AFGHANISTAN

## Republic of Afghanistan

### POWER POTENTIAL STATISTICS

Area: 253,861 square miles
Population: 14,541,000
Total Active Regular Armed Forces: 86,000 (.59%
  population)
Gross National Product: $2.8 billion ($130 per capita)
Annual Military Expenditures: $60.7 million (2.02%
  GNP)
Fuel Production:
  Coal: 187,000 metric tons
  Natural gas: 2.9 million cubic meters
  Electric Power Output: 585 million kwh
  Civil Air Fleet: 6 major transport aircraft

### DEFENSE STRUCTURE

In early 1980, Afghanistan had just sustained a Soviet-backed coup. Although poorly armed guerrilla rebels fought on, the country appeared to be under the effective control of Soviet troops and a Soviet-sponsored leader, Babrak Karmal. An estimated 3,500 troops were airlifted into Kabul on December 25, 1979, in an impressive demonstration of the USSR's new force projection capabilities. Another 50,000 reportedly crossed the border during the last days of December, and perhaps an equal number were massed on Afghanistan's border. Estimates of the total number of Soviet troops in the country range from 50,000–100,000.

Babrak replaced Hafizullah Amin, who in September 1979 had himself overthrown Noor Mohammed Taraki. The regimes of Taraki and Amin had been increasingly Soviet-controlled and increasingly unsuccessful at putting down uprisings by Islamic rebels.

## POLITICO-MILITARY POLICY

The principal traditional military policy of Afghanistan has been defense against larger and more powerful nations to the north and south.

The armed forces are recruited by conscription, and all men between the ages of twenty-two and forty-five are subject to two years' service and subject to reserve duty until age forty-two.

## STRATEGIC PROBLEMS

Relations between Afghanistan and Pakistan have been strained since 1947, when Pakistan achieved independence. The principal contention has been over the people and territory along the northwest frontier of Pakistan. Ex-President Daoud had taken conciliatory steps on this issue prior to the 1978 coup. Iran and Pakistan also fear Afghan subversion among the large Beluchi minorities astride the borders of the three states.

During most of the nineteenth century and the early decades of the twentieth, Afghanistan was threatened by Russian expansion in Central Asia. It is probable that only British warnings to Russia prevented absorption of Afghanistan into the Russian empire.

## MILITARY ASSISTANCE

Afghanistan has received over $260 million in military assistance from Russia since 1954, in the form of equipment, training support, and advice. Many officers are trained abroad, particularly in Russia, but also in Turkey. Afghanistan received $5.2 million in military assistance from the United States from fiscal year 1950 through fiscal year 1976; in addition, 453 students have been trained in the United States under the Military Assistance Program (MAP).

## ALLIANCES

Afghanistan is a member of the UN and several related specialized agencies. Except for the military assistance agreement with the USSR, it is not a member of any alliance or regional political grouping.

## ARMY

*Personnel:* 80,000

*Organization:*
   3 army corps, based regionally (Kabul, Kandahar, Gardez); General Reserve (Kabul)
   2 armored divisions
   5 infantry divisions (including 20 infantry battalions)
   3 mechanized brigades (Royal Bodyguard)

*Major Equipment Inventory:*
   500 medium tanks (200 T-34, 300 T-54/55, T-62)
   35 light tanks (PT-76)
   300 APC (BTR-40, -50, -60, -152)
   800 artillery pieces (76mm, 100mm, 122mm, 152mm guns and howitzers)
       ZSU-23/4 antiaircraft SP
   200 antiaircraft artillery pieces (37mm, 57mm, 85mm, 100mm)
       SAM missiles (SA-2 Guideline)
       Sagger, Snapper antitank missiles

*Reserves:* Organized, trained reserves number at least 250,000. Mobilization capability, equipment, and function are unknown. At least an additional 200,000 men in tribal levies are also available. Most of these are unquestionably fierce fighters, but organization and discipline are weak.

## AIR FORCE

*Personnel:* 6,000

*Organization:*
   3 fighter squadrons (MiG-21)
   2 fighter-bomber squadrons (Su-7)
   5 fighter-bomber squadrons (Mig-17)
   3 light bomber squadrons (Il-28)
   2 transport squadrons (Il-14, Il-18, Twin Otter)
   2 helicopter squadrons (Mi-1, Mi-4, Mi-8)
   1 support squadron (Yak-11, Yak-18, MiG-15, An-2)

## PARAMILITARY

There is a gendarmerie of 21,000 men for internal security; it is administered by the Ministry of Internal Affairs.

# ALBANIA

## People's Republic of Albania

### POWER POTENTIAL STATISTICS

Area: 11,100 square miles
Population: 2,597,000
Total Active Regular Armed Forces: 42,500 (1.6% population)
Gross National Product: $748 million ($300 per capita)
Annual Military Expenditures: $165 million (10.7% GNP)
Iron Ore Production: 500,000 metric tons
Fuel Production:
    Coal: 850,000 metric tons (all lignite)
    Crude Oil: 2.5 million metric tons
    Refined Petroleum Products: 1.6 million metric tons
Electric Power Output: 1.8 billion kwh
Merchant Fleet: (ships 1,000 tons and over): 9 ships; 48,000 gross tons

### DEFENSE STRUCTURE

The Albanian armed forces are under the Ministry of National Defense. The minister, who is both a senior military officer and a high ranking member of the Albanian Workers (Communist) party, exercises direct military and administrative control over the military establishment. All of the regular military forces are within the People's Army, although the air force and navy are treated separately because of their distinctive functions and equipment. Designations of rank were abolished in 1966. Position in the military hierarchy is based on responsibilities stipulated in the tables of organization of the armed forces.

About 80 percent of the military personnel are in the army, and many functions that apply to all of the services are administered by the army. Among them are the Main Political Directorate and the Rear Services (logistics).

Naval units are controlled by the Coastal Defense Command, which is operationally responsible directly to the Ministry of National Defense. The senior naval officer is commander of naval forces, deputy commander of

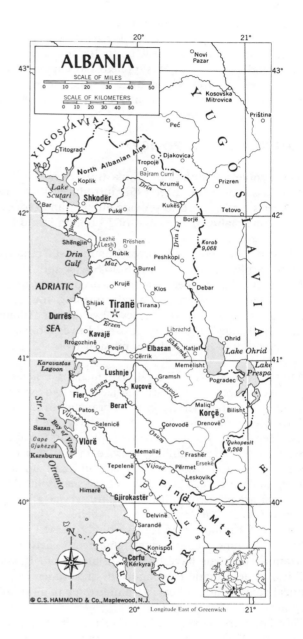

coastal defense, and deputy minister of defense for naval affairs. As deputy commander of coastal defense he coordinates naval operations with those of air defense and ground forces. The mission of the navy is to provide for military security of coastal waters, prevent submarines from approaching the coast, lay and sweep mines, intercept enemy forces, escort convoys, and, together with frontier guard and police, control entries to and exits from the country.

The commander of the air force is also a deputy minister of defense. About two-thirds of the air force strength is air defense artillery and missile units. Because the force is small, could not be easily resupplied, has exposed bases, and possesses no appreciable area in which to retreat, it could not be expected to contribute significantly to a sustained combat effort.

## POLITICO-MILITARY POLICY

The People's Republic of China took over the Soviet military assistance role after 1961, introduced its advisers and experts, and started to provide military and economic help. Peking claims that a total of $5 billion in aid of all kinds was given.

Albania consistently supported Communist China from the first public evidence of the Sino-Soviet split through 1977. Then relations between the two countries deteriorated, apparently because China's opening toward the West was unacceptable to the severely Marxist Albanian leadership, headed by seventy-year-old Enver Hoxha. The Chinese withdrew their military mission from Albania in 1978.

Military service is universal. All men of nineteen to thirty-five years of age are subject to two years of compulsory military service in most branches of the army, and for three years in the air force, navy, and frontier units. Men from thirty-five to fifty-five years of age are subject to obligatory military service in the reserve. In the event of mobilization Albania could call up about 500,000 males between sixteen and fifty years old. About 70 percent are physically fit for military service and about half have had military experience. It is believed that in case of war the Albanian armed forces would revert to guerrilla fighting. Training methods have remained Soviet. Almost all training manuals have been translated from Russian. Political indoctrination, conducted and supervised by political commissars, is heavily administered in all training programs.

Naval officers are required to have at least some university credits. They receive specialized courses before going to sea. Before 1961 most officers received training in the USSR. Since then some Albanian officers have gone to China for advanced training.

## STRATEGIC PROBLEMS

Albania's important strategic position at the southern entrance to the Adriatic, and its weakness and isolation, make it a potential target of any power which would strive for domination over the Adriatic. Thus in 1939 Albania was invaded and subjugated by Mussolini when he decided to turn the Adriatic into an Italian lake.

After Stalin's death in 1953, Albanian-Soviet relations gradually deteriorated to the extent that in December 1961 Khrushchev broke off diplomatic relations with Albania, ended Soviet economic assistance, withdrew Soviet military forces (which included a Soviet submarine base in Vlore Bay, garrisoned by some 3,000 Soviet sailors and harboring eight submarines), and excluded Albania from all meetings of the Warsaw Pact. Albania formally withdrew from the pact in 1968.

Historically and linguistically the Albanians form a relatively homogeneous nation. The Greeks (in the south) and the Yugoslavs (in the north) are numerically unimportant. In addition, 920,000 Albanians live in southern Yugoslavia, in the autonomous province of Kosovo, where they form a potential source of friction between the two countries. In this connection, Albania's birthrate (the highest in Europe) and fast-growing population (twenty-nine years to double) are significant. The Soviet Union would certainly welcome a new opportunity for use of a port at the mouth of the Adriatic, and Yugoslavia would certainly feel threatened by such a Soviet presence.

## MILITARY ASSISTANCE

The 1961 diplomatic break with the Soviet Union ended the supply of Soviet arms and equipment, and of spare parts to keep the Soviet tanks and planes running. This situation was alleviated in 1964–65 when Communist China began to provide spares for the MiG fighters and also furnished thirty Chinese-built MiG-17s.

## ALLIANCES

In September 1968, after the invasion of Czechoslovakia by troops of the Soviet Union and other Warsaw Pact powers, Albania formally withdrew from the pact. In fact it had not participated since 1961, when it sided with Communist China in the Sino-Soviet split. Now without allies, Albania has good relations with no Communist country except Vietnam. Its leaders have shown some interest in improving relations with Hungary and Bulgaria, and both Cuba and Vietnam have given strong verbal support to Albania's stand against China.

## ARMY

*Personnel:* 35,000

*Organization:*
    1 tank brigade
    8 infantry brigades
    2 tank battalions
    1 artillery regiment
    2 air defense regiments

*Major Equipment Inventory:*
  100 medium tanks (45 Soviet T-34 and T-54, 55
      Chinese T-59)
  122mm and 152mm guns and howitzers
  Su-76 self-propelled 76mm antitank guns
  APCs (BTR-40, BTR-50, BTR-152)
  Snapper antitank missiles
  45mm, 57mm, and 85mm antitank guns
  37mm, 57mm, and 85mm antiaircraft guns

*Reserves:* 75,000 to 80,000 trained reservists

## NAVY

*Personnel:* 3,000

*Organization:*
  Submarine Brigade
  Vlore Sea Defense Brigade
  Durres Sea Defense Brigade

*Major Units:*
  4 submarines (Whiskey class; 1 possibly inactive;
    SS)
  2 fleet minesweepers (T-43 class; MSF)
  6 inshore minesweepers (T-301 class; MSI)
  4 submarine chasers (Kronstad class; PCS)
  44 motor torpedo boats (12 P-4 class; 32 HU
    Chwan class; PT)
  6 fast patrol craft (Shanghai class; PCF)
  3 auxiliary ships (tankers, etc.)
  10 service craft (tugs, tenders, etc.)

*Naval Bases:* Durres, Vlore

*Reserves:* Over 5,000 trained reservists

## AIR FORCE

*Personnel:* 4,500

*Organization:*
  3 fighter-interceptor squadrons (2 MiG-21, 1
    MiG-19 AWX)
  3 fighter-bomber squadrons (MiG-17)
  1 transport squadron (An-2, Il-14)

*Major Aircraft Types:*
  80 combat aircraft (Chinese-built)
    16 MiG-17/F4 fighters
    32 MiG-19/F6 fighters (AGM)
    32 MiG-21/F8 fighters (Atoll AAM)
  97 other aircraft
    8 Il-14 transports
    4 An-2 transports
    65 trainers (MiG-15, Yak-11/18)
    20 helicopters (Mi-4)

*Missiles:* SA-2 Guideline SAMs (from China)

*Air Bases:* Tirane, Sazan, Vlore, Shijak, Kucove

*Reserves:* About 6,000 reservists

## PARAMILITARY

There is a Frontier Guard of five battalions, plus three battalions in reserve, and a Security Police of four battalions. These total about 12,500. Formal paramilitary training is obligatory for all young people.

# ALGERIA

## Algerian Democratic People's Republic

## POWER POTENTIAL STATISTICS

Area: 919,591 square miles
Population: 17,944,000
Total Active Regular Armed Forces: 63,300 (0.35%
  population)
Gross National Product: $19.6 billion ($1,100 per capita)
Annual Military Expenditures: $385 million (1.96%
  GNP)
Iron Ore Production: 3.2 million metric tons
Fuel Production:
  Crude Oil: 50 million metric tons
  Refined Oil: 5 million metric tons
  Gas: 9.5 billion cubic meters
Electric Power Output: 4.5 billion kwh
Merchant Fleet (ships 1,000 tons and over): 55 ships;
  945,000 gross tons
Civil Air Fleet: 43 major transport aircraft

## DEFENSE STRUCTURE

The president of the Council of Ministers is the chief of state and the supreme commander of the armed forces. Col. Houari Boumedienne, who seized power by a military coup in June 1965, occupied the positions both of president and of minister of national defense until his death at the end of 1978. He dealt directly with commanders of the armed forces, known collectively as the *Armee Nationale Populaire* (ANP) or National People's Army. The General Staff, under a chief of staff, is responsible for organizational, mobilization, budget, and employment planning of the four services: army, navy, air force, and National Gendarmerie.

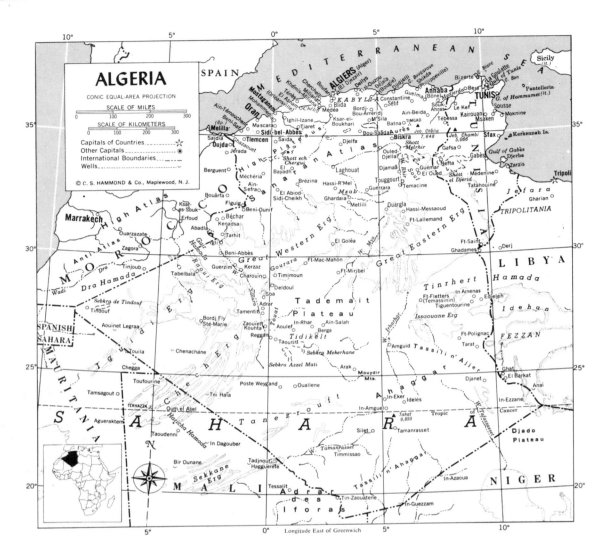

The Ministry of National Defense includes a Political Commissariat responsible to the Political Bureau of the nation's single party, the *Front de Liberation Nationale (FLN)*. There are party cells at all levels of the armed forces.

## POLITICO-MILITARY POLICIES

Algeria's foreign policy has been one of revolutionary idealism modified by caution. Algeria has actively and tangibly supported "wars of national liberation" throughout Africa against regimes that the Algerian government has considered reactionary, imperialistic, or racist. This policy, combined with difficulties with its more conservative neighbor, Morocco, has led to a relatively high rate of defense expenditures.

Originally the ANP was maintained by voluntary enlistments, and calls for volunteers were always over-subscribed. However, since 1968 there has been compulsive military service for all nineteen-year-olds. Initially it was for two years; now six months are required, and there is a training program in the university.

## STRATEGIC PROBLEMS

Algeria is situated between liberal, Western-oriented Tunisia and conservative, also Western-oriented, Morocco. Relations with Tunisia have improved, and there is no longer any dispute between the two countries. However, much of the border between Algeria and Morocco, which passes through an area rich in raw materials, was never precisely defined by the French. Moroccan-Algerian border clashes in 1962 and the fall of 1963 erupted into serious fighting in late October 1963; the ANP, still a guerrilla-type force, was defeated by the smaller Moroccan professional army. Members of the OAU mediated the dispute, and the frontier areas were demilitarized. The dispute was formally ended by agreements signed at the OAU annual meeting of 1972. The treaty of friendship and cooperation signed at that time has been ratified by Algeria but not Morocco, and the problem has not disappeared.

In 1975 a new dispute arose when Spain, its Western Sahara colony under threat of invasion by several hundred Moroccans, agreed to partition the territory between Mauritania and Morocco. Algeria promptly backed the small indigenous Polisario movement in its claim to be the legitimate government of an independent Saharan Arab Democratic Republic. Morocco and Mauritania broke relations with Algeria. The Polisario, with Algerian support, has conducted a guerrilla war in the Western Sahara. Algeria has promoted liberation for the Canary Islands in an attempt to pressure Spain into revoking the partition agreement. In 1978 French forces came to the aid of Morocco and Mauritania, who were hard pressed by the Algeria-based Polisario.

Boumedienne's coup of 1965 was the result of his concern about the dangerously unrealistic socialism and revolutionary interventionism of President Ben Bella. Boumedienne's somewhat more moderate policies have been opposed by doctrinaire extreme left idealists, including many Berbers and former members of the "internal" army. Dissidence still exists in the Berber mountain areas. A number of opposition groups, mostly in exile, continue to attack government policy. Several renewed their calls for the release of ex-President Ben Bella during the government-sponsored debate over the new national charter in 1976. Those inside Algeria were arrested, while Boumedienne and the charter won overwhelming electoral support.

## MILITARY ASSISTANCE

After independence Algeria fell heir to much French equipment. After the defeat by Morocco in 1963 the Soviet Union immediately made a loan of $100 million for arms to strengthen Algeria's defense. By mid-1971 this is believed to have reached a total of over $300 million. All classes of weapons were received: tanks, artillery, APCs, surface-to-air missiles, jet fighters and bombers, and submarine chasers and guided missile patrol craft. Three thousand Algerian officers have been trained in the Soviet Union, and about 1,000 Soviet military instructors are in Algeria. Because of Soviet control of spare parts Algeria is reported to have second thoughts about increased Soviet influence coupled with increased military aid.

Communist China aided the FLN with arms and training during the war for liberation. Since independence it has trained Algerian ground officers and pilots in China, conducted guerrilla training for dissidents from other African countries in Algeria, provided arms for African insurgents which are transshipped through Algeria, and begun to supply arms and training for an Algerian People's Militia. Communist Cuba has also participated in the guerrilla training in Algeria.

After Algeria's independence, a bilateral treaty permitted France to maintain several atomic test and space rocket launch sites, various civil aviation facilities, and the large modern naval base at Mers-el-Kebir. The French withdrew in 1967–68 but continued for a time to occupy the small airfield of Bou Sfer, near Mers-el-Kebir. France has a training mission with the National Gendarmerie and has equipped it with armored cars mounting antitank guns, machine guns, and other equipment.

## ALLIANCES

Algeria is a member of the Organization of African Unity (OAU), the Arab League, and the OAU Liberation Committee, which sponsors insurgent movements against the white and colonial regimes of southern Africa. Algeria actively supports the Arab conflict with Israel and opposes President Sadat's peace moves. Algeria also maintains membership in the Maghreb, and is a member of OPEC. It concluded a mutual defense pact with Libya in 1975.

## ARMY

*Personnel:* 55,000

*Organization:*
    4 motorized infantry brigades (with some armor)
    3 independent tank battalions
   50 independent infantry battalions
    5 independent artillery battalions
   12 companies of desert troops
    1 paratroop brigade
      antiaircraft troops
      engineer troops

*Major Equipment Inventory:*
  400 medium tanks (T-34, T-54/55)
   50 light tanks (AMX-13)
   50 assault guns (SU-100) SP
   10 assault guns (JSU-152) SP
  550 APCs (BTR-152)
  300 artillery pieces (140mm and 240mm rocket launchers, 85mm guns, 122mm and 152mm howitzers)
      antiaircraft guns (57mm, 85mm, 100mm)
      SSM (FROG)
      ATGM (Sagger)

*Reserves:* Perhaps as many as 100,000 men are experienced veterans of the ALN and postindependence ANP, and this number will be at least maintained as classes of conscripts pass through their two-year army training.

## NAVY

*Personnel:* 3,800

*Major Units:*
    2 fleet minesweepers (T-43 class)
    6 submarine chasers (SO-1 class; PCS)
    1 coastal minesweeper (MSC)
    3 guided missile patrol boats (Osa class; PTFG) (4 Styx SSM)
    6 guided missile patrol boats (Komar class; PTFG) (2 Styx SSM)
   14 torpedo boats (P-6 class; PT)
    1 trawler (possibly for intelligence collection; Sekstan class)
    6 patrol vessels (20 tons each)

*Major Naval Bases:* Mers-el-Kebir, Oran, Arzew, Algiers, La Senia, Philippeville, Bone

*Reserves:* About 9,000 trained reservists.

## AIR FORCE

*Personnel:* 4,500

*Organization:*
    2 fighter squadrons (MiG-21)
    7 fighter-bombers (Su-7, MiG-15, MiG-17)
    2 light bomber squadrons (Il-28)
    2 counterinsurgency (COIN) squadrons, (Magister)
    2 transport squadrons (An-12, Il-18)
    4 helicopter squadrons (Mi-1, Mi-4, Hughes 269, SA-330 Puma)
    1 (or more) SAM battalion (SA-2 Guideline)

*Major Aircraft Types:*
  198 combat aircraft
       52 MiG-21 fighters
       20 Su-7 fighter-bombers
       28 MiG-17 fighter-bombers
       40 MiG-15 fighter-bombers
       28 Magister armed trainers (COIN, ex-Luftwaffe)
       30 Il-28 light bombers
  156 other aircraft
       58 transports (An-12, Il-18, F-27)
       50 helicopters (Mi-1, Mi-4, Hughes 269, SA-330 Puma)
       48 training aircraft (T-28, Magister)

*Missiles:* 40 SAMs (SA-2 Guidelines)

*Major Air Bases:* Dar-el-Beider, Maison Blanche, Boufarak, Paul-Cazelles, Marine, Oukar, Biskra, Algiers, Oran, Sidi-bel-Abbes. There are thirty additional medium airfields and twenty minor ones.

*Reserves:* About 3,000 reservists

## PARAMILITARY

The French-trained and French-equipped National Gendarmerie numbers about 8,000 and is equipped with heavy weapons up to armored cars mounting cannon (about fifty AMLs).

After the 1962 military coup the People's Militia (about 30,000 Chinese-armed and Chinese-trained party leftists) was abolished, and it is doubtful that it has been re-established.

## FRENCH FORCES

    1 infantry company (Legionnaires); 1 air force detachment

# ANGOLA

## People's Republic of Angola

### POWER POTENTIAL STATISTICS

Area: 481,351 square miles
Population: 6,527,000
Total Active Regular Armed Forces: 31,500 (0.48% population)
Gross National Product: $2.8 billion ($440 per capita)
Annual Military Expenditures: $98 million (3.5% GNP)
Iron Ore Production: 5.6 million metric tons
Fuel Production:
    Crude Oil: 2.1 million metric tons
    Refined Petroleum Products: 720,000 metric tons
Electric Power Output: 1.3 million kwh
Merchant Fleet (ships 1,000 tons and over): 3 ships; 14,000 gross tons
Civil Air Fleet: 22 major transport aircraft

### POLITICO-MILITARY POLICIES AND POSTURE

Angola is ruled officially by the Popular Movement for the Liberation of Angola-Labor party (MPLA-PT). The MPLA-PT goals are to create a Marxist-Leninist regime and a unified nation based on "scientific socialism." The party administers the state through its Central Committee, with policy matters determined by the president and a

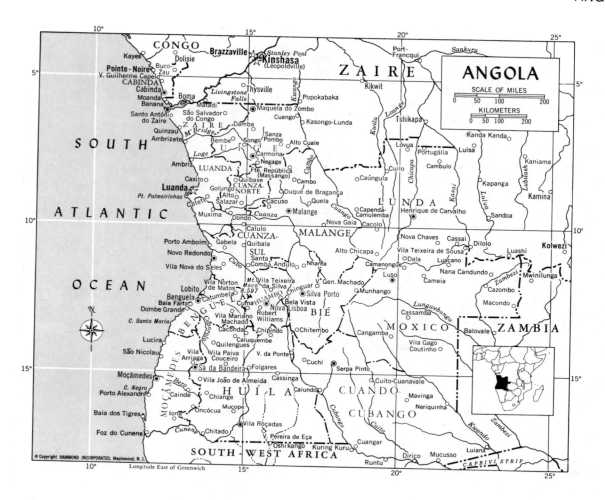

Political Bureau. After independence from Portugal, the MPLA, as it was called then, began converting its insurgent forces into a regular army.

Of its colonies in Africa, Portugal imposed its strongest control over Angola. Thus, when it suddenly became evident in 1974 that Angola would gain independence, there was little time to integrate the three main liberation movements—let alone the fragmented tribal groups on which they were based. Civil war broke out in 1975. The contending factions were: (1) the Soviet-backed MPLA with strength among the Kimbundu tribe (25 percent of the population); (2) the National Union for the Total Independence of Angola (UNITA), supported by China and later South Africa, with strength in the south among the Ovimbundu Tribe (33 percent of the population); and (3) the Angola National Liberation Front (FNLA), strong in the north among the Bakongo tribe (10 percent of the population) and supported by Zaire, France, and the United States. Three factors determined MPLA victory by March 1976—MPLA control of the region around Luanda,

the intervention of 15,000 Cuban troops and Soviet advisers, and the lack of countervailing Western support for UNITA and the FNLA. South Africa committed forces briefly to aid UNITA, but international condemnation and MPLA guarantees of security for the Cunene River hydroelectric project brought about their withdrawal.

Both UNITA and FNLA leaders have kept their vows to wage a continuing guerrilla war on the MPLA. UNITA, in particular, has been successful through 1978 in denying effective control of large areas of the south to the Luanda government. Cuba has had to increase its forces to 25,000 to maintain the regime. UNITA raids have prevented reopening of the key Benguela Railway to the copper mines of Zambia and Zaire. Another threat is posed by a liberation group operating against the MPLA in the Angolan enclave of Cabinda. Several thousand Cuban troops are securing this oil-rich area, separated from Angola proper by Zaire's narrow access to the Atlantic. Operated by a Gulf Oil Corporation subsidiary (majority ownership now Angolan), Cabinda's oil fields' production reached preindependence levels in 1977 and accounted for over half of Angola's export earnings.

The civil war and the departure of several hundred thousand Portuguese have crippled many sectors of the economy. Iron ore production ceased in 1975 and has not recovered. Diamond production has dropped by 80 percent. The war resulted in infestation of the coffee crop with disease and a 50 percent drop in production. Over half the country's food consumption had to be imported in 1977. The country's transport network is in need of much repair, with some 120 bridges destroyed or heavily damaged by the war and inadequate construction enterprises to rebuild them. This situation has forced the government to defer nationalizing foreign investments and to appeal to the West for aid.

The Luanda government has proclaimed itself nonaligned in world affairs, while recognizing a clear solidarity of purpose with the communist nations. President Neto has repeatedly maintained that no foreign bases would be established in Angola, but that Cuban and Soviet military assistance would continue as long as needed against anti-MPLA-PT forces. Angola and the USSR signed a twenty-year treaty of friendship and cooperation in October 1976. Russian fishing factories have assumed control of the disrupted Angolan fishing industry.

Angola serves as a base for the South-West Africa People's Organization (SWAPO) which operates against South African forces in Namibia. SWAPO has also cooperated with MPLA-PT and Cuban forces in fighting UNITA. SWAPO terrorist acts in Namibia brought on a highly destructive South African retaliatory raid within Angola in May 1978. From western Angola, secessionist Lunda tribesmen of Zaire's Shaba Province have launched two major invasions of the Zairean mining regions in 1977 and 1978. The second attack severely disrupted vital production in Kolwezi, Zaire, and brought accusations of Cuban complicity. Zaire, in turn, has supported FNLA forces in northern Angola. Zambia, once a supporter of UNITA, exchanged diplomatic recognition with Angola late in 1976 and subsequently expelled remaining UNITA elements. Most of the African states recognized the MPLA the same year. Angola became a member of the OAU in 1976.

The Luanda regime most likely faces a long-term civil war and an extensive period of consolidation should the conflict be ended diplomatically or by force. It must continue to rely on Soviet and Cuban support. Success in dealing with the insurgents will depend largely on the nature of the new government in Namibia and on reaching an understanding with Zaire. There are dissidents within the MPLA-PT and the military. In May 1977 one radical faction unsuccessfully attempted a coup. Its leaders have apparently been purged, however, and the Neto regime seems firmly entrenched in Luanda.

## ARMY

*Personnel:* 30,000

*Organization:*
    1 armored regiment
    8 infantry regiments

*Major Equipment Inventory:*
    130 medium tanks (T-34, T-54)
     50 light tanks (PT-76)
    165 APCs (BTR 40/152, BRDM-2, OT-62)
    120 guns (105mm, 122mm)
    100 BM-21 MRL
     82 120mm mortars
        75mm, 82mm, 107mm recoilless rifles
        Sagger antitank guided missiles (ATGM)
        23mm, 37mm antiaircraft guns
        SA-7 SAM

## NAVY

*Personnel:* 700

*Major Units:*
    4 patrol craft (Argos class; PC; 40mm guns)
    6 patrol boats (miscellaneous; PB; 20mm guns)
    2 utility landing craft (Alfange class; LCU)

## AIR FORCE

*Personnel:* 800

*Major Aircraft Types:*
    16 combat aircraft
        16 fighters (8 MiG-21, 8 MiG-17)
    43 other aircraft
         3 MiG-15 fighter/trainers
        11 transports (6 An-26, 5 C-47)
         2 PC-6A, STOL
         1 Alouette II helicopter

*Also left by Portugal (some are being flown):*
    2 RF-84 fighter/reconnaissance
    2 B-26 light bombers
    1 PV-2 patrol aircraft
    21 trainer/utility (3 Auster, 6 Do-27, 12 T-6)

# ARAB GULF STATES
## (Bahrain, Qatar, United Arab Emirates)

## POWER POTENTIAL STATISTICS

### BAHRAIN
#### State of Bahrain

Area: 231 square miles
Population: 289,000
Total Active Regular Armed Forces: 2,000 (0.69% population)
Gross National Product: $600 million ($2,430 per capita)
Annual Military Expenditures: $42.8 million (7.1% GNP)
Fuel Production:
 Crude Oil: 2.9 million metric tons
 Refined Petroleum Products: 10.9 million metric tons
Electric Power Output: 2.4 billion kwh
Civil Air Fleet: 2 major transport aircraft

### QATAR
#### State of Qatar

Area: 4,000 square miles
Population: 165,000
Total Active Regular Armed Forces: 2,000 (1.2% population)
Gross National Product: $4.0 billion ($25,320 per capita)
Fuel Production:
 Crude Oil: 25.5 million metric tons
 Refined Petroleum Products: 265,000 metric tons

Electric Power Output: 1 billion kwh
Merchant Fleet (ships 1,000 tons and over): 2 ships; 80,000 gross tons
Civil Air Fleet: 2 major transport aircraft

## UNITED ARAB EMIRATES*

Area: 32,000 square miles
Population: 656,000
Total Active Regular Armed Forces: 23,850 (3.63% population)
Gross National Product: $11.9 billion ($18,140 per capita)
Annual Military Expenditures: $66 million (0.55% GNP)
Fuel Production:
 Crude Oil: 94.3 million metric tons
 Refined Petroleum Products: 316,000 metric tons
Electric Power Output: 2.2 billion kwh
Merchant Fleet (ships 1,000 tons and over): 13 ships; 114,000 gross tons
Civil Air Fleet: 11 major transport aircraft

## POLITICO-MILITARY POLICIES AND POSTURE

The Persian Gulf (Arab Gulf to the Arabs) serves as Iraq and Iran's vital access to the open sea. It is important to the world because its bordering countries and its offshore waters contain more than half of the world's proven oil reserves. On the southern shore of this gulf are the small states of Kuwait, Bahrain, Qatar, and the United Arab Emirates.

To eliminate piracy, Britain concluded treaties with the sheikhdoms and Bahrain in the nineteenth century. Britain became responsible for foreign affairs and defense, gave some budget support, and advised on administration, while the sheikhdoms agreed to have dealings with no other country. A similar arrangement was made with Qatar when Turkish rule ended in 1916.

In discharging its responsibility for defense, Britain kept a joint force of over 9,000 in the area, until December 1971. At that time the United States concluded an agreement with Bahrain, which gave the United States home port facilities there. The U.S. facility was small, consisting of a few hundred naval personnel and three older ships. During the 1973 Arab-Israeli war, Bahrain informed the United States that it was cancelling the agreement.

Anticipating the British withdrawal, the nine sheikhdoms formed a loose federation in July 1968. Authority was vested in a council consisting of the nine sheikhs and a

*Abu Dhabi, Dubai, Sharjah, Ajman, Umm al Qaiwain, Ras al Khaimah, and Fujairah

Federal Council functioning as both cabinet and legislature. In 1971 the sheikhdoms of Abu Dhabi, Dubai,
Sharjah, Ajman, Umm al Qaiwain and Fujairah merged to
form a single nation, the United Arab Emirates. The
union's government was to be located in Abu Dhabi until a
new capital was built on the border of Abu Dhabi and
Dubai. It was not until early 1972 that the sheikhdom of
Ras al Khaimah, which had originally abstained from
joining, finally became the union's seventh member. The
UAE has been admitted to the UN and the Arab League.

Oil was discovered in Bahrain in 1932, in Qatar in 1949,
and in the sheikhdoms in 1959. The wealth from this oil
has been used for social services and economic development as deemed appropriate by the ruling sheikhs.

In January 1972 Sheikh Khalid of Sharjah was killed in
a coup attempted by his cousin, who had been deposed as
ruler in 1965. The sheikh was replaced by his younger
brother.

Bahrain declared its independence from Great Britain
on August 14, 1971, and was admitted to the UN on
September 21 of that year. Qatar declared independence
from Great Britain on September 1, 1971, and was admitted to the UN on September 21. Both states have joined the
Arab League. In February 1972, the prime minister of
Qatar, Sheikh Khalifa bin Hamad al-Thani, deposed his
cousin the emir, Sheikh Ahmed, in a bloodless coup.

Endemic problems include border disputes, conflicting
territorial claims, and traditional tribal rivalries. In 1970
Iran renounced its former claim to Bahrain. The most
serious problem facing the new state is subversion and
attacks by externally supported radical liberation
movements, feeding on internal dissatisfaction with
authoritarian rule. It is not always clear what ideologies
these movements prefer—nationalist, socialist (extreme),
or simply antiregime, but nearly all their support is
channeled from Communist countries through Iraq and
South Yemen. The most prominent of these organizations
is the Popular Front for the Liberation of Oman and the
Arab Gulf (PFLOAG). Its headquarters is in South
Yemen, and it is strongly opposed to Iranian hegemony in
the gulf region.

On November 30, 1971, Iranian troops seized the
Persian Gulf islands of Greater and Lesser Tunb and Abu
Musa. Ras al Khaimah, claiming the Tunb islands as its
own, protested the Iranian action. The takeover of Abu
Musa was peaceful since accord between Iran and Sharjah
had already been reached whereby Iranian troops were to
occupy specified areas of Abu Musa while Sharjah authorities retained control over the remainder of the island.

Bahrain has a total force of 1,100, equipped with
Saladin and Ferret armored and scout cars, antitank guns,
mortars, and two helicopters. Bahrain also has a 200-man
coast guard which operates about 20 small patrol boats
(PB).

Qatar has an armed force of 2,000, equipped with
Saladin and Ferret armored and scout cars, some artillery
and mortars, and six Hunter fighter-bombers. Qatar has a
400-man navy which operates the following units:
- 6 fast patrol craft (Vosper Thornycroft 103-ft. class;
  PCF; 20mm guns)
- 4 armed patrol boats (miscellaneous classes; machine
  guns; PB)
- 27 fast patrol boats (mainly Fairey Marine Spear class;
  unarmed; 26+ knots; PB)

## ARMY*

*Personnel:* 22,900

*Organization:*
- 1 royal brigade
- 6 infantry battalions
- 3 armored car battalions
- 3 artillery battalions
- 3 air defense battalions

*Major Equipment Inventory:*
- 100 Saladin and Ferret armored and scout cars
  light artillery
  antitank guided missiles (Vigilant)

## NAVY*

*Personnel:* 900

*Major Units:*
- 6 fast patrol craft (Vosper Thornycroft-built;
  30mm guns; PCF)
- 3 patrol boats (Keith Nelson-built; 20mm guns;
  PB)

(In addition, there are about 20 patrol boats (PB)
operated by a 90-man police force.)

## AIR FORCE*

*Personnel:* 550

*Major Aircraft Types:*
- 32 Mirage fighters
- 12 Hunter fighter-bombers
- 12 transports (4 C-130, 4 Caribou, 4 BN-2A)
- 27 helicopters (7 Alouette III, 5 Puma, 1 Iroquois,
  6 AB-206, 8 AB-205)

*Guided Missiles:*
- SS-11, SS-12 antitank guided missiles launched from
  Alouettes

*The United Arab Emirates Armed Forces include the former Union
Defense Force and armed forces of all 7 Emirates.

# ARGENTINA

## Argentine Republic

### POWER POTENTIAL STATISTICS

Area: 1,072,067 square miles (excluding claimed Antarctic and South Atlantic island areas of 481,177 square miles)

Population: 26,658,000

Total Active Regular Armed Forces: 146,000 (0.55% population)

Gross National Product: $48 billion ($1,840 per capita)

Annual Military Expenditures: $1.742 billion (3.63% GNP)

Crude Steel Production: 2.4 million metric tons

Fuel Production:

Coal: 615,000 metric tons

Crude Oil: 20.9 million metric tons

Refined Petroleum Products: 23 million metric tons

Natural Gas: 7.69 billion cubic meters

Electric Power Output: 27 billion kwh

Nuclear Power Production: 1,500 megawatts

Merchant Fleet (ships 1,000 tons and over): 167 ships; 1.6 million gross tons

Civil Air Fleet: 39 major transport aircraft

### DEFENSE STRUCTURE

The president of Argentina is commander in chief of the armed services. Administrative matters are handled through the Ministry of Defense.

### POLITICO-MILITARY POLICY

After seven years of military rule, the Argentines in 1973 chose as president former dictator Juan Peron, who had been living in exile since 1955. Peron died on July 1, 1974, and was succeeded by his widow, Isabel. Friction among warring factions of the Peronistas intensified, and a period of guerrilla activity by them and other groups, kidnappings for ransom, and assassinations, led to the declaration of a state of siege in November. Uncontrolled inflation, strikes, layoffs, and scandal among government officials, including an embezzlement charge against Isabel Peron herself, finally resulted in a bloodless coup, led by the commanders of the army, navy, and air force. Isabel Peron was deposed on March 24, 1976, in a move which also brought about the removal of all members of the Supreme Court, banned all organized political activity, and greatly restricted the existence and operations of labor unions. Army Chief of Staff Lt. Gen. Jorge Videla,

became president. Most of the cabinet members, including the minister of defense, are military officers.

Males between the ages of twenty and forty-five are required to serve in the armed forces. Ten years of service are required, usually one year of it in continuous active service or training in the army or air force, or two years in the navy. Another ten years are served in the National Guard, which is called out only in the event of war. The final five years are in the Territorial Guard. Naturalized citizens are exempt from military training for a period of ten years after naturalization. Reservists can be called up periodically for training.

### STRATEGIC PROBLEMS

Argentina's centuries-old claim to the British colony of the Falkland Islands (Islas Malvinas) off its southeast coast became more significant in 1976, when the British indicated an intention to develop the islands' economic potential and in particular to make a serious search for oil. The OAS in January 1976 supported Argentina's right to sovereignty, and the dispute resulted in the recall of both ambassadors. By late summer of 1978 representatives of Argentina and the United Kingdom had met several times to discuss the problem, with no resolution.

Another dispute of long duration, this one over possession of islands in the Beagle Channel, south of Tierra del Fuego, flared as both Argentina and Chile sought control over the 200-mile economic zone and its potential oil and gas resources. In 1977, a court of arbitration appointed by Queen Elizabeth II in 1971 in accordance with a long-standing treaty, ruled in favor of Chile. The Argentine government refused to accept the ruling, and both nations built up military strength in the area. After talks at the presidential level failed, the Vatican was asked to abritrate the matter.

Terrorism, some of it supported from outside the country, has been a continuing problem, with several groups conducting guerrilla activities against targets in government and business. Well over 2,000 people had died at the hands of one group or another by 1976. The military government has imposed harsh measures in an effort to control the dissidents, including the detention of many thousands.

### MILITARY ASSISTANCE

Deliveries of military equipment under the U.S. Military Assistance Program (MAP) from 1950 to 1977 were valued at $46.9 million. For 1977 the value was $740,000. As part of the Carter campaign for human rights, military aid for fiscal year 1978 was sharply reduced. The Argentine government responded by refusing to accept any military aid. Under the MAP, 4,023 students have been trained.

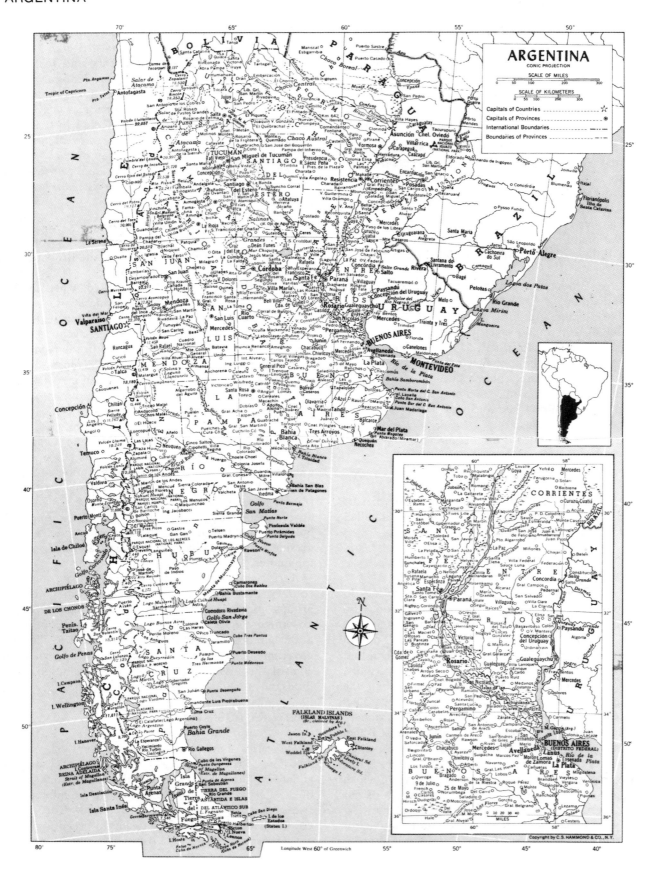

ARGENTINA
CONIC PROJECTION

SCALE OF MILES
0    50    100    200    300

SCALE OF KILOMETERS
0    50    100    200    300

Capitals of Countries ............... ☆
Capitals of Provinces ............... ◉
International Boundaries ...........
Boundaries of Provinces ...........

FALKLAND ISLANDS
(ISLAS MALVINAS)
(Br. claimed by Arg.)

Copyright by C.S. HAMMOND & CO., N.Y.

Longitude West 60° of Greenwich

## ALLIANCES

Argentina belongs to the OAS and its related agencies. In 1962 the government signed an agreement on cooperation and exchange of information with the European Atomic Energy Community.

## ARMY

*Personnel:* 85,000 (20,000 regulars; 65,000 national servicemen)

*Organization:*
- 2 armored brigades
- 4 infantry brigades (expandable to divisions upon reserve mobilization)
- 3 mechanized brigades
- 2 mountain brigades
- 1 airborne brigade
- 10 artillery regiments

*Major Equipment Inventory:*
- 120 light tanks (AMX-13)
- 240 medium tanks (M-4)
- 300 APCs (M-113)
- armored cars (Mowag)
- artillery:
  - 155mm self-propelled; 105mm, 155mm towed; 105mm pack
  - 120 mm mortars
  - 75mm, 95mm, 105mm recoilless rifles
  - 35mm, 40mm, 90mm antiaircraft guns
  - Tigercat SAMs
  - ATGMs
- 63 transport and liaison aircraft (T-39 Sabreliner, Twin Otter, T-41 and, Cessna 185; and Iroquois, Sioux, and FH-1100 helicopters)

*Reserves:* About 250,000 (trained), comprising the National Guard (200,000) and Territorial Guard (50,000).

## NAVY

*Personnel:* 33,000 (including naval air and marines)

*Major Units:*
- 4 submarines (2 Guppy class, 2 Salta class; SS)
- 1 light aircraft carrier (British Colossus class; CVL)
- 2 light cruisers (US Brooklyn class; CL; one armed with Seacat short-range SAM)
- 10 destroyers (2 British Type 42 class with Seadart SAM, DDG; 4 US Fletcher class, DD; 3 US Sumner class, DD; 1 US Gearing class, DD)
- 9 patrol ships (40mm+ guns; miscellaneous classes; PGF)
- 2 fast patrol craft (Type TNC 45 class; PCF; 40 knots; 3-inch gun torpedoes)
- 6 patrol boats (PB)
- 2 motor torpedo boats (Higgins class; PT)
- 2 missile attack boats (Mod-Type 148 class; PTG; Gabriel SSM)
- 5 landing ships (4 LST and 1 LSD)
- 6 coastal minesweepers (British Ton class; MSC)
- 28 landing craft (1 LCU, 27 LCVP)
- 15 auxiliary ships (transports, tankers, hydrographic, etc.)
- 15 service craft (tugs, dry docks, cranes, etc.)
- 4 naval aviation squadrons (distributed among three main shore bases and the carrier *25 de Mayo*)
- 61 combat aircraft
  - 14 A-4 attack aircraft (for service aboard *25 de Mayo*)
  - 12 MB-326GB, light attack
  - 25 T-28 armed trainers
  - 6 S-2 ASW aircraft (carrier-based)
  - 4 P-2 patrol aircraft
- 78 other aircraft
  - 29 transports (14 C-45 Beaver, 7 C-47, 5 C-54, 3 Electra)
  - 11 utility/trainers (5 Beech Queen Air, 4 PC-6 Porter, 1 Twin Otter, 1 HS-125)
  - 35 helicopters (S-31 Alouette, S-55, S-61 Sea King)
  - 3 Hu-16 Albatross maritime patrol

*Naval Bases:* Puerto Belgrano, Rio Santiago (La Plata), Darsena Norte (Buenos Aires), Mar del Plata, Ushaia

## AIR FORCE

*Personnel:* 22,000

*Organization:*

Air Operations Command is responsible for all flying operations of bombers, fighter-bombers, fighters, transport, search and rescue, interceptor aircraft, and antiaircraft guns. It has operational control over seven air brigades and seven air bases. Two of the bases are located in Antarctica and are assigned scientific activities only.

Personnel Command is responsible for administration, schools, and medical services.

Material Command is responsible for maintenance, logistics, industries related to the air force, and missile development activities.

Air Regions Command is responsible for the National Weather Service, and controls the operations of all airports.

*Major Aircraft Types:*
118 combat aircraft
    12 Canberra
    20 F-86F fighters
    47 A-4B fighter-bombers
    12 A-4C fighter-bombers
    15 Mirage III
    12 IA-58 Pucara (this program includes the delivery of 50 aircraft in the next three years)
246 other aircraft
    114 transports (C-130, B-707, F-28, DHC-6, C-47, HS-748, Merlin III, IA-50, and some single-engine light aircraft plus SA-16 for SAR)
    30 helicopters (H-500, UH-1H, S-60, Lama, etc.)
    102 trainers (Mentor, MS-760, IA-35)

*Major Air Bases:* Chamical, Rio Gallegos, Mar del Plata, El Palomar, Tandil, Parana, Comodoro Rivadavia, Reconquista, Moron, Reynold, Mendoza

## MARINE CORPS

*Personnel:* 6,000

*Organization:*
    1 command battalion
    6 infantry battalions
    1 artillery battalion
    1 service battalion
    1 air defense battalion
    1 communications battalion

*Major Equipment Inventory:*
    35 amphibious assault vehicles
    artillery:
        120mm mortars
        106mm mortars
        105mm howitzers
        105mm recoilless rifles
        75mm recoilless rifles
        88mm antiaircraft guns
        Bantam antitank missiles
        Tigercat SAMs

## PARAMILITARY

A gendarmerie of 17,000 men under army command is used mainly for frontier guard duties. There are 8,000 additional men in the National Maritime Prefecture (Coast Guard).

# AUSTRALIA

## The Commonwealth of Australia

### POWER POTENTIAL STATISTICS

Area: 2,967,909 square miles
Population: 14,298,000
Total Active Regular Armed Forces: 73,000 (0.51% population)
Gross National Product: $95.2 billion ($6,830 per capita
Annual Military Expenditures: $2.9 billion (3% GNP)
Crude Steel Production: 7.8 million metric tons
Iron Ore Production: 93 million metric tons
Fuel Production:
    Coal: 72.9 million metric tons
    Crude Oil: 20.5 million metric tons
    Refined Petroleum Products: 27.7 million metric tons
    Natural Gas: 5.9 billion cubic meters
    Manufactured Gas: 7.1 billion cubic meters
Electric Power Output: 84 billion kwh
Merchant Fleet (ships 1,000 tons and over): 79 ships; 1.3 million gross tons
Civil Air Fleet: 150 major transport aircraft

### DEFENSE STRUCTURE

Nominally the commander in chief of the armed forces of the Commonwealth of Australia is the governor general, representing the sovereign, who is also the sovereign of Great Britain. The federal government is parliamentary in form, with actual executive power—including that over the armed forces—vested in the cabinet and the prime minister, who are responsible to Parliament. Principal responsibility within the cabinet for the administration and control of the armed forces is exercised by the minister of defense. Each service is headed by a civilian minister, but none of these is in the twelve-member cabinet. The army, navy, and air force are administered, respectively, by the military, navy, and air boards, each consisting of the minister, the chief of staff, and four or five senior civilian officials and military officers. Joint operations are conducted by unified commands, and overall defense planning by a joint staff. Otherwise the three services remain separate.

### POLITICO-MILITARY POLICY

In 1957 Australia made a fundamental decision to relate the organization and the equipping of its armed forces to United States patterns, which was a major shift from Australia's traditional military relationship with the United Kingdom. While this did not mean any loosening of Australia's Commonwealth ties, it did mean that Australia was realistically conforming to the changed pattern of

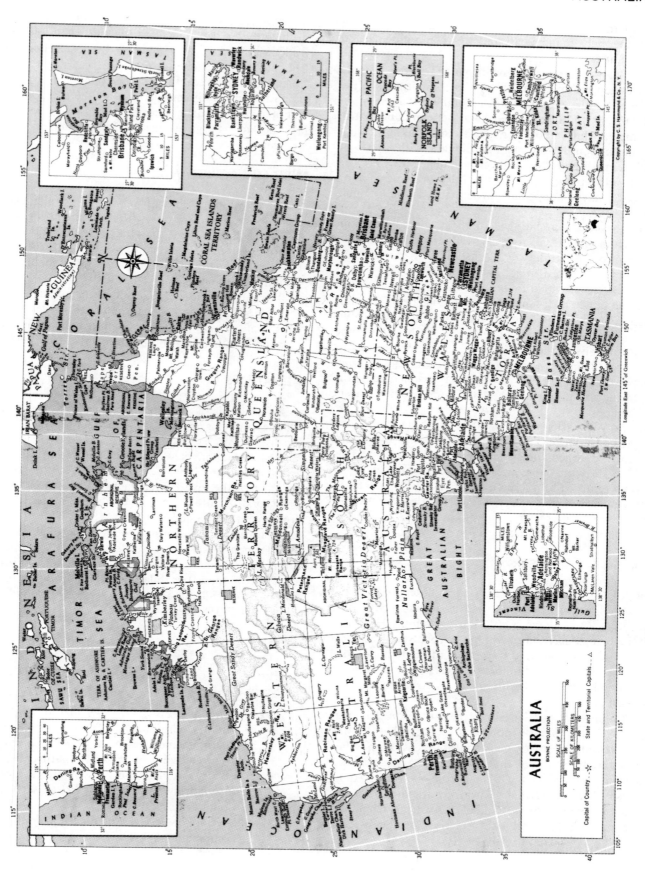

AUSTRALIA

BONNE PROJECTION

SCALE OF MILES

SCALE OF KILOMETERS

Capital of Country....★

State and Territorial Capitals....△

power in the Pacific and Southeast Asia, where Britain was deliberately reducing its military commitments and responsibilities.

Australia supported the now-disbanded Southeast Asia Treaty Organization (SEATO) and its commitment to the defense of South Vietnam against Communist aggression. It sent troops to fight beside the Americans and South Vietnamese, while at the same time undertaking a civil program in South Vietnam coordinated with those of the Vietnamese and American governments. In 1971 the Australian troop contingent was withdrawn. A new Labor Party government stopped all participation in the Vietnam effort in 1972.

The announced withdrawal of most United Kingdom forces from Southeast Asia by 1971 posed a difficult problem for Australia, with its limited population. However, the Five-Power Pact of 1971 (see United Kingdom) has provided a solution that appears satisfactory to all concerned: Australia, Malaysia, New Zealand, Singapore, and the United Kingdom. Australia's contribution to the Australia-New Zealand-U.K. (ANZUK) Force consists of units of the three services, some on permanent station and some on rotation. With headquarters in Singapore, units serve also in Malaysia. In emergency, the bulk of the five-power forces would come from Malaysia and Singapore.

Several years after World War II, Australia abandoned wartime conscription and returned to a policy of recruitment for the armed forces by voluntary enlistment. This failed to provide adequate manpower, and in 1965 Australia returned to a limited selective service system, in which young men over twenty served for eighteen months in the armed forces and three years in the reserve. Conscription was abolished again in 1972.

## STRATEGIC PROBLEMS

In general, because of Australia's remoteness from the conflicts of Europe and Asia and its insular geography, strategic problems have been relatively minor. However, with the British decision to withdraw from Southeast Asia and the Indian Ocean, and the impact of modern weapons and transportation technologies, Australia has become more directly concerned with affairs in Asia, particularly Southeast Asia.

Australians are worried about the attraction that their large, rich, and sparsely populated country has for the overpopulated nations of East and Southeast Asia. They are particularly concerned that Indonesia, having obtained West Irian (western New Guinea) from the Netherlands, may wish to extend farther eastward to threaten formerly Australian Papua New Guinea. Australia opposed Indonesian incorporation of formerly Portuguese East Timor, which occurred in July 1976.

There are also possibly long-term strategic implications in the growing dependence of the Australian economy on trade with Japan. In 1976 a Treaty of Friendship and Cooperation was signed with Japan.

Australia has recently become concerned about Soviet expansion in the Indian Ocean. In 1976 the new Liberal-National government began a five-year, $15 billion program to enlarge its armed forces and update their weapons.

## MILITARY ASSISTANCE

On a wholly cooperative basis, Australia exchanges students at military schools with the United Kingdom, New Zealand, Canada, and the United States, and exchanges information with these nations within existing alliances. Otherwise, Australia is not the recipient of any formal military assistance.

Australia provided $40.6 million in military assistance to both Malaysia and Singapore between 1964 and 1969. This was accomplished through training missions, by training in Australia, and by transfer of equipment.

## ALLIANCES

Australia is a member of four major overlapping alliance systems. First, as a member of the Commonwealth, Australia maintains close military ties with the United Kingdom, New Zealand, and, to a lesser extent, with Canada and other Commonwealth nations, and it is a member of the Five-Power Pact (see above).

Second, Australia has had a bilateral mutual assistance treaty with the United States since 1951. Third, there have been formal and informal cooperative bilateral defense arrangements between Australia and New Zealand, aside from their Commonwealth relationship, since World War II. Fourth, these two bilateral relationships were linked together formally in the Australia–New Zealand–United States (ANZUS) Treaty in 1952.

## ARMY

*Personnel:* 34,000 (includes about 2,500 Pacific Islands Regiment)

*Organization:*
    6 infantry battalions
    1 Pacific Islands Regiment (PIR; 2 battalions)
    1 armored regiment (tank: Leopards, Centurions)
    1 cavalry regiment, plus 2 separate cavalry
       squadrons (mechanized) (APC, scout
       and armored cars)
    1 Special Air Service Regiment (air-mobile
       commandos)

2 field artillery regiments
1 medium artillery regiment
1 light antiaircraft regiment
1 aviation regiment
4 engineer regiments
2 signal regiments
1 battalion group in ANZUK
350 men, all ranks, detached to Papua New Guinea
Defence Force

*Major Equipment Inventory:*
135 medium tanks (Centurion)
42 medium tanks (Leopard)
50 armored cars (Saladin)
265 scout cars (Ferret)
80 helicopters (Sioux, Kiowa, Jet Ranger)
25 light aircraft (Pilatus Porter)
675 APCs (M-113)
235 105mm howitzers
106mm recoilless rifle guns
antiaircraft pieces (40mm)
SAMs: Rapier, Redeye

*Reserves:* The Citizen Military Force, about 36,000 men, is available for rapid mobilization to form twenty-five additional battalions with supporting arms and services. There is also a 1,000-man Emergency Reserve Force. In addition, there are about 120,000 trained reservists.

## NAVY

*Personnel:* 16,300

*Major Units:*
6 submarines (Oxley class; SS)
1 light aircraft carrier (modified Majestic class; CVL)
3 guided missile destroyers (Perth class; DDG; Tartar SAMs)
2 destroyers (Daring class; DD)
6 frigates (River class; FF; has Seacat short-range SAMs)
3 coastal minesweepers (Ton class; MSC)
12 patrol craft (Attack class; PC; 40mm gun)
7 auxiliary ships (tankers, survey ships, etc.)
33 service craft (tenders, tugs, etc.)
6 utility landing craft (LCU)
20 Skyhawk attack aircraft
14 S-2 Tracker HS-748 ASW patrol aircraft
50 helicopters (including Wessex, Iroquois, Jet Ranger, Seal, and Wasp)
10 trainer/support aircraft (MB-236, TA-4, A-4)

*Major Naval Bases:* Sydney, Brisbane, Jervis Bay, Cairns, Darwin

*Reserves:* There are 4,330 men in the Citizen Naval Forces and 1,075 in the Emergency Reserve. In addition, there are 65–70,000 trained reservists.

## AIR FORCE

*Personnel:* 22,700

*Organization:*
Operational Command (headquarters, Sydney)
Support Command (headquarters, Melbourne)
3 fighter squadrons (Mirage III)
2 bomber squadrons (F-111)
1 light bomber reconnaissance squadron (Canberra)
2 maritime reconnaissance squadrons (P-2, P-3)
5 transport squadrons (2 C-130, 2 Caribou, 1 special transport squadron, BAC-111, C-47, HS-748)
3 helicopter squadrons (UH-1, CH-47)
1 SAM squadron (Bloodhound Mk1)

*Deployment:*
2 fighter squadrons ANZUK Force (Mirage III)

*Major Aircraft Types:*
171 combat aircraft
110 Mirage III fighters (Sidewinder AAM)
24 F-111C bombers
15 Canberra light bombers
12 P-2 Neptune patrol bombers
10 P-3 Orion maritime reconnaissance aircraft
302 other aircraft
84 Aermacchi MB-326 trainers
24 C-130 transports
22 Caribou transports
18 C-47 transports
12 miscellaneous transports (2 BAC-111, 10 HS-748)
55 helicopters (UH-1, CH-47)
87 trainer/support aircraft (CT-4, T-41)

*Major Air Bases:* Amberley, Point Cook, Bankstown, Canberra, Richmond, Tullarmarine, Woomera, Learmont, Laverton, Tindall, Darwin, East Sale, Williamtown, Fairbairn, Edinburgh, Townsville, Pearce.

*Reserves:* There are 950 men in the Citizens Air Force available for prompt mobilization, plus about 580 in the Emergency Reserve. In addition, there are about 45,000 trained reservists.

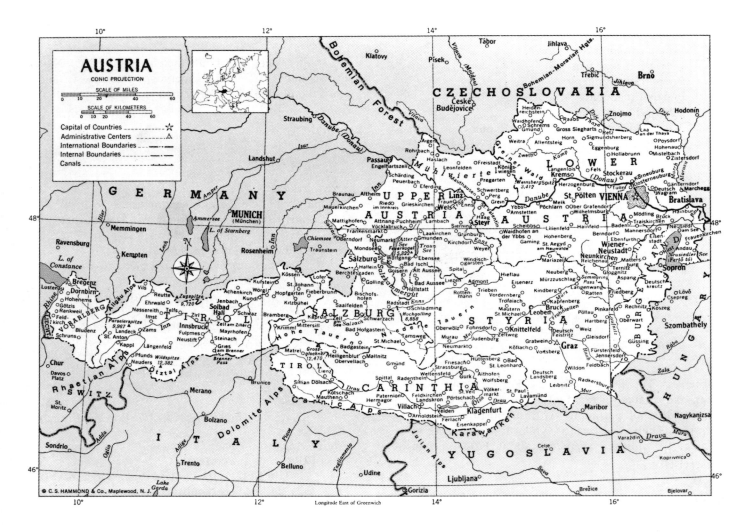

# AUSTRIA

## Republic of Austria

### POWER POTENTIAL STATISTICS

Area: 32,374 square miles

Population: 7,511,000

Total Active Regular Armed Forces: 37,000 (0.49%
population)

Gross National Product: $47.8 billion ($6,360 per capita)

Annual Military Expenditures: $529 million (1.12%
GNP)

Crude Steel Production: 4.9 million metric tons

Iron Ore Production: 3.9 million metric tons

Fuel Production:

Crude Oil: 2 million metric tons

Refined Petroleum Products: 10 million metric tons

Natural Gas: 2.1 billion cubic meters

Lignite: 3.2 million metric tons

Electric Power Output: 38.3 billion kwh

Nuclear Power Production: 700 megawatts

Merchant Fleet (Ships 1,000 tons and over): 14 ships;
59,000 gross tons

Civil Air Fleet: 14 jet and 2 piston transport aircraft

### DEFENSE STRUCTURE

The federal president nominally controls the armed
forces. Supreme administrative and operational authority
is exercised by the federal secretary of defense.

### POLITICO-MILITARY POLICY

The Austrian State Treaty, effective July 27, 1955,
ended the post–World War II four-power occupation and
gave full sovereignty to the Republic of Austria. Under the
treaty, Austria is prohibited from possessing nuclear or
other major offensive weapons. Austria's declaration of

permanent neutrality, made into law October 26, 1955, provides that Austria will never join any military alliance and will not permit the establishment of any foreign military base on its territory.

The armed forces are maintained by conscription. Service is for six months, followed by sixty days of reservist training and an additional thirty to ninety days of training for reservists in certain specialities.

## STRATEGIC PROBLEMS

Austria's size and location, the provisions of the state treaty, the declaration of permanent neutrality, and the federal Constitution (which commits the country to the principle of "comprehensive national defense") all dictate a strictly defensive military and strategic posture. Standing forces and militia forces are provided for effective crisis management, for fulfilling the obligations arising from Austria's neutral status, and for repelling direct military aggression. In 1972 reforms of the Austrian army's organization and deployment were initiated, with the aim of putting into effect a defense concept specifically designed to meet Austria's strategic position.

It must be noted that Austria's limited national space and military forces would make it difficult to resist full-scale aggression from the north or east. The mountainous terrain of the southern border would make effective defense there possible for at least a limited time. There is little risk of internal subversion.

## MILITARY ASSISTANCE

Between 1955 and 1977 Austria received $97.6 million in U.S. military assistance. The MAP in 1977, provided $24,000 and trained 429 students. Some air force training assistance is provided by Sweden.

## ALLIANCES

Military alliances are not permitted by the declaration of permanent neutrality. Austria is a member of EFTA and an associate member of the Common Market.

## ARMY

*Personnel:* 33,000, including 18,000 conscripts. (In addition, there are some 70,000 reservists called up for reserve training at some time during the year.)

*Organization:*
1 army headquarters
1 mechanized division
   3 mechanized brigades
2 corps

   9 territorial commands
     3 infantry brigades
     4 infantry regiments (to form 4 infantry brigades after mobilization)
     1 river boat group (supporting engineers)

*Major Equipment Inventory:*
270 medium tanks
   120 M-60
   150 M-47
150 Kuerassier tank destroyers
460 Saurer APC
108 105mm howitzers
 38 M-109 self-propelled 155mm gun-howitzers
 22 155mm SFK M-2 field guns
 24 155mm howitzers
 18 130mm rocket launchers
300 88mm mortars
100 107mm heavy mortars
 82 120mm heavy mortars
 70 35mm Oerlikon antiaircraft guns; Super Bat/ Skyguard air defense system
300 20mm Oerlikon antiaircraft guns
 60 40mm Bofors antiaircraft guns
240 85mm antitank guns
400 106mm recoilless antitank rifles
  1 river patrol boat (PBR; 20mm gun; 11 more planned)
 11 river launches

*Reserves:*
113,000:  4 reserve brigades
         16 territorial regiments
          4 territorial battalions of Landwehr (militia)
800,000 trained reservists available

## AIR FORCE

(Austrian air units, an integral part of the army, are listed separately for purposes of comparison.)

*Personnel:* 4,000, including 2,000 conscripts

*Organization:*
1 air division
   1 battalion headquarters
   3 air regiments
   1 radar regiment
   1 school wing

*Major Aircraft Types:*
 30 combat aircraft (Saab 105 OE fighter-bombers)
139 other aircraft

25 trainers (7 Saab 105 OE, 18 Saab-Safir)
74 helicopters (23 AB-204B, 13 AB-206A, 24 Alouette III, 12 OH-58B, 2 S-650E)
40 transports (23 Cessna L19, 3 Beaver L-20, 2 Skyvan, 12 Turbo Porters)

*Deployment:* Cyprus (UNFICYP): 1 infantry battalion (300 men); Syria (UNDOF): 1 infantry battalion (500 men); Force Commander (UNDOF); headquarters personnel (UNFICYP, UNDOF) and observers (UNTSO)

*Major Air Bases:* Langenlebarn, Hoersching/Linz, Zeltweg, Wiener Neustadt, Algen-Ennstal, and Graz-Thalerhof

# BAHAMAS

## Commonwealth of the Bahamas

### POWER POTENTIAL STATISTICS

Area: 4,404 square miles (land area)
Population: 229,000
Gross National Product: $758 million ($3,510 per capita)
Fuel Production:
    Refined Petroleum Products: 8.8 million metric tons
    Electric Power Output: 680 million kwh
Civil Air Fleet: 7 major transport aircraft

### POLITICO-MILITARY POLICIES AND POSTURE

The Bahamas is an archipelago of 700 islands, only 40 of which are inhabited. It became an independent nation under the Commonwealth on July 10, 1973. Britain continues to be responsible for external defense and internal security. There is no military force; the police force numbers about 900 and includes nine patrol boats (PB). There are U.S. missile tracking stations and U.S. Navy and Coast Guard installations, including a navy underwater research and development center.

# BANGLADESH

## People's Republic of Bangladesh

### POWER POTENTIAL STATISTICS

Area: 55,126 square miles
Population: 86,931,000

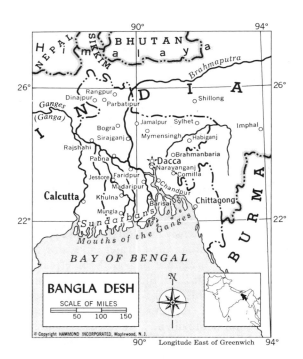

Total Active Regular Armed Forces: 34,000 (0.04% population)
Gross National Product: $7.2 billion ($90 per capita)
Military Expenditures: $145 million (2.0% GNP)
Crude Steel Production: 89,000 metric tons
Fuel Production:
    Refined Petroleum Products: 1.15 million metric tons
    Electric Power Output: 1.6 billion kwh
Merchant Fleet (ships 1,000 tons and over): 24 ships; 213,000 tons
Civil Air Fleet: 9 major transport aircraft

### POLITICO-MILITARY POLICIES AND POSTURE

Control of the government and the armed forces is exercised by the president (and chief martial law administrator), Gen. Zia ur Rahman. Though the armed forces have been divided in the past, they now appear united in supporting President Zia's course of gradual relaxation of martial law and restoration of democracy. The principal internal threat comes from dissident followers of the former prime minister, Sheikh Mujubur Rahman, and some of those who served as irregulars in the 1971 civil war.

Relations between Bangladesh and Pakistan have improved since the latter recognized the former's existence in February 1974. Relations between Bangladesh and India are correct, but disputes over division of the flow of the Ganges may cloud future relations. The pressure of

Muslim refugees from Burma, driven into Bangladesh from Arakan State in the spring of 1978, has soured relations between Bangladesh and Burma, although it is doubtful that this will lead to open conflict.

## ARMY

*Personnel:* 27,500

*Organization:*
    8 infantry brigades (each with 3 battalions)
    3 artillery regiments
    1 tank regiment
      engineer and signal corps support troops

*Major Equipment Inventory:*
    T-54 medium tanks
    105 mm howitzers, 25-pounder gun/howitzers
    81mm, 120mm mortars
    106mm recoilless rifles

## NAVY

*Personnel:* 3,500

*Major Equipment Inventory:*
    2 frigates (1 Salisbury class, 1 Leopard class; FF)
    4 patrol craft (PC: 40mm + guns)
    5 river patrol boats (PBR: 40mm + guns)
    1 training ship (armed with 40mm + guns)

*Naval Bases:* Chittagong, Kulna, Dacca, Kaptai, Juldia

## AIR FORCE

*Personnel:* 3,000

*Organization:*
    1 fighter squadron (MiG-21)
    1 helicopter squadron (Alouette III, Mi-8)
    1 transport squadron (An-24, An-26, F-27, Yak-40)

*Major Aircraft Types:*
    12 combat aircraft
      12 MiG-21 fighters
    15 other aircraft
      6 transports (1 An-24, 2 An-26, 2 F-27, 1 Yak-40)
      9 helicopters (6 Alouette III, 3 Mi-8)

*Airbase:* Tezgaon (Dacca)

# BARBADOS

## POWER POTENTIAL STATISTICS

    Area: 166 square miles
    Population: 260,000
    Gross National Product: $440 million ($1,840 per capita)
    Electric Power Output: 220 million kwh
    Civil Air Fleet: 6 major transport aircraft

## POLITICO-MILITARY POLICIES AND POSTURE

Barbados, the easternmost of the West Indies, is an independent, sovereign state within the Commonwealth. Although relatively stable economically and socially, the island has one of the densest populations in the world and a high annual birth rate. The island is a member of the OAS. Barbados agreed in March 1978 to participate in a multination guarantee of the territorial integrity of Belize.

Barbados has no regular military force, but maintains its own militia Territorial Force, the Barbados Regiment, consisting of one battalion equipped with light arms. There are four patrol boats (PB) for Coast Guard air/sea rescue duties. One former U.S. LST is used as a commercial ship. Internal security is provided by a police force of 675 men.

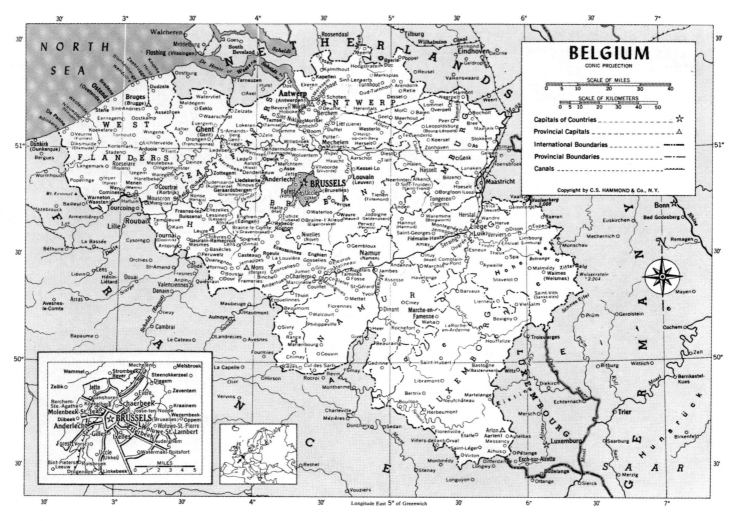

## BELGIUM

### Kingdom of Belgium

## POWER POTENTIAL STATISTICS

Area: 11,779 square miles

Population: 9,842,000

Total Active Regular Armed Forces: 95,700 (0.97% population)

Gross National Product: $79 billion ($8,040 per capita)

Annual Military Expenditures: $2.3 billion (2.9% GNP)

Crude Steel Production: 12 million metric tons

Fuel Production:

   Refined Petroleum Products:* 31.3 million metric tons

   Coal: 7.2 million metric tons

   Manufactured Gas: 2.5 billion cubic meters

Electric Power Output: 47.1 billion kwh

Nuclear Power Production: 3,500 megawatts

Merchant Fleet (ships 1,000 tons and over): 78 ships, 1.6 million gross tons

Civil Air Fleet: 55 major transport aircraft

## DEFENSE STRUCTURE

Constitutionally the armed forces are commanded by the king. Overall responsibility for the formulation of defense policy in a parliamentary government is exercised by the prime minister and his cabinet; specific defense decisions are made by the Ministerial Committee of Defense, over which the prime minister presides. Implementation of these decisions is the responsibility of the defense minister, who is assisted by a military staff system under the direction of the chief of the General Staff.

There are four armed forces—army, navy, air force, and gendarmerie. There are three elements within the integrated staff echelon of the armed forces: (1) The

*Belgium and Luxembourg

General Staff, which in turn has two echelons: a conventional, integrated general staff which coordinates the planning of the next echelon of separate army, navy, and air force general staffs; (2) The Gendarmerie General Staff, responsible for interior order; (3) The Central Administration, to provide administrative support to the operational forces. The operational echelon of the defense establishment includes the principal commands of the four services, the military instruction establishments, and the scientific establishments.

## POLITICO-MILITARY POLICY

Because traditional policy of neutrality proved unreliable protection against aggression in two world wars, Belgium has been a leading exponent of collective security since 1945. Belgium is a member of the Western European Union established by the Treaty of Brussels in 1948, and was one of the twelve original members of NATO. Belgium's basic defense policy is that of NATO: to prevent war through the deterrent effect of the common efforts of neighbors; if that fails, to defend the common territory by joint military action. The nation's convictions in this regard are demonstrated by the fact that all Belgian armed forces, except those required for internal security, have been fully integrated into NATO forces, and most are deployed in West Germany under NATO command. Further evidence is the fact that Belgium has provided lodgement for the seat of the NATO Council, and for the principal NATO military headquarters: Allied Command Europe.

Manpower for the armed forces is provided by a combination of long-term enlistment and conscription. Regular enlisted men, with terms of service varying from two to five years, make up about half of the army, two-thirds of the navy, and four-fifths of the air force. The remainder are conscripts. A new policy announced in 1973 makes it mandatory that Belgian NATO units be all volunteer. Draftees are to serve six months only, and only on homeguard assignments.

## STRATEGIC PROBLEMS

As demonstrated in two world wars, Belgium is vulnerable to invasion from all directions, with some natural security provided only by the short seacoast in the northwest and the rugged, forested Ardennes Mountains in the southeast. Some additional defensive capability is provided by the lines of the Meuse and Schelde rivers and many canals, and the potentiality for flooding extensive regions of the western portion of the country. Belgian space is so limited, however, that these natural and man-made obstacles can impose little delay upon the forces of a powerful aggressor. This is adequate reason for Belgium's adherence to the NATO strategic concept.

An internal stability problem is created by the ethnic and emotional division of the country between Dutch-speaking Flemings (about 55 percent of the population) and French-speaking Walloons (about 33 percent). About 11 percent are bilingual. Constitutional reforms in 1971 provided that the ministries be divided equally between the two groups. There have been mass demonstrations—and resulting injuries—by militants in the past, most recently in 1975 by Flemish-speaking demonstrators in Brussels against practices in the capital they claimed were anti-Flemish. However, the nationalist movements have been free of terrorism. In 1978 the government accepted a plan that would make Belgium a federated state by the mid-1980s. It would consist of two communities, French-speaking and Flemish-speaking, and three political-economic regions—Flanders, Wallonia, and Brussels.

The Communist party is weak and divided, and offers little threat of internal subversion.

## MILITARY ASSISTANCE

From 1950 to 1977 Belgium received $1.24 billion in military assistance from the United States. A U.S. Military Assistance and Advisory Group has provided training assistance to the Belgian armed forces in employment of American equipment. Students trained under MAP numbered 118.

Since 1960 Belgium has provided substantial military assistance to its former colonies, Zaire, Burundi, and Rwanda, at the request of their governments. While military assistance to Burundi ended in 1973, Belgian military cooperation with Zaire and Rwanda continues, concentrating on military training. This policy is reflected in military assistance expenditures of $7 million for 1974; military missions include 127 army and six gendarmerie officers and men for Zaire and 46 army and six gendarmerie officers and men for Rwanda; a total of 750 months of military training courses in Belgium for military personnel of Zaire and Rwanda is to be provided; and limited logistical support was to be provided to Rwanda only. In 1978, when rebels based in Angola invaded Zaire's Shaba Province and massacres of Europeans there were reported, Belgium cooperated with France in the rescue of about 2,500 Europeans from the area, contributing 1,750 troops to the operation.

## ALLIANCES

Belgium is a member of Western European Union, of BENELUX, of the European Common Market, and of NATO.

## ARMY

*Personnel:* 71,500

*Organization:*
    1 army corps (assigned to the Central European Command of NATO's Allied Command Europe—ACE)
    4 mechanized or armored brigades, forming 2 divisions (assigned to NATO)
    1 parachute-commando regiment (one battalion assigned to ACE Mobile Force)
    2 SSM battalions (Honest John)
    2 SAM battalions (Hawk)
    3 helicopter squadrons
    1 fixed-wing/helicopter mixed squadron
    3 infantry battalions for territorial defense (not assigned to NATO)
     logistical support units
    3 artillery battalions

*Major Equipment Inventory:*
    400 Leopard and M-47 medium tanks
    200 Scorpion, M-41, AMX-13 light tanks
    120 Striker with Swingfire antitank weapons
  1,200 M-75, AMX-VTP Spartan APCs
    120 Scimitar with 30mm Rarden cannon
     105mm, 155mm howitzers
     M-109 self-propelled 155mm howitzers
     M-44 self-propelled 155mm howitzers
     203mm howitzers
     M-108 self-propelled 105mm howitzers
     20mm, 40mm, 57mm antiaircraft guns

*Reserves:* Approximately 120,000 men, organized in two rapidly mobilizable brigades (one mechanized, one motorized), plus independent territorial defense battalions and logistical support units. (About 300,000 additional trained men are available for mobilization.)

## NAVY

The navy is essentially a minesweeping force, earmarked mostly for NATO's Channel Command, partly for coastal minesweeping.

*Personnel:* 4,200

*Major Units:*
    4 frigates (E-71 class; FF; Sea Sparrow SAM; Exocet SSM)
    7 minehunters (MSH)
    6 coastal minesweepers (MSC)
   14 inshore minesweepers (MSI)
    6 river patrol boats (PBR)
    6 auxiliary ships (research, transport, etc.)
   12 service craft (tugs, launches, etc.)
    4 helicopters (S-58 and Alouette III)

*Major naval bases:* Ostend, Zeebrugge, Nieupoort, Kallo

## AIR FORCE

All air force units except one transport squadron are assigned to NATO Allied Command Europe (ACE).

*Personnel:* 20,000

*Organization:*
    2 all-weather fighter squadrons (F-104)
    5 fighter-bomber squadrons (2 F-104, 3 Mirage 5)
    1 transport wing (1 tactical squadron of C-130s, 1 communications squadron of B-727, HS-728, Merlin IIIA, and Falcon 20)
    2 SAM wings (8 squadrons based in West Germany; 72 Nike-Hercules)
    1 tactical reconnaissance squadron (Mirage 5)
    1 helicopter flight (HSS-1)

*Major Aircraft Types:*
   210 combat aircraft
      90 F-104 fighters
     120 Mirage 5 fighters, fighter-bombers, fighter/reconnaissance aircraft
     Equipment on Order: F-16, Alpha Jet
   200 other aircraft
      12 C-130 transports
       2 Falcon 20 transports
      B-727 transports
      H-748 transports
      Merlin IIIA transports
      miscellaneous trainer/support aircraft
      11 HSS-1 helicopters

*Air Bases:* Beauvechain, Kleine Brohel, Florennes, Brustem, Koksyde, Bierset

## PARAMILITARY

National Gendarmerie: 15,000 men with 30 helicopters and light armored cars FN-4RM/62.

# BENIN

## People's Republic of Benin

### POWER POTENTIAL STATISTICS

Area: 43,383 square miles
Population: 3,333,000
Total Active Regular Armed Forces: 1,750 (0.05% population)
Gross National Product: $660 million ($200 per capita)

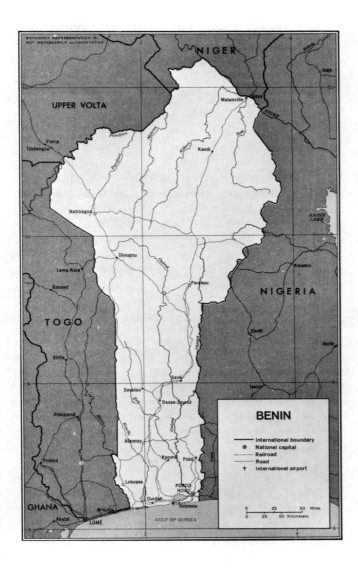

independence, a defense agreement was signed which provided for French assistance in maintaining internal security, base rights, and arms and training. France renewed its defense arrangements, albeit at reduced levels of aid, in December 1976. Despite constant anti-Western rhetoric, Benin continues to rely on commerce with France. Nationalization of foreign interests following the 1972 coup has discouraged foreign investors. Benin has not established particularly close relations with the Soviet bloc, although it has backed both the MPLA in Angola and the Polisario in Western Sahara. Benin's relations with Ivory Coast, Gabon, and Morocco are strained, following a brief and bizarre airborne raid into Benin in 1977. Benin belongs to the OAU, OCAM, *Conseil de l'Entente,* and the Economic Community of West African States.

Benin's weak economy and dense population were responsible for its dependence on France for an annual budget subsidy. Internal security problems have come mainly from tribal-regional divisions among politicians, civil servants, and the army. Three power centers exist: Abomey in the southwest, Porto-Novo in the southeast, and the politically and economically undeveloped north. There were six presidents in the first turbulent decade of independence, with the army playing the principal role in their selection and ousting. As of mid-1978, the Kerekou regime has survived five coup attempts. Large numbers of exiles live in Togo and France, while an active opposition group has offices in France, Ivory Coast, Gabon, and Senegal.

The army numbers about 1,750 men, organized into three infantry battalions. Voluntary enlistments are for eighteen months. Arms and equipment are mainly French and include a few armored cars. There is no navy, but about 100 army personnel man three patrol craft used for port control at Cotonou. The air force, part of the army, is 110 men strong, and operates one C-47 transport, one light transport, two liaison aircraft and one Alouette II helicopter. There is a gendarmerie of 1,200 men organized into eight companies.

Annual Military Expenditures: $10.9 million (1.65% GNP)
Electric Power Output: 55 million kwh
Civil Air Fleet : 1 major transport aircraft

## POLITICO-MILITARY POLICIES AND POSTURE

On October 26, 1972, an army junta headed by Maj. (now Lt. Col.) Mathieu Kerekou seized power. Control of the country is now firmly in the hands of President Kerekou and his Benin People's Revolutionary Party (PRPB). The PRPB is to be the vanguard of social revolution and is organized on Marxist-Leninist lines with a Central Committee and six-member Political Bureau. Kerekou heads both and acts as minister of defense. He has replaced most military men with civilians in the government in an attempt to broaden support.

Dahomey—renamed Benin in 1975—received its independence from France in 1960; initially, its armed forces consisted of former soldiers in the French army. Upon

# BHUTAN
## Kingdom of Bhutan

### POWER POTENTIAL STATISTICS

Area: 19,305 square miles
Population, 1,282,000
Total Active Regular Armed Forces: 4,000 (0.31% population)
Gross National Product: $90 million ($70 per capita)
Annual Military Expenditures: Unknown
Electric Power Output: 8 million kwh

## POLITICO-MILITARY POLICIES AND POSTURE

The Kingdom of Bhutan occupies a position of considerable strategic importance to both China and India because of its passes through the Himalayas, leading to Tibet in the north and debouching into the swampy lowlands north of the Brahmaputra River in the south.

India succeeded to the U.K. role of protecting power with Indian independence in 1947. In this role, India is providing military assistance: training the army of some 4,000 regulars and 15,000 militia, and building roads from India into the interior of Bhutan, as well as constructing an airfield at Paro, with auxiliary airfields elsewhere. Military service is obligatory for all males; liability extends from age eighteen to fifty.

# BOLIVIA

## Republic of Bolivia

## POWER POTENTIAL STATISTICS

Area: 424,162 square miles
Population: 5,149,000
Total Active Regular Armed Forces: 23,300 (0.45% population)
Gross National Product: $3.5 billion ($730 per capita)

Annual Military Expenditures: $90 million (2.57% GNP)
Fuel Production:
 Crude Oil: 1.94 million metric tons
 Refined Petroleum Products: 983,000 metric tons
Electric Power Output: 1.1 billion kwh
Civil Air Fleet: 48 major transport aircraft

## DEFENSE STRUCTURE

The president is ex-officio captain-general of the armed forces, which consist of an army, an air force, and a small semiautonomous river and lake force under a flag officer. He presides over a Supreme Council of National Defense and appoints the service commanders as well as the commander in chief of the armed forces. Administrative responsibility for the armed forces is in the hands of the minister of national defense.

## POLITICO-MILITARY POLICIES

Bolivia's history has been one of political unrest and repeated changes of government, with the military frequently involved. In 1964 a military government headed by Gen. Rene Barrientos deposed a revolution-imposed civilian government. After the death of Barrientos in an air accident in 1969, coup followed coup until 1971, when left-leaning Gen. Juan J. Torres was overthrown by a coalition of the military, the *Movimiento Nacionalista Revolucionaria* (MNR), and the *Falange Socialista Boliviana* (FSB), under Col. Hugo Banzer Suarez.

Food shortages and inflation caused increasing unrest, and Banzer tightened military controls. Miners' strikes in 1976 led to declaration of a state of siege and temporary proscription of the Miners' Federation. Elections of a new government, originally promised for 1974, were finally held in July 1978. The results were annulled, however, following exposure of widespread fraud. Still another coup (the 188th in 153 years) forced Banzer to turn over power to a military junta of the commanders of the army, air force, and navy, who in turn swore in as president Gen. Juan Pereda Asbun, who had been Banzer's candidate in the elections. After two more coups (November 1978 and November 1979) and an indecisive election (July 1979), Bolivia's first woman president was elected by the Congress in November 1979.

All male citizens between nineteen and forty-nine are subject to conscription, but in practice the size of the armed services is limited by Congressional appropriations.

Government decrees in 1972 established the Armed Forces Development Corporation, which gave the military a more active role in most areas of the economy, including mining, agriculture, and industry. Exploitation of the copper deposits in the Oruro region was a first concern.

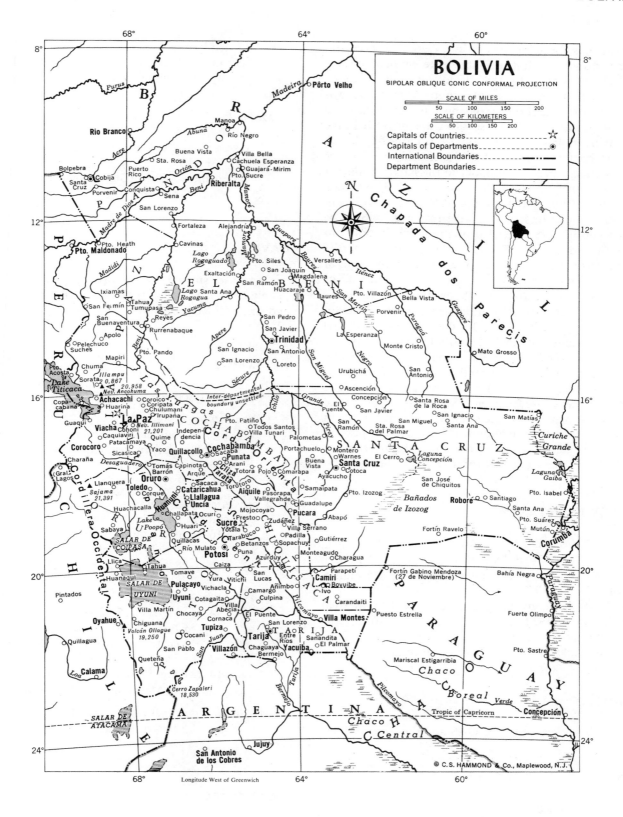

# BOLIVIA

BIPOLAR OBLIQUE CONIC CONFORMAL PROJECTION

SCALE OF MILES
0  50  100  150  200

SCALE OF KILOMETERS
0  50  100  150  200

Capitals of Countries ............................ ☆
Capitals of Departments ..................... ◉
International Boundaries ....................
Department Boundaries ....................

68°  64°  60°

8°  8°

12°  12°

16°  16°

20°  20°

24°  24°

68°  Longitude West of Greenwich  64°  60°

© C.S. HAMMOND & Co., Maplewood, N.J.

**Brazil**
Pôrto Velho
Manoa
Rio Branco
Abuná
Río Negro
Buena Vista
Sta. Rosa
Villa Bella
Cachuela Esperanza
Guajará-Mirim
Pto. Sucre
Bolpebra
Puerto Rico
Cobija
Santa Cruz
Porvenir
Conquista
Sena
Riberalta
San Lorenzo
Pto. Heath
Fortaleza
Alejandría
Versalles
Pto. Maldonado
Cavinas
Lago Rogaguado
Pto. Siles
San Joaquín
Magdalena
Madidi
Exaltación
San Ramón
Huacaraje
Baures
Pto. Villazón
Bella Vista
Ixiamas
Lago Rogagua
Santa Ana
Porvenir
San Feimin
Tahua Tumupasa
Reyes
Yacuma
San Pedro
San Javier
La Esperanza
Monte Cristo
Mato Grosso
San Buenaventura
Rurrenabaque
Apolo
Pto. Pando
San Ignacio
Trinidad
San Antonio
San Lorenzo
Loreto
Urubichá
San Antonio
Pelechuco
Suches
Mapiri
Apere
Sécure
Ascención
Concepción
Santa Rosa de la Roca
Pto. Acosta
Chuma
Sorata
Illampu 20,958
Nev. Ancohuma
Inter-departmental boundary unsettled
El Puente
San Javier
San Ignacio
San Matías
Copacabana
Achacachi
Coroico
Coripata
Chulumani
Irupana
Pto. Patiño
Grande
Concepción
Santa Rosa del Palmar
San Miguel
Santa Ana
Curiche Grande
Huarina
Todos Santos
Villa Tunari
Palometas
San Ramón
Lake Titicaca
La Paz
Nev. Illimani 21,201
Independencia
Portachuelo
Montero
Warnes
Laguna Concepción
Guaqui
Viacha
Caquiaviri
Quime
Buena Vista
Santa Cruz
Laguna Gaiba
Corocoro
Patacamaya
Sicasica
Yaco
Quillacollo
Cochabamba
Punata
Arani
Totora
Pojo
Cómarapa
Ayacucho
Cotoca
San José de Chiquitos
Pto. Isabel
Charaña
Desaguadero
Tomás Capinota
Arque
Samaipata
Pto. Izozog
Santa Ana
Gral. Lagos
Barrón
Tarata
Cliza
Toro Toro
Aiquile
Pasorapa
Vallegrande
Guadalupe
Abapó
Bañados de Izozog
Roboré
Santiago
Pto. Suárez
Llanquera
Oruro
Sacaca
Pucara
Mutún
Toledo
Corque
Challapata
Ocuri
Prestos
Mojocoya
Zudáñez
Fortín Ravelo
Corumbá
Huachacalla
Huari
Sucre
Yotala
Villa Serrano
Sajama 21,391
Lake Poopó
Tarabuco
Padilla
Sopachuy
Gutiérrez
Sabaya
Quillacas
Betanzos
Puna
Monteagudo
Charagua
Salar de Coipasa
Río Mulato
Potosí
Azurduy
Parapetí
Fortín Gabino Mendoza (27 de Noviembre)
Bahía Negra
Llica
Caiza
Tahua
Tomave
Yura
San Lucas
Camiri
Puesto Estrella
Huanaqui
Vitichi
Bovuibe
Fuerte Olimpo
Pintados
Salar de Uyuni
Pulacayo
Vichacla
Camargo
Ivo
Carandaiti
Villa Martín
Uyuni
Cotagaita
Culpina
Pilcomayo
Oyahue
Chocaya
Villa Abecia
El Puente
Villa Montes
Cornaca
San Lorenzo
Pto. Sastre
Chiguana
Tupiza
Mariscal Estigarribia
Quillagua
Volcán Ollague 19,250
Cocani
San Juan
Tarija
Entre Ríos
Sanandita
El Palmar
Chaco Boreal
Quetena
San Pablo
Villazón
Chaguaya
Yacuiba
Bermejo
Verde
Concepción
Loa
Calama
Cerro Zapaleri 18,530
Tropic of Capricorn
Pto. Sastre
Salar de Atacama
ARGENTINA
Chaco Central
Jujuy
San Antonio de los Cobres

**PERU**
Purus
Madeira
Acre
Ortón
Beni
Madre de Dios
Mamoré
Guaporé
Iténez
San Martín
Paraguá
Guaporé
Chapada dos Parecis
Iténez
Baures
Negro
San Miguel
Ichilo
Grande
Piray
Mamoré
Las Yungas
Cordillera Oriental
COCHABAMBA
SANTA CRUZ
EL BENI
PANDO
Cordillera Occidental
CHICHAS
CHUQUISACA
TARIJA
PARAGUAY
Pilcomayo
Pilaya
Tarija
Bermejo
San Juan
CHILE

## STRATEGIC PROBLEMS

Bolivia has been involved in several unsuccessful boundary disputes with its neighbors. Resentment at these losses is still strong. In 1884 it lost its only seaport, Antofagasta, to Chile. Recent reports that Chile was considering offering Bolivia the port of Arica aroused feelings in Peru, which had lost it to Chile in 1884. In the Chaco War, Bolivia lost not only most of the Chaco, reputed to contain some oil, but also its only port on the Paraguay River, an indirect outlet to the Atlantic. Earlier it had lost other areas to Peru and Brazil. Diplomatic relations with Chile were broken in 1962 over use of water of the Rio Lauca. In 1975 ties were resumed, only to be broken again in 1978, when negotiations for an outlet to the Pacific broke down. Troops were sent to the border area. In 1973 after Brazil took over a small strip of territory in Santa Cruz, there were reported threats of Brazilian expansion across the Abuna River, which forms Bolivia's northern boundary in the department of Pando.

Bolivia today has little need for concern about external aggression because of its high altitude and the natural defense barriers of the Andes Mountains. Internally, however, there remain substantial threats. The major center of opposition is in the tin-mining region, where strikes and violence are frequent. The miners are organized in a now unofficial people's militia, often turbulent and subject to leftist manipulation. A similar peasant militia is more generally supportive of orderly government. Guerrillas have been active in rural areas.

## MILITARY ASSISTANCE

United States military missions have been in Bolivia since 1942. In 1977 Bolivia received $1.65 million in U.S. grant-aid programs, making a total of $38.6 million between 1950 and 1977.

Brazil has been giving assistance to Bolivia in road building, and in 1972 it provided eight aircraft for the Bolivian military aviation college.

Bolivian students trained under MAP total 4,437.

## ALLIANCES

Bolivia is a member of the OAS and the Andean Pact.

## ARMY

*Personnel:* 20,000

*Organization:*
    2 infantry brigades

    2 motorized regiments
    1 paratroop regiment
    5 artillery regiments
    2 ranger battalions trained in antiguerrilla warfare
    5 engineer combat-construction battalions, largely used in civic action

*Major Equipment Inventory:*
    M-113 APCs
    M-3A scout oars, Commando armored cars, M-2 half-tracks
    light artillery, and 105mm howitzers and mortars
    57mm recoilless rifles

## NAVY

Comprises small 1,500-man patrol units with approximately 22 active river patrol boats (PBR) on Lake Titicaca and the Beni River. Another 14 PBR inactive.

## AIR FORCE

*Personnel:* 1,800

*Organization:*
    1 fighter-bomber squadron (F-51, T-33, F-86)
    1 counterinsurgency squadron (COIN T-28, T-25)
    1 transport squadron (C-47, C-54, Convair 440, C-130)

*Major Aircraft Types:*
  47 combat aircraft
    16 fighter-bomber/trainer (T-33, F-86)
    12 F-51 fighter-bombers
     6 T-28 armed trainers (COIN)
    13 T-25 Neiva
 123 other aircraft
    54 transports (15 C-47, 5 C-45, 2 C-54, 4 Convair 440, 2 C-130, 6 IAI-201, 1 Learjet, 1 Porter, PC-6, 18 F-23)
    32 trainers (6 T-41, 18 T-23, 8 Fokker S-11)
    14 helicopters (Hughes 500 M, 2 UH-1)
    25 utility and liaison (U-17, U-3)

*Major Air Bases:* La Paz, El Trompillo, Charana, Colcapima, Santa Cruz, La Florida, El Tejar, Puerto Suarez

## PARAMILITARY

The armed Corps of National Police and Carabineros numbers about 5,000.

# BOTSWANA

## Republic of Botswana

### POWER POTENTIAL STATISTICS

Area: 220,000 square miles
Population: 760,000
Total Active Regular Armed Forces: 400 (0.05%
  population)
Gross National Product: $300 million ($395 per capita)
Fuel Production: Coal 69,000 metric tons
Electric Power Output: 85 million kwh
Civil Air Fleet: 2 major transport aircraft

### POLITICO-MILITARY POLICIES AND POSTURE

Botswana is one of the few functioning multiparty democracies in black Africa. The elected president is chief of state, head of government, and commander in chief of the armed force. The police until 1977 were the only armed force, directly controlled by the minister for home affairs, who, like the other cabinet members, is appointed by the president from the Legislative Assembly. A Defense Force was set up in March 1977.

Formerly the British Protectorate of Bechuanaland, Botswana became independent in 1966. The last British troops left a year later. Botswana's defense then depended upon its police force, on whatever collective security might be afforded by membership in the UN, the Common-wealth, and the OAU, and on its continued good relations with Rhodesia and South Africa.

Botswana's politico-military posture is dominated by the tension between its economic dependence on South Africa and its political stands against apartheid and for majority rule in Rhodesia. In addition to the 30,000 or more Botswana temporary workers employed in South Africa, most of its export income derives from livestock shipped through South Africa. The two countries are further linked in the South African Customs Union. Botswana accepted several hundred refugees from the 1976 Soweto rioting in South Africa but continues to refuse to allow any South African rebel groups to use Botswana as a base.

Botswana's main security problem in the late 1970s is its northeastern border with Rhodesia. Botswana pursued an active diplomatic role against the Smith regime in Rhodesia as one of the five "front-line" states. In 1976 and 1977, when hundreds of Rhodesian refugees began entering the country, Botswana was subjected to frequent raids by Rhodesian security forces. Rhodesia has accused Botswana of harboring guerrillas from the Zambia-based Zimbabwe African People's Union. In response to these raids, Botswana began formation of a Defense Force. The country remains vulnerable, however, to invasion by either South Africa or Rhodesia.

Despite its weak economy, Botswana is fairly stable. The people are mostly Bantu, living in closely related tribal groupings. The party in power is moderate. Three minor opposition parties are all left-wing, Pan-African, and have ties with the African nationalist parties of South Africa, but have little popular support. The only major divisive issue is Tswana impatience at the continued presence of relatively wealthy white expatriates in the private and public sectors.

# BRAZIL

## Federative Republic of Brazil

### POWER POTENTIAL STATISTICS

Area: 3,286,470 square miles
Population: 122,602,000
Total Active Regular Armed Forces: 211,500 (0.17%
  population)
Gross National Product: $163 billion ($1,450 per capita)
Annual Military Expenditures: $2.15 billion (1.56%
  GNP)
Crude Steel Production: 9.1 million metric tons
Iron Ore Production: 66.6 million metric tons

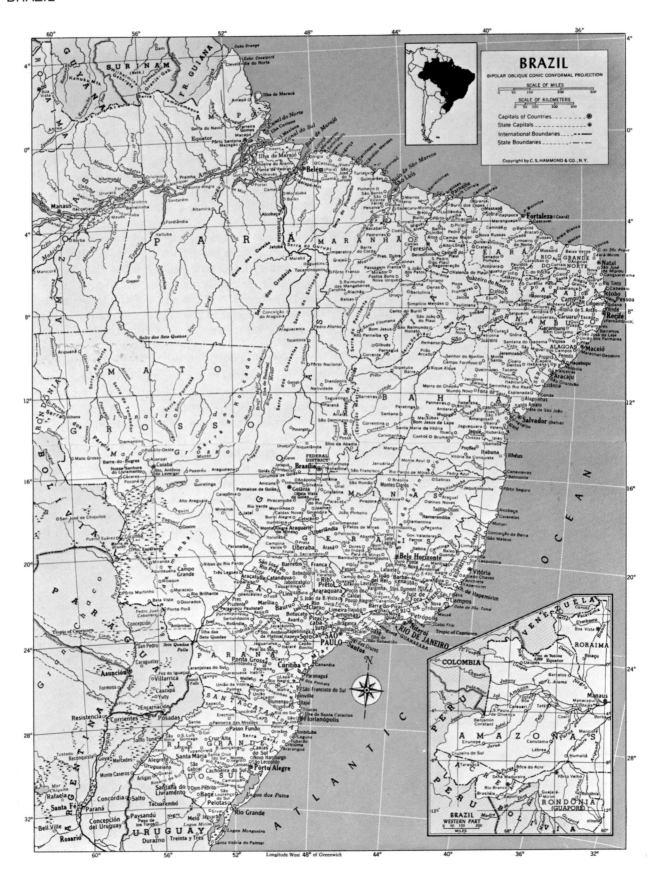

BRAZIL
BIPOLAR OBLIQUE CONIC CONFORMAL PROJECTION

SCALE OF MILES
0    50    100        200        300

SCALE OF KILOMETERS
0   50   100      200      300

Capitals of Countries . . . . . . . . ⊛
State Capitals . . . . . . . . . . . . ⊛
International Boundaries . . _ . . _ . .
State Boundaries . . . . . . . . . . _ . . _

Copyright by C.S. HAMMOND & CO., N.Y.

Fuel Production:
    Crude Oil: 8.5 million metric tons
    Refined Petroleum Products: 47.6 million metric tons
    Coal: 2.7 million metric tons
    Natural Gas: 1.6 billion cubic meters
Electric Power Output: 85 billion kwh
Nuclear Power Production: 600 megawatts
Merchant Fleet (ships 1,000 tons and over): 277 ships;
    3.45 million gross tons
Civil Air Fleet: 118 major transport aircraft

## DEFENSE STRUCTURE

The president of Brazil is supreme commander of the armed forces, with the assistance of a National Security Council, an Armed Forces General Staff, ministries of war, navy, and air force, and a personal staff known as the Military Household. The National Security Council is responsible for strategic defense planning. The General Staff develops war plans and organization. The ministries supervise and control their respective forces. The Military Household is responsible for the president's security and serves as liaison for him with the service ministries.

## POLITICO-MILITARY POLICY

Brazil has generally avoided foreign war, having been engaged in only five since becoming independent in 1822. In both world wars Brazil attempted to remain neutral but finally declared war on Germany after some of its ships were sunk by submarines. In World War II Brazil granted use of bases to the United States, collaborated in antisubmarine warfare, and sent some 20,000 men to fight in Italy.

A 1964 military coup ousted the left-wing government of Joao Goulart. Elections were held in 1966, and a civilian-military government was established under army Marshal Artur da Costa e Silva. In December 1968 da Costa e Silva, yielding to pressure by hard-line military leaders, assumed extraordinary powers, voided the Constitution, and prorogued Congress. After da Costa e Silva died in December 1969, Congress was convened by the junta of service ministers to confirm his successor, Gen. Emilio Garrastazu Medici. On March 15, 1974, Medici's successor, Gen. Ernesto Geisel, began his five-year term, after an election controlled by the military. Since 1969 the government has assumed the character of a military dictatorship, curbing civil liberties, notably freedom of the press, and taking extreme measures to root out opposition and control guerrillas. It is training officers to run the nation as well as the armed forces and proceeding to build up its arms industry and to improve land, sea, and air forces.

Military service is compulsory for all males at age twenty-one, and service in the reserves continues to age forty-five. The first nine years are served in the "first line," one on active duty, the remainder in the organized reserve. The next seven years are in the "second line," and the final years in the unorganized reserve. In order to qualify for public office a man must prove that he is a reservist, that he has fulfilled his military obligations, or has been officially exempted.

The armed forces participate in a variety of civic action projects. In the frontier regions of the north and west, the military provides the only educational and medical services available to civilians. In addition to maintaining two paramilitary training schools, the military provides literacy training for conscripts.

## STRATEGIC PROBLEMS

The northeastern portion of Brazil lies closer to the Eastern Hemisphere than any other Western Hemisphere country. Although this makes that area slightly vulnerable to trans-Atlantic attack, it also can assure a useful air link from the United States to the Middle East via Africa, as in World War II.

Because of jungles, mountains, and swamps, most of Brazil's frontiers—touching every South American nation except Ecuador and Chile—are physically inaccessible except by a few large rivers. The southern borders with Uruguay and Argentina, however, are less forbidding, and for many years Brazil has maintained half of its army in the southern third of the country.

Offshore, Brazil has declared a 200-mile territorial limit, and protection of fishing restrictions within it is a concern of the Brazilian navy, which is being built up with new ships designed for this purpose.

The Brazilian economy has been expanding rapidly as Brazilians and foreign investors have been developing some of Brazil's enormous natural resources. The construction of a hydroelectric plant on the Parana River has been a source of tension with both Paraguay and Argentina, who share the river as a border with Brazil. Brazil has provided assistance to other nations of Latin America, some of it military but most of it economic or industrial.

There is continuing internal unrest and violence in Brazil. Successful insurgency to the extent of overthrow of the government is, however, highly unlikely. Inflation, labor troubles, government controls on commercial credit, a high population gain, and urban migration are all important problems. Until 1969 the poverty-stricken northeast section of Brazil was considered the most vulnerable to insurgency, but leftist group efforts to organize the peasantry were unsuccessful. The focus of insurgency shifted to urban guerrilla activity: robbing banks for funds, attacks on government buildings, seizure of radio stations, and kidnapping of foreign diplomats. Government antiterrorist efforts and action against opponents of the incumbent regime have led to charges of torture and inhumane treatment of prisoners, including a report by the United States State Department to the Congress that resulted in Brazilian rejection of U.S. military aid.

The government reported in January 1973 that the urban guerrilla movement, the Popular Revolutionary Vanguard, had been virtually "dismantled," but at the same time a Marxist-Leninist guerrilla group in the jungles of the Amazon claimed it was gaining popular support.

## MILITARY ASSISTANCE

The United States sent a joint service mission to Brazil in 1948 to establish an advanced school for senior officers. Following a State Department report to the United States Congress in 1978 charging widespread violations of human rights in Brazil, the Brazilian government withdrew its request for $55 million in military aid and cancelled the 1952 military assistance treaty. During the period 1950–77, the United States had provided $223.58 million in aid, $33,000 in the last year, and trained 8,657 students under MAP.

## ALLIANCES

Brazil is a member of the OAS and related organizations. Brazilian units formed part of the UNEF in Suez, and Brazilian air force units participated in the United Nations transport operation in the Congo. In 1965, Brazil supported the United States in its action in the crisis in the Dominican Republic, and was among the first to send troops to the Inter-American Peace Force. By resolution of the OAS, overall command of the IAPF was given to a Brazilian.

## ARMY

*Personnel:* 180,000

*Organization:*
   8 infantry divisions
   4 mechanized divisions
   1 armored division
   1 airborne brigade

*Major Equipment Inventory:*
   250 medium tanks (M-4, M-47)
   200 light tanks (M-41, M-3)
   500 APCs (M-113, M-59)
   120 armored cars (M-8), scout cars (M-3), and half-tracks (M-2)
   200 light and medium artillery pieces (75mm, 105mm self-propelled, 155mm)
    50 antiaircraft guns (M-117 90mm, M-1 40mm)
       Hawk surface-to-air missiles (9 batteries)

   49 liaison aircraft (L-42, O-1E)
   15 helicopters (Bell 206A and UH-1D)

## NAVY

*Personnel:* 45,500 (includes 1,000 marines)

*Organization:* 6 naval commands and 1 fleet command

*Major Units:*
   3 diesel submarines (Oberon class; SS)
   7 diesel submarines (Guppy classes; SS)
   1 light aircraft carrier (CVL)
  20 destroyers (DD); 4 Niteroi class with short-range Seacat SAMs; 2 Niteroi class with short-range Exocet SSMs; 7 Fletcher class, one with short-range Seacat SAMs; 7 miscellaneous classes, one with short-range Seacat SAMs
  10 patrol ships (Imperial Marinhero class; PGF; 3-inch gun)
   6 patrol boats (PB; machine guns and mortar)
   6 coastal minesweepers (MSC)
   4 transport (APA)
   2 landing ships (LST)
  48 landing craft (LCV, LCM, LCVP, etc.)
   5 river patrol boats (PBR)
   1 river monitor (PM)
  10 harbor patrol boats (PSB)
  17 auxiliary ships (including survey ships, oilers, etc.)
  33 service craft (tugs, tenders, etc.)
   7 C-95 patrol aircraft (operated by Air Force)
  50 helicopters (S-55, Wasp, SH-3D)
   8 S-2E ASW aircraft (operated by Air Force)

*Naval Bases:* Rio de Janeiro, Araeu, Belem, Natal, Recife, Salvador, Ladario (at Corumba on the Paraguay River), and Sao Pedro da Aldeia Naval Station

## AIR FORCE

*Personnel:* 36,000

*Organization:*
   6 air zones (headquarters at Belem, Recife, Rio de Janeiro, Sao Paulo, Porto Alegre, Brasilia)
   1 fighter squadron (Mirage III)
   4 fighter-bomber squadrons (2 AT-26, 2 F-5)
   5 COIN/reconnaissance squadrons (3 AT-26, 2 T-25)
   8 transport squadrons (C-47, C-130, Boeing 737, Buffalo, C-119, HS-748/125, C-95)
   3 liaison-observation squadrons (Jet Ranger, O-1, UH-1, L-42, T-25)
   1 search and rescue SAR or RCM (HU-16, C-95/130, Bell 47 helicopter)

*Major Aircraft Types:*
    160  combat aircraft
        32  F-5 fighter-bombers
        32  AT-26 Xavante fighter-bombers
        16  Mirage III fighters
        80  armed trainers (T-25/ AT-26)
    550  other aircraft
        150  transports (C-130/47, Boeing 737, Buffalo,
                 C-119, HS-748/125, C-95 Bandeirante)
         40  maritime patrol and ASW (S-2, PBY,
                 HU-16, C-95)
         50  liaison-observation (L-42)
         80  helicopters (OH-1, UH-1, Jet Ranger)
        230  trainer/miscellaneous support aircraft
                 (T-23, Fokker S-11, T-37)

*Air Bases:* Rio de Janeiro, Sao Paulo, Recife, Belem,
Galeao, Cumbica, Santarem, Balterra, Cachijo,
Jacareacanga, Salvador, Guarantinqueta, Campos do
Alfonsos, Fortaleza, Porto Alegre, Natal, Manaus

## PARAMILITARY

Public security forces of various kinds total about
120,000. They also serve as an auxiliary reserve force for
the army. In addition, militia organizations exist in some
states. Sao Paulo's, the largest, comprises about 250,000
men.

Because they feel inadequately protected, some large
landholders have developed their own security forces, and
former policemen have formed death squads to eliminate
those they adjudge to be criminals.

## BRITISH DEPENDENT AND ASSOCIATED STATES IN THE WESTERN HEMISPHERE

Six former British colonies in the Caribbean area have
become independent states within the Commonwealth
since 1962, the Bahamas, Barbados, Guyana, Jamaica,
Trinidad and Tobago, and Grenada. Of the still dependent
colonies, five are associated states, i.e., have control over
their internal affairs, but not over foreign relations and
defense. All of the associated states and two of the dependencies (British Virgin Islands and Montserrat) have their
own separate police force. Britain maintains only a small
force in the area (two frigates and a battalion and a half of
men).

## ASSOCIATED STATES

*Antigua (State of Antigua)*
One of the Leeward Islands, Antigua (together with the

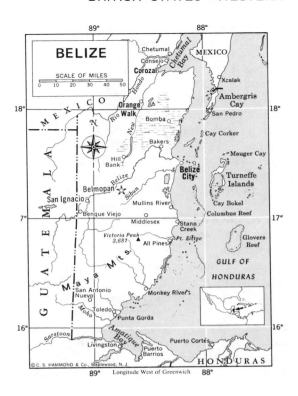

nearby island of Barbuda) has an area of 171 square miles
and a population of about 73,000. It will become independent in 1978. The GNP is $52 million ($720 per capita).

*St. Christopher–Nevis (State of St. Christopher–Nevis)*
These two islands in the Leewards have a combined area
of 118 square miles and a population of about 57,000
(including Anguilla). Anguilla, formerly associated with
them, and still legally joined, has been administered
separately since 1971, and will probably not rejoin when
St. Christopher–Nevis becomes independent. The gross
national product is $30.4 million ($210 per capita).

*St. Lucia (State of St. Lucia)*
One of the Windward Islands, St. Lucia has an area of
238 square miles and a population of 120,000. The gross
national product is $57 million ($475 per capita).

*St. Vincent (State of St. Vincent)*
One of the Windward Islands, St. Vincent, including the
northern Grenadines, has an area of 250 square miles and a
population of 112,000. The gross national product is $335
million ($2,991 per capita).

## DEPENDENCIES

*Anguilla*
One of the Leeward Islands, Anguilla, while legally
associated with St. Christopher–Nevis, since 1971 has been

administered separately, and has reverted to Crown colony status.

### Bermuda (Colony of Bermuda)

Bermuda is a close cluster of seven main islands (the only ones permanently inhabited), all connected by bridges, and perhaps 150 islets, with a total area of 21 square miles and a total population of 60,000. The gross national product is $430 million ($7,540 per capita). There is a local defense militia force of 360 and a police force of 350. The United States maintains a naval air base and a NASA tracking station.

### Belize (Colony of Belize)

Area: 8,867 square miles
Population: 154,000
Gross National Product: $96 million ($700 per capita)

Formerly British Honduras, Belize remains a dependent British territory with Britain responsible for external affairs, defense, internal security, and the civil service. Guatemala claims sovereignty over at least part of Belize, particularly the north, where oil has been discovered. Belize's proven offshore oil reserves are extremely rich. When Guatemala has threatened to invade, most recently in 1977, British military reinforcements have been sent to the area. Illegal immigration from Guatemala is a constant problem. The government of Belize has refused to accept independence, which the British are eager to give, until security against invasion is guaranteed. In March 1978 Barbados, Guyana, and Jamaica agreed to participate in such a guarantee. Most Latin American nations support independence.

Belize has a coastal patrol of fifty volunteers with two patrol boats (PB).

### British Virgin Islands (Colony of the Virgin Islands)

The British Virgin Islands, which lie to the east of the U.S. Virgin Islands, have an area of 50 square miles and a population of 11,000. There are thirty-six islands, of which sixteen are inhabited. The islands are economically interdependent with the U.S. Virgin Islands.

### Cayman Islands

Formerly administered by the governor of Jamaica, the Caymans became dependencies when Jamaica became independent. The islands have an area of 93 square miles, with a population of 11,000. A local airline operates two light transport planes.

### Falkland Islands (Colony of the Falkland Islands and Dependencies)

Located in the South Atlantic Ocean, about 480 miles northeast of Cape Horn, the islands and their dependencies, South Georgia and South Sandwich, have a total land area of 6,280 square miles and a total population of about 2,000.

Although Britain originally colonized West Falkland, Argentina colonized East Falkland, which Britain seized and occupied in 1833. Argentina has continued to protest British occupation of this territory. In recent years British moves toward making a serious search for oil have aggravated the situation, and both nations recalled their ambassadors in 1976. The OAS supports Argentina's right to sovereignty. The problem is under discussion.

### Montserrat (Colony of Montserrat)

One of the Leeward Islands, Montserrat has an area of 32 square miles and a population of about 12,000.

### Turks and Caicos Islands (Colony of the Turks and Caicos Islands)

Geographically, these islands are two southeastern groups of the Bahamas. There are over thirty small islands, with a total area of 166 square miles. Only six of the islands are inhabited, by about 6,000 people. On Grand Turk Island the United States maintains a missile-tracking station and a naval base.

# BRUNEI

## POWER POTENTIAL STATISTICS

Area: 2,226 square miles
Population: 190,000
Total Active Regular Armed Forces: 2,600 (1.37% population)
Gross National Product: $460 million
Fuel Production:
  Crude Oil: 9.3 million metric tons
  Refined Petroleum Products: 53,990 metric tons
  Natural Gas: 5 billion cubic meters
  Electric Power Output: 230 million kwh
  Civil Air Fleet: 4 major transport aircraft

## POLITICO-MILITARY POLICIES AND POSTURE

Intruding into the Malaysian state of Sarawak, on the island of Borneo, is the small sultanate of Brunei. The sultanate relies for defense on the Royal Brunei Malay Regiment of 2,600 men, commanded by the sultan as commander in chief, and on a British Gurkha battalion, stationed in Brunei at the sultan's expense.

The Royal Brunei Regiment has an air wing with eight Jet Ranger and Iroquois helicopters and one transport. Its 350-man naval forces are based at the Muara marine base. The newest acquisition is a 99-foot, fast (57-knot) patrol boat (PB) with eight SS-12 short-range SSMs on two launchers. There are six smaller PB armed with two 20mm guns, 3 machine gun–armed river patrol boats (PBR), 2

mechanized landing craft (LCM), and 24 small assault boats.

Brunei may eventually reconsider its decision not to join Malaysia, but this is unlikely as long as the present sultan's father lives. At any rate, little Brunei is no military threat to East Malaysia, and the Malaysian government has given no hint of changing its diplomatically correct attitude toward Brunei.

# BULGARIA

## People's Republic of Bulgaria

### POWER POTENTIAL STATISTICS

Area: 42,829 square miles
Population: 8,871,000
Total Active Regular Armed Forces: 151,000 (1.7% population)

Gross National Product: $20.9 billion ($2,360 per capita)
Annual Military Expenditures: $1.81 billion (8.66% GNP)
Crude Steel Production: 2.5 million metric tons
Iron Ore Production: 2.3 million metric tons
Fuel Production:
 Coal: 288,000 metric tons
 Lignite: 25.5 million metric tons
 Natural Gas: 180 million cubic meters
 Crude Oil: 120,000 metric tons
Electric Power Output: 29.7 billion kwh
Nuclear Power Production: 1,701 megawatts
Merchant Fleet (ships 1,000 tons and over): 112 ships; 965,000 gross tons
Civil Air Fleet: 7 jet, 23 turboprop, and 6 piston transports

### DEFENSE STRUCTURE

The minister of defense is the commander and highest ranking officer of the fully integrated Bulgarian armed forces, known as the Bulgarian People's Army, which consists of the Ground Forces, air force, Air Defense Force, and navy. Under the Ministry of National Defense are the General Staff, the Main Inspectorate of Training, the Rear Services (logistics), the military districts, and frontier troops. The chief of the Main Political Directorate, responsible for political indoctrination of the forces, reports not only to the minister of defense, but to the Central Committee of the Bulgarian Communist party. There are three military districts, with headquarters in Sofia, Plovdiv, and Sliven.

## POLITICO-MILITARY POLICY

The internal, foreign, and military policies of Bulgaria follow those of the USSR. Bulgaria's close association with the Soviet Union reflects not only Bulgarian ideological and economic ties with that country, but also traditional Bulgarian friendship for Russia rooted in Bulgaria's struggle for independence in the nineteenth century. In 1968 troops took part in the military intervention in Czechoslovakia.

There is compulsory military service for all male citizens upon reaching the age of nineteen. The period of service for privates and noncommissioned officers is two years for the army, air force, and air defense forces, and three years for the navy. The treaty of peace signed by Bulgaria in 1947 limits the overall size of its armed forces to 65,000 men. But with Soviet backing, the Bulgarian military establishment has grown beyond the treaty size and now totals 193,000.

## STRATEGIC PROBLEMS

Like the other small Balkan countries, Bulgaria has little strategic space. This, combined with other inadequacies of resources, means that Bulgaria cannot play an important role in a major European war.

Otherwise, Bulgaria's principal strategic problems stem from longstanding frontier controversies with its neighbors. Bulgaria shares ancient Macedonia with Greece and Yugoslavia; it has long been a Bulgarian dream to unite all of Macedonia with Bulgaria, a dream which has contributed to a number of wars and incidents over the past century.

Bulgaria also has irredentist claims on the southern portion of Romania's Dobruja—the region lying east of the lower Danube—which was lost to Romania in 1913 as a result of the second Balkan War. But while relations between Bulgaria and Romania are relatively cool, the Dobruja issue does not seem to be as critical as the Macedonian problem. Relations with Greece and Turkey, members of NATO and historical antagonists, have been marked by a prolonged tension for many years but have recently improved.

## MILITARY ASSISTANCE

Bulgarian armed forces are organized, trained, and equipped along Soviet lines, with the benefit of substantial Soviet assistance.

Bulgaria, like all of the other Warsaw Pact countries, has received heavy weapons and complex equipment from the USSR, but much of this equipment is of older vintage. Ground forces have Soviet-made tanks, artillery, antitank guns, and antitank wire-guided missiles, and short-range surface-to-surface missles. There are very few weapons manufactured locally. All combat aircraft are from the USSR.

## ALLIANCES

In addition to a 1955 Treaty of Friendship and Mutual Assistance with the USSR, Bulgaria is a member of the Warsaw Pact and the Council of Mutual Economic Assistance (CEMA). It has also signed bilateral treaties of friendship, cooperation, and mutual assistance with all other members of the Warsaw Pact.

## ARMY

*Personnel:* 119,000

*Organization:*
    3 armies (military regions), with headquarters at
        Sofia, Plovdiv, and Sliven
    8 motorized rifle divisions (3 in cadre form)
    5 tank brigades
    1 parachute regiment
    4 antiaircraft regiments

*Major Equipment Inventory:*
    2,000 medium tanks (T-34/54/55/62)
          light tanks (PT-76)
    1,000+ light, medium, and heavy artillery pieces,
          MRL, mortars, Snapper, Sagger and
          Swatter anti-tank guided missiles and RCL
      250 BTR-40P
    1,500 APCs (BTR-50/60/152)
          SSMs (Frog and Scud)
          SU-100 and JSU-122 self-propelled guns
          ZSU-57/2 self-propelled antiaircraft, 57mm,
          85mm towed antiaircraft guns

*Reserves:* over 500,000 trained reservists

## NAVY (includes a small Danube flotilla)

*Personnel:* 10,000

*Major Units:*
    4 submarines (2 Whiskey class, 2 Romeo class; SS)

2 frigates (Riga class; FF)
6 submarine chasers (SO-1 class; PC)
3 coastal escorts (Poti Class; PCE)
3 missile attack boats (Osa class; PTG; SS-N-2/ Styx missiles)
14 motor torpedo boats (6 Shershen, 8 P-4 class; PT)
2 fleet minesweepers (T-43 class; MSF)
12 inshore minesweepers (4 Vanya, 8 T-301 class; MSI)
12 minesweeping boats (Po-2 class; MSB)
20 utility landing craft (10 Vydra class; 10 MFP class; LCU)
7 auxiliary ships
21 service craft (tugs, tenders, etc.)
8 helicopters (Hound)

*Major Naval Bases:* Varna, Burgas, Sozopol

*Reserves:* About 40,000 trained reservists

## AIR FORCE (including Air Defense Force)

*Personnel:* 22,000

*Organization:*
12 fighter-interceptor squadrons (MiG-21/19/17)
6 fighter-bomber squadrons (MiG-17/23)
3 fighter/reconnaissance squadrons (MiG-21/17)
3 transport squadrons (Il-14, An-24, Tu-134)
4 helicopter squadrons (Mi-2/4/6/8)

*Major Aircraft Types:*
248 combat aircraft
  12 MiG-23 fighter-bombers
  58 MiG-21 fighter/interceptors
  36 MiG-19 fighter/interceptors
 132 MiG-17 fighter-bomber/interceptors
  10 MiG-21/25/15 fighter/reconnaissance
265 other aircraft
  10 Il-14 transports
   3 Tu-134 transports
   2 An-24 transports
 200 trainer/support aircraft (L-29, MiG-15/17/21)
  50 helicopters (Mi-2/4/6/8)
SAM (SA-2/6/7)

*Air Bases:* Sofia, Yambol, Burgas, Balchik, Tolbukhin, Ignatiev, Plovdiv, Karlovo

## PARAMILITARY

There are five brigades of border guards, totalling about 15,000 men. There is a Security Police Force of about 10,000 organized in eight regiments. A People's Militia of 150,000 is available for local defense in the event of war.

# BURMA

## Socialist Republic of the Union of Burma

### POWER POTENTIAL STATISTICS

Area: 261,789 square miles
Population: 33,123,000
Total Active Regular Armed Forces: 142,900 (0.43% population)
Gross National Product: $3.7 billion ($120 per capita)
Annual Military Expenditures: $149 million (4.0% GNP)
Fuel Production:
  Crude Oil: 1.16 million metric tons
  Refined Petroleum Products: 1.1 million metric tons
Electric Power Output: 890 million kwh
Merchant Fleet (ships 1,000 tons and over): 8 ships; 48,000 gross tons
Civil Air Fleet: 20 major transport aircraft

### DEFENSE STRUCTURE

President Ne Win (erstwhile Defense chief of staff) exercises command of the armed forces through the Ministry of Defense, with an integrated Defense Forces staff. Operational control of the forces in the field is unified and is exercised by the appropriate vice chief of staff and five army area commands and three naval regions.

### POLITICO-MILITARY POLICY

Burma's foreign policy since independence has been one of neutrality and nonalignment. In part, this policy has been dictated by Burma's relatively isolated geographic position between South and Southeast Asia, by the interior position of the ethnic majority Burman population, surrounded by ethnic non-Burman groups on the periphery, and by the looming presence (since 1949) of People's Republic of China forces along the 1,300 mile border between the two states.

Burma has been free to pursue friendly policies toward its neighbors, and toward both the USSR and the United States. However, it has had to be sensitive to China's propinquity, the overwhelming military potential of its People's Liberation Army, and China's propensity to create mischief in difficult border areas occupied, in the main, by ethnic minorities resenting Burman rule. Relations with China deteriorated markedly during the Great Proletarian Cultural Revolution in China and only recently have been restored to a relatively stable and friendly basis.

Going it alone and plagued by internal dissension and incipient or active insurgencies, Burma has given priority

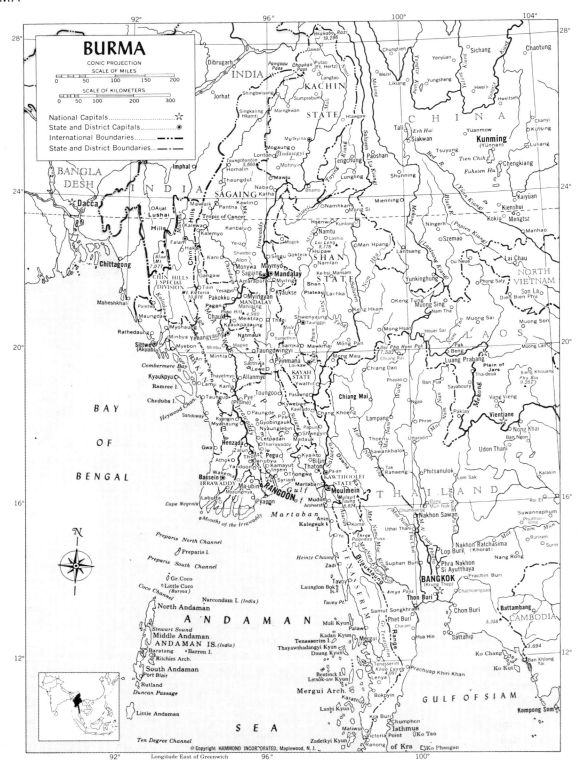

## BURMA

CONIC PROJECTION

SCALE OF MILES

0    50    100    150    200

SCALE OF KILOMETERS

0    50    100    200    300

National Capitals..........................☆
State and District Capitals................◉
International Boundaries..........━ ━ ━
State and District Boundaries...━ ∙ ━ ∙ ━

© Copyright HAMMOND INCORPORATED, Maplewood, N.J.

Longitude East of Greenwich

to internal defense forces consisting of a large, lightly equipped army, an air force structured for ground support, and a navy organized for coastal and river patrol. The recent creation of a 200-mile economic zone in the Bay of

Bengal and Andaman Sea requires larger forces than Burma can support if the zone is to be patrolled effectively.

The Defense Services are maintained at strength largely by voluntary enlistments of two years, but a National

Service Law prescribes conscription of all citizens between eighteen and forty-five, and of physicians, engineers, and technicians to age fifty-six. This ensures adequate manpower in an emergency and the availability of scarce skills at all times.

## STRATEGIC PROBLEMS

Burma offers strategic routes from northeastern India and the Indian Ocean into southwestern China, and vice versa. The importance of these routes was demonstrated by the World War II experience. In addition, the inability of the government of the Union of Burma to control large tracts adjacent to Burma's borders with Bangladesh (East Pakistan), India, China, and Thailand, has invited meddling, if not invasion, by neighbors.

Withal, Burma's major security problems have been, and are, internal. Domestic Communists of various colors, ethnic minorities, and former nationalist Chinese all have mounted threats to Burma's internal security at times. Although some of these groups have formed temporary coalitions, their general inability to coalesce has minimized their threat to Burman stability. Support of such groups from the outside, chiefly from China and Thailand, however, has greatly exacerbated Burma's external relations and kept the level of violence in the border areas at a fairly high level. Recent Thai restraint has contributed to some easing of the situation. At the same time, for the past twenty years the Defense Services have been relatively successful in keeping serious conflict away from the main centers of Burman population, where disaffection could become a major threat to the regime.

## MILITARY ASSISTANCE

Burma has received military assistance from a variety of sources: the Federal Republic of Germany, India, Israel, the United Kingdom, the United States, and Yugoslavia. There are now no major external sources of supply. Although U.S. assistance is now limited to support in suppressing opium and heroin activities, a total of $76.4 million in assistance has been provided since 1958, and 878 students have been trained under MAP.

## ALLIANCES

Burma consistently has refused to enter into any alliance relationships, including ASEAN, preferring to rely on its own resources, supplemented by membership in the UN and a number of international consultative and economic organizations. Burma did send a small staff detachment to join UN operations in the Congo in 1960, and there are border agreements with China and Thailand. There is evidence of a tacit understanding with India over combined defense of the Assam–northern Burma area in the event of a Chinese move in that quarter.

## ARMY

*Personnel:* 130,000

*Organization:* 5 area commands (Central, Eastern, Southeast, Southwest, and Northwest)
    100 infantry battalions (organized into 3 divisions)
      2 armored battalions
      5 artillery battalions
      1 engineer battalion

*Major Equipment Inventory:*
    medium tanks (M-4, Sherman)
    light tanks (Comet)
    armored cars (Humber)
    scout cars (Ferret)
    light artillery pieces (25-pounder guns, 105mm, 75 mm howitzers)
    medium artillery pieces (155mm howitzers)
    120mm mortars
    antitank guns
    antiaircraft guns

## NAVY

*Personnel:* 6,300 (includes 800 marines)

*Major Units:*
    2 patrol escorts (PG; 4-inch gun; obsolescent frigates)
    4 patrol ships (PGF)
   21 patrol craft (PC)
   15 patrol boats (PB)
   35 river patrol boats (PBR)
    8 mechanized landing craft (LCM; now used as transports)
    1 utility landing craft (LCU; used as transport)
    2 hydrographic survey ships
    1 service craft (transport)

*Naval Bases:* Seikyi, Sinmalaik, Sittwo (Akyab), Moulmein, Mergui, and Bassein.

## AIR FORCE

*Personnel:* 6,600

*Organization:*
    3 fighter-bomber/COIN squadrons (T-33, T-37, Provost, SF-260)
    1 transport squadron (C-45, C-47, Otter)
    1 helicopter squadron (Alouette III, Huskie, Sioux)

*Major Aircraft types:*
   60 combat aircraft
     20 armed jet trainer/ground attack (15 T-37, 5 T-33)

40   armed piston trainer/ground attack (30
       Provost, 10 SF-260 Warrior)
94   other aircraft
       27   transports (6 C-45, 15 C-47, 6 Otter)
       27   helicopters (8 Alouette III, Huskie, Sioux)
       40   utility/liaison aircraft and trainers
               (including 10 U-17)

*Air Bases:* Mingaladon (Rangoon), Meiktila (2),
Hmawbi, Mandalay, Myitkyina, and Kengtung

## PARAMILITARY

The People's Police Force numbers 10,000 and is under
the minister of home affairs. Armed village defense and
local militia exist under the aegis of the Burma Socialist
Program party (BSPP).

# BURUNDI

## Republic of Burundi

## POWER POTENTIAL STATISTICS

Area: 10,739 square miles
Population: 4,263,000
Total Active Regular Armed Forces: 7,000 (0.16%
    population)
Gross National Product: $450 million ($120 per capita)
Annual Military Expenditures: $21.3 million (4.73%
    GNP)
Electric Power Output: 25 million kwh
Civil Air Fleet: 5 major transport aircraft

## POLITICO-MILITARY POLICIES AND POSTURE

Lt. Col. Jean-Baptiste Bagaza led a bloodless coup on
November 1, 1976, overthrowing the ten-year-old regime
of Col. Michel Micombero. Bagaza and his allies in the
army seem to have been motivated by multiple desires to
end seriously destabilizing intra-Tutsi factionalism, to
improve the position of the military, to curtail rampant
corruption, and to reduce Hutu-Tutsi social conflict. In
rapid succession Bagaza became military chief of staff,
head of the new Revolutionary Supreme Council (SRC)
and, finally, president. Significantly, the Burundi cabinet
is composed mostly of civilians.

Ethno-tribal divisions in Burundi have been a source of
internal security problems and led in 1965, and again in
early 1972, to widespread massacres. The Nilotic Tutsi
(Watusi) tribe, comprising about 15 percent of the population, has traditionally ruled over the much more numerous
peasant Bantu Hutu (Bahutu) tribe. The Tutsi are further
divided into Big Tutsi, including the royalty and high
government officials who tend to be moderate and conciliatory toward the Hutu, and the Little Tutsi, who tend to
be leftist and anti-Hutu. President Micombero comes from
this extremist group. In October 1965 Hutu officers in the
army and gendarmerie, aided by some Tutsi soldiers and
police, staged an abortive coup. Hutu in the countryside
also massacred several thousand Tutsi, and bloody
reprisals by the Tutsi followed. In March 1972, young King
Ntare V, deposed by Micombero in 1966, was allowed to
return to Burundi, but was arrested and, in April, was
killed during an attempt by monarchists to free him and
overthrow the government. An estimated 20,000 people,
most of them Tutsi, were killed in the uprising, and an
estimated 100,000 Hutu were killed in the suppression of
the uprising and the reprisals that followed. Zaire sent
troops to assist the government in suppressing the uprising.
In May 1973 there was another abortive Hutu attempt to
seize power, begun by Hutu raiders from Tanzania and
Rwanda, and followed by the killing of 10,000 or more
Hutu.

President Bagaza has made socioeconomic equality for
the Hutu the centerpiece of his domestic and foreign
policies. About 150,000 Hutus exiled in Rwanda and
Tanzania have been encouraged to return. Some land
reform favorable to Hutu tenant farmers has been initiated. These programs have improved relations considerably with Tanzania and Rwanda (under Hutu majority
rule). In September 1976 Burundi signed a treaty of
friendship and cooperation with Zaire and Rwanda. At the
same time the three established an Economic Community
of the Great Lakes.

Burundi reestablished relations with China in 1971. It
was one of the first states to recognize the Neto regime in
Angola and has ties with the USSR and Cuba. Most of

Burundi's foreign aid (about $40 million in 1975) comes from the West, however, and the new government has been successful with its new image in attracting increased EEC, UN, World Bank, and bilateral aid (France, West Germany, and Belgium). Nevertheless, Burundi remains an overwhelmingly pastoral society, whose dense population and low literacy and infrastructure levels will retard its economic and military potential for the foreseeable future.

Estimates of the size of the Burundian army (all-Tutsi) range from 6,000 to 10,000 men, organized into five battalions and several paramilitary units. The air force consists of three small transports and several helicopters. Belgium and Zaire have assisted in army training programs.

# CAMBODIA

## Democratic Kampuchea

### POWER POTENTIAL STATISTICS

Area: 69,898 square miles
Population: 8,087,000*
Total Active Armed Forces: 62,000 (0.77% population)
Gross National Product: $500 million (estimate; $50 per capita)
Annual Military Expenditures: $68 million (13.6% GNP)
Electric Power Output: 260 million kwh
Civil Air Fleet: 1 jet and 7 piston transport

*Since the accession of Pol Pot this figure has been greatly reduced. In 1979 authoritative estimates were approximately 5,000,000.

### DEFENSE STRUCTURE

Under the regime of 1975–79, control of the Cambodian armed forces nominally was vested in the prime minister and discharged through a deputy prime minister. In reality, control appeared to be through a shadowy chimera known as Angkra ("The Organization"), possibly synonymous with the Communist party of Kampuchea, and regional commands thought to be generally amenable to central control by the prime minister, Pol Pot.

### POLITICO-MILITARY POLICIES

After the seizure of Phnom Penh in 1975 and the explusion of the Lon Nol regime, the new Cambodian government worked to establish an independent position in Indochina and maintain the integrity of its borders vis-a-vis both Thailand and Vietnam. The borders, though partially demarcated in both cases, remained in doubt. Conflicts or potential conflicts derived in part from (1) differences over the accuracy of maps, as in the case of Thailand, (2) questions about the propriety of French administrative decisions, in the case of Vietnam, (3) charges concerning the arbitrary movement of border markers, and (4) the existence of large ethnic Khmer minorities in some regions astride the international borders. The situation is complicated by very old Thai claims (not really asserted officially) to the western border areas and by the relatively sparse Khmer presence in certain areas adjacent to the nominal border with Vietnam. Cambodian reliance on economic, military, and political support from China to restrain Vietnam, itself increasingly involved in real or potential conflict with China, exacerbated the situation. Increases in Vietnamese military control and presence in Laos near the Laos-Cambodia border did not ease tension.

To all of this must be added the historical Khmer-Thai and Khmer-Vietnamese antipathies, deriving from the long-term (since the thirteenth century at the latest) expansion of Thai and Vietnamese power at Khmer expense.

The Cambodian regime deliberately adopted a two-pronged policy of attempting to eliminate all possible foci of internal dissent through ruthless killing of uncertain but clearly large numbers of intellectuals, former and potential political opponents, military officers, common soldiers, and others, as well as pursuing border conflicts with both Thailand and Vietnam. To some degree, it is true, Cambodia attempted to placate the Thai as the military conflict with Vietnam escalated.

The raids against the Vietnamese were marked by savage attacks on civilians. In an all-out military confrontation, there was no doubt the Vietnamese would prevail, and at the turn of the year 1979 they made their move, quickly seizing Phnom Penh and, with the help of the rebel Kampuchean United Front for National Salvation, gaining control of the country. A new government was installed in Phnom Penh. A treaty with Vietnam provided for stationing of Vietnamese troops in Cambodia. Remnants of the Pol Pot forces continued resistance in pockets scattered across the country. Civil war was continued through 1979.

The attack by Soviet-supported Vietnam on the China-supported government in Cambodia soon led to a Chinese invasion of Vietnam. (See China and Vietnam)

## STRATEGIC PROBLEMS

The role of Cambodia as a strategic buffer between Thailand and Vietnam was suspended by the arrival of the French in the nineteenth century, and the suspension was in some degree prolonged by the U.S. presence in the Indochinese peninsula until 1972. The ability of any Cambodian regime to maneuver between its two more powerful neighbors today takes on renewed significance. The reliance of the recent regime (1975–79) on Chinese support, and the strained relations between Vietnam and China, did little to ease the problems.

Additionally, Cambodia lacks strategically defensible and defined frontiers, except perhaps in the north along the Phanom Dong Raek, and there the Thai hold the more advantageous terrain.

Protection of Cambodia's rights in the Gulf of Thailand and the South China Sea in the era of 200-mile economic zones has complicated already difficult issues over fisheries and control of islands.

## MILITARY ASSISTANCE

Under previous regimes, Cambodia relied for military assistance on various sources, including China, France, the United States, the USSR, and Vietnam. During the period preceding the all-out Vietnamese invasion, the Cambodians were presumably making use of weapons and materiel supplied earlier.

## ALLIANCES

Cambodia has eschewed adherence to any formal military alliance, but its position after 1975 forced heavy reliance on China.

NOTE: Relatively little is known of details of organization, strength, and equipment of the Cambodian armed forces. Following are the best estimates available of the situation as of late 1978:

## ARMY

*Personnel:* numbers unknown

*Organization:*
   infantry and commando units (battalions)
   armored car units
   tank units
   parachute units

*Major Equipment Inventory:*
   light tanks (M-24, AMX-13)
   armored cars (M-8 and M-20)
   half-tracks (M-2)
   scout cars (M-3)
   APCs (BTR-40, BTR-152, M-113)
   M-109 self-propelled 155mm howitzers
   M-101, M-102 105mm howitzers
   M-1, A-1 155mm howitzers
   76mm and 122mm guns (Soviet)
   81mm mortars
   light and medium antiaircraft guns and field artillery
      (Soviet, French, and Chinese)
   106mm recoilless rifles
   Cessna O-1 liaison aircraft

## NAVY

*Personnel:* 11,000 (includes 4,000 marines)

*Major Units:*
   19 patrol boats (PB; all ex-U.S.)
   68 river patrol boats (65 U.S. Mark I and II classes;
         3 miscellaneous classes; PBR)
    1 river monitor (Edic class; PM; mortar and
         machine guns)
    6 utility landing craft (LCU)
    3 service craft (tugs, floating dry docks)

*Major Naval Bases:* Ream, Chran Changvar (Phnom Penh), Kompong Som

## AIR FORCE

*Personnel:* numbers unknown

*Organization:* estimate, based upon equipment
   jet ground attack units (T-37)
   turboprop ground attack units (AU-24)
   piston ground attack units (T-6, T-28, C-47 gunships)
   helicopter ground attack units (UH-1 gunship)
   transport units (C-47, C-54)
   helicopter units (UH-1, Alouette III, H-34, Mi-4)
   utility liaison units (Beaver, O-1, An-2)

*Major Aircraft Types:*
   combat aircraft
      T-37 jet ground attack aircraft
      AU-24 turboprop ground attack aircraft
      T-28 piston ground attack aircraft
      C-47 gunships

UH-1 gunships
other aircraft
    helicopters (UH-1, H-34, Alouette III, Mi-4)
    transports (C-47, C-123)
    utility/liaison aircraft (Beaver, O-1, An-2)
    trainers (GY-80, T-6, T-41, Magister)

*Major Air Bases:* Seam Reap, Battambang, Pochentong
(Phnom Penh)

## PARAMILITARY

Lightly armed police and home guard type units.

# CAMEROON

## United Republic of Cameroon

## POWER POTENTIAL STATISTICS

Area: 183,568 square miles
Population: 8,088,000
Total Active Regular Armed Forces: 5,600 (0.07%
    population)
Gross National Product: $2.5 billion ($301 per capita)
Annual Military Expenditures: $62.5 million (2.5%
    GNP)
Electric Power Output: 1.35 billion kwh
Civil Air Fleet: 2 jet transports and 3 piston transports

## POLITICO-MILITARY POLICIES AND POSTURE

The president is chief of state and commander of the armed forces. This command is exercised through a minister of the armed forces. Although officially nonaligned in the world ideological struggle, Cameroon is Western-oriented. Cameroon was established in 1961 from former British Cameroon and the much larger and more populous French Cameroun. The French portion, upon independence in 1960, retained close ties with the French Community and entered into certain thus-far unpublished mutual defense arrangements and a technical military assistance arrangement with France. These continued following the unification of the two Cameroons. In 1974 a new cooperation agreement was signed which contained some military provisions but placed the two countries on a more equitable footing. Cameroon, however, continues to rely on French aid, which still is not sufficient to compensate for a large trade imbalance in France's favor.

Cameroon is a one-party state—Cameroon National Union—with a reputedly efficient secret police. Throughout the 1960s it fought and defeated an insurgent group based on the *Union des Populations du Cameroon (PUC)*. The PUC leader was executed in 1971. The party offers little threat to the regime now, though it has a large exile population. President Ahidjo won an overwhelming electoral victory to a fourth five-year term in 1975. He has since announced his intention to retire in 1980, which could cause political turmoil.

A potential for internal instability is inherent in the ethno-religious diversity of the people. There are about 200 tribes speaking twenty-four major languages. In the north, where the Moslem 15 percent of the country's population is concentrated, the Fang and Fulani tribes predominate. One-third of the population, mainly the southern Bantus, profess Christianity, and the remainder are animist. The core of former insurgency came from the Bamileke, about 20 percent of the population, in the central highlands area. So far the north-south split on ethno-religious grounds, so prevalent in West African states, has not manifested itself.

French military assistance has continued since 1960 at a rate of about $7 million annually. Until recently, French officers commanded Cameroonian units, while others trained, staffed, and performed technical services. A small instructor-adviser detachment continues to work with the military and police forces. Training of Cameroonian officers and NCOs is conducted in France, also. Between 1960 and 1964 some 10,000 French troops were in Cameroon, assisting the government against the insurgency. The troops have been evacuated, except for the training detachment.

The United States in 1962–63 provided $277,000 in military assistance, but none since then.

Cameroon, which withdrew in 1972 from the French-oriented OCAM, is a member of the Organization of

African Unity (OAU) and the Central African Customs and Economic Union. It has also withdrawn from *Air Afrique,* French-backed and shared by OCAM nations, and now has its own successful Cameroon Airlines.

In a region plagued by military coups, Cameroon's relative stability is perhaps due to a military balance of power. There is a gendarmerie of 3,000 men and a mobile police force (the Cameroonian Guard) of 2,000 in addition to an army of 5,000. All three forces are said to watch each other jealously and all are under close observation by the president's own special security police. The army is organized as three infantry battalions, an armored car company, and engineer and support companies. There is a navy of 600 men operating out of Douala. Craft included three patrol craft (PC), with 40mm or larger guns; five patrol boats (PB); one mechanized landing craft (LCM); five personnel landing craft (LCP); and nine support craft. The 300-man air force operates four Magister armed jet trainers, two C-47 transports, four light aircraft, and two Sud SA-1221 Djinn helicopters. There are air bases at Batouri, Douala, Foumban, Garoua, Kaele, N'Gaoundere, Maroua Salak, Port Pouet, Yaounde, and Tiko.

# CANADA

## POWER POTENTIAL STATISTICS

Area: 3,851,809 square miles
Population: 23,712,000
Total Active Regular Armed Forces: 74,200 (0.19% population)
Gross National Product: $195.3 billion ($8,330 per capita)
Annual Military Expenditure: $3.47 billion (1.8% GNP)
Crude Steel Production: 13.1 million metric tons
Iron Ore Production: 56 million metric tons
Fuel Production:
    Coal: 20.8 million metric tons
    Lignite: 4.7 million metric tons
    Crude Oil: 63.8 million metric tons
    Refined Products: 84 million metric tons
    Natural Gas: 74.5 billion cubic meters
Electric Power Output: 316.5 billion kwh
Nuclear Power Production: 7,200 megawatts
Merchant Fleet (ships 1,000 tons and over): 79 ships; 576,000 gross tons
Civil Air Fleet: 551 major transport aircraft

## DEFENSE STRUCTURE

Canada is the only important nation in the world to have a completely unified defense structure, in which there are no separate or distinct services within the armed forces, but rather (in the words of the legislation by which this was accomplished) "One service called the Canadian Armed Forces." Civilian control over the Canadian Armed Forces is exercised by the prime minister and the cabinet, with the minister of defence having direct responsibility. Under him the senior military man of the armed forces is the chief of the Defence Staff, who in 1964 replaced the former four-man Chiefs of Staff Committee, and who is responsible for administering the armed forces through Canadian Forces Headquarters.

## POLITICO-MILITARY POLICY

Canada has, for all practical purposes, linked its security requirements with those of the United States. Thus Canada has become a junior—but important and independent—partner in integrated defense arrangements for the North American continent. This does not imply that Canada feels obligated to follow the lead of the United States in foreign or military policy. But it does represent Canadian convictions that the principal objectives of the two nations are parallel, and many of their defense problems mutual.

Canada has been one of the leading proponents of the establishment of peacekeeping forces by the UN in instances where internal disorders, or danger of war, pose threats to international peace. Canadian forces have participated in all of the various UN forces and observer groups that have been established by the UN Security Council.

There were three principal reasons why the Canadian government made the policy decision first to integrate, then to unify, its armed forces. The first reason was budgetary; a study of the nation's force structure concluded that there was much unnecessary duplication of functions, personnel, and equipment among the three armed services. Second was the belief that Canada's future military obligations, either for the defense of North America or for peacekeeping forces, would be in terms of relatively small mission forces including components of two, or all three, of the conventional services. Third, and aside from the likelihood of requirements for mission forces, was a belief that in modern war all military functions for large forces, as well as small ones, involve joint operations of the conventional services.

In 1968 unification had become a fact, and there is now only one service of the Canadian Armed Forces. All personnel have a common uniform for duty (other than special purpose clothing) and off duty; a common grade structure has been established on a single promotion list.

Manpower for the Canadian Armed Forces is obtained by voluntary enlistment.

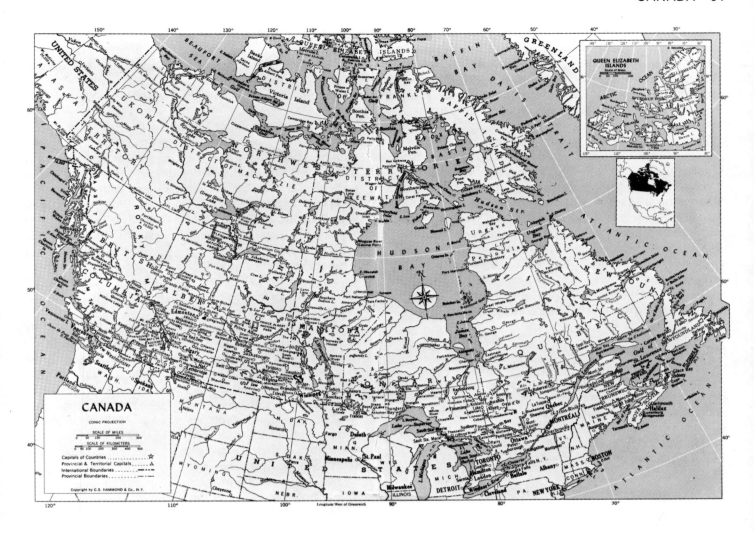

## STRATEGIC PROBLEMS

Canada's principal strategic problems are geographical. First and most importantly, Canada lies athwart most of the likely paths of Soviet attack on the United States, either by manned aircraft or by ICBM. Second, most of Canada's relatively small population is concentrated in the far southern strip of the nation, close to the American border. Canada does not have the population or other resources to provide adequate defense against Soviet attacks, which would also threaten Canadian population and industrial centers. Thus, it is in Canadian interest to have the assistance of the United States in establishing passive and active defense means along the far-flung northern and northeastern periphery of the continent; it is in American interest to have Canadian cooperation in the establishment of early warning and interceptor bases along this same periphery, most of which is on Canadian soil.

The great bulk of Canada (second largest nation in the world) in relation to the size of the population, and in relation to its far-northern location, has other strategic implications. It is difficult for Canada to maintain naval forces sufficiently large to provide protection for one seacoast; without American help it is impossible to protect two seacoasts on the opposite shores of a great continent.

Similarly, Canada would be indefensible against attack from the south (the experience of the War of 1812 is no longer valid) were it not that both Canada and the United States, since the Treaty of Washington in 1871, have acted on the assumption that war between the two nations would be unthinkable, and both are proud that theirs is the longest unfortified frontier in the world.

About one-fourth of Canada's population is French-speaking, and there is a strong movement for Quebec separatism, that is, the independence of predominantly French-speaking Quebec Province. A tiny (probably one hundred members or fewer) pro-separatist extremist group carried out terrorist acts, including the kidnapping and murder of a cabinet minister, in 1970. The *Parti Quebecois*, committed to independence, now controls the provincial government of Quebec. More scattered terrorist acts by extremist separatist groups may be expected, and while the seccession of Quebec is unlikely, the growing cleavage in Canadian society is inevitably eroding national morale.

## MILITARY ASSISTANCE

Canada has no foreign assistance program as such, nor is it the recipient of any such programs. However, Canadian military personnel attend service schools and staff colleges in the United States and Great Britain, and students from the United States, Britain, and other members of NATO attend Canadian military schools.

## ALLIANCES

Canada is a member of three overlapping alliances. First, as a member of the Commonwealth, Canada retains close and cordial military ties with the United Kingdom, and with a number of other Commonwealth countries, particularly Australia and New Zealand. The importance of Commonwealth ties has lessened in the years since World War II, however, as Canada has ever more firmly related its defense requirements and arrangements to those of the United States.

Canada was one of the original members of NATO. Until 1969, in addition to one brigade group and six tactical air squadrons stationed in Germany, committed to NATO's Allied Command Europe, approximately half of the remainder of Canada's combat forces was earmarked for NATO in the event of war or grave emergency. However, the land force contingent in Germany has been reduced, but in emergency will be reinforced by airlift from Canada.

Canada's relationship with the United States is perhaps the closest military alliance in the world between fully sovereign nations. This dates back to August 18, 1940, when at Ogdensburg, N.Y., President Franklin D. Roosevelt and Prime Minister William L. Mackenzie King announced the

consider in a broad sense the defense of the north half of establishment of a Permanent Joint Board of Defense to the Western Hemisphere. This Ogdensburg Declaration was considered by Canada to be a treaty, although in the United States, for constitutional reasons, it is classed as an executive agreement.

The Permanent Joint Board on Defense, with mixed civilian-military membership representation from both nations, is still the primary instrument for integrating the defense efforts of the two nations. It does not make decisions, but rather prepares recommendations to the two governments. Other bilateral consultative bodies have been established since World War II, including: the Military Cooperation Committee, established in 1946; the Senior Policy Committee on the Canada-United States Defense Production and Development Sharing Program, established in 1958; and the Canada-United States Ministerial Committee on Joint Defense, also established in 1958.

One of the most significant aspects of the alliance is the Defense Development Sharing Program. The origins of this also go back to the period just before American entry into World War II when, on April 20, 1941, President Roosevelt and Prime Minister Mackenzie King agreed at Hyde Park on cooperation in defense production. This close cooperation continued until 1958, when the governments of the two nations agreed upon the virtual integration of their weapons systems design, development, and production procedures, to assure the most complete possible coordination of their defense economies.

The most significant of the various operational military cooperative programs between the two nations is the North American Air Defense Command (NORAD) which was established in 1958 by a ten-year agreement which brought about the virtual integration of the air defense commands of the two nations. The agreement has been renewed since, most recently in 1975 for five years.

Canada, while recognizing the necessity for close military, political, and economic ties with the United States, is careful to maintain and proclaim its complete sovereign independence from its giant neighbor. Prime Minister Pierre Elliott Trudeau visited Moscow and signed consultation agreements with the USSR a year before President Nixon's 1972 visit, and Canada also established cordial relations with the People's Republic of China well in advance of U.S. moves.

Canada participated in the three-nation International Commission of Control and Supervision (ICCS) set up to supervise the Vietnam ceasefire in 1973 but withdrew July 31, citing the ICCS's inability to cope with constantly occurring truce violations.

*The Canadian Armed Forces are organized within functional commands.*

# NATIONAL DEFENSE HEADQUARTERS

National Defense Headquarters and organizations and units under its command and control (such as Canadian Forces colleges and Defence Liaison): Ottawa.

# MARITIME COMMAND

Headquarters, Halifax. Commands all surface and subsurface naval forces and has operational control of the maritime patrol aircraft of the forces.

*Personnel:* 9,000 Regulars; 3,200 Reserves

*Organization:*
   Maritime Forces, Pacific Region
   Maritime Forces, Atlantic Region
   Maritime Forces, Canadian Atlantic Sub-Area, a sub-ordinate command of NATO's Allied Command Atlantic (SACLANT)

*Major Units:*
   3 submarines (SS, Oberon class)
   4 guided missile destroyers (DDG, DD280 class; Sea Sparrow SAMs)
   4 guided missile frigates (FFG; improved Resti-gouche class; Sea Sparrow SAMs)
   12 frigates (FF)
      2 Annapolis class
      4 Mackenzie class
      6 St. Laurent class
   3 replenishment oilers (AOR)
   10 auxiliary ships (tugs, tankers, etc.)
   19 service craft
   1 hydrofoil ASW ship (experimental)

*Major Bases:* Halifax, Esquimalt

# MOBILE COMMAND

Headquarters, St. Hubert, Quebec. Provides operation-ally ready land and tactical air forces to meet defense commitments. Command and control of all resources assigned to the command are exercised from St. Hubert. Has operational control over Air Command's Tactical Air Group headquarters located at St. Hubert.

*Personnel:* 17,700 Regulars; 15,700 Reserves

*Organization:*
   3 combat groups
   1 airborne regiment
   1 combat training center

*Major Equipment Inventory:*
   250 medium tanks (215 Centurion, 35 Leopard)
   100 scout cars (Ferret)
   800 APCs (M113)
   100 armored reconnaissance vehicles (Lynx)
   70 M-109 self-propelled howitzers (155mm)
   250 105mm howitzers
   500 106mm recoilless antitank guns
      ATGM (SS11B, TOW)
      SAM (Blowpipe)
   2,848 trucks (489 5 ton, 1¼ ton, 1/4 ton)
On order: 128 Leopard tanks

# AIR COMMAND

Headquarters, Winnipeg. Provides operationally ready regular and reserve air forces to meet national, continental, and international commitments.

*Personnel:* 22,780 Regulars; 730 Reserves

*Organization:*
   Maritime Air Group
      4 maritime patrol squadrons (Argus)
      1 maritime surveillance squadron (Tracker)
      2 ASW helicopter squadrons (Sea King)
      2 utility squadrons (Tracker, T-33, Dakota, Iroquois)
      1 training squadron (Tracker, Sea King)
   10 Tactical Air Group
      4 tactical helicopter squadrons (Iroquois, Kiowa)
      1 helicopter training squadron (Iroquois, Kiowa)
      1 helicopter support squadron (Chinook, Iroquois)
      2 tactical fighter squadrons (CF-5)
   Air Transport Group
      2 transport squadrons (Hercules)
      1 transport and refuelling squadron (Boeing 707)
      1 utility transport squadron (Cosmopolitan, Falcon)
      1 operational training squadron (Hercules)
      4 transport/rescue squadrons (Buffalo, Labrador, Iroquois, Twin Otter)
   Air Defense Group
      3 fighter-interceptor squadrons (Voodoo)
      1 operational training squadron (Starfighter)
      1 electronic warfare squadron (Canuck, T-33)
      29 long-range radar squadrons
      4 auxiliary radar sites
   Flying Training Schools
      3 schools (Musketeer, Tutor, Dakota, Kiowa, T-33, CF-5)
   Air Reserve Group
      4 reserve wings (Otter, Dakota, Twin Otter)

1 Canadian Air Group (assigned to Canadian Forces Europe)
3 tactical fighter squadrons (Starfighter, T-33)

*Major Aircraft Types:*
266 combat aircraft
    164 fighter-bombers (91 Starfighter, 73 CF-5)
    44 fighter-interceptors (13 Starfighter, 31 CF-5; 15 Voodoo in storage)
    30 maritime patrol (Argus)
    28 ASW helicopters (Sea King)
449 other aircraft
    70 transports (24 Hercules, 6 Boeing 707, 7 Cosmopolitan, 7 Falcon, 14 Buffalo, 12 Twin Otter)
    137 helicopters (6 Labrador, 48 Iroquois, 68 Kiowa, 7 Sea King, 8 Chinook)
    242 trainers and utility (9 Canuck, 36 T-33, 25 Musketeer, 100 Tutor, 10 Dakota, 30 Otter, 32 Tracker)
Equipment on Order: 18 P-3 Orion maritime patrol aircraft

## COMMUNICATION COMMAND

Headquarters, Ottawa. Provides information services in the form of strategic communications to the Canadian Forces and Emergency Government.

*Personnel:* 3,300 Regulars; 1,560 Reserves

*Organization:*
    76 Communications Group
    764 Communications Squadron
    763 Communications Regiment
    2 Department of National Defence data centers
    Communications Reserve
    21 communications reserve units

## CANADIAN FORCES EUROPE

Canadian Forces Europe are equipped and trained for full-scale military defensive operations on the European central front. CFE is a national entity under commander of Canadian Forces Europe. It is directly responsible to chief of Defence Staff Ottawa.

*Personnel:* 8,800 Regulars

*Organization:*
    4 Canadian Mechanized Brigade Group
    1 Canadian Air Group

## CANADIAN FORCES TRAINING SYSTEM

Headquarters at Trenton, Ontario; plans, conducts, and controls all recruit, trades, specialist, and officer classifications common to more than one command of Canadian Forces.

*Personnel:* Permanent personnel and 11,000 recruits annually

Other overseas deployments of Canadian Forces:
    UN Force in Cyprus (UNFICYP), 515 officers and men
    UN Emergency Force (Israeli-Egyptian border) (UNEF)
    UN Disengagement Observer Force (Israeli-Syrian border) (UNDOF) UNEF and UNDOF, 1,050 officers and men
    Ghana, 3 officers
    Tanzania, 1 officer
    UN Truce Supervisory Organization (UNTSO)
    UN Military Advisory Commission (UNCMAC)
    UN Military Observer Group in India and Pakistan (UNMOGIP)

## PARAMILITARY

The Royal Canadian Mounted Police, approximately 8,000 strong, performs internal security as well as regional police functions, mostly in the lightly inhabited northern territories. The force is equipped with thirteen aircraft, approximately 2,000 vehicles, and thirty-two patrol boats (PB) in the marine division of 245 men.

The provinces of Quebec and Ontario have provincial police forces, totaling about 5,000 men. Most of these perform routine regional police functions.

Finally, there is a Coast Guard, which operates 146 ships, including some twenty-five icebreakers and twelve cutters which have defense implications.

# CENTRAL AFRICAN REPUBLIC

## POWER POTENTIAL STATISTICS

Area: 241,313 square miles
Population: 1,934,000
Total Active Regular Armed Forces: 700 (0.04% population)
Gross National Product: $394 million ($220 per capita)

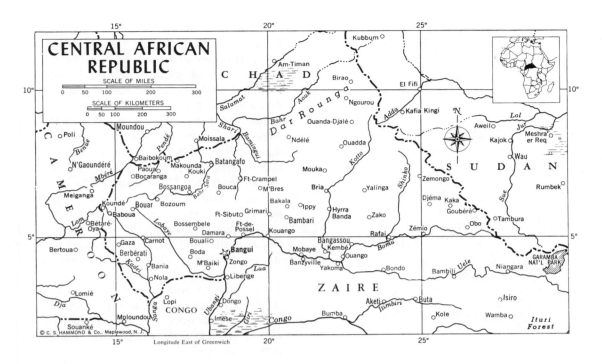

Annual Military Expenditures: $7.5 million (1.9% GNP)
Electric Power Output: 106 million kwh
Civil Air Fleet: 2 jet, 1 turboprop, and 1 piston transport

## POLITICO-MILITARY POLICIES AND POSTURE

In December 1976, President Bokassa proclaimed the country, then a republic, to be an empire. A year later he crowned himself Emperor Bokassa I. The former chief of staff of the army had deposed his predecessor on January 1, 1966, assumed the offices of president, prime minister, and minister of defense, and promptly abolished the Constitution and dissolved the National Assembly. He ruled by decree, assisted by the Council of Ministers. Among reasons advanced for the military coup were economic stagnation, discovery of vast uranium ore deposits in which France was much interested, army-gendarmerie rivalry, and growing Chinese Communist influence. Bokassa broke diplomatic relations with Peking and publicized Chinese Communist plans for increased control. He was himself disposed in September 1979 by his cousin David Dacko, with the help of 800–1,000 French troops. Dacko restored the republic.

Upon independence from France in 1960, the CAE signed a defense agreement with France which included internal security matters, base rights, transit and overflight privileges, and military assistance. Ubangi veterans of the French army formed the army. French officers were seconded as instructor-advisers. France has furnished equipment as well as training, has kept garrisons at Bangui and Bouar, and in November 1967, at the request of Bokassa during a governmental crisis, deployed a paratroop company to the Bangui airfield.

The CAR is a member of the OAU, the OCAM, and the Central African Customs and Economic Union (UDEAC).

The CAR's strategic location and its reserves of uranium have attracted the close attention of France. French companies own much of the country's enterprises, and France makes up the CAR's budget deficit.

The CAR maintains good relations with all its neighbors. Relations with Peking were restored in 1976. Bokassa had a particularly close friendship with Presidents Mobuto of Zaire and Amin of Uganda. Clandestine economic and political exchange occurs with South Africa.

Israel assisted the country to establish a youth organization on the lines of its own, a paramilitary organization for pioneering new agricultural settlements, and a preliminary training and indoctrination organization. Several thousand youths have passed through the training programs given by a team of twenty Israeli officers.

The army consists of 700 men, organized as an infantry battalion with a supporting engineer company. The equipment includes French EBR-75 armored cars and EBR-ETT armored personnel carriers. The air force of 100 men operates two C-47, ten Noratlas and ten AL-60 transports, and ten Sikorsky H-34 and Alouette II helicopters. Air bases are Bangui, Bouar, Bambari, and Berberati. There is a gendarmerie with a strength of 500 and a *Garde Republicaine* of 700 men.

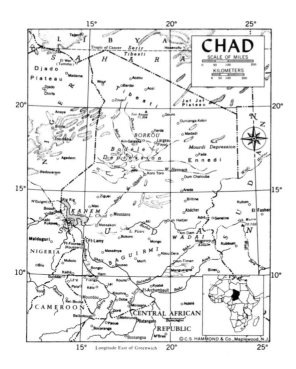

# CHAD

## Republic of Chad

### POWER POTENTIAL STATISTICS

Area: 495,752 square miles
Population: 4,472,000
Total Active Regular Armed Forces: 5,200 (0.12%
  population)
Gross National Product: $296 million ($70 per capita)
Annual Military Expenditures: $22.2 million (7.76%
  GNP)
Electric Power Output: 60 million kwh
Civil Air Fleet: 4 piston transports

### POLITICO-MILITARY POLICIES AND POSTURE

In March 1979 an agreement mediated by Nigeria ostensibly brought an end to civil warfare in Chad and replaced President Felix Malloum with a coalition government headed by Goukouni Oueddi, chief of the strictly Islamic Toubou tribe. The new government was not initially able to take control of the government and restore order, and there were reports of widespread massacres of Moslems in southern Chad, where they are a minority and where many are merchants and small businessmen. The separatist United Front of the South was also calling for secession of the southern provinces.

Upon independence from France in 1960 the army of Chad was formed from Chadian veterans of the French army. It inherited a stock of French arms and equipment, and a bilateral military technical assistance agreement provided additional equipment and some 500 French officers and men as instructor-advisers. This agreement, similar to those executed between France and other former African colonies, provides also for French assistance in maintenance of internal security, base rights, and transit and overflight privileges. The French army continued to control northern Chad until 1965. France maintained a regional military force in Chad, which was used for intervention—at the request of the governments concerned —in Congo (Brazzaville) in 1963, Gabon in 1964, and in Chad itself in 1968. The strength of French troops stationed in Chad was reduced in June 1971 to about 900 officers and men, apart from advisers attached to the Chad army. Chad ordered all French forces to leave the country in 1975, but good relations and a 300-man advisory force were reestablished the following year. In June 1978 there were reportedly 1,800 French troops in Chad, and in early 1979 more were flown in, to a total of about 2,500, to support the government of President Malloum in the civil warfare then going on. All French troops were to be withdrawn as a result of the March peace agreement, but in April they were still in Ndjamena, the capital, along with Nigerian troops, attempting to maintain order.

Chad's recent troubles stem in large part from the same north-south split along lines of race, religion, and living patterns that threatens the domestic tranquillity of many Sudanic African countries. The sedentary animist and Christian people of the south accepted education and training from the French, and controlled the government from independence until 1979. The nomadic Moslems of the north retain their traditional ways under feudal leaders and maintain close ties with kinsmen in Libya and Sudan.

There was serious insurgency in the northern and central regions from 1963 to 1968, leading the president in August 1968 to request and obtain military assistance from the French Government to put down the rebellion. This effort was not fully successful, and several rebel groups continued to fight the government in the north and east.

The northern rebels are composed of several divergent factions linked in name as the Chad National Liberation Front, or FROLINAT. The two main factions differ sharply on relations with Libya, which has laid claim to and in April 1979 made an abortive attempt to occupy the 27,000-square-mile, mineral-rich Aouzou strip in northern Chad. In 1977, FROLINAT launched an offensive that overran some three-fourths of Chad. Malloum, who had just broken relations with Libya over the Aouzou, was forced to accept Libyan, Niger, and Sudanese mediation for a ceasefire early in 1978. The ceasefire did not hold, and Chad accepted the intervention of some 1,700 French troops in March 1978.

Chad is a member of the OAU. It withdrew from OCAM in 1973. Chad is an active participant in the Lake Chad Basin Commission. Good relations are maintained with Zaire, Nigeria, and the Central African Republic. Chad's military weakness stems from its ethnic divisions, a desert the size of Texas, and one of the world's poorest economies. The subsistence sector comprises 96 percent of the population, and one product, cotton, accounts for 80 percent of the perennially deficient export earnings.

The army of 5,200 men consists of two infantry battalions and supporting light artillery batteries. There is an air force of 200 men with one C-47, ten Noratlas transports, and ten Sikorsky H-34 and ten Alouette II helicopters. Air bases are Abeche, Fada, Largeau, Fort Archambault, N'Djamena, Mongo, Moudou, Pala, and Bongor.

There is also a gendarmerie of 6,000 men. In 1965 it was planned, with French assistance, to recruit and train six brigades of gendarmerie to be stationed in the disaffected areas. The extent of implementation of this plan is not known.

# CHILE

## Republic of Chile

### POWER POTENTIAL STATISTICS

Area: 286,396 square miles
Population: 10,770,000
Total Active Regular Armed Forces: 87,500 (0.08% population)
Gross National Product: $10.3 billion ($970 per capita)
Annual Military Expenditures: $732.6 million (7.11% GNP)
Crude Steel Production: 450,000 metric tons
Iron Ore Production: 10.4 million metric tons
Fuel Production:
  Crude Oil: 1.1 million metric tons
  Refined Petroleum Products: 4.2 million metric tons
  Coal: 1.2 million metric tons
  Natural Gas: 3.6 billion cubic meters
Electric Power Output: 9.7 billion kwh
Merchant Fleet (ships 1,000 tons and over): 43 ships, 393,000 gross tons
Civil Air Fleet: 33 major aircraft

### DEFENSE STRUCTURE

Since the military coup in September 1973, Chile has been ruled by a military junta composed of the commanders in chief of the army, navy, air force, and National Police (Carabineros), with the commander in chief of the army, Gen. Augusto Pinochet Ugarte, as president of the junta. Operational and policy matters concerning all the services are the responsibility of the junta. Administration of the armed services is through the Ministry of Defense.

### POLITICO-MILITARY POLICY

After a period of increasing unrest in the 1960s, in the 1970 elections Sen. Salvador Allende, an avowed Marxist and a Socialist party leader, formed a coalition of leftist parties—Socialist, Communist, radical and splinter groups—which won the election as the Popular Unity movement, although receiving only 37 percent of the popular vote. With both houses of the Chilean Congress controlled by the opposition parties, however, Allende had great difficulty in obtaining support from the Congress. He nationalized the copper industry and instituted land reforms, which failed because leftist guerrillas took over farmlands by force. The economic situation became disastrous, as Chile's reserves of foreign exchange were exhausted and loans of additional funds were refused, or negotiated only with great difficulty. Widespread dissatisfaction with the government, the enormous increase in the cost of living (238 percent May 1972 to May 1973), inflation, and shortages of consumer goods, including food, led to frequent and prolonged strikes. A truckers' strike in the summer of 1973, which was joined by numerous sympathy strikes and demonstrations, finally brought the downfall of the government in a military coup in September. (An attempted coup in June had been crushed.) The four-man military junta declared a state of siege. Most provisions of the constitution were suspended. The strict measures taken to eradicate dissidents and disperse foreign revolutionary elements, including mass arrests and torture, resulted in censure by and strained relations with the United States and many other nations. Although restrictions have been eased a little and many political opponents have been granted amnesty, no real moves toward restoring constitutional government have been made. Political parties and most labor union activity are banned.

### STRATEGIC PROBLEMS

Relations with Bolivia, broken in 1962 when Chile threatened to divert water from the Lauca River, were resumed in 1975, only to be broken again in 1978, with the failure of negotiations for the outlet to the sea that Bolivia has been seeking since the War of the Pacific (1879-83). A dispute with Argentina concerning sovereignty over three islands in the Beagle Channel and related control of the sea 200 miles from the coastline (including any oil that might be found in that area) was arbitrated in Chile's favor in 1977 by a board appointed by Queen Elizabeth II.

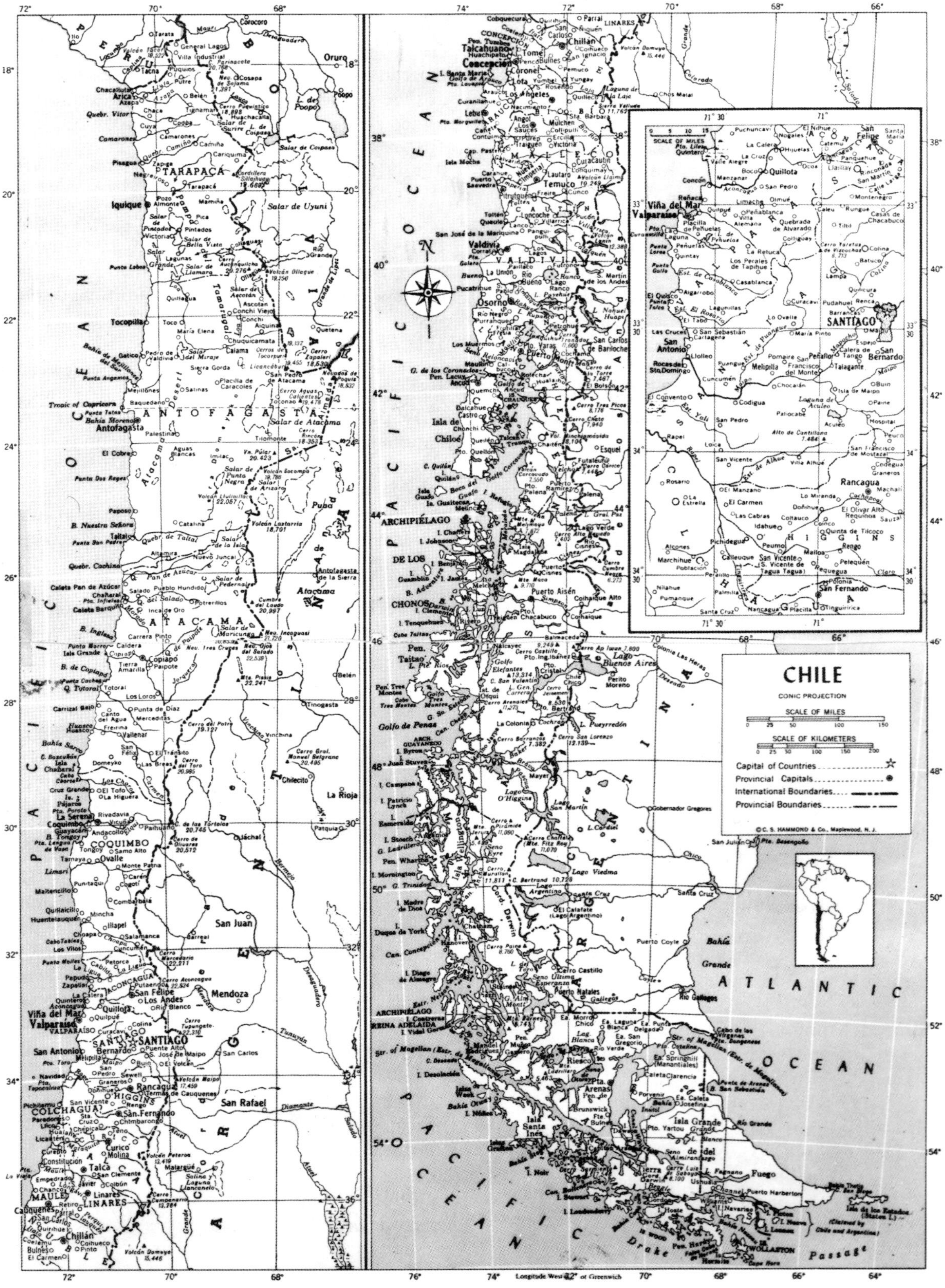

CHILE
CONIC PROJECTION
SCALE OF MILES
SCALE OF KILOMETERS
Capital of Countries
Provincial Capitals
International Boundaries
Provincial Boundaries
©C. S. HAMMOND & Co., Maplewood, N. J.
PACIFIC OCEAN
ATLANTIC OCEAN
TARAPACÁ
ANTOFAGASTA
ATACAMA
COQUIMBO
ACONCAGUA
VALPARAÍSO
SANTIAGO
O'HIGGINS
COLCHAGUA
MAULE
LINARES
CONCEPCIÓN
VALDIVIA
Arica
Iquique
Tocopilla
Antofagasta
Copiapó
La Serena
Valparaíso
Viña del Mar
San Antonio
Rancagua
Talca
Chillán
Concepción
Temuco
Valdivia
Osorno
Puerto Montt
Isla de Chiloé
Puerto Aisén
Golfo de Penas
Punta Arenas
Isla Grande de Tierra del Fuego
Cape Horn
Drake Passage
Str. of Magellan
Tropic of Capricorn
Longitude West of Greenwich

Argentina has refused to accept the decision and the Vatican has undertaken arbitration.

## MILITARY ASSISTANCE

American military grant aid from 1950 to 1977 totalled $97.4 million. Under the MAP, 6,883 students have been trained. In 1977 Chile refused further military aid.

## ALLIANCES

Chile is a member of the OAS and related organizations. It withdrew from the Andean Pact in 1976.

## ARMY

*Personnel:* 52,000

*Organization:*
- 7 Divisions
- 20 infantry regiments
- 4 horse cavalry regiments
- 2 armored cavalry regiments
- 8 artillery regiments
- antiaircraft artillery battalions

*Major Equipment Inventory:*
- 75 medium tanks (M-4, M-48)
- 70 light tanks (M-3, M-41)
- 150 APCs (M-113, M-2 half-tracks)
- 150 light artillery (105mm howitzers)
- antiaircraft guns (20mm, 40mm)
- 120mm mortars
- 106mm recoilless rifles
- 20 liaison aircraft and helicopters

*Reserves:* There are about 300,000 men in the reserves.

## NAVY

*Personnel:* 25,500, including Marines and coast artillery

*Major Units:*
- 2 submarines (2 Oberon class; 1 Balao class; SS)
- 2 light cruisers (Brooklyn class; CL)
- 1 light cruiser (Gota Lejon class; CL)
- 6 destroyers (DD; 2 Fletcher class; 2 Sumner class; 2 Almirante class with Sea Cat SAMs and Exocet SSMs, both short-range
- 5 frigates (FF; 2 Leander class with short-range Sea Cat SAMs and Exocet SSMs; 3 Charles Lawrence class
- 2 patrol escorts (PG; 3-inch guns)
- 3 patrol craft (PC; 20mm + guns)
- 4 motor torpedo boats (Luerssen class; PT)
- 3 tank landing ships (LST)
- 7 landing craft (1 LCU; 6 LCP)
- 6 auxiliary ships (oilers, survey ships, etc.)
- 9 service craft (tugs, dry docks, etc.)
- 4 P-2 ASW patrol aircraft
- 3 PBY ASW patrol aircraft
- 5 HU-16 ASW patrol aircraft (3 C-95 ASW patrol)
- 5 C-47 transports
- 11 trainer aircraft (5 C-45, 6 T-34)
- 4 Bell 206A Jet Ranger ASW/SAR helicopters

## AIR FORCE

*Personnel:* 10,000

*Organization:*
- 3 fighter-bomber squadrons (2 Hunter, 1F-5 Tiger II)
- 1 COIN squadron (T-25, A-37)
- 1 transport squadron (C-118/95/47, Beech 99, Beaver, Otter, Twin Otter)
- 1 training squadron (T-25/34/37, Vampire)

*Major Aircraft Types:*
- 80 combat aircraft
  - 18 F-5 fighter-bombers
  - 36 Hunter fighter-bombers
  - 26 A-37, T-25 trainer light ground attack aircraft
- 244+ other aircraft
  - 73 transports (C-118/45/47, Beech 99, C-130, Otter, Twin Otter)
  - 5 HU-16 SAR aircraft
  - 10 liaison aircraft (O-1, U-17)
  - 126 trainer aircraft (T-34/37/25, Vampire)
  - 30+ helicopters (Bell 47 and UN-1, Sikorsky UH-19, Hiller UH-12)

*Air Bases:* Los Cerrillos, Puerto Moutt, Cerro Moreno, Antofagasta

## PARAMILITARY

The national military police, *Carabineros,* number about 22,500. This force is elite, competent, and respected. Its equipment and training include the latest available for control of urban disorders. It has been heavily engaged in civic action such as medical services, social services, and literacy programs.

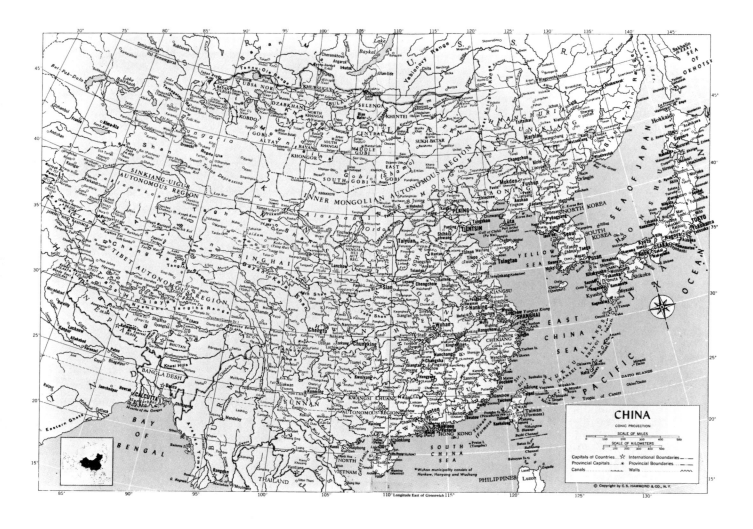

# CHINA, PEOPLE'S REPUBLIC OF

## POWER POTENTIAL STATISTICS*

Area: 3,691,501 square miles (including Tibet)
Population: 934,600,000
Armed Forces: 4,300,000 (0.46% population)
Gross National Product: $299 billion ($320 per capita)
Annual Military Expenditures: $23.8 billion (10.9% GNP)
Steel Production: 25 million metric tons

Fuel Production**:
  Coal: 401 million metric tons
  Crude Oil: 78 million metric tons (export 6 million metric tons)
  Refined Petroleum Products: 35 million metric tons (export 2.5 million metric tons)
Electric Power Output: 115 billion kwh
Grain Production: 255 million metric tons
Merchant Fleet (ships 1,000 tons and over): 610
Machine Tools (units): 50,000

*These figures represent a generally conservative consensus from reliable sources.

**The oil production sources and capacity of the People's Republic of China (PRC), and the uses to which they might be put, are the subjects of intense study and speculation. It has been suggested that the PRC might find oil to be the prime vehicle for financing economic growth.

Civil Air Fleet: 30 jets, 18 turboprop, and 70 piston transports

## DEFENSE STRUCTURE

The name People's Liberation Army (PLA) designates all the armed forces of the People's Republic of China. This includes ground, sea, and air elements. The ground army is further divided into first-line strategic forces and regional elements. Finally, there are specialized border and construction units and several categories of militia. The training of these latter units is usually assigned to the army.

The PLA answers to two separate authorities. On the government side there is a Ministry of National Defense (MND) of the State Council. MND also oversees the Academy of Military Science. The State Council, under the Standing Committee of the People's Congress, appears above the MND in the command structure but actually seems to have little function.

As in most one-party nations, the party actually controls the armed forces. In China the Politburo of the Communist party Central Committee, via the Politburo's Standing Committee, controls the Central Military Commission (CMC), which is the working military authority. This body's small membership (not more than ten or eleven) and their assignments to other powerful bodies ensure some measure of coordinated central command and control. CMC also controls and directs the National Defense Scientific and Technological Commission, an agency whose importance is growing in the new era of modernization.

The PLA proper, under the CMC, is directed by three major departments: the General Staff Department (whose chief of staff is the operating chief of the PLA), the General Logistics Department, and the General Political Department. These departments control and direct general military matters, logistics, and political matters, respectively, for the service arms: air force, navy, Armored Corps, Artillery Corps, Engineer Corps, Railway Engineer Corps, Capital Construction Corps, and the Second Artillery Corps. This last element is generally believed to be in charge of nuclear weapons matters. It is noteworthy that there is no separate and comparable agency for ground forces in general or for infantry as a combat arm. This may be attributed to the strong traditional need for an army that is the creature of the party and is controlled directly by the central political authority. The General Political Department, seriously weakened during the Great Proletarian Cultural Revolution, has more recently reestablished its status and stature as the instrument of political life in the PLA.

Geographically, the PRC is divided into eleven military regions, within which are the major strategic forces, under strong control from Peking, and the regional forces that answer to the political and military authorities of their regions. The boundaries of subordinate military districts usually coincide with those of provinces. In general, air and naval forces are at the disposition of regional authorities only under carefully controlled conditions.

## POLITICO-MILITARY POLICY

During the revolutionary period, from 1927 until 1949, the People's Liberation Army and the Chinese Communist party were virtually one. While there was some separation of function between political and military leadership, every man was considered to be a soldier, and the army was celebrated as the army of the people. The role of the senior military people has always been substantial, but it has generally conformed to the political line. When it has not, the politicians and ideologues have prevailed.

During the Great Proletarian Cultural Revolution the range of PLA activities was expressed in the slogan: "Support the Left, Support Industry, Support Agriculture; Exercise Military Control, Give Military and Political Training." Although charged with the task of supporting the left, the institutional biases and affiliations of the PLA often led to support of more moderate groups when the Red Guards became too violent or extreme. First-line troops were also used with some force in July of 1967 when a serious mutiny threatened in the Wuhan garrison. The army moved in January 1974 when local militia units, apparently controlled by the Gang of Four, became troublesome in Hangchow. Army units have been sent to perform relief work in such places as the earthquake-stricken city of Tangshan. Soldiers are used in public works and to help farmers, as well as in growing substantial amounts of the army's own food.

As the Cultural Revolution wound down, the discredited or demoralized party cadres who had been in charge were replaced by the so-called revolutionary committees, which took over control of most civil functions. The great majority of these bodies were firmly in the hands of military people. Although PLA power is now less strong and less obvious, it persists in internal affairs, and control over its direction is still at the center of much of the political struggle in Peking.

During the last years of the fighting against Nationalist forces in the revolutionary period, the PLA was involved in sizable operations over extended areas. Communist forces in the climactic battle of Huai Hai, for example, numbered over half a million men. Other experience includes massive participation in the Korean War, several campaigns in Tibet, several actions in the Taiwan Strait, the 1962 border fight with India, and the taking of the Paracel Islands.

The situation with the USSR has led Peking to promote the Russians to first place among dangerous enemies. The

Chinese have not forgotten that the Soviet action in Czechoslovakia in 1968 was justified as an act in the interest of the socialist camp. Although the United States is still seen as an imperialist power, the recognition of the PRC by President Carter and the withdrawal of American military support from Taiwan have made the United States almost an ally of Peking in its quarrel with Moscow.

The conventional force structure and deployment of the strategic army divisions and air and naval forces shows realistic response to perceived threats, to the degree that physical capabilities permit. The great strategic policy purpose is to make it clear that the cost of conventional attack on the territory of the PRC will be too high for the returns expected. Almost all attention now goes to the Soviet threat, although the positioning of forces indicates some interest in the actions of India and Taiwan and the new hostility toward Vietnam. One interesting element of the deployment in the north is the positioning of main-force units at some distance from the actual borders, with second-line and militia forces filling the areas closer to the border. This is a visible application of the concept of People's War—the involvement of the entire nation in the national military effort.

There is little attention directed at development of substantial amphibious or airborne capability, further suggesting that large offensives requiring such preparations are not contemplated at this time. The steady general improvement does imply that the PRC might be able to take significant military action over its borders, particularly in Southeast Asia. This is not likely, however, in the light of support for these areas, expressed or implied, by the superpowers and in consideration of Peking's fears of a two-front war.

Physical action to "liberate" Taiwan is less likely at this time, particularly in light of the new relations between the PRC and the United States. Peking's use of force will probably continue to be contained below a level that might get out of hand. The seizure of the Paracels in 1974 came at a time when no one was likely to give physical support to other claims over the territory. The islands may have substantial oil resources or value as a position from which to track Soviet naval movements, but their seizure was not a signal for strong reaction from anyone other than the helpless government in Saigon. The possible presence of oil has more recently produced some demonstrations by PRC fishing boats in the area of Senkaku (or Tiao Yu Tai) Islands, which are claimed by Japan as well.

The PRC is a late comer on the nuclear weapons scene and lacks the resources to mount a program that could in any way hope to match those of the United States or the Soviet Union. Consequently, Peking's nuclear weapons policies have aimed at getting maximum returns in both the political and military fields from modest resources.

On the political side, the PRC asserts that it will never be the first to use nuclear weapons—a prudent policy, given the damage-inflicting potential of the superpowers. The Chinese program is celebrated as an encouragement for the poorer nations and as a protection for them. Proliferation of nuclear weapons is touted by the Chinese as desirable in breaking the monopoly of the great powers. China has also held that all nations, large or small, must have a voice in disarmament discussions and agreements. Huang Hua, the PRC's foreign minister, delivered a lengthy address at the Tenth Special Session of the UN General Assembly on Disarmament on May 29, 1978. The general thrust suggested that the superpowers are defrauding the rest of the world in an attempt to maintain their own power position, and that the great powers must reform their policies and goals before any useful international agreements can be reached.

On the military side the nuclear weapons program has involved some twenty-six tests of devices with yields from about 20 kilotons to 3 megatons. One or more were underground, and one was missile-borne. The missile reportedly has a range of some 3,500 miles and is referred to as a "reduced range" ICBM.

Numbers of ballistic missiles seem to have changed little since 1972, when there were an estimated 50 medium-range missiles, and 100 intermediate. The nature of the force in being suggests that weapons are deployed to strike targets in European Russia. This strategy, and the time and resource constraints of the Chinese economy, probably account for the slow movement toward a sea-launch capability and retention of some eighty obsolescent TU-16 and 400 Il-28 bombers as delivery vehicles.

The Chinese ICBM continues to be the subject of speculation. A large device, comparable in size to the U.S. TITAN II or the Soviet SS-9, has been known since 1973. An instrumented down-range ship has been sighted and what look to be tracking stations on the north slope of the Himalayas and the east coast of Africa have been reported. As of mid-1978, there still has not been a full range test of this weapon.

Since April 1970 the PRC has launched seven satellites and achieved the "soft" return of one. One of these launches was performed with solid fuel. The chairman of the U.S. Joint Chiefs of Staff now says that a capability exists to field a small number in silos by the early 1980s.

There is no antiballistic missile program, a severe shortage in all-weather interceptors, limited numbers of surface-to-air missile sites, and outmoded command and control systems for air defense.

Current strategic thinking is reflected in present force improvement efforts. Ground force programs look to increased firepower and mobility, with great effort going to the problem of antitank defense and close air operations in support of ground troops. The air force is concentrating on high-performance defense aircraft and navy efforts concentrate on new missile-firing destroyers and close-in defense vessels, including substantial numbers of hydrofoil boats. Production of Whiskey and Romeo class submarines continues, although the exact role of the diesel-driven submarine in a modern antisubmarine environment is not clear. There is one Golf class boat of missile-firing type, and a nuclear submarine is under test.

The doctrine of self-reliance as preached by Mao Tsetung has been substantially breached by the new leadership in its preliminary efforts toward military improvement. Chinese delegations abroad, particularly in western Europe, have shown strong interest in certain weapons, including French antitank HOT missiles, French aircraft and helicopters, British Harrier V/STOL aircraft, German aircraft and helicopters, and, in a number of places, advanced ASW materiel, communications and electronics gear, and advanced computers. This last item caused some concern in Washington because, while the computer in question is part of a system used for exploration for oil and minerals, it also has significant value for antisubmarine purposes. These interests seem to show efforts to make badly needed defense improvements, and many suggest ambitions as a regional power, but indicate no aspirations for global capabilities at this time.

The PLA has gone through periods when the privileges and prerequisites of rank were exercised, but the egalitarian and revolutionary ethic has generally prevailed. There are no ranks; people are addressed as Soldier-Fighter Li, or Comrade Platoon Leader Wang, or Army Commander Chang. The differences of rank are more subtly shown, however. For example, an officer's tunic is not only made of better cloth; it also has more pockets. From time to time there are attacks on officers for such imperialistic sins as elaborate banqueting or use of government cars for family transport. Such programs as the one sending officers to the ranks for a period of service and education no longer operate, but the effort to keep military officials in line is a continuing one.

There is a political officer in every unit of the PLA down to and including the company or equivalent. The political officer is, by Mao's fiat, superior to the tactical unit commander. The General Political Department of the PLA headquarters in Peking is the ultimate source of precepts for political and ideological conduct. Teng Hsiao-ping's man in this office will probably foster ȝse cooperation with the General Staff Department.

All fit males eighteen or older are subject to military duty. Candidates are screened and given initial training in their home areas and then shipped to their units. Six to seven million young people come into the age zone each year; so the PLA can be highly selective. Service in the army is for three years, with the air force service four years, and the navy five. The troops receive massive political indoctrination and are constantly reminded that they are the friends and protectors of the Chinese people.

## CHINA IN PASSAGE

The previous discussion deals directly with the nature of military power in the affairs of the People's Republic of China. At this writing (late 1979) the overall Chinese condition is ambiguous. Two years after the deaths of Mao and Chou, the leadership that won out over the Gang of Four in the contest for central power seems well protected against any renewed attack from the radical left. There continues to be talk about serious differences between Hua Kuo-feng and Teng Hsiao-ping, but no major rupture has appeared. Massive programs, interior and exterior, have been announced and begun. The roles and weights of ideological considerations as against material ones are apparently not fully agreed upon, but a new and realistic thrust toward modernization is clearly dominant. The four modernizations call for improvements in agriculture, industry, military forces, and science and technology.

In interior affairs there has been movement toward some use of pay incentives and material rewards. Schools have reopened and normalized. Advanced education has been reinstated. There is substantial interest in science and technology. The idea is accepted that military improvement can best be made by the prior construction of the industrial base. Thrift and economy in military and administrative costs are enjoined. The modernization effort will make massive demands on China's store of distributable resources.

The new face of China is most apparent in foreign affairs. The concern over the Soviet Union continues undiminished. China has broken with Vietnam and its former close friend, Albania. On the other hand, Peking engages Asian nations in new and closer relations. ASEAN has been endorsed, relations with India are better, and there has even been cautious endorsement of the temporary continuance of United States–Japan mutual security arrangements. China has now normalized relations with the United States, and cultivates closer relations with NATO and others in the West. The containment of the Soviet Union is clearly the most important task on the PRC's agenda, but the new actions also represent some deviation from Mao's doctrine of self-reliance. The tools and technology of the modern state are being sought from outside sources, and Chinese distaste for long-term financing arrangements is diminishing somewhat.

The leaders in Peking face a most complex problem. Some political and ideological faithfulness is necessary to hold the nation together. Progress must take place with this in mind. The leadership will be sorely tested as it tries to manage both broad-front modernization and the task of denying its interior rivals and enemies abroad opportunities to displace it. There is a tendency to treat China today as a truly powerful entity. That position still lies in the future. It will take skillful management and political talent to bring reality to Peking's goal of front-rank status.

## STRATEGIC PROBLEMS

The Great Proletarian Cultural Revolution was devised by Mao Tse-tung to give Chinese youth a revolutionary experience (however synthetic), to uncover and put out of office or reeducate those party cadres who had lost their revolutionary zeal, and to purge officials suspected of trying to lead China down the "capitalist road." From August of 1966 until the Ninth Party Congress in April 1969, the country was torn by the violence and militancy of the youthful Red Guards and their backers.

The PLA faced two strategic problems. First, there was the continuing need to provide visible evidence of readiness to deal with an invader. The American presence and activity in Vietnam were disquieting, and Peking's fears focused on the possibility that the war would overflow into the territory of the PRC. The concern over the USSR, always present, moved to a higher level after two armed clashes on the Ussuri River in March 1969, and the later withdrawal of American forces from Vietnam.

After March 1969 both sides began to build up military forces along their border. Peking has accused the Soviets of stationing sixty-four to sixty-seven divisions with 15,000 tanks and several thousand aircraft, and building several dozen missile bases along the border. The tension shows no signs of reducing as of late 1979. The quarrel involves old territorial claims, Marxist-Leninist doctrinal differences, and probably some rivalry over leadership in the "socialist camp."

In May 1978 a peculiar event occurred in which a Soviet patrol penetrated several kilometers into Chinese territory. Accounts of the event are contradictory and confused, but Moscow did apologize for what it insisted was a mistake, and the event led to nothing larger. Brezhnev and his defense minister had toured the area in late March and early April and had witnessed extensive military maneuvers. No reason was given for the visit, but it was clearly meant to reassure Soviet forces in the area that they were not forgotten and probably also to set a lesson for the Chinese. There was no overt connection with the later raid.

The second strategic problem facing the PLA was one of interior strategy. The PLA had to defend itself against efforts at takeover by such militant groups as that clustered around Chiang Ching (Madam Mao) while carrying out the difficult task of establishing control over a divided nation. The PLA's ability to form revolutionary committees and generally to maintain some level of stability demonstrated that it was indeed the most reliable and efficient element in the national system.

During five days in late 1973 eight of the eleven regional commanders were moved to new posts. They kept their command positions in the PLA structure, although removed from their party posts and shuffled about in a way that seemed designed to break up any local alliances.

As the Cultural Revolution slowed and halted, the revolutionary committees became more conspicuously the organs of control and direction. The move to include peasants and rehabilitated political cadres gave a broader base, but the primacy of the PLA was clear. The extreme left lost some, but not all, of its influence. Extensive reindoctrination campaigns were launched. Young people by the million were "sent down to the countryside," where they were to learn from the peasants and find a new life away from the cities and universities.

The PRC's technical military problem goes beyond the question of numbers. At the end of the Korean War the PLA was a reasonably modern force in terms of equipment, almost all of which came from the Soviet Union or had been made in China to Russian specifications. After the split in the early 1960s the Chinese were faced with the problem of maintaining an increasingly obsolescent force. Over time there have been some small improvements— home-designed destroyers and patrol craft, at least one nuclear-powered submarine, and modest improvement on the MiG-19. In the main, however, there has been continued production of copies of earlier equipment, except in the nuclear field, where Peking has been obliged to build from the ground up. In 1974 CIA officials reported a sharp downturn in Chinese military spending due either to economic or political conditions or to recognition that continuing production of last-generation weapons was not an effective policy. Awareness of this problem was apparent in the 1975 deal for fifty to sixty Rolls Royce Spey jet engines plus a plant in China to build more. It is believed that the plan is to fit this engine to a Chinese-designed airframe and thus to upgrade the seriously inadequate air defense system. Peking's crucial problem is the fact that the superpowers have substantial leads in technology, in production facilities, and in resources available for military programs. A broad-front modernization of the PLA would be unbearably costly and time consuming; so the PLA must be committed to selective programming. The concept of People's War, while subject to many functional variations, will continue to have an important part in the total strategy. People are one abundant resource for China.

A significant event managed by Chou En-lai shortly before his death was the U.S. presidential visit to the PRC in early 1972 and the ensuing "Shanghai Communique," which eventually produced the shift of American recognition from Taipei to Peking. This shift seems to have put the Taipei government in a more precarious position and has strengthened the PRC's position with respect to the Soviet Union. The Chinese interest in European weapons suggests that Peking hopes that Washington will not invoke COCOM, the agreement under which many non-Communist countries have promised not to sell military equipment to Communist countries without consulting each other.

On the international stage, Peking has begun to seek multiple contacts. The PRC replaced Nationalist China in the United Nations in 1971. After Nixon's trip to China, Japan withdrew recognition of Taipei and opened full relations with Peking. The PRC has become very active in relations with NATO nations and repeatedly tells them that Western Europe, not China, is the real target of Soviet aggression.

It would be unwise to attribute too much of Peking's current activity to a change in ideology or goals. The changes are tactical and in the sense of military strategy perfectly logical. The gathering of allies, the relief of pressure by the gaining of a new front, and the improvement of one's own fighting capability are all perfectly reasonable military actions, and China's behavior must be seen as realistic prudence.

Chou's death on January 8, 1976, brought forward an intense struggle for political ascendancy in China. The leftist element, personified by Madam Mao and the Gang of Four, appealed for support on grounds of ideological devotion to the principles and beliefs of Chairman Mao—as interpreted by them. An opposition group, less clearly defined, took a more moderate stand and strongly supported Chou's modernization plans. After Mao's death in September 1976, Hua Kuo-feng, the new, little-known party chairman, was represented as having been chosen as successor by Mao himself. Teng Hsiao-ping, who had been in and out of trouble several times, survived two purges and emerged as second-ranking official in the nation. The venerable and respected military figure Yeh Chien-ying was moved to the high but largely ceremonial post of president of the Republic. Teng, considered by many to be the real locus of power, has installed his men as minister of defense and director of the General Political Department, while retaining his post as chief of staff.

The new leadership has initiated major changes in all aspects of Chinese life and affairs. The Gang of Four is a handy scapegoat for anything bad that has happened in the past. Pains have been taken to portray Mao as an enthusiastic advocate of military force improvement, while still invoking the mystique of People's War. Some powerful military figures have apparently lost favor and position, but the active support of the PLA has gone to the new leadership. The people now in power have carried on and

even intensified the animosity toward the Soviet Union and continue to stress the need to arm against this threat.

The strategic situation that China faces today is dominated by the physical threat posed by the Soviet Union. There are many reasons why the Soviet Union might choose *not* to strike China, but the capability does exist, and the animosity between the two countries is real. Visitors to China have discussed the possibility of a Russian blitzkrieg through Sinkiang, but the gains from such an attack, including the destruction of China's nuclear test site, would not necessarily induce Peking's capitulation or willingness to bargain. A war fought over larger areas, particularly in the industrial sections of the northeast, would do more immediate damage, but would also be much more costly. If the Soviet Union should use nuclear weapons, the hard-won Chinese industrial superstructure would vanish. Chinese damage in retaliation would not be vast, but, if a second strike capability could be maintained, some damage to Russian cities would ensue. China would not initiate the use of nuclear weapons, because the maximum damage of which the Chinese force is capable would do little to reduce Soviet ability to devastate China in return. It is probably true that neither side at the moment sees war as a useful solution, particularly when the reactions of the rest of the world are uncertain, and there are dangers of a conflict spreading.

There is little possibility that either Chinese side can, or will try, to solve the Taiwan question by force of arms, particularly when, for Peking, the possibility of a two-front war exists. For the present, China and India have put aside their dispute over borders, and relations are improving. Tibet is still rebellious, and there is still a need to deal with that situation, but it does not imply any real menace to PRC national security. Relations with North Korea are good, but the Chinese appear to be very careful, at least in public, to avoid anything that looks like the physical commitment of the Korean War. Japan, in its present mood and state of armament, represents no physical threat to the mainland. There have for some time been tensions between China and Vietnam, and China supported the Khmer Rouge government in Cambodia in its conflict with Hanoi. On February 17, 1979, Chinese troops invaded Vietnam and advanced over forty miles in some places before Peking announced on March 5 that China's goals had been attained and the troops were being withdrawn. No further explanation was forthcoming.

China's major problem in any attempt to become a global, or even a major regional military power is economic. It remains true that over 80 percent of the Chinese people live on and draw their living from the earth. China may come close to its goal of standing in the first rank of modern socialist nations by the year 2000, but not if any real attempt to equal Soviet or American military strength is permitted to draw off limited resources.

## MILITARY ASSISTANCE

China, limited by its own poverty, has tended to select and operate its military assistance programs with extreme care. In many cases clients are reminded of the 1965 exhortation to make revolution at home with the resources available there. Leftist insurgents have received some weapons support, training assistance, and political backing. Some success was gained in picking up with Egypt when that nation broke with Moscow. Several African nations or rebel groups have been given help, but the Russian-Cuban entry into that area has overwhelmed the Chinese contributions. For example, China formerly maintained a cadre of about 100 instructors in Zaire, working with Angolan dissidents. This effort was over-shadowed when Cuba and the Soviet Union became involved. China's major client for military hardware has probably been Pakistan, but after the Bangladesh affair the flow seems to have diminished. The PRC's largest aid program has been directed to the building of the Tan-Zam Railway, from Zambia to the Tanzanian coast, which involved as many as 15,000 Chinese workers and some $400,000,000. Military assistance in the form of a squadron of older MiG aircraft and some tanks went to Tanzania. Relations between the two nations have deteriorated recently, despite Chinese help and friendship. In general it may be said that Peking operates at the fringe of military assistance, trying to maintain some appearance as an active participant in international politics.

## ALLIANCES

Despite their present antagonism, neither China nor the USSR has denounced their Treaty of Friendship, Alliance, and Mutual Assistance, which runs until 1980. Unless either nation became involved in conflict with the United States, it is unlikely that the treaty would be invoked or honored. Similar treaties with North Korea and Mongolia would probably have the same fate. The PRC's close alliance with Albania has suffered extremely since Peking began its move to enter the global community. Albania, feeling insecure with its only real ally, has been harsh in criticism of China, and the PRC has cut off all assistance, but the final, formal break has not yet occurred.

## ARMY

In this and the following sections the figures used represent a rough average from several sources. The PRC does not publish useful information in this area. This is equally true with regard to the deployment of units.

*Personnel:* 4.3 million, including railway engineer troops

*Organization:*

|  |  |
|---|---|
| 11 | military regions (each usually has 2 or 3 military districts; generally there is one army in each district) |
| 30 | armies (rough equivalents of Western army corps, usually of 2 or 3 divisions each; 3 artillery regiments; plus, in some cases armor and cavalry units) |
| 120+ | infantry divisions* |
| 10–12 | armored divisions |
| 3 | cavalry divisions |
| 2 | airborne divisions |
| 1 | mountain division (in Tibet) |
| 35–40 | artillery divisions (component regiments are usually attached to infantry divisions and include antitank and antiaircraft units as well as field artillery.) |
| 15 | railway engineer and construction divisions |

Independent Regiments:

|  |  |
|---|---|
| 17 | artillery regiments |
| 5 | antitank artillery regiments |
| 30 | antiaircraft artillery regiments |
| 5 | armored regiments |
| 67 | engineer regiments |
| 2 | signal regiments |
| 34 | motor transport regiments |

In addition, there are some 7,000,000 armed militia.

*Deployment:*

Since the Ussuri River incidents in March 1969, there has been a continuous, albeit slow, increase in the size and nature of PLA deployments. Estimates of the strength now facing the northern borders run from 40 percent to 55 percent of the entire PLA. Most of the armored strength is so positioned. Military regions in which major forces are located include Shenyang, Peking, Lanchou, Sinkiang, and Tsinan. There seems to have been a slight increase—four or five divisions—in the east and southwest to cope with the Vietnam situation, but no really large change has appeared. Interior regions are relatively stable. In addition to main-force units there are some seventy-five regional-type divisions. These are used for interior purposes as much as possible and are seen as augmentation for the strategic forces when required. Regional units are lightly armed.

The PLA has, from time to time, shown the ability to field combined-arms forces such as that involved in the capture of the Paracels. United States officials have commented on larger training ventures which have included extensive air-ground cooperation. Nationalist officials on Taiwan have noted extensive airfield and infrastructure building as well as active unit rotation in

---

*Average 12,000–14,000 men; armored, cavalry, and airborne divisions are slightly smaller.

and out of the area opposite Taiwan. A South Seas Command based at Canton, Kunming, and Hainan has been reported, but little is known about it.

During the active period of the Vietnam War the PRC had several railway engineer units helping to maintain facilities in the area. This activity has of course ceased. Roadbuilding in Southeast Asia has been cut back, and a program in Laos is apparently the only active effort of any real size.

*Major Equipment Inventory:*
8,000–9,000 tanks
      1,200+ T-59 tanks (Chinese-built T-54)
      JS-2/3 heavy tanks
      T-34 medium tanks
      T-60 amphibious tanks
      T-69 light tanks
2,000–3,000 APC (Chinese-designed and Chinese-built)
15,000–18,000 light, medium, and heavy artillery pieces
5,000–6,000 heavy mortars
1,200+ antiaircraft guns
SAM launchers SA-2 Guideline
SSM launchers
300–400 helicopters

*Reserves:* Militia units were formed by the Chinese Communists as early as 1928. During the active fighting periods these units did intelligence work and conducted small-scale operations. The actual number of militia has been difficult to establish. Estimates run up to 200,000,000, but this is obviously a count of people eligible for service. The actual strength of militia people who are armed and receive some training is estimated at between 7,000,000 and 10,000,000. Units have border security and internal public safety tasks. The Gang of Four organized highly politicized "urban militia" formations in places where their political strength permitted, but these have of course disappeared. The general debate over military affairs in Peking includes some differences over the amount of time and effort that should go into militia forces. They do give muscle to the operating concepts of People's War and constitute a readily available manpower pool. Mobilization plans recognize the separate identity of militia units, and they could be used as such in operations in the rear or on the flanks of an invader.

## NAVY

*Personnel:* 180,000 (including 25,000 naval air force and 28,000 marines)*

*Organization:*
3 fleets: North Sea—about 20 percent of naval strength, deployed between Yalu River and Lien Yuen Kang. East Sea—about 55 percent of naval strength, between Lien Yuen Kang and Chao An Wan. South Sea—about 25 percent of strength, based from Chao An Wan to Hainan. This force is likely to expand in response to growing Soviet activity in Southeast Asia.
3 escort squadrons (one per fleet)
4 landing craft squadrons—2 in East Sea fleet
2 submarine squadrons
4 minesweeper squadrons
2 torpedo boat squadrons
2 auxiliary ship squadrons
6 naval air divisions**
1 independent naval air regiment**
10 marine and 4 amphibious tank units
10 coast artillery units

*Major Vessels:*
    1 ballistic missile submarine (G class, diesel, SSB)
   65 submarines (W & R class, SS)
  1–3 submarines, nuclear-powdered (SSN)
    3 coastal submarines
   10 destroyers (4 Soviet Gordy class, 6 new construction Chinese-design Luta class, missile-firing)
10–12 destroyer escorts
   40 corvettes
30–40 submarine chasers, Kronstadt class
 140 missile patrol boats, Osa and Komar class, surface-to-surface missiles
   21 fleet minesweepers (20 T-43, 1 Bathurst type)
    6 coastal minesweepers
250–275 torpedo boats (80 P-6, 70 P-4, 100+ hydrofoil)
 350 patrol gunboats, Shanghai class
  50 fast patrol craft, Swatow type
  15 landing ships tank (LST)
  15 landing ships medium (LSM)
   6 landing ships, infantry, large (LSIL)
 450 landing craft, utility, and landing craft, mechanized (LCU & LCM), plus 17 LCT
  12 river gunboats
400+ miscellaneous support ships and craft
 500 fighter aircraft (MiG15/17/19, F-6, F-9)

---

*There has been no actual verification of the existence of a marine corps as such. These are probably army units that receive amphibious training and contingency assignments on a cyclic basis.

**In actual operations naval air defense units enter the command and control system of the National Air Command. Rescue and sea combat forces operate under naval command.

130  light bombers (Il-28, Tu-16, Tu-2)
 20  medium bombers (Tu-4)
 50  helicopters (Mi-4)
      miscellaneous utility, trainer, and rescue
      aircraft

*Major naval bases:* Tsingtao, Lushan, Taku, Shanghai, Huang Pu, Chou Shan, Amoy, Foochow, Whampoa, Changkiang, Tsamkong

*Reserves:* Reserves are estimated at 350,000.

## AIR FORCE

*Personnel:* About 400,000, including over 100,000 in air defense units

*Organization:*
 20  fighter and fighter-bomber divisions (3 air regi-
      ments per division, 3 squadrons per regiment)
  6  bomber divisions
  1  transport division (by co-opting civil aircraft
      perhaps one division could be landed.)
  5  independent air regiments
      trainer, support, and helicopter units
 32  independent antiaircraft artillery regiments
      manning 1,000+ weapons of all types
  9  radar regiments
      miscellaneous ground security and support
      elements

*Major Aircraft Types:*
  approximately 5,000 combat aircraft
    80  Tu-16 bombers, light
   400  Il-28 bombers, light
        a few Tu-2 and Tu-4
   300  MiG-21 and F-9
 3,000  fighters, MiG-17 and MiG-19
   600  MiG-15 and F-6 fighter-bombers (MiG-15s
        also used as trainers)
   350  helicopters (Mi-4, Frelon, Mi-8)
   450  transports of all types (An-2, Il-12/14,
        Il-18)

*Major Air Bases:* There are some 170 air bases and fields, over half of which are jet-capable, within 450 miles of Taiwan. Construction has also been recently focused on fields sited for defense of the Sino-Soviet border. Principal bases include Luchiao, Foochow, Tenghai, Tsaochiao, Liencheng, Pingtan, Hungchiao, Chienchiao, Changsha, Hsincheng, Nanhai, Shenyang, Peking, Nanking, Canton, Sian, Kwangchan, Kunming, Wuhan, Chengchow, and Lhasa.

*Reserves:* There are about 500,000 trained reservists.

## PARAMILITARY

In addition to the militia described earlier, the military establishment includes production and construction corps units which may number several million. These elements are lightly armed and organized on military lines.

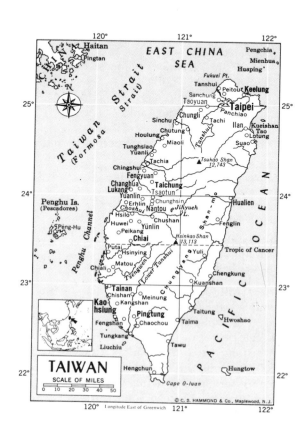

# CHINA, REPUBLIC OF (TAIWAN)

## POWER POTENTIAL STATISTICS

Area: 13,892 square miles
Population: 16,831,000
Total Active Armed Forces: 450,000–500,000 (2.67–
  2.97% population)
Gross National Product: $19.5 billion ($1,150 per capita)
Annual Military Expenditures: $1.5 billion (6.9% GNP)
Crude Steel Production: 1.27 million metric tons
Fuel Production:
  Coal: 2.96 million metric tons
  Crude Oil: 215 million metric tons (import 13.57
    million metric tons)

Refined Petroleum Products:
Import 3.32 million metric tons
Export 1.52 million metric tons
Natural Gas: 1.6 billion cubic meters
Electric Power Output: 29.7 billion kwh
Nuclear Power Production: 2,900 megawatts
Merchant Fleet (ships 1,000 tons and over): 153 ships;
1.4 million gross tons*
Civil Air Fleet: 10 jets, 12 turboprop (phasing out), and
37 piston transports

## DEFENSE STRUCTURE

Chiang Ching-kuo, son of Generalissimo Chiang Kai-shek, succeeded his father in April 1975 as president of the Republic of China (ROC) and commander in chief of the armed forces. The Ministry of Defense (MND) is a cabinet-level agency with a minister and a military chief of staff who is also chief of staff to the president (as commander in chief) and is the operational head of the armed forces. The MND General Staff resembles western models to a considerable degree and holds a good deal of authority in day-to-day as well as long-term affairs. There is a Combined Service Force that manages supply and manufacture of materiel on an integrated basis. A separate political department furnishes political officers to units of the forces, oversees political training and indoctrination, and performs a variety of personnel services.

## POLITICO-MILITARY POLICY

While eventual return to the mainland is the stated central goal of the Nationalist leaders, the prospects of accomplishing this by a classical invasion decrease. The government now emphasizes the capability of fast-moving special units that could reach the mainland and cooperate with anti-Communist or non-Communist risings against the Peking regime. This would take place in a time of turbulence and internal strife on the mainland and would be the first step in the reunion of all China under Nationalist leadership.

Meantime, attention goes to the assurance of economic progress and the maintenance of strong armed forces

*The China Shipbuilding Corporation is growing steadily. Its construction target for 1978 is 37 vessels totalling 500,000 tons. Repair work will be done on a further 4,000,000 tons. A second supertanker of 450,000 tons is under construction. Foreign sales account for much of this output, but additions are being made to the national merchant fleet as well.

which, while they now seem to be oriented toward effective defense, would be able to act offensively under proper conditions. The defense costs borne and the commitments made testify to the realism of the Nationalist view. (It is noteworthy that, despite its defense burden, Taiwan —making good use of U.S. economic assistance—has prospered in the last two decades and no longer asks for American aid.)

Having survived the ravages of World War II, in which China's manpower losses were exceeded only by those of the USSR, Germany, and Japan, the Nationalist government was defeated in a bitter civil war (1945–49) and fled to Taiwan. Social, political, and psychological factors, as well as serious military errors, contributed to this defeat. A major objective of military policy has been to correct these shortcomings. With U.S. military assistance and advice, this effort has been substantially successful.

The strength of the armed forces is maintained by conscription, with military service mandatory for all male citizens over the age of nineteen. Service is for two years. The percentage of soldiers of mainland origin steadily decreases, but they still dominate the upper levels in the officer and NCO ranks. The majority of troops in the lower ranks is now of Taiwan origin. The growing prosperity and rapid industrialization in Taiwan are making it more difficult to interest youth in the service as a career, whether they be of mainland or Taiwan parentage. The government is coping with this problem in good part by maintaining a well-trained and readily available reserve which now has perhaps 1,200,000 members. There are also local militia units numbering about 175,000.

## STRATEGIC PROBLEMS

The strategic problem facing the Republic of China is massive in size, but straightforward. There is only one enemy and, in essence, only one national policy goal. The governments in Taipei and Peking agree that there is one China, of which Taiwan is a part. The United States acknowledged the existence of this condition in the Shanghai Communique, issued at the end of the Nixon visit to the mainland in February 1972, and reaffirmed it in the joint communique issued to announce U.S. recognition of the Peking government in December 1978. Taipei now enjoys full recognition from fewer than twenty nations, and the number is likely to decrease.

Although outsiders may have trouble understanding the essence of the Chinese conflict, both sides see quite simply that within that one China there exists an unfinished civil war. The Communist government wants to bring under central control the last element holding out against it. The stated goal of the Nationalists has been the recovery of the mainland where once they ruled. However the probability of a return to the mainland may be assessed, the *idea* of return has been the driving force in Taipei's strategic concepts. With this, of course, is the perception of the need to withstand any Communist attack.

Obviously, the abrupt withdrawal of U.S. diplomatic recognition of Taiwan in December 1978 shocked military officials there. President Carter also announced the withdrawal of U.S. troops from the island of Taiwan and abrogation of the Mutual Defense Treaty of 1955. Peking, for its part, insists that the settlement of the Taiwan question is a purely Chinese matter and has made no open commitment not to use force. Washington has implied, however, that there is a tacit understanding to this effect. American officials also stated that the sale of certain weapons to Taipei would continue. The Communist leaders have not accepted this condition, but have not allowed the American statements to stand in the way of the new relationship with the United States.

Under the circumstances, the Nationalist authorities strive to maintain and improve their military forces. They say that they will not negotiate with Peking, nor will they seek help from the Soviet Union. This latter course is not without its attractions, since it exposes the PRC to the threat of a major two-front conflict.

It is evident to the ROC that a major attack on the mainland cannot be undertaken without massive support and assistance from abroad. The plan for spot use of special forces at points of turbulence or revolt recognizes the need for an alternative to massive conventional action.

Taipei's determination to retain control over the offshore islands—the Quemoy and Matsu groups—has posed a major strategic problem for the government. Nationalist determination, a strongly fortified position, and extensive American help have combined to keep the islands in ROC hands. This was accomplished despite repeated and massive bombardments (which ceased temporarily after normalization of United States-Peking relations) and numerous threats of Communist offensives. The political importance of the islands lies in the fact that the Nationalists still hold more than just one province in the unresolved civil war; Quemoy and Matsu are parts of Fukien Province. The islands also have some strategic value, particularly Quemoy, which controls entry to the port of Amoy and sea traffic in the area. It would be extremely difficult and costly to use Amoy as a mounting area for an assault on Quemoy or Taiwan.

Moving to more specific strategic problems, the Nationalists face a mainland army that, despite its relative backwardness, is very large. The problems of maintaining an acceptable air situation are paramount. Neither side has the naval capability to execute a sizable amphibious or airborne assault on the other without previous attrition operations of considerable magnitude.

The narrow width of the island of Taiwan poses a significant defense problem. Taiwan's military planners recognize and prepare to cope with this situation. Air bases, all on the west coast, might be subjected to saturation attacks from the mainland, but hardened shelters, modern air-to-air weapons, and superior aircraft promise a very costly undertaking for the PRC. The Communist navy is largely a close-in coastal force, and could not undertake decisive surface or submarine engagements. In summary, it can be said that, at the operational level, both sides have serious problems in the development of an offensive strategy. Defensive measures offer better returns on the strategic investment.

There is now the additional factor of Communist nuclear weapons. Their use would change the prospects absolutely, since the destruction of comparatively few targets would severely cripple Taiwan. An intangible is the question of how Peking would view the use of these weapons against their brethren on Taiwan whose ''liberation'' is their avowed purpose.

## MILITARY ASSISTANCE

Since 1950 the United States has provided $2.64 billion in military assistance to the ROC. An American military mission has been stationed in Taiwan since 1951 to help the Chinese in their utilization of the equipment furnished. This support has now disappeared, and with it some measure of reassurance. Nevertheless, the military competence of the Nationalist forces is high, and the economy will support substantial military spending.

ROC assistance to others has been modest, although the high capability of Taiwan to repair damaged equipment was substantially used during the Vietnam War.

## ALLIANCES

The only full alliance of the ROC has been the Mutual Security Treaty with the United States. In the past the United States has availed itself of the treaty and collateral agreements (of which there are about sixty) to base air force units on Taiwan and to use naval facilities there. There has been some combined training. Intelligence sharing has been routine, and the ROC has been supplied U-2 aircraft for extended reconnaissance. Several important U.S. communications facilities have been maintained. The island was a major forward supply and support base for American forces in Vietnam. At the war's peak, about 9,000 U.S. troops were stationed in Taiwan. The United States declined offers of ROC military participation in the Vietnam War, as it did in the Korean War. However, several civic action groups worked in South Vietnam, assisting the government in rural development projects. All such arrangements are now terminated.

## ARMY

*Personnel:* 350,000 (This includes three divisions in the Quemoy garrison and one in Matsu.)

*Organization:*
    4 armored brigades
   12 infantry divisions
    6 light divisions
    4 special forces groups
    2 airborne brigades
    3 armored cavalry regiments
    1 SSM battalion (Honest John)
    3 SAM battalions (1 Hawk, 2 Nike-Hercules)

*Major Equipment Inventory:*
    480 medium tanks (M-47 and M-48)
    500 light tanks (M-24 and M-41)
        tank destroyers (M-18)
        APC (M-113)
        SSM (Honest John)
        SAM (Hawk and Nike-Hercules)
        helicopters (UH, H-34, KH-3)*
        PL-10 trainers (Chinese-built light training aircraft)
        Artillery includes 105mm, 155mm, 203mm howitzers and antiaircraft weapons.

*Reserves:* The army has over 1,000,000 trained reserves, and equipment is on hand for training and for mobilization, if required.

## NAVY

*Personnel:* 36,000

*Major Units:*
    5 submarines (2 US Guppy types for ASW training; 3 midget; SS)
   20 destroyers (DD)
   14 destroyer escorts and frigates (DE)
    3 patrol craft, escort (MSF)
   15 fast attack vessels, missile-armed (PTFG)
    6 motor torpedo boats (PT)
   22 mine vessels (MSO, MSC, MSI)

*Major Amphibious Vessels:*
    2 LSD
    1 LST converted to AGC
   20 LST
   15 LSM
   30 LSU
    5 LSIL

There are a number of support and auxiliary vessels performing routine naval tasks.

*Naval Bases:* Tainan, Taitung, Chi-lung, Tsoying, and the Penghus

*Reserves:* The navy has some 50,000–60,000 trained reservists.

## AIR FORCE

*Personnel:* 80,000

*Organization:*
    8 fighter-bomber squadrons (F-100, F-5)
    4 fighter-interceptor squadrons (F-104)
    2 fighter/reconnaissance squadrons (RF-101, RF-104)
    1 ASW squadron (S-2)
    1 SAR squadron (HU-16, PBY)
    1 transport wing (C-46, C-47, C-119, C-123, Boeing 720)
    1 helicopter wing (H-13, H-19, Hughes 500, UH-1)
    1 trainer support wing (PL-1, PL-2)

*Major Aircraft Types:*
    275–300 combat aircraft
        190 fighter-bombers (90 F-100, 100 F-5)*
         60+ fighter-interceptors (F-104)
         17 fighter/reconnaissance aircraft (4 RF-101, 13 RF-104)
          9 ASW aircraft (S-2)
        300 other miscellaneous aircraft, including about 150 transports, 10 SAR, 46 helicopters, and trainers and general support types

*Air Bases:* Taipei, Hsinchu, Taoyuan, Taichung, Chiai, Tainan, Ping-tung, Kung Kuang

*Reserves:* over 125,000 trained reserves

## MARINE CORPS

*Personnel:* 36,000

*Organization:* 2 divisions and FMF headquarters

*Reserves:* about 70,000 trained reservists

## PARAMILITARY

There is a militia force of 150,000–200,000 which receives some training.

---

*The ROC is building UH helicopters under license. The five-year plan (now well under way) calls for 200 helicopters.

*The F-5E is now being built in Taiwan, and eventually this aircraft will be the principal system in the ROC Air Force.

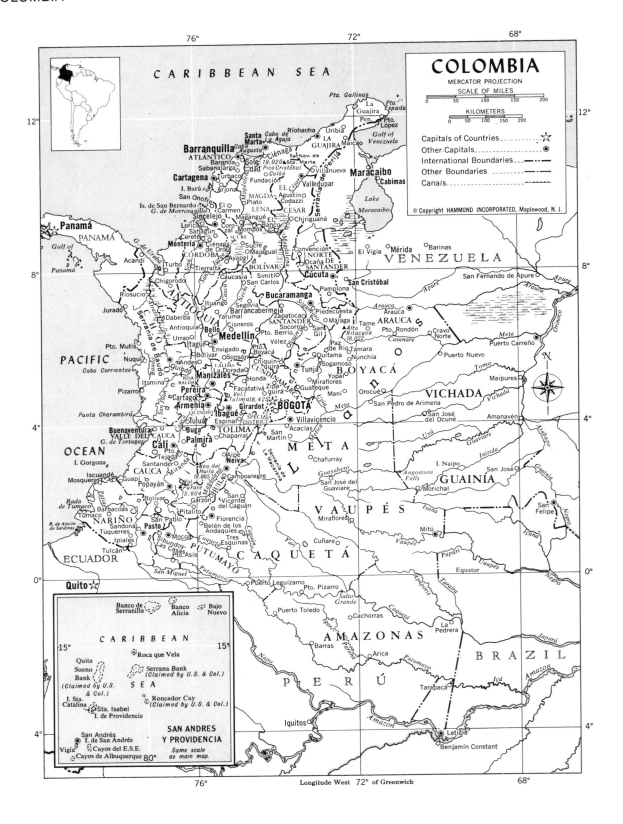

COLOMBIA
MERCATOR PROJECTION
SCALE OF MILES
0  50  100  150  200
KILOMETERS
0  50  100  150  200

Capitals of Countries ........ ☆
Other Capitals ............... ◉
International Boundaries ...... 
Other Boundaries .............
Canals .......................

© Copyright HAMMOND INCORPORATED, Maplewood, N. J.

CARIBBEAN SEA

Pta. Gallinas
La Espada
Pta. Espada
Pto. López
Gulf of Venezuela

Santa Marta
Barranquilla
Cartagena
Panamá

ATLÁNTICO
Baranoa
Sabanalarga
Cabo de la Aguja
Ríohacha
Uribia
LA GUAJIRA
Maicao

La Guajira Pen.

Soledad
Sta. Marta
Pico Cristóbal Colón 19,020
Sn. Nev. de

Fundación
Villanueva
Valledupar
Maracaibo
Cabimas

Turbaco
I. Barú
Arjona
San Onofre
Is. de San Bernardo
G. de Morrosquillo
Sincelejo
Lorica
Sahagún
Cereté
Montería
Ciénaga de Oro
Ayapel
Majagual
Sucre
Corozal
SUCRE

El Plato
MAGDA-LENA
El Carmen
Magangué
Mompós
El Banco
Agustín Codazzi
EL CESAR
Chiriguaná
CESAR

El Vigía
Mérida
Barinas
VENEZUELA

San Fernando de Apure
Apure
Arauca

PANAMA
Gulf of Panamá
Acandí
Turbo

CÓRDOBA
BOLÍVAR
Simití
San Carlos
Caucasia
Chigorodó

Convención
NORTE DE SANTANDER
Ocaña
Cúcuta
San Cristóbal
Pamplona

Riosucio
Juradó
Dabeiba
Ituango
ANTIOQUIA
Yarumal
Segovia
Barrancabermeja
Zapatoca
Piedecuesta
Bucaramanga
Málaga
ARAUCA
Arauca
Pto. Rondón
Casanare
Cravo Norte
Puerto Carreño

Antioquia
Cisneros
SANTANDER
Socorro
San Gil
Alto Ritacuva 18,022
Tame

Urrao
Bello
Itaguí
Medellín
Envigado
Pto. Berrío
Vélez
Paz de Río
Duitama
Nunchía
Puerto Nuevo

PACIFIC
Pto. Mutis
Nuquí
Cabo Corrientes
Andes
Sonsón
Bolívar
Chiquinquirá
Yopal
Miraflores
Sogamoso
Tomo
Maipures

Quibdó
CALDAS
La Dorada
Honda
CUNDINAMARCA
Tunja
BOYACÁ
VICHADA
Vichada
Amanavén

Itsmina
Pizarro
Manizales
RISA-RALDA
Vol.
Pereira
Cartago
Facatativá
Zipaquirá
Orocué
San Pedro de Arimena
N

Punta Charambirá
Armenia
QUINDÍO
Tolima 18,428
BOGOTÁ
SPECIAL DISTRICT
Mani
San José del Ocuné
Amanavén

Ibagué
Girardot
Espinal
Acacías
Villavicencio
Meta
Uvá
Guaviare

Buenaventura
VALLE DEL CAUCA
Buga
Palmira
TOLIMA
Chaparral
San Martín
META
Inirida
I. Naipo
San José
Guainía
San Felipe

G. de Tortugas
Cali
Pto. Tejada
Aipe
Neiva
Chafurray
Angostura Falls
GUAINÍA
Morichal
Guainía

OCEAN
I. Gorgona
CAUCA
Santander
Miranda
Campoalegre
Guayabero
San José del Guaviare
Negro

Iscuandé
Mosquera
Guapi
Popayán
HUILA
Nev. del Huila 18,865
Vol. Puracé 15,604
VAUPÉS
Miraflores
Isana
Mitú
Vaupés
Icána

Rada de Tumaco
Bolívar
Garzón
San Vicente del Caguán
Cuñare
Papurí
Guainía

Barbacoas
Tumaco
B. de Ancón de Sardinas
Pitalito
Belén de los Andaquíes
Florencia
Tres Esquinas
Yarí
Apaporis
La Pedrera

NARIÑO
Sandoná
Túquerres
Pasto
San Pablo
Mocoa
Sibundoy-Las Casas
Pto. Asís
PUTUMAYO
CAQUETÁ
Caguán
Caquetá

Ipiales
Tulcán
ECUADOR
San Miguel
Putumayo
Puerto Leguízamo
PTO. Pizarro
Salto Grande
Equator
Taraira
Vaupés

Quito ☆

AMAZONAS
Puerto Toledo
Cachorras
La Pedrera
Caquetá
Japurá

Barras
Arica
BRAZIL
Japurá

PERÚ
Napo
Tarapacá
Icá
Amazon

Iquitos
Leticia
Benjamín Constant

— Inset (bottom left) —

Banco de Serranilla
Banco Alicia
Bajo Nuevo

CARIBBEAN
15°
15°
Roca que Vela
Quita Sueno Bank (Claimed by U.S. & Col.)
Serrana Bank (Claimed by U.S. & Col.)
I. Sta. Catalina
Sta. Isabel
I. de Providencia
SEA
Roncador Cay (Claimed by U.S. & Col.)

SAN ANDRÉS Y PROVIDENCIA
Same scale as main map

San Andrés
I. de San Andrés
Vigía
Cayos del E.S.E.
Cayos de Albuquerque
80°

Longitude West 72° of Greenwich

# COLOMBIA

## Republic of Colombia

## POWER POTENTIAL STATISTICS

Area: 455,355 square miles

Population: 25,837,000

Total Active Regular Armed Forces: 64,700 (0.25%
    population)

Gross National Product: $13.5 billion ($523 per capita)

Annual Military Expenditures: $181.8 million (1.35%
    GNP)

Crude Steel Production: 255,000 metric tons

Fuel Production:

    Crude Oil: 7.5 million metric tons

    Refined Petroleum Products: 8.4 million metric tons

    Coal: 3.15 million metric tons

    Natural Gas: 1.7 billion cubic meters

Electric Power Output: 13.8 billion kwh

Merchant Fleet (ships 1,000 tons and over): 36 ships;
    234,000 gross tons

Civil Air Fleet: 79 major transport aircraft

## DEFENSE STRUCTURE

The president is commander in chief of the armed
forces. The minister of defense, who is the senior general
officer of the army, has supervision over the three services
and the National Police.

## POLITICO-MILITARY POLICY

Internally, the history of Colombia has often been
characterized by bloody strife. For twenty years (1958–78),
under a formal agreement, the president's cabinet included
six members from each of the two major parties and a military officer. Although this arrangement put an end to ten
years of exceedingly fierce competition, unrest has grown
in recent years, and guerrilla operations and labor strikes
have resulted in an almost constant state of siege. The
guerrilla groups, with considerable support from Communist nations, continue to be active. Largest of them is the
Colombian Revolutionary Armed Forces (FARC), which
is pro-Soviet. The National Liberation Army (ELN),
which is pro-Cuba, People's Liberation Army (EPL),
which is pro-China, and various other guerrilla groups
have also conducted terroristic activities.

Externally, boundary disputes with its neighbors,
Panama, Peru, Ecuador, and Venezuela, have resulted in
bad feelings but not in open warfare. Following the
breaking away of Panama in 1903, and the prompt recognition of its sovereignty by the U.S. Government (eager to

proceed with construction of the Panama Canal), relations
between Colombia and the United States were strained for
many years. Increasing economic ties, since the ratification
of a treaty between the two nations in 1921, have produced
a generally amicable relationship.

The armed forces of Colombia are among the most
modern in Latin America. All males are obligated for
military service between the ages of eighteen and forty-
five. At least one year of active duty is served between
eighteen and thirty. For the last fifteen years men are in a
reserve status.

Colombia is the only Latin American country that
participated actively in the Korean War. A battalion of
1,000 men served in the United Nations forces, and two
Colombian patrol escorts operated in the area.

## STRATEGIC PROBLEMS

Colombia's position, straddling the Isthmus of
Panama, with coastlines on both the Pacific Ocean and the
Caribbean Sea, is a strategic one with respect to the
approaches to the vital Panama Canal. In September 1972
the United States agreed to abandon to Colombia claims to
sovereignty over the islet of Quitasueno and the lighthouse
it had maintained there and to the keys of Roncador and
Serrana in the San Andres-Providencial Archipelago,
retaining fishing rights. Nicaragua promptly announced its
claim to the territory. Colombia and Venezuela have
disputed claims to the undersea platform extending north
from Guajira Peninsula.

## MILITARY ASSISTANCE

From the time of Colombia's independence, foreign
advisers from a number of European countries have
assisted in the organization and training of the armed
forces. Since 1939 U.S. missions have been active, and
Colombian officers have received training at U.S. service
schools. A Mutual Assistance Treaty with the United
States was signed in 1952.

In the period 1950–77 Colombia received $96.84 million
worth of military equipment from the United States. A
total of 7,392 students were trained under the MAP.

## ALLIANCES

Colombia is a member of the OAS and its subsidiary
organizations, and of the Andean Pact.

## ARMY

*Personnel:* 50,000

*Organization:* 8 infantry brigades, with light armor,
motorized artillery, and engineer detachments

*Major Equipment Inventory:*
light tanks (M-3)
armored cars (M-8)
light artillery pieces (105mm)
antiaircraft guns (40mm)

*Reserves:* About 250,000 men but with no mobilization organization

## NAVY

*Personnel:* 8,700 (including 1,500 marines)

*Major units:*
 2 submarines (SS; type 209 class)
 3 midget submarines (SSM; for attack swimmers)
 4 destroyers (DD)
   2 modified Halland class
   1 Sumner class
   1 APD class
 8 frigates (FF)
   4 Joao Coutinho class
   1 Courtney class
   3 Cherokee class
 6 patrol craft (PC)
 12 patrol boats (PB)
 1 tank landing ship (LST)
 4 river patrol boats (PBR)
 2 auxiliary ships (oiler, survey ship)
 23 service craft (tugs, docks, workshops, etc.)

*Naval Bases:* Barranquilla, Balanquero, Cartagena, Santa Marta

## AIR FORCE

*Personnel:* 6,000

*Organization:*
 1 fighter-bomber squadron (Mirage 5)
 1 bomber squadron (B-26)
 1 reconnaissance and rescue squadron (PBY)
 1 transport squadron (C-130, C-47, C-54, HS-748, F-28)

*Major Aircraft Types:*
 17 combat aircraft
   6 Mirage 5 fighter-bombers
   3 B-26 light bombers
   8 PBY maritime patrol aircraft
 140 other aircraft
   50 transports (C-130, Fokker F-28, C-54, C-47, C-45, Beaver, Otter, HS-748)
   45 trainers (T-34, T-37, T-41, T-6, T-33)
   45 helicopters (Bell 47, UH-23, UH-1, HH-43, OH-6A)

*Air Bases:* Barranquilla, Cali, Buenaventura, Bogota, Medellin, Cucuta, Cartagena, Leticia, Santa Marta, Bucaramanga, Paranquero.

## PARAMILITARY

The National Police Force of about 35,000 men is headed by a commandant, who is responsible to the commanding general of the armed forces. The police force is organized in divisions, one for each department of the country. It operates thirty-six helicopters.

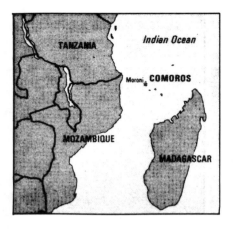

# COMOROS

## Republic of the Comoros

## POWER POTENTIAL STATISTICS

Area: 693 square miles
Population: 320,000
Gross National Product: $69.5 million ($240 per capita)
Electric Power Output: 3 million kwh
Civil Air Fleet: 3 major transport aircraft

## POLITICO-MILITARY POLICIES AND POSTURES

The Comoros are four small islands, formerly administered by France, lying between the East African coast and the northern tip of Madagascar. In July 1975 they unilaterally declared their independence, but one of the four, Mayotte, withdrew and is a French territorial community. Comoros continues to claim sovereignty over Mayotte, but it is not included in the area and population figures given here. France stations 2,000 troops on Mayotte as part of its contingency intervention force for Africa.

Comoros's brief history since independence has been troubled. In September 1975 the four opposition parties overthrew the first president in a bloodless coup. His successor, Ali Soilih, governed without a legislature and caused confusion by destroying the civil service and replacing it with a group of apparently ineffective "people's committees." There were also charges that he was interfering with the religious observances of the largely Moslem population. Soilih was overthrown in May 1978 by a group led by Belgian Robert Denard, who served as commander in chief of the nation's armed forces until asked to leave in September, apparently because of opposition from other African nations. A new constitution was approved in October.

Comoros received $10 million in aid from the Arab League in 1976.

# CONGO

## People's Republic of Congo

### POWER POTENTIAL STATISTICS

Area: 132,046 square miles
Population: 1,484,000
Total Active Armed Forces: 3,400 (0.23% population)
Gross National Product: $700 million ($490 per capita)

Annual Military Expenditures: $37.5 million (5.35% GNP)
Fuel Production: Crude Oil: 12.0 million metric tons
Electric Power Output: 130 million kwh
Civil Air Fleet: 4 major transport aircraft

### POLITICO-MILITARY POLICIES AND POSTURE

The military has played a predominant role in Congo's postindependence governments. In 1968, then Capt. Marien Ngouabi led a coup that seized power. As president, Ngouabi established a single-party state under the Congolese Labor party (PCT). In March 1977 a small group of the regime's opponents assassinated Ngouabi. He was succeeded by Brig. Gen. Yhomby-Opango, who suspended the country's fourth constitution since 1960 and transferred all political authority to an eleven-member Military Committee.

A mutual defense agreement with France has been superseded by a training and logistics pact. France retains major commercial investments in Congo and is the country's main trading partner and a principal aid donor, despite the regime's Marxist ideology. Cuban and Soviet presence has increased in recent years. The Soviets have assisted in gold and phosphate mining. Cuba has technical and military advisory programs and an estimated 400 people in the country. This tie has become closer because of strong Congolese backing of the MPLA in Angola and the problem Congo shares with the MPLA of dealing with Cabindan rebels who seek autonomy from Angola.

Congo has good relations with most of its neighbors. It cooperates with Gabon, Cameroon, and the Central African Empire in the Central African Customs and Economic Union. Zaire and Congo have periodically accused each other of supporting hostile guerrilla movements, but relations are generally satisfactory.

The chief security problems are internal. Deep-seated tribal jealousies, poor economic performance, and radical urban elements have plagued the country with coup attempts, assassinations, and purges since independence. Before his assassination, Ngouabi had suppressed several coup attempts and a general strike led by radicals in the trade union and student movements. The new government has sharply curtailed the activities of the PCT and the unions. An opposition party in exile was formed in Paris in 1976 by former Vice President Moudileno-Massengo.

The army has a strength of about 3,000 and consists of an armored battalion, two infantry battalions (one parachute-commando), a support battalion which includes T-62 and PT76 tanks, armored cars, artillery, antiaircraft, antitank, and combat engineer units, a communications company, and a transportation company. French weapons are being replaced with more modern Soviet and Chinese equipment. Service is voluntary and for two years. The navy numbers about 200, has three Shanghai class fast patrol craft (PCF) and four river patrol craft (PBR) on the Congo and Oubangui rivers. The air force is also about 200-strong and operates eight MiG-15 fighters, two C-47 transports, two liaison aircraft, and three helicopters. Air bases are at Brazzaville, Dolisie, and Pointe Noire.

There is a People's Militia (under the command of the army), and a gendarmerie of 1,400 in twenty companies.

Congo is a member of the OAU. It withdrew from OCAM in 1972.

# COSTA RICA

## Republic of Costa Rica

### POWER POTENTIAL STATISTICS

Area: 19,653 square miles
Population: 2,144,000
Total Active Regular Armed Forces: none (Civil Guard only)
Gross National Product: $2.8 billion ($1,370 per capita)
Fuel Production: Refined Petroleum Products: 253,000 metric tons
Electric Power Output: 1.7 billion kwh
Civil Air Fleet: 18 major transport aircraft

### POLITICO-MILITARY POLICIES AND POSTURE

The Costa Rican army was abolished in 1948 and replaced by a Civil Guard of about 1,200, which has paramilitary capabilities. There are about 3,000 other police. For revenue purposes the nation maintains three patrol boats (PB) manned by fifty personnel. Service in the Civil Guard is voluntary. Costa Rica claims exclusive fishing rights within 200 miles of its coasts.

The United States has furnished $1.83 million in military assistance in the years 1950–77 for use by the Civil Guard and various police units. Under the MAP, 696 Costa Rican students have been trained.

Costa Rica is a member of the ODECA and OAS and is a vigorous supporter of an inter-American defense and economic system.

# CUBA

## Republic of Cuba

### POWER POTENTIAL STATISTICS

Area: 44,218 square miles
Population: 9,874,000
Total Active Regular Armed Forces: 122,500 (1.2% population)
Gross National Product: $8.0 billion ($840 per capita)
Annual Military Expenditures: $949 million (11.9% GNP)
Fuel Production: Crude Oil: 140,000 metric tons
Electric Power Output: 6.6 billion kwh
Merchant Fleet (ships 1,000 tons and over): 81 ships; 584,000 gross tons
Civil Air Fleet: 37 major transport aircraft

### DEFENSE STRUCTURE

The Revolutionary Armed Forces includes the army, the air force, the navy, and the militia. Fidel Castro is prime minister, first secretary of the Cuban Communist party, and commander in chief of the Revolutionary Armed Forces. His brother Raul is vice premier, minister of the Revolutionary Armed Forces, and party second secretary.

### POLITICO-MILITARY POLICY

The history of Cuba for more than a century has been one of instability, unrest, and revolution. On January 1, 1959, after three years of insurgency against the dictatorship of Fulgencio Batista, Fidel Castro and his guerrilla forces took over the government in what they termed a nationalist revolution. In 1961, the Castro regime became avowedly Communist.

The state of Cuba's economy has improved in recent years, with expansion of industry, substantial income from the sugar crops, and considerably increased tourism,

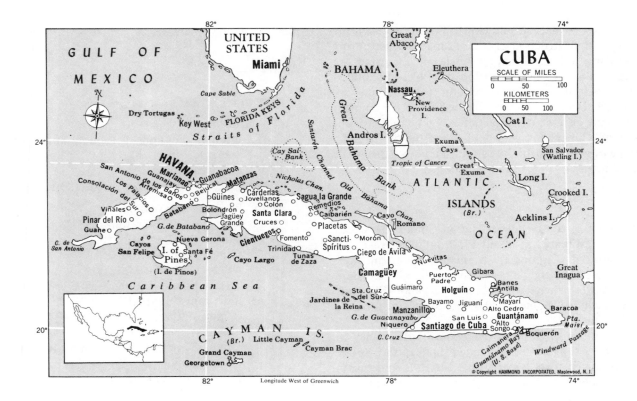

including tourists from the United States. However, Cuba is still dependent upon the Soviet Union for enormous amounts of financial support. In 1975 the OAS voted to lift the economic and diplomatic sanctions that had been imposed on Cuba in 1964, legitimizing the action of seven members which had already resumed relations. The United States and Cuba have moved toward normalizing relations, to the extent of exchanging missions, but U.S. inclinations toward rapprochement slowed as Cuban troops took an active part in African conflicts.

Cuban military experts and guerrilla fighters since the advent of Castro have been sent clandestinely to other Latin American nations to give advice and assistance to revolutionary movements. Since 1965 Cuba has become increasingly involved in assisting revolutionaries in Africa. In as many as fifteen countries Cubans have trained soldiers in guerrilla warfare and the use of such weapons as the mortar and the recoilless rifle. In Angola, approximately 15,000 Cuban troops participated in 1975–76, fighting with forces of the Soviet-supported Popular Movement for the Liberation of Angola (MPLA). Cuban troops also fought in Ethiopia against Somalia and against the rebels in Eritrea.

The volunteer guerrilla army with which Castro seized power proved inadequate as a permanent force. On November 13, 1963, conscription was introduced. Men between seventeen and forty-five years of age are required to serve for three years. Women between seventeen and thirty-six may volunteer for two years of duty. Women are admitted to armed forces officers' schools, to be trained principally as antiaircraft artillery and signal corps officers. Military personnel are assigned to agricultural duties during the cane-cutting season, probably with a detrimental effect on military efficiency.

## STRATEGIC PROBLEMS

Cuba's location makes the island vulnerable to attack from several directions. Its proximity to the United States (only 90 miles from Florida) makes Cuba an easy target for the overwhelming U.S. military power. The presence of the U.S. Navy base at Guantanamo Bay makes Cuba even more vulnerable. Proximity to Caribbean islands, Central America, and northern South America increases Cuba's strategic security problems. Castro has repeatedly used this vulnerability as a propaganda theme to unify the nation behind his government.

Cuba's location on the other hand has the advantage of rendering it a useful base for an attack on any of these same places. Thus, the stationing there of Russian missiles in 1962 was immediately interpreted by the U.S. Government as a clear threat to the United States and its Latin

American allies and led to the so-called Cuban Missile Crisis. In the fall of 1970, the United States protested the evident USSR construction of a base capable of harboring and servicing missile-equipped nuclear submarines in Cienfuegos Bay. Cuba's location has also facilitated Castro's policy of exporting revolution to Latin America.

So stringent are the controls of the Castro government that internally generated insurgency is highly unlikely. But millions of Cuban refugees still stand ready to take advantage of any opportunity to return and overthrow the government.

## MILITARY ASSISTANCE

Soviet military aid began arriving in Cuba in 1960 and by 1972 was estimated at about $150 million a year. All types of ground weapons from small arms to medium tanks, the latest jet fighters, surface-to-air missiles, land and sea tactical surface-to-surface missiles, and ASW craft have been included. Some 5,000 Soviet instructor-advisers still are in Cuba.

In 1962, in an attempt to overcome its deficiency in ICBMs targeted against the United States, the Soviet Union introduced forty-two IRBMs, MRBMs and thirty-six IL-28 nuclear-capable jet light bombers into Cuba. Their crews, plus protective ground units, and armored units to stiffen the Cuban army, numbered 25,000. As a result of the United States-Soviet confrontation of October 1962, the missiles and bombers were immediately withdrawn. A large number of troops, claimed by the Cubans to be a training unit, remain.

Many of the smaller Soviet weapons have been reexported with instructor-advisers to Cuban-supported insurgent movements in Latin America and Africa. A Cuban SAM battery was reported serving in North Vietnam. In 1978, 11,400 military advisers were reported in Angola, 310 in Guinea, and 50 in Somalia. Numbers in other countries are unknown.

## ALLIANCES

Cuba's membership in the OAS was suspended by the other members at Punta del Este in February 1962. To further its attempts to export revolution, Cuba sponsored the Latin America Solidarity Organization (OLAS), a federation of left-wing groups, particularly of those sympathetic to violent revolutionary methods.

A treaty of friendship and mutual defense with the Soviet Union governs economic and military assistance and presumably defense arrangements. In July 1972 Cuba was admitted as the ninth member of COMECON (Council 1 for Mutual Economic Assistance), the Soviet-led economic alliance, which may be expected to result in

less direct aid from the Soviet Union as aid from the other member nations increases.

## ARMY

*Personnel:* 96,000

*Organization:*
   12 infantry divisions (probably little more than brigade strength)
    2 armored brigades
    8 independent regiments (battalion strength)

*Major Equipment Inventory:*
  580 heavy and medium tanks (JS-2, T-34/54/55/62) light tanks (PT-76)
  100 assault guns (SU-100)
  200 APCs (BTR-40/60/152)
      BRDM armed reconnaissance vehicles
   45 short-range SSMs (Frog)
      152mm, 130mm, 122mm, 85mm, 76mm artillery pieces
      23mm, 37mm, 57mm, 85mm, 100mm antiaircraft guns
      Snapper antitank missiles

*Reserves:* 85,000 trained reserves can be mobilized within two to three days to bring the divisions to full combat strength (see Paramilitary, below).

## NAVY

*Personnel:* 10,000

*Major Units:*
    2 submarines (1 Foxtrot class; 1 Whiskey class; SS)
   18 submarine chasers (6 Kronstadt, 12 SO-1 class; PCS)
   25 missile attack boats with SS-N-2/Styx SSM (18 Komar, 7 Osa class; PTG)
   20 motor torpedo boats (12 P-4, 6 P-6, 2 Turya class; PT)
   17 patrol boats (PB)
    6 mechanized landing craft (T-4 class ; LCM)
    3 auxiliary ships
   24 service craft
   50 Samlet SSMs for coastal defense

*Naval Bases:* Mariel, Havana, Varadero, Cienfuegos, and Cabanas

## AIR FORCE

*Personnel:* 16,500

*Organization:*
12 fighter-bomber/interceptor squadrons
24 SAM battalions (SA-2 Guidelines, 144 launchers
    —6 per battalion)

*Major Aircraft Types:*
210 combat aircraft
    80 MiG-21 interceptors
    30 MiG-19 interceptors
    30 Su-7 fighter-bombers
    70 MiG-17 fighter-bomber/interceptors
241 other aircraft
    70 transport (An-2, An-24, Il-14)
    71 helicopters (Mi-1 Hare and Mi-4 Hound)
    100 trainer/support aircraft (MiG-15/17, Zlin
        326)

*Missiles:*
600 VK750 SAMs (SA-2 Guideline)
Atoll AAMs (on MiG-21 interceptors)

## PARAMILITARY

Cuba has a well-armed People's Militia of about 200,000. These can perform home guard functions, and also serve as a reserve for the army. They are feared as block-wardens, having the duty of informing on citizens who may make statements or commit acts deemed disloyal to the regime. There is also a body of about 13,000 state security troops and border guards. In addition, units known as Youth Technical Brigades, in uniform and armed, serve as technicians in industry and agriculture to make sure that the workers produce and that they are loyal to the regime.

# CYPRUS

## Republic of Cyprus

### POWER POTENTIAL STATISTICS

Area: 3,572 square miles
Population: 642,000 (523,400 Greek; 120,800 Turkish)
Total Active Armed Forces: 20,000-man Greek Cypriot
    National Guard (3.1% population)
Gross National Product: $789.3 million ($1,580 per
    capita)
Annual Military Expenditures: $43.2 million (5.47%
    GNP)
Fuel Production: Refined Petroleum Products: 400,500
    metric tons
Electric Power Output: 888 million kwh

Merchant Fleet (ships 1,000 tons and over): 502 ships;
    2.51 million gross tons (most are foreign-owned, with
    convenience registry)
Civil Air Fleet: 6 major transport aircraft

### STRATEGIC BACKGROUND

Historically, possession of Cyprus assured the occupying power control of the eastern Mediterranean, and in particular the shores of southern Anatolia and Syria-Palestine. Typical of the significance of Cyprus as a base for operations on these shores was its seizure by Richard I in 1190 before he began land operations in the third Crusade. Its value as a base was repeatedly proved by British use in World Wars I and II and in the mounting of the ill-fated Suez expedition of 1956. This value has been enhanced by the advent of airpower, and this is one reason Britain retained substantial base areas on the island at the time of granting independence and Commonwealth membership to Cyprus in 1959.

This strategic location has made disorders on Cyprus of special concern to the United States and other NATO powers. If a hostile power should establish a foothold on Cyprus, it would pose a serious threat to NATO's position in the Mediterranean, as well as to the CENTO defense posture.

There has been endemic unrest and violence in Cyprus for more than twenty-five years. A British colony until 1960, Cyprus has a population that is 80 percent Greek and 18 percent Turkish, and both groups have strong national feelings. The Greeks have long aspired to *enosis* (union with Greece), and in the early 1950s began a guerrilla war against the British and the Turkish minority in hopes of achieving it. The guerrilla forces, called EOKA, were led by Col. George Grivas, a Cypriot officer in the Greek army. The Turkish Cypriots opposed *enosis,* and at that time favored continued British rule. The resulting tension between Greece and Turkey almost split the NATO alliance.

Independence was achieved in 1960 under terms forbidding *enosis* and safeguarding the security and rights of the Turkish minority. Britain retained two military enclaves at Akrotiri and Khekelia, with a combined area of 99 square miles. The first president of the new republic was Archbishop Makarios, who had been the principal popular leader in the earlier struggle for *enosis,* but who tried to restrain its militant proponents after he became president. Civil war broke out between Greek and Turkish factions in late 1963, with each receiving aid from its home country. Establishment of a UN force in Cyprus (UNFICYP) in March 1964 resulted in only a temporary and uneasy peace. There were new crises, and new violence, each year from 1964 through 1967. After Turkish aircraft intervened in August 1964, President Makarios sought and received promises of military assistance from the USSR. United States pressure on the governments of Cyprus and Greece led to a limitation on this assistance, but considerable Soviet military equipment is believed to have been received.

In November 1967, Turkey and Greece again came to the brink of war as violence flared on Cyprus. Mediation by the UN, and primarily by the United States, resolved this crisis in December 1967. Greece and Turkey agreed to withdraw all of their national armed forces on the island (about 10,000 Greek, more than 2,000 Turkish) except for training contingents of 950 and 650. This withdrawal was completed early in 1968. Internal security remained the responsibility of UNFICYP.

In late 1971, a new guerrilla pro-*enosis* organization, EOKA-B, was formed under the leadership of Grivas, by then a lieutenant general. He died in early 1974, but his followers continued their terrorist activities. The situation was complicated by the fact that the Makarios government was on friendly terms with both Cypriot Communists and Communist nations, while the Greek junta government was strongly anti-Communist. Also, Greek-Turkish relations were already edgy over disputed sovereignty in the eastern Aegean Sea, where oil had been discovered earlier in the year.

In July 1974, the Cypriot National Guard, which was led by Greek officers and included EOKA-B members, overthrew Makarios in a violent coup and took control of the country. Turkey responded with a full-scale invasion in July that seized the northeast portion of the island, and another invasion in August. The Turks eventually took 38 percent of the island. The outcome of Greece's Cyprus adventure brought the fall of its junta government, and a return of democratic rule there. (See Greece.) Angered at the use of U.S. arms by the invading Turks, the United States Congress imposed an arms embargo on Turkey. (See Turkey.)

Meanwhile, Turkey consolidated its hold on northeast Cyprus. About 200,000 Greek Cypriot refugees fled the Turkish-held portion and were reportedly not allowed to return, while Turkey colonized the area with Turks from the mainland. The Turks on Cyprus set up a government of the "Turkish Federated State of Cyprus," which the Greek Cypriots refused to recognize. Makarios was restored to power in Greek Cyprus (December 1974), continuing in office until his death in 1977. His government (and that of his successor) is recognized by the United States and most other countries as the government of all Cyprus.

## CURRENT MILITARY SITUATION

Cyprus remains in a condition of de facto partition. Turkey made additional troop withdrawals in 1978 which, according to Turkish statements, brought its forces on the island down to 22,750 (August 1978) from 40,000 at the end of 1974. After six rounds of talks since 1975, aimed at reaching a settlement and conducted under UN auspices at Vienna, efforts have remained at stalemate since spring 1977. In spring 1978 the Turks made a proposal for two "federated" states, each with its own legislature and president, and offered to relinquish 7 percent to 10 percent of the land they held and to divide the important port city of Famagusta, which they had seized in 1974. The Greeks refused to accept the plan, which they said would make the results of the 1974 invasion, and the partition of the island, permanent and official. There was no significant military activity and no terrorism related to Cypriot problems in 1978. EOKA-B disbanded and agreed to turn in its weapons, although some individuals and splinter elements undoubtedly did not cooperate.

UNFICYP has continued to maintain a force on the island. The national contingents in UNFICYP include small, mostly battalion-sized units, plus supporting elements, from Britain, Canada, Denmark, Sweden, and Austria, under command of an Irish general. Austria also provides a field hospital, and Australia provides a small civilian police unit.

Britain maintains in its enclaves on Cyprus a 2,000-man ground force, consisting of two armored reconnaissance squadrons, two infantry battalions, and the headquarters of the Near East Air Force, based at Akrotiri, with one transport squadron of Hercules, and one battalion of Bloodhound surface-to-air missiles. During the 1974 crisis this force was strengthened to an estimated total of more than 8,000 air and ground personnel.

## GOVERNMENT (GREEK CYPRIOT NATIONAL GUARD) FORCES

*Personnel:* about 20,000

*Organization:* Unknown

*Major Equipment Inventory:*
35 BTR-50P APC
40mm Bofors antiaircraft guns
artillery pieces (105mm and 155mm howitzers, 25-pounder guns)
106mm jeep-mounted recoilless rifles
infantry heavy weapons and small arms
6 motor torpedo boats (P-4 class, PT)

## TURKISH FORCES ON CYPRUS

*Personnel:* about 30,000

*Organization:*
2 infantry divisions

*Major Equipment Inventory:*
1,000 tanks (M-47, M-48), armored cars (Commando), and APCs (M-59, M-113)
106mm and 75mm recoilless rifles
infantry heavy weapons and small arms

# CZECHOSLOVAKIA

## Czechoslovak Socialist Republic

### POWER POTENTIAL STATISTICS

Area: 49,371 square miles
Population: 15,189,000
Total Active Regular Armed Forces: 185,000 (1.22% population)
Gross National Product: $63.2 billion ($4,200 per capita)
Annual Military Expenditures: $3.46 billion (5.47% GNP)
Crude Steel Production: 14.7 million metric tons
Iron Ore Production: 1.9 million metric tons
Fuel Production:
Coal: 28.3 million metric tons
Lignite (brown coal): 89.5 million metric tons
Crude Oil: 131,000 metric tons
Manufactured Gas: 7.9 billion cubic meters
Electric Power Output: 66.4 billion kwh
Nuclear Power Production: 2,131 megawatts
Merchant Fleet (ships 1,000 tons and over): 13 ships: 144,000 gross tons (operates from Szczecin (Stettin), Poland)
Civil Air Fleet: 18 jet, 7 turboprop, and 27 piston transports

### DEFENSE STRUCTURE

The Czechoslovakian armed forces consist of the Czechoslovak People's Army (CPA), plus internal and border troops. The CPA comprises the Ground Forces, air force, and the Air Defense Force. The president of the republic is commander in chief of the armed forces and titular head of the defense establishment. The Council of Defense, which exercises policy and budgetary control over national defense and security organizations, is nominally responsible to the Federal Assembly, but the Politburo of the Communist party is in de facto control over its activities.

The armed forces are commanded by the minister of defense, a high-ranking military officer, who is responsible to the prime minister, the effective head of the government. Under the minister of defense are the General Staff, Inspector General, Main Political Directorate, Main Directorate for the Ground Forces, Main Directorate for the Air and Air Defense Forces, Personnel Directorate, Rear Services, and frontier and interior troops. Organizationally the country is divided into military districts whose headquarters administer ground forces and support units within their boundaries.

Effective party domination over the military establishment is assured by placement of high Communist party officials in positions of control over the Ministry of National Defense. Political officers, under the Main Political Directorate of the Ministry of National Defense, are assigned to all units. The party organization and Communist youth groups are also represented at all levels and in all branches of the military services.

The Ground Force is by far the largest and most important of the services. Its officers hold most of the higher staff positions, and its support units provide the common services that are required by all branches of the armed forces. Like the chiefs of the other main directorates, the Ground Force commander is a deputy minister of national defense.

After those of the Soviet Union and Poland the Czechoslovak air forces are the largest and the best equipped of the Warsaw Pact members. Air defenses include aircraft detection and surveillance stations, antiaircraft artillery and surface-to-air missile units. Most of the surveillance

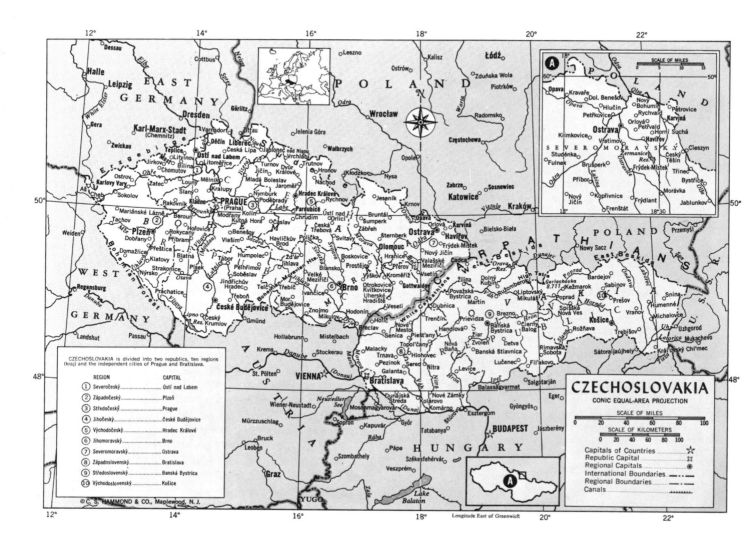

CZECHOSLOVAKIA is divided into two republics, ten regions (kraj) and the independent cities of Prague and Bratislava.

| | REGION | CAPITAL |
|---|---|---|
| 1 | Severočeský | Ústí nad Labem |
| 2 | Západočeský | Plzeň |
| 3 | Středočeský | Prague |
| 4 | Jihočeský | České Budějovice |
| 5 | Východočeský | Hradec Králové |
| 6 | Jihomoravský | Brno |
| 7 | Severomoravský | Ostrava |
| 8 | Západoslovenský | Bratislava |
| 9 | Středoslovenský | Banská Bystrica |
| 10 | Východoslovenský | Košice |

## CZECHOSLOVAKIA

CONIC EQUAL-AREA PROJECTION

SCALE OF MILES
0  20  40  60  80  100

SCALE OF KILOMETERS
0  20  40  60  80  100

| | |
|---|---|
| Capitals of Countries | ☆ |
| Republic Capital | ☆ |
| Regional Capitals | ◉ |
| International Boundaries | — ·· — |
| Regional Boundaries | — · — |
| Canals | ╌╌╌ |

stations are located on the northwestern and southwestern borders of Bohemia, where they would be the first to spot planes approaching the Czechoslovakian airspace from west and southwest. Antiaircraft artillery is assigned to the defense of military formations or targets that might be attacked by low-flying aircraft. Surface-to-air missile units, because of their better capability against high-flying planes, are usually responsible for city and outer perimeter defenses.

The Main Directorate for Rear Services (logistics) procures and distributes most of the weapons, ammunition, military equipment, and other supplies to all components of the armed forces. Uniformity of organization and procedures, and standardization of many items of armament and equipment in the various Warsaw Pact forces, allow easier interchange of materiel.

Until 1965 the frontier forces serving on the country's borders were under the Ministry of Interior. In 1965 they were transferred to the Ministry of National Defense and placed within the armed forces.

## POLITICO-MILITARY POLICY

On the night of August 20–21, 1968, a massive invasion of Czechoslovakia by Soviet and Warsaw Pact armed forces ended the Czech ''spring'' of that year, a period of more liberal and independent communism. The invasion forces numbered approximately 500,000 Soviet troops, plus an additional 150,000 from other Warsaw Pact countries, but none from Romania. On orders from the Czech government, the overwhelmingly outnumbered Czechoslovak armed forces did not resist. The country was forced to revert to orthodox communism and Soviet control. A new Czechoslovak government signed an agreement with the Soviets that justified the invasion, accepted the Brezhnev doctrine of limited sovereignty, and acknowledged that the stationing of Soviet troops in Czechoslovakia was essential to the security of the country.

Of the Soviet forces that invaded Czechoslovakia in August 1968, five divisions and other units totaling 65,000 men remained ten years later. Czechoslovak political and military leaders rationalize that the continued presence of, and requirement for, Soviet troops in their country reflects a joint decision of the Warsaw Pact leadership in response to world and central European instability. A Soviet withdrawal in the foreseeable future cannot be anticipated. From the standpoint of the Czechoslovak forces, the accommodation of the large body of Soviet troops in the already marginally adequate military installations creates some inconvenience. In general, relations between Soviet troops and the Czechoslovaks are reasonably good, but resentments surface at times and incidents occur occasionally.

Czechoslovakia is one of the countries of the Mutual and Balanced Force Reductions "reduction area," and is a direct participant in the talks in Vienna toward reduction of forces in central Europe (see Western Europe Regional Survey).

Military service is universal. Persons eighteen to sixty are subject to military service, and the call-up age is nineteen.

There are two draft calls annually, one in the spring, the other in the fall. The basic tour of conscript duty is two years. Discharged conscripts usually remain on reserve status until age fifty. Nearly 40 percent of the total force is replaced each year, creating a potential trained reserve of about 1,000,000 men under thirty-five years of age who have had active service within about fifteen years.

## STRATEGIC PROBLEMS

As evidenced by the Soviet takeover in 1968, as well as the German occupation in 1939, Czechoslovakia's principal strategic problems are its small size and the elongated shape that puts the vital regions of the country within easy striking distance of the frontiers, and provides little opportunity for effective air defense. This vulnerability is only slightly offset by the mountainous nature of the frontier regions on the Polish and German borders.

Since the establishment of the Czechoslovakian state in 1918, there have been divisive tensions between the more numerous and dominant Czechs of Bohemia and Moravia, and the minority Slovaks of Slovakia. A major issue has been the justified claim of the Slovaks that they have not been adequately represented in the central government. This tension has unquestionably weakened Czech governments in the past, but it is notable that Czechs and Slovaks were united in support of their liberal government at the time of the Soviet invasion of August 1968.

## MILITARY ASSISTANCE

Like the other Eastern European Communist countries, Czechoslovakia has been the recipient of massive Soviet military assistance. The Soviet Union continues to supply combat aircraft, tanks, heavy artillery, and similar weapons. However, Czechoslovakia produces significant quantities of military equipment, spare parts, and weapons systems, including a lightweight, wire-guided antitank missile, a jet trainer, cargo aircraft, the RM-70 multiple rocket launcher, and other weapons.

The advanced technology and efficiency of Czechoslovakia's arms industry has resulted in Czechoslovakia's playing a leading role in the Communist military assistance program. A substantial proportion of the Communist arms, equipment, and training advisers that have been provided to underdeveloped clients have come from Czechoslovakia.

## ALLIANCES

In addition to a mutual assistance treaty of friendship with the USSR and all other Eastern European countries, Czechoslovakia is a member of the Warsaw Treaty Organization and the Council of Mutual Economic Assistance. All of its allies (if that is the right term), with the exception of Romania, participated in the 1968 invasion of Czechoslovakia.

## ARMY

*Personnel:* 145,000

*Organization:*
  2 military districts: (headquarters: Prague and Trencin)
  3 armies (headquarters: Prague, Brno, and Olomouc)
  4 tank divisions*
  8 motorized rifle divisions (2 cadres)
  1 airborne brigade
  3 SSM brigades (Scud)
  2 artillery brigades

*Major Equipment Inventory:*
  3,500 medium tanks (T-55 and T-62, some T-54 and T-34 models remain)
    light tanks (PT-76)
    scout cars (OT-65 and FUG-1966)

---

*One division is full combat strength. The others average 30 to 70 percent full strength.

2,000  APCs (BMP, BTR-50P, OT-62, OT-64, BTR-152)
150  152mm self-propelled guns (JSU-152)
180  heavy artillery pieces
360  medium artillery pieces
600  light artillery pieces
300  240mm rocket launchers
200  antitank guns (82mm guns and recoilless rifles)
  Snapper, Swatter, and Sagger antitank missiles
  ZSU-57/2, ZSU-23-4 self-propelled anti-aircraft guns
  SSMs (FROG and Scud)

*Reserves:* About 750,000 trained reserves

## AIR FORCE (including Air Defense Force)

*Personnel:* 40,000

*Organization:*
  18  interceptor squadrons (MiG-21/19)
  12  fighter-bomber squadrons (MiG-17/15, Su-7)
  6  reconnaissance squadrons (MiG-21, L-39)
  1  transport air division (Il-18, Il-14, An-2, Mi-4, Mi-8)
  SAMs (SA-2 Guideline)

*Major Aircraft Types:*
  525  combat aircraft
    200  MiG-21 interceptors/fighter reconnaissance
    85  MiG-19 interceptors
    60  MiG-17 fighter-bombers
    30  MiG-15 fighter-bombers
    120  Su-7B fighter-bombers
    30  L-39 reconnaissance
  465  other aircraft
    65  transports (Il-14, Il-18, Li-2, An-12)
    100  helicopters (Mi-1/4/6/8)
    300  trainer/support aircraft (including 150 L-29s)

*Other Equipment:*
  300  antiaircraft guns
  SAMs (SA-2/3/4/6/7)

*Air Bases:* Prague, Kosice, Zatec

*Reserves:* 90,000 trained reservists

## PARAMILITARY

There are approximately 25,000 frontier guards and internal security troops on active duty as well as a 120,000-man volunteer People's Militia.

# DENMARK

## Kingdom of Denmark

## POWER POTENTIAL STATISTICS

Area: Metropolitan Denmark, 16,615 square miles; Greenland, 840,000 square miles; Faroe Islands, 540 square miles
Population: 5,112,000
Total Active Regular Armed Forces: 34,300 (0.67% population)
Gross National Product: $42.2 billion ($8,290 per capita)
Annual Military Expenditures: $1.3 billion (3.1% GNP)
Crude Steel Production: 722,000 metric tons
Fuel Production:
  Crude Oil: 195,000 metric tons
  Refined Petroleum Products: 8 million metric tons
  Manufactured Gas: 330 million cubic meters
Electric Power Output: 23.9 billion kwh
Merchant Fleet (ships 1,000 tons and over): 351 ships; 4.9 million gross tons
Civil Air Fleet: 66 major transport aircraft and 21 helicopters

## DEFENSE STRUCTURE

The monarch (Queen Margrethe II) is a nominal commander in chief of the armed forces. Civilian control in the conventional parliamentary government of a constitutional democratic monarchy is exercised by the defense minister, responsible to the prime minister. Full command of the three services rests in the chief of defense, the ranking military officer. He and his Chief of Defense staff and the army, navy, and air force commanders (with appropriate staff) form an integrated Defense Command. The defense minister is advised by a Defense Council of the above officers, plus a chief of Danish Operational Forces.

## POLITICO-MILITARY POLICY

For three-quarters of a century prior to World War II, Denmark adhered to a policy of strict neutrality in European power politics. After having been a victim of German aggression in World War II, Denmark espoused the concept of collective security, and was an original member of NATO.

The armed forces consist of regulars and conscripts serving nine months. The annual call-up is about 20,000 men. After active service, they may be recalled for refresher training.

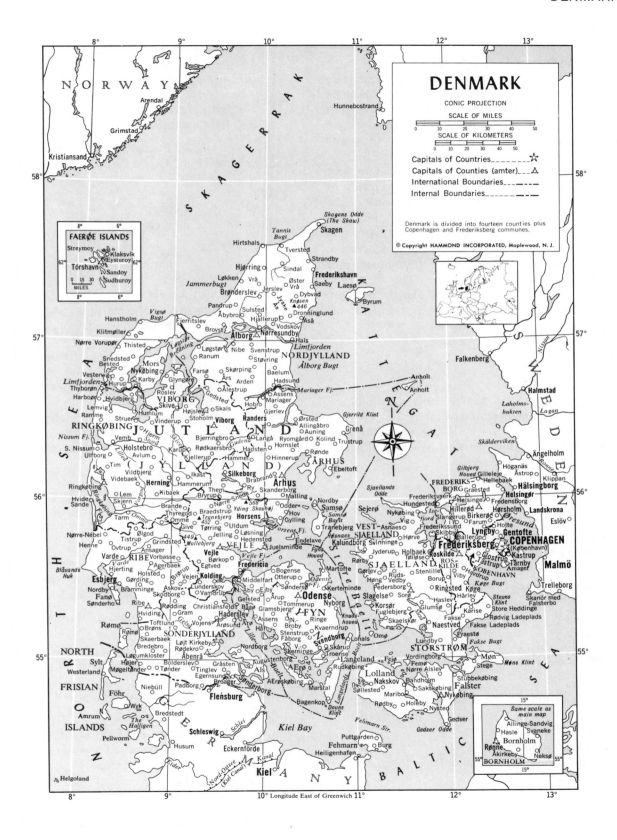

DENMARK

CONIC PROJECTION

SCALE OF MILES

SCALE OF KILOMETERS

Capitals of Countries_____☆
Capitals of Counties (amter)____△
International Boundaries_____
Internal Boundaries_____

Denmark is divided into fourteen counties plus
Copenhagen and Frederiksberg communes.

© Copyright HAMMOND INCORPORATED, Maplewood, N. J.

FAERØE ISLANDS

Streymoy
Klaksvík
Eysturoy
Tórshavn
Sandoy
Sudhuroy
MILES

## STRATEGIC PROBLEMS

Denmark's position astride the entrance to the Baltic Sea makes it one of the most strategically located nations of the world. Its small size and the lack of natural obstacles (save for restricted channels between the islands) make it vulnerable to invasion from the south, both overland through Jutland and by amphibious attack from the coasts of East Germany and Poland.

Greenland is a special strategic problem. This vast frozen land mass lies athwart possible trajectories of intercontinental missile exchange between the USSR on the one hand, and Canada and the United States on the other. There is a small Danish Greenland Defense Force. A bilateral agreement exists with the United States concerning the defense of Greenland. Thule and Sondre Stromfjord are United States-Danish bases.

Denmark is ethnically homogeneous, and there are no significant internal security problems. The Communist party has an estimated 5,000 members.

Denmark is a member of the EEC.

## MILITARY ASSISTANCE

Denmark received about $617.7 million in military assistance from the United States from 1950 to 1977. A small U.S. Office of Defense Cooperation (formerly Military Assistance Advisory Group, MAAG) is in the American embassy at Copenhagen.

## ALLIANCES

Denmark is a NATO member. The Danish armed forces are earmarked for the Northern Europe Command, within which the combined Danish-German Allied Command Baltic Approaches (ACBA) under the command of COMBALTAP (Command Baltic Approaches) has been established.

## ARMY

*Personnel:* 22,000 (peacetime)

*Organization:*
    3 major commands (Western Land Command, Eastern Land Command, Army Materiel Command)
Field Army (mobilized) (54,000)
    5 armored brigades and defense forces of Bornholm
Local Defense (mobilized) (24,000)
    21 infantry battalions
    7 artillery battalions
    7 engineer companies
    6 tank destroyer squadrons

*Major Equipment Inventory:*
    200 medium tanks (Centurion)
        medium tanks (Leopard) under procurement
    650 armored personnel carriers (M-113)
    72 self-propelled howitzers (155mm M-109)
    48 light tanks (M-41)
    276 light and medium artillery pieces

*Reserves:* 65,000 (includes local defense) plus a volunteer Army Home Guard of approximately 55,000.

## NAVY

*Personnel:* 5,300 (peacetime)

*Major Units:*
    6 diesel submarines (2 Nornvalen class; 4 Delfinen class; SS)
    2 guided missile frigates (Peder Skram class; Sea Sparrow SSMs, Harpoon SAMs; FFG)
    5 patrol ships (Hvidbjoernen class; PGF; 3-inch guns)
    3 patrol escorts (Triton class; PG; 76mm guns; officially typed corvettes)
    4 missile attack boats (Willemoes class; PTG; 4–8 Harpoon SSMs)
    10 motor torpedo boats (PT; 6 scheduled for retrofit to missile attack boats)
    23 patrol craft (PC; 20mm guns or larger)
    4 minelayers (MM)
    3 coastal minelayers (MMC)
    8 coastal minesweepers (MSC)
    23 patrol boats (PB)
    6 auxiliary ships (tankers, icebreakers, etc.)
    8 helicopters (Alouette III)

*Major Naval Bases:* Copenhagen, Frederikshavn, Korsoer, and shore installations at Stevns and Langeland; Groennedal in Greenland.

*Reserves:* 3,000 plus a volunteer Navy Home Guard of 5,000.

## AIR FORCE

*Personnel:* 7,000 (peacetime)

*Organization:*
    2 major commands (Tactical Air Command, Air Materiel Command)
    4 Nike Hercules squadrons
    4 Hawk squadrons
    2 all-weather fighter interceptor squadrons (F-104)
    3 fighter-bomber squadrons (F-35, F-100)
    1 fighter-reconnaissance squadron (RF-35)
    1 transport squadron (C-130, C-47)

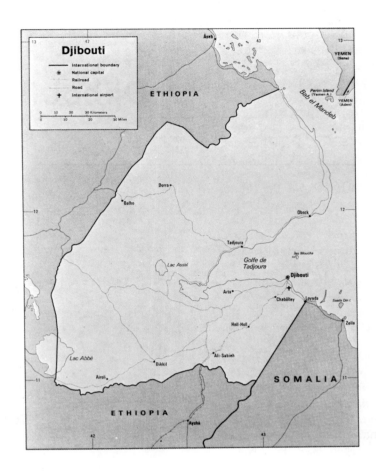

1 rescue squadron (S-61 helicopters)

*Major Aircraft types:*
116 combat aircraft
    40 F-104 all-weather fighter interceptors
    40 F-100 fighter-bombers
    20 F-35 fighter-bombers
    16 RF-35 fighter reconnaissance
19 other aircraft
    3 C-130 transports
    8 C-47 transports
    8 S-61 helicopters
58 F-16 aircraft under procurement (to replace
    F-100)

*Major Air Bases:* Karup, Aalborg, Skrydstrup, Vandel, Tirstrup, Vaerloese; on Greenland: Thule, Soendre Stroemfjord, Narssarssuaq

*Reserves:* 7,500 plus a volunteer Air Force Home Guard of 11,000 divided into Ground Observer Corps and Air Station Corps

# DJIBOUTI

## Republic of Djibouti

### POWER POTENTIAL STATISTICS

Area: 8,996 square miles
Population: 180,000
Total Active Regular Armed Forces: 4,400 (2.44% population)
Gross National Product: $65 million ($361 per capita)
Electric Power Output: 55 million kwh
Civil Air Fleet: 1 major transport aircraft

### POLITICO-MILITARY POLICIES AND POSTURE

Djibouti became independent of France on June 27, 1977, following an overwhelming referendum in favor of independence. Its military force is under the command of the president. France continues to assume responsibility for Djibouti's security, with over 4,000 troops based there and an aircraft carrier stationed off coast. France is training 3,700 men for the Djibouti army.

Djibouti's strategic problems are a combination of significant location and internal ethnic divisions. Located at the Indian Ocean entrance to the Red Sea, it is a trade crossroads, entrepot, and refueling point, and also a base for air transport between Europe, East Africa, Arabia, and India. This strategic position assured French influence in the Middle East and East Africa. The modern port of Djibouti is connected by rail to Addis Ababa, the capital of Ethiopia, and half of that country's external trade travels by this route. Ethiopia, therefore, has a vital interest in the country. During the 1977–78 Ogaden conflict, Somali forces cut the rail line in Ethiopia, severely disrupting the economies of both Djibouti and Ethiopia. France increased its assistance to the chronically impoverished country.

Internally, the indigenous population is about equally divided between the Afars, related to the Ethiopian Danakil tribe, and the Issas, a Somali tribe. However, the Somali presence is artificially increased by an influx of tribesmen seeking jobs in more prosperous Djibouti. On this ethnic basis, Somalia claimed the former French territory. In response, Ethiopia claimed that the area was part of its nineteenth century empire.

Issa leaders constituted the majority in Djibouti's first government. Six months after independence the government faced its first crisis when five Afar ministers resigned in protest over mass arrests of Afar tribesmen following a terrorist incident. The government also banned the leftist Afar party, MPL, which actively supported the Ethiopian regime. Many Issas and transient Somalis (Somali refugees increased substantially at the end of the Ogaden war) favor unification with Somalia. The government, however, is committed to a neutralist position. In February 1978, a new cabinet was formed, balanced between Afars and Issas.

Djibouti became a member of the OAU and the Arab League shortly after independence. Its prospects for an independent future depend on continued French presence and aid, and on Ethiopian and Somali restraint. There are about 4,150 French troops in Djibouti.

## ARMY

*Personnel:* 3,600

*Organization and Equipment:*
  1 mixed regiment
  1 infantry regiment (Foreign Legion)
  1 artillery regiment
    AMX-13 light tanks
    Ferret scout cars

## NAVY

*Personnel:* 300

*Equipment:*
  2 minesweepers
    some landing craft

## AIR FORCE

*Personnel:* 500

*Organization and Aircraft Types:*
  1 squadron of A-1s
  1 transport squadron with Noratlas piston transports and H-34 and Alouette II helicopters

## PARAMILITARY

There is a gendarmerie of 500.

# DOMINICA
## State of Dominica

Dominica, one of the Windward Islands, became fully independent on November 2, 1978. Since 1967 it had been an autonomous British associated state, with the United Kingdom having responsibility for its foreign affairs and defense only. The country received $18.5 million in aid from the United Kingdom in the ten years preceding independence. The new government was controlled by the Dominica Labor Party and proclaimed that Dominica would be a socialist state. It lies between the French islands of Guadeloupe and Martinique, and it was expected that in the future most of its foreign aid would come from France. Dominica has an area of 290 square miles and a population of 78,000. It has an armed force of fewer than 100 men, with a few submachine guns. The GNP is $32 million ($410 per capita).

# DOMINICAN REPUBLIC

## POWER POTENTIAL STATISTICS

Area: 18,704 square miles
Population: 5,466,000

Total Active Regular Armed Forces: 19,500 (0.36%
population
Gross National Product: $4.4 billion ($880 per capita)
Annual Military Expenditures: $66 million (1.5% GNP)
Fuel Production: Refined Petroleum Products: 1.7
million metric tons
Electric Power Output: 2 billion kwh
Merchant Fleet: 1 ship; 1,000 gross tons
Civil Air Fleet: 18 major transport aircraft

## DEFENSE STRUCTURE

The president is supreme chief of the armed forces. He
appoints the secretary of state for the armed forces, whose
job is primarily policy-making and supervision. Administration is exercised by the chiefs of staff of the several
services.

## POLITICO-MILITARY POLICIES

During the civil war in 1965, the United States landed
troops in the Dominican Republic to protect the lives of
the resident Americans and to prevent the possibility of a
Castro-like Communist takeover of the government. Since
that time, the Dominican Republic has weathered plots
to overthrow the administration of President Joaquin
Balaguer, numerous episodes of political violence, and
clashes between police and politically motivated guerrillas.
A program of economic and social reform initiated in 1972
has provided a basis for somewhat increased internal
stability.

Males between eighteen and fifty-four are eligible for
service in the armed forces; they are enlisted up to the
number the budget will support. Since many enlisted men
remain on active duty for years, often until retirement age,
the number of applicants regularly exceeds the number of
available billets. A law requires those not enlisted to do
two months a year service in the reserves. This provision is
apparently not universally applied.

The army is involved in several civic action programs. It
runs a civilian school for adults and children, cooperates
with other governmental agencies on highway construction
and maintenance, and participates in social assistance
programs with medical and other supplies.

## STRATEGIC PROBLEMS

The Dominican Republic occupies the eastern portion of the island of Hispaniola, having a common border of 193 miles with Haiti. Historically the two nations have been hostile, and have been close to war several times in the past decade. The security of the border, and particularly of the narrow valleys that provide access from Haiti, is a prime objective of military planning.

The proximity of Cuba presents a threat of invasion by sea, or infiltration by dissident elements or guerrillas. Consequently another major objective is defense of the coastline and elimination of the small number of dissidents who operate in the mountainous central region of the island.

## MILITARY ASSISTANCE

Military assistance from the United States has totaled $30.8 million since 1950. Under the MAP, 4,021 students have been trained.

## ALLIANCES

The Dominican Republic is a member of the OAS.

## ARMY

*Personnel:* 10,500

*Organization:*
    4 infantry brigades of 2 battalions each
    1 artillery regiment
    1 antiaircraft regiment

*Major Equipment Inventory:*
    20 light tanks (AMX-13)
    armored cars
    75mm, 105mm, 122mm howitzers

## NAVY

*Personnel:* 4,000

*Major Units:*
    8 patrol ships (PCF; 3-inch+ gun; 2 may be in reserve)
    2 patrol escorts (PG; multiple 3-inch guns; 2 may be in reserve)
    5 patrol craft (PC; 20mm+ guns)
    10 patrol boats (PB)
    1 medium landing ship (LSM; used as a transport)
    2 utility landing craft (LCU)
    3 auxiliary ships (tugs, tankers, etc.)
    10 service craft (tugs, survey ships, etc.)
    2 patrol aircraft (Catalina PBY)
    14 helicopters

*Naval Bases:* 27 de Febrero, Las Calderas

## AIR FORCE:

*Personnel:* 3,500

*Organization:*
    1 fighter squadron (Vampires)
    1 fighter-bomber/light bomber squadron (F-51/B-26)
    1 transport squadron (C-47, C-46, Beaver)

*Major Aircraft Types:*
    43 combat aircraft
        15 Vampire fighters
        20 F-51 fighters
        6 B-26 light bombers
        2 PBY maritime patrol craft
    60 other aircraft
        20 transports (C-47, C-46, Beaver)
        30 trainers and utility (T-6, T-11, BT-13, PT-17, Cessna 172)
        10 helicopters (Bell 47, H-19, and OH-6)

*Air Bases:* San Isidoro, Santo Domingo, Puerta Plata, Santiago, La Romana, Saibo, Barahona, La Vega, Monte Cristi, Azua

## PARAMILITARY

The Dominican Republic has a gendarmerie of about 10,000 men.

# ECUADOR

## Republic of Ecuador

## POWER POTENTIAL STATISTICS

Area: 105,685 square miles
Population: 7,665,000
Total Active Armed Forces: 20,800 (0.27% population)
Gross National Product: $5.6 billion ($780 per capita)
Annual Military Expenditures: $169.8 million (3.03% GNP)
Fuel Production:
    Crude Oil: 8.2 million metric tons
    Refined Petroleum Products: 2.0 million metric tons

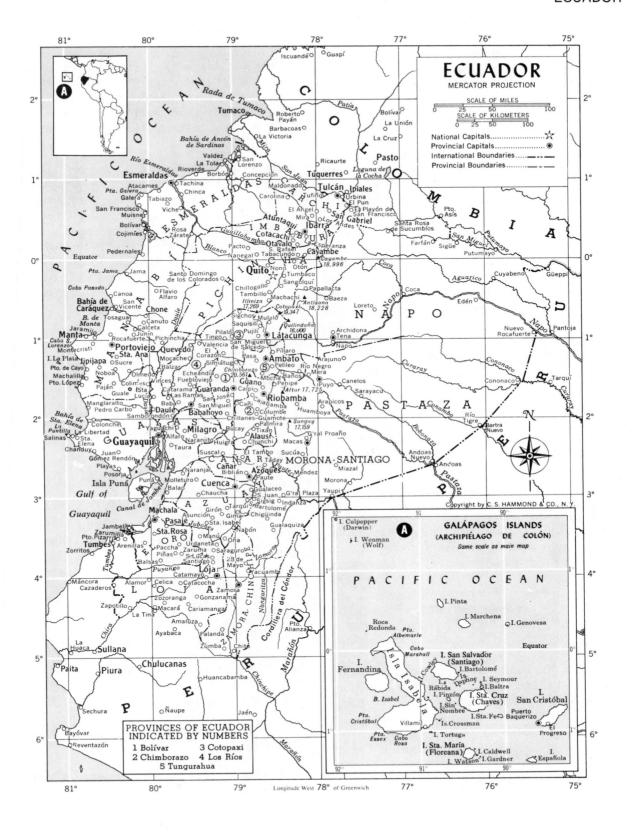

ECUADOR
MERCATOR PROJECTION

SCALE OF MILES
0    25    50    100
SCALE OF KILOMETERS
0    25    50    100

National Capitals....................☆
Provincial Capitals..................◉
International Boundaries.........._._._
Provincial Boundaries............._.._.._

GALÁPAGOS ISLANDS
(ARCHIPIÉLAGO DE COLÓN)
Same scale as main map

PACIFIC OCEAN

Copyright by C. S. HAMMOND & CO., N. Y.

PROVINCES OF ECUADOR
INDICATED BY NUMBERS
1 Bolívar        3 Cotopaxi
2 Chimborazo   4 Los Ríos
        5 Tungurahua

Longitude West 78° of Greenwich

Electric Power Output: 2.1 billion kwh
Merchant Fleet (ships 1,000 tons and over): 24 ships; 196,000 gross tons
Civil Air Fleet: 25 major transport aircraft

## DEFENSE STRUCTURE

The military dictatorship of Gen. Guillermo Rodriguez Lara was overthrown in a military coup in 1976. A military junta restored the constitution of 1945 and gradually moved toward civilian government. A new constitution was approved by popular vote in January 1978 to become effective after a president is elected. First-round elections were held in mid-July. The president is commander in chief of the armed forces, responsible for internal order and external security. He is advised by the National Security Council and the General Staff of the armed forces. The minister of national defense is responsible for matters affecting external security, with the assistance of the chief of the Armed Forces General Staff.

The country is divided into four defense zones with headquarters in Quito, Guayaquil, Cuenca, and Pastaza.

## POLITICO-MILITARY POLICY

The army has been involved in politics almost continuously throughout Ecuador's history. Traditionally the army has considered itself the guardian of democratic institutions, although it has overthrown numerous elected heads of state.

A border dispute of many years' standing with Peru flared into open conflict in July 1941. Under pressure from the United States, Argentina, and Brazil, a ceasefire was imposed, and in January of 1942 an arbitration agreement (generally known as the Rio Protocol) gave Peru most of the disputed territory. Ecuadorians, however, have continued to hope for access to the Maranon River, which is a major tributary of the Amazon; they continue to regard Peru as an aggressor who stole half of their national territory.

Ecuador claims jurisdiction over the Pacific Ocean 200 miles from its coast, and defense of this area is a prime function of the military forces. Since 1968, naval patrol boats have seized many American fishing vessels within this 200-mile limit and imposed fines on them.

Military training for one year is compulsory for all men when they reach the age of twenty. However, because of lack of vacancies, actual conscription is determined by lottery.

There are extensive military civic action programs. The military maintains a secondary school and has special literacy classes for conscripts. A military institute trains officers in the skills and disciplines of civilian administration.

## STRATEGIC PROBLEMS

The Communist party is weak and divided among pro-Moscow, pro-Peking, and pro-Cuba elements. All of these groups have influence in labor and student circles. The Indians, who make up over half of the population, have shown little susceptibility to subversion.

## MILITARY ASSISTANCE

Since Ecuador signed the Treaty of Rio (Inter-American Treaty of Reciprocal Assistance) of 1947, its armed forces have been reorganized and reequipped with U.S. aid, a total of $43.4 million since 1950. A total of 5,123 students were trained under the MAP. Israel has given assistance to the civic action program. An attempt by Israel to sell Ecuador twenty-four Kfir jet aircraft with U.S. engines in 1977 was blocked by the U.S. government.

## ALLIANCES

Ecuador is a member of the OAS.

## ARMY

*Personnel:* 12,800

*Organization:*
    11 infantry battalions
    1 parachute battalion
    3 artillery groups
    3 mechanized reconnaissance squadrons
    2 engineer battalions
    2 antiaircraft battalions
    3 signal companies
       independent infantry companies

*Major Equipment Inventory:*
    80 light tanks (M-3, AMX-13, M-41)
    50 light artillery pieces (105mm)
       light antiaircraft pieces
    16 light aircraft (T-41A, IAI-201, Cessna 172, Skyvan)

## NAVY

*Personnel:* 3,800 (includes 700 naval infantry in Galapagos Islands)

*Major Units:*
    2 diesel submarines (Type 209 class; SS)
    1 destroyer (Gearing class; DD)
    2 patrol escorts (PG; multiple 4-inch + guns)
    3 patrol ships (PGF; single 3-inch + gun)

2 patrol craft (PGM-71 class; PC; 40mm gun)
3 missile attack boats (PTG; Exocet SSMs)
3 motor torpedo boats (PT)
5 patrol boats (PB)
1 tank landing ship (LST)
2 medium landing ships (LSM)
12 service craft (tugs, tankers, etc.)
1 cargo ship (AKL)
6 patrol aircraft
2 helicopters (Alouette III)

*Naval Bases:* Guayaquil, Salinas, San Lorenzo, Galapagos

## AIR FORCE

*Personnel:* 3,500

*Organization:*
1 fighter/fighter-bomber squadron (Jaguar)
1 fighter/reconnaissance squadron (Meteor)
1 light bomber squadron (Canberra)
1 COIN squadron (BAC-167, A-37)
1 transport squadron (C-47, Learjet, DC-6, HS-748)

*Major Aircraft Types:*
51 combat aircraft
   12 fighter/fighter-bomber (Jaguar)
    8 fighter/reconnaissance (Meteor)
    6 light bombers (Canberra)
   25 COIN/trainer (BAC-167, A-37)
91 other aircraft
   37 transports (5 Buffalo, 12 SF-260, 3 HS-748, 1 Skyvan, 2 Learjet, C-47, DC-6)
   45 trainers (T-28, T-33, T-34, T-41)
    7 helicopters (OH-13, Lama)
    2 liaison aircraft (Cessna 180, O-2)

*Air Bases:* Quito, Loja, Latacunga, Manta, Riobamba, Salinas

## PARAMILITARY

The National Civil Police, under the minister of government, number 5,800. In case of national emergency they can be transferred to the minister of defense.

# EGYPT
## Arab Republic of Egypt

### POWER POTENTIAL STATISTICS

Area: 386,872 square miles

Population: 40,424,000
Total Active Regular Armed Forces: 318,500 (0.79% population)
Gross National Product: $14.5 billion ($380 per capita)
Annual Military Expenditures: $1.10 billion (7.59% GNP)
Iron Ore Production: 1.2 million metric tons
Fuel Production:
   Crude Oil: 8.4 million metric tons
   Refined Products: 10.4 million metric tons
Electric Power Output: 14 billion kwh
Merchant Fleet (ships 1,000 tons and over): 69 ships; 362,000 gross tons.
Civil Air Fleet: 27 major transport aircraft

### DEFENSE STRUCTURE

The president of the Arab Republic of Egypt, with strong executive powers, is the supreme commander of the unified armed forces, and presides over both the National Security Council (a kind of standing war cabinet) and the smaller National Defense Council, which is more closely concerned with defense strategy and politico-military planning. Under the president there is a single military commander in chief of the armed forces, who in recent years has also been the minister of war, the administrative director of the armed forces. In October 1978 in a change of top-level military personnel, the designation of minister of war was changed to minister of defense.

Egypt has four armed services: army, navy, air force, and air defense force. The commanders in chief of these four services report to the commander in chief of the armed forces through the chief of staff of the armed forces.

### POLITICO-MILITARY POLICY

Four missions have influenced the design of the Egyptian armed forces: accomplishment of the officially announced military goal of recapturing all territories lost to the Israelis; defense against attempts to impose foreign domination; defense against intra-Arab hostilities or threats thereof; and control of internal disturbances. Under President Gamal Nasser stress was placed on gaining hegemony, or at least preeminence, over the Arab states of the Middle East and nearby Africa. This apparent objective was pursued in part to obtain access to the income of the rich oil-producing Arab states, in part to secure strategic positions surrounding Israel, and in part to secure the headwaters of the life-giving Nile. With much support from the USSR, Nasser's government sponsored subversion and coup attempts in Libya, Sudan, Saudi Arabia, Iraq, and Jordan, supported and participated in military operations in Yemen, and backed subversion

134    EGYPT

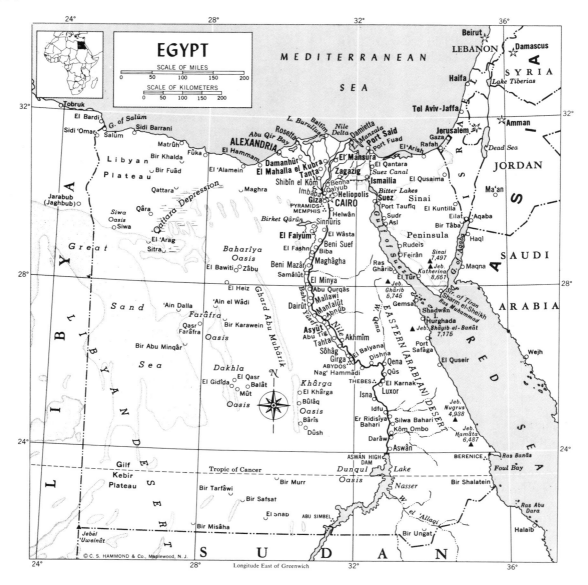

among the Arab populations of Ethiopian Eritrea and the Persian Gulf regions of Iran.

President Nasser died in September 1970 and was succeeded by Anwar Sadat, a relatively unknown former officer who, like Nasser, had played a role in the 1952 overthrow of King Farouk. Sadat has sought to moderate the activist role in the Arab world that Egypt had taken upon itself under Nasser. He also reduced Egypt's dependence on the USSR and, in July 1972, sent home Soviet military advisers.

In the years after the October War, Sadat further reduced, then completely ended, Egyptian dependence on the USSR. Basically he has sought to reduce Soviet prominence in an area where it does little except provide arms to the Arabs and, in his view, meddle in their internal affairs, contributing to instability. President Sadat has also lifted

many of the oppressive security measures enacted under Nasser, courted close ties with the United States, promoted Western investment, and, more recently, undertaken dramatic, almost irreversible steps toward establishing a modus vivendi with the state of Israel, steps strongly opposed by the radical Arab states. Sadat's position in Egypt and the region has been somewhat imperiled by these policies, as well as by Egypt's chronically infirm economic condition.

After the disastrous and humiliating defeat that Egypt suffered at the hands of the Israelis in four days of fighting in 1967, the major objective of Egyptian leaders was to rebuild strength, efficiency, confidence, and morale in the armed forces. To that end, Egypt's Communist allies, led by the USSR, provided military aid, both in materiel and in training. Not only was lost equipment replaced, but the forces were reorganized, and officers and men were trained to operate the most sophisticated modern hardware.

Thanks to the buildup and training, and to imaginative planning, Egypt achieved immediate, although transitory, success in the surprise attack on Israel on October 6, 1973. Israel's recovery from the initial losses, however, not only reduced the scope of the Egyptian gains, but also was marked by a dramatic Israeli crossing to the west bank of the Suez Canal—as well as Israeli repulses at Suez and Ismailia—before the ceasefire on October 24 finally ended the fighting. United States diplomatic efforts helped produce the Sinai I and II agreements, which achieved a withdrawal of troops by both Egypt and Israel and provided for U.S. involvement in monitoring the disengagement zones.

President Sadat's peace initiative late in 1977, which, with strong assistance from the United States, resulted in a peace treaty with Israel in the spring of 1979, marked a major step toward resolution of the very basic problems between the two nations. However, it was achieved at the cost of severed relations with all other Arab nations of the Middle East. The Arab League voted to expel Egypt, and moved its headquarters from Cairo to Tunis. Thus isolated from its former sources of financial support Egypt is forced to rely for assistance on the United States and other non-Arab nations.

Military service in Egypt is compulsory for all men eighteen years and over. University students may postpone their service until they finish school or reach the age of twenty-eight. The length of service is one year for university graduates, eighteen months for high school graduates, and three years for all others. Enlisted men serve nine years more in the reserves. About 80,000 to 100,000 men are inducted per year, most of them into the army.

There are four officer-training colleges. The Military Academy in Cairo graduates army line officers and trains naval, air defense, and air force officers for one year, after which they report either to the Naval College at Ras al-Tin, the Air Force College at Bilbeis, or the Air Defense College at Alexandria. Besides these, there are two engineering and technical officer-training institutions: the Military Technical College in Cairo graduates engineer officers, and the Military Technical Institute in Cairo graduates technical officers.

All reserve officers are trained after university graduation at the Reserve Officers' College in the Suez Canal Zone. Officers then attend a particular course at their own specialty institute.

## STRATEGIC PROBLEMS

The population of Egypt is compressed within the narrow Nile River Valley, which constitutes only 3.6 percent of Egypt's total area, resulting in a density of over 2,200 people per square mile, one of the highest in the world. This concentration of people and productive capacity—particularly intense in Cairo, with 8,000,000 inhabitants—makes Egypt vulnerable to threat or vital damage by hostile foreign power. Although the Aswan high dam increased productivity and slightly enlarged the arable area of Egypt, it is also vulnerable. Israeli air attacks on Egyptian targets in 1967 and a helicopter-borne commando raid of November 1968 against Nile bridges and power plants clearly demonstrated Israel's ability to exploit this vulnerability.

While the reopening of the Suez Canal (1975) has provided a source of income to the perennially hard-pressed Egyptian economy, it is also vulnerable to hostile attack. Recent discoveries of oil in the western desert may somewhat reduce Egypt's dependence upon the oil-rich Arab nations for economic support, a dependence that inevitably influences Sadat's peace negotiations. The existence of a vast subterranean river under the western desert also offers promise for the future, if funds to exploit the resource can be obtained.

## MILITARY ASSISTANCE

Before the October War, Egypt was almost completely dependent upon the USSR and other Warsaw Pact nations for military equipment and for training its forces in the use of modern weaponry. An estimated $4.5 billion in aid was received from the USSR between June 1967 and 1972, and another $1.5 billion before 1967. The 20,000-man Soviet mission then in Egypt was expelled in 1972, including Soviet pilots who had flown reconnaissance missions from Cairo in MiG-25s over Israeli positions in the Sinai Peninsula.

Since 1973 Egypt has sought and received assistance from a number of Western nations and from the United States.

## ALLIANCES

Egypt is a member of the Organization of African Unity (OAU). Before being expelled, Egypt was the leading member of the Arab League and the principal force behind the United Arab Command, the league's military organization, which is not in fact a command, and does not even have a military headquarters.

Egypt also has a joint military command relationship with Sudan. In May 1971 Egypt and the Soviet Union signed a fifteen-year treaty of friendship and cooperation. Sadat curtailed this agreement in July 1972 and terminated it in September 1975.

## ARMY

*Personnel:* 276,000

*Organization:*
- 3 armored divisions
- 5 infantry divisions
- 5 mechanized infantry divisions
- 16 artillery brigades
- 2 airborne brigades
- 20 battalion combat groups

*Major Equipment Inventory:*
- 1,400 medium tanks
  - 1,300 T-54/55, T-62
  - 100 T-34
- 100 light tanks (PT-76)
- 150 assault guns (SU-100 and JSU-152)
- 1,200 APCs (BTR-40P, BTR-50P, BTR-152, BTR-60P, BMP)
  - K-61 amphibious assault vehicles
- 2,200 light, medium, and heavy artillery pieces (122mm, 130mm, and 152mm guns and howitzers, and 160mm and 240mm mortars)
  - self-propelled antiaircraft guns (ZSU-57/2 and ZSU-23/4)
  - 203mm howitzers
  - RPG-7 antitank weapons
  - 57mm, 85mm, and 100mm antitank guns
- 24 SSMs (FROG 3/7)
- 25 SSMs (Samlet)
- 24 SSMs (Scud)
- 1,000 Snapper, Sagger, and Swatter antitank missiles SA-7 Grail missiles
- 1,000 vehicle-mounted rocket launchers
  - 20mm, 23mm, 37mm, 57mm, 85mm, and 100mm antiaircraft guns integrated with air force interceptors

*Reserves:* Approximately 600,000 trained reservists

## NAVY

*Personnel:* 17,500 (organized in four commands: Destroyer, Submarine, Minesweeper, and Torpedo)

*Major Units:*
- 12 submarines (6 R class; 6 W class; SS)
- 5 destroyers (4 Skory class; 1 British Z class; DD)
- 3 frigates (British Hunt class, Black Swan class, River class; DE)
- 12 corvettes (SO-1 class; PCS)
- 10 fleet minesweepers (6 T-43, 4 Yurka class; MSF)
- 4 inshore minesweepers (2 T-301 class, 2 K-8 class; MSI)
- 16 guided missile patrol boats (6 Osa, 10 Komar class with Styx SSM; PTFG)
- 30 torpedo boats (20 P-6, 6 Shershen class, 4 P-4 class; PT)
- 25 miscellaneous Syrian and Yugoslavian patrol craft (YP)
- 3 landing craft (Let Polnocny class)
- 11 landing ships (10 Vydra; 1 SMB-1 class; LS)
- 10 landing craft (LCM)
- 9 miscellaneous (tugs, training ships, auxiliaries, etc.)
- 3 hovercraft

*Note:* Some vessels equipped with Otomat SSM

*Naval Bases:* Ras al-Tin, Port Tawficq, Port Said, Mersa Matruh

*Reserves:* About 25,000 trained reservists

## AIR FORCE

*Personnel:* 25,000

*Organization:*
- 11 fighter-interceptor squadrons (9 MiG-21, 2 MiG-23)
- 21 fighter-bomber squadrons (9 Su-7, 3 MiG-17, 6 MiG-21, 3 Mirage)
- 1 medium bomber squadron (Tu-16)
- 5 transport squadrons (Il-14, An-12, C-130)
- 150 SAM battalions (Sa-2, 3, 6)

*Major Aircraft Types:* *
- 511 combat aircraft
  - 200 MiG-21 fighter-interceptors/fighter-bombers
  - 38 Mirage fighter-bombers
  - 23 MiG-23 fighter-interceptors
  - 130 Su-7 fighter-bombers
  - 100 MiG-17 fighter-bombers
  - 20 Tu-16 medium bombers
- 474 other aircraft
  - 76 transports (40 Il-14, 30 An-12, 6 C-130)
  - 250 trainer/support aircraft (MiG-15, L-29, Saeta)
  - 138 helicopters (60 Mi-8, 42 SA-341, 36 Sea King/Commando)

*Missiles:*
- 650 SAM launchers (SA-2 Guideline, SA-3 Goa, SA-4 Ganef, SA-6 Gainful)
  - ASM-5 Kelt carried by Tu-16 bombers
  - AAM K-13 Atoll carried by fighter-interceptors

*Equipment on Order:* 44 Mirage F-1

*Interceptors, shown under Air Force, and antiaircraft and SAMs shown under Army and Air Force are organized under an independent Air Defense Command similar to that of the Soviet organizational system. Here they are grouped functionally by weapons types.

*Reserves:* 35,000 trained reservists

*Major Air Bases:* Almaza, Cairo West, Bilbeis, Beni Suwayf, Luxor, El Minya, Ras Banas, Hurghada

## PARAMILITARY

The National Guard is a poorly armed and poorly equipped home guard type of force of about 200,000, under army command.

# EL SALVADOR

## Republic of El Salvador

### POWER POTENTIAL STATISTICS

Area: 8,260 square miles
Population: 4,580,000
Total Active Regular Armed Forces: 5,630 (0.12% population)
Gross National Product: $2.6 billion ($610 per capita)
Annual Military Expenditures: $42.2 million (1.6% GNP)
Fuel Production: Refined Petroleum Products: 715,400 metric tons
Electric Power Output: 1.2 billion kwh
Merchant Fleet (ships 1,000 tons and over): 1 ship; 2,000 gross tons
Civil Air Fleet: 8 major transport aircraft

### POLITICO-MILITARY POLICIES AND POSTURE

The president is commander in chief of the armed forces with control exercised through the minister of defense, an army officer. Men between eighteen and thirty are all eligible for service but are called on a selective basis for one-year service. The National Assembly annually sets the strength of the army, which must have at least 3,000 men. During peacetime El Salvador utilizes its armed forces in nation-building through military civic action.

The nineteenth and twentieth century history of El Salvador has been characterized by violence, chaos, and military intervention. The combination of a very dense population and high population growth rate (3.3% yearly) with the concentration of large landholdings in the hands of a very small percentage of the population creates widespread poverty and endemic unrest. With considerable Communist encouragement, these conditions foster the growth of numerous revolutionary organizations, and extreme repressive action by the government and government-supported groups. The result has been a constant state of tension and action and reaction, with large-scale arrests, kidnappings, murders, and assassinations for which both sides are responsible and for which there is no simple solution. Long-promised agrarian reform might be helpful. Riots and protests following the election of Gen. Carlos Humberto Roberto (the third successive military president) in 1977 led to declaration of a state of siege from February until the end of June. In October 1979 Humberto Romero was ousted and a reform-oriented military government was installed.

Boundary disputes with Honduras developed into a brief military clash in 1969. There have been several incidents since then. In 1976 the two nations agreed to arbitration.

United States financial military assistance for 1977 was $647,000, making a total of $10.3 million since 1950. In addition, 1,972 students have been trained under the MAP. El Salvador has renounced further U.S. military aid.

El Salvador is a member of the OAS and ODECA. The headquarters of ODECA is in San Salvador.

The 4,500-man army is organized in three infantry battalions, one cavalry squadron, two artillery battalions, and one parachute company. These are expandable to regimental size upon mobilization of reserves, the Territorial Service, which has 30,000 men organized to produce twelve additional infantry units. The 130-man navy has four patrol boats (PB). The air force, reorganized in 1954 with U.S. assistance, has 1,000 men, one fighter-bomber squadron and one transport squadron. Equipment includes eighteen Ouragan Magisters and four Arava transports (all from Israel), one FH-1100 helicopter, and about thirty trainers, mainly T-34 and T-11. The only air base is at Ilopango, but airstrips exist throughout the country.

The National Guard, a constabulary, has 2,500 men.

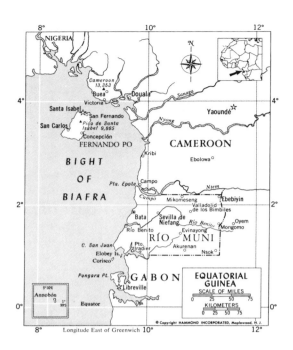

# EQUATORIAL GUINEA

## Republic of Equatorial Guinea

### POWER POTENTIAL STATISTICS

Area: 10,832 square miles (10,040 Rio Muni, 779
Fernando Po, 15 minor islets)
Population: 339,000
Total Active Regular Armed Forces: 5,000 (1.47%
population)
Gross National Product: $70 million ($240 per capita)
Annual Military Expenditures: $3.5 million (5.0% GNP)
Electric Power Output: 17 million kwh
Civil Air Fleet: 3 major transport aircraft

### POLITICO-MILITARY POLICIES AND POSTURE

Spanish colonies since 1778, the island of Fernando Po
and mainland Spanish Guinea (Rio Muni) received
independence as Equatorial Guinea on October 12, 1968.
Included in Fernando Po are adjacent islets and the island
of Annobon, and in Rio Muni the island of Corisco, the
Elobey Islands, and adjacent islets. The country was ruled
for ten years by President-for-life Marcias Nguema, a
brutal, absolute, and apparently paranoid dictator, who
seized emergency powers in 1969. He was overthrown in
August 1979 by a military junta headed by Nguema
Mbazogo.

Before independence Fernando Po's strategic location,
combined with the presence of 40,000 Ibos (Biafrians) on
the island, and Spain's permissive policies, had caused the
island to become an air base for arms and food flights to
Biafra in the Nigeria-Biafra civil war (1967–70).

Before Spain granted independence, Nigeria had
contemplated annexation or purchase of Fernando Po.
Also, Cameroon had claimed both Fernando Po and Rio
Muni, and Gabon had claimed Rio Muni. Since independence Cameroon and Gabon have each renounced these
claims, contingent on a like restraint by the other.

Although the minority, the wealthier Bubis of Fernando
Po fear diversion of their island's economic resources to
development of poorer Rio Muni, whose population is
predominantly of the Fang tribe. Upward of one-fourth of
the population has left the country for refugee camps in
neighboring countries. In Gabon, they have become a
significant problem. An opposition organization, ANRD,
was created among exiles in 1974.

Equatorial Guinea's currently depressed economy is
based on cocoa, coffee, and timber, grown on large plantations that were formerly worked by imported Nigerian
labor. The departure of most of the Nigerians after
disputes over wages and working conditions has sharply
cut production of all crops, reducing timber production to
near zero. Marcias has decreed compulsory labor for all
over fifteen years of age and has shipped some 25,000
mainlanders to what amounts to slave labor plantations on
Fernando Po (Marcias) Island.

Spain contributes substantially to Equatorial Guinea's
economy, both through subsidies and as a trading partner;
80 percent of the country's trade is with Spain. Spain
suspended diplomatic relations with Equatorial Guinea in
March 1977.

The armed forces have received training from Spain,
some Communist countries (especially China and Cuba),
and other African countries.

Equatorial Guinea is a member of the OAU.

# ETHIOPIA

### POWER POTENTIAL STATISTICS

Area: 457,142 square miles
Population: 31,341,000
Total Active Regular Armed Forces: 44,500 (0.14%
population)
Gross National Product: $2.89 billion ($100 per capita)
Annual Military Expenditures: $104.4 million (3.61%
GNP)
Electric Power Output: 500 million kwh

Fuel Production: Refined Petroleum Products: 559,000
  metric tons
Merchant Fleet (ships 1,000 tons and over): 4 ships;
  19,000 gross tons
Civil Air Fleet: 19 major transport aircraft

## DEFENSE STRUCTURE

Since 1974 the Provisional Military Administrative
Council (PMAC), more popularly known as the Dergue,
has exercised governmental powers. In early 1977 Lt. Col.
Mengistu Haile-Mariam emerged from a long and bloody
struggle for power within the PMAC as chairman.
Mengistu became head of each level of the Dergue's
new three-tiered heirarchy—General Congress, Central
Committee, and Standing Committee. The Standing
Committee, consisting of thirteen to sixteen military
officers, effectively controls policy matters. Mengistu also
became chairman of the civilian (and relatively powerless)
Council of Ministers and commander in chief of the armed
forces. Subsequent military reorganization in August 1977
established a National Revolutionary Campaign Command

(NRCC), which plans and controls all military operations
and administration.

## POLITICO-MILITARY POLICY

Traditionally, Ethiopia has assumed an independent,
nonaligned position. It has supported collective security
efforts, including, since 1945, the United Nations. This
policy of independence and nonalignment goes back far
before World War II, and, except for the Italian conquest
and occupation of 1935–41, it has been notably successful.
In implementation of its collective security approach,
Ethiopia contributed to UN forces in Korea (1951–53) and
the Congo (1960–64). It also took a lead in the African
unity movement, was a founder of OAU, and built the
OAU headquarters in Addis Ababa.

Independence has been maintained over the centuries
against neighboring enemies by the relative inaccessibility
of the high (6,000–10,000 feet) central plateau. For more
than a millenium, predominantly Christian Ethiopia's
traditional enemies have been Arabs and other Moslems,
whose nations surround it on three sides.

When revolutionary change came to Ethiopia, which had been ruled by the Emperor Haile Selassie I since 1931, it was triggered not by the separatist movements that have long threatened the heterogeneous nation, but rather by inflation following the severe famine of 1973, a famine that was apparently unnecessarily devastating because of mismanaged governmental relief efforts. Strikes and riots in Addis Ababa in early 1974 were followed by army units' taking over the principal cities. By mid-1974 the army controlled the government, and in September the military officially deposed Haile Selassie; he was kept under virtual arrest until his death in 1975.

Coincident with the death of the emperor, the Ethiopian state collapsed into anarchy in 1975 and 1976. The new rulers' attempts at mobilizing a national revolution against the forces of "feudalism, imperialism, and bureaucratic capitalism" degenerated into a series of violent struggles between the government and several independent elements of Ethiopian society. By mid-1976 ethnic and regional rebel groups contended with government forces in most areas of the country. The capital itself became the scene of murderous struggles both within the Dergue and between it and urban radical groups demanding, among other things, return to civil rule. In Eritrea liberation groups extended their control to some 80 to 90 percent of the province and seriously threatened the Ethiopian garrison at Asmara. In 1977 Somalia assisted the ethnic Somali liberation movement (WSLF) in seizing most of the Ogaden region of southeastern Ethiopia.

Mengistu responded to these multiple challenges by intensifying the campaign of terror against the domestic opposition and by ending the long-standing American relationship in favor of economic assistance and military forces from the USSR and Cuba. The Dergue may have been successful in eradicating most of the underground Marxist Ethiopian People's Revolutionary Party (EPRP) in 1977. At the same time it alienated a splinter group of the EPRP, the All-Ethiopia Socialist movement (MAESON). MAESON was initially allied with the Dergue and was favored by Cuba and the USSR as the base for an eventual civilian Marxist-Leninist party. A third party, the London-based Ethiopian Democratic Union (EDU), enjoys considerable popularity and strength in several provinces along the Sudanese border.

## STRATEGIC PROBLEMS

Ethiopia faces a complex set of strategic problems. These revolve around three interrelated sets of issues: internal ethno-religious antipathies, the dislocations of government-inspired socioeconomic revolution, and Ethiopia's encirclement by hostile Arab and Moslem neighbors.

Ethiopia contains some forty different tribes of mostly Semitic or Hamitic origin. The ruling Amharas and Tigreans of the highlands comprise 40 percent of the population and are mostly Coptic Christians; the coastal and lowland peoples are mostly Moslems. The concentration of power and wealth in the Amharas is a long-standing source of jealousy and mistrust among other groups.

Early Dergue attempts at land reform met with considerable resistance from disparate groups, including local police, disaffected military units, landowners, and opposition political parties. Even a force of students mobilized to implement Dergue reforms became rebellious at government inaction. Clearly, a sizable portion of the Ethiopian military will be involved in establishing and keeping internal order (Eritrea and Ogaden aside) for a number of years to come.

Russian arms and Cuban troops ended the immediate threat of Somali annexation of the Ogaden. By mid-April 1978 Somalia had pulled its defeated troops back across its border and had given assurances that it would not claim Ethiopian territory. However, Somali irredentism runs strong. Half a million Somali nomads live in the Ogaden, and the WSLF can be expected to continue guerrilla operations from the rugged southwestern provinces for an indefinite period. Somalia once before (1968) renounced its claims to the area, but launched the invasion in 1977. It could seek again to exploit internal weakness in Ethiopia.

Ethiopia's chief security problem in recent years had lain in the Eritrean liberation movements. The former Italian colony of some two million, half Coptic Christians and half Moslems, was federated with Ethiopia in 1952. In 1962, Ethiopia annexed the area as a province, sparking a liberation struggle that has persisted ever since. Three groups, the Eritrean Liberation Front (ELF), the Eritrean Popular Liberation Front (EPLF), and the Eritrean Liberation Front—Popular Liberation Forces (ELF-PLF), claimed in mid-1978 a combined strength of 45,000 soldiers. The three groups have fought among themselves over ideological and religious issues but may unify in the face of a determined Ethiopian offensive. The Eritreans have received considerable assistance from Arab states. Notable exceptions include Libya and Southern Yemen, who chose ideological partnership with the Mengistu regime over support for their former Eritrean friends. This places Libya and Southern Yemen solidly behind Soviet and Cuban support of the Mengistu government. In November 1978 Ethiopian troops retook Asmara, the Eritrean capital, and Keren, the last rebel stronghold. Rebel forces continued strong in the countryside.

There has been a tremendous influx of Eastern European economic aid since 1976. Signs of tension between Ethiopia and its new benefactors have arisen over two issues. The Cubans and Soviets, former backers of Eritrean independence, have preferred a negotiated federal solution to the conflict, rather than a lengthy war. They also want to see a viable civilian one-party Marxist government succeed the PMAC.

Ethiopia's relations with Sudan have never been close. The two agreed in 1965 to prevent their territories from being used for hostile purposes against each other. In 1972 Haile Selassie helped mediate an end to the Sudanese civil war, which brought a few years of stable relations. However, Sudan has always supported the Eritrean cause, and it renewed its active hostility toward Ethiopia following Ethiopian attacks on Eritrea in 1975. Sudan accused Ethiopia and Libya of backing a coup attempt against President Numayri in 1976. Sudan has loudly denounced the presence of Soviet and Cuban military personnel in Ethiopia.

Half of Ethiopia's trade passes by rail through the port of Djibouti on the Gulf of Aden. This vital link was a key target of the Somali invasion of 1977. Maintenance of the rail line depends upon control of the northern Ogaden and continued neutrality of the newly independent (1977) Djibouti government.

## MILITARY ASSISTANCE

Since World War II Ethiopia has received assistance from many nations. The British, who drove out the Italians in 1941, conducted military training from 1947 to 1951. Sweden helped organize and train the air force, organized a cadet school in 1946, and helped establish the office of the chief of staff of the Imperial Armed Forces in 1956. France, India, Israel, and Norway have helped train the navy. Prior to rupture of diplomatic relations Israeli advisers conducted special infantry training, and provided advisers for the Frontier Guard and the Commando Police. West Germany has provided equipment for police field units. India has helped with training of the Imperial Bodyguard and the Military Academy. Most of this assistance was by contract, paid for by Ethiopia.

Military assistance from the United States comprised armament, equipment, and supplies of all kinds, worth $204.1 million from 1953 through 1977 ($3.8 million in 1977) and the training of about 3,929 Ethiopians in the United States. In the face of the Marxist rhetoric and violence of the new regime, the United States announced a reduction in aid to Ethiopia in February 1977. Total suspension of sales and aid followed Ethiopia's closing of most U.S. services in the country, including the Kagnew communications center at Asmara. Simultaneously, the Soviet Union began supplying Ethiopia heavily with weapons and advisers.

As the Ogaden conflict worsened, Mengistu sought and received Soviet and Cuban assistance. Between November 1977 and March 1978, some 17,000 Cuban troops, 1,000 Soviet advisers, and an estimated $1 billion in equipment poured into Ethiopia and turned the tide of the Ogaden war.

For its part, Ethiopia has in the past provided pilot and supporting aviation training for students from other African countries, including Sudan, Kenya, and Nigeria.

## ALLIANCES

Ethiopia is a member of the OAU. In 1963, in response to armed incursions of Somali nomadic tribesmen across the borders of both countries, Ethiopia and Kenya concluded a treaty of mutual defense, directed against Somalia. In November 1978 Ethiopia and the USSR signed a twenty-year treaty of friendship and cooperation that contained a pledge of military consultation.

## ARMY

*Personnel:* 40,000

*Organization:*
    4 infantry divisions (each of 3 brigades of 3
        battalions; 8,000 men per division; 1 division
        is the Imperial Bodyguard)
    4 artillery battalions
    5 antiaircraft batteries
    1 armored battalion
    1 airborne (parachute) infantry battalion
    2 combat engineer battalions
    8 training battalions
    1 armored car squadron

*Major Equipment Inventory:*
    35 medium tanks (M-60, T-34)
    80 light tanks (M-41 and M-24)
  150 light APCs (M-113, BTR-152, M-59)
    60 armored cars (AML-245, M-8, M-20
        Commando)
  150 105mm howitzers, 155mm guns, M100 SP
        155mm howitzers, M-114 155mm howitzers
    6 helicopters UH-1
        antiaircraft guns

## NAVY

*Personnel:* 1,500

*Major Units:*
    2 patrol ships (PGF)
    9 patrol craft (PC)
    4 harbor patrol boats (PSB)

2 mechanized landing craft (LCM)
2 personnel landing craft (LCP)

*Naval Bases:* Massaua, Asab

## AIR FORCE

*Personnel:* 3,000

*Organization:*
1 bomber squadron (Canberra)
2 fighter/fighter-bomber squadrons (F-5, F-86)
2 COIN squadrons (T-33, T-28)
1 transport squadron (C-119, C-54, C-47, Dove)

*Major Aircraft Types:*
40 combat aircraft
  15 F-5 fighters
  12 F-86 fighters
   9 T-33, T-28 armed trainers
   4 Canberra light bombers
82 other aircraft
  30 transports (C-54, C-47, Dove, Il-14, C-119)
  30 Saab 91 Safir trainers
   8 T-28 trainers
  14 Alouette II/III, Mi-8, UH-1 helicopters

*Military Air Bases:* Debre Zeit, Bishiftu, Jijiga, Harar

## PARAMILITARY

The National Police Force is about 28,000 strong with 4,000 of these committed against the insurgency in the province of Eritrea, as are the 3,000 special Commando Police. The Frontier Guard numbering some 1,500 men patrols the Somalia border against the incursions of the *shifta* (gangs of bandits).

# FIJI

## Dominion of Fiji

## POWER POTENTIAL STATISTICS

Area: 7,055 square miles
Population: 615,000
Gross National Product: $644 million ($1,130 per capita)
Electric Power Output: 270 million kwh
Merchant Fleet (ships 1,000 tons and over): 2 ships; 4000 gross tons
Civil Air Fleet: 1 DC-3; 1 light aircraft

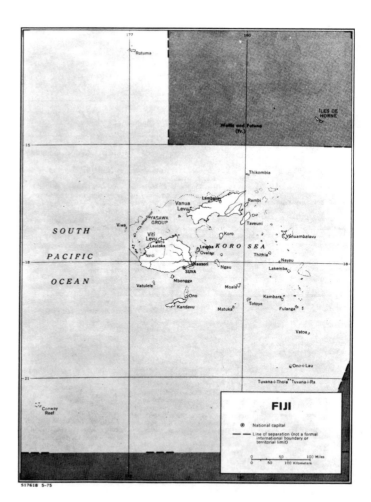

517618 5-75

## POLITICO-MILITARY POLICIES AND POSTURE

Fiji lies centrally among the islands of the South Pacific. Since achieving independence in 1970, it has become a leader among South Pacific states. It holds dominion status within the Commonwealth, acknowledges the British sovereign, and is represented by a governor general as head of state. The island is governed by its own Parliament and prime minister. The population of Fiji is slightly more than half Indian and slightly less than half native Fijian (of mixed Melanesian and Polynesian ancestry). Its constitution reflects this fact, with equal numbers of seats in the House of Representatives reserved for each group. There are some tensions between the two ethnic communities, but the government and society appear stable. Fiji played a leading role in negotiating an agreement that made it and forty-five other African, Pacific, and Caribbean nations associate members of the European Economic Community. Several UN agencies have their regional headquarters at Suva, Fiji's capital.

# FINLAND

## Republic of Finland

## POWER POTENTIAL STATISTICS

Area: 130,119 square miles
Population: 4,755,000
Total Active Regular Armed Forces: 39,500 (0.83% population)
Gross National Product: $29 billion ($6,110 per capita)
Annual Military Expenditures: $520 million (1.79% GNP)
Crude Steel Production: 1.6 million metric tons
Iron Ore Production: 597,000 metric tons
Fuel Production:
   Refined Petroleum Products: 10.8 million metric tons
   Manufactured Gas: 26.8 million cubic meters
Electric Power Output: 33 billion kwh
Nuclear Power Production: 1,500 megawatts
Merchant Fleet (ships 1,000 tons and over): 184 ships; 2.1 million gross tons
Civil Air Fleet: 41 major transport aircraft

## DEFENSE STRUCTURE

The president of the Republic of Finland is the commander in chief of the Finnish armed forces, and as the nation's chief executive has considerably more direct personal authority and responsibility for military affairs than does the head of state or of government in most other nations. The defense minister has no command authority; his is an essentially administrative position. The armed forces are integrated, and the nation's senior military officer, with the title of commander of the defense forces, is responsible directly to the president. The prime minister acts as chairman of the National Defense Council (comparable to the U.S. National Security Council), which includes the minister of defense, four other ministers, the commander of the defense forces, and the chief of the General Staff.

## POLITICO-MILITARY POLICY

Finland's location has forced it to shape its military policy and strategy with primary reference to the Soviet Union. The events of World War II proved conclusively to the Finns that no amount of Finnish valor and military skill can deny Russian might. Thus, Finnish foreign policy is designed to preserve independence, while assuring Russia that (1) Finland is firmly neutral in international affairs, and will not attempt to thwart or to oppose Soviet interests, (2) Finland poses no military threat to Russia, and (3) its defenses are strong enough to make it unlikely that any other power will be able to establish an anti-Soviet base in Finland easily before the USSR can intervene.

Finland's armed forces are limited in size by the 1947 post–World War II peace treaty with the Allied and Associated Powers (USSR, U.K., Australia, Canada, Czechoslovakia, India, New Zealand, and the Union of South Africa).

Under the treaty the maximum strength allowed for the army is 34,400; the navy is limited to 10,000 tons and 4,500 men; the air force cannot exceed sixty combat aircraft and 3,000 men. Among the prohibitions of the treaty are nuclear weapons, guided missiles, submarines, motor torpedo boats, and aircraft with internal bomb-carrying capability. Conscript service is for eight to eleven months. By treaty, no military training may be conducted outside the service.

## STRATEGIC PROBLEMS

Finland's principal strategic problem is proximity to the power centers of the USSR. Because of its far northerly location, Finland has traditionally stressed the development of a capability to operate efficiently in cold weather. This capability had much to do with the initial and dramatic successes that the Finns won over the Russians in the early weeks of the 1939–40 war with the USSR. Finland's defensive capability is enhanced by the obstacles created by the Arctic north, and a vast area of forests and lakes in the east and central portions of the country. The obstacles are less formidable, however, on the direct but narrow approaches to Finland's heartland from the Soviet power center of Leningrad.

## ALLIANCES AND MILITARY ASSISTANCE

Under the MAP Finland has received $179,000 in assistance from the United States and MAP training for forty-nine students. Finland has contributed contingents or observers to UN forces or missions in Cyprus, Kashmir, Jerusalem, and Lebanon. Finland is a member of EFTA.

## ARMY

*Personnel:* 34,000 (about 10,000 are permanent, regular cadre; the remainder are conscripts)

*Organization:*
   1 armored brigade (about half strength)
   6 infantry brigades (about 35% of full strength)
   8 independent infantry battalions (reduced strength)
   2 field artillery regiments

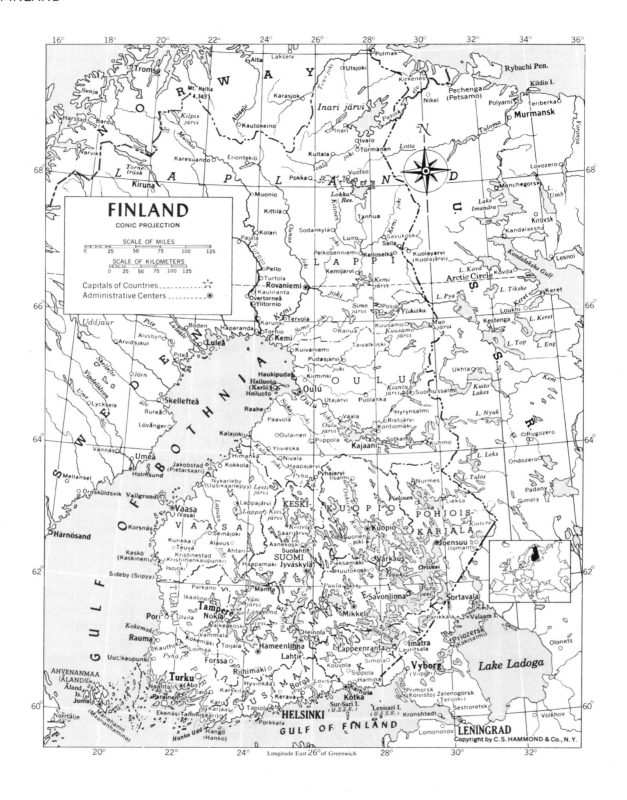

# FINLAND

CONIC PROJECTION

SCALE OF MILES

0   25   50   75   100   125

SCALE OF KILOMETERS

0   25   50   75   100   125

Capitals of Countries ............ ☆
Administrative Centers ............ ◉

Copyright by C.S. HAMMOND & Co., N.Y.

8 coast artillery battalions
1 antiaircraft regiment
4 antiaircraft battalions

*Major Equipment Inventory:*
medium tanks (T-54, T-55)
light tanks (PT-76)
APCs (BTR-50P)
guns (105mm, 122mm, 130mm)
howitzers (122mm, 152mm)
mortars (81mm, 120mm)
antiaircraft guns (ZSU-57/2 SP; 35mm Oerlikon,
40mm Bofors, 30mm Hispano-Suiza, and 23mm
Soviet towed)
antitank missiles (Vigilant, SS-11)

*Reserves:* About 150,000 trained reserves; could be increased to over 500,000

## NAVY

*Personnel:* 2,500

*Major Units:*
2 frigates (Riga class; FF)
2 patrol ships (PGF)
14 fast patrol boats (PCF)
5 missile attack boats (Styx SSM; mainly Soviet OSA class; PTG)
5 patrol craft (PC)
1 coastal minelayer (MMC)
6 inshore minesweepers (MSI)
13 utility landing craft (LCU)
10 icebreakers (AGB)
65 service craft (transports, tugs, etc.)

*Major Naval Bases:* Hanko, Helsinki, Turku

*Reserves:* About 8,000 trained reservists

## AIR FORCE

*Personnel:* 3,000

*Organization:*
3 regional wings: Hame, Satahunta, and Karjala
3 fighter squadrons (1 MiG-21, 2 Draken)
1 transport squadron (C-47, Pembroke, Beaver)

*Major Aircraft Types:*
54 combat aircraft
54 fighters (18 MiG-21, 36 Draken)
131 other aircraft
17 transports (10 C-47, 4 Cessna 310, 3 Beaver)
103 trainer aircraft (4 MiG-15, 4 MiG-21, 5 PA-28, 55 Magister, 35 Safir)
11 helicopters (1 AB204, 1 AB206, 1 Alouette II, 3 Mi-4, 4 Mi-8)

*Major Air Bases:* Dissala, Pori, Luonetjarvi, Parote, Kuopio, Jyvaskyla, Utti, Tampere, Kauhava

*Reserves:* About 11,000 men

## PARAMILITARY

The National Police Force of 5,000 provides for internal security. There is a frontier guard organization numbering 3,000 men. The frontier guard operates three patrol ships (PGF), three patrol craft (PC), and ten patrol boats (PB).

# FRANCE

## French Republic

### POWER POTENTIAL STATISTICS

Area: 212,973 square miles (including Corsica)
Population: 53,536,000
Total Active Regular Armed Forces: 495,500 (0.93% population)
Gross National Product: $381 billion ($7,150 per capita)
Annual Military Expenditures: $17.6 billion (4.62% GNP)
Crude Steel Production: 23.2 million metric tons
Iron Ore Production: 45.2 million metric tons
Fuel Production:
Crude Oil: 1.1 million metric tons
Refined Petroleum Products: 123.8 million metric tons
Coal: 21.9 million metric tons
Natural Gas: 7.1 billion cubic meters
Manufactured Gas: 6.5 million cubic meters
Electric Power Output: 211 billion kwh
Nuclear Power Production: 20,400 megawatts
Merchant Fleet (ships 1,000 tons and over): 416 ships; 11.75 million gross tons
Civil Air Fleet: 300 major transport aircraft

### DEFENSE STRUCTURE

The president of France is the commander in chief of the armed forces. He also presides over the Council of Ministers, the High Defense Council, and the Defense Committee. The Council of Ministers defines defense policy as part of the general national policy. The High Defense Council is the decision-making body for general defense policies within the framework established by the Council of Ministers, and includes the premier, the

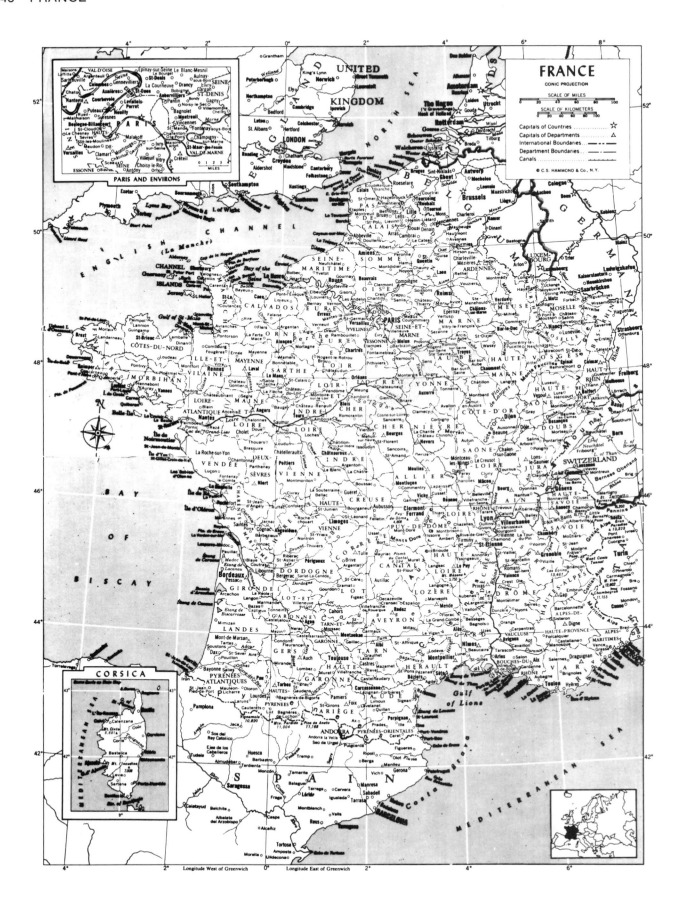

ministers of foreign affairs, national defense, interior, and finance, and the general secretary for national defense. The High Defense Council advises the Council of Ministers.

The premier is responsible for overall defense management, the coordination of defense activities, and the implementation of the decisions of the Council of Ministers and the Defense Council. The minister of national defense, who functions as the executive of the premier, has authority over the three integrated services and is responsible for their preparedness. He is assisted by the chief of staff of the armed forces and the general staffs of the three services. The French armed forces are organized on the basis of three task-oriented operational systems (the Nuclear Strategic Force, the Forces of Maneuver, and the Territorial Defense Force), each including elements of all three services.

## POLITICO-MILITARY POLICY

The structure and missions of the French armed forces reflect the government's basic conviction that for reasons of national security and national prestige France should remain responsible for its own defense, and that it should retain a substantial degree of independence of the two superpowers. The French government also believes that with its own nuclear force France contributes to a more stable international environment. Because of its diminished confidence in the U.S. commitment to invoke its deterrent on behalf of a European ally, France believes that it has to possess its own nuclear forces to deter attack by another power. The French feel, therefore, that their nuclear capability complements the U.S. nuclear deterrent. France hopes that eventually a European security system will evolve, built around the French nuclear forces.

The Strategic Force forms France's major deterrent and is capable of attack over intercontinental range. It consists of Mirage IV bombers armed with 100-kiloton nuclear bombs; intermediate range, ground-to-ground, solid-fuel ballistic nuclear missiles stationed in southern France; and four nuclear-powered submarines with Polaris-type missiles. All are now fully operational. In 1973 the government announced construction in southeastern France of sites for an additional group of intermediate-range ballistic missiles equipped with thermonuclear warheads of almost megaton strength. The Strategic Force operates directly under the president.

The Forces of Maneuver have as their mission the containment of a nuclear or conventional attack inside or outside Europe. They include the bulk of the army, the navy, and the tactical air force units.

The Territorial Defense Forces (DOT) are responsible both for the defense of national territory and for internal security. An Alpine brigade, which is entrusted with the protection of the strategic missile silos in southeastern France, twenty-five other army battalions, and gendarm-

erie units, constitute the core of the DOT. Light air force squadrons support the DOT.

France's independent defense policy led in 1966 to French withdrawal from NATO's military structure, even though it remained a member of the North Atlantic Alliance. France has also retained its membership in the Western European Union. Two French mechanized divisions continue to be stationed in West Germany under a bilateral arrangement; one independent brigade remains in West Berlin. Despite France's withdrawal from ACE, it cooperated in Mediterranean naval exercises in 1970, and has never left NATO's air defense communications system. A cautious movement toward reestablishing closer ties with NATO began after the 1974 elections, and has continued.

Because of France's determination to establish its own nuclear capability, it refused to sign the Limited Test Ban Treaty. France has continued nuclear and thermonuclear tests at its Pacific test range near Tahiti, despite a call from the International Court of Justice in mid-1973 to stop them. After 1974, France did shift from atmospheric to underground tests.

Economic, military, and cultural treaties with former French colonies in Africa maintain France's influence there. France has favored the creation of a Western-backed inter-African strike force to respond to threats similar to the 1978 invasion of the Kolwezi area of Zaire from Angola, but the United States and United Kingdom have demurred.

Universal military service, modified by exception of certain classifications, provides the majority of the armed forces. Active service lasts twelve months and is followed by three and one-half years of availability, with another twelve years of reserve service. Draftees are not used in such overseas operations as the 1978 Zaire rescue.

Beginning in Jaunary 1975, with the appointment of a new minister of national defense, efforts have been made to improve the effectiveness and morale of the armed forces, which, although among the largest in the West, have been relatively ill paid and somewhat weak in weaponry, with much of France's defense budget going into its nuclear force.

## STRATEGIC PROBLEMS

The country's geographic situation provides a marked contrast in defensive strengths and vulnerabilities. The Pyrenees and the southern Alps, combined with the existence of a determinedly neutral Switzerland, provide protection from land attack on the southern and southeastern frontiers. Although the Rhine from Switzerland to north of Strasbourg is a difficult obstacle, it is not impassable. From the Rhine to the North Sea, the northern border is rugged in places and subject to inundation in a few, but is nevertheless demonstrably passable to troops.

The ocean borders—Channel, Atlantic, and Mediterranean—while they strengthen France's economic position in seaborne trade, are not invulnerable to modern amphibious assault. French realization of this geographic situation goes far to explain the incompleteness of France's separation from the North Atlantic Alliance, despite its insistence both on political independence and on rejection of NATO military command.

France's internal political situation has in the past been fraught with dissension among a multiplicity of parties, but since Charles de Gaulle assumed leadership twenty years ago, France has enjoyed greater stability. In 1974 and again in 1978, legislative elections gave the Gaullist and moderate (led by President Valery Giscard d'Estaing) factions enough seats to form a coalition government. Press and poll predictions had earlier given the 1978 election to the Socialists and Communists, but their coalition broke apart in fall 1977. The Communist party of 400,000 members (the second largest in the West) has the capability of weakening the national effort in the fields of politics, economics, and defense, but French Communist leaders, part of the Eurocommunism movement, currently assert their independence of Moscow and, in a 1977 reversal of their earlier position, now support the French nuclear deterrent.

France's relations with its strongest neighbor and traditional enemy, (West) Germany, are now very cordial. The two countries form a stable central core for Western Europe. A 1963 French–West German friendship treaty provides for semiannual meetings of the countries' leaders.

In January 1974 the government banned four separatist movements: two rival Breton groups, the Liberation Front of Brittany (FLB-ARB) and the left-wing Liberation Front of Brittany for National Liberation and Socialism (FLB-LNS); the Corsican Peasant Front for Liberation (FPCL); and Basque Enbata. These groups were believed to have foreign support.

Agreement was reached with Spain in January 1974 on the limits of each country's claims to the continental shelf in the Bay of Biscay.

## MILITARY ASSISTANCE

The United States has not provided France with military aid since 1966.

France has 12,000 to 13,700 troops stationed in Africa and is committed by bilateral treaty to help many of the Francophone African countries if they are attacked. In 1978, in shaky cooperation with Belgium, France sent 600 to 1,000 French Foreign Legion troops to Kolwezi, Shaba Province, Zaire, to rescue Europeans from the area, which had been overrun by Zairean rebel raiders based in Angola.

French naval, army, and air units participate in joint exercises with indigenous troops in Africa. Some 3,000 French officers and NCOs are serving on secondment or on contract with African armed forces.

The French armament industry has become a major pillar of the French economy, and France now sells arms worldwide.

## ALLIANCES

France is a member of the Western European Union, NATO (limited), SEATO, and the European Common Market. It also has bilateral treaties with most of its former colonies.

## ARMY

*Personnel:* 331,000

*Organization:* (reorganization not completed)
  1 army consisting of 2 army corps plus supporting
    elements
      1 army corps (5 armored divisions)
      1 army corps (3 armored divisions, in
        Germany)
      1 Alpine division
      1 parachute division (2 paratroop brigades)
      1 independent brigade (in Berlin)
      3 infantry divisions (separate, in France)
      3 regiments SAM (Hawk)
      5 regiments SSM (Pluton) (tactical nuclear)

*Deployment:* France remains responsible for the protection and security of its overseas departments and territories, which have been organized into four defense zones: the Antilles and Guiana zone in the Caribbean (one battalion); the Indian Ocean zone with headquarters in La Reunion Island (one regiment); the Pacific Ocean zone (divided into two zones, New Caledonia and Polynesia; two battalions). Additional units are stationed in independent Africa: Senegal, Ivory Coast.

*Major Equipment Inventory:*
  960 AMX-30 medium tanks
  800 AMX-13 light tanks (with 90mm guns and 4
      SS-11 antitank missiles)
      EBR heavy armored cars
      AML light armored cars
  400 AMX-10
      APCs (AMX-VTT)
      AMX 105mm and 155mm self-propelled
       howitzers
      AMX twin 30mm self-propelled antiaircraft
       guns
      155mm field artillery
   40 fixed-wing aircraft
  550 helicopters (including 130 SA-330 Puma)

*Missiles:* SSM: Pluton; SAM: Hawk, Crotale, Roland; ATM: Nord SS-11, Entac, Nord/Bolkow, Milan

*Reserves:* There are approximately 300,000 trained reservists available for mobilization that can add fourteen divisions to the sixteen divisions listed above.

## NAVY

*Personnel:* 68,500 (includes a Naval Air Force of 11,500 and some 900 marines). About 90,000 trained reserves.

*Major Units:*

  5 nuclear-powered ballistic missile submarines (SSBN; 1,860 n.m. missiles)
  1 diesel-powered ballistic missile submarine (SSB; 1,860 n.m. missiles)
 23 diesel submarines (SS)
  2 aircraft carriers (Clemenceau class; CV; 40 aircraft)
  1 guided missile cruiser (CG; Masurca SAMs)
  1 helicopter light cruiser (CLH; 8 helicopters; Exocet short-range SSMs)
 24 frigates (FF; 15 fitted with Exocet short-range SSMs; 3 additional in reserve.)
 10 guided missile destroyers (DDG)
      3 Type C 70 class; SM-1 SAMs; Exocet SSMs; Crotale ASMs; others building)
      2 Suffren class; Masurca SAMs; Malafon ASM
      4 Type T 47 class; Tartar SAMs
      1 Type F 67 class (Crotale SAMs; Exocet SSMs, Malafon ASMs)
 12 destroyers (DD; 4 fitted with Exocet short-range SSMs)
  2 dock landing ships (LSD)
  5 missile attack boats (PTG; most with SS-12 short-range SSMs)
 21 patrol craft (PC; 4 others in reserve)
  6 patrol boats (PB)
 13 fleet minesweepers (MSF)
  6 minehunters (MSH; others under construction)
 23 coastal minesweepers (MSC)
  7 tank landing ships (LST)
 13 utility landing craft (LCU)
 36 mechanized landing craft (LCM)
 28 auxiliary ships (tugs, oilers, survey, etc.)
185 service craft

*Major Naval Bases:* Brest, Toulon, Cherbourg, Lorient

## NAVAL AIR FORCE

*Organization:*
  2 fighter-bomber squadrons (Etendard IV-M)
  2 interceptor squadrons (F-8E Crusader)
  1 reconnaissance squadron (Etendard IV-P)
  2 ASW squadrons (Alize)
  5 maritime reconnaissance squadrons (Neptune and Atlantique)
  6 helicopter squadrons (Super Frelon, SH-34, Alouette II and III)

*Major Aircraft Types:*
246 combat aircraft:
     90 Etendard IV-M and IV-P fighter-bomber and reconnaissance aircraft
     37 F-8E Crusader interceptors
     58 Alize ASW aircraft
     26 P-2E/H Neptune maritime reconnaissance aircraft
     35 BR 1150 Atlantique maritime reconnaissance aircraft
300+ other aircraft:
     17 Super Frelon helicopters
     43 SH-34 helicopters
     38 Alouette II and III helicopters
135+ miscellaneous trainer/support aircraft (Nord 262, C-47, CM-175, Falcon, C-54, Navajo, DC-6, Walleye)

*Missiles:* (air-to-air): Sidewinder and Matra D530; air-to-surface: Nord AS20, Nord AS37 Martel, and Nord S210

*Major Naval Air Bases:* Lann Bihoue, Nimes Garons, Landivisiau, Hyeres, San Raphael, Lanveox, Poulmic, Dax, Aspretto, St. Mandrier

## AIR FORCE

*Personnel:* 96,000

*Organization:*
  Strategic Air Command (CFAS): subject to president's command
      1 IRBM group (2 squadrons of 9 missiles each)
      3 strategic bomber wings (3 squadrons per wing; Mirage IV-A)
      3 tanker squadrons (1 per bomber wing; KC 135 F)
  Tactical Air Command (FATAC)
      2 tactical air commands
     16 fighter-bomber squadrons (1 Mirage III-B, 7 Mirage III-E, 6 Jaguar, 2 Mirage V)
      3 tactical reconnaissance squadrons (Mirage III-R and III-RD)
  Air Defense Command (CAFDA): coordinated by the automatic STRIDA II air defense system
      3 interceptor squadrons (Mirage III-C)
      5 all-weather interceptor squadrons (F-1)

1 fighter squadron (Mystere IV-A, Super
    Mystere B-2)
Military Air Transport Command (COTAM)
    1 squadron DC-8
    4 squadrons Nord 2501 Noratlas transports
    3 squadrons C-160 Transall
    2 mixed squadrons
    4 helicopter squadrons (Alouette II)
Air Force Schools Command (CEAA)
Air Communications Service (CTAA)

*Overseas Deployment:* 1 squadron of F-100, 1 squadron of Alouette II helicopters and Noratlas transports in the Republic of Djibouti

*Major Aircraft Types:*
    452  combat aircraft
        40  Mirage IV-A strategic bombers
        12  Vautour 2B light bombers
        30  Mirage III-C light bombers
        160  Mirage III-B and III-E fighter-
            bombers
        30  Mirage V fighter-bombers
        60  Mirage III-R reconnaissance aircraft
        15  Super Mystere B-2 fighter-bombers
        105  Jaguar fighter-bombers
    1,960  other aircraft
        11  KC-135 F tankers
        5  DC-8 transports
        70  Noratlas transports
        37  Transall C-160 F transports
        123  miscellaneous transports
        82  helicopters (Alouette II and III)
        1,435  miscellaneous trainers/support aircraft

*Missiles:* AAM: Matra R-511 and R-530; ASM: Matra Martel, Nord AS-12, AS-20, AS-30, and AS-33; SAM: Crotale; SSM: SSBS (IRBM)

*Major Air Bases:* Metz, Bordeaux, Aix, Bretigny, Tours, Orange, Strasbourg, Cognac, Reims, Toulouse, Dijon, Nimes, Villacoublay, Limoges, Cambrai, Etampes, Creil, Mont de Marsan, Luxeuil, Nancy, Avord

## PARAMILITARY

The gendarmerie of some 70,000 men plus 85,000 more in reserve is administered by the Ministry of the Armed Forces and can augment the regular forces. There is also a Republican Security Force *(Compagnies Republicaines de Securite)* of 17,000 men, under the Ministry of the Interior.

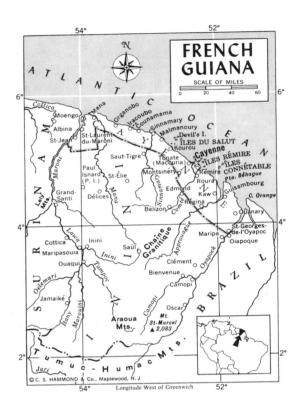

# FRENCH ANTILLES AND GUIANA

## POWER POTENTIAL STATISTICS

Area: French Guiana: 35,135 square miles
    Guadeloupe: 686 square miles
    Martinique: 431 square miles
Population: French Guiana: 60,000
    Guadeloupe: 324,000
    Martinique: 319,000
Total Active Armed Forces: none (French responsibility)
Gross National Product: French Guiana: $100 million
    ($800 per capita)
    Guadeloupe: $470 million ($1,340 per capita)
    Martinique: $1.2 billion ($3,660 per capita)
Civil Air Fleet: 4 major transport aircraft (0 French
    Guiana, 3 Guadeloupe, 1 Martinique)

## POLITICO-MILITARY POLICIES AND POSTURE

French Guiana, Guadeloupe, and Martinique are all overseas departments of France and thus have representation in the Senate and the National Assembly in Paris; their people have full rights as French citizens. While there has been some support for more self-rule in all three departments, there is no serious movement toward complete independence from France. During the 1940s and early 1950s Communist parties had considerable local influence; in Martinique they received 60 percent of the vote for local representation. The Communists still remain strong in Guadeloupe but have lost influence in Martinique.

Martinique and Guadeloupe both have essentially two-crop economies, based on sugar and bananas; the only real industries are sugar refineries and rum distilleries. Because France buys its sugar about 20 percent above the world price, and because the government gives the islands more financial support per capita than any of the other departments, the per capita GNP remains high.

Most of the inhabitants of French Guiana live along the coast; the interior is largely wilderness. Agriculture is primitive and the population is so small that Guianans are fully dependent on France. In 1975 there was a border dispute with Surinam.

Defense is the responsibility of the French government. The area comprises the French Antilles and Guiana Defense Zone, headquartered in Fort-de-France, the capital of Martinique. France maintains 2,500 troops in the zone, under a joint service command *(Commandement Superieur Interarmees du Groupe Antilles-Guyane)*. There is one marine battalion stationed on Guadeloupe. One naval squadron with a patrol escort ship and two minesweepers are stationed on Martinique, plus a small air detachment of transport and trainer aircraft.

France operates a space research center in French Guiana which is a launching site for sounding rockets and satellites.

# GABON
# Gabonese Republic

## POWER POTENTIAL STATISTICS

Area: 102,317 square miles
Population: 575,000
Total Active Regular Armed Forces: 1,100 (0.19% population)
Gross National Product: $2.8 billion ($4,990 per capita)
Annual Military Expenditures: $52.6 million (1.88% GNP)
Fuel Production:
 Crude Oil: 11.4 million metric tons
 Refined Products: 1.55 million metric tons
Electric Power Output: 376 million kwh
Merchant Fleet (ships 1,000 tons and over): 1 ship; 74,000 gross tons
Civil Air Fleet: 24 major transport aircraft

## POLITICO-MILITARY POLICIES AND POSTURE

President Bongo assumed leadership of Gabon after the death of his predecessor in 1967. He declared the country a one-party state a year later. President Bongo holds several ministerial posts in the government, including that of national defense.

Upon independence from France in 1960, Gabon entered into a series of mutual defense and military assistance agreements with France relating to internal security, base rights, transit and overflight privileges, and military assistance. In February 1964 the internal security agreement was implemented when a military coup led by dissatisfied junior officers of the army and gendarmerie sought to depose the regime in power. A reinforced French regiment was flown in, with fighter support from bases in Dakar and Brazzaville, crushed the revolt, and restored the government.

Gabon is rich in raw materials: timber, petroleum, iron, manganese, and uranium. This, together with foreign technical assistance and investment, and relative stability, has permitted one of the highest per capita incomes in Africa. France's nuclear program is largely dependent upon uranium from Gabon.

France provides most of Gabon's imports, aid and investment. Ties remain close despite increased Gabonese requirements for a state share of corporate ownership. There is a large French civilian community in Gabon, which constitutes a problem in the amount of capital repatriated to France. Gabon generally supports French policy in Africa, as in the case of French intervention in Mauritania and Zaire.

Gabon has good relations with its neighbors. In 1972 Gabon and Equatorial Guinea disputed rights to two offshore islands, but this problem was peacefully settled. Relations with Cameroon have improved since a 1976 border post incident. Gabon is a member of the OAU and Central African Customs and Economic Union. An OPEC member, Gabon has seen its economy boom since 1974. However, its oil reserves are expected to be depleted by the mid-1980s.

The Gabonese army was formed in 1960 around a nucleus of French army veterans. France has continued to supply arms and equipment and instructor-advisers. French military assistance costs about $800,000 annually. The army numbers 900 and is organized as a two-company infantry battalion. Service is voluntary and for one year. The navy has 100 men, six fast patrol craft (PCF), and a small patrol boat (PB) based at Libreville and Port Gentil. The air force of 100 operates one C-130, three C-47 transports, three Broussard liaison aircraft, a Fokker F-28, three Alouette III and an SA-330 Puma helicopter. Six Mirage fighters are on order. There are international airports at Libreville and Port Gentil. The Gendarmerie has a strength of about 600, including 60 French officers and NCOs. French forces in Gabon consist of 400 army personnel, including a paratroop company. A small coast guard operates seven patrol boats (PB).

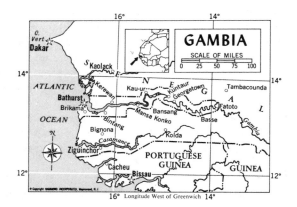

# THE GAMBIA
## Republic of the Gambia

## POWER POTENTIAL STATISTICS

Area: 4,003 square miles
Population: 576,000
Total Active Armed Forces: none (police only)
Gross National Product: $115 million ($210 per capita)
Electric Power Output: 30 million kwh

## POLITICO-MILITARY POLICIES AND POSTURE

The Gambia was granted independence by Britain in 1965; in April 1970 it was proclaimed a republic within the Commonwealth with the president/prime minister as head of state.

The Gambia, a 300-mile strip along both banks of the Gambia River, is bounded on all sides except the river mouth, by Senegal. Because of this unusual geographical relationship, as well as tribal and religious (Moslem) affinities, very close ties are maintained with Senegal, including a mutual defense pact and joint economic development of the Gambia River Valley.

The Gambia is a member of the OAU, and the Commonwealth of Nations. An agreement with Britain provides for police and paramilitary training, advisers, and equipment. The defense agreement with Senegal provides for a joint Defense Committee with a permanent secretariat, and Senegalese assistance in training any Gambian military unit should it be required. One of the few African multi-party states, the Gambia held legislative elections in 1977. The ruling People's Progressive Party, in power since independence, won a large majority of seats. The Gambia maintains good relations with all African states (except Rhodesia and South Africa) and received aid from many nations, East and West.

The Gambia has no armed forces as such. Within the 580-man, British-trained, British-led police force is a field force of 170 men and two British officers, which operates as a mobile military company. There is also a small patrol craft (YP).

# GERMANY, EAST
## German Democratic Republic

## POWER POTENTIAL STATISTICS

Area: 40,646 square miles
Population: 16,783,000
Total Active Regular Armed Forces: 135,000 (0.80% population)
Gross National Product: $69.2 billion ($4,120 per capita)
Annual Military Expenditures: $3.33 billion (4.80% GNP)
Crude Steel Production: 6.7 million metric tons
Iron Ore Production: 51,000 metric tons
Fuel Production:
    Coal: 456,000 metric tons
    Lignite: 246.9 million metric tons
Electric Power Output: 92 billion kwh

Nuclear Power Production: 4,143 megawatts
Merchant Fleet (ships 1,000 tons and over): 157 ships;
  1.27 million gross tons
Civil Air Fleet: 7 jet and 18 turboprop transports

## DEFENSE STRUCTURE

The People's Chamber, a unicameral legislature, is the supreme organ of the state. In practice, the executive branch of the government, consisting of the Council of State and the Council of Ministers, is the center of official power. The executive is itself controlled by the ruling Socialist United party of Germany (Communist party), and the same individuals hold power in both party and government. The Council of State is an administrative organ of the People's Chamber operating between the parliamentary sessions. The executive powers granted to the Council of State include control over the defense and security forces of the country and responsibility for the fundamental decisions regarding defense and security matters. In the administration and organization of military affairs the Council of State is assisted by the National Defense Council.

The National Defense Council serves as directing agency in matters of defense and state security, and exercises control over the Ministry of National Defense. The minister of national defense is the highest ranking active military officer. He has several deputies, among whom are the chiefs of the Main Staff, Training Directorate, Main Political Directorate, and Rear Services Directorate. The armed forces comprise the Ground Forces, navy, air force, and air defense force. Top area and tactical commanders are responsible directly to the minister and to the chief of the Main Staff. The Main Staff also controls several directorates that have functions common to all service branches.

Each of the service branches has its own military school, which offers a university level curriculum and provides the service with the bulk of its officers. Cadets are young men who have completed general or technical secondary schools, or conscripts who have performed well and have been able to meet entrance requirements. Political reliability is the most important consideration for admission to military schools. The Friedrich Engels War College in Dresden, directly under the Ministry of National Defense, provides advanced military and political courses for officers of all services. Senior and midcareer training is made available to a substantial number of East German officers at several of the war colleges and specialized military schools in the Soviet Union.

## POLITICO-MILITARY POLICY

East Germany is more rigidly and more directly controlled by Moscow than any of the other Eastern European states (with the possible exception of Czechoslovakia). It appears to be serving increasingly as a proxy for the Soviet Union in such foreign ventures as assistance to various warring factions in Africa.

The task of the armed forces is officially stated to be not only to defend the state, but also to protect the "Socialist achievement." Defending Communist policies and objectives against possible dissidence is thus considered as important as defense of the country. To the extent that the government of East Germany has independent policy objectives, they are essentially defensive. First, and foremost, is internal security—since external security is adequately guaranteed by the Soviet occupation forces. Second, the GDR, for its own purposes, as well as in support of Soviet foreign policy, wishes to establish itself in the eyes of the world, and particularly nearby neighbors, as a sovereign equal of the Federal Republic of Germany (West Germany).

The German Democratic Republic is one of the countries of the Mutual and Balanced Force Reductions "reduction area," and is a direct participant in the talks in Vienna toward a reduction of forces in central Europe (see Western Europe Regional Survey).

The armed forces are maintained by conscription. The term of service for young men between the ages of eighteen and twenty-five is two years for the army, three years for the navy and the air force. To meet normal peacetime personnel requirements, it is necessary to draft about two-thirds of the eighteen year-old group. The average conscript has a good educational background and has had enough preinduction military training to make for easy transition to service life. About 95 percent of the officers, more than 50 percent of the noncommissioned officers, and about 20 percent of the enlisted personnel are members of the Socialist Unity [Communist] Party.

After completion of active duty obligations, all personnel remain in reserve status until the age of fifty and officers until the age of sixty. Of some 2,500,000 individuals that are the military-age mobilization potential, most could step into military units with a minimum of basic training.

## STRATEGIC PROBLEMS

Because the Soviet Union has clearly assumed responsibility for the external security of East Germany as a geographic component of the Communist bloc, East Germany has little concern or responsibility for strategic planning, save as a minor partner and contributor within the Warsaw Pact. The principal strategic concern of the government, therefore, is to avoid the possibility of political isolation from the sources of its power in Russia. Thus any change of regime in Czechoslovakia or Poland would be extremely threatening to East Germany, as it was in 1968; party chairman and head of state Walter Ulbricht then reportedly urged Soviet intervention in Czechoslovakia.

## MILITARY ASSISTANCE

East Gemany has received massive Soviet assistance in arms, equipment, and training, and the East German armed forces are organized along Soviet lines. Soviet military advisers occupy key positions in the staff of the Ministry of National Defense, and at lower echelons.

## ALLIANCES

East Germany has bilateral treaties of friendship and mutual assistance with the USSR and other Eastern European states, and is also a member of the Warsaw Treaty Organization and of the Council of Mutual Economic Assistance.

As the westernmost area of the Warsaw Treaty Organization, East Germany has the strongest concentration of Soviet troops outside the USSR. These forces, called the Group of Soviet Forces in Germany, are among the best in the Soviet military establishment. The Soviet contingent is vastly superior to East German forces in numbers and equipment. Soviet ground forces, about 350,000 strong, are organized into twenty divisions (ten motorized rifle and ten tank) maintained at combat strength. They have over 7,500 tanks, many of them new T-72s. Tactical aviation units supporting and providing air defense for the Soviet forces total 1,000 aircraft, including about 800 interceptors and fighter-bombers and several hundred transport planes. The operation of the air warning and air defense systems is a joint Soviet-East German effort.

## ARMY

*Personnel:* 90,000 regular army (another 46,000 are frontier guards)

*Organization:*
    Border Command (controlling the border troops; organized into brigades and independent regiments)
2   mobile army corps (1 tank division, 2 motorized rifle divisions each); headquarters: Leipzig and Mecklenburg
2   tank divisions (3 tank regiments, 1 motorized rifle regiment, 1 artillery regiment each)
4   motorized rifle divisions (3 motorized rifle regiments, 1 tank regiment, 1 artillery regiment each)
    Tank and motorized rifle divisions also have engineer, signal, antiaircraft artillery, medical and missile battalions plus rear services, armored reconnais-

sance, and nuclear decontamination companies.
1   security guard regiment East Berlin (provides security for installations and buildings of the government in East Berlin)

*Major Equipment Inventory:*
2,200   medium tanks (T-55, T-54, T-34)
  125   light tanks (PT-76)
        Snapper and Sagger antitank guided missiles
 700+   APCs (BTR-152, BTR-50P, BTR-60P)
  850   light, medium, and heavy artillery pieces
        ZSU-57/2 self-propelled antiaircraft guns
        ZSU-23/4 self-propelled antiaircraft guns
        SSMs (FROG and Scud)

*Reserves:* About 250,000 trained reserves

## NAVY

*Personnel:* 16,000

*Major Units:*
 1   frigate (Riga class; FF)
14   submarine chasers (Hai class; PCS)
 4   submarine chasers (SO-1 class; PCS)
15   missile attack boats (Osa class with SS-N-2/Styx SSM; PTG)
34   coastal minesweepers (Kondor class; MSC)
69   motor torpedo boats (PT)
35   patrol boats (PB)
12   medium landing ships (10 Robbe class; 2 Froesch class; LSM)
12   utility landing craft (Labo class; LCU)
10   auxiliaries (tenders, training ships, etc.)
55   service craft
 8   helicopters (1 squadron; Mi-4/Hound)

*Major Naval Bases:* Rostock, Warnemuende, Sassnitz, Peenemuende, Stralsund, Dranske-Bug

*Reserves:* No more than 40,000 trained reservists

## AIR FORCE (including Air Defense Forces)

*Personnel:* 29,000 (including 9,000 antiaircraft troops)

*Organization:*
18   interceptor squadrons (MiG-21)
11   fighter-bomber squadrons (MiG-17, Su-7)
 3   transport squadrons (Tu-124/134, Il-14, An-14/24)
 2   helicopter squadrons (Mi-1/4/8/24)
 1   training division (L-29)
 1   antiaircraft division (5 antiaircraft regiments and 21 SAM battalions)

*Major Aircraft Types:*
510   combat aircraft

360 MiG-21 interceptors
20 MiG-17 fighter-bombers
130 Su-7 fighter-bombers
415 other aircraft
75 transports (An-14/24, Il-14, Tu-124/134)
40 helicopters (Mi-1/4/8)
300 trainer/support aircraft (L-29, Yak-18, MiG-15/21)

*Major Antiaircraft Equipment:*
126 SAM launchers (SA-2 Guideline; 21 battalions)
162 antiaircraft guns (57mm and 100mm)

*Reserves:* There are 45,000 to 50,000 reservists.

*Air Bases:* Eggersdorf, Cottbus, Jacksdorf, Neubrandenburg, Annahutte, Kamenz, Bautzen, Brandenburg-Breis, Marxwald, Odenbruch, Janischwelk-Ost, Drewitz, Dresden, Frankfurt-Oder, Gross-Dollen, Dessau, Vogelsang, Gorlitz, Peenemunde, Preschen, Orewitz

## PARAMILITARY

Within the organization of the national *Volkspolizei* (People's Police) are eighteen battalions of separately caserned *Bereitschaftpolizei* (alert police). These highly mobile, politically reliable units can be committed to assist local police forces in situations requiring an increased level of strength. They number about 10,000. In addition, there are about 8,500 Transport Police, organized in company-style units, who provide security for the national railroad system. The *Betriebskampfgruppen* (Battle Groups) are the workers' militia—armed, trained, uniformed, and equipped in *Volksarmee* style, including some crew-served antitank and antiaircraft weapons. The *Kampfgruppen* number between 350,000 and 400,000, and are capable of performing home guard functions and securing industrial installations.

# GERMANY, WEST

## Federal Republic of Germany

## POWER POTENTIAL STATISTICS

Area: 95,815 square miles
Population: 61,262,000
Total Active Regular Armed Forces: 493,300 (0.80% population)
Gross National Product: $517 billion ($8,400 per capita)

Annual Military Expenditures: $91.1 billion (3.7% GNP)
Crude Steel Production: 42.4 million metric tons
Iron Ore Production: 2.3 million metric tons
Fuel Production:
Coal: 89 million metric tons
Lignite: 134.5 million metric tons
Crude Oil: 5.5 million metric tons
Refined Petroleum Products: 113.6 million metric tons
Natural Gas: 19 billion cubic meters
Manufactured Gas: 15.6 billion cubic meters
Electric Power Output: 335 billion kwh
Nuclear Power Production: 19,100 megawatts
Merchant Fleet (ships 1,000 tons and over): 590 ships; 8.9 million gross tons
Civil Air Fleet: 181 major transport aircraft

## DEFENSE STRUCTURE

The president of the Federal Republic as chief of state is the titular head of the armed forces of West Germany; actual control is exercised by the chancellor (prime minister) through the minister of defense in typical parliamentary governmental fashion. Under existing law the minister of defense is commander in chief of the armed forces in peacetime, the chancellor in wartime. Parliamentary authority is exercised by a Defense Committee with power to investigate any aspect of military affairs.

There is no overall military command structure in the West German armed forces. The rearmament of West Germany was begun while the nation was still nominally occupied by the Western Allies of World War II. The purpose was to integrate West German forces into the NATO defense structure so that they could participate in the defense of their own country as part of Western Europe. This philosophy is still the basis of West Germany's defense policy, partly to continue to reassure its allies, and partly as a key element in the determination of modern West Germany to maintain unquestioned civilian control over the armed forces. Thus the West German armed forces can operate effectively only as elements of an integrated international NATO army. There is no national general staff, although a General Staff Corps provides officers for operational headquarters. The senior military officer in the West German defense structure is the inspector general. There is no West German operational command larger than an army corps or air wing (although German officers can, and do, serve as army and regional commanders and staff officers in the international command structure of NATO's Allied Command Europe).

There are three territorial defense commands—Schleswig-Holstein, North, and South— and six military regions under these commands. The Territorial Defense

Organization is under army command but staffed by all three services.

## POLITICO-MILITARY POLICY

One of the most important features of the deliberate and carefully structured renunciation of traditional German militarism is the effort to make the armed forces truly democratic without seriously impairing military efficiency. In a series of laws beginning with the initial authorization of German armed forces in 1955, the West German Bundestag (Parliament) has included measures to assure the maintenance of civilian control and to guarantee the rights of all citizens who are members of the armed forces.

The present German military policy of eschewing nationalistic, aggressive military operations, and of participating in war only as an integral element of an international army is a dramatic reversal of one of the most consistent national policies in history. West Germany's relations with its western neighbor and traditional enemy, France, are now very cordial, with these two nations forming a strong, stable core for Western Europe.

Over half of the manpower of the armed forces (Bundeswehr) is obtained through conscription under the compulsory Military Service Law of 1956. The present term of service is fifteen months.

## STRATEGIC PROBLEMS

Except for the south, where Germany's frontier is secured by the Alps, all of its frontiers are vulnerable to attack. Participation in NATO eases the situation on the west and to some extent on the north, although the military weakness of Denmark and Norway, combined with Soviet Baltic strength, makes the northern coast less secure. With Soviet forces stationed near its 1,700-kilometer borders in East Germany and Czechoslovakia, West Germany remains highly vulnerable to attack from the east, across the North European Plain. Soviet armored forces are deployed in peacetime less than 100 miles east of the Rhine River, across West Germany's narrow waist. NATO's problem for the defense of Europe is essentially how to stop a westward thrust by Soviet forces before they reach the Rhine. West Germany's dilemma is how to contribute to defense in that highly vulnerable area without assuring the devastation of its national territory. Effective intelligence and reconnaissance are stressed in West Germany's defense policy.

Officially accepting the division of Germany, in 1970 the Federal Republic signed a treaty with the Soviet Union affirming the permanence of the existing boundary between East and West Germany and of the Oder-Neisse boundary between Poland and East Germany, as well as mutually renouncing the threat or use of force. A similar treaty was signed the same year with Poland. In 1972, a traffic treaty between West and East Germany resolved many of the problems of access to Berlin and of intra-Berlin transit that had caused the Berlin crises of 1948–49 and 1961, plus many lesser episodes. A second treaty that year established normal diplomatic relations between the two Germanies.

West Germany maintains a small but efficient navy and has special military arrangements with Denmark, through NATO, whose purpose is primarily to maintain the security of West Germany's northeastern flank on the Baltic Sea. A further objective is to deny the Warsaw Pact the approaches from the Baltic to the North Sea. Such denial is vital not only for protection of sea lanes but also for guarding the petroleum resources of the North Sea. The size of West German ships is limited by the Paris Agreements of 1954. In September 1973 West Germany was authorized by the Council of Western European Union to build conventionally powered submarines up to 1,800 tons (almost twice the earlier limit), to permit greater responsibility for surveillance of the North Sea and the Atlantic Ocean.

West Germany is a homogeneous nation, without any significant minorities that might assist a hostile invader. There is, however, evidence of some perpetuation in a small minority of the German people of the ultra-nationalistic, reactionary philosophy that brought Hitler to power. Of more immediate danger to internal stability have been the small bands of radical terrorists who have carried out assassinations, kidnappings, bombings, and airplane hijackings in recent years. The abridgement of liberties and due process to which the government has sometimes resorted in dealing with these groups has aroused concern within Germany and conceivably could lead to a dangerous polarization of German society, providing fertile ground for a reactionary revival. However, terrorist incidents have dropped sharply since 1975.

## MILITARY ASSISTANCE

Germany has not received military assistance from the United States since 1967.

West Germany has offered assistance to a number of African countries on both a sales and a grant basis. This has included aircraft and pilot training, patrol craft and naval training, police training and equipment, and military transport.

## ALLIANCES

West Germany is a member of three overlapping alliances: the fifteen-member NATO alliance, the Western European Union (with Britain, France, and Benelux), and a bilateral alliance with the United States. With these alliances West Germany has undertaken several collaborative projects. The continuing presence of forces of the United States, Britain, Canada, France, and Belgium on German soil, as part of the NATO shield forces, has created an acute shortage of training facilities in Germany. The West German government has reached agreements with Portugal and France whereby the *Bundeswehr* can send contingents to train on the territory of those NATO partners. Also, joint research and development has been done with NATO allies. Military aircraft have been jointly produced by West Germany and France, and a number of military items have been designed and produced in cooperation with the United States. West Germany was admitted to the United Nations in 1973.

## ARMY

*Personnel:* 345,000, including 35,000 in a territorial force which is held for rear-area duties, and not assigned to NATO

*Organization:*
 3 army corps
 16 armored brigades
 12 armored infantry brigades
 3 infantry brigades
 2 mountain brigades
 3 airborne brigades
 15 SSM battalions (Honest John/Sergeant/Lance)

*Major Equipment Inventory:*
 1,050 medium tanks (M-48A2)
 2,600 medium tanks (Leopard)
 280 105mm howitzers
 80 155mm howitzers
 600 155mm self-propelled howitzers
 150 175mm self-propelled guns
 80 203mm self-propelled howitzers
 210 multiple rocket launchers
 310 40mm/30mm self-propelled antiaircraft guns (Gepard)
 2,100 APCs (Marder)
 600 APCs (HS-30)
 3,350 APCs (M-113)
 1,110 tank destroyers (90mm *Kanonpanzer* or SS-11 mounted on APCs)
 36 light aircraft (mostly Do-27; some OV-10)
 550 helicopters (UH-1, Alouette II, CH-53)
 90 SSM Sergeant, Honest John, Lance

*Reserves:* There are approximately two million *Bundeswehr* reservists, including all men who have actually served in the *Bundeswehr*. Of these, 540,000 are available for immediate mobilization. Enlisted reservists are subject to recall up to the age of forty-five in peacetime and up to sixty in wartime. Officers and noncommissioned officers are subject to recall at any time up to age sixty; those who have been members of the professional regular cadre of the *Bundeswehr* can be called back up to age sixty-five, regardless of rank. There is a regular reserve training program, part obligatory and part voluntary, which has been only partially implemented to date due to shortages of facilities.

## NAVY

*Personnel:* 38,300 (including 6,000 naval air)

*Major units:*
 24 diesel submarines (18 Type 210; 6 Type 205; SS)
 3 guided missile destroyers (Charles F. Adams class; DDG; Tartar SAMs)
 8 destroyers (4 Hamburg class, Exocet short-range SSMs; 4 Fletcher class; DD)
 6 frigates (Koeln class; FF)
 6 patrol ships (PGF)
 30 missile attack boats (PTG; Exocet SSMs)
 10 motor torpedo boats (PT)
 7 patrol boats (PB)
 18 coastal minesweepers (MSC)
 43 inshore minesweepers (MSI)
 22 utility landing craft (LCU)
 19 mechanized landing craft (LCM)
 34 auxiliary ships
 92 service craft
 115 F-104/TF-104 (four fighter-bomber/reconnaissance squadrons)
 22 Sea King
 20 Do-28 liaison aircraft

*Reserves:* 36,000 for direct mobilization

*Main naval bases:* Flensburg, Wilhelmshaven, Kiel, Olpenitz

## AIR FORCE

*Personnel:* 110,000

*Organization:*
 2 tactical air divisions (each with ground attack, reconnaissance, and guided missile wings)
 2 air defense divisions
 1 air transport command (with 3 wings)
 8 tactical fighter squadrons (F-4F)
 8 fighter-bomber squadrons (F-104G)
 6 light ground attack squadrons (2 normally used for training, G-91)
 4 reconnaissance squadrons (RF-4)
 4 transport squadrons (C-160 Transall)
 24 SAM batteries (Nike-Hercules, 9 launchers each)
 36 SAM batteries (I-Hawk, 6 launchers each)

2 SSM wings (Pershing, 36 launchers each)
2 helicopter squadrons (UH-1 D)

*Major Aircraft Types:*
  630 combat aircraft
     80 RF-4E reconnaissance
   170 F-4F tactical fighters
   200 F-104G fighter-bombers
    70 TF-104G training
   180 G-91 light ground attack
  733 other aircraft
     89 C-160 Transall transports
      4 Boeing 707 transports
   120 miscellaneous transports (C-140, Hansa-Jet, VFW 614)
   400 miscellaneous trainer/support aircraft (Do-27, Do-28, L-4, T-37, P-149, T-38)
   120 helicopters (UH-1)

*Reserves:* 100,000 for direct mobilization

## PARAMILITARY

In addition to the Territorial Force, and reservists for that force, there are approximately 18,500 Border Police (equipped with Saladin armored cars, patrol boats, and helicopters) and 15,000 internal security forces.

# GHANA

## Republic of Ghana

### POWER POTENTIAL STATISTICS

Area: 92,100 square miles
Population: 11,553,000
Total Active Regular Armed Forces: 19,600 (0.17% population)
Gross National Product: $8 billion ($790 per capita)
Annual Military Expenditures: $68 million (0.85% GNP)
Fuel Production: Refined Petroleum Products: 1.15 million metric tons
Electric Power Output: 4 billion kwh
Merchant Fleet (ships 1,000 tons and over): 22 ships; 136,000 gross tons
Civil Air Fleet: 12 major transport aircraft

### POLITICO-MILITARY POLICIES AND POSTURE

After the ousting and exile of Ghana's dictatorial President Nkrumah in 1966 by a military coup, the country was ruled for three years by a seven-man National Liberation Council. Following promulgation of a new Constitution, civilian rule was restored in September 1969 but was ended in January 1972 by a bloodless coup led by Col. Ignatius Acheampong (who later became a general). The military junta withdrew the Constitution, dissolved Parliament, and established a National Redemption Council as the governing body. In 1975 a seven-member Supreme Military Council (SMC) became the main policy-making body, consisting of the chairman (who is defense minister), chief of Defense Staff, and the heads of the three armed services, police, and border guards. In July 1978, Acheampong resigned as chairman in favor of Lt. Gen. Fred W. K. Akuffo, who had been chief of Defense Staff, and in June 1979 another coup placed Flight Lt. Jerry Rawlings in power.

Up until the 1966 coup, the Soviet Union had given an estimated $10 to $50 million in military aid including ground arms and ammunition, aircraft, training of cadets in Russia, and training of Nkrumah's Presidential Guard Regiment. When the Presidential Guard resisted the February 1966 coup, eleven Russian instructor-advisers were reportedly killed.

Pilot training has been conducted in Ghana by Indians, Israelis, and Canadians, and in Britain and Italy. United States military assistance, 1950–77, amounted to $606,000; $81,000 was provided in 1977. In addition, 238 students have been trained in the United States under the MAP. Pakistan has provided limited training assistance. Arms have been purchased from New Zealand and Australia, and aircraft from the Soviet Union (only civil aircraft for Ghana Airways), Italy, and Canada. Yugoslavia assisted in the construction of a naval base.

Ghana possesses strategic mineral wealth which could, with effective management, ensure a viable economy and place it among the economic leaders of Africa. It exports substantial amounts of manganese, bauxite, gold, and diamonds. Cocoa, however, is the major export commodity. The 850,000-kw Volta hydroelectric power project, completed before Nkrumah's overthrow, has permitted an increased production of refined aluminum. When Nkrumah left, the country had heavy foreign debts. The new government has repudiated most of the debts or declared a moratorium on them. The loss of foreign credit, the government's nationalization of foreign assets, and inflation rates of 50 to 100 percent in the mid-1970s have created an economic crisis exacerbated by rampant smuggling and corruption.

Ghana has established satisfactory relations with all of its neighbors in recent years and has aggressively pursued trade links bilaterally and through the founding of the Economic Community of West African States. Relations with the USSR, which had waned after Nkrumah's ouster, have improved substantially in recent years. Ghana was an early supporter of the Soviet-backed MPLA in Angola. Western nations provide substantial aid but in the Ghanaian view have not been forceful enough in ending white minority rule in southern Africa. Ghana remains a Commonwealth member.

Internally, the government is beset by ethnic strife, especially from Ewe tribesmen within the military and those pressing for the liberation and reunification of Western Togoland. Togo does not support the movement, however. Former chairman of the SMC, Acheampong, survived three coup attempts. His resignation followed more than a year of protests from professional groups against the SMC's plans for transition to a unity government of military and civilian leaders without parties.

## ARMY

*Personnel:* 16,500

*Organization:*
    2 brigade groups (3 infantry battalions each with
        support troops of reconnaissance, artillery,
        engineers, transport)
    1 paratroop battalion

*Major Equipment Inventory:*
    Saladin armored cars (British)
    Ferret scout cars (British)
    76mm guns (USSR)
    infantry crew-served and individual weapons
        (USSR and British)

*Reserves:* 500 Army Volunteer Force; 2 reconnaissance squadrons

## NAVY

*Personnel:* 2,000

*Major Units:*
    2 patrol ships (PCF)
    8 patrol craft (PC)
    1 coastal minesweeper (MSC)
    1 training ship
    1 maintenance repair craft

*Major Naval Bases:* Secondi, Tema

*Reserves:* 200

## AIR FORCE

*Personnel:* 1,500

*Organization:*
    1 fighter-bomber squadron (MB-326B)
    2 transport squadrons (Otter, Caribou, Skyvan,
        Heron)
    1 communication/liaison squadron (Beaver,
        BN-2A)
    1 helicopter squadron (S-58 Wessex, Hughes 269
        Osage, Whirlwind)
    1 training squadron (Bulldog)

*Major Aircraft Types:*
    6 combat aircraft
    6 MB-326GB fighter-bombers
    67 other aircraft
        25 transports (7 Otter, 8 Caribou, 6 Skyvan, 3
            Heron, 1 HS 125)
        19 communication/liaison (11 Beaver, 8
            BN-2A)
        13 trainers (Bulldog)
        10 helicopters (3 Wessex, 3 Osage, 4 Whirl-
            wind)

*Air Bases:* Accra, Takoradi, Kumasi, Temaie

# GREECE
## Hellenic Republic

### POWER POTENTIAL STATISTICS

Area: 50,547 square miles
Population: 9,372,000
Total Active Regular Armed Forces: 160,000 (1.71%
    population)

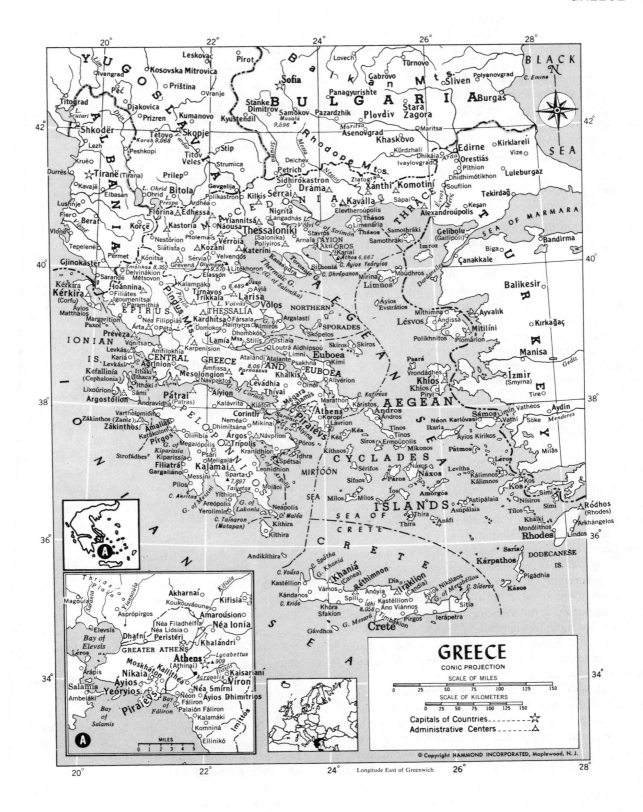

GREECE
CONIC PROJECTION

SCALE OF MILES

0   25   50   75   100   125   150

SCALE OF KILOMETERS

0  25  50  75  100  125  150

Capitals of Countries ━━━━━━━ ☆
Administrative Centers ━━━━━━━ ⌂

© Copyright HAMMOND INCORPORATED, Maplewood, N. J.

Longitude East of Greenwich

Gross National Product: $26.7 billion ($2,920 per capita)
Annual Military Expenditures: $1.6 billion (6% GNP)
Fuel Production:
    Refined Petroleum Products: 11.4 million metric tons
    Lignite: 22.2 million metric tons
Electric Power Output: 18 billion kwh
Merchant Fleet (ships 1,000 tons and over): 2,379 ships;
    29.5 million gross tons
Civil Air Fleet: 33 major transport aircraft

## DEFENSE STRUCTURE

Since the military government of Greece (established by coup in 1967) fell in 1974, partly as an immediate result of the Cyprus crisis of that year, Greece has had a moderate democratic government led by veteran statesman Constantine Karamanlis. A new constitution, modeled on the current French system and adopted in 1975, makes Greece a republic with a strong president.

The three services are integrated under the Ministry of National Defense. Under the defense minister is a commander in chief, armed forces, who heads a staff composed of the chiefs of staff of the army, the navy, and the air force.

## POLITICO-MILITARY POLICY

During much of the century and a half existence of the modern Greek state, its military policy has reflected traditional hostility to Turkey, the former occupying power, and this hostility continues, despite the fact that Greece and Turkey are allies in NATO. Discovery of oil off the island of Thasos, at the northern end of the Aegean Sea, in early 1974 exacerbated a long-standing rivalry over maritime sovereignty in that area. Tensions between the two nations were already high when the coup d'etat in Cyprus, supported if not engineered by the Greek military junta, brought them to the brink of war in July 1974. With almost 40,000 Turkish troops ashore on the island, the Greek government realized the futility of sending units to attempt to resist them.

In January 1973 U.S. and Greek representatives signed an agreement granting the United States home port facilities for the Sixth Fleet in the Athens area, but the installation was subsequently postponed indefinitely by the Greek government. Karamanlis announced the withdrawal of Greek units from NATO during the crisis in 1974, and Greece is still not participating militarily in NATO. A U.S. NATO air base and communications bases remain in Greece.

The armed forces are supported by conscription, with all able-bodied men between the ages of twenty-one and fifty subject to twenty-four months' service. In the navy, which has many volunteers, conscript service is eighteen months. The annual call-up is about 50,000.

## STRATEGIC PROBLEMS

Greece commands a significant geographic position from which to control the eastern basin of the Mediterranean, and consequently the maritime communications to and from the Black Sea and the Middle East. It was because of this that foreign armies invaded Greece in two world wars, and NATO now considers Greece a fundamental link in its defenses of southeastern Europe.

Although the long northern frontier of Greece is largely mountainous, the corridors and natural communications lines are generally perpendicular to the frontier, and thus the mountains do not form an effective barrier to invasion. This is compounded by the narrowness of northeastern Greece. The vulnerability of this frontier was not only amply demonstrated in World Wars I and II; it was successfully exploited by Greece's northern Communist neighbors during the Greek civil war of 1945–49.

The emotional and political involvement of Greece in the bitter dispute between Greek and Turkish Cypriots brought Greece and Turkey to the threshold of war twice (1963 and 1964) before the military coup in Cyprus in July 1974 resulted in Turkish invasion of the island and caused a military and political crisis in Greece. Weakened by the upheavals and forced retirements of military leaders in recent years, Greece refrained from a military response and in Geneva sought a solution through the UN, NATO, and meetings of the foreign ministers of Great Britain, Turkey, and Greece.

## MILITARY ASSISTANCE

The original stimulus to the American foreign aid program was provided when the United States decided, in 1947, to replace faltering British military and economic assistance to Greece. This resulted in the Truman Doctrine, followed by the Marshall Plan, and the subsequent U.S. worldwide military assistance programs to underdeveloped Free World nations threatened by Communism. In fiscal year 1977 Greece received $1.07 million under MAP. It has received a total of $1.6 billion in military assistance since 1950. A total of 14,408 students have been trained under MAP. United States military assistance to Greece was briefly suspended after the 1967 coup d'etat, but otherwise has continued under various Greek governments.

Under the terms of the Zurich-London Agreements of 1959 Greece is committed to assist (in concert with Turkey) in the establishment and training of the armed forces and internal security forces of Cyprus. This agreement was never fully implemented, and was completely ended by the mid-1974 events in Cyprus.

# ALLIANCES

Greece is a member of NATO, although it is not now participating militarily.

# ARMY

*Personnel:* 120,000

*Organization:*
      3 corps
     11 infantry divisions (some mechanized)
      1 armored division
      1 commando brigade (marines)
     12 artillery battalions
      6 SSM battalions (Honest John)
      3 SAM battalions (Hawk)
        aviation companies (light aircraft and
          helicopters)

*Major Equipment Inventory:*
    500   medium tanks (M-48)
    300   medium tanks (M-47)
     50   medium tanks (AMX-30)
    450   light tanks (M-24, M-41)
    650   APCs (M-2, M-59, M-113)
     60   armored cars (M-8, M-20)
     50   scout cars (M-3)
     15   175mm SP guns
    800   105mm, 155mm, 203mm howitzers, SP and
            towed
     24   Honest John SSM
          76mm SP antitank guns
  1,500   TOW antitank missiles (88 launchers)
          Milan antitank missiles
          57mm, 75mm, 106mm recoilless rifles
            (antitank)
          66mm LAW, 3.5-inch rocket launchers
            (antitank)
          60mm, 81mm, 4.2-inch mortars
    324   Hawk SAM (12 batteries)
    500   Redeye SAM
    100   light aircraft and helicopters (U-17, I-21,
            UH-1, Bell 47, AB-204, AB-205)

*Reserves:* About 300,000 reservists available for mobilization

# NAVY

*Personnel:* 17,000

*Major Units:*
      7 diesel submarines (4 Clavkos class; 2 Guppy
          class; 1 Balao class; SS)
     12 destroyers (1 Sumner class; 5 Gearing class; 6
          Fletcher class; DD)
      4 patrol escorts (PG; 3-inch guns)
      4 guided missile patrol combatants (PGG; Exocet
          SSMs)
      6 missile attack boats (PTG; Exocet or SS-12
          SSMs; 6 more under construction)
     19 motor torpedo boats (PT)
      4 patrol craft (PC)
     13 patrol boats (PB)
      2 minelayers (MM)
      5 minesweepers (MSC; used as corvettes, PCE)
     15 coastal minesweepers (MSC)
      1 dock landing ship (LSD)
     10 tank landing ships (LST)
      5 medium landing ships (LSM)
      8 utility landing craft (LCU)
     13 mechanized landing craft (LCM)
     48 personnel landing craft (LCP)
     14 auxiliary ships (survey research, tankers,
          tenders, etc.)
     27 service craft
     14 helicopters (HU-16B Albatross)

*Major Naval Bases:* Piraeus, Salonika, Valos, Mitilini

*Reserves:* About 25,000 trained reservists

# AIR FORCE

The 28th (Hellenic) Tactical Air Force is made up of seven combat squadrons and one transport squadron and has been assigned to NATO's Sixth Allied Tactical Air Force.

*Personnel:* 23,000

*Organization:*
      6 fighter-bomber squadrons (1 F-104, 2 F-4, 3 A-7)
      5 interceptor squadrons (4 F-5, 1 Mirage, F-1)
      2 reconnaissance squadrons (RF-84F, and RF-5)
      3 transport squadrons (Noratlas, C-47, C-119,
          Do-28)
      3 helicopter squadrons (Alouette II, Bell 47,
          AB-204, H-19)
      1 maritime reconnaissance/search and rescue
          squadron (under navy control; Hu-16)
      1 SAM wing (3 battalions of Nike-Hercules)

*Major Aircraft Types:*
    262 combat aircraft
        136 fighter-bombers (36 F-104, 40 F-4, 60 A-7)
         80 F-5A fighter-interceptors
         38 fighter/reconnaissance aircraft (18 RF-5,
              20 RF-84F)
          8 HU-16 maritime reconnaissance/rescue
              aircraft
    318 other aircraft
         80 transports (27 C-47, 30 Noratlas, 8 Cl-215,
              12 C-130, 3 Aero Commander)

73 helicopters (14 Bell 47, 22 AB-204/205, 12 H-19, 25 UH-1)

165 trainer/support aircraft (T-37, T-33, T-34, T-41, T-2, TA-7, F-5, TF-104, L-21, U-17)

Equipment on Order: F-16 fighters

*Missiles:* AAM Falcon, Sidewinder; ASM Bullpup

*Reserves:* About 30,000 trained reservists

## PARAMILITARY

There is a National Gendarmerie of 25,000 men for internal security and a National Guard of 50,000. The latter is manned by reservists from all three services between the ages of nineteen and fifty, and is also open to volunteers up to age sixty; it is organized on a regional basis, all its members serving a minimum of six months and training on Sundays and holidays.

# GRENADA

## State of Grenada

One of the Windward Islands, Grenada became an independent nation under the Commonwealth in February 1974, after which defense ceased to be a British responsibility. It has a total area of 133 square miles (144 with the Grenadines, which are attached to Grenada) and a population of 106,000. The GNP is $54 million ($500 per capita).

In March 1979, the New Jewel Movement, led by Maurice Bishop, seized power from the former government of eccentric and sometimes autocratic Sir Eric Gairy, the leading political figure in Grenada since the early 1960s. Only two persons were killed in this first coup d'etat in an English-speaking Caribbean country. The political orientation of the new government was not clear; early elections were promised.

# GUATEMALA

## Republic of Guatemala

### POWER POTENTIAL STATISTICS

Area: 42,042 square miles
Population: 6,716,000
Total Active Regular Armed Forces: 9,400 (0.14% population)
Gross National Product: $5.4 billion ($880 per capita)

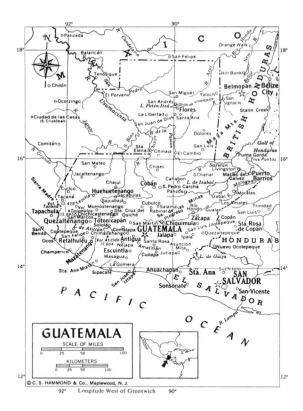

Annual Military Expenditures: $58.5 million (1.08% GNP)
Fuel Production: Refined Petroleum Products: 730,000 metric tons
Electric Power Output: 1.5 billion kwh
Merchant Fleet (ships 1,000 tons and over): 5 ships; 17,000 gross tons
Civil Air Fleet: 8 major transport aircraft

### POLITICO-MILITARY POLICIES AND POSTURE

The president is commander in chief of the armed forces, exercising his control through the minister of defense in his cabinet. The minister of defense appoints most of the officers of the armed forces.

Since the overthrow of the Arbenz government in 1954, the Communist party has been outlawed, and there have been numerous guerrilla incidents in the countryside and, since a concerted effort by the army to break up guerrilla groups in the late 1960s, much terrorist activity in Guatemala City. Chiefly responsible are the Communist *Fuerzas Armadas Rebeldes,* but there are other terrorist groups as well, both leftist and rightist.

Guatemala has long claimed sovereignty over the bordering British colony of Belize (British Honduras) on the grounds that it inherited Spanish sovereignty. Britain asserts that an 1859 treaty voids that claim. The UN General Assembly and most Latin American nations support independence for Belize. Guatemalan troops were deployed close to the border in 1972 and 1977, and on both occasions additional British military forces were sent to the area. In 1977, when Panama's president expressed support for Belize, Guatemala broke diplomatic relations.

In 1977 the United States provided $595,000 in military assistance, making a total of $23.6 million since 1955. Guatemala has renounced further U.S. military aid. Under the MAP program 3,339 students have been trained.

Guatemala is a member of the OAS and ODECA.

Military service in Guatemala is compulsory for two years for men between ages eighteen and fifty. Until age thirty, men are in a special reserve force. The armed forces have a program for education of illiterates and work on communications, agriculture, and reforestation.

The army numbers 8,000 and is organized in ten infantry battalions, an artillery battery, an armored cavalry troop, an engineer battalion, a parachute battalion and a medical battalion. All weapons and vehicles are U.S.: 105mm howitzers, M3A1 scout cars, M3A1 light tanks, M8 armored cars, and M-113 armored personnel carriers.

The 400-man navy operates fourteen patrol boats (PB) (all armed with machine guns of different calibers) and a variety of service craft. There is a marine rifle company of 210 men.

The 1,000-man air force has one fighter-bomber squadron equipped with eight A-37 light ground attack jet aircraft and T-33 armed jet trainers, one light bomber squadron of B-26 light bombers, one reconnaissance squadron of light aircraft, one transport squadron of C-47s and nine IAI Aravas, and one helicopter squadron of 10 UH-12, H-19, and UH-1 helicopters. Air bases are at La Aurora in Guatemala City, Puerto Barrios on the Atlantic coast and Puerto San Jose on the Pacific coast.

The younger generation of army officers are all graduates of the Guatemalan Military Academy, and most have taken specialized courses in foreign service schools, principally in the United States, but also in France, Italy, Spain, and West Germany. About 80 percent of all company grade officers are qualified parachutists.

The *Policia Nacional* has a strength of 3,000 men. In the event of a national emergency, they automatically come under control of the army. There is also a secret or judicial police, strength unknown. These police as well as the *Policia Nacional* are used in counter-terrorist activities.

# GUINEA

## Republic of Guinea

### POWER POTENTIAL STATISTICS

Area: 94,925 square miles
Population: 5,973,000

Total Active Regular Armed Forces: 6,150 (0.10% population)
Gross National Product: $1.1 billion ($240 per capita)
Annual Military Expenditures: $6.1 million (0.55% GNP)
Electric Power Output: 500 million kwh
Merchant Fleet (ships 1,000 tons and over): 2 ships; 14,000 gross tons
Civil Air Fleet: 10 major transport aircraft

## POLITICO-MILITARY POLICIES AND POSTURE

Since independence from France in 1958 President Sekou Toure has headed a strongly centralized one-party government. As chief of state he commands the armed forces through the minister of the People's Army.

At the time of independence Guinea chose not to remain a member of the French Community; as a result all French interests were withdrawn, and no French military assistance was provided. All French military equipment and stores were removed, leaving Guinea with no military force except an ill-equipped gendarmerie. Guinea claims that its request to purchase 500 small arms from the United States was turned down. Communist block assistance began in March 1959, and a year later a Soviet military mission arrived. Since March 1960 Soviet arms shipments are said to have exceeded $50 million. An army of 5,000 has been built on the French-trained gendarmerie and French army veterans selected for political reliability. Additional military aid has been received from China (about $5 million) and Cuba, which has several hundred advisers in Guinea.

Having rejected French ties, Guinea has in the past supported the overthrow of the governments of those former French African colonies which do maintain close relationships with France. As one of the radical block of African states, Guinea provided sanctuary and training for exile insurgent groups from Portuguese Guinea (now Guinea-Bissau) and Angola during their fights for independence. Similarly, a force was dispatched to Benin in early 1977 following that government's report of a mercenary invasion. The Soviet Union, China, and Cuba aided this effort with funds, training, and arms. A Guinea-Sierra Leone mutual defense pact, negotiated in 1970, was invoked by the Sierra Leone government in March 1971, when its overthrow was threatened; Guinean troops responded.

Guinea reestablished diplomatic relations with France in 1976 after an eleven-year break. Commercial exchanges between the two have increased so that France rivals the USSR as Guinea's major trading partner. Guinea supported the French position in the 1978 conflict with Algeria over the Western Sahara and is a militant supporter of the Arab cause in the Middle East.

Guinea has good relations with its neighbors Sierra Leone, Guinea-Bissau, and Liberia, and is expanding transport links with Mali. In 1976 Toure accused Senegal and Ivory Coast of conspiring in a coup and insurgent invasion of Guinea. The long-standing hostility toward the two showed signs of moderating in 1978.

Guinea's mineral wealth assures a substantial future economic potential and considerable strategic importance, despite the currently poor economic situation. Almost one-third of the world's known reserves of bauxite are in Guinea, and several million metric tons a year are being exported, constituting 95 percent of export earnings. Guinea also has reserves of iron ore estimated at eight billion tons. Gold and diamonds are mined in significant quantities, and oil has been discovered.

Due to economic stagnation and tensions arising from President Toure's harsh one-man rule, there is a substantial potential for insurgency. Perhaps as many as 1,000,000 Guineans have moved to neighboring countries, mostly in search of jobs. Opposition parties have been established by these expatriates in Paris, Dakar, and Abidjan. In Ivory Coast, 5,000 have formed the Guinean National Liberation Front and are cooperating with Guinean expatriates elsewhere. Elements of the army, police, and Toure's own Democratic Party of Guinea are said to be dissatisfied with alleged government mismanagement. On November 11, 1970, an anti-Toure force of about 300 men landed from four ships and attacked Conakry, capital of Guinea. After three days of fighting, the invaders and their local supporters were defeated. A UN Security Council mission, after investigating Toure's charges, accused Portugal of being actively involved in the attempt to overthrow Toure. An alleged coup attempt in 1976 resulted in reprisals against the leadership of the Fulani tribe.

From 1950 through 1977 the United States provided $899,000 in military assistance and excess defense materials, and trained four students in the United States.

Guinea's army of 5,000 is organized into five infantry battalions supported by an armored battalion, an artillery battalion, and three engineer companies. Military service is compulsory for two years, although not all eligible men are called up. Equipment includes Soviet T-34 and T-54 tanks, PT-76 light tanks, a few BTR-152 armored personnel carriers, 100mm antitank guns, 122mm howitzers, and 14.5mm ZPU-1 antiaircraft machine guns. The army, however, has been diverted largely to civic action tasks, major diversions which must adversely affect combat efficiency. Reserves number about 15,000.

The main combat units of the 350-man navy are two ex-Soviet P-6 motor torpedo boats (PT) received in 1967. There are also four ex-Chinese Shanghai class fast patrol craft (PCF), four patrol boats (PB) and two landing craft. Ports are Conakry and Kakande.

The Guinean air force numbers about 800 men. Some Soviet transports, Il-14, Il-18, and An-14 have been received. There are also eight MiG-17 and three MiG-21 fighters, Soviet Yak-18 piston primary trainers, and L-29 and MiG-15 jet trainers.

There is a 900-man gendarmerie. The People's Militia, some 5,000 men from the party youth organization, was formed in 1966 officially to shield Guinea against invasion, but generally assumed to be a counterforce against the possibility of an army coup. Units are assigned to the main population centers and have actually taken over internal security tasks from the army. Republican Guards number 1,600 men.

Guinea is a member of the Organization of African Unity.

# GUINEA-BISSAU
## Republic of Guinea-Bissau

### POWER POTENTIAL STATISTICS

Area: 13,948 square miles
Population: 625,000 (includes 3,000 Europeans)
Total Active Regular Armed Forces: 5,000 (0.80% population)
Gross National Product: $112 million ($179 per capita)
Annual Military Expenditures: $1 million (0.89% GNP)
Electric Power Output: 17 million kwh
Civil Air Fleet: 3 major transport aircraft

### POLITICO-MILITARY POLICIES AND POSTURE

After 500 years of Portuguese rule and eleven years of guerrilla warfare, Guinea-Bissau became independent in September 1974. The country is administered by the Council of State, headed by the president. More important is the control exercised over government affairs by the Marxist-type PAIGC party (African Party for the Independence of Guinea and Cape Verde), which conducted the war against Portuguese rule. The PAIGC leader is

president and controls the military through a commissioner of the armed forces.

Strategically, Guinea-Bissau occupies a significant position in the bulge of West Africa close to central Atlantic sea lanes. The country has close ties with the Cape Verde islands, 600 miles to the northwest. The PAIGC rules in both countries, and the major foreign policy goal remains eventual unity.

Guinea-Bissau's chief problems are internal consolidation and economic development. The post independence warfare disrupted what little investment the Portuguese had made in the former colony. The PAIGC encountered some difficulty in establishing support in urban Bissau. Finally, over 10 percent of the population was newly returned from refugee camps in Senegal and Guinea. Although the PAIGC had received nearly all its preindependence military aid from China and the Soviet bloc (several hundred Cuban advisers arriving as early as 1971), it has been more successful in the West in obtaining development aid.

Relations with Portugal have been strained over financial matters since 1976. All Portuguese troops and most civilians left shortly after independence. Guinea-Bissau maintains excellent relations with Guinea and Senegal. Senegal and Guinea-Bissau have concluded a joint defense pact. Guinea-Bissau is a member of the OAU and ECOWAS.

# GUYANA
## Cooperative Republic of Guyana

### POWER POTENTIAL STATISTICS

Area: 83,000 square miles
Population: 818,000

Total Active Regular Armed Forces: 2,000 (0.24% population)
Gross National Product: $418 million ($510 per capita)
Annual Military Expenditures: $9 million (2.15% GNP)
Electric Power Output: 370 million kwh
Civil Air Fleet: 6 major transport aircraft

### POLITICO-MILITARY POLICIES AND POSTURE

Guyana was granted independence by Great Britain in May 1966 as a member of the Commonwealth. Since 1968 the government has been in the hands of the almost wholly black Marxist-Leninist People's National Congress. The main opposition party is the People's Progressive Party, largely East Indian in membership, and also Marxist-Leninist. A referendum in July 1978 approved the writing by the National Assembly of a new constitution which would transform the government from a parliamentary one to a strong presidential government, in which the president would be both head of state and head of the government. Industries and schools have been nationalized.

Despite aid received from the United States (in 1964–71 Guyana was the largest per capita recipient in the Western Hemisphere), and considerable technical assistance from other nations, including China and East Germany, Guyana is still a poor country. The economic situation suffered severely from a strike in the sugar industry in 1977–78 that lasted 135 days. The government unsuccessfully used troops to try to break the strike.

Guyana's strategic significance, especially to the United States, is twofold. First, its position relative to the South Atlantic puts it on the best air route between the United States and Africa. Second, there are large deposits of bauxite (4.7 million tons mined annually) and manganese (200,000 tons mined annually).

Guyana has been involved in border disputes with Surinam and Venezuela, the former claiming 6,000 square miles of bauxite-rich land, and the latter claiming three-fifths of Guyanese territory. The long-standing dispute with Venezuela has been put in abeyance by the 1970 Protocol of Trinidad whereby the two nations agreed not to press claims to each other's territory for twelve years. An armed clash in 1969 with Surinam was stilled after a mixed commission agreed that both forces would quit the disputed area. A brief Amerindian revolt fomented by white ranchers was suppressed in 1969. Troops were sent to the Brazilian border in 1972 after guerrilla incidents there.

The Guyana Defense Force has a strength of over 2,000, with a women's corps of 60. It is organized in two infantry battalions and has two U-10 and two BN-2A STOL liaison aircraft and four 45-foot armed patrol boats (PB) armed with machine guns.

The Guyana National Service, which trains approximately 1,500 Guyanese between fourteen and twenty-four years of age in such things as history and culture, agricultural methods, and socialist doctrine, also gives some paramilitary instruction.

# HAITI

## Republic of Haiti

## POWER POTENTIAL STATISTICS

Area: 10,714 square miles
Population: 5,600,000
Total Active Regular Armed Forces: 6,000 (0.11% population)
Gross National Product: $1.1 billion ($230 per capita)
Annual Military Expenditures: $13.8 million (1.25% GNP)
Electric Power Output: 175 million kwh
Civil Air Fleet: 6 major transport aircraft

## POLITICO-MILITARY POLICIES AND POSTURE

Before his death in 1971, President Francois Duvalier, absolute dictator for fourteen years, made his son, Jean-Claude, his successor and president-for-life. He is nominal commander in chief of the armed forces.

Haiti shares the island of Hispaniola with the Dominican Republic. The boundary has been a cause of friction between the two nations, partly because of Haitians crossing into the more prosperous and productive Dominican Republic. Communist Cuba, to the west, has occasionally attempted the landing of exiles and Cuban guerrillas to overthrow the regime.

Haiti is a member of the OAS. The United States has provided military assistance totaling $3.4 million from 1950 through 1977. Six hundred and ten students have been trained under the MAP.

Haiti's army has a total of about 6,000 men, most of whom perform a constabulary function. There is a Presidential Guard of about 265 men; an elite counter-insurgency battalion; the Leopard Corps (with 569 men); and the Dessalines Battalion, of about the same size, which has tactical capabilities. The National Security Volunteers, a sort of civilian militia into which the infamous Tontons Macoutes were merged, has lost most of its military aspects and serves primarily as a labor source for government projects.

Equipment includes armored personnel carriers and ten light artillery pieces. The Coast Guard of 300 men operates two patrol motor gunboats (PGM) and seven patrol boats (PB). The 250-man air force operates a composite squadron with the main function of maintaining internal air service. Aircraft are six F-51 piston fighters, ten trainers, two C-45 light transports, three C-47 medium transports, and six helicopters.

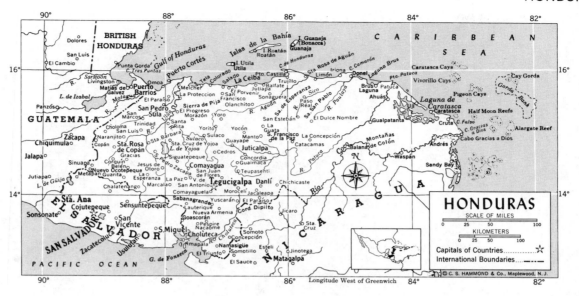

# HONDURAS

## Republic of Honduras

### POWER POTENTIAL STATISTICS

Area: 43,277 square miles
Population: 3,578,000
Total Active Regular Armed Forces: 4,700 (0.13%
    population)
Gross National Product: $1.4 billion ($490 per capita)
Annual Military Expenditures: $31.4 million (2.24%
    GNP
Fuel Production: Refined Petroleum Products: 485,600
    metric tons
Electric Power Output: 450 million kwh
Merchant Fleet (ships 1,000 tons and over): 15 ships;
    84,000 gross tons
Civil Air Fleet: 16 major transport aircraft

### POLITICO-MILITARY POLICIES AND POSTURE

Honduras has been governed by military leaders for
many years. In August 1978, Col. Juan Alberto Melgar
Castro, who himself had been made president by a military
coup in 1975, was overthrown by a junta of the
commanders of the three armed forces, after a series of
scandals involving members of the government. The actual
seat of power resides in the Armed Forces Council,
composed of twenty-eight colonels and lieutenant colonels.

Honduras has in the past been involved in boundary
disputes with its neighbors, Guatemala and Nicaragua. In
1969 a dispute with El Salvador flared in the brief and
indecisive "Soccer War." After occasional incidents and
futile talks, in July 1976 a series of border clashes led to an
agreement to arbitrate.

Agrarian reform has been the chief cause of unrest
in Honduras, with the government repeatedly promising to
divide large, uncultivated holdings. In 1975 an uprising
by members of the National Peasants Union (UNC),
supported by the General Labor Federation (CGT) and the
National Peasants Association (ANACH), resulted in the
arrest of the leaders of the UNC and the CGT and virtual
dissolution of those organizations. Under stricter military
control unrest is minimal.

Honduras belongs to the ODECA and the OAS.
Honduran troops participated in the Inter-American Peace
Force sent to the Dominican Republic in 1965. In 1977 the
United States provided $826,000 in military aid, making a
total of $12.8 million since 1950. Under the MAP 3,004
students have been trained.

Every male citizen is liable for eight months of service
between the ages of eighteen and fifty-five, but the army is
adequately filled with volunteers. Between ages thirty-two
and fifty-five, men may be in a reserve status. The army of
men is organized as three infantry battalions and about
twenty infantry companies with a supporting light artillery
battery (eight pieces) and light tank company (seventeen
tanks). The coast guard of fifty men operates five coastal
patrol boats (PB). There are 1,200 men in the air force,
which is organized as two fighter-bomber squadrons and
one transport squadron. There are a few armed jet trainers
(F-86 and RT-33), twelve jet fighter-bombers (Super
Mystere B-2), three Arava 201 transports, three helicopters,
and twenty-seven other aircraft, including T-41 trainers.
Airfields are at Tegucigalpa and San Pedro Sula. There is a
Civil Guard of 2,500.

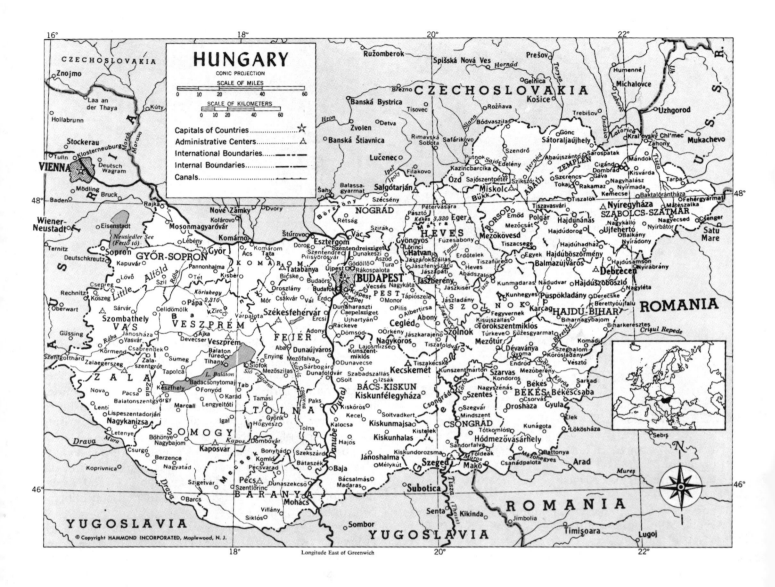

# HUNGARY

## Hungarian People's Republic

### POWER POTENTIAL STATISTICS

Area: 35,919 square miles

Population: 10,715,000

Total Active Regular Armed Forces: 103,000 (0.96%
  population)

Gross National Product: $29.4 billion ($2,750 per capita)

Annual Military Expenditures: $762 million (2.59%
  GNP)

Crude Steel Production: 3.65 million metric tons

Iron Ore Production: 602,000 metric tons

Fuel Production:

  Coal: 2.9 million metric tons

  Lignite: 22.3 million metric tons

  Natural Gas: 6.1 billion cubic meters

  Crude Oil: 2.1 million metric tons

  Refined Petroleum Products: 1.7 million metric tons

Electric Power Output: 23.4 billion kwh

Nuclear Power Production: 408 megawatts

Merchant Fleet (ships 1,000 tons and over): 19 ships;
  65,000 gross tons

Civil Air Fleet: 5 jet, 8 turboprop, and 8 piston
  transports

## DEFENSE STRUCTURE

The Hungarian People's Army consists of the Ground Forces, the Air Defense Force (which includes military aviation—this former Axis-allied state was denied an air force by the peace treaty of 1947), border troops, and units of river vessels. As in the other Eastern European Communist republics, the armed forces of Hungary are controlled through the interlocking hierarchies of the Communist party and the government. The minister of national defense is the senior military officer, the commander of the armed forces, and a member of the cabinet and the defense council. Under the Ministry of Defense are the General Staff, the Main Political Directorate, the Training Directorate, the Directorate of Rear Services, and the Personnel Directorate. The chief of the Main Political Directorate is deputy minister of defense. He reports to the party's Central Committee and is responsible for political indoctrination. All military units have deputy commanders for political affairs.

## POLITICO-MILITARY POLICY

Hungary's foreign and military policies are largely directed by Moscow, although the strict Soviet control established after Russian troops suppressed the Hungarian Revolution of 1956 has somewhat relaxed. Despite obvious reluctance, Hungary contributed troops for the 1968 invasion of Czechoslovakia, and the presence of Soviet troops in Hungary underlines ultimate Soviet control. However, Hungary is developing internal economic and political structures of its own, including the "New Economic Mechanism" which, beginning in 1968, has decentralized economic planning. Since the Helsinki Agreement of 1975, Hungary has been a leader in Eastern Europe in implementing its provisions, including those on human rights and trade. The United States' return to Hungary of the crown of St. Stephen and signing of a most-favored-nation trade agreement, both in 1978, indicate U.S. efforts for warmer relations with Hungary.

The peace treaty of 1947 restricted the armed forces to ground forces of 65,000 men and an air force of 5,000 men and ninety aircraft (seventy combat), and limited their functions to the defense of frontiers. In total disregard of these limitations the numbers are well over these figures.

The armed forces are maintained by compulsory military service, which begins at age eighteen. The term of service is generally two years, but can be three years in certain specialist branches.

## STRATEGIC PROBLEMS

Hungary's size and strategic location have resulted in its present subservience to the Soviet Union. Its freedom of action is further limited by the presence of 60,000 Soviet troops, the four divisions of the Southern Group of Forces and a Tactical Air Army (referred to as the Soviet Air Force, Hungary), which have maintained strict, although relatively unobtrusive, military control over Hungary since 1956. Soviet ground and air units are based near major Hungarian military installations.

## MILITARY ASSISTANCE

Hungarian armed forces are organized, trained, and equipped along Soviet lines, and with the benefit of substantial Soviet assistance in provision of equipment and training personnel. Soviet control is facilitated by the presence of Russian advisers at several echelons in the Hungarian staff and command system.

## ALLIANCES

Hungary has bilateral treaties of friendship and mutual assistance with the USSR and all other Eastern European Communist countries. Hungary is a member of the Warsaw Pact and the Council for Mutual Economic Assistance.

## ARMY

*Personnel:* 80,000

*Organization:*
    4 military districts (Budapest, Debrecen, Kiskunfelegyhaza, and Pecs)
    1 tank division (3 tank regiments, 1 motorized rifle regiment, 1 artillery regiment, and support)
    5 motorized rifle divisions (3 motorized rifle regiments, 1 tank regiment, 1 artillery regiment, engineer, antitank, signal)
    1 airborne regiment
    1 river flotilla (see Navy)

*Major Equipment Inventory:*
    1,600 medium tanks (T-34, T-54, T-55)
       50 light tanks (PT-76)
          armored cars (FUG-A)
          scout cars (OT-65)
          APCs (OT-64, OT-66, and BTR-152)
      400 field artillery pieces
          light artillery rocket launchers
          SU-100 and JSU-122 self-propelled guns
          antiaircraft guns
          ZSU-57/2 self-propelled antiaircraft
          Snapper, Swatter, and Sagger antitank missiles
          SSMs (FROG, Scud)

*Reserves:* There are approximately 100,000 trained reserves.

## NAVY

There is no navy as such. The Danube flotilla, part of the army, has 500 men, and ten patrol craft (PC), and five landing craft on the river.

## AIR FORCE (AIR DEFENSE FORCE, including military aviation)

*Personnel:* 12,500

*Organization:*
    10 fighter-interceptor squadrons (MiG-21/19)
    4 fighter-bomber squadrons (MiG-17/19, Su-7)
    2 transport squadrons (An-2, Il-14, An-24, Li-2)
    3 helicopter squadrons (Mi-2/4/8)

*Major Aircraft Types:*
    184 combat aircraft
        100 MiG-21 interceptors
        24 MiG-19 fighters
        12 MiG-17 fighter-bombers
        48 Su-7 fighter-bombers
    165 other aircraft
        10 Il-14 transports
        10 An-2 transports
        4 An-24 transports
        6 Li-2 transports
        45 helicopters (Mi-2/4/8)
        90 trainers (L-29, Yak-18, MiG-15)
        84 SAM launchers (SA-2, 14 battalions)

*Air Bases:* Budapest (3), Miskolc, Pecs, Debrecen, Kiskunfelegyhaza, Nyiregyhaza, Estergom, Szolnok, Kaposvar, Szeged, Dombova, Tokol, Gyor, Papa, Szombathely, Szekesfehervar. Soviet air force units (approximately 300 aircraft) are stationed at some of these bases.

*Reserves:* 30,000 trained reservists

## PARAMILITARY

The Security Police, some 25,000 strong, include border guards and internal security forces. Since the revolution of 1956 these units have been under the Ministry of the Interior.

There is a Workers' Militia, about 35,000 strong, for home guard functions.

# ICELAND

# Republic of Iceland

## POWER POTENTIAL STATISTICS

Area: 39,702 square miles
Population: 224,000
Total Active Armed Forces: None
Gross National Product: $1.4 million ($6,350 per capita)
Electric Power Output: 2.5 billion kwh
Merchant Fleet (ships 1,000 tons and over): 29 ships; 54,000 gross tons
Civil Air Fleet: 22 major transport aircraft

## POLITICO-MILITARY POLICIES AND POSTURE

A member of NATO, Iceland maintains no military forces, although there is an internal security police force of about 500 men, and a Coast Guard of six vessels and 170 men. Iceland provides its NATO allies with air and radar base sites on its territory; there are 3,300 U.S. Air Force and Navy personnel in Iceland, stationed at the NATO air base of Keflavik.

Iceland is a member of the Council of Europe.

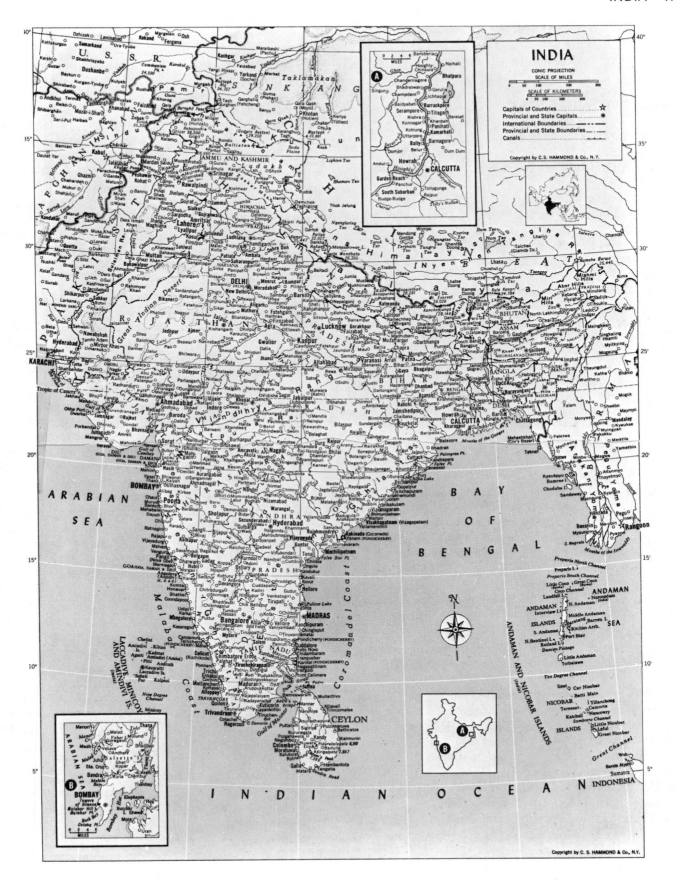

INDIA

CONIC PROJECTION
SCALE OF MILES

SCALE OF KILOMETERS

Capitals of Countries ............................... ☆
Provincial and State Capitals ..................... ◉
International Boundaries ........... ▬ ▪ ▬ ▪ ▬
Provincial and State Boundaries ... ▬ ▪▪ ▬ ▪▪
Canals ..................................................

# INDIA

## Republic of India

## POWER POTENTIAL STATISTICS

Area: 1,229,737 square miles
Population: 667,907,000
Total Active Regular Armed Forces: 1,006,000 (0.15%
population)
Gross National Product: $88 billion ($140 per capita)
Annual Military Expenditures: $3.6 billion (4.09%
GNP)
Crude Steel Production: 9.14 million metric tons
Iron Ore Production: 42.65 million metric tons
Fuel Production:
Coal: 101 million metric tons
Lignite: 3.9 million metric tons
Crude Oil: 8.8 million metric tons
Refined Petroleum Products: 23 million metric tons
Electric Power Output: 99.6 billion kwh
Nuclear Power Production: 4,200 megawatts
Merchant Fleet (ships 1,000 tons and over): 363 ships;
5.5 million gross tons
Civil Air Fleet: 93 major transport aircraft

## DEFENSE STRUCTURE

The president is the supreme commander of the
armed forces. Actual responsibility for national defense
rests with the cabinet, presided over by the prime minister,
assisted by the standing Defence Committee, and advised
by the top level National Defence Council. The minister
of defence is head of the defense organization and is
responsible to Parliament and the prime minister for the
administrative and operational control of the armed forces
and for implementation of the government's defense policy.
There are three services—army, navy, and air force—each
under its own chief of staff.

## POLITICO-MILITARY POLICIES AND POSTURE

India's international stance since independence in 1947
had been nonalignment in the East-West confrontation.
This traditional policy was altered in 1971 by a mutual
assistance treaty with the USSR and by strained relations
with the United States in regard to the 1971 war with
Pakistan. Save to the extent they have related to India's
troubles with Pakistan, India has consistently supported
and participated in UN peacekeeping functions.

Despite its hitherto determined neutralism and peaceful
protestations, India's other policies have been to some
extent responsible for a series of small wars and three
serious armed confrontations. Since independence India
has firmly resolved (1) to maintain its boundaries as drawn
in colonial days and by the 1947 partition, (2) to hold
Jammu and Kashmir against Pakistan's claims, (3) to
unify and rule its diverse population, and (4) to eliminate
remaining foreign enclaves along its coast. Small-scale
guerrilla warfare interspersed with major hostilities against
Pakistan has been taking place in Jammu and Kashmir since
1949. The Portuguese enclaves, including Goa, were seized
in 1961. Naga and Mizo tribesmen along the border with
Burma have been in revolt since the early 1960s, apparently
aided and abetted by both Pakistan and Communist China.
Border incidents with Communist China, beginning in
1959, culminated in October 1962 in major hostilities in
Ladakh and a successful limited objective Chinese offensive in the North East Frontier Agency.

The defeat by China caused a complete reappraisal of
Indian defense policy and a massive buildup of its armed
forces and defense industries. The armed forces were nearly
doubled in size. For the first time, military aid was sought
from the United Kingdom, United States, and (mainly
since 1965) the USSR. MiG-21 fighters are being produced
under a Soviet license. The first was delivered to the air
force in February 1973. A tank—the Vijayanta—based on
the Chieftain main battle tank, is being manufactured with
British assistance.

This buildup, resulting from the confrontation with
China, may well have stimulated Pakistan's 1965 efforts to
gain Kashmir before India became too powerful. For a
time, British and U.S. military aid were withheld from
both parties, with India turning to the Soviet Union, and
Pakistan to Communist China. While India's military
buildup was primarily intended to deter Chinese aggression, it thus developed also into an arms race with
Pakistan. That race was undoubtedly ended for the
foreseeable future by India's 1971 victory in a two-front
war with Pakistan, resulting from Indian support of the
Bengali rebels in what has become Bangladesh.

Faced with a nuclear-armed China across the Himalayas,
and with the tremendous expense of developing its own
nuclear deterrent, India's policy is to keep its options
open. This includes rejection of the Nuclear Non-Prolifer-
ation Treaty, and continued nuclear and delivery-system
research and development, as well as construction of
domestic (i.e., without foreign controls of nuclear fuel)
reactors. On May 18, 1974, India fired an underground
nuclear device of some 10–15 kilotons yield. Indian
officials and defense intellectuals claimed that this test was
directed toward the peaceful use of nuclear explosions for
such purposes as mining and massive earth-moving.
International reaction was skeptical and, in some cases,
outraged. It remains to be demonstrated just what future

course India will follow. In 1978, the Indian government continues to state that it will use nuclear explosives for peaceful purposes only.

Services in the Indian armed forces is voluntary for a term of ten to fifteen years, depending upon the degree of technical training required, followed by five or three years in the reserve.

## STRATEGIC PROBLEMS

India's primary problem is the reconciliation of defense needs that consume over 40 percent of the budget and over 3 percent of the GNP, with the insatiable demands for developing the economy of a poor country in the midst of a population explosion. While expenditures are heavy, the Indian defense effort appears to be the minimum acceptable on a risk basis.

The Himalayan defensive barrier covering India's northern border is complicated by the existence of the three independent Himalayan states in the center of the frontier. Direct passes from Tibet run through Nepal and Bhutan, and the two most important, Nathu and Cho, through Sikkim. A mere 60 miles south of these latter passes is the Siliguri Neck, a strip of India between Sikkim and Bangladesh through which run the land communications from central India to oil-rich Assam and strategic Arunachal Pradesh (formerly the North East Frontier Agency). A collective security agreement was in effect in Nepal until 1969, and India has special treaty rights in both Bhutan and Sikkim. Nepal has recently built up its army. The army of Bhutan has been strengthened with Indian help, and Indian troops are stationed in Sikkim. Roads and airfields have been built in all three.

The World War II route from India to China through north Burma—the Ledo and Burma roads—is another potential invasion route. An understanding apparently exists between India and Burma on arrangements for mutual defense of this area.

Nagaland is in the rugged mountain frontier region between Upper Assam and northern Burma, and just to the south is the home of the Mizo tribes. Both are in revolt against Indian sovereignty, demanding full autonomy. They have several thousand armed insurgents, and the Nagas receive training and weapons from China. Arms are packed across north Burma from Yunnan Province. India has had 36,000 troops deployed against these insurgents and is pursuing a fullfledged counterinsurgency campaign of political compromise and reconciliation, rural redevelopment, and civic action, as well as direct military force.

Communist-led disorders throughout India, on the rise in recent years, pose further threats to internal security. Communist strength is particularly great in South India and among poverty-stricken city dwellers.

Since Chinese airfields in Tibet are relatively close to Indian cities, and Chinese cities are remote from Indian air bases, India's air defenses have been extensively overhauled. An air defense radar and command control system has been installed with U.S. help; Soviet MiG-21 interceptors and SA-2 Guideline surface-to-air missiles provide the active defense.

## MILITARY ASSISTANCE

Soviet military assistance began about 1960, and accelerated after 1965. All classes of arms, tanks, artillery, aircraft, and ships, as well as production facilities, have been delivered. Indian military personnel are trained in the Soviet Union, and there are several hundred Soviet officers in India.

United States aid under the Miltary Assistance Program amounted to $90.3 million from 1950 through 1967, but only $4.9 million since that time. Since 1962 both the United States and Great Britain have provided substantial aid in grants and on favorable credit terms. United States aid was mainly in transport aircraft, air defense detection and control equipment, and light weapons for mountain operations. The agreement was for $200 million, but only $85 million had been delivered by the September 1965 India-Pakistan war, when deliveries were stopped. Under the MAP 580 students were trained in the United States.

India provided military aid to Burma in the form of small arms and ammunition during Burma's first wave of insurgency in 1950. India has also provided military advisers to, and accepted military students from, a number of Asian, Middle Eastern, and African countries.

## ALLIANCES

India is a member of the UN and the British Commonwealth. In August 1971 a treaty of peace, cooperation, and friendship with the USSR was made, which contains clauses calling for consultation in case of attack or threat thereof by a third party.

## ARMY

*Personnel:* 860,000

*Organization:* 4 commands (Eastern: headquarters, Calcutta; Western: headquarters, Simla; Central: headquarters, Lucknow; Southern: headquarters, Poona)

    2 armored divisions
    5 independent armored brigades
   15 infantry divisions
   10 mountain divisions

   1 independent infantry brigade
   1 parachute brigade
 20 antiaircraft groups

*Major Equipment Inventory:*
medium tanks
     200 Centurion Mk.5/9
     500 Vijayanta
      26 M-47
     150 M4 Sherman
  1,000 T-54/55/62
       light tanks
     150 PT-76
  700 APCs (OT-62, Mk.2/4a, BTR 50/152)
  350 armored cars (Daimler and Humber)
3,000 artillery pieces (including 350 100mm and 105mm SP and towed howitzers, 130mm and 140mm guns, 203mm howitzers—Soviet and British—57mm and 3.5-inch rocket launchers)
     40mm antiaircraft guns
     ZSU-23/4 guns
     SAM 6,7
     SS-11 and Entac missiles
   70 liaison aircraft (HS-748, Auster, Krishak)
   50 helicopters (Lama, Alouette III)

*Reserves:* At least 100,000 (includes 44,000 in the Territorial army)

## NAVY

*Personnel:* 46,000

*Major Units:*
   8 submarines (Foxtrot class; SS)
   1 light aircraft carrier (CVL; 22 aircraft)
   2 light cruisers (one each Fiji and Leander classes; CL)
 13 frigates (FF)
     6 Leander class fitted with Seacat short-range SAMs
     7 miscellaneous (one fitted with SS-N-2/Styx SSMs)
 12 light frigates (Petya class; FFL)
   3 patrol escorts (PG)
   4 guided missile patrol combatants (Nanuchka class; SS-N-2/Styx SSMs; PGG)
   4 coastal minesweepers (MSC)
   4 inshore minesweepers (MSI)
 16 missile attack boats (Osa class with SS-N-2/Styx SSM; PTG)
   4 fast patrol craft (PCF)
   1 patrol craft (PC)
   2 patrol boats (PB)
   1 tank landing ship (LST)
   6 medium landing ships (Polnocny class; LSM)
   8 auxiliary ships
   7 service craft
 25 Sea Hawk fighter-bombers (1 squadron)
 15 Alize ASW aircraft (1 squadron)
 15 Alouette III helicopters (SAR; 1 squadron)
 15 Sea King helicopters (ASW; 1 squadron)
   6 Il-38 maritime reconnaissance (1 squadron)
 75 trainer aircraft (HT-2, HJT-16, Hughes 300, Alouette, Alize)

*Naval Bases:* Bombay (including Jamnagar and Lonavaia), Cochin (including Calicut and Coimbatore), Calcutta (including Vishakahapatnam), Goa (including Dabolim), Port Blair

## AIR FORCE

*Personnel:* 100,000

*Organization:* 5 commands (Western, Central, Eastern, Training, and Maintenance)
   3 light bomber squadrons (Canberra)
 13 fighter/interceptor squadrons (MiG-21 with Atoll AAM)
   8 fighter/interceptor squadrons (Gnat)
   4 fighter-bomber squadrons (Su-7)
   3 fighter-bomber squadrons (Marut)
   4 fighter-bomber squadrons (Hunter)
   1 maritime reconnaissance squadron (Constellation)
   1 photo reconnaissance squadron (Canberra)
 12 transport squadrons (4 C-47, 3 C-119, 2 An-12, 2 Otter, 1 Caribou)
   1 communications squadron (Tu-124, HS-748, VIP flight)
   9 helicopter squadrons (6 Mi-4, 3 Mi-8, also units of Alouette III, SA-315)

*Major Aircraft Types:*
803 combat aircraft
   45 Canberra light bombers
 435 fighter/interceptors (235 MiG-21, 200 Gnat)
 310 fighter-bombers (140 Su-7, 60 Marut, 110 Hunter)
    5 Super Constellation maritime reconnaissance aircraft
    8 Canberra photo reconnaissance aircraft
850 other aircraft
 209 transports (50 C-47, 45 C-119, 6 Il-14, 3 Tu-124, 30 An-12, 30 Otter, 20 Caribou, 25 HS-748)
 383 trainers (10 Su-7, 8 MiG-21, 10 Canberra, 50 Iskra, 20 Hunter, 130 HT-2, 155 Kiran)

258 helicopters (100 Mi-4, 50 Mi-8, 100 Alouette III, 2 HH-52, 6 SA-315)

*Missiles:*
20 SA-2 Guideline sites, SAM
40 Tigercat SAM

*Reserves:* These consist of the Regular Reserves (former regular air force personnel), the Air Defense Reserves (personnel in civil aviation) and the Auxiliary Air Force.

*Air Bases:* The air force operates from sixty air fields oriented mainly to the northwest and the northeast.

## PARAMILITARY

The Border Security Force numbers 100,000 men organized as light infantry. Civil police throughout the country total some 550,000.

The National Volunteer Force (Lok Sahayak Sena) gives elementary military training to segments of the population at large with no liability for active military service.

# INDONESIA

## Republic of Indonesia

## POWER POTENTIAL STATISTICS

Area: 735,368 square miles
Population: 145,958,000
Total Active Regular Armed Forces: 269,000 (0.18% population)
Gross National Product: $43 billion ($310 per capita)
Annual Military Expenditures: $1.7 billion (3.95% GNP)
Fuel Production:
    Crude Oil: 74 million metric tons
    Refined Petroleum Products: 11.3 million metric tons
    Coal: 206,000 metric tons
Electric Power Output: 8.7 billion kwh
Merchant Fleet (ships 1,000 tons and over): 209 ships; 853,000 gross tons
Civil Air Fleet: 110 major transport aircraft

## DEFENSE STRUCTURE

The president of the Republic of Indonesia is minister of defense and security and the supreme commander of the armed forces. National defense policies are determined by the cabinet presidium in which the minister of defense and security serves as chairman. The chiefs of the army, navy, air force, and police carry ministerial rank and advise and report to him.

## POLITICO-MILITARY POLICY

The so-called New Order government of President Suharto took power in 1966, following a bloody military coup in October 1965 that ousted the Communist-dominated government of former President Sukarno. The Sukarno government had been engaged in a confrontation with neighboring Malaysia (then including Singapore) before the coup and was strongly anti-Western. The new Suharto government conducted massacres of Communists and persons suspected of Communist sympathies, established friendly relations with Malaysia, and emphasized economic recovery and stability at home.

Relations with Malaysia continued warm, and the two countries are working together to standardize their common language. Relations with Singapore are correct and becoming more cordial. At the same time, the government's anti-Communist stance is softening to the extent that relations with the Soviet Union are more friendly, and Indonesia has been receiving Soviet economic aid.

A selective service system and volunteers provide the manpower for the armed forces.

The Indonesian army's relative lack of armor reflects both a doctrine that emphasizes guerrilla warfare and Indonesia's terrain, which is ill suited to heavy vehicles.

## STRATEGIC PROBLEMS

There are still a few hard-core Communists in Indonesia, but a recent U.S. estimate suggests only about 1,000 members and about 100 activists; before the 1965 coup, membership was estimated at 1.5 million. Indigenous Communists are still of concern to the government, however. Diplomtic relations with China were to have been established in 1977 or 1978, but China's approaches to Indonesian Communists delayed this move. When East Timor was promised independence by the new Portuguese government, and civil war broke out there between opposing liberation groups in 1975, Indonesia intervened militarily with "volunteers." Fear of East Timor as a base and refuge for Indonesian Communists, always strong in nearby east Java, was reportedly one reason for Indonesian intervention. In July 1976 East Timor became Indonesia's twenty-seventh province, a move opposed by Australia, concerned over Indonesian expansion.

The South Moluccan separatists, who have carried out terrorist actions in the Netherlands, have been relatively quiet in Indonesia. There is a West New Guinea liberation movement carrying out sporadic guerrilla activities aimed at ousting Indonesia from that province, officially called

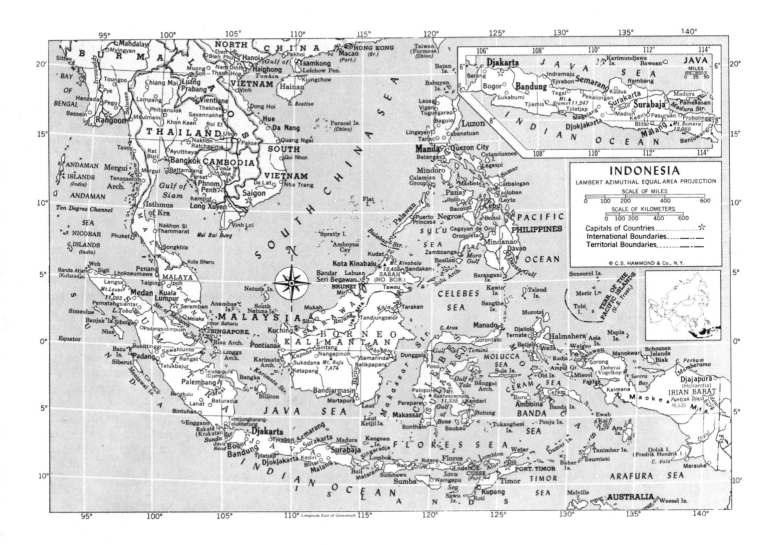

Irian Barat. Papua New Guinea, an independent country formerly under Australian mandate, occupies the other half of the island of New Guinea.

Activist student groups are a chronic internal security problem. They were important in ousting Sukarno, and incidents of student unrest and riots continue. Resentment of Indonesia's economic dependence on Japan, viewed as "colonialism" or "neoimperialism" by activist students, led to violent student demonstrations during Prime Minister Tanaka's 1974 visit.

Indonesia is a major producer of petroleum. In 1976 the financial collapse of the government oil conglomerate set back development plans and threatened Indonesia with bankruptcy, but the economic situation has been stabilized, and oil revenues should reduce the country's economic problems.

## MILITARY ASSISTANCE

Between 1958 and 1965 Indonesia received some $1.2 billion in Soviet and Eastern European military aid. The navy and air force are still almost entirely equipped with Soviet craft, but much of this equipment has reached the end of its usefulness. An unknown but substantial number of Indonesian officers has been trained in the Soviet Union. Until 1965 a Soviet military technical mission of at least 400 experts was stationed in Indonesia. Since the October 1965 coup, no new weapons aid has been provided, although Indonesia has been allowed to buy limited quantities of spare parts.

The United States in 1967 resumed a limited military aid program, which had been suspended in early 1965 over displeasure with former President Sukarno's "Crush Malaysia" policy. United States military aid has totaled $165 million from 1950 through 1977. Under the MAP, 5,206 students have been trained.

## ARMY

*Personnel:* 200,000

*Organization:*
- 15 infantry brigades (organized into about 100 infantry battalions)
- 4 mixed paratroop-infantry brigades
- 8 armored battalions

*Major Equipment Inventory:*
- 300 light tanks (PT-76, AMX-13, M-3 Stuart)
- 130 armored cars (Saladin, Commando)
- 50 scout cars (Ferret)
- 100 APCs (Saracen and BTR-152)
- 100 M-2 half-tracks
    light and medium artillery pieces (105mm howitzers)
    antiaircraft pieces (40mm, 57mm)
    recoilless rifle antitank guns (106mm)
    rocket launchers (3.5 inch)
    mortars (81mm and 60mm)
    aircraft:
        Aero Commander, C-47, Wilga
        helicopters (Alouette III, UH-1)

## NAVY

*Personnel:* 25,000, including naval air; 14,000 Marine Corps *(Korps Kommando—KKO)*

*Major Units:*
- 2 marine brigades
- 4 submarines (Soviet Whiskey class; SS; about 8 more in reserve)
- 11 frigates (4 Claud Jones class; 3 Riga class; 4 miscellaneous; FF)
- 9 submarine chasers (6 Kronstadt class; 3 PC-461 class; PCS)
- 17 patrol craft (PC)
- 6 fleet minesweepers (Soviet T-43 class; MSF)
- 5 coastal minesweepers (MSC)
- 5 motor torpedo boats (German; PT)
- 10 missile attack boats (Komar class with SS-N-2/Styx SSM; PTG)
- 8 patrol boats (PB)
- 9 tank landing ships (U.S. Country class; LST)
- 3 utility landing craft (LCU)
- 25 mechanized landing craft (LCM)
- 25 personnel landing craft (LCP)
- 14 auxiliary ships
- 10 service craft
- 6 maritime patrol aircraft (GAF Nomad 22)
- 10 maritime patrol aircraft (HU-16)
- 6 transports (C-47)
    helicopters (4 Bell 47, S-61)
- 6 GAF Nomad 22 on order

*Major Naval Bases:* Surabaja, Kemajaran (Djakarta), Gorontalo

## AIR FORCE

*Personnel:* 30,000

*Organization:*
- 1 COIN Squadron (OV-10)
- 2 fighter-bomber squadrons (Sabre A-7)
- 2 transport squadrons (Aero Commander, C-140, C-130, C-212 Aviocar, Skywagon, C-47)
- 3 helicopter squadrons (Alouette II, Kiowa, Iroquois, S-58)

*Major Aircraft Types:*
- 67 combat aircraft
    - 16 fighters (Sabre)
    - 35 fighter-bombers (A-7, F-51)
    - 16 COIN aircraft (OV-10)
- 166 other aircraft
    - 23 medium transports (9 C-21 Aziocar, 8 C-130, 6 C-47)
    - 20 helicopters (S-58, O-58, Alouette II, Iroquois)
    - 132 light transport, trainer, support aircraft (V-140, Otter, Cessna 310, L-4, T-6, Aero Commander, Cessna Skywagon)

*Equipment on Order:* 12 F-5, 6 SA-330 Puma, 8 Hawk, 8 F-27

*Major Air Bases:* Medan, Palembang, Djakarta, Husein (Bandung), Iswahjudi, Denpasar, Semerang, Lombok, Balikpapan, Amboina

## PARAMILITARY

The Indonesian National Police of 110,000 is a separate service under the minister of defense. The 20,000-man Mobile Brigade supplements the army's internal security mission and is trained in amphibious and airborne operations. The Sea Police, a paranaval force, assists the navy in port and close inshore security missions. In time of martial law the police is under operational control of the army. The police force is organized into eleven territorial units and the Djakarta metropolitan area. There is also a militia of about 100,000.

# IRAN

## Islamic Republic of Iran

## POWER POTENTIAL STATISTICS

Area: 635,363 square miles
Population: 35,808,000
Total Active Regular Armed Forces: 322,000 (0.9%
  population)
Gross National Product: $75.9 billion ($2,170 per capita)
Annual Military Expenditures: $7.83 billion (10.32%
  GNP)
Fuel Production:
  Coal: 1.15 million metric tons

Crude Oil: 295.5 million metric tons
Refined Petroleum Products: 34.65 million metric
  tons
Natural Gas: 21.8 billion cubic meters
Electric Power Output: 7 billion kwh
Merchant Fleet (ships 1,000 tons and over): 59 ships; 1.1
  million gross tons
Civil Air Fleet: 25 major transport aircraft

## DEFENSE STRUCTURE

In February 1979 a Provisional Revolutionary Islamic
Council was named as the supreme governing body.
Establishment of an Islamic Republic was endorsed in a
nationwide referendum at the end of March; the government remained subordinate to the religious council. A

defense minister heads the armed forces, with chiefs of staffs of the services under him.

The provisional government promptly announced a policy of removing all senior army officers associated with the shah and replacing them with junior ones. A number of senior officers were executed. The 30,000-man Imperial Guard was disbanded. Many of the noncommissioned men in the armed forces, most of whom were serving a compulsory two-year period of military service, deserted during the period of unrest, but a majority of them drifted back as the situation was clarified. The government, meanwhile, announced a policy of drastically cutting the size of the armed forces.

## POLITICO-MILITARY POLICY

After World War II and until 1979, Iranian policy was oriented mainly toward the West. The departure of the shah and installation of the government of Ayatollah Ruhollah Khomeini resulted in severance of the previously close ties of the Iranian military organization with the United States, cancellation of contracts for more U.S. weapons, and announcement of a nonalignment policy. The new government also severed ties with Israel and recognized the Palestine Liberation Organization. The occupation of the U.S. embassy in November 1979 triggered a serious international crisis.

## STRATEGIC PROBLEMS

Iran is strategically located along the Persian Gulf and astride vital land and air routes connecting Asia, Europe, and Africa. Iran is a land-bridge between the countries of East and West Asia and between the Soviet Union and the warm waters of the Indian Ocean. Defense against land attack would be aided by rugged mountain ranges rimming the north and the west and by deserts and lesser ranges to the east.

The country's greatest concerns are the 1,100 miles of common land boundary with the Soviet Union, and what Iran considers threats to the region's oil resources.

As to the first of these concerns, Iran has had several centuries' experience of intermittent contact and conflict with Russia, which steadily pushed its frontiers southward on both sides of the Caspian Sea, at Iranian expense. The latest such experience was shortly after World War II when Soviet forces occupying provinces in northern Iran departed only as a result of great pressure from the United Nations and the United States.

Under the shah's rule, Iran's second strategic concern was the threat to the region's oil resources and the stability of the moderate traditional regimes controlling oil production in the Persian Gulf. Iran displayed its intention to act forcefully against dissident and subversive activity in the

region by dispatching combat ground, air, and naval forces in 1975–76 at the request of Sultan Qabus of Oman to that country's Dhofar Province. There rebel tribesmen were attempting, with the help of South Yemen, to establish an autonomous region under the banner of the Popular Front for the Liberation of Oman and the Arab Gulf (PFLOAG). The rebellion was at least superficially suppressed in late 1976 through the combined actions of the sultan's armed forces and Iranian troops, with minor Jordanian military support. While the Pan-Arab socialist (Baath) regime in Iraq and the monarchy in Iran remain suspicious and mistrustful of each other, their lingering disputes were settled in 1975. Iraq accepted Iran's claim to the Shat al Arab estuary up to its western bank. Iran simultaneously stopped supporting the Kurdish dissidents attempting to achieve autonomy inside Iraq. Both countries still observe each other cautiously as they acquire sophisticated armaments in great numbers for their respective armed forces. The Iraqi penchant for supporting revolutionary extremist groups in the area, and Iran's clear intentions to discourage them, could be a harbinger of future conflict in the Gulf region.

Relations with Saudi Arabia have on the whole been good, and both countries assisted the Royalist regime in Yemen during the fighting against Egyptian forces (see Yemen). However, disputes have arisen with Saudi Arabia over the division of offshore oil interests in the Gulf. Iran formerly stated its claim to Bahrain, but relinquished this when Bahrain, with UN approval, announced its desire for full independence in May 1970. When the British vacated the Persian Gulf, Iran occupied three small islands in the Strait of Hormuz, which it had long claimed.

There are a number of minority nationalities in Iran, including Kurds, Azerbaijani Turks, and several other tribal groups. In March 1979, shortly after the return of Khomeini to Iran, the Kurds in northwest Iran revolted, demanding autonomy. After several days of violence the army restored order. The Khomeini government granted the Kurds the right to appoint security forces and to operate Kurdish-language schools, and appointed a Kurd as governor general of Kurdistan. A few days later the Turkomans in northeast Iran rebelled. After eight days of fighting government security forces restored order.

Throughout 1978 Shah Mohammad Riza Pahlevi was forced to deal with an increasing level of broad-based opposition to his regime, caused by disapproval of his authoritarian rule and disenchantment with forced-pace modernization. The dissidents included radical terrorists, liberals, and traditionalists, but the strongest element was focussed on the exiled Ayatollah Ruhollah Khomeini. The opposition drew strength from large numbers of people at the lower levels of society who had great difficulty coping with inflation, the uprooting effects of urbanization, industrialization, and the assault of contemporary culture on traditional values. By late 1978 terrorist violence and mass demonstrations had forced the imposition of martial law in most Iranian cities. With Khomeini directing from Paris, nationwide strikes, particularly in the oil industry, and increasing opposition finally caused the shah to depart on an extended vacation.

The return of Khomeini was followed by a period of transition, accompanied by protests, reprisals, and executions, as the various factions sought satisfaction for their causes. By national referendum at the end of March, establishment of an Islamic republic was voted. Nevertheless opposition on religious, political, and social grounds continued, with increasing intensity as 1979 drew to an end.

## MILITARY ASSISTANCE

Until the departure of the shah, Iran relied almost exclusively on the United States for most sophisticated weapons, and the United States maintained sensitive observation positions in the country for monitoring the Soviet Union. This assistance came to an end with the advent of Khomeini. The new government has announced a policy of treating equally with all nations. With the departure of U.S. technicians and cancellation of maintenance and spare-parts contracts, much military equipment has become inoperable.

## ALLIANCES

Iran's only formal alliance, its membership in CENTO, was rescinded by the Khomeini government. Iran is a member, along with Pakistan and Turkey, of Regional Cooperation for Development, established in 1964.

## ARMY

*Personnel:* 200,000

*Organization:*
　3 corps with headquarters at Kermanshah in the northwest, Tehran in the northeast, and Shiraz in the south
　3 infantry divisions
　3 armored divisions
　4 independent brigades (2 infantry, 1 special forces, 1 airborne)
　5 divisional artillery groups
　1 aviation battalion
　1 SAM battalion (Hawk, Rapier)

*Major Equipment Inventory:*
　800 heavy tanks (Chieftain)

　920 medium tanks (M-47, M-60A1, M-48, M-4)
　250 light tanks (M-24, M-41, Scorpion)
　200 armored cars (M-8, M-20)
2,000 APCs (M-113, BTR-50, BTR-60)
　　　antiaircraft artillery (Soviet ZU-23, 57mm, and 85mm, and Bofors 40mm)
　700 guns and howitzers
　　　130mm, 155mm, 175mm guns
　　　105mm, 155mm, 203mm self-propelled and towed howitzers
　　　antitank recoilless rifles (57mm, 75mm, 106mm)
　　　antitank guided missiles (Dragon, TOW)
　　　SAMs (Hawk and Rapier, SA-7, SA-9)
　　　SSMs (SS-11, SS-12, TOW)
　　　light aircraft (L-18, U-17, O-2, Beagle Pup)
　295 helicopters (5 H-43, 14 CH-47, 52 AB-205, 24 AB-206, 100 AH-1, 100 Bell 214)

*Reserves:* About 500,000 men of prior service fit for duty

## NAVY

*Personnel:* 22,000

*Organization:*
　3 fleets: Indian Ocean, Caspian Sea, and Persian Gulf. There is no naval aviation or marine corps, but there is a battalion of naval infantry, used mainly to guard shore installations.

*Major Units:*
　2 submarines (SS; Tang class)
　3 destroyers (all 3 with Standard SAMs, and 1 with Seacat short-range SAMs; 1 Battle class; 2 Sumner class; DD)
　4 frigates (FF; Saam class; Sea Killer SSM and Seacat SAMs, both short-range; DEG)
　4 patrol escorts (PG; PF-103 class; 3-inch guns)
　6 missile attack boats (PTG; Kaman class; Harpoon SSMs)
　7 patrol craft (PC)
　3 coastal minesweepers (MSC)
　2 inshore minesweepers (MSI)
　2 tank landing ships (LST)
　1 utility landing craft (LCU)
　14 hovercraft
　7 auxiliary ships (tankers, tugs, supply ships, etc.)
　10 service craft
　15 helicopters (7 AB-212, 8 SH-3)
　2 maritime patrol aircraft (P-3)
　4 transport (F-27)
　4 Aero Commanders

*Missiles:* SAMs: Standard, Seacat; SSM: Sea Killer, Harpoon

*Naval Bases:* Khorramshahr (major base), Bandar Pahlavi, Bushire, Kharg Island, Bandar Abbas, Chahbahar (tri-service)

## AIR FORCE

*Personnel:* 100,000

*Organization:*
    3 fighter-interceptor squadrons (F-14)
  10 fighter-bomber squadrons (F-5)
  10 fighter-bomber/interceptor squadrons (F-4)
    2 fighter/reconnaissance squadrons (RF-4, RF-5)
    8 transport squadrons (C-130, Boeing 707, F-27, Aero Commander)

*Major Aircraft Types:*
449 combat aircraft
    77 fighter-interceptors (F-14)
  190 fighter-bomber/interceptors (F-4; interceptors carry Sidewinder and Sparrow AAM, fighter-bombers Maverick ASM)
  166 fighter-bombers (F-5)
   16 fighter/reconnaissance (RF-5)
186 other aircraft
    6 tankers (Boeing 707)
  100 transports (57 C-130, 6 747, 14 F-27, 10 C-47, 9 Aero Commander, 4 Falcon)
  143 trainers (T-6, T-41, T-33, F-33)
   95 utility (O-2, U-17, L-18)
   38 helicopters (10 AB-206, 6 AB-212, 2 CH-47, 4 H-43, 16 Super Frelon)

*Missiles:* 2,500 Maverick ASM, 1,900 Sidewinder AIM-9

*Equipment On Order:*
250 F-18
 40 F-14 fighters with Phoenix AAM
110 F-5 Tiger II fighters
140 F-16 fighters
 10 E-3A AWACS
287 Bell 214 utility helicopters (service assignment unknown)
 11 Boeing 707 tankers
  6 Boeing 747 transports

*Air Bases:* Tehran, Hamadan, Dezful, Doshen-Tappeh, Mehrabad, Galeh-Marghi, Zahidan, Mashad, Shiraz, Ahwaz, Isfahan, Tabriz, Faharabad, Chahbahar

*Reserves:* No more than 35,000 men of prior service fit for duty

## PARAMILITARY

There are three paramilitary organizations: the Imperial Iranian Gendarmerie, the National Police, and the Resistance Forces. The gendarmerie of 80,000 men consists mainly of volunteers, and a few conscripts. Its units generally correspond to the boundaries of the country's provinces. The gendarmerie has a light aircraft (FW/RW) and shore patrol unit. Equipment includes wheeled vehicles and armored cars, helicopters, Cessna-185 light aircraft, and patrol craft. In peacetime the gendarmerie is under the direction of the minister of the interior. In wartime it comes under the Ministry of War. Selected units of the National Police may be used for special assignments. The mission of the Resistance Forces is to prepare the people to defend their homes, villages, and regional industries, and to cooperate with the armed forces in case of aggression or internal unrest.

During the international crisis following seizure of the U.S. embassy in November 1979, a national program was inaugurated to arm and train all citizens.

# IRAQ

## The Republic of Iraq

### POWER POTENTIAL STATISTICS

Area: 172,000 square miles
Population: 12,689,000
Total Active Regular Armed Forces: 125,000 (0.98% population)
Gross National Product: $19 billion ($1,610 per capita)
Annual Military Expenditures: $1.6 billion (8.42% GNP)
Fuel Production:
  Crude Oil: 112.4 million metric tons
  Refined Products: 5 million metric tons
Electric Power Output: 7 billion kwh
Merchant Fleet (ships 1,000 tons and over): 35 ships; 1.2 million gross tons
Civil Air Fleet: 25 major transport aircraft

### DEFENSE STRUCTURE

Iraq is a republic controlled by the Pan-Arab, socialist Baath party (whose name means renaissance, or rebirth), which has dominated the politics and policies of the country since the overthrow of a military dictator in 1968.

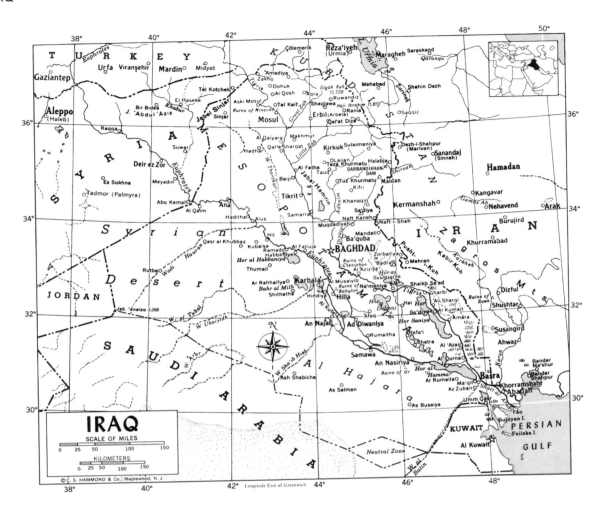

The Revolutionary Command Council (RCC) of the Baath Party governs the country in an absolute manner, with strong security and intelligence measures. The president of the RCC, Hassan Bakr, is head of state and commander in chief of the armed forces. His chronically poor health has placed real power in the hands of an ambitious son-in-law, Saddam Hussein Tikriti, who is vice president of the RCC and has assumed the rank of major general in the army. Upon Bakr's death, Tikriti is expected to take the preeminent position in both civil and military affairs.

Most high-ranking military officers owe their promotions to membership in the Baath party. There is a joint command structure, but the army has predominance over the air force and navy.

## POLITICO-MILITARY POLICY

The Communist party of Iraq (CPI) has at times sought to form a National Progressive Front with the Baath party, but the Baathists, who themselves lack broad support in Iraq, consider such an alliance inimical to Arab unity and socialism. Despite extensive Soviet involvement in Iraq, especially in the military, the CPI is held in check.

In spite of considerable oscillation in national and international policies, traditional Arab-Israeli hostility has kept Iraqi policy consistent in opposition to Israel. One consequence of this policy since 1958 has been to keep the successive military governments more or less aligned with the USSR. Iraq depends heavily on the Soviet Union for military equipment and economic assistance, and in exchange is a staunch supporter of Soviet policy. Iraq contributed armored and air (MiG-21 and Hunter) units to the October 1973 Arab-Israeli war. One air squadron operated from Syria and one from Egypt.

Iraq is undergoing a massive military buildup. Army and air force personnel strengths have expanded significantly. Modern and sophisticated weapons have been provided for them by the Soviet Union, and by some Western nations as well.

Military service for two years is compulsory for all male citizens over the age of eighteen; liability for service continues through age forty. More than 70,000 males reach military age annually, more than enough to keep units up to their authorized strengths.

Most commissioned officers are graduates of the Military College at Rustamiyah or the Air Force Flying College at Shaiba air base near Basra. The army also maintains a staff college for the training of selected army and air force officers for high command and staff positions. Iraqi officers are also sent abroad, primarily to the Soviet Union, for specialized training.

## STRATEGIC PROBLEMS

Iraq's major strategic problems are internal. Although Iraq is potentially one of the largest producers of crude oil in the world, the general populace has one of the lowest standards of living. The present regime is attempting, although slowly, to undertake social and economic reform.

In a country of many cultural and ethnic groups, Shi'a Moslems make up over half the population, and materially, socially, and educationally, they are in poor condition. More prosperous and better educated are the Sunni Moslems, who control the government through the Baath party. About one-fifth of the total population are Kurds. They have clashed bitterly with the central government for over a generation, seeking to establish an autonomous region for themselves in the north, bordering Turkey and Iran. In 1975 Iran withdrew its support of the Kurdish tribal leader, Mustafa Barzani, and this action resulted in the collapse of the Kurdish rebellion. Although terrorism and small-unit guerrilla operations continue, it is unlikely that any Kurdish uprisings in force could be successful.

Externally, Iraq has to contend with the rival center for Baath power in Damascus, Syria. The Iraqi Baathists have handled this problem badly, and there is deep mutual hostility and suspicion between the two Arab capitals. Border problems with Iran and Kuwait are also of some concern. In an effort to improve its position in the Persian Gulf, Iraq must deal effectively with the conservative Arab monarchs along the littoral, primarily in Kuwait and Saudi Arabia, where the Baathist Pan-Arab brand of socialism is not popular. Iraq would like to annex from Kuwait the islands of Bubiyan and Warbah, which control access to Iraq's port at Um Qasr.

## MILITARY ASSISTANCE

Until July 1958 Iraq's armed forces were largely British-trained and equipped, although there had been some U.S. military assistance. Since 1958 Soviet arms deliveries have been made under a series of agreements. The early shipments may have been grant aid; more recently Iraq has paid cash and has also invested some surplus oil revenues in the USSR and Eastern European nations.

At various periods Iraq has had military assistance agreements with India and Pakistan. There also are military advisers from both Eastern and Western Europe in the country.

Iraq assists Palestinian extremists financially and allows them to train in the country. The government also strongly supports the Popular Front for the Liberation of Oman and the Arab Gulf.

## ALLIANCES

Iraq is a member of the Arab League. It was a charter member of the Baghdad Pact (now CENTO) but withdrew after the coup of 1958. In 1972 Iraq signed a fifteen-year friendship and cooperation agreement with the Soviet Union.

## ARMY

*Personnel:* 100,000

*Organization:*
- 4 armored divisions
- 2 mechanized divisions
- 4 infantry divisions (each with 3 brigades plus an artillery regiment, engineers, and support troops)
- 1 independent armored brigade
- 2 independent infantry brigades
- 2 heavy antiaircraft regiments

*Major Equipment Inventory:*
- 1,000 medium tanks (T-62, T-54, and T-55; some T-34; AMX-30)
- 100 light tanks (M-24, PT-76)
- 1,500 APCs (BTR-40/50/60/152, BMP)
- 500 guns and howitzers (85mm, 100mm, 122mm, 130mm, 152mm)
- antitank guns
    - 100mm self-propelled (SU-100, 40 JSU-122)
    - 82mm recoilless
- antitank guided missiles (Sagger, SS-11)
- 115 armored cars (AML-60)
- SSMs (FROG, Scud)
- antiaircraft guns
    - towed (23mm, 57mm, 85mm, 100mm)
    - self-propelled (ZSU-23-4, ZSU-57-2)
- SAM SA-7

*Reserves:* 260,000 trained reservists

## NAVY

*Personnel:* 3,000

*Major Units:*
- 3 submarine chasers (SO-1 class; PCS)
- 14 Osa class missile attack boats with SS-N-2/Styx SSM (PTG)

10  motor torpedo boats (P-6 class; PT)
30  patrol boats (PB)
 2  fleet minesweepers (MSF)
 3  medium landing ships (LSM; Polnocny class)
 3  inshore minesweepers
 3  service craft

*Reserves:* Approximately 3,000

*Naval Bases:* Basra, Umm Qasr

## AIR FORCE

*Personnel:* 22,000 (10,000 are Air Defense Forces)

*Organization:*
  1  bomber squadron (Tu-16)
  5  fighter-interceptor squadrons (MiG-21, MiG-23, MiG-19)
 12  fighter-bomber squadrons (Su-7, MiG-17, MiG-23, Hunter)
  4  transport squadrons (Tu-124, An-12, An-24, Il-14)
  8  helicopter squadrons (Mi-4, Mi-8, Wessex, Alouette III, Mi-6, Super Frelon, Gazelle)
  1  trainer/support group (L-29, L-39, Jet Provost, Yak-18, MiG-15)
The L-29, L-39, and Jet Provost have a COIN capability

*Major Aircraft Types:*
290  combat aircraft
  100  MiG-21 fighters
   20  MiG-23 fighters
   30  MiG-17 fighters
   20  MiG-19 fighters
   48  Su-7 fighter-bombers
   33  MiG-27 fighter-bombers
   30  Hunter fighter-bombers
    9  Tu-16 medium bombers
283  other aircraft
   31  transports (2 Tu-124, 5 An-12, 12 An-24, 12 Il-14)
  158  helicopters (16 Mi-6, 35 Mi-4, 30 Mi-8, 12 Wessex, 40 Alouette III, 10 Super Frelon, 15 Gazelle)
   95  trainer/support (16 Jet Provost, 28 L-29, 20 L-39, 15 Yak-18, 15 MiG-15)

*Missiles:* SAMs (SA-2, SA-3)

*Air Bases:* Habbaniya, Shaiba, Kirkuk, Raschid, Basra, Mosul

*Reserves:* Over 18,000 trained reservists

## PARAMILITARY

There are miscellaneous security units, including a border guard. Most prominent is the People's Army, which may number between 100,000 and 200,000 and can best be described as an increasingly well organized militia of the Baath party.

# IRELAND

## Irish Republic

### POWER POTENTIAL STATISTICS

Area: 26,600 square miles
Population: 3,242,000
Total Active Regular Armed Forces: 15,153 (0.47% population)
Gross National Product: $9.3 billion ($2,930 per capita)
Defense Budget: $182 million (1.95% GNP)
Fuel Production:
  Coal: 48,000 metric tons
  Refined Petroleum Products: 1.96 million metric tons
  Natural Gas: 277 million cubic meters
Electric Power Output: 9.3 billion kwh
Merchant Fleet (ships 1,000 tons and over): 21 vessels; 166,000 gross tons
Civil Air Fleet: 28 major transport aircraft

### DEFENSE STRUCTURE

Under Ireland's republican, parliamentary form of government, the Permanent Defence Force (including army, air force, and navy) is administered by the minister of defence, assisted by the chief of staff, the adjutant general, and the quartermaster general.

### POLITICO-MILITARY POLICY

Irish national foreign policy and military policy are traditionally neutral. With respect to the East-West confrontation since World War II, however, Irish policy has been retitled independent, rather than neutral, in view of Ireland's ideological commitment to Western democracy. Implicitly Ireland relies upon the armed forces of the West for its security, and thus maintains armed forces totally inadequate for effective self-defense. In international affairs Ireland has increasingly offered members or elements of its armed forces (recruited from the Reserve Force) for peacekeeping activities, almost exclusively through the United Nations.

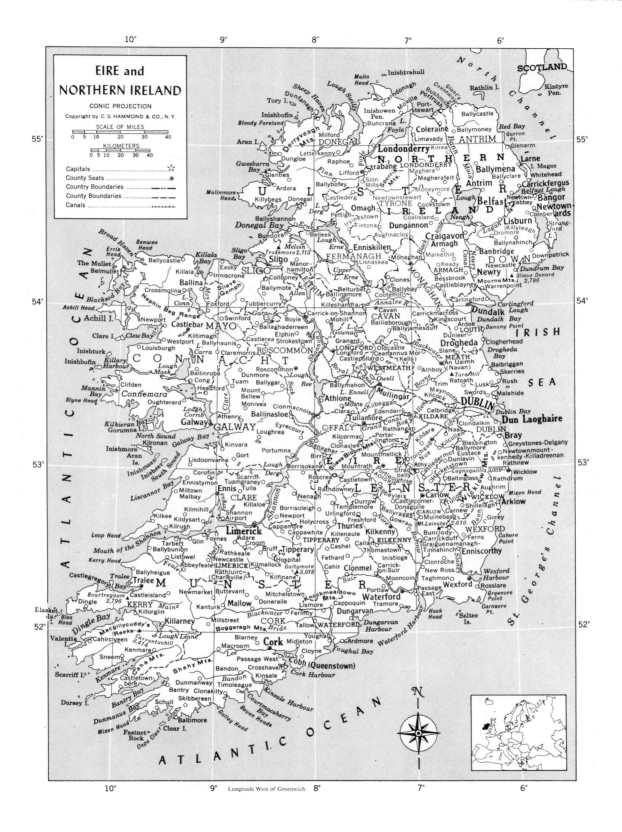

EIRE and NORTHERN IRELAND

CONIC PROJECTION

Copyright by C. S. HAMMOND & CO., N.Y.

SCALE OF MILES
0  5  10    20    30    40

KILOMETERS
0  5 10   20    30    40

Capitals .................................... ☆
County Seats ............................. ◉
Country Boundaries ............... — · — · —
County Boundaries ............... — — — —
Canals ..................................... ······

Longitude West of Greenwich

ATLANTIC OCEAN

Under current Irish law, the Permanent Defence Force is limited to a total strength of 15,600 men, and the reserves to 22,800. All personnel of the active and reserve armed forces are volunteers; the term of service is three years for the army followed by nine years in the Reserve, four years in the Naval Service and Air Corps, followed by six years in the Reserve.

## STRATEGIC PROBLEMS

In Northern Ireland, where the majority of the population (largely Protestant) favors a retention of the political link with Great Britain, the problem of violence continues to be a major cause of concern to the government of Ireland. This violence is carried on by a very small minority among the Catholic and Protestant communities in the North through the agency of illegal organizations such as the Provisional I.R.A. (mainly Catholic), the Ulster Volunteer Force (Protestant), and many smaller, outlawed paramilitary groups. These groups are opposed to any political settlement which does not meet their demands in full; that is, the I.R.A. is committed to the establishment of an all-Ireland Socialist Republic while the Protestant extremists are determined to exclude the Catholic community from participation in the governing of Northern Ireland. Ireland, with the cooperation of the government of the United Kingdom, has worked actively toward finding a peaceful solution to the problems in Northern Ireland which would take into account the legitimate aspirations of both communities, but at present the political situation is in something of a stalemate. In the absence of political progress violence continues sporadically, but the passage of stringent laws in Ireland to deal with illegal organizations and the vigorous pursuit of these groups by the Irish and British security forces have resulted in significant losses for the violent elements in the North.

## MILITARY ASSISTANCE

Ireland trains officer cadets from Zambia.

## ALLIANCES

Ireland is a member of the EEC. It actively supports UN peacekeeping efforts and maintains a detachment battalion with the UN Force headquarters in Cyprus. To date over 16,000 Irish soldiers have served on UN missions in Kashmir, Lebanon, the Congo, New Guinea, and the Middle East.

## ARMY

*Personnel:* 13,484

*Organization:*
    9 infantry battalions
    4 cavalry squadrons
    6 field artillery regiments
    1 antiaircraft regiment

*Major Equipment Inventory:*
    armored cars, Panhard, AML 60 and AML 90
    APC, Panhard and Unimog
    light field artillery, 25-pounder
    Bofors antiaircraft guns

*Reserves:* There are approximately 22,800 volunteers formally enrolled in the Reserve Defence Force.

## NAVY (Naval Service)

*Personnel:* 800

*Major Units:*
    1 patrol ship (PGF)
    3 patrol craft (PC; fisheries protection ships)
    1 auxiliary ship
    5 service craft

## AIR FORCE

*Personnel:* 869

*Organization:*
    1 tactical reconnaissance squadron (FR-172, Vampire)
    1 support squadron (Dove, Alouette III)

*Major Aircraft Types:*
     8 FR-172 light ground attack aircraft
     3 Vampire armed trainers
     3 Dove transports
     5 Alouette III helicopters
     3 Magister armed trainers
    10 SF 260, Warriors

## PARAMILITARY

Constabulary and civil police number 8,502.

# ISRAEL

## State of Israel

## POWER POTENTIAL STATISTICS

Area: 8,017 square miles*

*Does not include territories occupied since June 1967

Population: 3,712,000
Total Active Regular Armed Forces: 164,500 (4.43%
  population)*
Gross National Product: $13.3 billion ($3,720 per capita)
Annual Military Expenditures: $4.32 billion (32.48%
  GNP)
Fuel Production:
  Crude Oil: 37,000 metric tons
  Refined Petroleum Products: 7.35 million metric tons
Electric Power Output: 13.5 billion kwh
Merchant Fleet (ships 1,000 tons and over): 39 ships;
  395,000 gross tons
Civil Air Fleet: 25 major transport aircraft

## DEFENSE STRUCTURE

The Israel Defense Force (IDF) originated in the Haganah, a Jewish underground defense organization started during the Palestine Mandate in the 1920s. Palmach was its elite combat force of full-time regulars. The transformation of these forces into the IDF reserve and regular components upon independence in 1948 was conceptually and organizationally simple. Not only had these forces considerable experience in guerrilla warfare against the British and Arabs in Palestine, but they were augmented after World War II by Jewish veterans of the British, American, and other armies, including a number of highly trained and experienced middle to senior-level officers. With the popular determination to establish and defend Israel tempered by the modern war experience of others, a highly effective military instrument appropriate to the defense needs of the country evolved during the early years of independence. The form of these forces has been shaped by Israel's geographic location, the close identification of the Israeli citizen-soldier with the state, his skill, ingenuity, and motivation, acquired from four major conflicts with Arab regulars (1948, 1956, 1967, and 1973), and numerous border clashes with irregular forces. The IDF has demonstrated a substantial and consistent combat effectiveness superiority over all of its Arab enemies.

Actual control of the IDF is vested in the prime minister and the cabinet. Direct responsibility for administering the armed forces is exercised by the minister of defense. The chief of the General Staff is also chief of staff of the army and presides over the tri-service unified Defense Forces. The General Staff directs activities and operations of the combat commands (navy, air force, three territorial commands, the Paratroop Command, and the Armored Command), the Training Command, and NAHAL (Fighting Pioneering Youth, a paramilitary organization).

*Not including mobilized reserves; the total can be raised to about 409,500 within 48 to 72 hours.

## POLITICO-MILITARY POLICY

All Israeli military planning concentrates on the Arab threat. While some Arab states reluctantly acknowledge the permanent existence of Israel, it is extremely difficult to allay Israeli fears that the Arabs ultimately intend to render Israel politically, militarily, and economically impotent. Israel expends a crushing percentage of its resources on security and defense. Since the 1967 Six Day War, Israeli dependence on the United States for purchase of weapons has markedly increased.

Military service is universal for men and women (except the Arab 10 percent of the population); men eighteen to twenty-nine years of age serve thirty-six months and unmarried women eighteen to twenty-six serve twenty months from their eighteenth birthday. Service in the reserves is required up to age fifty-five for men and thirty-four for women.

The IDF comprises a regular professional nucleus of about 25,000 to 30,000, with two yearly conscript classes of about 25,000 each. About 75,000 are normally on active duty at any one time. This active force has two major elements: (1) a mobilization base (including a training cadre and recruits in training), and (2) first-line defense units such as air defense and sea patrols and units along the border.

The senior service school is the National Defense College, a tri-service institution which conducts a ten-month course in strategy and politico-military affairs. The Command and General Staff College has a course focusing on General Staff operations, technique, and procedures. Many officers are also sent to foreign staff colleges and war colleges for training, mostly to the United States.

The logistical system is adequate and efficient, principally because of the Israelis' high level of managerial and technical skill and their wide scale adoption of modern business machines and methods. An important handicap is the continuing dependence on foreign sources for major items of combat equipment. Modern, large, defense-related industries are being developed for the purpose of rendering Israel more self-reliant and relatively independent of foreign sources of military hardware.

In the field, responsibility for logistical operations devolves primarily upon the territorial commanders. They are responsible for arming and equipping mobilized reserve forces in their areas and for providing logistical support to all units coming under their control. Supply depots are located at key points to provide arms, equipment, and field rations in the event of mobilization and to furnish base support for combat operations. Maintenance is conducted as far forward as resources and the situation permit.

As an extremely small state surrounded by much larger, well-armed neighbors with varying degrees of hostility, Israel has considered retention of lands occupied in the

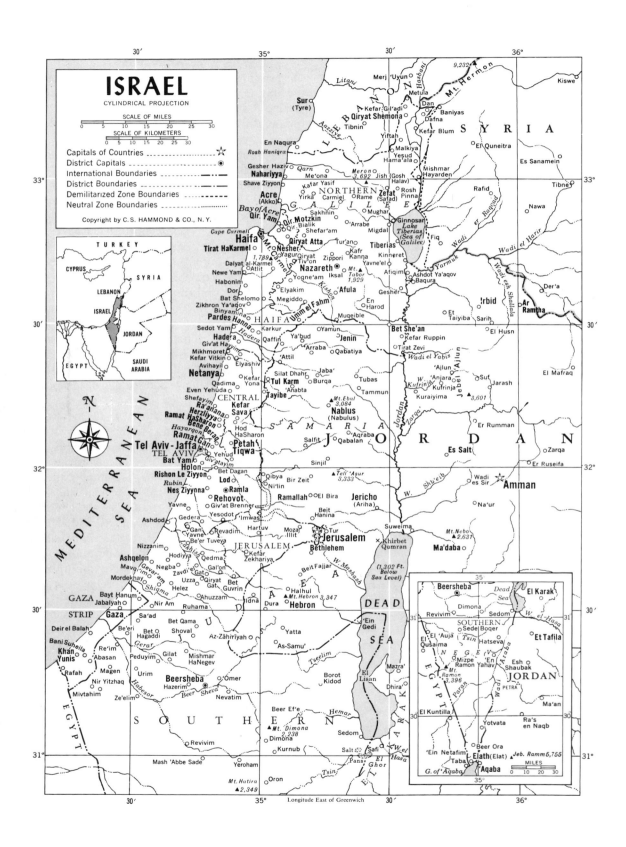

# ISRAEL

CYLINDRICAL PROJECTION

SCALE OF MILES

0  5  10  15  20  25  30

SCALE OF KILOMETERS

0  5  10  15  20  25  30

Capitals of Countries ................. ☆
District Capitals ..................... ◉
International Boundaries .............. — — —
District Boundaries .................. —·—·—
Demilitarized Zone Boundaries ....... — — — —
Neutral Zone Boundaries ............. ..........

Copyright by C.S. HAMMOND & CO., N.Y.

1967 war essential for its security. The treaty signed with Egypt in early 1979 will turn over the Sinai, but the future of the Gaza Strip, the west bank of the Jordan River, and the Golan Heights that border Syria remains unsettled. With the Arab states united in opposition to the treaty and to Egypt, the possibility of a peaceful agreement about these areas seems remote. Unless a future Egyptian government renounces the treaty and joins its military forces with those of the other Arabs, a direct attack in force on Israeli territory is unlikely. However, the militant Palestinians in the Palestine Liberation Organization (PLO), with varying degrees of support from the Arab nations and the ayatollah's government in Iran, and bases in Lebanon pose a constant threat of guerrilla attack on Israeli targets near the border.

A prime threat to Israeli security is posed by the Palestine Liberation Organization (PLO), the militant Palestinians who claim title to all Israeli territory and maintain refugee and guerrilla camps in Lebanon from which attacks on Israeli objectives are launched.

Israel's situation has led to a strategy based on preemptive offensive strikes by closely coordinated modern land, air, and sea forces against any seriously threatening Arab forces. Border incidents and infiltrations prompt instant, severe Israeli reaction. Border police and fortified farms along the border provide the tripwire against incursions and are backed up by mobile army units. Surface-to-surface missiles are available as retaliation for any possible Egyptian missiles delivering high explosives against Israeli cities.

A number of factors permit this strategy. First is the high literacy and technical competence of Israeli manpower, plus physical fitness derived through good nutrition, rural life, and fitness programs. Also contributing is the military experience of the leaders, going back to World War II and enriched by further experience in the successful major campaigns against Arab armies. These factors plus the motivation of self-survival have resulted in very high morale and *esprit de corps* in a relatively homogeneous and united population. All of this permits utilization of the most modern weapons, bold, rapid, and sometimes complex maneuvers, and an extremely rapid mobilization.

## MILITARY ASSISTANCE

Since 1967 the United States has been the principal supporter of Israel. United States military assistance since the end of the October 1973 Arab-Israeli war has averaged about $1.8 billion per year. About half of this sum, including forgiven loans, must be considered grant aid. (U.S. aid to Israel is funded under the Foreign Military Sales Program and the Security Supporting Assistance Program.) Israel has received some of the most modern and sophisticated U.S. weapons. Israel's indigenous industry complements the U.S. aid program significantly. It has developed some weapons systems, notably aircraft, missiles, boats, tanks, electronic materiel, and small arms. Israeli industry has exported arms to South Africa, Taiwan, and some Latin American countries. Some African states would probably welcome Israeli assistance, as they have in the past, if a settlement with the Arabs were to relax the Arab political pressures that have led most of them to break diplomatic relations with Israel.

## ALLIANCES

During the 1967 hostilities France terminated a previous de facto alliance with Israel, in which it had been Israel's source of modern aircraft and heavy weapons. The United States demonstrated during and after the 1973 war that it will provide Israel with whatever military support is necessary to offset Soviet aid to the Arab countries, in order to maintain a Middle East balance of power.

## ARMY

*Personnel:* 140,000 (20,000 regulars and about 120,000 conscripts); total is 375,000 when fully mobilized

*Organization:*
- 6 infantry brigades (includes paratroop brigades)
- 8 armored brigades
- 4 mechanized brigades
- 25 artillery battalions
  regional defense cadres and border guards training command and reserve cadres (see below) announcement was made in November 1979 that a field command would be formed.

*Major Equipment Inventory:*
- 3,610 medium tanks
  - 850 M-48, M-47 Patton (105mm gun)
  - 1,200 Centurion, Ben Gurion, and Sabra (105mm gun)
  - 550 T-54 and T-55, T-62 (105mm gun)
  - 810 M-60 main battle tanks
  - 200 Super Sherman or Isherman (105mm gun)
- 100 light tanks (AMX-13 and PT-76)
- 490 self-propelled artillery pieces (including heavy mortars, 105mm, 155mm, and 203mm howitzers, and 175mm gun)
- 2,300 APCs (M-113)
- 1,300 half-tracks (M-2, M-3)
- 96 recoilless rifles (106mm, jeep-mounted)
- 50 self-propelled guns (90mm)
  SS-11 missiles on weapons carriers
- 15 armored cars (AML-90)

armored cars (Staghound and AML-60)
SSM Lance
antitank missiles (Cobra, Swingfire, TOW, Sagger, Dragon)
980 antiaircraft guns (20mm Vulcan and Chaparral, 30mm, 40mm)
1,200 SAMs (Redeye)

*Equipment on Order:*
Lance and Zeev SSM

*Reserves:* Approximately 200,000 available for immediate mobilization, to activate approximately:
14 infantry brigades (including paratroop)
20 armored brigades
11 mechanized brigades
60 artillery battalions

*Training:* Reserves are called up for training fourteen to thirty-one days per year, plus one day per month; officers and NCOs receive special courses an additional week per year.

*Mobilization:* Reserves are mobilized within forty-eight hours; individuals report to depots where they join their unit cadres, obtain their weapons and equipment, and are ready for operations.

## NAVY

*Personnel:* 3,500 regular and conscripts (9,500 total when fully mobilized); includes 500 naval commandos

*Major Units:*
3 submarines (SS; Type 206 class)
12 missile attack boats (PTG; Saar class, Gabriel SSMs)
2 missile attack boats (PTG; Dvora class; Gabriel SSMs)
6 missile attack boats (PTG; Reshef class; Harpoon and Gabriel SSMs)
35 patrol boats (PB)
3 roadstead large patrol boats (PBR)
3 patrol launches (PSB)
3 medium landing ships (LSM)
6 utility landing craft (LCU)
3 mechanized landing craft (LCM)
5 service craft

*Naval Bases:* Haifa, Ashdod, Eilat

## AIR FORCE

*Personnel:* 21,000 (20,000 regulars and about 1,000 conscripts; 25,000 when fully mobilized)

*Organization:*
13 fighter/fighter-bomber squadrons (Mirage III, F-15, F-4, Kfir) armed with AAM Shafrir, R-530 Matra, Sidewinder, Sparrow
8 ground attack squadrons (A-4)
1 tactical reconnaissance squadron (RF-4, OV-1)
*Note.* Fighter-bomber and ground attack squadrons are armed with AGM Bullpup, Shrike, Standard ARM, Rockeye, Walleye, Maverick, and LUZ-1.
4 transport squadrons (C-47, C-130, C-97, Boeing 707, Arava, Do-28, Noratlas, IAI Arava)
1 helicopter wing (CH-53, AB-205, S-65, CH-47, S-61, H-19, Super S-58, Super Frelon, Alouette II, Iroquois)
1 training wing (Queen Air, Magister, Super Mystere, Ouragan, Mirage, TA-4)

*Major Aircraft Types:*
740 combat aircraft
5 F-15 fighters
40 Mirage III fighters
100 Kfir fighters
265 F-4, RF-4 fighter-bombers/reconnaissance
10 OV-10 electronic reconnaissance aircraft
320 A-4 ground attack aircraft
646 other aircraft
115 transports (10 C-47, 26 C-130, 12 C-97, 15 Do-28, 38 Noratlas, 14 Arava)
286 helicopters (28 CH-53, 95 AB-205, 16 S-65, 44 S-65, 32 AH-1, 8 CH-47, 8 Super Frelon, 5 Alouette II, 24 S-58, 12 H-19, 14 S-61)
177 trainers (80 Magister, 18 Super Mystere, 30 Ouragan, 20 Mirage, 9 Queen Air, 20 TA-4)
68 utility craft (60 L-18, 8 L-23)

*Missiles:* 600 Hawk SAMs and 15 Hawk batteries

*Major Air Bases:* Lod, Ekron, Hatzerim

*Equipment on Order:* 250 F-16, 20 F-15, P-6A

## PARAMILITARY

Virtually the entire Israeli population, excluding Arabs, is assigned civil defense and home guard duties. Communal farms are well organized for defense with fortifications and stocks of arms and ammunition. Older men, youths, and women are well trained to man these positions; many are veterans of the Defense Forces or participated in the guerrilla struggle in Palestine before 1948.

The principal paramilitary force is called NAHAL. (Fighting Pioneering Youth), an organization that combines military service with agricultural training. NAHAL's prime military mission is to serve as first line of defense against ground attack along the borders and to prevent infiltration. A secondary mission is to assist and support the army in performing duties in the occupied territories.

# ITALY

## Italian Republic

### POWER POTENTIAL STATISTICS

Area: 116,303 square miles

Population: 56,867,000

Total Active Regular Armed Forces: 355,000 (0.65% population)

Gross National Product: $196 billion ($3,470 per capita)

Annual Military Expenditures: $4.96 billion (2.53% GNP)

Crude Steel Production: 23.4 million metric tons

Iron Ore Production: 524,000 metric tons

Fuel Production:

Lignite: 1.2 million metric tons

Crude Oil: 1.1 million metric tons

Refined Petroleum Products: 106.7 million metric tons

Natural Gas: 15.37 billion cubic meters

Manufactured Gas: 3.5 billion cubic meters

Electric Power Output: 166.5 billion kwh

Nuclear Power Production: 1,400 megawatts

Merchant Fleet (ships 1,000 tons and over): 603 ships; 10.7 million gross tons

Civil Air Fleet: 123 major transport aircraft

### DEFENSE STRUCTURE

Italy has a parliamentary republican government; the president is the nominal commander of the armed forces.

Actual civilian control of the armed forces is exercised by the government through the minister of defense, who in turn is advised by the Chiefs of Staff Committee, consisting of the chief of the Defense Staff, the chiefs of staff of the three services and the defense secretary general.

### POLITICO-MILITARY POLICY

Since World War II, despite an increasing political trend toward socialism and the influence of the most powerful Communist party in Western Europe, Italy has aligned itself consistently with the Western European democratic powers, and was a charter member of NATO.

The armed forces of Italy are raised and maintained through conscription. For the army and the air force the term of conscript service is twelve months; for the navy it is eighteen months.

### STRATEGIC PROBLEMS

Italy's relatively large population is densely concentrated in the narrow coastal lowlands and river valleys of this mountainous peninsula. Thus its population and industrial centers are particularly vulnerable to air attack.

As demonstrated in World War II, Italy's elongated coastline is vulnerable to hostile amphibious operations. The mountain barrier of the Alps to the north, and the central spine of the Apennines, create effective obstacles to military movement in all directions on the Italian peninsula.

There are three principal and traditional overland invasion routes across the Alpine barrier: from France along the Mediterranean coast and across the Maritime Alps; from Germany and Austria through the Brenner Pass; and from Yugoslavia through the Ljubljana Gap and the Julian Alps. A number of other passes have been successfully exploited by the innumerable invasion forces that have been attracted to Italy through the course of history.

Hostility has existed in the past because of an irredentist dispute with Yugoslavia involving the Istrian Peninsula, the major Italian city of Trieste, and the Yugoslav city of Rijeka (Fiume), where a mixed population (including about 200,000 Slavs) inhabits a strategic invasion route region. The Osimo Agreements of 1976 set the precise boundary lines between Trieste and the Yugoslavian territory that almost surrounds it, and have effectively solved the Trieste question for the present.

In the past, Italy's Communist party, with approximately 25 percent of the electorate, has appeared to be the nation's most serious internal security problem. However, the party has been increasingly independent of Moscow in recent years, and has cooperated with the moderate Christian Democrats in seeking to provide government stability and to attack Italy's serious economic problems, including very high inflation rates and unemployment. A grave internal problem is the Red Brigades, an extremist, terrorist left-wing guerrilla group, whose maimings and killings of moderate journalists, politicians, labor leaders, and businessmen escalated sharply to forty incidents in 1977 and culminated in the kidnapping and murder of former Christian Democratic premier, Aldo Moro, in 1978. The shootings in 1977 were among 450 terrorist attacks that year by the Red Brigades, other leftists, and rightist extremists. One rightist group is the neo-Fascist New Order party. Concurrently there was a resurgence of Mafia activity, including kidnappings and murders, concentrated in Sicily and the southern province of Calabria, and also many mass demonstrations and strikes. Italy appeared vulnerable to a breakdown in order and possible takeover by an extremist group in 1978, but the murder of Moro served at least temporarily to unite the great majority of Italians in hostility to the Red Brigades and determination to maintain their democratic republic.

Italy's main strategic problem is the protection of maritime lines of communications on which it depends for a very large part of its supply. For this reason Italy is extremely sensitive to what is going on around the Mediterranean and follows with great concern any event which may upset the politico-military balance in that area.

## MILITARY ASSISTANCE

Italy has received no military assistance from the United States since 1968. Partly as a result of the offshore procurement policies of the United States, and partly through Italian and joint allied research and development projects, Italian industry has benefited greatly, and has become a major supplier of American and Italian-designed weapons within the NATO alliance.

## ALLIANCES

Italy is one of the four major contributors of military forces to NATO; Italian forces, together with those of Greece and Turkey, form the southern flank of the alliance. Within the NATO alliance the United States maintains in Italy a small combat force headquarters and the necessary logistical support elements: the South European Task Force, or SETAF. The principal mission of SETAF is to provide nuclear artillery and missile support to Allied Forces, Southern Europe, in Italy. In 1973 the United States opened a submarine base on La Maddalena Island, north of Sardinia.

## ARMY

*Personnel:* 243,000

*Organization:*
    1 armored division
    3 mechanized divisions
    1 independent mechanized brigade
    5 independent motorized brigades
    5 Alpine brigades
    1 airborne brigade
    1 amphibious regiment
    1 missile brigade with one Lance battalion
    4 SAM battalions with HAWK

*Major Equipment Inventory:*
1,700  medium tanks (746 M-47s, 300 M-60s, 654 Leopards)
4,500  APCs (M-106, M-113, M-548, M-577)
        self-propelled guns (M-109 155mm, M-107 175mm)
        howitzers (105mm, 155mm, 203mm)
        antitank guided missiles (Mosquito, Cobra, TOW, SS-11)
        SSM (Lance)
        SAM (HAWK)

*Army Aviation:*
    159 aircraft (40 L-19, 39 L-21, 80 SM-1019)
    377 helicopters (70 AB-47, 36 AB-204, 99 AB-205, 141 AB-206, 26 CH-47C, 5 A-109)

*Reserves:* About 550,000 trained reservists are available to bring active units to full combat strength, to create new units, or to act as replacements.

## NAVY

*Personnel:* 42,000 (including marines)

*Major Units:*
    10 submarines (2 Sauro class; 4 Toti class; 2 Tang class; 2 Guppy class; SS)
     1 guided missile cruiser (Vittorio Veneto class; CG; Terrier SAMs, 9 ASW helicopters)
     2 guided missile cruisers (Andrea Doria class; CG; Terrier SAMs; 4 ASW helicopters)
     4 guided missile destroyers (2 Audace class; 2 Impravido class; DDG; Tartar SAMs)
     3 destroyers (1 San Giorgio class; 2 Impetuoso class; DD)
     3 guided missile frigates (Lupo class; FFG; Otomat SSMs, Seasparrow SAMs)
    10 frigates (2 Alpino class; 4 Bergamini class; 4 Centauro class; FF)
     4 patrol escorts (De Cristofaro class; PG; 3-inch guns)
     4 patrol ships (PGF)
     6 motor torpedo boats (PT)
     3 fast patrol boats (PB)
     2 missile attack boats (PTG; Sparviero class; Otomat SSMs)
     4 fleet minesweepers (MSF)
    31 coastal minesweepers (MSC)
    10 inshore minesweepers (MSI)
     2 tank landing ships (LST)
     5 auxiliary ships
   175 service craft
     1 marine infantry battalion

ITALY
CONIC PROJECTION
SCALE OF MILES
0  20  40  60  80  100  120
SCALE OF KILOMETERS
0  20  40  60  80  100  120
Capitals of Countries _____ ☆
Regional Capitals _____ ◉

Copyright by C. S. HAMMOND & Co., N.Y.

12° Longitude East of Greenwich 14°

*Naval Aviation:*
   64 ASW helicopters (27 AB-204 and 13 A-106 embarked; 24 SH-3D shore based)

*Principal Naval Bases:* La Spezia, Naples, Taranto, Ancona, Brindisi, Genoa, Leghorn, Augusta, Venice

*Reserves:* 116,000 men available for rapid mobilization.

## AIR FORCE

*Personnel:* 70,000

*Organization and Major Aircraft Types:*
   3 air regions (headquartered at Rome, Milan, and Bari)
   6 fighter-bomber squadrons (1 with 18 F-104-G, 3 with 54 F-104-S, and 2 with 36 G-91-Y)
   3 light attack/reconnaissance squadrons with 54 G-91-R
   6 AWX squadrons with 72 F-104-S
   3 fighter/reconnaissance squadrons with 54 RF-104-G
   3 maritime reconnaissance squadrons, 2 with 14 Atlantique and 1 with 8 S-2 Tracker
   1 ECM reconnaissance squadron with 6 PD-808
   3 transport squadrons (2 with 28 C-119 [being replaced by G-222] and 1 with 12 C-130 Hercules)
   2 SAR squadrons with 11 HU-16 aircraft and 15 AB-204 helicopters
   10 training squadrons (TF-104-G, G-91-T, MB-326, P-166-M aircraft and AB-47, AB-204 helicopters)
   8 SAM groups (Nike-Hercules)

*Equipment on Order:* 44 G-222, 20 SF-260, and 20 HH-3F helicopters

## PARAMILITARY

There is an 85,000-man Carabinieri. This superbly trained force performs internal security, frontier guard, and military police duties. The Carabinieri should not be considered generally available to reinforce the army; however, as demonstrated in World War II, the combat potentialities of this corps are probably superior to any comparable number of army infantry troops.

# IVORY COAST

## Republic of the Ivory Coast

## POWER POTENTIAL STATISTICS

Area: 124,503 square miles

Population: 7,365,000
Total Active Regular Armed Forces: 4,540 (0.06% population)
Gross National Product: $6.7 billion ($940 per capita)
Annual Military Expenditures: $142.7 million (2.13% GNP)
Electric Power Output: 1.2 billion kwh
Merchant Fleet (ships 1,000 tons and over): 19 ships; 151,000 gross tons
Civil Air Fleet: 20 major transport aircraft

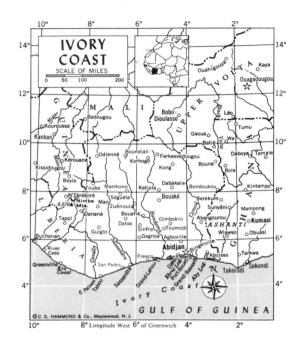

## POLITICO-MILITARY POLICIES AND POSTURE

The elected president is head of government, as well as chief of state and commander in chief of the armed forces. President Houphouet-Boigny, one of Africa's most distinguished statesmen, has ruled the country since independence in 1960. There is constitutional separation of powers between the elected executive, the National Assembly, and the judiciary.

The country is committed to a paramilitary civic action effort in support of nation building. The *Service Civique* and a youth organization promote literacy, modern agricultural methods, basic technical skills, health and sanitation, and social services. The armed forces, however, have not been performing a civic action role. Military service is compulsory but selective—six months in the army or two years in the *Service Civique*.

Ivory Coast has enjoyed relative internal stability since its independence. Several cabinet ministers and army officers were arrested in 1963 for plotting against the government, but there have been no overt rebellious acts. President Houphouet-Boigny is a member of the Baoule tribe, largest in the country, and other tribes fear its domination. Should the president die in office, transfer of power is likely to be contested. Another potential source of trouble is the fact that about one-quarter of the population are recent immigrants from neighboring states, attracted by the burgeoning economy.

There appears to be no significant external threat. The radical leaders of Ghana and Guinea were evidently plotting to overthrow Houphouet-Boigny until Nkrumah was deposed in 1966. Subsequently, the new government in Ghana professed its friendship. Guinea, after a brief threat to cross Ivory Coast to restore the radical regime in Ghana apparently restricts itself to vitriolic denunciations of Ivorian "submission to neocolonialism."

For its own part Ivory Coast adheres to the principle of nonintervention in the internal affairs of other African states and subscribes to an orderly approach to African unity rather than an early continental union. Houphouet-Boigny has strongly condemned Communist-supported subversive efforts in Africa. He has supported French intervention in Zaire (1977 and 1978) and Mauritania (1978) as essential to counter what he views as Soviet imperialism. Relations with the USSR were broken in 1969 following student unrest in Ivory Coast. No ties have ever been established with China. Unlike most African states, Ivory Coast has friendly relations with Israel and a moderate policy toward South Africa.

Ivory Coast has the second highest per capita GNP (after Gabon) and the most highly developed economy in black Africa. Close military and economic ties have been maintained with France since independence in 1960, and French developmental assistance is largely responsible for Ivory Coast's growth and relative prosperity. Mutual defense and military assistance agreements relate to internal security, base rights, transit and overflight privileges, and military training and aid. Over 30,000 Frenchmen are in Ivory Coast in business and in advisory posts. France maintains an air and naval base at Port Bouet. About 500 French troops are stationed in the country. In October 1976, French and Ivorian army and air force units held joint exercises near Bouake. Ivory Coast supports the concept of a French-backed Pan-African or West African military force.

The United States provided $158,000 in military aid through 1977, and fifty students have been trained in the MAP. Israel has had a training mission in Ivory Coast since 1963 with the *Service Civique,* and with a women's army unit.

Ivory Coast is a member of the OAU, and was instrumental in furthering the discussions that led to forming the OCAM in 1965. It is a member of the *Conseil de l'Entente* with Niger, Upper Volta, Dahomey, and Togo. Ivory Coast has also joined the Economic Community of West African States (ECOWAS) and the West African Economic Community (CEAO). CEAO members—Ivory Coast, Senegal, Mali, Mauritania, Upper Volta, and Niger—signed a nonaggression and mutual assistance pact in 1977.

The army numbers 4,000 and is organized into three infantry battalions, one armored squadron, one reconnaissance squadron, one paratroop company, two artillery batteries with 105mm howitzers and 40mm antiaircraft guns, and one engineer company. Reserves number from 12,000 to 15,000 men. Equipment is French and includes five AMX-13 light tanks, armored cars, and infantry heavy weapons. The 240-man navy operates three patrol craft (PC) with short-range SSMs; six patrol boats (PB); and three landing craft. Seaports are Abidjan, Sassandra, Tabou, and a new port in the southwest, San Pedro. The 300-man air force operates seven light transports (four Broussard, one C-45, one Falcon, one Aero Commander), three C-47 transports, five helicopters (four Alouette II and one Puma), and some trainers. Principal airfields are at Port Bouet (Abidjan), Bouake, Man Daloa, Sassandra, Korhogo, Tabou, and Odienne.

The gendarmerie is 2,000 strong. The *Service Civique* and the youth organization receive military training, but their strengths and the extent to which they are armed are not known. There is reputed to be an armed militia of loyal party militants created for the purpose of ensuring an orderly transfer of power within the party in the event of the president's death. Its strength is not known.

# JAMAICA

## POWER POTENTIAL STATISTICS

Area: 4,411 square miles
Population: 2,217,000
Total Active Regular Armed Forces: 2,000 (0.09% population)
Gross National Product: $3.4 billion ($1,610 per capita)
Annual Military Expenditures: $26.6 million (0.78% GNP)
Fuel Production: Refined Petroleum Products: 1.17 million metric tons
Electric Power Output: 2.6 billion kwh
Merchant Fleet (ships 1,000 tons and over): 1 ship; 6,000 gross tons
Civil Air Fleet: 10 jet transports

JAMAICA
SCALE OF MILES
0 10 20 30 40 50

© C. S. HAMMOND & Co., Maplewood, N. J.

Longitude West of Greenwich

## POLITICO-MILITARY POLICIES AND POSTURE

Jamaica is an independent nation (since 1962) within the Commonwealth, with a governor general representing the sovereign. The prime minister also holds the portfolio of minister of defence, and commands the Jamaica Defence Force through the major general.

Jamaica endorses all efforts to ensure the stability and security of the Western Hemisphere. In international affairs Jamaica's policy is that of nonalignment, while internally the philosophy is democratic socialism. Jamaica, with Barbados and Guyana, has an agreement to protect an independent Belize. Jamaica is a member of the OAS, CARICOM, and SELA.

Jamaica is the world's second largest producer of bauxite and alumina, and has a policy of increased public sector involvement in bauxite processing. This is also the case in the tourist industry, the second largest foreign exchange earner. Jamaica's foreign exchange position is crucial to the country's economic health, and strict monetary restrictions have been introduced.

The initial outfitting of the army upon independence was British; some specialist training is still done in the United Kingdom. Jamaica has received $1.1 million in military assistance since 1950 from the United States. Eleven students have been trained under the MAP.

The Jamaica Defence Force numbers 2,000 and is organized as two infantry battalions and headquarters and supporting units. There is also one reserve infantry battalion. The air wing operates seven helicopters (Bell 206B and 212) and seven light fixed-wing aircraft (Cessna, Islander, Twin Otter, etc.) for coastal patrol, reconnaissance, and liaison. It is headquartered at Up Park Camp, Kingston. There are international airports at Palisadoes (Kingston) and Montego Bay. The Coast Guard is based at Kingston and operates six patrol boats (PB).

There is an air wing and a Coast Guard Reserve. Including the constabulary, armed personnel would total 7,676.

# JAPAN

## POWER POTENTIAL STATISTICS

Area: 143,574 square miles
Population: 115,493,000
Total Active Regular Armed Forces: 255,446 (0.22% population; authorized 0.24%)
Gross National Product: $685 billion ($6,010 per capita)
Annual Military Expenditures: $9.5 billion (1.39% GNP)
Crude Steel Production: 107.4 million metric tons
Iron Ore Production: 770,000 metric tons
Fuel Production:
    Coal: 18.4 million metric tons
    Crude Oil: 580,000 metric tons
    Refined Petroleum Products: 228.6 million metric tons
    Natural Gas: 2.8 billion cubic meters
    Manufactured Gas: 6.5 million cubic meters
Electric Power Output: 537 billion kwh
Nuclear Power Production: 17,000 megawatts
Merchant Fleet (ships 1,000 tons and over): 1,846 ships; 36.5 million gross tons
Civil Air Fleet: 241 major transport aircraft

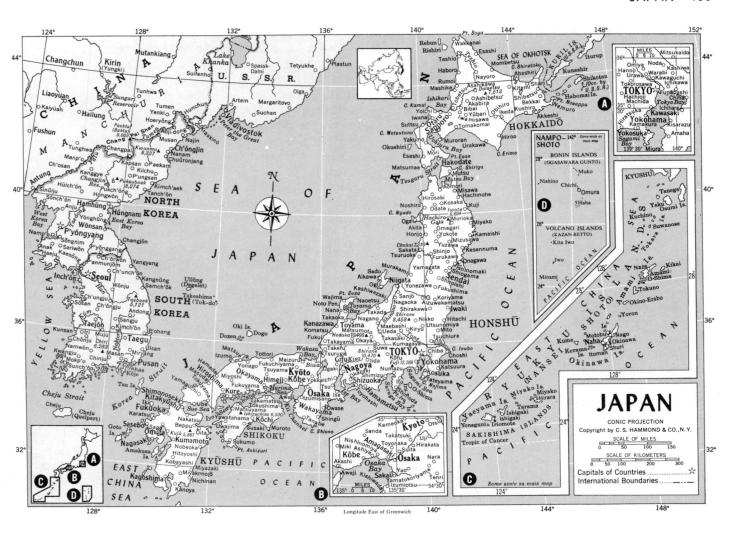

## DEFENSE STRUCTURE

Japan is a constitutional monarchy, with a parliamentary government. The prime minister exercises supreme civilian authority over the armed forces—which in Japan are referred to collectively as the Self Defense Forces. He does this through the Japan Defense Agency, which is directly under his office and is not a cabinet ministry, although its director general functions in the same way as the minister of defense in other governments. There are formal party and cabinet bodies that examine and act upon major military proposals, and a central, integrated military staff, serving the director general, to coordinate the plans and operations of the otherwise independent Self Defense Forces.

## POLITICO-MILITARY POLICY

Japan's basic military policy is to assure its independence and territorial integrity by the maintenance of forces solely for defensive purposes. It relies strongly on its firm mutual security treaty with the United States, ratified in 1960 for a period of ten years, after which either side could denounce it with one year's notice. This is a reflection of the Constitution of May 1947, approved by the American occupation authorities under Gen. Douglas MacArthur, which rejects war or the threat or use of armed force as instruments of national policy. It quite clearly represented the views of a majority of the Japanese people in the immediate years after World War II.

In July 1950, when American forces in Japan had been

greatly reduced by movement to Korea, General MacArthur authorized the establishment of a National Police Reserve of some 75,000 men. In 1952, when the Japanese–United States treaties became effective, the force was reorganized to include a 110,000-man National Self Defense Force and a Maritime Self Defense Force of some 7,590. From these beginnings, and with much debate at every step, the Japanese Defense Agency has grown to its present size.

The members of the Self Defense Forces are considered to be civil servants; there is no separate military legal authority such as is found in the armed forces of practically every other nation in the world. Crimes or offenses committed by Japanese military men are tried in civilian courts.

There is no conscription, which is further evidence of the firmness of Japanese intentions to avoid anything that could be construed as militarism. Enlistment in the Self Defense Forces is entirely voluntary. Only a very small proportion of the civilian population has had any military experience since World War II.

Consistent with its general policy pattern, and also reflecting its experience as the only nation to have suffered atomic attack, Japan has consistently refused to consider the development of nuclear weapons. Japanese scientists, however, are active in research on uses of nuclear energy for peaceful purposes. The emergence of a nuclear capability in Communist China has forced some reexamination of weapons policy in Tokyo. There have been some tentative suggestions that Japan might find it legal under the Constitution and desirable for defense to have some purely defensive nuclear weapons, but this idea has not gained great support. The final decision is not likely to be made soon, and will depend in part on U.S. involvement in East Asia.

The Japanese people are ambivalent about military power as an instrument of national policy. On one hand they feel some disquiet over the fact that their current influence is not commensurate with their position as the third largest economic power in the world. On the other hand, they suffered massive defeat in World War II; they uniquely know the meaning of nuclear weapons, and in the climate of today's weapons and power arrays they perceive the frightening vulnerability of their supply lines and homeland. Furthermore, low defense expenditure permits the application of most of Japan's GNP to maintain the phenomenal rate of growth of the economy.

## STRATEGIC PROBLEMS

Today, as during and before World War II, Japan's greatest strategic weakness is the poverty in material natural resources. Save for coal, Japan is dependent upon imports for almost all of the raw materials required for its mighty industrial complex. The worldwide energy crisis has had a particularly heavy impact on Japan, relying as it does on oil imported from Arab nations for 42 percent of total requirements, and on imports in general for 99.7 percent of consumption. In addition almost all of the iron and copper needs of Japanese industry come by sea. Although Japan responded quickly to demands of Arab states for support in their quarrel with Israel in 1973, and has been rewarded with some assurance regarding supply, the steep rise in price threatens Japan's economic position. And Japan remains vulnerable to future Arab demands. Japan is particularly concerned about maintaining a friendly situation in South Korea and is uneasy about the possibility that U.S. troops will be withdrawn.

Another vulnerability is the concentration of the Japanese population and of the industrial complex. This concentration was a major factor in the successful American strategic bombing of Japan in 1945. The Japanese heartland is within easy range of air bases and missile bases in Siberia, North Korea, and Communist China, to say nothing of missile submarines in the waters surrounding the Japanese islands. Japan's recent installation of a comprehensive air defense system can only partially offset this severe vulnerability. Terrorism has become a significant problem within Japan, with both rightist and leftist groups active in opposition to the government.

## MILITARY ASSISTANCE

Since the establishment of the first Police Reserve Force in 1950, the United States has provided Japan with $855 million in military aid, mostly in the form of weapons. Because of Japan's well developed economy, U.S. military assistance has been mainly in terms of permitting Japan to purchase American weapons and equipment, and to develop local industrial facilities for the continued production of such material. At the same time, the United States has maintained a small military advisory group in Japan, to assist the Self Defense Forces in becoming familiar with American equipment and the techniques of employing it. Also, over 15,000 Japanese men have been sent to the United States for schooling and training.

## ALLIANCES

Japan's only foreign alliance is that with the United States under the Treaty of Mutual Cooperation and Security. It provides not only for U.S. military assistance to Japan, but also for the maintenance of a number of U.S. military bases that were originally established as part of the U.S. occupation of Japan after World War II. In 1970 Japan announced its intention to continue the treaty in force indefinitely. The question of Okinawa was deferred until 1971, when a treaty was signed calling for the reversion of the Ryukyus to Japanese sovereignty by 1972. Under its terms, the United States retains certain bases. Nuclear weapons have been withdrawn, not to be replaced without consultation between the two parties.

## ARMY (Ground Self Defense Force)

*Personnel:* 168,871

*Organization:*

- 5 army areas; 2–4 divisions per army; headquarters at Sapporo, Sendai, Tokyo, Itami (near Osaka), Kumamoto
- 12 infantry divisions (7,000–9,000 men per division)
- 1 mechanized division
- 1 airborne brigade
- 1 independent artillery brigade and two independent artillery groups
- 1 helicopter brigade
- 5 independent engineer brigades
- 1 signal brigade
- 2 SAM brigades (Hawk) and 2 SAM groups (Hawk)

*Major Equipment Inventory:*

- 800 light and medium tanks (M-24, M-41, M-4, M-47, Type 61, and Type 74)
- 650 APCs (M-113, Type 60, SU, and SX)
- 64 heavy artillery pieces (203mm howitzers)
- 250 medium artillery pieces (including 155mm self-propelled guns)
- 580 light artillery pieces (mostly 105mm howitzers) self-propelled antitank guns (SS-4 twin 106mm recoilless rifles)
- 50 antiaircraft pieces SAMs (Hawk)
- 140 light aircraft (LM-1, LM-2, O-1, T-34)
- 252 helicopters (50 OH-6, 40 H-13, 90 UH-1, 28 H-55, 42 V-107)

*Reserves:* There are approximately 39,000 trained, organized reservists.

## NAVY (Maritime Self Defense Force)

*Personnel:* 42,000

*Major Units:*

- 16 diesel submarines (7 Uzushio class; 5 Ooshio class; 4 Hayashio class; SS)
- 3 guided missile destroyers (2 Tachikaze class, with Tartar and Standard RIM SAMs; 1 Amatsukaze class, with Tartar; DDG)
- 2 ASW helicopter destroyers (Haruna class; DDH; 3 helicopters)
- 11 destroyers (4 Takatsuki class, each with 2 HSS-2 ASW helicopters; 3 Murasame class; 2 Akizuki class; 2 Harukaze class; DD)
- 16 frigates (all under-armed destroyers with 3-inch guns: 6 Yamagumo class; 3 Minegumo class; 7 Ayanami class; FF)
- 15 light frigates (4 Chikugo class; 4 Isuzu class; FFL)
- 15 submarine chasers (PCS)
- 5 motor torpedo boats (PT)
- 10 patrol boats (PB)
- 3 mine countermeasures support ships (MCS)
- 30 coastal minesweepers (MSC)
- 6 minesweeping boats (MSB)
- 6 tank landing ships (LST)
- 10 auxiliary ships
- 50 service craft
- 38 S-2 ASW patrol aircraft (3 squadrons)
- 86 P-2 patrol bomber/ASW aircraft (4 squadrons)
- 3 US-1 rescue flying boats
- 15 PS-1 ASW flying boats
- 68 helicopters (60 HSS-2 + 8 Vertol 107; 4 squadrons, one for minelaying)

*Major Naval Bases:* Omimoto, Yokosuka, Maizuru, Kure, Sasebo

## AIR FORCE (Air Self Defense Force)

*Personnel:* 44,575

*Organization:*

- 4 regional commands: Northern Air Defense Force, Central Air Defense Force, Western Air Defense Force, Southwestern Composite Air Division
- 3 fighter-bomber squadrons (F-86)
- 6 fighter-interceptor squadrons (F-104)
- 4 fighter-interceptor squadrons (F-4)
- 1 fighter/reconnaissance squadron (RF-4E and RF-86)
- 1 transport wing (YS-11, C-1)
- 4 training wings (T-34, T-1, T-33, T-2)
- 1 rescue wing (T-34, MU-2, V-107)
- 5 SAM battalions (Hawk)
  Base Air Defense Ground Environment System (BADGES): a centralized, computerized air defense system with 4 command centers and 24 radar stations

*Major Aircraft Types:*

- 491 combat aircraft
  - 299 fighters (74 F-4, 225 F-86)
  - 174 F-104 fighter-interceptors
  - 4 RF-86 fighter/reconnaissance aircraft
  - 14 RF-4E fighter/reconnaissance aircraft

430 other aircraft
    32  transports (13 YS-11, 19 C-1)
   356  trainers (57 T-1, 185 T-33, 83 T-34, 31 T-2)
    15  Mu-2 light transport/utility
    27  helicopters (7 S-62, 20 V-107)

*Equipment on Order:* F-4, T-2, F-1 aircraft

*Major Air Bases:* Matsushima, Hofu, Tsuiki, Hama-matsu, Chitose, Miho, Komaki, Iruma, Hyakuri, Komatsu, Naha (Okinawa), Misawa, Shizuhama, Ashiya, Nyutabaru, Gifu

## COAST GUARD (Maritime Safety Agency)

*Personnel:* 11,200

*Major Units:*
    55  patrol ships (PGF)
    25  patrol craft (PC)
    50  patrol boats (PB)
   155  roadstead patrol boats (PBR)
     6  auxiliary ships
   160  service craft
    34  aircraft

# JORDAN

## The Hashemite Kingdom of Jordan

## POWER POTENTIAL STATISTICS

Area: 37,297 square miles*
Population: 3,008,000
Total Active Regular Armed Forces: 68,800 (2.3% population)
Gross National Product: $1.9 billion ($870 per capita)
Annual Military Expenditures: $266 million (14% GNP)
Fuel Production: Refined Petroleum Products: 1.3 million metric tons
Electric Power Output: 700 million kwh
Civil Air Fleet: 15 major transport aircraft

## DEFENSE STRUCTURE

The king exercises principal political and military authority in this constitutional monarchy. A constituent assembly of both appointed and elected members renders advice to the appointed cabinet. The king is in fact, as well

*Includes West Jordan, approximately 2,185 square miles, occupied by Israel since June 1967.

as nominally, the commander in chief of the armed forces. He exercises his administrative authority generally through the minister of defense, but retains a direct, personal command relationship with the Jordan Arab Army.

In addition to the Jordan Arab Army, the armed forces include the Royal Air Force and a small Royal Navy, which is an integral part of the army. The Public Security Force is under the Ministry of Interior, but is operationally subordinate to the army, and during war is part of the military service.

### POLITICO-MILITARY POLICY

Military service, based on conscription, is for three years.

Since its establishment as an independent kingdom in 1946, the Hashemite Kingdom of Jordan has been a conservative pro-Western Arab state. The people share the general Arab hostility toward Israel. Jordan's military policy, like its foreign policy, has been to a considerable degree ambivalent. On the one hand, in company with its Arab neighbors, Jordan's policy is to be ready for defense against possible Israeli aggression while at the same time preparing for an ultimate offensive war to regain occupied territories. On the other hand, Jordan has sought (certainly indirectly, and possibly directly) to reach some sort of accommodation with Israel, probably with the ultimate aim of accepting and diplomatically recognizing Israel's presence in the region formerly known as Palestine, and probably with some compromise sharing of sovereignty over the now-occupied West Bank.

The Arab Summit Conference in Rabat, Morocco, in 1974 relieved the Hashemite monarch of his responsibility to negotiate with Israel concerning the status of a Palestinian homeland. The conference endorsed the Palestine Liberation Organization (PLO) to act for Palestinian interests in the conflict with Israel.

British influence has been strong in the armed forces, because of the long period of British control. British officers organized and trained the Arab Legion, predecessor of the Jordan Arab Army, and British doctrine and staff organization have carried over.

The army's logistical system is modern and effective. Growing stocks of U.S. arms, equipment, and spare parts, and adoption of U.S. record and maintenance procedures have made it increasingly American in character. All weapons and major equipment for the armed forces are imported.

The most important source of officers is the Royal Military Academy in Amman. It offers a two-year course of military and academic subjects. The Royal Staff College, also in Amman, offers a two-year course for the higher education of selected officers. In addition, the armed forces rely on foreign staff and technical schools for specialized training.

The Bedouin inhabitants of the area east of Amman continue to be the most numerous element in the armed forces, particularly in the infantry armored units. Palestinian Arabs are predominant in the National Guard, technical services, and air force.

Jordan, along with Syria, supports a non-PLO Palestine Liberation Army, one battalion of which is stationed in Jordan, near Amman.

## STRATEGIC PROBLEMS

The principal strategic problem for Jordan is the threat to its viability as a nation as a result of the loss of West Jordan (the richest region of the country) to Israel in June 1967. This region may be returned to Jordan in some eventual peace settlement, but meanwhile the economic and political strains on Jordan are tremendous.

Related to the problem of the future of West Jordan is the question of the orientation of the total population. Almost half are native inhabitants of West Jordan. Nearly 700,000 are refugees, or children of refugees, from those portions of Palestine that became incorporated in the boundaries of Israel in 1948–49. Most of the refugees are militant in their hatred of Israel, and in their incitement of Arab action to destroy Israel and to permit them to return to their ancestral homes in an Arab Palestine. With some significant exceptions, the refugees feel little loyalty to Jordan or to its monarch. The loyalty and support of the Palestinian Arab inhabitants of eastern Jordan have probably increased somewhat as they have adapted

themselves to and gained positions in the kingdom.

Because of the anti-Israel militancy of a majority of Jordan's inhabitants, the government was long forced to permit the establishment of guerrilla bases near the Jordan River, from which raids were periodically mounted against Israel and Israeli-occupied West Jordan. The presence of these bases, and the continuation of the raids, provoked Israel to frequent retaliation, which neither the Jordanian armed forces nor the guerrillas could oppose effectively.

Government attempts to curb guerrilla activities led in 1969 and 1970 to clashes between government forces and Palestinian commandos and resulted, in September of 1970, in complete defeat of the commandos, and reestablishment of government control throughout the country. During this fighting Syrian troops crossed into Jordan, apparently intending to link up with Palestinian commandos and to overthrow the king. They were defeated, however, by combined Jordanian air and armored units; fear of Israeli intervention apparently forced Syria to accept this defeat, and to withdraw from Jordan.

Jordan did not open a front against Israel at their common border during the October 1973 war, but did send Jordanian army units to fight under Syrian command on the Syrian front.

Since the 1973 war significant improvements have been made in Jordan's armored and mechanized forces. Work is now in progress in the army and the air force to upgrade air defense.

## MILITARY ASSISTANCE

The United States is Jordan's principal supplier of arms, having replaced the United Kingdom. At the end of 1977, U.S. military aid had reached $236.9 million. Under the MAP, 1,533 students had been trained. The oil-rich Arab states provide financial support. Decisions taken in Khartoum in 1967 and Rabat in 1974 guaranteed that Saudi Arabia, Kuwait, the UAE, and Libya would contribute annual subsidies. Jordan provides military advisers and training to military units of the skeikhdoms of the Arabian Peninsula.

## ALLIANCES

Jordan is a member of the Arab League.

## ARMY

*Personnel:* 62,000

*Organization:*
    2 armored divisions
    2 infantry divisions
    1 mechanized division

1 antiaircraft regiment (Tigercat SAMs, Hawk SAMs)

1 Royal Guards brigade (mechanized)

*Major Equipment Inventory:*
650 medium tanks
150 M-60
300 M-47 and M-48
200 Centurion Mk.5
300 armored cars (Saladin, Ferret)
700 APCs (M-113, Saracen)
200 M-42 Duster self-propelled 40mm antiaircraft guns
100 M-63 Vulcan self-propelled antiaircraft guns recoilless rifles (M-40 106mm)
35 M-55.50 cal. antiaircraft guns
150 light artillery pieces (105mm howitzers and 25-pounder guns; M-52 SP, M-7 SP, M-101 towed)
100 medium and heavy artillery pieces (155mm and 203mm howitzers, M-109 SP, M-44 SP, M-115 towed, M-1A1 towed, M-114 towed)

*Missiles:*
940 TOW 58 antitank launchers
2,500 M-47 Dragon and 380 trackers (antitank)
SAMs: 300 Redeye; 6 batteries of Hawks

*Reserves:* There are over 70,000 trained reservists; mobilization plans and capabilities are unknown.

## NAVY

*Personnel:* 300

*Major Units:* 10 patrol boats (PB)

*Naval Base:* Aqaba

## AIR FORCE

*Personnel:* 6,500

*Organization:*
4 fighter squadrons (3 F-5, 1 F-104)
1 transport squadron (C-130, CASA 212)
1 helicopter squadron (Alouette III, Whirlwind, Scout)

*Major Aircraft Types:*
74 combat aircraft
56 F-5 fighter/fighter-bombers
18 F-104 fighter-interceptors
65 other aircraft
12 transports (4 C-130, 4 CASA 212)
8 light transports (Devon, Dove, Herald, Varsity, and Twin Bonanza)

20 trainers (Hunter, T-37, Bulldog)
25 helicopters (Alouette III, Whirlwind, and Scout)

*Equipment on Order:*
22 F-5 Tiger II

*Air Bases:* Amman, Aqaba, Al Mafraq

## PARAMILITARY

Jordan has an 8,750-man gendarmerie (including the camel-mounted Desert Patrol).

# KENYA

## Republic of Kenya

## POWER POTENTIAL STATISTICS

Area: 224,960 square miles
Population: 15,096,000
Total Active Regular Armed Forces: 7,270 (0.05% population)
Gross National Product: $3.9 billion ($270 per capita)
Annual Military Expenditures: $201.6 million (5.17% GNP)

Fuel Production: Refined Petroleum Products: 2.6
  million metric tons
Electric Power Output: 1.3 billion kwh
Merchant Fleet (ships 1,000 tons and over): 4 ships;
  11,000 gross tons
Civil Air Fleet: 18 major transport aircraft

## POLITICO-MILITARY POLICIES AND POSTURE

The president is commander in chief of the armed forces
which he controls through the minister of defence. The
armed forces are integrated under the commander of the
army, who is also commander, Kenya Military Forces. He
reports directly to the minister of defence without intermediate joint staff organization.

The Kenyan army grew out of three battalions of the
former King's African Rifles, at the time of independence
in 1963. Africanization of the army proceeded much faster
in Kenya than in neighboring Tanganyika and Uganda.
However, British officers still held top command positions
in January 1964, when a strike or mutiny occurred at the
headquarters of the 11th Battalion of the Kenya Rifles near
Nakuru in protest against continued British presence and
also against inadequate pay. At the request of President
Jomo Kenyatta, British forces intervened to suppress the
outbreak. Kenyatta disciplined the mutineers with long
prison sentences, and intensified ongoing efforts to develop
a modern force with professional, nonpolitical elan.

Kenya relies on a voluntary recruitment program for its
armed forces; because of ample manpower it is able to be
rigidly selective. The Kenyan army enjoys a standard of
health and education considerably higher than that existing
in the country as a whole. Service is for nine years.

The foremost defense problem facing Kenya today is
that posed by separatist elements among some 300,000
Somali peoples who are presently living in the northeastern
section of Kenya. Since independence Kenya has been
concerned about Somali ambitions to establish a Greater
Somalia embracing parts of Kenya and Ethiopia. Kenya's
1963 defense treaty with Ethiopia stems from this fear. (On
June 9, 1970, the border with Ethiopia was delineated and
accepted by both countries.) In 1967 Somalia and Kenya
concluded a peace agreement, but periodic border incidents
have occurred.

Kenya expressed support for Ethiopia and provided very
limited nonmilitary logistical support during Ethiopia's
Ogaden conflict with Somalia. However, Kenya remains
concerned over the Marxist nature of the Ethiopian regime.

Relations with Uganda and Tanzania, marked by the
collapse of the East African Community (EAC), have
deteriorated sharply since 1975. Uganda apparently
claimed a part of western Kenya in early 1976. Kenya's
assistance to Israeli commandos and rescued passengers
after the Entebbe raid in July 1976 resulted in reprisals

against Kenyans in Uganda and massing of troops by both
nations along their border. Tensions eased by the end of
the year. In February 1978 the two nations established
bilateral diplomatic relations outside the EAC. Bitter
ideological invective and a commercial war with Tanzania
accompanied the demise of the EAC. The border was
closed early in 1977. Each country seized assets and
expelled citizens of the other during 1977. The two began
reestablishing commercial relations in 1978.

Internal politics have centered mainly around jockeying
within the governing KANU party for succession to the
octogenarian President Kenyatta. Elected to his third five-
year term in 1974, Kenyatta had conducted a government
crackdown on dissidents in Parliament since 1975. The
immediate transition following Kenyatta's death in August
1978 was smooth, with the presidency passing to Daniel
arap Moi, who had served as vice president for almost ten
years. Longer term prospects remained uncertain.

Tensions persist between the dominant Kikuyu tribe and
the Luo, whose most popular leader, Tom Mboya, was
assassinated in 1969. The 1975 assassination of government critic Joshia Mwangi Kariuki appeared government-
inspired and reflected factional strife within the Kikuyu
elite. Though KANU elections were postponed in 1976 and
1977, the government, through the professional Kenya
Police, has maintained order.

Upon independence the Kenyan army, already equipped
by Britain, was given $9.8 million in additional arms and
equipment plus another $23.8 million in military assets,
mainly installations. To establish a navy with patrol craft,
Britain has provided a base at Mombasa, training, and
$3.64 million in equipment. Over 300 British military men
continue on duty with the Kenyan armed forces in a
training role. Kenyans receive training in Britain. Joint
training exercises of British and Kenyan units are held
annually in Kenya. By a 1964 agreement Britain granted
Kenya $140 million in development and military aid.

In addition to British assistance, Kenya has received
aircraft from Canada, and Kenyans have been trained in
Bulgaria, Ethiopia, and Israel. In 1964 some members of
KANU were reported to have received military training in
Eastern European Communist countries and others to
have had guerrilla training in Communist China. Kenya
has received military assistance from the United States of
$1,200,000 since 1975. Training has been given to fifty-one
students.

Kenya is a member of the Commonwealth, the OAU,
and the East African Community. A 1964 agreement with
Britain permits the British army to train in Kenya and the
RAF and RN to use Kenyan bases.

The army of 6,300 is organized as four infantry
battalions, one parachute company, a support battalion,
and one armored reconnaissance platoon. Equipment
includes Saladin armored cars and Ferret scout cars; 81mm

and 120mm mortars and 107mm recoilless rifles. There is a navy of 350 men operating seven patrol craft (PC). The air force of 620 men has ten F-5, four Hunter jet fighters, and six BAC 167 Strikemaster light jet attack aircraft, two C-47, seven Beaver and six Caribou transports, five Bulldog trainers and five Bell 47 helicopters. Major air bases are at Eastleigh (Nairobi), Nanyuki, Embakasi, Nyeri, Mombasa, and Kisumu.

The 11,500-man police force is the largest and best equipped in East Africa. Approximately half perform internal security functions; the force is well trained in riot control and includes an air unit and constabulary-type general service units (1,800 men).

# KOREA, NORTH

## Democratic People's Republic of Korea

### POWER POTENTIAL STATISTICS

Area: 46,768 square miles
Population: 18,421,000
Total Active Regular Armed Forces: 490,000 (2.66% population)
Gross National Product: $10 billion (estimated $590 per capita)
Annual Military Expenditures: $1.27 billion (12.7% GNP)
Crude Steel Production: 2.8 million metric tons
Iron Ore Production: 3.8 million metric tons
Fuel Production: Coal: 35 million metric tons
Electric Power Output: 28 billion kwh
Merchant Fleet (ships 1,000 tons and over): 11 ships; 50,000 gross tons
Civil Air Fleet: 9 piston transports

### DEFENSE STRUCTURE

The Communist leader of The Democratic People's Republic of Korea (DPRK), Premier Kim Il-Sung, has ruled since 1945. He exercises all real power; he heads both the government and party apparatus and is also the supreme commander of all the armed forces. He is assisted by seven vice premiers, one of whom is also minister of defense.

The Ministry of Defense consists of a General Staff, the Main Political Administration (for troop indoctrination), Forces Inspectorates (artillery, engineer, armor, etc.), navy, air force, and Rear Service Administration (logistics). All top Defense Ministry chiefs are members of the Korean

Labor Party (KLP) Central Committee. North Korea is divided into military districts, each headed by a commander and his deputy for political affairs. Nearly all officers in the armed forces are party members. Thus centralized KLP control is assured at all levels of the military organization.

### POLITICO-MILITARY POLICY

The DPRK's overriding aim has been to overthrow the anti-Communist government of South Korea (the Republic of Korea) and to unify the country under a Commuist government. The DPRK came close to achieving this after invading the South in the summer of 1950, but was soon overrun itself until the Chinese Communists intervened in the autumn. The armistice of July 1953 set a demarcation line approximating the original 38th parallel artificial boundary of 1945. Peace talks have been revived from time to time between the two Koreas, but actual peace is no closer than it was when the war ended.

Since the armistice, there have been over 2,000 incidents, most of them in or near the demilitarized zone, presumably aimed at discouraging the United States from maintaining troops in South Korea. Most serious have been the commando attempt in January 1968 to assassinate the ROK president, the seizure of the U.S.S. *Pueblo* later the same month, the shooting down of an American EC-121 electronic reconnaissance aircraft on April 15, 1969, and the murder of two U.S. officers who were trimming trees in the demilitarized zone in August 1976.

Since 1956, the DPRK has indicated an ambition to direct its own policies free of either Russian or Chinese Communist control. Harsh austerity controls and ruthless industrialization have brought the DPRK near this goal. North Korea is no longer totally dependent economically upon Soviet Russia. However, the DPRK is still dependent upon both of its major allies for military and other support. The Pyongyang regime has steered a cautious course through the Sino-Soviet dispute, and currently is pursuing a policy of friendly nonalignment with both Communist giants.

### STRATEGIC PROBLEMS

The DPRK's basic strategic problem is its geographic proximity to a highly armed and hostile non-Communist nation (the Republic of Korea, South Korea (ROK), which regards the North Korean government as an illegal occupier of half of the Korean peninsula). The DPRK is within easy striking range of powerful U.S. aircraft stationed in Japan and Okinawa, as well as nearby aircraft in the ROK. North Korean factories, hydroelectric plants, and population centers are highly concentrated, and such targets are well known to opposing intelligence. The DPRK railroad and road system is highly vulnerable to air attack. The long east and west coasts necessitate maintenance of an active patrol force.

The DPRK faces a continuing strategic and military problem in walking a diplomatic tightrope between the feuding Communist giants who share its northern borders. The DPRK needs Russian backing to discourage incursions from Red China, which touches most of its northern boundary, as well as to provide economic and military support. Friendly relations with the contiguous Chinese People's Republic, which once came to North Korea's rescue, are equally vital. The DPRK still depends on the back-up of nearby Chinese troops in a renewed war with South Korea, for North Korea's population is less than half that of the ROK, and its army, although supported by a stronger air arm, remains numerically inferior.

## MILITARY ASSISTANCE

The principal supporter of the DPRK's large military organization and of its growing economy has been the Soviet Union. Due to this aid, the DPRK was able to mount its nearly successful attack upon the ROK in June 1950. The Soviet Union was also chiefly responsible for rebuilding the DPRK's military strength and war-shattered economy following the July 1953 armistice. Since then, Communist China, which supplied almost a million-man army in the war, has also contributed significantly to DPRK military armaments, although China is incapable of providing the heavy support received from the USSR.

When North Korea began openly supporting Chinese policy in 1963, Soviet Premier Khruschev cut off military and economic aid, which included fuel and parts for the Soviet-supplied MiG jet fighters and Ilyushin bombers. But in 1965, when the DPRK changed its pro-Peking position and drew closer again to the USSR, military aid was renewed and increased, including the supply of antiaircraft missiles.

## ALLIANCES

The DPRK has signed military aid treaties with the Soviet Union and Communist China.

## ARMY

*Personnel:* 420,000

*Organization:*
  2 armored divisions
 23 infantry divisions (3 motorized or mechanized)
  5 independent infantry brigades (probably mechanized or partly mechanized)
  5 independent armored regiments
 20 artillery regiments
    special commando groups (15,000 men)
20–25 SAM battalions (SA-2 Guideline)

*Major Equipment Inventory:*
1,700 medium tanks (T-34, T-54/55, T-59)
  150 light tanks (PT-76)
  200 self-propelled guns (SU-76, SU-100)
6,000 mortars and light and medium guns and howitzers
3,000 heavy artillery pieces (up to 152mm guns)
1,500 antitank guns (82mm RCL, 57mm, 100mm)
3,000 antiaircraft pieces (37mm, 57mm, 85mm, 100mm, and ZSU-5N-2SP guns)
  900 APCs (BTR-40, BTR-152, BA-64)
  300 SAMs (SA-2 Guideline)
   10 FROG SSM

*Reserves:* Approximately 1,000,000 trained reservists

## NAVY

*Personnel:* 30,000

*Major Units:*
 15 submarines (4 Soviet Whiskey class; 4 Romeo class, 7 miscellaneous; SS)
  3 light frigates (Najin class; FFL)
  5 patrol escorts (PGF)
 15 submarine chasers (PCS)
 10 missile attack boats (Komar class with SS-N-2/ Styx SSM; PTG)
  8 missile attack boats (Osa class with Styx SSM; PTG)
160 motor torpedo boats
 20 fast patrol craft (PCF)
 10 patrol craft (PC)
100 patrol boats (PB)
100 landing craft
100 support craft

*Major Naval Bases:* Chinnamp'o (west coast), Wonsan (east coast)

*Reserves:* About 15,000 reservists

## AIR FORCE

*Personnel:* 40,000

*Organization:*
  3 light bomber squadrons (Il-28)
  9 interceptor squadrons (MiG-19/21)
 18 fighter-bomber squadrons (MiG-15/17, Su-7)

*Major Aircraft Types:*
- 630 combat aircraft
- 70 Il-28 light bombers
- 150 MiG-21 interceptors
- 30 MiG-19 interceptors
- 30 Su-7 fighter-bombers
- 50 MiG-15 fighter-bombers
- 300 MiG-17 fighter-bombers
- 350 other aircraft
- 200 transports (An-2, Li-2, Il-12, Il-14)
- 50 helicopters (MI-4, MI-8)
- 100 trainer/support aircraft (Yak-11, Yak-18, MiG-15, Il-28)

*Missiles:* Atoll AAM

*Major Air Bases:* Pyongyang, Pyongyang East, Taechon, Wonsan, Pyong-ni, Viji, Sunan, Sinuiju, Saamcham

*Reserves:* About 40,000 trained reservists

## PARAMILITARY

There are 35,000 security forces and border guards. A people's militia claims an additional strength of 1,250,000.

# KOREA, SOUTH

## Republic of Korea

## POWER POTENTIAL STATISTICS

Area: 38,031 square miles

Population: 39,206,000

Total Active Regular Armed Forces: 632,000 (1.64% population)

Gross National Product: $31.5 billion ($880 per capita)

Annual Military Expenditures: $3.2 billion (10.16% GNP)

Crude Steel Production: 2.7 million metric tons

Iron Ore Production: 621,000 metric tons

Fuel Production:
  Coal: 16.4 million metric tons
  Refined Petroleum Products: 18 million metric tons

Electric Power Output: 26.5 billion kwh

Nuclear Power Production: 1,200 megawatts

Merchant Fleet (ships 1,000 tons and over): 241 ships; 2.2 million gross tons

Civil Air Fleet: 17 jet, 11 turboprop transports

## DEFENSE STRUCTURE

The Republic of Korea (ROK) has a strong presidential form of government. The ROK president is the constitutional commander of the nation's armed forces; he also heads the State Council (cabinet) which is the highest administrative organ and includes the minister of national defense.

The president is assisted by the National Security Council, of which he is chairman and which includes the prime minister, the ministers of national defense, economic planning, foreign affairs, home affairs, and finance, and the director of the Central Intelligence Agency. The chairman of the Joint Chiefs of Staff also participates in NSC meetings. General control over the armed forces is exercised by the Joint Chiefs of Staff, who are administratively responsible to the national defense minister.

## POLITICO-MILITARY POLICY

The current primary objective of the Republic of Korea (ROK) is to maintain its independence in the face of an ever-present invasion threat from Communist North Korea. A less realistic goal is to overthrow the North Korean regime (Democratic People's Republic of Korea), regarded as the illegal occupier of the north, and reunite the Korean peninsula under the South Korean government. The first policy is strongly supported by the United States. The United Nations, which is pledged to defend the ROK from aggression, also supports Korea's peaceful reunification under UN-supervised free elections, but not by force.

Any such peaceful reunification seems precluded in the foreseeable future. North Korea's independence and military strength are supported by both the Soviet Union and the People's Republic of China. The military establishments of North and South Korea, backed up by alliances with the world's greatest powers, are poised in an uneasy deadlock which neither dares break. High-level discussions between representatives of the two Korean governments in July 1972 were not fruitful for a variety of reasons, all rooted in the almost total distrust that each side feels for the other.

Meanwhile, South Korea seeks to increase its military and economic strength and decrease its dependence on the United States. The 1968 North Korean attempt to kill the ROK president, the capture of the U.S. intelligence ship *Pueblo,* and the shooting down by North Korean aircraft of a U.S. EC-121 aircraft over international seas on April 15, 1969, caused a rapid remodernization of the South Korean and American forces defending the ROK, especially the neglected air arm. The ROK also benefited from its contribution of 50,000 troops in Vietnam, which resulted in increased U.S. aid and promises of profitable reconstruction in South Korea.

The control of all aspects of political activity in the ROK is becoming increasingly severe. The kidnapping from Japan in August 1973 of Kim Dae Juk, a political opponent of the late President Park's, and the subsequent refusal to permit him to go to the United States for an academic appointment, created unfavorable reactions among the ROK's friends, particularly Japan. The extent of political changes following the assassination of President Park in late 1979 is not yet clear.

Military service is compulsory for all physically fit adult males. After completing service (thirty-three months for army and marines, thirty-six months for navy and air force), the individual is automatically a member of the reserve force.

## STRATEGIC PROBLEMS

South Korea's chief strategic vulnerability is the proximity of all ROK targets, including concentrated industries and population centers, to air attacks from North Korea, Communist China, and the Soviet Maritime Provinces. Second is the vulnerability of South Korea to ground infiltration or attack from the north. The ROK has taken energetic steps against continuing North Korean infiltration and sabotage, including special counter-insurgency forces, intensive coastal patrols, and a home guard militia. In view of the strong anticommunism of most South Koreans, and their general support of the ROK government, there is no likelihood of indigenous guerrilla warfare arising, although disturbances are not uncommon. With continued U.S. military commitment and the maintenance of a strong ROK defense structure, the chances of an all-out attack from Pyongyang are slight. Should the Korean War be renewed, there is little possibility of either side mounting a quick knockout blow.

The artificial division of the Korean peninsula in 1945 left the South with the agricultural, unindustrialized part of the country and the less educated and more unskilled part of the population. Movement from rural to urban areas subsequently increased economic problems. In recent years, however, there has been a boom in exports, which has helped to reduce the large gap in balance of payments.

## MILITARY ASSISTANCE

The ROK military forces are totally dependent on U.S. aid. American military assistance from 1946 through 1977 amounted to $4.9 billion. The United States has improved the weapons of the ROK armed services and enlarged and updated the ROK Air Force, which is still far weaker than that of North Korea. More than 34,000 students have been trained under the MAP.

The United States maintains military advisory groups in Korea which equip and train all four ROK services. Most of South Korea's military units are under operational control of the United Nations Command, which is Korea's senior military headquarters. The UN commander is also the commanding general of the U.S. Eighth Army, which has one infantry division, 38th Artillery Brigade (Air Defense), 4th Missile Command (surface-to-surface), and various support units in Korea, numbering 43,000 Americans. More than 100 up-to-date U.S. jets are stationed on five Korean airfields, with at least another 100 in Japan with B-52 bombers in Okinawa. The U.S. Seventh Fleet periodically has a carrier task force patrolling Korean waters.

In 1977 President Carter announced the intention of withdrawing 32,000 U.S. troops from South Korea over a four or five-year period. The announcement proved very unpopular in the United States, and in April 1978 it was announced that the timetable would be considerably slowed, and that withdrawal would be contingent upon transfer of $800 million in military equipment and $275 million in credits to South Korea. By the end of 1978, moreover, there would be seventy-four instead of sixty-two F-4 fighters there.

## ALLIANCES

The continuing ROK-U.S. alliance is embodied in the Mutual Defense Treaty of November 1954, which provides that the parties will consult with each other if threatened by external attack. The pact also states that an armed attack on the Pacific territories controlled by either signatory would be dangerous to the security of the other.

Soviet and U.S. opposition has kept both Koreas out of the United Nations. The ROK is a member of the Asian and Pacific Council (ASPAC), the Economic Commission for Asia and the Far East (ECAFE), the Food and Agriculture Organization of the United Nations (FAO), and the World Health Organization (WHO). The ROK also helped found the Asian Nations Anti-Communist League.

## ARMY

*Personnel:* 560,000

*Organization:*
    2 armies
   19 infantry divisions
    2 armored divisions (armor is also found in
       infantry divisions)
  80 artillery battalions (most with infantry divisions)
    1 SSM battalion (Honest John)
    4 SAM battalions (3 Hawk, 1 Nike-Hercules)
      cadres for 10 divisions

*Major Equipment Inventory:*
  1,200 medium tanks (M-60, M-48, M-47, M-4)

2,400 APCs (M-113)
  80 light tanks (M-3)
  50 armored cars (M-8)
1,400 howitzers (105mm and 155m towed)
  64 203mm howitzers (SP and towed)
  24 155mm guns (towed)
 255 antitank guns (76mm, 90mm, SP)
    recoilless rifle antitank guns (106mm, 75mm,
      57mm)
    rocket launchers (3.5-inch, 66mm LAW)
    mortars (2.2-inch, 81mm, 160mm)
    SAMs (Hawk, Nike-Hercules)
    SSMs (Honest John)
    TOW antitank guided missiles

*Reserves:* There is a trained manpower pool of approximately 1,500,000 men being organized into a militia force for home defense. Currently available for mobilization are personnel and equipment for four tank battalions and ten infantry divisions.

## NAVY

*Personnel:* 20,000

*Major Units:*
  7 destroyers (4 Gearing, 3 Fletcher, 2 Sumner
    class; DD)
  1 frigate (Rudderow class; FF)
  6 patrol ships (Charles Lawrence and Crossley
    class ex-APD; PGF)
  6 submarine chasers (PCS)
 10 missile attack boats (PTG)
 30 patrol boats (PB)
  8 coastal minesweepers (MSC)
  1 minesweeping boat (MSB)
  1 landing ship dock (LSD)
  8 tank landing ships (LST)
 12 medium landing ships (LSM)
  1 utility landing craft (LCU)
  5 auxiliary ships
 15 service craft
  1 ASW squadron (20 S-2)

*Major Naval Bases:* Chinhae, Pusan, Inchon

*Reserves:* There are 30,000 to 35,000 trained reservists

## MARINE CORPS

*Personnel:* 20,000

*Organization:*
  1 division (3 brigades)
  2 independent brigades

*Reserves:* About 60,000 trained reservists

## COAST GUARD (Maritime Safety Agency)

*Personnel:* 11,212

*Major Units:*
  94 patrol ships
 214 patrol craft
  7 surveying vessels
  5 tenders
  5 miscellaneous
 34 aircraft

## AIR FORCE

*Personnel:* 32,000

*Organization:*
 14 fighter-bomber squadrons (7 F-5, 2 F-4, 5 F-86)
  1 fighter reconnaissance squadron (RF-86, RF-5)
  1 transport group (C-46, C-47, C-54 Aero-
    commander)
  1 training group (PL-1, PL-2, O-1, T-28, T-6)

*Major Aircraft Types:*
 364 combat aircraft
 170 F-5 fighter bombers
  54 F-4 fighter bombers
 120 F-86 fighters
  10 RF-5 fighter reconnaissance aircraft
  10 RF-86 fighter reconnaissance aircraft
 328 other aircraft
  55 transports (C-46, Aero Commanders, C-47,
    C-54)
 128 trainer/support aircraft (T-28, T-6, T-33, PL-2,
    O-1)
  95 utility, light reconnaissance aircraft (T-37,
    OV-10, U-17, O-2)
  50 helicopters (H-19, UH-1N, UH-1, SH-3, KH-4)
    Missiles (AAM Sidewinder, Sparrow; ASM,
    Maverick Bullpup)
    On order: 100 Hughes 500, 90 F-16, 6 C-130,
    CH-47

*Major Air Bases:* ROK: Saechon, Chinhae, Osan, Chongju, Taegu, Suwon, and about 10 small strips; USAF: Seoul, Kimpo, Pusan, Kusan, Kananung, Pohang, Chunchon, Pyong-taek, Hoengson

*Reserves:* There are 35,000 trained reservists.

## PARAMILITARY

In addition to the militia force (see above, Army, Reserves), civilians are also being formed into local counterespionage and defense units (based on Israel's example and with the guidance of Israeli advisers).

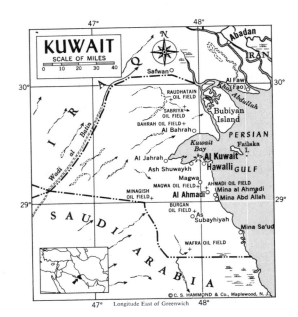

# KUWAIT

## State of Kuwait

## POWER POTENTIAL STATISTICS

Area: 7,780 square miles
Population: 1,241,000
Total Active Regular Armed Forces: 12,000 (0.97%
   population)
Gross National Product: $13.9 billion ($13,080 per
   capita)
Annual Military Expenditures: $845 million (6.08%
   GNP)
Fuel Production:
   Crude Oil: 108.6 million metric tons
   Refined Petroleum Products: 22.3 million metric tons
   Natural Gas: 5.6 billion cubic meters
Electric Power Output: 7 billion kwh
Merchant Fleet (ships 1,000 tons and over): 74 ships;
   1.97 million gross tons
Civil Air Fleet: 18 major transport aircraft

## POLITICO-MILITARY POLICIES AND POSTURE

Kuwait is a constitutional monarchy, but the authority
of the monarch (emir) is close to absolute. In 1976 the
National Assembly was dissolved by the emir because of
the ruling family's serious concern over the left-wing and
communist tendencies of some representatives of labor
groups and a few academicians who were criticizing the
royal family.

Kuwait has one of the highest per capita incomes in the
world. The country is a member of the Arab League.

There is a continuing border dispute with Iraq, which
has sought to expand its very short coastline on the Persian
Gulf by annexing Kuwaiti territory, especially the islands
of Bubiyan and Warbah, which control access to Iraq's
port at Um Qasr.

Kuwait participates in a broad range of financial aid
and investment activities bilaterally, multilaterally through
Arab organizations, and with international institutions.

Kuwait is a member of the Arab League.

## ARMY

*Personnel:* 10,000

*Organization:*
   1 armored brigade
   2 composite brigades (armored/infantry/artillery)

*Major Equipment Inventory:*
   100 medium tanks (50 Chieftain, 50 Centurion)
   100 armored cars (Saladin)
   100 APCs (Saracen)
   20 scout cars (Ferret)
   10 25-pounder artillery pieces
   20 howitzers (M-114, 155mm)
   32 TOW SSM antitank launchers, 1,800 missiles
   14 Hawk SAM batteries, 360 missiles

*Equipment on Order:*
   Hawk SAMs
   M6 tanks

## NAVY (Coast Guard)

*Personnel:* 500

*Major Units:*
   28 patrol boats (PB)
   3 mechanized landing craft (LCM)

## AIR FORCE

*Personnel:* 1,500

*Organization:*
   2 fighter-bomber/fighter-interceptor squadrons
      (Hunter, Mirage I)
   2 ground attack squadrons (A-4)
   1 COIN ground attack squadron (Strikemaster)
   1 helicopter squadron, antitank (Gazelle, with
      HOT missiles)
   1 helicopter squadron (AB-205, AB-206, Whirl-
      wind, Puma, Gazelle)

*Major Aircraft Types:*
    67 combat aircraft
        12 Mirage fighters
        6 Hunter fighter-bombers
        20 A-4 ground attack aircraft
        9 Strikemaster ground attack (COIN) aircraft
        20 Gazelle antitank helicopters with HOT
            missiles
    68 other aircraft
        2 Caribou light transports
        2 C-130 medium transports
        2 DC-9 transports
        42 helicopters (6 AB-205, 4 AB-206, 10 Puma,
            2 Whirlwind, 20 Gazelle)
        20 trainers (Jet Provost, Lightning; in storage)

*Missiles:* 50 SAMs (Hawk)

*Equipment on Order:*
    Mirage fighters
    A-4 ground attack aircraft
    HOT antitank missiles

## PARAMILITARY

A constabulary of 2,000 men provides internal and border security.

# LAOS

## Lao People's Democratic Republic

### POWER POTENTIAL STATISTICS

Area: 91,428 square miles
Population: 3,587,000
Total Active Regular Armed Forces: 46,000 (1.28% population)
Gross National Product: $250 million ($70 per capita)
Annual Military Expenditures: $28 million (11.2% GNP)
Electric Power Output: 295 million kwh
Civil Air Fleet: 1 turboprop, 7 piston transports

### POLITICO-MILITARY POLICY

The present regime in Laos long has been allied with, some believe subordinate to, the ruling party in Vietnam. In attempting to assert its control over the territory called Laos, the government has had difficulty with its own ethnic minorities (primarily the Meo), Lao insurgents (some based in and possibly supported by Thailand), and a large foreign presence (Chinese in the far north and northwest, Vietnamese elsewhere). The Lao government fundamentally is in the position of ruling a state searching for a nation, heavily dependent on outside support. It is increasingly reliant on force to attain its internal objectives and requires the forbearance (Thailand, China) or support (Vietnam, and perhaps Cambodia) of its neighbors to permit it to do so.

### STRATEGIC PROBLEMS

In precolonial times, Laos served as a buffer between growing power centers in Thailand and Vietnam, as well as between an expanding Thai kingdom and China. In more recent times, Laos was a conduit for North Vietnamese expansion south of the 17th parallel, a buffer between China and Vietnam and Thailand and Vietnam, and a pawn between the United States and the USSR (1961–62). Lao governments, lacking the power to impose their will over the territory nominally assigned to them on various (mostly French-drawn) maps, have been unable to control their lands in the passes through the Annamite Cordillera where Vietnamese interests are strong, or the Mekong Valley where the Thais have serious interests. The situation is the same in the north and northeast (with traditional Chinese interest and more recent interposition between Burma and Vietnam). If this were not sufficiently disconcerting, U.S. and USSR intervention in Laos, directly and indirectly, at times has upset delicate local balances.

## ALLIANCES

The current regime in Laos is bound to alliances with Vietnam extending back at least to 1946, and the Vietnamese presence in Laos is pervasive. Indeed, the alliance is so strong as to call into doubt the independent existence of the state except as the Vietnamese may choose to manipulate the government in articulating their policy with respect to other powers.

## ARMY (Liberation Army)

*Personnel:* 44,000

*Organization:*
    60 infantry battalions
     1 artillery regiment (4 batteries)
       support troops

*Major Equipment Inventory:*
       light tanks (M-24 and PT-76)
       armored cars (M-8)
       scout cars (M-3)
       APCs (BTR-40 and M-113)
    60 artillery pieces (105mm and 155mm howitzers, heavy mortars)
       light aircraft (O-1)

## NAVY (of the Liberation Army)

*Personnel:* 500

*Major Units:*
     9 patrol boats (PB; plus 10 in reserve)
     4 mechanized landing craft (LCM; plus 3 in eserve)
     1 cargo transport

## AIR FORCE (of the Liberation Army)

*Personnel:* 1,500

*Major Aircraft Types:*
    72 combat aircraft
       12 MiG-21 fighters
       50 T-28 armed trainers
       10 AC-47 gunships
    50 other aircraft
       10 T-28 trainers
       10 C-47 transports
       10 Beaver and Aero Commander light transports
       10 trainer/support aircraft (U-17, T-41)
       10 helicopters (Alouette II and III, UH-19, Mi-8, H-34)

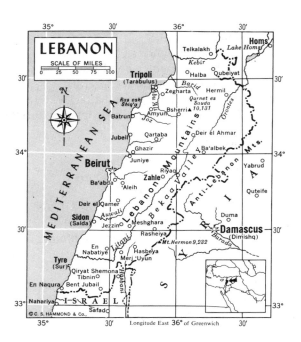

# LEBANON

## The Republic of Lebanon

## POWER POTENTIAL STATISTICS

   Area: 4,015 square miles
   Population: 2,568,000
   Total Active Regular Armed Forces: 11,250* (0.44% population)
   Gross National Product: $3.93 billion** ($1,530 per capita)
   Annual Military Expenditures: $141 million (3,43% GNP**)
   Fuel Production: Refined Petroleum Products: 2 million metric tons
   Electric Power Output: 1.2 billion kwh
   Merchant Fleet (ships 1,000 tons and over): 53 ships; 178,000 gross tons
   Civil Air Fleet: 34 major transport aircraft

## POLITICO-MILITARY POLICIES AND POSTURE

Lebanon has been in a state of severe crisis and turmoil since mid-1975. Many factions must bear a degree of responsibility for the assault made on Lebanese institutions.

---

*Armed forces decreased during the civil war from prewar 15,000; figure given here is for early 1978. Numbers have again declined since then.
**1975 figures for GNP last available

The outlook for this country of proud, confident people, once the center of Middle East commerce and finance, stability, and representative government, is clouded. In the last thirty years, sectarian troubles have brewed close to the surface constantly, yet a delicate balance among diverse ethnic, cultural, social, and religious groups prevailed until the mid-1970s. Periods of tension and inter-ethnic conflict were generally dealt with by the Lebanese themselves, although the United States did act in 1958, in a show of force to support the central government. Since the influx of more than a quarter-million Palestinian refugees following the 1967 Arab-Israeli war, however, foreign intervention and external stimuli have had a strong impact.

In 1975 fighting broke out between Christians and extreme Moslem leftists, who were joined by Palestinian refugees. Intervention by the Syrian army in mid-1976 temporarily reduced sectarian fighting, but deep-seated mistrust and animosity remained from the savage and brutal encounters of the previous year. In the process the Lebanese armed forces virtually disintegrated. Military personnel had largely joined rival militia units.

After the Syrian government sent troops into Lebanon, the Arab League authorized formation of an Arab Deterrent Force (ADF), with the Syrian army as its principal component, joined by troops from other Arab nations. By early 1977 the ADF had restored a semblance of control over most of Lebanon in the name of the central government. However, the fragile truce did not hold. Small-scale terrorism and sectarian conflict continued. The central government made conscientious efforts to restore vital municipal services and industry in and around severely damaged Beirut and undertook to reestablish the nucleus of a security force. For the most part, however, central authority has not been extended throughout the country.

North of Beirut the major Christian elements have consolidated their territory around the town of Jounieh. There is a strong Christian Maronite desire to establish a separate Christian enclave there. However, the most powerful Christian militia, Phalange, and the central government leaders oppose the idea and have thus far prevented an official proclamation of partition. Clashes between these Christian and Syrian troops have added to the horror of Lebanon's strategic catastrophe.

The Israeli military invasion into southern Lebanon in the spring of 1978 was aimed at enlarging the Christian-controlled buffer zone between Israel's northern border and Lebanon's Palestinian-controlled Fatahland (generally along the Litani River). Opinion is divided as to whether the invasion was stabilizing in its effect, or merely exacerbated the bitter conflict tearing the state apart. In any event, several thousand additional inhabitants left their homes and streamed northward. Israel appeared determined not to allow a sizable Palestinian presence back into the south, where PLO military units could threaten Israel's border areas. The United Nations quickly sent an Interim Force in Lebanon (UNIFIL), charged with securing the zone and preventing infiltration of armed Palestinians back into it after Israeli withdrawal across the border.

All that can be said at this point is that the character of Lebanon, as it existed during the previous generation, has changed irretrievably. Syria has obtained a significant degree of influence over the country by virtue of its military presence. The resilient, enterprising nature of the Lebanese people holds out hope that some of the losses the country has suffered may be recouped, providing a degree of calm and stability are restored. However, the large Palestinian presence and ingrained bitter rivalries among Lebanese sects argue against steady progress toward stability. A mood of despair pervades Lebanon's leadership and people.

## MILITARY ASSISTANCE

With the exception of the air force, the armed forces have few remaining materiel assets. The Christian militias and PLO military units have taken over much of the army's equipment. The United States and France were formerly main sources of military assistance.

Lebanon is a member of the Arab League.

## ARMY

*Note:* All armed forces figures are as of early 1976. See discussion above.

*Personnel:* 10,000

*Organization:*
    2 armored battalions
    6 infantry battalions (one motorized)
    3 field artillery battalions
    2 reconnaissance battalions
    1 commando battalion
    1 antiaircraft battalion

*Major Equipment Inventory:*
    40 Centurion Mk 5 medium tanks
    40 AMX-13 light tanks
    18 M-41 light tanks
    48 armored cars (Staghound, Commando, AEC Mk 3)
    24 APCs (M-113, M-706, M-59)
    32 self-propelled antiaircraft guns (M-42)
     6 tank destroyers (M-50 Ontos)
       guns (75mm)
    40 howitzers (122mm, 155mm)
       recoilless rifles (106mm)
 1,050 TOW missiles (18 launchers)

## NAVY

*Personnel:* 250

*Major Units:*
　　4　patrol boats (PB)
　　1　utility landing craft (LCU)

*Naval Base:* Beirut

## AIR FORCE

*Personnel:* 1,000

*Organization:*
　　1　fighter/fighter-bomber squadron (Hunter)
　　1　transport squadron (Dove)
　　1　trainer/support squadron (Bulldog, Magister)
　　1　helicopter squadron (Alouette II/III, UH-1N)

*Major Aircraft Types:*
　　13　combat aircraft
　　　　13　Hunter fighter-bombers
　　51　other aircraft
　　　　12　Mirage fighters (in storage—for sale)
　　　　　3　transports (Dove)
　　　　25　trainer/support aircraft (Bulldog, Magister)
　　　　11　helicopters (Alouette II/III, UH-1N)

*Air Bases:* Beirut (Khalde), Riyaq, Tripoli

## PARAMILITARY

The National Gendarmerie numbers 4,000 men. Other internal security units total about 850 men.

# LESOTHO

## Kingdom of Lesotho

### POWER POTENTIAL STATISTICS

Area: 11,716 square miles
Population: 1,291,000
Total Active Police Forces: 2,500 (0.19% population)
Gross National Product: $315 million ($270 per capita)
Annual Police Expenditures: $3.12 million (0.99% GNP)
Civil Air Fleet: 9 piston transports

### POLITICO-MILITARY POLICIES AND POSTURE

Lesotho, the former British protectorate of Basutoland and homeland of the Basotho people, became independent

in 1966. The king is constitutional monarch; the prime minister is the leader of the majority in the National Assembly and thus head of the government. A power struggle between these two shortly after independence revealed basic factional and ideological divisions within the country. In January 1970, the prime minister, Dr. Jonathan, suspended the constitution and announced a state of emergency, arresting the leaders of the opposition party and placing the king under house arrest. A majority of the College of Chiefs refused to depose the king, and he was instead given permission to leave for the Netherlands. He returned after six months and took a new oath to abstain from involving the monarchy in politics. Dr. Jonathan, in addition to being prime minister, holds the positions of minister of defense and internal security. Although Lesotho belongs to the Commonwealth and the OAU, its external security is completely dependent on friendly relations with South Africa, by which it is totally surrounded.

Both the UN and Britain have warned South Africa not to attempt to annex Lesotho. Nevertheless, Lesotho could be effectively and easily blockaded by South Africa and could offer little resistance to punitive measures directed against any insurgent movements based there. Accordingly, as early as 1965, before independence, attempts to use Lesotho as an insurgent base were broken up by the government, and some political refugees from South Africa were encouraged to leave. Despite Lesotho's open criticism of *apartheid,* its policy of cooperation with South Africa was continued with little prospect for change.

Lesotho is also dependent on South Africa economically: as a source for all imports, as a market for its exports of livestock and animal products, and as employer for 200,000 workers who send home $3 million annually. Lesotho originally received one-half its annual budget from Britain, but recent revenue increases, largely from Lesotho's share in the South Africa Customs Union pool, have made possible a balanced budget. Britain still contributes capital development funds. Mineral exploration has generally been unfruitful, although some diamonds are mined and exploration continues for oil and additional diamond deposits. The only other prospect for earning additional foreign exchange is the Malibamatso (formerly Oxbow) hydroelectric project.

Lesotho increased its polemical attacks on South African racial policies in the mid-1970s and has come into line with the "front-line" presidents. Yet never was Lesotho's dependence on South Africa more evident than in the dilemma posed by Transkei independence in 1976. Lesotho supported the OAU position against recognizing Transkei, which abuts Lesotho's southern border. Transkei required the thousands of Basotho migrant workers who must cross to South Africa through Transkei to carry border permits. Compliance would signify de facto recognition, and Dr. Jonathan instead declared the border closed and requested and received UN aid. Following shooting incidents at border checkpoints, Lesotho announced in 1977 that it would form an army.

# LIBERIA

## Republic of Liberia

## POWER POTENTIAL STATISTICS

Area: 43,000 square miles
Population: 1,761,000
Total Active Regular Armed Forces: 4,200 (0.24% population)

Gross National Product: $923 million ($600 per capita)
Annual Military Expenditures: $8.5 million (0.92% GNP)
Iron Ore Production: 16.9 million metric tons
Fuel Production: Refined Petroleum Products: 499,200 metric tons
Electric Power Output: 980 million kwh
Merchant Fleet (ships 1,000 tons and over): 2,627 ships; 81.85 million gross tons (most of these are foreign-owned and registered under the Liberian flag as a convenience)
Civil Air Fleet: 4 major transport aircraft

## POLITICO-MILITARY POLICIES AND POSTURE

Governmental structure is patterned on that of the United States, with the president commander in chief of the armed forces. Control is exercised through a minister of national defense who directs the chief of staff of the army and the Coast Guard commander.

Government power is centralized. Liberia effectively has been a one-party state (True Whig Party) since 1878. President William Richard Tolbert took office in June 1971 following the death of W. V. S. Tubman, who had been president for twenty-five years. The Honorables, some 25,000 to 50,000 descendants of Afro-American colonizers from the United States, dominate political and economic affairs, at the expense of the interior tribes. This situation provides a potential for instability. Alleged governmental corruption, indebtedness, and lack of economic development despite rich iron and rubber resources, are further causes of unrest. President Tolbert has instituted a series of social, educational, and economic programs aimed at unifying Liberian culture.

Tubman was one of the guiding founders of the OAU; Liberia remains staunchly Pan-Africanist in outlook. It was an original member of the Economic Community of West Africa and has participated in other efforts toward African economic cooperation. President Tolbert has chastised the West for not taking a stronger role in ending minority rule in southern Africa. Liberia has close economic ties with Sierra Leone to its north. The special relationship with the United States, Liberia's largest trading partner, was reaffirmed during the brief visit by President Carter to Monrovia in April 1978.

The U.S. Military Aid Program from 1950 through 1977 has given Liberia $8.8 million in arms and equipment; in fiscal year 1977 MAP totalled $131,000. A small military assistance and advisory group helps with the training of the Liberian forces. From 1950 through 1977, 648 Liberian military students were trained in the United States under MAP. An agreement signed in 1959 provides for consultation if either Liberia or the United States is attacked or threatened.

The army, known as the National Guard, is 4,000 strong, organized into three infantry battalions, one engineer battalion, and a heavy weapons support company. Equipment includes a few armored cars and light artillery pieces and two Cessna trainer and two C-47 transport aircraft. The naval force is the Coast Guard, with 200 men operating four motor boats (PB) and the presidential yacht. The principal base is at Monrovia. There is no air force, but the airports of Robertsfield and Spriggs Payne are near Monrovia.

The armed forces are maintained by voluntary enlistment. However, a law rendering male citizens liable for military service between the ages of sixteen and forty-five years is used to maintain the militia. This paramilitary force, perhaps 20,000 strong, is organized in two divisions, each with two brigades of four regiments. It is lightly armed and used mainly for security in the interior and in border areas.

# LIBYA

## Socialist People's Libyan Arab Jamahiriya

### POWER POTENTIAL STATISTICS

Area: 679,536 square miles

Population: 2,816,000

Total Active Regular Armed Forces: 25,000 (0.89% population)

Gross National Product: $16.6 billion ($6,260 per capita)

Annual Military Expenditures: $439 million (2.64% GNP)

Fuel Production:

Crude Oil: 92.8 million metric tons

Refined Petroleum Products: 2.6 million metric tons

Electric Power Output: 2.1 billion kwh

Merchant Fleet (ships 1,000 tons and over): 24 ships; 830,000 gross tons

Civil Air Fleet: 39 major transport aircraft

### DEFENSE STRUCTURE

In March 1977 the Libyan government was reorganized, and the country's name was changed. Abolished were the Revolutionary Command Council (RCC) and the Constitution established after the 1969 coup that deposed King Idris. The general secretariat of the General People's Congress, headed by Secretary General (formerly president) Colonel Qadhafi, replaced the RCC. Some members of the RCC have been made members of the secretariat. The cabinet was replaced by the General People's Committee. Quadhafi continues to rule by decree, with the army and security services as his power base.

### POLITICO-MILITARY POLICIES

The 1969 coup signaled an immediate change in the former kingdom's relatively moderate stance within the Arab League. The RCC lost no time in announcing that it was in full support of Egyptian President Nasser's anti-Israel policies and that it planned to achieve a socialist society.

Qadhafi has become something of a leader in inter-Arab affairs, pushing for the use of oil to exert stronger pressure on the United States and other Western powers to stop support of Israel. With promises of economic aid he has also persuaded five black African states (Uganda, Niger, Chad, Mali, and Burundi) to break diplomatic relations with Israel. Qadhafi's long-term potential for Arab and African leadership has been diminished, however, by his reputation for unpredictable and sometimes imprudent statements and actions.

As early as September 17, 1969, Libya began to cut former economic and military aid ties with the United States and the United Kingdom. Late that year Libya turned to France and the Soviet Union for military assistance. France agreed to sell 110 Mirage 5 aircraft, electronic equipment, and tanks. Arms shipments from the USSR began in July 1970.

Libya's principal strategic importance derives from its modest yet significant distribution of high-quality, low-sulfur crude oil to Europe. Its reserves are also modest, but are more than adequate to insure the under-populated country abundant revenue in excess of its absolute needs. Libya has either completely nationalized or gained majority control of the oil companies extracting its oil.

Libya has been involved increasingly, both overtly and covertly, in support of international radicals and terrorists. Libya's current (1978) support of Chadian rebel tribal elements may well result in Libyan annexation of the northern portion of Chad. Tunisia has accused Libya of assisting terrorists there, and in May 1978 Zaire charged Libya with supporting the rebel invasion of Shaba Province. Libya's aid to terrorists and insurrectionists has included assistance to Palestinian extremists, terrorist groups in Spain, the Moro movement in the Philippines, and probably the Irish Republican Army.

Underlying much of Qadhafi's activity are two basic goals: Arab unity and anti-Zionism that seeks the elimination of Israel from the region. His attempts at Arab unity have all ended in failure, but this has not discouraged him. Unions of Libya with Tunisia, Egypt, Syria, and Algeria have been proposed.

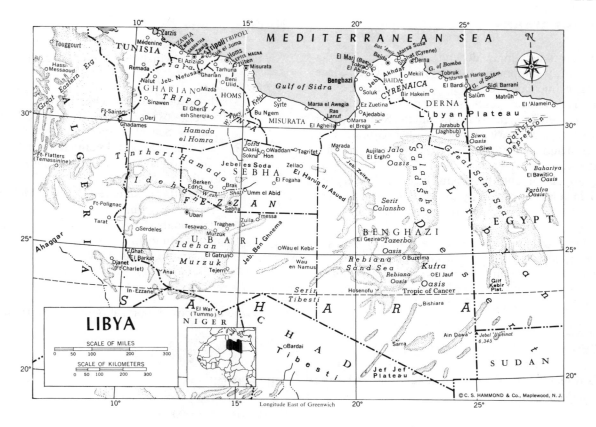

Qadhafi views old regimes as tired and decrepit. He has attempted to overthrow Moroccan King Hassan, Egypt's President Sadat, Tunisia's Prime Minister Nouira, and Sudan's President Numayri. Qadhafi believes that the replacement of these leaders with regimes favorable to him would facilitate Arab union.

Qadhafi seeks an influential role in Arab military matters and a prominent position in Mediterranean and African affairs. To this end he is acquiring large quantities of modern armaments, utilizing the Soviet Union as a primary, but not exclusive, supplier. Although Libya's armed forces are poorly trained and lack experienced leaders, staffs, and troops, this situation could well change in the future. Intensive training is under way. This, coupled with increased manpower conscription, will lead to some improvement in combat capabilities. Libya's military supply and training connection with the Soviets permits Moscow a degree of influence in the region. Although Communist atheism is antithetical to Qadhafi's Islamic ideology, the Libyan leader, for the present, obviously perceives communism as a lesser evil than so-called Western economic imperialism, and he has acted as a major agent of the Soviet Union in Middle East and African affairs. Qadhafi apparently remains confident that he can prevent the Soviets from gaining the upper hand over his Pan-Arab aspirations.

While Qadhafi's control of Libya is close to absolute, he seems to be facing growing opposition, although there does not appear to be any possibility that he could be removed by popular uprising. The most likely possible change in power would appear to be a move by hostile neighbors and conservative Arab elements to remove Qadhafi and change the extremist nature of the current regime. In the event of simple assassination, Maj. Abdel Salaam Jullud, somewhat less an idealist and more pragmatic than Qadhafi, would probably replace him.

Libya's relations with Egypt have been strained for several years, with Libya a leader in the strong rejection by hard-line Arab states of Sadat's peace initiatives toward Israel. In July 1977 a series of incidents between the two countries culminated in serious border clashes, including air and armor attacks.

## MILITARY ASSISTANCE

Libya is overwhelmingly dependent upon the Soviet Union for military equipment, training, and services. Since the Qadhafi regime came to power, several billion dollars worth of arms have been purchased for cash. The Libyans have also acquired French, British, Italian, Spanish, and Brazilian weapons. Military advisers, while predominantly Soviet, also include Turks and Pakistanis. There appears to be some Cuban involvement.

Qadhafi appears intent upon acquiring a nuclear energy program, which in all probability would have to be entirely operated by foreign personnel brought in and paid with Libyan money.

Libya's large weapons stockpiles can be a significant factor in reequipping the Arab armies in the event of another war with Israel, and their distribution would give Qadhafi an opportunity to favor those radical countries that share his political aims.

## ALLIANCES

Libya is a member of the Arab League, the OAU, the Maghreb, and OPEC.

## ARMY

*Personnel:* 20,000

*Organization:*
  1 armored brigade
  2 infantry brigades (mechanized)
  3 artillery battalions (U.S.-equipped)
  2 antiaircraft battalions

*Major Equipment Inventory:*
  medium tanks
        500  T-45/55
         15  T-34
      1,000+  T-62
      1,000+  T-72
  200 armored cars (Saladin) and scout cars (Ferret and Shorland)
  250 APCs (Saracen, BTR-60, BMP, M-113)
  150 guns (122mm) and self-propelled and towed howitzers (105mm, 155mm)
      antiaircraft guns (40mm Bofors)
  100 antitank missiles (Vigilant and Sagger)
   12 helicopters (AB-206, Bell 47G, Alouette)
      SAMs: Crotale, SA-2, SA-3, SA-6 (8 batteries in all)
      SSMs: 25 Scud B

## NAVY

*Personnel:* 2,000 (including Coast Guard)

*Major Units:*
  3 submarines (Foxtrot class; SS)
  1 frigate (Vosper Thornycroft Mark 7 class; FF; carries Seacat short-range SAMs)
  1 guided missile patrol combatant (PGG; OTO-Oerlikon SSMs; others building)
  8 patrol craft (PC)
  10 missile attack boats (PTG; PTO-Melara or SS-N-2/Styx missiles)
  10 patrol boats (PB)
  1 dock landing ship (LSD)
  2 tank landing ships (LST)
  1 medium landing ship (LSM)
  3 service craft

*Naval Base:* Tripoli; ports at Benghazi, Darnah, Tobruk, and Burayqah

## AIR FORCE

*Personnel:* 3,000

*Organization:*
  1 bomber squadron (Tu-22)
  2 fighter squadrons (MiG-23)
  4 fighter-bomber squadrons (Mirage)
  1 transport squadron (C-47, C-130)

*Major Aircraft Types:*
  125 combat aircraft
       15  bombers (Tu-22)
      110  fighters (80 Mirage, 30 MiG-23)
   86 other aircraft
       26  transports (9 C-47, 1 C-140, 16 C-130)
       25  jet trainers (3 T-33, 12 Magisters, 10 Galeb)
       35  helicopters (9 Super Frelon, 7 Alouette II/III, 2 AB-206, 3 OH-13, 14 Mi-8)

*Missiles:* SAMs (Thunderbird and Rapier)

*Air Bases:* Wheelus and Idris (Tripoli), Benina (Benghazi), El Adem, El Awai

## PARAMILITARY

A paramilitary force has been organized. Its composition and strength are unclear.

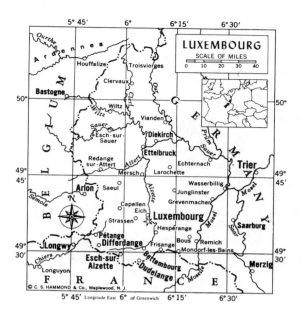

# LUXEMBOURG

## Grand Duchy of Luxembourg

### POWER POTENTIAL STATISTICS

Area: 999 square miles
Population: 358,000
Total Active Regular Armed Forces: 550 (0.15% population)
Gross National Product: $2.5 billion ($6,900 per capita)
Annual Military Expenditures: $32 million (1.28% GNP)
Crude Steel Production: 4.6 million metric tons
Iron Ore Production: 2.1 million metric tons
Petroleum Production is lumped with Belgium
Electric Power Output: 1.3 billion kwh
Civil Air Fleet: 10 major transport aircraft

### POLITICO-MILITARY POLICIES AND POSTURE

The government of Luxembourg abandoned its traditionally neutral policy at the close of World War II, and has since been an enthusiastic partner in all Western European mutual security agreements as a member of the Benelux bloc. A member of NATO, Luxembourg maintains only a nominal armed force, composed of one light infantry battalion of 550 men. U.S. military assistance to Luxembourg since 1950 has totaled slightly more than $8 million, most of which was provided in the early 1950s. Military service is voluntary; enlistment is for three years. The gendarmerie is 450 strong.

# MADAGASCAR

## Democratic Republic of Madagascar

### POWER POTENTIAL STATISTICS

Area: 230,035 square miles
Population: 8,258,000
Total Active Regular Armed Forces: 5,000 (0.06% population)
Gross National Product: $2.0 billion ($250 per capita)
Annual Military Expenditures: $38 million (1.9% GNP)
Fuel Production: Refined Petroleum Products: 577,700 metric tons
Electric Power Output: 465 million kwh
Merchant Fleet (ships 1,000 tons and over): 9 ships; 33,000 gross tons
Civil Air Fleet: 3 jet transports

## POLITICO-MILITARY POLICIES AND POSTURE

In May 1972, student protests triggered extensive rioting and arrests that led to a transfer of power to Gen. Philibert Ramanantsoa, army chief of staff. A referendum in October gave Ramanantsoa full control of the country, with military rule to be maintained for five years. However, three changes in government in 1975 brought Comdr. Didier Ratsiraka to power. He formally became president in January 1976. He has ruled through a Supreme Revolutionary Council and a Military Development Committee. A National Assembly was elected in 1978.

Upon independence in 1960, Madagascar concluded mutual defense and military assistance agreements with France which provided for aid in maintaining internal security, military training and aid, and base rights, transit, and overflight privilege for France. Under the agreements the French retained the headquarters of Overseas Zone 3 (Indian Ocean) and a garrison of about 2,500 men at Diego Suarez Naval Base, plus detachments at Ivato and Antsirabe. Madagascar signed an agreement with France in June 1973 under which all 4,000 French troops remaining in the country would be phased out, and this has been done. French military assistance amounted to about $12.5 million annually. West Germany has also provided military assistance, including thirty light military vehicles and the training of seamen in Germany. Israel has trained 500 security police and provided their weapons. The United States has furnished about $200,000 worth of equipment for the gendarmerie and police.

Before the 1972 coup the policies of Madagascar were generally pro-West. Since then, the government has been more strongly anticolonial and independent, breaking several ties with France, and also breaking diplomatic relations with South Africa. Madagascar is a member of the OAU, but, although it lies only 250 miles off the southeast African coast, its population is mainly of Malay descent, and its interest in African affairs has been slight. It withdrew from OCAM in 1973. It also withdrew from the franc zone, issuing its own currency. Despite the nationalization of numerous French concerns, Madagascar receives much foreign aid from France and trades more with France than any other nation.

There is internal friction between the Protestant highland peoples of Malay stock and the Catholic coastal peoples of mixed Malay, African, and Arab background. The government is endeavoring to unify these divergent groups. A more serious potential danger to internal stability lies in tensions resulting from the slow economic growth rate coupled with a high birth rate.

In 1976 there was a massacre of more than a thousand Comoros Islanders in Madagascar, followed by the repatriation of thousands more to Comoros.

All male citizens are subject to eighteen-month conscription either for military or for civic service. The army is 4,000 strong and organized into two mixed regiments (each consists of four infantry companies), one paratroop company, one reconnaissance squadron, one engineer unit, one artillery battery, and headquarters and support units. The navy of about 600 men operates seven patrol vessels, one utility landing craft, and one company of marines. The major naval base is Diego-Suarez with ports at Tamatave, Majunga, Tulear, Nossi Be, Fort Dauphin, and Manakara. The air arm has 400 men and operates three C-47, three Flamant, and seven Broussard transports, five helicopters (Bell 47 and Alouette II/III), and some trainers. Main air bases are Arivoniamamo (Tananarive), Ivato (Tananarive), Diego-Suarez, Fort Dauphin, Tamatave, Majunga, and Tulear. There is a gendarmerie numbering 4,100 men.

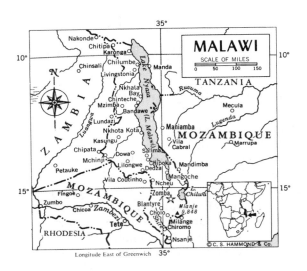

# MALAWI

## Republic of Malawi

## POWER POTENTIAL STATISTICS

Area: 45,747 square miles
Population: 5,777,000
Total Armed Regular Armed Forces: 1,200 (0.02% population)
Gross National Product: $683 million ($130 per capita)
Annual Military Expenditures: $20.6 (3.02% GNP)
Electric Power Output: 315 million kwh
Civil Air Fleet: 4 major transport aircraft

## POLITICO-MILITARY POLICIES AND POSTURE

Malawi, a member of the Commonwealth, is a republic governed by a president who dominates a one-party parliament, and who is the commander in chief of the nation's armed force. Malawi's strategic problems are twofold: maintaining internal and external security against dissidents at home and abroad; and maintaining a balance of political and economic relations with both South Africa and the surrounding "front-line" states of Mozambique, Tanzania, and Zambia.

Although nominally nonaligned, the government of President H. K. Banda has in recent years severed relations with Communist nations and established relations with South Africa. Although a member of the OAU, Malawi has advocated realism in expectations of African unity, and restraint in achieving Pan-African aims. President Banda's official visit to South Africa in 1971 and the visit of President Fouche of South Africa to Malawi in 1972 were the first official visits exchanged by South Africa and any independent black African state.

In 1964 several dissident ministers fled the country and fomented a liberation movement among the 20,000 Malawians working in Tanzania. This movement received support from Algeria, Egypt, Cuba, and Communist China, and was provided sanctuary and bases in Tanzania and Zambia. From these countries raids against Malawi have been mounted periodically, but the rebels have gained little support from the population and have been quickly rounded up. In the past several years two groups—the 25,000-member Jehovah's Witnesses sect and some 7,000 Asians—have suffered persecution. Five thousand Jehovah's Witnesses have been held in detention camps since 1975; thousands of others fled to Mozambique. Expulsion of several hundred Asians with British passports aroused the ire of the United Kingdom in 1975. Nevertheless, the policy continued.

For export of its agricultural produce and import of essential goods, landlocked Malawi depends upon rail traffic from the port of Beira in Mozambique. South Africa has provided a loan to build an additional rail link to the line running to the port of Nacala in Mozambique. Communications by road exist with similarly landlocked Zambia and with Tanzania, but these are tenuous, longer, and do not have the capacity of the routes through Mozambique. Some 200,000 Malawians work in Rhodesia and 100,000 in South Africa, remitting part of their wages to families at home. This represents a significant contribution to the national income which could be terminated at any time by the host countries.

Thus, Malawi's economy is dependent on both sides of the conflict in southern Africa. Malawi's diplomacy reflects this duality. South African aid helped in the 1975 relocation of the capital to Lilongwe. Yet Malawi condemns apartheid and refuses to recognize the Transkei or other homelands. In 1976 Malawi closed its frontier with Rhodesia.

Malawi's borders were determined by colonial fiat and do not match either ethnic divisions or old tribal boundaries. Because of ethnic realities and tribal history —and also probably as a counterirritant to Tanzania and Zambia's suport for Malawian dissidents—Dr. Banda has laid claim to three districts in Tanzania and to three districts in Zambia. However, no efforts appear to be in progress to force these claims.

Malawi was formerly dependent upon Britain for about 40 percent of its budget, but Britain and Malawi agreed in 1972 to terminate this support. Some fifty British officers and noncommissioned officers who were seconded to Malawi in both command and training posts were to be replaced as fast as Malawian officers became trained and qualified. It is not clear whether or not British military personnel still remain in Malawi. The army, some 1,200 strong, consists of the First Battalion Malawi Rifles, plus supporting services, four patrol boats (PB) on Lake Nyasa, and an air unit. The air unit operates two HS-748 Andover and two Britten-Norman BN-2 aircraft. Airfields are Blantyre-Limbe, Lilongwe, Mzimba, Mzuzu, and Karonga.

The Young Malawi Pioneers, a youth organization, is believed to have paramilitary functions; the League of Malawi Women augments the security services.

# MALAYSIA

## POWER POTENTIAL STATISTICS

Area: 128,328 square miles
Population: 13,099,000
Total Active Regular Armed Forces: 61,500 (0.47% population)
Gross National Product: $12.4 billion ($990 per capita)
Annual Military Expenditures: $689 million (5.56% GNP)
Iron Ore Production: 308,000 metric tons
Fuel Production:
    Crude Oil: 8 million metric tons
    Refined Petroleum Products: 4.5 million metric tons
Electric Power Output: 7.6 billion kwh
Merchant Fleet (ships 1,000 tons and over): 49 ships; 533,000 gross tons
Civil Air Fleet: 26 major transport aircraft

## DEFENSE STRUCTURE

This federated monarchy, with thirteen separate compo-

nent states, is a member of the British Commonwealth, and has a parliamentary form of government. The elected paramount ruler is the commander in chief. The services are independent but are closely coordinated by the Armed Forces Council, under the chairmanship of the minister of defence. The present prime minister (Datuk Hussein Onn) serves concurrently as minister of defence and takes a close personal interest in defense matters.

The armed forces are maintained by voluntary recruitment.

## STRATEGIC PROBLEMS

Strategic problems facing Malaysia are: (1) the ethnic division of the population, especially between ethnic Chinese and Malays; (2) dangers of a revival of insurgency, particularly by ethnic Chinese; (3) the long sea-air lines of communication (about 400 miles by air) between peninsular West Malaysia and insular East Malaysia (the states of Sarawak and Sabah in Borneo).

Political power in Malaysia traditionally has been in Malay hands, while economic power has been held by others, chiefly the Chinese, who are nearly equal in number to the Malays in West Malaysia. From time to time, ethnic violence between the two groups threatens to erupt over imagined or real grievances. The most recent widespread violence broke out in 1969, leading to imposition of a state of emergency lasting until February 1971, and the danger of renewed violence always lurks close to the surface. The ethnic split extends, in part, into the army, where the Royal Malay Regiment recruits exclusively among Malay.

During the Communist insurgency in Malaya, from 1947 to 1960, most of the insurgents were ethnic Chinese. The remnants of the insurgents retreated north of the Thai border in 1959–60, and they have been recruiting, training,

and conducting propaganda efforts since. The terrorist groups now contain large numbers of ethnic Malay and Chinese recruited and based in Thailand. Cooperation between Malaysian military and police and various Thai authorities has been less than satisfactory from Malaysia's perspective, although combined operations in 1977–78 did succeed in penetrating long-time insurgent base areas. The Communist Party of Malaya (CPM) split into three groups, each attempting with modest success to penetrate back into West Malaysia and to recruit there. The Chinese Communist Party continues to support the CPM, mostly through propaganda, although the Chinese government has declared the Malaysian insurgency an internal problem of the Malaysian government.

East Malaysia has generally presented no major problems since the end of the confrontation with Indonesia in 1966. Small, isolated bands of terrorists near the Sarawak-Kalimantan boundary have limited mischief value. The strategic problems of providing for the defense of the two widely separated parts of the country may be complicated further if Indonesia succeeds in winning acceptance of the archipelago principle at the Law of the Sea Conference. The Philippine claim to Sabah may be resolved if President Marcos can find a politically feasible formula for renunciation; in any case, it is not likely to lead to open conflict. The issue of Malaysian support of Moro insurgents in the southern Philippines could again complicate Malaysian-Philippine relations, but it is dormant for the time being.

The Five-Power Defence Pact in truth leaves Malaysia fully responsible for its own security, although the modest Australian–New Zealand presence is welcome. Political problems continue to prevent full defense cooperation between Malaysia and Singapore, even under the Five-Power Agreement.

## MILITARY ASSISTANCE

Malaysia in the past received substantial assistance from the United Kingdom and Australia, as well as $2.3 million in military aid from the United States, and the training of 552 Malaysians under the MAP. Malaysia is currently purchasing a variety of military equipment abroad.

## ALLIANCES

Malaysia is a member of the Five-Power Defense Pact. It also is a member of ASEAN.

## ARMY

*Personnel:* 50,000

*Organization:*
  9 infantry brigades
27 infantry battalions
  3 reconnaissance regiments (M-2 half-track, Ferret scout cars, Commando V150 APC)
  3 artillery regiments (105mm howitzers)
  1 special service unit

*Major Equipment Inventory:*
    scout cars (40 M-2 half-tracks, Ferret, 200 Commando V150 APC)
54 105mm howitzers (M-101)
30 40mm antiaircraft guns, 3.5-inch Commando rocket launcher (Bazookas)

*Reserves:* There are approximately 45,000 trained reservists in the Army Volunteer Forces (national militia). The militia units are prepared to take the field at short notice, either beside the regular forces, or for home defense.

## NAVY

*Personnel:* 6,000

*Major Units:*
  2 frigates (Yarrow class; FF; 1 with Seacat short-range SAMs)
  4 missile attack boats (PTG; with Exocet SSMs)
28 fast patrol craft (PCF)
  6 coastal minesweepers (MSC)
  3 tank landing ships (LST)
  3 service craft

*Naval Bases:* Johore Straits, Labuan

## AIR FORCE

*Personnel:* 5,500

*Organization:*
  1 fighter squadron (F-5)
  2 ground attack squadrons (CL-41G)
  4 transport squadrons (Caribou, C-130, Herald, Dove, Cessna 402)
  4 helicopter squadrons (S-61, Bell 205, Bell 47, Alouette III)
  1 training squadron (Bulldog, Cessna 402, Provost)

*Major Aircraft Types:*
  36 combat aircraft
    16 F-5 fighters
    20 CL-41G ground attack aircraft
199 other aircraft
     6 C-130 transports
     8 Herald transports
    14 DHC-4 Caribou transports
    36 light transports (Dove, Cessna 402, HS-125)
     8 Bell 205
    35 S-61A helicopter troop carriers
    12 Bell 47 helicopters
    25 Alouette III helicopters
    55 trainers (Provost, Cessna 402, Bulldog)

*Major Air Bases:* Kuala Lumpur, Imph, Paya Lebar, Labuan, Kuantan, Alor Star, Gong, Kedak.

## PARAMILITARY

There is a field police force, some 10,000 men in fourteen companies with the primary mission of maintaining internal security. There are about 30 police boats (PB).

# MALDIVES

# Republic of Maldives

## POWER POTENTIAL STATISTICS

Area: 115 square miles
Population: 143,000
Gross National Product: $17.4 million ($150 per capita)
Electric Power Output: 6 million kwh
Merchant Fleet (ships 1,000 tons and over): 35 ships; 101,000 gross tons
Civil Air Fleet: 2 piston transports

## POLITICO-MILITARY POLICIES AND POSTURE

A sultanate under British control until 1965, Maldives became independent in that year and became a republic in

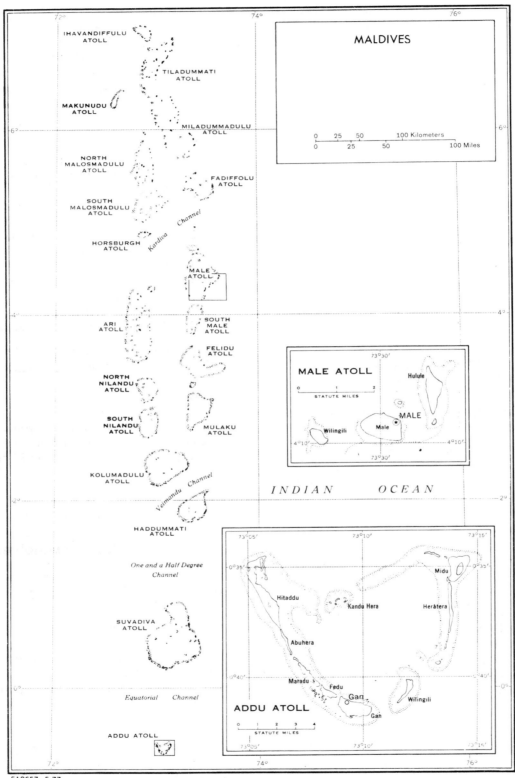

### MALDIVES

0   25   50   100 Kilometers
0   25   50   100 Miles

IHAVANDIFFULU ATOLL

TILADUMMATI ATOLL

**MAKUNUDU ATOLL**

MILADUMMADULU ATOLL

NORTH MALOSMADULU ATOLL

FADIFFOLU ATOLL

SOUTH MALOSMADULU ATOLL

HORSBURGH ATOLL

*Kardiva Channel*

MALE ATOLL

ARI ATOLL

SOUTH MALE ATOLL

FELIDU ATOLL

**NORTH NILANDU ATOLL**

**SOUTH NILANDU ATOLL**

MULAKU ATOLL

KOLUMADULU ATOLL

*Veimandu Channel*

INDIAN        OCEAN

HADDUMMATI ATOLL

*One and a Half Degree Channel*

SUVADIVA ATOLL

*Equatorial      Channel*

ADDU ATOLL

#### MALE ATOLL

73°30'

0       1       2
STATUTE MILES

Hulule

MALE

Wilingili    Male

4°10'                          4°10'
73°30'

#### ADDU ATOLL

73°05'      73°10'      73°15'

0°35'                              0°35'

Midu

Hitaddu          Kandu Hera      Heràtera

Abuhera

0°40'                              0°40'

Maradu    Fedu        Wilingili
Gan
Gan

0       1       2       3       4
STATUTE MILES

73°05'      73°10'      73°15'

518657  5-77

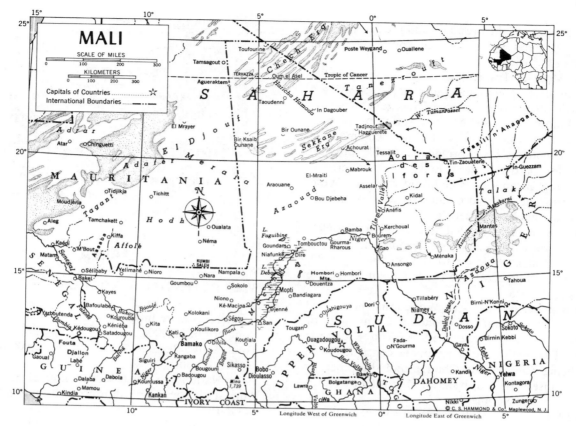

**MALI**

*(Map of Mali showing scale of miles, capitals of countries, and international boundaries)*

1968. It has a presidential form of government with much power vested in the president. The country is a 500-mile chain of 2,000 islands, only about 215 of which are inhabited, lying about 400 miles southwest of Sri Lanka and off the southern tip of India. It is among the least developed countries in the world, with fish its principal export. The population of the Maldives is almost entirely Moslem, and its closest international ties are with the Moslem states of the Middle East, which have provided economic aid.

Strategically significant is the former British military and air base of Gan Island at the southern tip of the island chain. The air facility there was closed by the British in 1976 as part of their withdrawal from military commitments in Asia. Maldives received four patrol boats (PB), four mechanized landing craft (LCM), and two service craft at that time. The Gan base lies 450 miles north of Diego Garcia, the British-administered island where the United States has recently expanded its air, naval, and communications base. In 1977 the Soviet Union attempted to rent Gan, ostensibly as a base for its fishing fleet in the area, but the offer was rejected.

There were reports that some of the Middle East states had opposed the arrangement, and also various unconfirmed reports that Iran, India, Saudi Arabia, or the United States had made a more acceptable counter-offer.

# MALI

## Republic of Mali

### POWER POTENTIAL STATISTICS

Area: 464,873 square miles
Population: 6,287,000
Total Active Regular Armed Forces: 3,950 (0.06% population)
Gross National Product: $645 million ($110 per capita)
Annual Military Expenditures: $29 million (4.50% GNP)
Electric Power Output: 105 million kwh
Civil Air Fleet: 1 jet and 2 turboprop transports

### POLITICO-MILITARY POLICIES AND POSTURE

In June 1960 the French colonies of French Sudan and Senegal became independent as the Federation of Mali. Two months later Senegal withdrew from the federation, and the former French Sudan proclaimed itself the Republic of Mali on September 22, 1960. Under a leftist government Mali severed its ties with France and remained outside the French Community. Ruinous economic policies and the growing power and truculence of the Popular

Militia, military arm of the president and the party, led to a military coup d'etat by a group of young officers in November 1968.

President Moussa Traore heads an eleven-member Military Committee of National Liberation. Following a purge of Soviet-oriented members of the government in early 1978, Traore also assumed the position of minister of defense and internal security. Military commanders administer the country's six provinces. Mali's political leanings are less leftist under Traore. The country is officially nonaligned and has sought aid from the West, especially during the Sahel drought. France customarily makes up the annual budget deficit.

In 1976 the regime created the Malian People's Democratic Union as the nation's sole political body. It also announced plans to revert to civilian rule by 1980. Meanwhile, Mali appeared to be headed again for severe food shortages in 1978.

Mali is a member of the OAU. While it has not joined OCAM, it is a member of the Economic Community of West African States and the West African Economic Community. Two major dams are under construction in Mali, one being built by the Chinese and the other by Western and conservative Arab states. Mali will be a major recipient of Sahel development funds.

Between 1961 and 1971 Mali received over $20 million in military assistance from the Soviet Union. This included MiG-17 fighters, T-34 tanks, armored personnel carriers, artillery, military vehicles, small arms, training in the Soviet Union, and a Soviet military mission in Mali. Until the 1968 coup, Communist China armed and trained the Popular Militia. In 1964, the United States sent a military mission to Mali to train engineer units for civic action and in 1966 to train a paratroop company; about $2.8 million in American military assistance was provided from 1961 to 1967, and sixty-seven military students have been trained under MAP.

Tribal divisions are not so serious in Mali as in many other African countries since about 60 percent of the population is from the Mande tribe. The Berber Tuaregs have traditionally opposed the central government authority and police action against them is occasionally necessary, but they represent less than five percent of the population.

The army has a strength of about 3,500 and is organized into three infantry battalions, one paratroop company, and service support units. Equipment is largely Soviet. There is a river patrol force of about 50 men operating three patrol boats (PB) on the Niger River. The air force has about 400 men and operates six MiG-17 jet fighters, two MiG-15 jet fighter-trainers, two C-47 transports, two Il-14 transports, two Broussard liaison aircraft, and two Mi-4 helicopters. Air bases are at Bamako and Gao with other fields at Mopti, Kayes, Nioro, Tombouctou, and Yelimane. There is a gendarmerie of 1,200.

# MALTA

## POWER POTENTIAL STATISTICS

Area: 122 square miles
Population: 326,000
Total Active Regular Armed Forces: 2,600 (0.8% population)
Gross National Product: $609 million ($1,850 per capita)
Annual Military Expenditures: $9.4 million (1.54% GNP)
Electric Power Output: 420 million kwh
Merchant Fleet (ships 1,000 tons and over): 13 ships, 84,000 gross tons
Civil Air Fleet: 4 jets

## POLITICO-MILITARY POLICIES AND POSTURE

Malta holds a strategic position in the Mediterranean, lying midway between Sicily and North Africa and possessing several fine harbors and an important dockyard. From 1814, when it voluntarily became part of the British Empire, it has been a British military and naval fortress and the headquarters of the British Mediterranean fleet. Malta is now preparing to disengage itself from this role, and from its economic dependence on the presence of foreign military facilities and personnel. This growing independence poses problems for the United Kingdom and NATO. Recent indications are that the ruling Malta Labour Party may be moving to make its power authoritarian and permanent by intimidating and suppressing opposition groups. These actions have caused concern about the future stability and political orientation of Malta.

Politically, Malta gained independence within the British Commonwealth in 1964, and at that time signed a defense agreement with the United Kingdom that allowed British forces to remain in Malta for ten years. Britain agreed to pay, during that period, grants and loans amounting to $118 million to help diversify the economy and assist emigration. (Malta is one of the world's most densely populated countries, with 2,480 persons per square mile.) When the Malta Labour party won the elections of 1971, the new socialist government negotiated another agreement with Britain and the NATO Council, to run until March 31, 1979. It provided increased compensation for Malta—$33 million yearly in rent payments, plus a lump sum of $16.5 million (part grant and part loan), $5.9 million in economic aid from Italy, and technical help from other NATO countries. Under the agreement, the United Kingdom and other NATO countries accepted the principle that Malta was offering part of its territory for use by foreign powers for military purposes, so that in the shortest possible time, it might be able to reconstruct its economy to be free of the economic need for a foreign military presence. The agreement also stipulates that Malta's military facilities may not be used against any Arab country. Malta has long-standing ties with the Arab peoples; Maltese is basically a Semitic language, and Arabs ruled Malta for 200 years in the early Middle Ages.

The Constitution was revised in 1974, making Malta a republic with its own president within the Commonwealth.

In early 1978, press reports indicated that the Malta Labour Party regime of Premier Dom Mintoff was harassing the courts, police, legal profession, and political opponents in order to maintain control of the country; the party held a bare majority of seats in the legislature. Offices of the opposition Nationalist Party were wrecked during the most recent general election campaign, and there have been many unsolved bombings, most of them aimed at opponents of the government.

Malta receives considerable foreign aid in addition to the payments from NATO countries, especially from Libya and China.

# MAURITANIA

## Islamic Republic of Mauritania

### POWER POTENTIAL STATISTICS

Area: 419,229 square miles
Population: 1,562,000
Total Active Regular Armed Forces: 1,000 (0.06% population)
Gross National Product: $328 million ($240 per capita)
Annual Military Expenditures: $29 million (8.84% GNP)
Iron Ore Production: 8.6 million metric tons
Electric Power Output: 100 million kwh
Civil Air Fleet: 7 major transport aircraft

### POLITICO-MILITARY POLICIES AND POSTURE

The president of the republic commands the armed forces through an appointed minister of defense. The National Assembly passes upon the defense budget submitted by the minister.

The army was formed from Mauritanian-manned French army units upon independence in November 1960. The following year mutual defense and military assistance agreements were signed with France which provided for help in maintaining internal security base rights, transit and overflight privileges, and military aid and training. All French troops were withdrawn by January 1966.

Morocco formerly claimed sovereignty over Mauritania on dubious historical grounds. In 1957 French troops had to suppress an invasion by Moroccan irregular forces. Morocco abandoned the claim and recognized Mauritania in 1969, but suspicions persisted in Mauritania over Moroccan designs on it and Spain's colony of Western Sahara. The two countries cooperated to reach a partition agreement with Spain in 1975 giving them joint administration over Western Sahara. In 1976 Spain withdrew. Mauritania and Morocco agreed on a border giving Mauritania one-third of the territory. The situation was complicated by the guerrilla war waged by Polisario rebels who claim to be the legitimate government of the Saharan Arab Democratic Republic (Western Sahara). Backed by Algeria, the Polisario has made numerous attacks in Mauritania since 1976. Mauritania has received French and Moroccan air and troop support and financial backing from conservative Arab states. In July 1978, apparently dissatisfied with the conduct of the war, army Chief of Staff Col. Ould Salek deposed President Ould Daddah, who had ruled Mauritania since independence. In August

1979 Mauritania signed an agreement with the Polisario Front renouncing its claims to Western Sahara.

Mauritania's eastern border with Mali was under dispute until largely settled in favor of the latter in 1968. However, this still vaguely defined border remains a potential source of irritation.

The most important of a number of relatively minor internal tensions is the ethnic division between the Arabic-speaking Moorish-Arab-Berber majority (80 percent of the population) and the black minority. Proportionally more blacks than Arabs sought an education during the French regime. Blacks have been represented out of proportion to their numbers in the bureaucracy and business, but politi-cally the country is Arab. Mauritania joined the Arab League in 1973.

Substantial natural resources provide most of Mauritania's foreign exchange earning. There are several iron ore deposits, and a large copper ore reserve has been discovered. The fishing industry has great potential and is being developed to a catch of 250,000 tons per year. Trawlers are built in France, and smaller fishing craft are built locally.

Mauritania is a member of the OAU and the Arab League. In 1965 it withdrew from the French-oriented OCAM and adopted a policy of nonalignment. In June 1973 the franc was replaced by the gold-backed ouquiya.

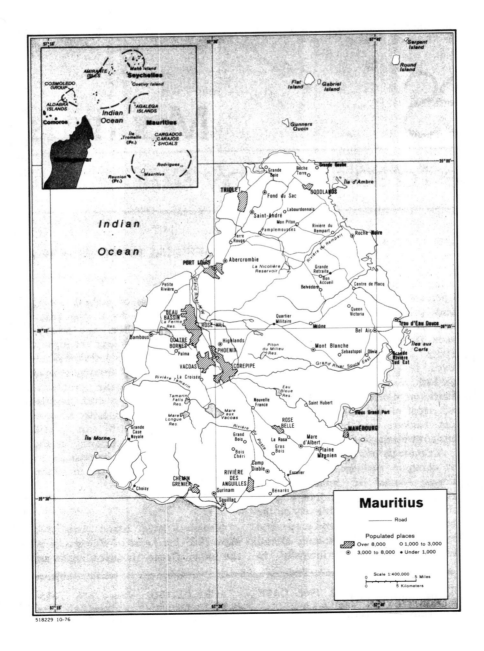

518229 10-76

To demonstrate its solidarity with the Arab world at the time of the June 1967 Arab-Israeli war, it broke diplomatic relations with the United States; they were resumed in December 1969. The United States has provided substantial aid for Sahel drought relief and future agricultural development.

The army numbers 900 men and is organized in one parachute-commando company, several mechanized reconnaissance squadrons, an artillery battery, and a camel corps. Equipment is French, including light artillery and EBR-75 armored cars. Military service is voluntary and is for two years. There is a 100-man coast guard–type force that operates six patrol craft (PC) and five patrol boats (PB) at Port Etienne for port control and customs. The air force has a strength of about 100 and operates one C-47 transport, two Broussard utility aircraft, and six light trainers. Airfields are at Atar, Nouakchott, Port Etienne, Fort Gouraud, Fort Trinquet, Akjoujt, Kaedi, Rosso, Kiffa, and Aioun-el-atrous.

## MAURITIUS

### POWER POTENTIAL STATISTICS

Area: 787 square miles
Population: 927,000
Total Active Regular Armed Forces: 3,000 (0.3% population)
Gross National Product: $570 million ($640 per capita)
Annual Military Expenditures: $4 million (0.7% GNP)
Electric Power Output: 312 million kwh
Merchant Fleet (ships 1,000 tons and over): 6 ships; 35,000 gross tons
Civil Air Fleet: 1 major transport aircraft

### POLITICO-MILITARY POLICIES AND POSTURE

Mauritius is an independent parliamentary democracy within the Commonwealth, acknowledging Elizabeth II as head of state. It was ruled by Great Britain from 1810 until independence in 1968, but the dominant culture, language, and influences on the legal system are all French—descended, like the island nation's elite social and economic class, from French settlers of the eighteenth century. This Creole elite, racially an African-European mixture, constitutes 28 percent of the population, while 67 percent of the population are Indians, most of whose ancestors were brought to Mauritius in the nineteenth century as indentured servants to perform as laborers in place of the emancipated slaves. Mauritius is one of the most densely populated countries in the world, primarily because malaria was eradicated there during World War II. Current birth and population growth rates are low for Africa. A minor addition to the population numerically, but one that caused criticism of the U.K. government when it was revealed ten years later, was the resettlement in Mauritius in 1965 of 1,000 residents of Diego Garcia, displaced for the new U.S. naval base. Overpopulation and unemployment are probably the most serious internal problems. Government and society appear stable.

Mauritius attends the annual Franco-African summit meetings. It has been active in the United Nations in working for stronger sanctions against South Africa.

Mauritius operates one patrol craft (PC).

## MEXICO

### United Mexican States

### POWER POTENTIAL STATISTICS

Area: 761,600 square miles
Population: 66,938,000
Total Active Regular Armed Forces: 91,400 (0.14% population)
Gross National Product: $74.2 billion ($1,150 per capita)
Annual Military Expenditures: $632.8 million (0.85% GNP)
Crude Steel Production: 5.1 million metric tons
Iron Ore Production: 3.65 million metric tons
Fuel Production:
   Coal: 5.1 million metric tons
   Crude Oil: 40.8 million metric tons
   Refined Products: 38.5 million metric tons
   Natural Gas: 24 million cubic meters
Electric Power Output: 50.1 billion kwh
Nuclear Power Production: 700 megawatts
Merchant Fleet (ships 1,000 tons and over): 52 ships; 548,000 gross tons
Civil Air Fleet: 117 major transport aircraft

### DEFENSE STRUCTURE

The president is commander in chief of the armed forces. The army and the air force are administered by the Ministry of National Defense, the navy by the Ministry of the Navy.

The nation is divided into thirty-three military zones. Zone commanders are responsible for maintaining order, particularly during elections.

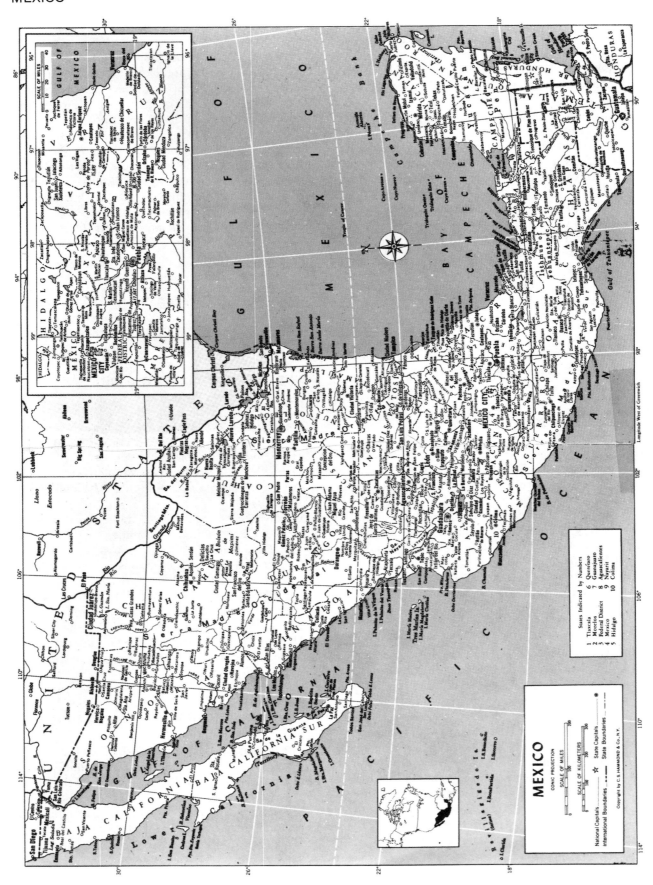

## MEXICO
### CONIC PROJECTION
#### SCALE OF MILES
#### SCALE OF KILOMETERS

National Capitals ● ● ● ● ● ● ● ● ● ● ● ● ● ● ● ● ●
International Boundaries ─ ─ ─ ─ ─ ─
State Capitals ☆
State Boundaries ─ ─ ─ ─

Copyright by C. S. HAMMOND & Co., N.Y.

States Indicated by Numbers
1 Tlaxcala
2 Morelos
3 Federal District
4 Mexico
5 Hidalgo
6 Querétaro
7 Guanajuato
8 Aguascalientes
9 Nayarit
10 Colima

## POLITICO-MILITARY POLICY

Beginning in 1920 after a decade of revolutionary turmoil, a strong executive initiated measures to break the political strength of the revolutionary generals and produce a loyal, professional army. At the same time social and economic reforms stabilized the government. Today the Mexican army is among the least militaristic and most nonpolitical in Latin America. It has been modeled on that of the United States and is modern in organization, training, discipline, and proficiency. Military personnel surrender their political rights and may not even express political opinions in public without incurring penalties under the law.

The army is composed of volunteers. Military training is compulsory for all eighteen-year-old male citizens for one year, but generally is accomplished by Sunday drill. There appears to be no organized reserve system, although the Marine Corps lists a small reserve unit.

## STRATEGIC PROBLEMS

Like its neighbors in Central America, Mexico affords a base for potential attack on the United States and so might conceivably serve as a preliminary objective in such an attack.

In the past half century, Mexico's relations with its neighbors have been good. However, there has been some tension in relations with Guatemala regarding alleged trespassing in territorial waters; Guatemala has also charged that Mexico has harbored political exiles and has supported subversion.

With the decline of Mexican militarism, the potential for revolution and coup d'etat was greatly reduced. Mexico is still considered politically stable, but it is experiencing heavy pressures from extremely rapid population growth, high unemployment (almost half the labor force estimated unemployed), soaring inflation (23 percent to 30 percent annually), and a gap between incomes of rich and poor that is wide even in relation to other Latin American countries. There appears to be some danger of worker and student protests violent enough to trigger a coup by right-wing factions and the military, despite the latter's traditionally nonpolitical character. In 1977 the army was used to suppress political disturbances in the heavily socialist province of Oaxaca.

The vast new oil fields in the Yucatan can be expected to bring Mexico, in the next few years, economic gains that may have a politically stabilizing effect.

The Communist movement is small and divided. There is some terrorist activity, but the terrorist groups are small and apparently uncoordinated.

## MILITARY ASSISTANCE

In 1976 Mexico received $128,000 in military assistance from the United States, making a total of $2.4 million since 1950. Under the MAP 868 students have been trained.

## ALLIANCES

Mexico is a member of the UN and the OAS and their various committees. It has never severed diplomatic relations with Cuba and adheres firmly to a policy of self-determination and nonintervention.

The Joint Mexican-U.S. Defense Commission was established by executive agreement in 1942, and is the only means for bilateral military discussion and planning between the United States and Mexico. In 1941 the United States was given the use of bases in Mexico in return for help with the reorganization and modernization of the Mexican air force. This reciprocal base-use privilege still exists.

## ARMY

*Personnel:* 73,500

*Organization:*
    2 infantry brigades (1 paratroop)
    1 mechanized brigade
  60 independent infantry battalions
  20 independent cavalry regiments
    1 artillery regiment
      antiaircraft, engineer, and support units

*Major Equipment Inventory:*
  medium tanks (M-4)
  armored cars, armored personnel carriers (MAC 1, Humber MKIV)
  75mm, 105mm howitzers

## NAVY

*Personnel:* 11,000 (includes 1,300 marines)

*Organization:*
  4 naval districts in the Gulf coast command
  4 naval districts in the Pacific coast command

*Major Units:*
    2 destroyers (Fletcher class; DD)
    6 patrol escorts (frigate-size but lack special capabilities; 3-inch + guns; PG)
  34 patrol ships (single 3-inch gun main armament; PGF)

```
 22 patrol craft (PC)
 17 fleet minesweepers/patrol frigates (some used in
      each capacity)
  6 patrol boats (PB)
  8 river patrol boats (PBR)
  2 tank landing ships (LST)
 25 auxiliaries and service craft (tankers, tugs,
      transports, etc.)
  5 maritime reconnaissance aircraft (HU-16)
 10 helicopters (OH-13/Alouette III)
 30 light support aircraft
```

*Marine Corps* (part of Navy): 3 companies with an additional 3 companies in reserve.

*Major Naval Bases:* Veracruz, Tampico, Acapulco, Puerto Cortes, Guaymas, Manzanillo, Islas Mujeres, Ciudad del Carmen

## AIR FORCE

*Personnel:* 6,000 (including 1,800 paratroops)

*Organization:*
```
  1 fighter-bomber squadron (T-33)
  5 COIN/training squadrons (T-28, T-6)
  1 reconnaissance/training squadron (T-11)
  1 SAR squadron (LASA-60)
  2 transport squadrons (C-118, C-54, C-47,
      IAI-201, BN-2, C-140)
  2 training squadrons (Musketeer, Beech F-33,
      T-34)
  1 paratroop battalion
```

*Major Aircraft Types:*
```
102 combat aircraft
     15 T-33 fighter-bombers
     30 T-28 armed trainers
     45 T-6 armed trainers
     12 T-11 reconnaissance/trainers
141 other aircraft
     35 transports (2 C-118, 4 C-54, 6 C-47, 10
         IAI-201, 12 BN-2 1 C-140)
     38 helicopters (13 OH-13, 1 OH-23, 9 Alouette
         III, 5 Bell 205, 10 Bell 206)
     68 trainer, support, rescue (20 Musketeer, 10
         T-34, 18 LASA-60, 20 Beech F-33)
```

## PARAMILITARY

Police forces are about 60,000 strong, including the *Rurales,* a constabulary.

# MONGOLIA

## Mongolian People's Republic

### POWER POTENTIAL STATISTICS

Area: 604,247 square miles
Population: 1,612,000
Total Active Regular Armed Forces: 25,000 (1.55% population)
Gross National Product: $1.2 billion ($820 per capita)
Annual Military Expenditures: $130.2 million (10.85% GNP)
Fuel Production:
    Coal: 171,000 metric tons
    Lignite: 2.5 million metric tons
    Crude Oil: 10,000 metric tons
Electric Power Output: 995 million kwh
Civil Air Fleet: 3 turboprop, 3 piston transports

### DEFENSE STRUCTURE

As in all Communist countries, military forces are controlled by the party. Control is accomplished by individuals holding dual membership in corresponding party and government positions. A Central Committee conducts party affairs; its secretariat handles organizational, executive, and administrative work through functional departments, one of which is the military department. On the government side, two-thirds of the Council of Ministers are also Central Committee members. The Council of Ministers exercises general guidance in defense matters and the organization of the armed forces; under it the Ministry of Defense is concerned with the detailed organization of defense matters. Usually, as at present, the minister of defense is also commander of the Mongolian People's Army (MPA). In addition, he is a member of the party's Central Committee.

### POLITICO-MILITARY POLICY

Mongols have always been warriors; from before the days of Genghis Khan in the twelfth century, military service has been universal for all males, and Mongolia's territorial militia organization has been the basis for national administration. This military attitude was somewhat attenuated from the late sixteenth to early twentieth centuries when Tibetan Buddhism and Chinese suzerainty tended to reduce the Mongols to passivity. More recently the revolutionary fervor of communism, and the threats of Japanese imperialism in the 1930s and 1940s, and of Chinese Communist imperialism since 1960, have

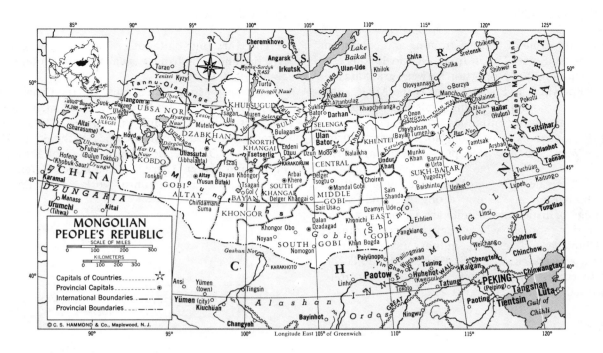

restored a considerable war-like spirit among the Mongols. Today, according to the Constitution, military service in the Mongolian People's Revolutionary Army is considered "a fundamental and honorable duty of all citizens." Active service for two years is compulsory and universal.

All units of the Mongolian People's Army have political officers and Communist Party organizations on the Soviet army model. From the founding of the MPR the army has been considered an important vehicle for modernizing measures, technical training, patriotism, and political consciousness. More recently, the army has been heavily engaged in construction work at the new industrial complex of Darkhan.

## STRATEGIC PROBLEMS

Mongolia's strategic situation is characterized by its buffer state role, giving defensive depth to the Soviet Union's central Siberia against an irredentist China. China has not given up its claim to Mongolia, which is based on the suzerainty of the Manchu Dynasty. This claim is rejected by Mongolia, which asserts that allegiance was to the Manchus, not to China. Should China expand into sparsely populated Mongolia, Soviet communications (Trans-Siberian Railroad) to its Pacific coast would be within close range (100 miles) of an unfriendly frontier.

Mongolia is obliged to guard some 2,500 miles of Chinese border and to provide forces to ensure the internal security of a large area with the lowest population density of any country in the world. Mongolia can accomplish these defense tasks against a serious threat only with outside help. Thus Soviet troops entered the MPR in 1923 to assist in putting down a counterrevolution and remained until 1956, first because of the Japanese threat and then to help maintain internal security. They returned in the early 1960s after the Sino-Soviet split. Mongolia provides forward defensive positions for Soviet military units, and areas for forward deployment of Soviet missile forces. China complained in 1973 about the addition of more Soviet troops.

The rigorously controlled existence in a Communist state is the antithesis of the free nomadic life previously enjoyed by the Mongols. This, combined with an abortive pan-Mongol movement, and the preference of some Mongolians for China over Russia, caused some dissension in the 1920s and early 1930s, resulting in repressions and repeated purges. However, the Mongols, now enjoying one of the highest living standards in Asia, appear to have become resigned to modernization under communism, and are committed to alignment with the Soviet Union; there is little likelihood of serious insurgence. Communist China, however, continues to employ the MPR's Inner Mongolian cousins for harassment, reconnaissance, and subversion along the Sino-Mongolian border.

## MILITARY ASSISTANCE

The monetary value of military training and equipment received from the Soviet Union from 1967 to 1976 is estimated at $30 million; the proportion between grant aid and sales is not known. The Soviet Union is the MPR's sole source of arms and training. Training missions and technical assistance have been continuous since 1921.

The MPR sent troops to assist the North Koreans during the Korean War, and has been providing aid to North Vietnam.

Soviet SA-2 missile units guard the key communications hub of Choibalsan in eastern Mongolia, and Soviet medium-range ballistic missile units are farther east, near the Manchurian border, where they can cover greater areas of China as well as U.S. military installations in South Korea and Okinawa. Soviet Forces, Mongolia, are estimated to consist of one army with supporting units, including 10,000 military engineers.

## ALLIANCES

An alliance of friendship and mutual defense with the Soviet Union was signed in 1936. It has been periodically renewed, the latest renewal in 1966 for twenty years. This pact provides for assistance in the event of attack by a third party. Under it Soviet and Mongolian forces fought the Japanese in the 1930s and 1940s; Mongolia sent horses, food, and winter clothing to the Soviet Union during World War II. There are also mutual defense agreements with other Communist countries in the Soviet orbit. Mongolia is not a Warsaw Pact member, but is a member of COMECON. (See Eastern Europe Regional Survey.)

## ARMY

*Personnel:* 24,000

*Organization:*
    2 infantry divisions (including armor units)
    1 (or more) SAM battalions
    cadres for reserve units

*Major Equipment Inventory:*
  140 medium tanks (T-34, T-54/55)
   10 SU-100 self-propelled guns
   90 APC (BTR-152 and BTR-60)
      antitank missiles (Snapper)
      130mm howitzers, 152mm gun/howitzers
      SAMs (SA-2 Guideline; at least 1 battalion)

*Reserves:* Probably personnel for one mechanized infantry division in cadre form. Most adult males have had military service; about 10 percent, or perhaps 30,000, could be quickly mobilized.

## PARAMILITARY

There are four battalions of security police and two to five battalions of frontier guards with a total strength of about 18,000.

There is a Mongolian Society for the Promotion of the Army, founded in 1961, with 100,000 members between the ages of eighteen and thirty-five. It is a pre-military training organization on the lines of the Soviet DOSAAF (Voluntary Organization for Support of the Army, Air Force, and Navy). There is also a Labor Defense Association which is a communist worker's militia of armed factory workers.

# MOROCCO

## Kingdom of Morocco

## POWER POTENTIAL STATISTICS

Area: 171,953 square miles
Population: 19,199,000
Total Active Regular Armed Forces: 60,000 (0.31% population)
Gross National Product: $9.7 billion ($530 per capita)
Annual Military Expenditures: $353 million (3.65% GNP)
Iron Ore Production: 343,000 metric tons
Fuel Production:
    Coal: 702,000 metric tons
    Crude Oil: 10,000 metric tons
    Refined Petroleum Products: 2.7 million metric tons

Electric Power Output: 3.1 billion kwh
Merchant Fleet (ships 1,000 tons and over): 39 ships;
    268,000 gross tons
Civil Air Fleet: 21 major transport aircraft

## DEFENSE STRUCTURE

In this constitutional monarchy the king rules as well as reigns. Despite such trappings of democracy as a unicameral legislature and a prime minister, the king dominates the government. He is chief of the General Staff and supreme commander of the Royal Armed Forces (FAR). A general appointed by the king coordinates the armed forces, gendarmerie, Royal Police Force, and Auxiliary Force. Another general, the army chief of staff, acts as the king's adjutant in his role as chief of the General Staff. A military cabinet advises the king on defense matters. The king personally appoints trusted officers to key posts.

The nation is divided for defense into three military zones and one independent sector: Littoral Zone with headquarters at Casablanca, Central Zone with headquarters at Meknes, Independent Sector with headquarters at Marrakech, and Saharan Zone, controlled from the overall headquarters at Rabat. Upon independence in 1956 the army was formed mainly from Moroccan veterans of the French and Spanish colonial armies, with the further addition of about 5,000 former guerrillas of the Moroccan Army of Liberation.

## POLITICO-MILITARY POLICIES

Morocco has followed a policy of nonalignment in East-West relations and of moderation with regard to the burning issues of the Pan-Arab movement. These policies, as well as a dispute over mineral-rich portions of southwestern Algeria claimed by Morocco, together with the heavy arming of Algeria by the Soviet Union, resulted in tensions between Morocco and Algeria. Soviet assistance to Algeria has given that nation an advantage over Morocco, which has sought additional military aid from the United States with a view to reducing Algeria's preponderance. In January 1969 Algeria's President Boumedienne and Morocco's King Hassan II concluded a Treaty of Solidarity and Cooperation, apparently upon the initiative of the former. In May 1970, agreement was reached on demarcation of the disputed frontier. These conciliatory moves dampened tensions between the two countries until 1975.

Morocco's own irredentism is far from defensive. One of many ancient Moroccan empires included what is now southwestern Algeria, Spanish Sahara, Mauritania, and parts of Mali. The king, both on this basis and in his role as hereditary religious leader of this region, laid claim to these territories for Morocco through the 1960s. However, he overcame rightist pressure to make the agreement with Algeria and also in 1969 renounced sovereignty over Mauritania.

Morocco has pursued its claim to the Spanish (or Western, Sahara. In 1975 it organized 350,000 peasants for a "Green March" on the territory. Though the march itself was forestalled, Spain turned over control of the area to Morocco and Mauritania. They divided it in 1976, the rich phosphate mines going to Morocco. In that same year, however, Algeria supported the Polisario movement, which claimed to be the government of the territory. Morocco and Mauritania, who broke relations with Algeria and formed a defense assistance pact, have been involved in a costly guerrilla war with the Algerian-based Polisario since 1976. France has provided air support to the Moroccan/Mauritanian side. Mauritania renounced its claims to Western Sahara in August 1979, leaving Morocco facing the Polisario Front alone.

The army is 80 percent Berber in composition, but most officers are urban Arabs. The ranks were filled by volunteers until 1966, when a royal decree prescribed conscription of all eighteen-year-olds for eighteen months' service. Two coup attempts by military elements took place in 1971 and 1972. The result was a purging of antiroyalists from the officer corps.

Despite its relatively moderate stance toward Israel, several contingents of Moroccan troops—perhaps 5,000 in all—and some tanks were sent to Syria on Soviet ships in the spring and summer of 1973.

## STRATEGIC PROBLEMS

As both an Atlantic and a Mediterranean power occupying one side of the Straits of Gibraltar, Morocco's strategic situation is significant. Its Western orientation and its location on the fringe of Europe, yet behind a water barrier, led to the United States-French agreement to establish four U.S. Strategic Air Command advanced B-47 bomber bases in French Morocco in 1951. These were continued after independence, but abandoned in 1963 as a result of a change in Moroccan policy, and the phase-out of the B-47. The United States still maintains two naval stations in Morocco.

Besides the continuing conflict over Western Sahara, Morocco's chief security problem has been internal unrest. Unable to secure the cooperation of opposition parties in 1972, King Hassan dissolved the legislature. Elections were postponed until 1977. In the context of the trials of 176 Marxist revolutionaries and the crisis in Western Sahara, the royalists won the majority of seats locally and in the Chamber of Representatives. The king engineered a political coup by bringing the major opposition party, Istiqlal, and one other party into the new cabinet.

In 1968 Spain ceded the small enclave of Ifni to Morocco. In 1973 shooting erupted between Spanish and Moroccan naval forces over a fishing dispute. Spain holds the towns of Ceuta and Melilla plus three other tiny areas on the Moroccan coast, all of which are claimed by Morocco.

Morocco dispatched troops to Zaire in 1977 and 1978 to help secure mineral-rich Shaba Province from Katangese rebels. French and American planes transported the army units. Several thousand troops directly aided Mauritania in fighting the Polisario guerrillas. In January 1977 Benin accused Morocco of conducting a mercenary raid against Benin's capital.

## MILITARY ASSISTANCE

At independence France turned over some $40 million in military equipment; Spain also contributed a significant amount. Spain has since contributed further by training Moroccan officers. French military aid and arms sales continued until 1966, when they were terminated, except for the continued training of 200 officers. Support against the Polisario has been provided since 1976.

Soviet military assistance began in late 1960. Finding Algeria more willing to cooperate in return for arms, the Soviets soon stopped aid to Morocco, but in October 1966 they sold Morocco spare parts for the aircraft, tanks, and artillery previously provided. Total Soviet grants and sales have amounted to nearly $20 million. In 1968, through a barter exchange with Czechoslovakia for $16 million in primary products, Morocco obtained eighty reconditioned T-54 tanks.

From 1956 through 1977 the United States provided $41.9 million in military assistance. In early 1967, following a visit to the United States by the king, $14 million additional assistance was promised, and delivery began on F-5 jet fighters and antitank weapons. A substantial U.S. military mission was established. Approximately 2,351 students have been trained under MAP.

## ALLIANCES

Morocco is a member of the OAU, the Arab League, and the less formal Maghreb (Northwest Africa) grouping. In support of UN peacekeeping operations, Morocco sent a brigade to the Congo from August 1960 to March 1961.

After the 1963 cancellation of the air base agreement with the United States, the Americans retained a major communication center at Kenitra. About 1,500 U.S. military personnel are stationed there.

## ARMY

*Personnel:* 52,000

*Organization:*
      1 armored brigade
      3 motorized infantry brigades
      1 light security brigade
      1 parachute brigade
     15 independent infantry battalions
      4 artillery groups
      2 desert cavalry groups
      4 camel corps battalions

*Major Equipment Inventory:*
    100 medium tanks (M-48)
    120 medium tanks (T-54)
    120 light tanks (AMX-13)
     40 half-tracks (M-3)
     95 APCs (Czech-built)
    300 APCs (M-113)
    100 self-propelled guns and howitzers (M-109, SU-100, M-56 Scorpion, AMX-105, M-50 SP tank destroyers)
     80 armored cars (AML-245, EBR-75, and M-8)
    200 light artillery pieces (75mm and 105mm howitzers, 76mm, 85mm, and 105mm guns, 37mm, 100mm, and Vulcan 20mm antiaircraft guns)
      6 helicopters (Alouette II, Gazelle SA-342)
     37 batteries Hawk SAM
        Chaparral SAM

*Reserves:* About 160,000 trained reservists

## NAVY

*Personnel:* 2,000 (includes marines)

*Major Units:*
      2 patrol craft (PC)
      2 fast patrol craft (PCF; additional units on order)
     10 patrol boats (PB; additional units on order)
      1 coastal minesweeper (MSC)
      3 medium landing ships (LSM)
      1 utility landing craft (LCU)

## AIR FORCE

*Personnel:* 6,000

*Organization:*
      1 fighter squadron (F-5)
      2 ground attack squadrons (Magister)
      2 transport squadrons (C-47, C-130, C-119)
      1 utility/liaison squadron (Broussard)
      6 helicopter squadrons (AB-204/205/212, H-34, OH-13, H-43)

*Major Aircraft Types:*
  56 combat aircraft
    24 F-5 fighters
    32 Magister armed trainer/light attack aircraft
  216 other aircraft
    8 C-119 transports
    10 C-47 transports
    12 C-130 transports
    21 utility/liaison aircraft (Broussard)
    65 helicopters (AB-204/205/212, H-34, OH-13, H-43)
    100 trainers (T-6, SF-260, T-34, T-28)

*Air Bases:* Sale (Rabat), Meknes, Marrakech, Nouasseur; other fields at Fez, Ville, Agadir, Khouribga, Anfa (Casablanca), Larache, Sidi Slimane, Ben Guerir, Boulhout, Solon, Oujda, Kenitra

*Reserves:* About 5,000 trained reservists

## PARAMILITARY

There are 2,250 gendarmerie plus 20,000 auxiliaries. The gendarmerie maintains two mobile security battalions and mans posts spread over the country. The Royal Guards are basically palace guards at the king's various residences. The function of the auxiliaries is unknown. All are subordinate to the Defense Ministry, except the palace guards, who traditionally are Senegalese.

# MOZAMBIQUE

## Peoples Republic of Mozambique

## POWER POTENTIAL STATISTICS

Area: 303,073 square miles
Population: 9,987,000 (includes 50,000 Europeans)
Total Active Regular Armed Forces: 17,500 (0.17% population)
Gross National Product: $2.0 billion ($220 per capita)
Annual Military Expenditures: $82.6 million (4.13% GNP)
Fuel Production:
  Coal: 300,000 metric tons
  Refined Petroleum Products: 372,000 metric tons
Electric Power Output: 558 million kwh
Merchant Fleet (ships 1,000 tons and over): 6 ships; 13,000 gross tons
Civil Air Fleet: 3 jet and 3 turboprop transports

## POLITICO-MILITARY POLICIES AND POSTURE

Mozambique attained independence from Portugal in June 1975. The Front for the Liberation of Mozambique (FRELIMO), which had been fighting Portuguese rule for thirteen years, formed the new government and became the country's sole political party. Samora Machel, FRELIMO president, became president of Mozambique and acts as head of government and commander in chief of the armed forces. Following independence, the estimated 10,000–15,000 FRELIMO troops were reorganized into a national army, and a state police agency, the National Service of Popular Security, was established.

The Machel regime seeks to establish a Marxist socioeconomic structure in Mozambique. During the preindependence era, it administered portions of the country along socialist lines. Since 1975 it has nationalized health services, education, the oil and insurance industries, funeral services, the legal profession, and all rental property, and has sought to reorganize the agricultural sector into communal and state farms. Portuguese remaining in the country were required to undergo "reeducation" and become citizens of Mozambique or leave.

Mozambique has adopted a policy of nonalignment in world affairs but has affirmed a commonality of interests with the Soviet Union and Cuba, both of which provide substantial aid. In 1977, the USSR and Mozambique signed a twenty-year treaty of friendship and cooperation.

Relations with Mozambique's six neighbors range from close cooperation (Tanzania) to outright hostility (Rhodesia). Tanzania has provided two battalions of troops to help control refugee groups. The two nations have agreed to cooperate on settling problems with the Makonde tribe on their border, on commercial ventures, and on studies toward establishing common policy and ideology. Relations with Zambia are also excellent, and a major item under discussion are plans for a rail link. Tanzania, Zambia, Mozambique, Angola, and Botswana cooperate politically as the five "front-line" states in the struggle against white rule in southern Africa. Both Malawi and Swaziland market most of their exports through Mozambique's ports. Political relations with those nations have improved since independence, but are limited by their extensive economic relations with South Africa.

Mozambique's fundamental security problems relate to its posture vis à vis Rhodesia and South Africa. Though favoring majority rule in both countries, Mozambique has pragmatically refrained from breaking with South Africa. The economic cost would be too high. Upwards of 100,000 Mozambicans work in South Africa under contracts extremely beneficial to Mozambique's economy. Rail freight from the Transvaal to the port (and capital) of Maputo provides another critical source of revenue. In

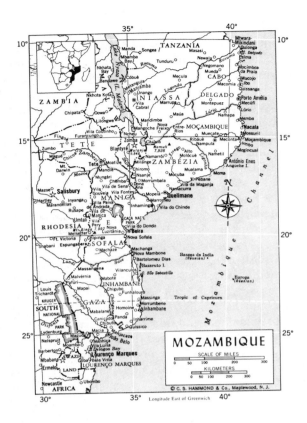

1977 Mozambique allowed sale of electrical output from the Cabora Bassa dam to South Africa. On the other hand, political relations have been strained over Mozambique's closed border with Rhodesia, its anti*apartheid* policy, and the presence in Mozambique of Soviet and Cuban advisers, as well as the headquarters for the African National Congress, a South African opposition group.

Mozambique has provided refugees camps for Rhodesian exiles and has become the headquarters for the Zimbabwe African National Union (ZANU). ZANU has rejected the internal solution for Rhodesian majority rule and has conducted increasingly destructive raids on Rhodesian rural areas from bases in Mozambique. One result has been several Rhodesian reprisals against camps in Mozambique which the government has been unable to prevent. In March 1976 Mozambique, at great economic cost, closed the border with Rhodesia to commerce and communications. Rhodesia has accused FRELIMO forces of joining ZANU's incursions across the border.

A number of factors will hinder Mozambique's evolution into a power of any great substance in the near future. Colonial development was restricted to isolated pockets along the elongated (1,700-mile) coast and inland to service transport routes from South Africa and Rhodesia. Much

of the populace is engaged in subsistence farming. The developed sectors of the economy underwent severe decline with the exodus of skilled whites. In addition to a substantial drop in GNP since 1974, huge trade imbalances and an unattractive investment climate imply a slow recovery from independence dislocations. Some foreign aid from a variety of sources has come as a result of the border-closing with Rhodesia, but this has not offset the revenue losses. Nevertheless, the Machel regime appears to be stable and to enjoy considerable popular support.

## ARMY

*Personnel:* 15,000

*Organization:*
   1 tank battalion
   9 infantry battalions
   2 artillery battalions

*Major Equipment Inventory:*
   35 medium tanks (T-34/54/55)
      light tanks (PT-76)
      APC (BTR-40/60/152)
      light artillery, 85mm, 100mm, 122mm guns/ howitzers BM-21 MRL
      antitank guns, 82mm, 100mm, Sagger ATGM
      antiaircraft guns
      SA-6, SA-7 SAM

## NAVY

*Personnel:* 500

*Major Units:*
   2 patrol boats (PB)

## AIR FORCE

*Personnel:* 2,000

*Organization:*
   1 fighter squadron (MiG-21)
   1 transport squadron (C-47, Noratlas)

*Major Aircraft Types:*
   8 combat aircraft
      8 MiG-21 fighters
   31 other aircraft
      8 C-47, Noratlas transports
      12 T-6 trainers
      8 Zlin liaison aircraft
      3 Alouette II helicopters

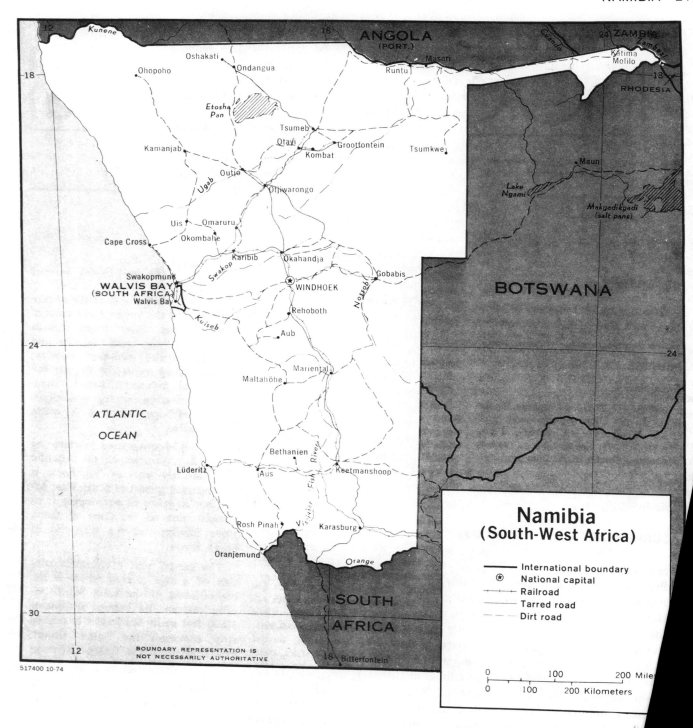

## Namibia
## (South-West Africa)

——— International boundary
(*) National capital
+−+−+ Railroad
——— Tarred road
- - - - Dirt road

0        100        200 Miles
0   100      200 Kilometers

BOUNDARY REPRESENTATION IS
NOT NECESSARILY AUTHORITATIVE

517400 10-74

# NAMIBIA

## POWER POTENTIAL STATISTICS

Area: 318,261 square miles

Population: 978,000
Gross National Product: $800 million ($818
Electric Power Output: 1.1 billion kwh
Civil Air Fleet: 4 major transport aircraft
    South Africa)

## STRATEGIC BACKGROUND

Namibia is the name adopted by Africans and the UN for the territory of South-West Africa. It is a vast arid land with large stretches of desert along its coastal and eastern regions. The area is rich in minerals and has well-developed livestock and fishing industries. The population consists of some 100,000 whites (mostly Afrikaaners), 50,000 "coloreds," and over 700,000 blacks. The black population resides mainly in the north, the whites in the central and southern regions. Whites control the mining, fishing, and agricultural concerns and own most of the productive land.

South-West Africa was a German colony from 1884 to 1920, when a League of Nations mandate placed it under South African administration. In 1946 the UN declared it a trust territory. Failing to get South African cooperation in preparing the territory for independence, the UN unilaterally revoked the mandate and set up a council for Namibia in 1967. A 1971 International Court of Justice ruling verified the illegality of South Africa's rule.

South Africa imposed in Namibia both a system of ocial *apartheid* and a homelands scheme similar to those South Africa itself. It established internal districts for whites and ten black tribal groups. Representatives the ten tribal groups and the white National Party ook constitutional talks in 1975 and reached an ent in early 1977. This "Turnhalle Accord" for the rt confirmed the separate development concept. e, South Africa responded to a Security Council v declaring that it would grant independence to 1979. However, this has not yet occurred.

### NT SITUATION (Mid-1978)

South-West Africa People's Organization onducted a guerrilla war against South s won recognition from the UN as the ative of the Namibian people. SWAPO gth from the Ovambo tribe, which ). SWAPO has rejected the Turnhalle stepped up its campaign of attacks ces and assassinations of tribal the 1977 agreement. Militarily, d greatly since 1976 because of its Nonetheless, it remains inferior in forces, who conducted a raid on e Angola in May 1978, killing

per capita)
registered in

uncil members (the United rance, West Germany, and lly for South African abanlution. In April 1978 South ised one-man, one-vote elecof most of its 15,000-man

military force. Under pressure from the Western nations and from the five front-line African presidents, Sam Nujoma, the SWAPO leader, indicated his acceptance of the proposal in July 1978.

However, hostilities continued and UN ceasefire efforts were unsuccessful. Following increased SWAPO raids and sabotage, South Africa carried out arrests of 39 SWAPO leaders in April 1979. Rejecting the UN plan for independence, South Africa established a national legislative assembly for Namibia in May 1979, but withheld independence. (See also South Africa.)

# NEPAL

## POWER POTENTIAL STATISTICS

Area: 54,362 square miles
Population: 13,854,000
Total Active Regular Armed Forces: 20,500 (0.15% population)
Gross National Product: $1.3 billion ($100 per capita)
Annual Military Expenditures: $16.4 million (1.26% GNP)
Electric Power Output: 144 million kwh
Civil Air Fleet: 5 turboprop transport aircraft

## POLITICO-MILITARY POLICIES AND POSTURE

The renowned, and possibly the most important, resource of this small Himalayan kingdom is its fierce Gurkha manpower. For more than a century Gurkha regiments were prominent in the British Indian Army, with a combat potential proportionately much greater than their numerical ratio within that army. In 1947, upon the partition of British India and Pakistan and the division of the army between the two new countries, India retained six Gurkha regiments while the British kept four as the Brigade of Gurkhas, thus perpetuating a great military tradition. Both governments are permitted to recruit Gurkhas in Nepal, and India has subsequently raised another regiment.

Nepal, situated between two major powers, must maneuver and placate to survive. It formerly had a collective security agreement with India, with whom it has substantial defense, political, and economic ties. These included supply of arms and training. However, in June 1969 Nepal cancelled the mutual security agreement and called for withdrawal of Indian troops, but accepted Indian aid in training officers and men. Cordial relations are maintained with Great Britain, the United States,

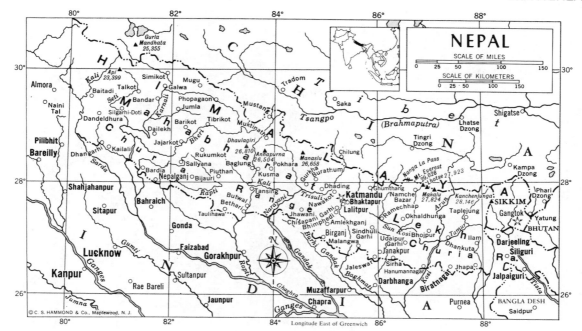

Communist China, and the Soviet Union. All of these have provided Nepal with varying forms of economic assistance, that of the United States being the most significant. Britain and the United States also have provided military assistance. The United States gave $2.0 million through 1976 and trained fifty-seven students under the MAP.

The regular Nepalese army of about 20,000 men (mostly Gurkhas), is organized as two understrength divisions. A militia reserve of trained military veterans, some 24,000 to 30,000, can be mobilized to bring these divisions to full combat strength. There is a small but growing air force, currently about 500 men, equipped with British aircraft— two Skyvan and three HS748 light transports and SA33J Puma and Indian-built Alouette III helicopters. Its mission is to provide reconnaissance and logistical support for the army, particularly for internal security, and to undertake border patrol.

# NETHERLANDS

## Kingdom of the Netherlands

## POWER POTENTIAL STATISTICS

Area: 13,967 square miles
Population: 13,976,000

Total Active Regular Armed Forces: 109,500 (0.78% population)

Gross National Product: $105.3 billion ($7,590 per capita)

Annual Military Expenditures: $4.2 billion (3.99% GNP)

Crude Steel Production: 7.7 million metric tons

Fuel Production:

Coal: 765,000 metric tons

Crude Oil: 1.37 million metric tons

Refined Petroleum Products: 70.4 million metric tons

Natural Gas: 97.3 billion cubic meters

Manufactured Gas: 1.0 billion cubic meters

Electric Power Output: 59 billion kwh

Nuclear Power Production: 500 megawatts

Merchant Fleet (ships 1,000 tons and over): 443 ships; 4.8 million gross tons

Civil Air Fleet: 97 major transport aircraft

## DEFENSE STRUCTURE

The queen is nominal commander in chief of the armed forces. The Council of Ministers is responsible to the prime minister for the preparation and implementation of all defense plans. The minister of defense, as member of the council and assisted by his three service secretaries of state, is responsible for military preparedness and the organization of the armed forces. A Military Committee, consisting of the three chiefs of staff and a chairman (general or admiral), advises the civilian authorities. Command authority is vested in the individual chiefs of staff, who are directly accountable to the government.

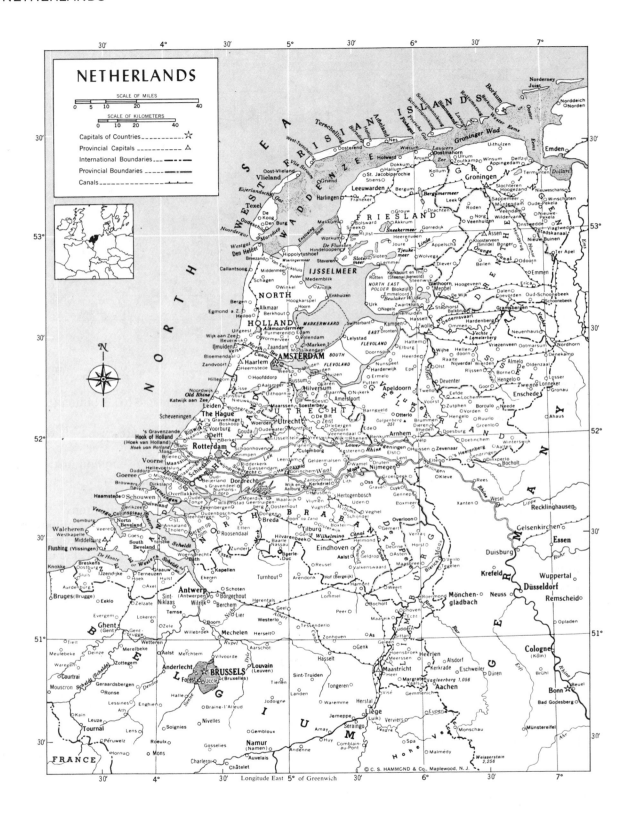

## POLITICO-MILITARY POLICY

The Netherlands is a charter member of the North Atlantic Treaty Alliance, and its commitment to NATO is reflected in the missions of the armed forces. Most of the Dutch army is assigned to the Northern Army Group of NATO's AFCENT Command. Only a few ground units are retained for the territorial defense of the country. The Dutch air force is largely integrated into NATO's Second Allied Tactical Air Force. The bulk of the Dutch navy is divided between two NATO commitments: the Eastern Atlantic Command (part of ACLANT) and the Channel Command (ACCHAN).

The Dutch armed forces are also responsible for the defense of the overseas territories in the West Indies.

Universal military service provides the bulk of the manpower for the armed forces *(Krijgsmacht)*. Some 50,000 men annually are called to the colors for a term of sixteen to twenty-one months, depending on the branch of service.

There is a strong draftees' union, and partly as a result, Dutch troops may wear their hair long, omit salutes, dress casually, and ignore many aspects of traditional military discipline. They also receive unusually high pay, plus compensation for overtime work. Despite their informal appearance, Dutch troops consistently perform well in NATO fall exercises.

## STRATEGIC PROBLEMS

The location of the country and the lack of territorial and air-space depth render the Dutch dependent on the NATO alliance for their security.

In 1949, when Indonesia became independent, about 5,000 residents of the South Moluccan Islands, west of New Guinea, which became part of Indonesia, emigrated to the Netherlands. Many had fought on the side of the Dutch in the Indonesian war for independence. They remain an unassimilated but generally peaceable minority, now numbering about 40,000. A small number of militants, dedicated to the dream of an independent South Moluccan republic and demanding that the Netherlands government support their claims, have perpetrated at least four terrorist incidents since 1975. Their seizure of a train and an elementary school in 1977 and of a government building in 1978 were effectively handled, with minimum loss of life, by special antiterrorist units of Dutch marines.

## MILITARY ASSISTANCE

The Netherlands has received no military aid from the United States since 1968.

## ALLIANCES

The Netherlands is a member of NATO, Western European Union, Benelux, and the European Economic Community.

## ARMY

*Personnel:* 73,000

*Organization:*
- 1 corps (assigned to NATO)
- 2 armored brigades
- 4 armored infantry brigades
- 2 SSM battalions (Honest John)

*Major Equipment Inventory:*
- 900 medium tanks (500 Centurion, 400 Leopard)
- 120 light tanks/tank destroyers (AMX-13 with 105mm gun)
- 2,300 APC's (AMX-VTT, M-113, AIFV, DAF-YP-408, M-106, M-577)
- 260 self-propelled guns/howitzers (203mm M-11, 175mm M-107, 105mm and 155mm AMX-105 and M-109)
- SSM launchers (Honest John)
- 100 helicopters (see Air Force)

*Reserves:* Approximately 40,000 men are immediately available for mobilization into one infantry division plus combat and service support corps troops earmarked for NATO. Privates are subject to recall up to the age of thirty-five, NCOs up the the age of forty, and officers can be recalled up to forty-five years of age. Trained reservists total about 350,000.

## NAVY

*Personnel:* 17,000 (including 3,000 marines and 2,000 naval air force)

*Major Units:*
- 6 diesel submarines (2 each Zwaardis, Potvis and Dofijn classes; SS)
- 2 guided missile destroyers (Tromp class; DDG; Tartar and Seasparrow SAMs)
- 9 destroyers (8 Friesland class; 1 Holland class; DD)
- 6 frigates (Van Speijk class; FF; Seacat short-range SAMs fitted)
- 1 guided missile frigate (Kortenaer class; FFG; Harpoon SSMs and Seasparrow SAMs; 11 more planned)
- 6 patrol ships (Wolf class; PGF)

5 patrol craft (Halder class; PC)
2 fast combat support ships
4 mine countermeasures support ships (MCS)
18 coastal minesweepers (MSC)
16 inshore minesweepers (MSI)
11 personnel landing craft (LCP)
3 hydrographic/oceanographic ships
5 auxiliary ships
20 service craft
2 long-range maritime patrol squadrons
2 ASW helicopter squadrons

*Major Aircraft Types:*
8 Breguet Atlantiques
15 P2V7 Neptunes
12 Westland Wasp helicopters (carried on FF's)
6 Lynx helicopters

*Major Naval Bases:* den Helder and Vlissingen

*Naval Air Stations:* Valkenburg and De Kooy

*Reserves:* About 10,000 reservists (including naval air and marine personnel)

## AIR FORCE

*Personnel:* 19,500

*Organization:* All air force units are assigned to NATO
2 interceptor squadrons (F-104)
5 fighter-bomber squadrons (F-104, F-5)
1 reconnaissance squadron (RF-104)
1 transport squadron (Fokker F-27)
3 light aircraft squadrons (Alouette III and Bo-105C)
12 SAM squadrons (8 Hawk, 4 Nike-Hercules)

*Major Aircraft Types:*
172 combat aircraft
72 F-104 interceptors/fighter-bombers
18 RF-104 fighter/reconnaissance aircraft
82 F-5 fighter-bombers/fighter trainers
117 other aircraft
12 F-27 transports
105 helicopters (Alouette III and Bo-105C)

*Major Air Bases:* Deelen, Eindhoven, Gilse Rijen, Leeuwarden, Soesterberg, Twenthe, Volkel

## PARAMILITARY

The State Police Corps, numbering 4,600, includes water, mounted, and motor police and is under the Ministry of Justice. The Royal *Marechausse* (gendarmerie) numbers about 3,200 men.

# NETHERLANDS ANTILLES

## POWER POTENTIAL STATISTICS

Area: 317 square miles
Population: 249,000
Gross National Product: $652 million ($2,680 per capita)
Fuel Production: Refined Petroleum Products: 33.15 million metric tons
Electric Power Output: 1.7 billion kwh
Civil Air Fleet: 3 jet, 2 turboprop, and 7 piston transports

## POLITICO-MILITARY POLICIES AND POSTURE

The Netherlands Antilles consist of two sets of islands: northern (St. Martin, Saba, St. Eustatius) and southern (Curacao, Aruba, Bonaire); they form one of the two components of the Kingdom of the Netherlands, the other being the Netherlands proper. The queen is represented by an appointed governor, who is chief of state and head of government. Responsibility for foreign policy and defense resides in the Council of Ministers at The Hague. The Antilles islands have full autonomy in internal affairs. They are organized as four territories—Aruba, Bonaire, Curacao, and the Windward Islands.

Curacao is the principal island, with a per capita income of $1,090. The major economic activity of Curacao and Aruba is refining crude oil from Venezuela.

Netherlands naval units, based on Aruba and Curacao, consist of two escorts, one landing craft utility, one squadron of Tracker antisubmarine patrol aircraft, and two companies of marines.

# NEW ZEALAND

## POWER POTENTIAL STATISTICS

Area: 103,736 square miles
Population: 3,176,838
Total Active Regular Armed Forces: 12,490 (0.39% population)
Gross National Product: $12.8 billion ($4,060 per capita)
Annual Military Expenditures: $281.8 million (2.20% GNP)
Fuel Production:
Coal: 460,000 metric tons
Lignite: 2.0 million metric tons
Crude Oil: 136,000 metric tons

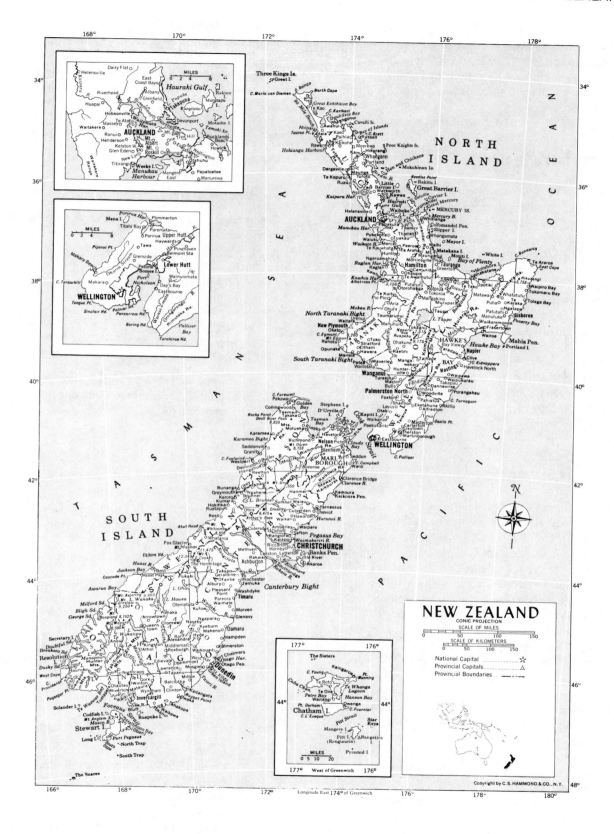

NEW ZEALAND
CONIC PROJECTION
SCALE OF MILES
SCALE OF KILOMETERS

National Capital ............ ☆
Provincial Capitals ............ △
Provincial Boundaries ............ ———

Copyright by C. S. HAMMOND & CO., N.Y.

Refined Petroleum Products: 3.4 million metric tons
Natural Gas: 876 million cubic meters
Manufactured Gas: 78 million cubic meters
Electric Power Output: 22.1 billion kwh
Merchant Fleet (ships 1,000 tons and over): 24 ships; 160,000 gross tons
Civil Air Fleet: 20 jets and 20 turboprop transports

## DEFENSE STRUCTURE

Nominally, the commander in chief of the armed forces of New Zealand is the governor general, who is the representative of the queen in New Zealand. In New Zealand's parliamentary government, however, executive power—including authority over the armed forces—is vested in the prime minister and the cabinet, who are responsible to Parliament. Principal responsibility for defense matters within the cabinet rests with the minister of defence, who presides over the Ministry of Defence and who is chairman of the Defence Council, which directs the administration and command of the armed forces. The Defence Council also comprises the chief of the Defence Staff, who is the principal military adviser to the minister; the secretary of defence, who is the permanent head of the Ministry of Defence and principal civilian adviser to the minister; and the chiefs of the general (army, navy, and air) staffs.

## POLITICO-MILITARY POLICY

New Zealand seeks as far as possible to maintain independent means of self-defense. The defense relationship with the United States and Australia, which finds formal expression in the ANZUS Treaty, is the most significant factor in New Zealand's defense policy. There are additional well-developed defense ties with Australia which reflect shared strategic interests as well as a close identity of national character and outlook.

With the approval of the governments of Malaysia and Singapore, New Zealand maintains military forces in Singapore, under the Five-Power (Malaysia, Singapore, Australia, New Zealand, and United Kingdom) Defence Arrangements.

In the absence of any direct defense threat, New Zealand is placing increasing stress on the potential of its armed forces to carry out civilian aid activities, both within New Zealand and as part of aid programs to developing nations. However, such tasks are not performed at the expense of military capabilities.

New Zealand's defense forces are composed of regular servicemen, backed by an Army Territorial Force and small air force and naval reserves. All military service is on a voluntary basis.

## MILITARY ASSISTANCE

New Zealand is not the recipient of any foreign military aid. Extensive training and reciprocal exchange programs are arranged with the United Kingdom, Australia, and the United States. Some training assistance is provided for Malaysian, Singaporean, Indonesian, and Papuan New Guinea students to attend service courses in New Zealand.

## ARMY

*Personnel:* 5,441

*Organization:* 2 brigade groups (a mix of Regular Force operational units plus Territorial units)

*Deployment:* 1 infantry battalion (light) in Singapore

*Major Equipment Inventory:*
    10 light tanks (M-41)
     9 scout cars (Ferret)
    59 APCs (M-113)
    40 howitzers (105mm)
     8 field guns (5.5-inch)

*Reserves:* The active Territorial Force numbers 5,861 and is available for rapid mobilization to fill out the regular army units.

## NAVY

*Personnel:* 2,760

*Major Units:*
    4 frigates (2 Leander and 2 Whitby class; FF; Seacat short-range SAMs fitted)
    4 patrol craft (PC)
    6 patrol boats (PB; 4 used for reservists training)
    1 survey ship (AGS)
    1 research ship
    5 service craft
    3 helicopters (Wasp)

*Major Naval Base:* Auckland

*Reserves:* There are about 1,000 naval reservists.

## AIR FORCE

*Personnel:* 4,289

*Organization:*
    Air Staff in Defense Headquarters
    1 operations group
    1 support group
    1 ground attack squadron (A-4)
    1 maritime patrol squadron (P-3)
    3 transport squadrons (C-130, Andover C MK1)

*Major Aircraft Types:*
18 combat aircraft
   13 attack aircraft (A-4)
    5 maritime reconnaissance aircraft (P-3)
88+ other aircraft
   18 transports (5 C-130, 10 Andover C MK1,
      3 Devon)
   45 trainers (16 Strikemaster, 5 Devon, 20
      Airtrainer, 4 Airtourer)
   25 helicopters (11 Sioux, 14 Iroquois)

*Deployment:* A helicopter support flight is permanently based in Singapore as part of the New Zealand Force, Southeast Asia. It is equipped with Iroquois helicopters. No. 75 Squadron (A4K Skyhawks), based in New Zealand, makes periodic deployments in the area.

*Major Air Bases:* Ohakea, Auckland (Whenuapai and Hobsonville), Wigram, Woodbourne.

# NICARAGUA

## Republic of Nicaragua

## POWER POTENTIAL STATISTICS

Area: 57,143 square miles
Population: 2,447,000
Total Active Regular Armed Forces: 7,100 (0.29%
  population)
Gross National Product: $2.24 billion ($980 per capita)

Annual Military Expenditures: $56.2 million (2.51%
  GNP)
Fuel Production: Refined Petroleum Products: 681,000
  metric tons
Electric Power Output: 1.2 million kwh
Merchant Fleet (ships 1,000 tons and over): 9 ships;
  22,000 gross tons
Civil Air Fleet: 12 major transport aircraft

## POLITICO-MILITARY POLICIES AND POSTURE

During the period of American military occupation of Nicaragua (1912–33) the U.S. Marines established and trained a professional *Guardia National* designed to maintain internal order in Nicaragua and to promote democratic government. However, this elite body took advantage of its position and, under Gen. Anastasio Somoza, soon took control of the country, which was dominated by the Somoza family and the *Guardia* until 1979. The *Guardia* serves as army and police force, and includes a coast guard and the air force.

On May 1, 1972, President Anastasio Somoza resigned in favor of a three-man junta. Somoza retained command of the *Guardia Nacional.* Following a severe earthquake, which levelled Managua in December 1972, Somoza made himself president of the National Emergency Committee and declared martial law, thereby becoming the country's chief executive. In 1974, after a constitutional change, he was elected president.

The Communist-backed Frente Sandinista de Liberación Nacional, which had been conducting guerrilla-type activities against the government for several years, developed strong forces by 1978 and in 1979 increased its operations to the proportions of a civil war.

The OAS attempted mediation between the government and the Broad Opposition Front (FAO), a fourteen-party anti-Somoza coalition, with the United States, Guatemala, and the Dominican Republic serving as mediators, but the mediators' efforts for agreement on a plebiscite failed. With U.S. military assistance cut off, Somoza sought aid (December 1978) from the leaders of Guatemala, El Salvador, and Honduras, while Venezuela, Costa Rica and Panama were apparently aiding the Sandanista forces. The United States tried to discourage this aid, focusing its efforts on a political solution.

Months of bloody fighting between Sandinista guerrillas and National Guard troops—during which city after city fell to the rebels—climaxed in June 1979 as the rebels consolidated their power in the south and began the final push toward Managua.

The Sandinista rebels announced the formation of a five-member provisional government intended to replace Somoza after his defeat. Originally, the U.S. position had been to avoid recognizing the junta while pursuing

Somoza's replacement by the Nicaraguan congress. However, when the congress failed in its attempts to legislate a change in the country's government, the United States agreed to pressure Somoza to resign and, to facilitate an orderly transfer of power and to avoid anarchy, agreed to give economic aid to the junta if the rebels added more moderates to their ranks and refrained from inflicting vengeance upon the National Guard.

The United States and the Sandinistas began direct negotiations in June. Although the Sandinistas refused to expand the junta, they did agree not to subject the National Guard to reprisals and to allow some of Somoza's supporters to leave the country.

Somoza resigned on June 17. The civil war ended on June 19 with the rebel capture of Managua and the subsequent surrender of the National Guard.

Much of the fighting was near the Costa Rican border. Costa Rica broke off relations with Nicaragua (November 1978), and Somoza closed the Costa Rican border (December 1978). The northern city of Esteli changed hands between the Sandinistas and National Guard several times in 1978 and 1979.

The United States provided Nicaragua $649,000 in military assistance in 1977, making a total of $18.2 million since 1950. Under the MAP 5,401 students have been trained. The United States cut off all military assistance in 1978.

Nicaragua is a member of the OAS and ODECA. The ground arm of the *Guardia* is about 5,400 strong, consisting of volunteers enlisted for three years. It is organized in twenty infantry companies, a motorized detachment, engineers, and an antiaircraft battery. It is equipped with U.S. materiel, including armored personnel carriers and two Cessna U-17A liaison aircraft. There is a *Guardia* reserve of 4,000. The Coast Guard numbers about 200 and operates six patrol craft (YP) divided between Pacific and Caribbean coasts. The air force has about 1,500 men. It has six T-33 armed jet trainers, six B-26 light piston bombers, six T-28 light armed piston trainers, and fourteen transports (C-47, Arava 201, Cessna 180). There are also about fifteen trainers (PT-13, PT-19, T-6). Air bases are at Managua and Puerto Cabeza with small strips throughout the country. There is a gendarmerie of 4,000 men.

# NIGER

## Republic of Niger

### POWER POTENTIAL STATISTICS

Area: 489,206 square miles
Population: 5,064,000
Total Active Regular Armed Forces: 2,100 (0.04% population)

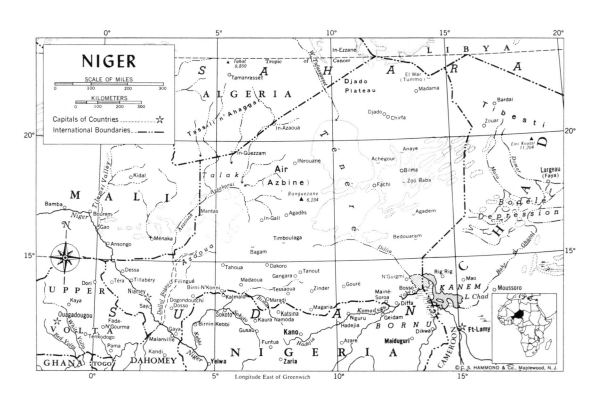

Gross National Product: $510 million ($100 per capita)
Annual Military Expenditures: $16.8 million (3.29%
  GNP)
Electric Power Output: 70 million kwh
Civil Air Fleet: 3 major transport aircraft

## POLITICO-MILITARY POLICIES AND POSTURE

Constitutional government fell victim in April 1974 to
the Sahelian drought, which has been especially severe in
Niger. A military coup, led by Lt. Col. Seyni Kountche,
seized control from Hamani Diori (who had served compe-
tently as president since 1960), dissolved the National
Assembly, and outlawed all political activity. Kountche
laid the whole blame for the former government's fall on
its allegedly inadequate response to the famine. The
president heads the Supreme Military Council, which runs
the country by decree.

Following the 1974 coup, Niger ordered home the
270-man French garrison, but it has since allowed an
estimated 100 French soldiers to return. France continues
to have substantial investments in uranium mining. Niger
has established closer ties with Communist states since
1974.

Niger is a member of the OAU and OCAM, and has
joined both the West African Economic Community and
the Economic Community of West African States. In 1976
Niger, Libya, and Algeria formed a Tripartite Commission
to study closer regional cooperation. Libya and Niger have
a defense and security treaty dating from 1974.

Niger is the terminus of two trans-Saharan caravan and
motor routes from Algeria. One military problem is the
protection of these routes from the occasional bandits
among the nomadic tribesmen in the north.

Former President Diori probably had been the most
successful leader of the region in containing internal
dissidence; Kountche's government has had more
difficulty. There have been at least three coup attempts
since 1974. With a low per capita income, a high birth rate,
and the tensions between Negro and Berber peoples
common to the northern sub-Sahara Africa, Niger can
expect continuing socioeconomic problems. The country's
large high-grade uranium ore deposits and large iron
deposits not only make Niger strategically significant, but
can be expected eventually to provide income to offset
current budget deficits, and perhaps to ameliorate internal
strife.

Upon independence Niger entered mutual defense and
military assistance agreements with France covering base
rights, transit and overflight privileges, and military
training and equipping. It also entered into a quadripartite
defense agreement with France, Dahomey, and Ivory
Coast; and joined the *Conseil de l'Entente,* a political-
economic grouping of Dahomey (now Benin), Ivory Coast,
Togo, and Upper Volta.

The army is about 2,000 strong and is maintained by
selective two-year conscription. It is organized into five
infantry companies, one armored car company, and a
para-commando platoon. The air force has a strength of
about 100 and operates four Noratlas transports, one C-47
transport, and three Broussard utility aircraft. Air bases
are Niamey, Zinder, Agadez, Tahoua, and Maradi. There
is a river patrol with two river patrol boats (PBR) on the
Niger River operating from Niamey. The gendarmerie has
a strength of 1,300. Under the MAP Niger has received
$63,000 from the United States, and four students have
received training.

# NIGERIA

## Federal Republic of Nigeria

## POWER POTENTIAL STATISTICS

Area: 356,699 square miles
Population: 69,492,000
Total Active Regular Armed Forces: 208,000 (0.30%
  population)
Gross National Product: $33 billion ($500 per capita)
Annual Military Expenditures: $2.1 billion (6.36%
  GNP)
Fuel Production:
  Crude Oil: 102.7 million metric tons
  Refined Petroleum Products: 2.86 million metric tons
  Natural Gas: 661 million cubic meters
Electric Power Output: 4 billion kwh
Merchant Fleet (ships 1,000 tons and over): 26 ships;
  307,000 gross tons
Civil Air Fleet: 39 major transport aircraft

## DEFENSE STRUCTURE

A federal republic and member of the Commonwealth,
Nigeria, following the termination of its civil war in 1970,
remained under the Federal Military Government which
conducted the war against the Biafran secession. At the
head of this government is a Supreme Military Council
(SMC) under Lt. Gen. Olusegun Obasanjo, the commander in chief of the armed forces. The council controls all
government, including military affairs, by decree, the
Constitution having been in abeyance since 1966. The
chiefs of staff of the three services are members of the
council, which has a general staff modelled on the British
system.

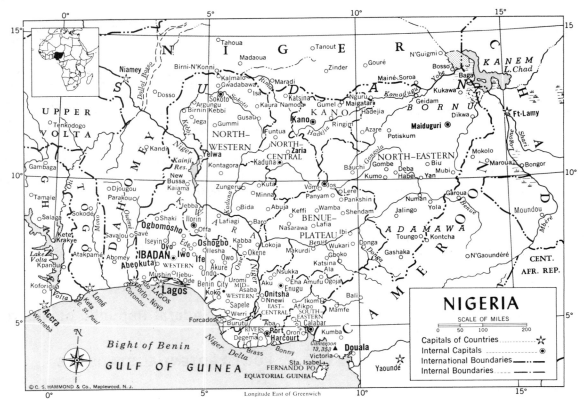

## POLITICO-MILITARY POLICIES

Nigeria has made an excellent economic and psychological recovery from the civil war, and is now resuming the leadership role in Africa that is suggested by its size, economic resources, and military establishment.

Upon independence from Britain in 1960 the army was formed from Nigerian elements of the Royal West African Frontier Force. At the time 25 percent of the officers were Nigerian; the rest were seconded from the British army. As a result of increased officer training in Britain, Canada, Australia, India, Pakistan, Israel, Ethiopia, and in U.S. university ROTC, the last British officers were relieved in 1966.

The original civilian government of the shaky, ethnically divided federation was overthrown in a military coup in January 1966. The new head of government and about half of the army officers were Ibos—a progressive tribe of southeastern Nigeria, constituting about 12 percent of the population, whose energy and education had given them leadership in Nigerian business and government far out of proportion to their numbers. Tribal resentment of Ibo influence, combined with widespread political unrest, resulted in a counter-coup in July, which triggered nation-wide attacks against Ibo government officials and businessmen. Growing alienation from the rest of Nigeria

led the Ibos of the Eastern Region to secede from Nigeria in May 1967. The federal government refused to permit this. A long, bloody, civil war followed, in which the federal government finally overcame desperate Ibo resistance in January 1970. The rebel leader, General Ojukwu, fled to Ivory Coast, where he was granted asylum.

During the civil war the Nigerian forces expanded from 12,000 to over 180,000, with consequent dilution of trained leaders. In 1978 the military numbered over 200,000. Defense expenditures consumed one-sixth of government spending. Having by far the largest black African army, Nigeria admits a lack of trained officers, modern equipment, and adequate bases. The SMC has cautiously initiated plans for demobilization of 60,000 to 100,000 soldiers. Military service is voluntary.

Immediately after victory, the Nigerian Federal Government, then under Maj. Gen. Yakubu Gowon, proclaimed a policy of reconstruction, rehabilitation, and reconciliation. Gowon had made little progress toward the promised return to civil rule when he was ousted in a bloodless coup led by Brigadier Muhammad in 1975. Muhammad, himself assassinated in 1976, set Nigeria on a course for return to civilian government by October 1979. His successor, Obasanjo, followed through with these plans, which included reorganizing the country into nineteen states, drafting a U.S.-style constitution, and holding elections for a constituent assembly to revise and adopt the constitution. Political parties were banned until October 1978. They emerged for elections in 1979 for president, vice president, and the bicameral National Assembly. The capital was to be moved to Abuja, in the center of the country. Shehu Shagari was elected president and was inaugurated October 1, 1979.

Relations between the Ibos and the rest of the population have improved. The most important factor in this recovery is oil. With an output of about 2.3 million barrels a day, Nigeria had become the world's eighth largest oil producer by fall 1973. Nigeria's oil became even more important with the Arab oil embargo of 1973–74, and Nigerian oil revenues exceeded $9 billion in 1977, accounting for 95 percent of Nigeria's foreign exchange earnings. The government has allocated large amounts to reconstruction of the Ibo areas, construction of roads, railroads, and airports, and to aid to agriculture.

Nigeria is also using its new power, with moderation, in foreign affairs. The country stands steadfastly behind efforts to end white minority rule in southern Africa. Nigeria supports the Patriotic Front in its guerrilla war against the Rhodesian "internal settlement" regime. Obasanjo has proclaimed his readiness to aid black opposition movements in South Africa, and he condemns the West for not imposing a boycott to force majority rule. Nigeria has approved of Cuban intervention in Angola. It was a prime founder, with Togo, of the Economic Community of West African States, which Nigeria hopes will bridge Francophone and Anglophone economies. The leadership recognizes that Nigeria will play a major role in Africa and has offered mediation in several disputes. Relations with most of its neighbors are friendly as are ties with the East and West globally.

Nigeria's main strategic problem is avoidance of internal conflict. The defeated Ibos, now somewhat reduced in numbers through casualties and noncombat military and civilian deaths, are not likely again to attempt to secede. However, they do remain the most progressive, energetic, and educated segment of the population, and the oil fields in the Eastern Region will tend to provide resources and incentive to their more rapid advancement and development. The Yorubas of the Western Region may again become jealous of the Ibos, as may the somewhat less educated and more warlike Moslem Hausa-Fulanis of the Northern Region. Realignment of the federal states is intended to introduce a regional-tribal pluralism. Re-creation of political parties, constitutional autonomy for states, and a carefully designed electoral system may further diffuse tribal pressures.

More serious internal problems than intertribal rivalries appear to be urban blight, agricultural depression, and the increasing gap between the extremely wealthy beneficiaries of Nigeria's new economic riches and the great number of Nigerians living in poverty. As indicated above, some government efforts are being made to attack these problems.

## MILITARY ASSISTANCE

After independence, Britain provided arms, naval craft and navy training, while two ships were supplied by the Netherlands. West Germany trained the air force. Italian trainers, German liaison aircraft, and French transports were purchased. The United States granted $1.5 million in military assistance from 1960 through mid-1977, and trained 472 students under MAP.

During the civil war, many countries kept a hands-off policy, but Britain, the Soviet Union, and for a time France, responded to cash offers for needed arms. From Britain came armored cars, artillery, small arms, and ammunition. The Soviet Union and Czechoslovakia sent jet fighters and transport aircraft. The United States reduced its military assistance to military medical training only, but renewed assistance after hostilities ceased.

## ALLIANCES

Nigeria is a member of the Commonwealth, OAU, and OPEC. In support of UN peacekeeping operations Nigeria provided a two-battalion force for the UN operation in the Congo from December 1960 to June 1963, and one battalion thereafter to June 1964.

## ARMY

*Personnel:* 200,000

*Organization:*
    4 infantry divisions
    4 reconnaissance regiments
    4 artillery regiments

*Major Equipment Inventory:*
    20 armored cars (AML-60/90)
    150 armored cars (Saladin)
        scout cars (Ferret)
        APCs (Saracen)
        light artillery (25-pounder gun, 76mm gun, 105mm howitzer, 122mm gun/howitzer)

*Reserves:* Over 100,000

## NAVY

*Personnel:* 3,000

*Major Units:*
    1 frigate (Nigeria class; FF)
    2 patrol escorts (2 MK3 class; 4-inch guns; PG)

8 patrol craft (PC)
4 patrol boats (PB)
1 utility landing craft (LCU)
1 survey ship
1 training ship
1 tug
8 police roadstead patrol boats (PBR)

*Reserves:* Possibly 2,500

*Naval Bases:* Lagos, Calabar

## AIR FORCE

*Personnel:* 5,000

*Organization:*
1 light bomber squadron (Il-28)
1 fighter squadron (MiG-21)
2 fighter-bomber squadrons (MiG-17)
1 light ground attack squadron (L-29)
3 training squadrons (P-149, Bulldog, MiG-15)
2 transport squadrons (C-47, Do-27, C-130, F-27)
1 helicopter squadron (Whirlwind and Alouette II)

*Major Aircraft Types:*
45 combat aircraft
    15 MiG-17 fighter-bombers
    14 MiG-21 fighters
    10 L-29 armed trainer/light ground attack
       aircraft
    6 Il-28 light bombers
109 other aircraft
    3 C-130 transports
    6 C-47 transports
    12 F-27 Friendship transports
    20 Do-27/28 utility aircraft
    18 helicopters (Whirlwind and Allouette II)
    50 trainers (P-149, Bulldog, MiG-15)

*Reserves:* Over 4,000

*Air Bases:* Lagos, Kaduna, Ikeja, Maiduguri, Kano

# NORWAY

## Kingdom of Norway

## POWER POTENTIAL STATISTICS

Area: 149,150 square miles (includes Svalbara)
Population: 4,067,000
Total Active Regular Armed Forces: 38,400 (0.94%
    population)

Gross National Product: $35.8 billion ($8,850 per capita)
Annual Military Expenditures: $1.4 billion (3.9% GNP)
Crude Steel Production: 898,000 metric tons
Iron Ore Production: 3.9 million metric tons
Fuel Production:
    Coal: 545,000 metric tons
    Crude Oil: 13.7 million metric tons
    Refined Petroleum Products: 8.5 million metric tons
    Manufactured Gas: 25 million cubic meters
Electric Power Output: 72.5 billion kwh
Merchant Fleet (ships 1,000 tons and over): 978 ships;
    29.5 million gross tons
Civil Air Fleet: 49 major transport aircraft

## DEFENSE STRUCTURE

Norway is a constitutional monarchy; the king is the nominal commander in chief of the armed forces. Control is exercised by the parliamentary cabinet, with the minister of defense responsible for administering the three independent military services.

## POLITICO-MILITARY POLICY

Before World II, Norway adhered to the traditional Scandinavian policy of neutrality. The experience of that war convinced Norwegians that neutrality will not deter an aggressor, and that Norwegian defense policy must be built upon a mutual security alliance, since Norway cannot possibly muster the military strength to defend itself against a major aggressor. Thus Norway has been a wholehearted participant in the NATO alliance, but, to avoid offense to its Soviet neighbor (Norway is the only NATO country, except Turkey, having a mutual frontier with Russia), it has consistently refused to allow allied troop units, or bases, or stored nuclear weapons, on Norwegian soil.

NATO maintains a regional headquarters, that of Commander in Chief North (CINCNORTH) at Kolsaas near Oslo. Officers of various NATO nations are represented on the staff. NATO units visit Norway to participate in maneuvers.

Norway furnished a unit for the UN Emergency Force in the Gaza Strip until evacuated in June 1967. At present Norway contributes twenty UN observers in the Middle East and Kashmir.

Norway's armed forces are maintained by conscription, with an annual call-up of more than 20,000 young men. Service is for twelve months in the army, and fifteen months in the navy and air force. Most of the Norwegian armed forces are earmarked for AFNORTH (Allied Forces Northern Europe).

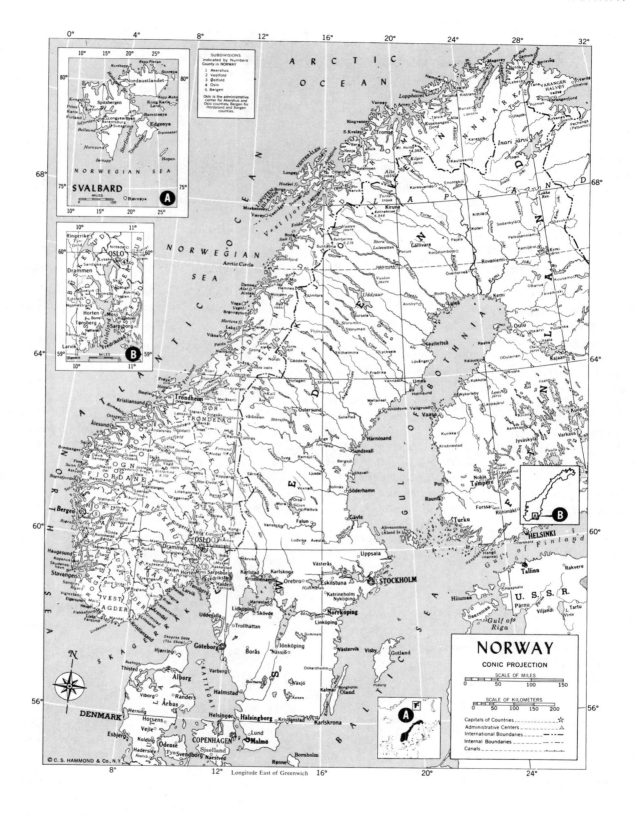

## STRATEGIC PROBLEMS

Norway's extreme length (its eastern boundary is over 1,600 miles long), the rugged nature of the interior of the country (particularly in the north), and the near total absence of a ground communications network in the north, pose almost insuperable defense problems, particularly near the Soviet border. Problems of defense are compounded by the Arctic climate, and by a deeply indented, sparsely inhabited coastline more than 2,000 miles long, very vulnerable to surprise amphibious attack.

Introduction of Soviet submarines into the numerous ice-free fjords would facilitate interdiction of North Atlantic sea lanes, and thus the loss of even northern Norway would represent a severe setback to NATO. In addition to the coastal invasion route from Kerkenes near the Soviet-Norwegian border, a serious threat is posed by the Finnish wedge, a salient of Finland with a good road which stretches close to the coast in the strategic Bardufoss-Tromso-Harstad area. A Soviet offensive on this axis could quickly seize northern Norway.

Near the Soviet Union on the strategic polar route from the United States, the archipelago of Spitsbergen (Svalbard) was awarded to Norway in 1920 by an international treaty, which also prohibited establishment of naval or military bases. There are a number of active coal mines on the islands, worked by some 700 Norwegians and 2,000 Russians. Beginning in 1944 Russia sought revision of the treaty to include joint Soviet-Norwegian defense measures. Norway has refused to consider this without the concurrence of all treaty signatories, which has not been forthcoming. The two nations make overlapping claims to the continental shelf of the Barents Sea between Spitsbergen and the Soviet Union, where extensive oil and gas deposits are believed to exist.

## MILITARY ASSISTANCE

Since 1950 Norway has received $893.8 million in American military aid, the most recent contribution in 1971. The U.S. Military Advisory Group in Norway numbers about thirty.

## ALLIANCES

Norway is a member of the NATO alliance.

## ARMY

*Personnel:* 20,000 (16,000 conscripts)

*Organization:*
   1 brigade group of 3 infantry battalions in
       northern Norway
   independent armored squadrons, infantry
       battalions, and artillery regiments

*Major Equipment Inventory:*
   78 medium tanks (Leopard)
   38 medium tanks (M-48)
   70 NM-116 light tanks (M-24/90)
      armored cars (M-8)
  130 155mm howitzers (M-109 SP)
      107mm mortars
      75mm artillery pieces
      Carl Gustav 84mm antitank guns
      106mm recoilless guns
      Entac, TOW antitank guided weapons
      antiaircraft guns (RH-202 20mm, L/60 and
          L/70 40mm)
   40 light aircraft (O-1E, L-18)

*Reserves:* About 120,000 men who will be organized into eleven RCTs (brigades), supporting units, and territorial defense forces.

## NAVY

*Personnel:* 8,400 (including 1,600 coast artillerymen and 5,000 conscripts)

*Major Units:*
   15 submarines (Type 207 Class; SS)
    5 guided missile frigates (Oslo class; FFG; fitted
          with Seasparrow SAMs and Penguin SSMs)
    3 patrol ships (PCF)
   20 motor torpedo boats (PT)
   27 missile attack boats (PTG; fitted with Penguin
          SSMs; 12 more on order)
    2 minelayers (MM)
   10 coastal minesweepers (MSC)
    1 coastal minelayer (MMC)
    7 utility landing craft (LCU)
    5 auxiliary ships and service craft
   36 coastal artillery batteries

*Reserves:* 22,000. Coast Guard would be incorporated into the navy in wartime.

## AIR FORCE

*Personnel:* 10,000 (4,000 conscripts)

*Organization:*
    3 fighter-bomber squadrons with 75 F-5A
    1 fighter-bomber squadron with 22 CF-104G
    1 all weather fighter-interceptor squadron with 16
          F-104G
    1 reconnaissance squadron with 13 RF-5A
    1 maritime reconnaissance squadron with 5 P-3B
    1 operational conversion unit with 14 F-5B
    2 transport squadrons (1 with 6 C-130H, 1 with 5
          DHC-6)
      electronic countermeasure aircraft (2 Falcon 20)

1 search and rescue squadron with 10 Sea King
   Mk 43 helicopters
2 helicopter squadrons with 32 UH-1B

*Major Aircraft Types:*
145 combat aircraft
17 Saab Safir trainers
4 light antiaircraft battalions with L/70 40mm
   guns
4 SAM batteries with Nike-Hercules
   (72 F-16 fighters, 40 Roland II SAM on order)

*Reserves:* 18,000. 7 light antiaircraft battalions with
L/60 40mm guns for airfield defense

*Major Air Bases:* Stavanger, Bodo, Bardufoss, Andoya
(Lofoten Islands)

## PARAMILITARY

There is a highly organized Home Guard consisting of
80,000 individuals. Most of them are in army units, linked
to the nation's territorial defense area commands. There
are also a few navy and air force Home Guard units. All
these are organized in small groups and platoons with
specific defense missions in their home localities. Weapons
are kept at home, and a fairly high state of readiness is
maintained by periodic drills and alerts.

The 360-man Coast Guard operates thirteen patrol ships
(PGF), three patrol aircraft and six helicopters.

# OMAN

## The Sultanate of Oman

## POWER POTENTIAL STATISTICS

Area: 82,000 square miles (northwest border not
   demarcated)
Population: 558,000
Total Active Regular Armed Forces: 15,000 (2.68%
   population)
Gross National Product: $2.6 billion ($4,880 per capita)
Annual Military Expenditures: $844 million (32.46%
   GNP)
Fuel Production: Crude Oil: 18.3 million metric tons
Electric Power Output: 380 million kwh
Merchant Fleet (ships 1,000 tons and over): 1 ship; 1,000
   gross tons
Civil Air Fleet: 21 jet transports

## POLITICO-MILITARY POLICIES AND POSTURE

This absolute monarchy was known until 1970 as the
Sultanate of Muscat and Oman. On July 23, 1970, a coup
carried out by the Palace Guard replaced Sultan Said bin
Taimur with his son, Qabus bin Said. The new ruler
immediately introduced a more modern form of government and sought to hasten the country's development in all
fields. Legislation is by decree; the sultan rules with the
advice of his cabinet.

The Buraymi Oasis, in the undefined border zone of
Saudi Arabia, Abu Dhabi, and Oman, has in the past been
the scene of violent clashes because of conflicting claims.
These have abated in recent years, and the division of the
oasis has been agreed upon. Since 1966 internal unrest in
Oman has been instigated by the Marxist-led Dhofar
Liberation Front and the Popular Front for the Liberation
of Oman and the Arab Gulf (PFLOAG). These radical
groups have received indirect support and training from
the People's Republic of China. For the past several years,
however, most aid has originated in the Soviet Union and
has been funneled through South Yemen and Iraq.

From 1974 through 1976 the Sultan's Armed Forces
(SOAF), with the help of Iranian army and air force units,
fought a counterguerrilla war against Dhofari tribal
elements in the border area next to South Yemen. The
SOAF suppressed the rebellion, and troops are now
engaged in rural development work with the Dhofaris,
aimed at improving their standard of living and integrating
them into Omani national life. However, there is still some
unrest in the region.

Before asking Iran for help in the Dhofari crisis, the sultan had first approached Saudi Arabia, but received no truly timely and useful response. Oman maintains cordial relations with Saudi Arabia, is appreciative of Saudi aid, and seeks Saudi cooperation in developing its oil resources. However, it takes a uniquely independent stance among nations in the southeastern portion of the Arabian Peninsula, and does not accept Saudi dominance of the area.

The sultan of Oman's defense forces are commanded by a British brigadier. Many of the personnel are mercenaries of various nationalities from the region, personnel seconded from the United Kingdom Royal Air Force, or contract personnel hired for maintenance and other technical work.

Oman is a member of the Arab League.

## ARMY

*Personnel:* 12,000

*Organization:*
  6 battalions (composite infantry and armored cavalry)
  1 Royal Guards Regiment
  1 artillery regiment
  engineers, signal companies

*Major Equipment Inventory:*
  60 armored cars (40 Saladin, 20 Commando)
  scout cars (Ferret)
  light artillery (75mm howitzers, 25-pounder, and 5.5-inch guns)
  mortars (4.2-inch)

*Missiles:*
  120 TOW missiles
  10 TOW launchers

## NAVY

*Personnel:* 450

*Major Units:*
  3 patrol ships (PGF)
  7 fast patrol craft (PCF, to be retrofitted with Exocet SSMs)
  4 patrol boats (PB)
  2 roadstead patrol boats (PBR)
  3 mechanized landing craft (LCM)
  2 auxiliary ships

## AIR FORCE

*Personnel:* 2,500

*Organization:*
  1 fighter squadron (Jaguar)
  2 strike squadrons (Strikemaster, Hunter)
  3 support squadrons (Skyvan, BN Defender)
  1 transport squadron (Viscount, BAC III, Caribou)
  1 helicopter squadron (AB-205, AB-206, AB-214)
  2 SAM squadrons (Rapier)

*Major Aircraft Types:*
  46 combat aircraft
    10 fighters (Jaguar)
    36 ground attack aircraft (20 Strikemaster, 16 Hunter)
  60 other aircraft
    33 STOL transports (16 Skyvan, 1 PC-6A, 3 Caribou, 13 BN-2)
     5 medium transports (3 BAC-III, 2 Viscount)
    22 helicopters (17 AB-205, 4 AB-206, 1 AB-214)

*Missiles:*
  AAMs (Matra R-550 on Jaguar fighters)
  28 SAMs (Rapier, 2 1/3 batteries)

*Air Bases:* Bait-al-Falaj (Muscat), Salalah, Azaiba

## PARAMILITARY

The sultan of Oman has a gendarmerie of 300.

# PAKISTAN

## Islamic Republic of Pakistan

### POWER POTENTIAL STATISTICS

Area: 342,750 square miles (includes Pakistan-held part of Jammu and Kashmir)
Population: 78,978,000
Total Active Regular Armed Forces: 394,000 (0.50% population)
Gross National Product: $15 billion ($200 per capita)
Annual Military Expenditures: $996 million (6.64% GNP)
Fuel Production:
  Lignite: 1.11 million metric tons
  Crude Oil: 341,000 metric tons
  Refined Petroleum Products: 3.4 million metric tons
  Gas: 5 billion cubic meters
Electric Power Output: 13.5 billion kwh
Nuclear Power Production: 100 megawatts

Merchant Fleet (ships 1,000 tons and over): 50 ships; 448,000 gross tons

Civil Air Fleet: 27 major transport aircraft

## DEFENSE STRUCTURE

The present regime is federal and presidential in form, but the president is titular. The army commander in chief is chief martial law administrator and administers military affairs through the Ministry of Defence, presumably in coordination with his counterparts in the other services.

## POLITICO-MILITARY POLICY

Although other issues have come to the fore from time to time since independence, Pakistan's politico-military policy has been dominated by its interest in Kashmir and fear of India. Since the loss of East Pakistan (Bangladesh) in 1971, some attention has been devoted to preservation of unity in the remainder of the country and to prevention of the growth of separatist tendencies among various ethnic groups and subgroups. The original concept of Pakistan as a homeland for all Muslims in the subcontinent is now somewhat shaken by the existence of three states with large Muslim populations.

## STRATEGIC PROBLEMS

One of the original strategic problems of Pakistan—how to defend two wings of a state separated by India—was solved when India defeated Pakistan in 1971 and Pakistan recognized Bangladesh in 1974.

The problem of Kashmir is no nearer actual solution than it was in 1947–48, but the status quo has become a semipermanent solution. India's preponderant military position on the subcontinent prompts Pakistani fears that a new war between India and Pakistan could lead to elimination of Pakistan as an independent state.

The issue of Pushtan independence along the northwest frontier, played down by the previous regime in Afghanistan, could arise again, and Pakistan also is apprehensive of possible Afghan espousal of the cause of Beluchi independence (or union with Afghanistan) in the southwest.

India's nuclear explosion understandably disturbed Pakistan, and the latter has made a concerted effort to gain access to the technology and raw material that would make a future nuclear weapons development program at least feasible.

## MILITARY ASSISTANCE

Pakistan has received military assistance from a wide variety of sources in the past. These have included China, France, Indonesia, Iran, Jordan, Turkey, the United Kingdom, the United States, and the Soviet Union. Currently, Pakistan plans to purchase military equipment from both France and the United States and seeks financial support from Arab states to permit additional acquisitions. United States military aid from 1950 to 1976 totaled $674 million, and 4,699 Pakistanis received U.S. military training.

## ALLIANCES

Pakistan is a member of the Commonwealth. It withdrew from SEATO even before the scrapping of the organizational arm of that treaty, and its membership in CENTO may be termed nominal.

## ARMY

*Personnel:* 365,000 (including 25,000 Azad Kashmir troops)

*Organization:*
  2 armored divisions
  14 infantry divisions
  2 independent armored brigades
  2 independent infantry brigades
  2 air defense brigades

*Major Equipment Inventory:*
  795 medium tanks
      75 T-54/55
    200 M-60
    200 T-59
    300 M-47/M-48
     20 M-4 Sherman
  170 light tanks
    100 M-24
     50 M-41
     20 PT-76
  350 APCs (M-113)
  1,200 artillery pieces (25-pounders, 105mm howitzers, 155mm howitzers SP, 130mm guns)
  90mm antitank SP guns
  75mm recoilless rifles
  650 antitank TOW missiles
    3.5-inch rocket launchers
    90mm, 60mm, 45mm, and 50-caliber anti-aircraft artillery guns

  Cobra ATG
  Crotale SAM
  80 light aircraft and helicopters (O-1, H-19, H-13, Mi-8, Alouette III, Beaver)

## NAVY

*Personnel:* 11,000

*Major Units:*
  3 submarines (Daphne class; SS)
  6 midget submarines (SX 404 class; SSM; 40 tons)
  1 training cruiser (CT; only 5.25-inch guns)
  2 destroyers (Gearing class; DD)
  4 substandard destroyers (DD; with under 5-inch guns; 1 Battle, 1 CH, and 1 CR class)
  1 frigate (Type 16 class; FF)
  2 patrol escorts (Hainan class; PG; 3-inch guns; more expected)
  1 patrol craft (PC)
  12 fast patrol craft (Shanghai class; PCF)
  1 motor torpedo boat (Hu Chwan class; hydrofoil; PT)
  7 coastal minesweepers (MSC)
  1 survey ship (ex-DE)
  5 auxiliary ships (tankers, tugs, etc.)
  5 service craft
  4 patrol aircraft (HU-16A, 3 Atlantique)
  12 helicopters (H-19, Alouette III, Seaking)

## AIR FORCE

*Personnel:* 18,000

*Organization:*
  1 light bomber squadron (B-57)
  7 fighter-bomber squadrons (Sabre, F-5)
  8 fighter squadrons (MiG-19, Mirage)
  1 fighter/reconnaissance squadron (Mirage)
  1 transport squadron (F-27, C-130, Falcon 20)
  1 helicopter squadron (Alouette III, H-13, H-19, H-43, Mi-8, S-61)

*Major Aircraft Types:*
  320 combat aircraft
    15 B-57 light bombers
   130 fighter-bombers (80 Sabre, 50 F-5)
   160 fighters (100 MiG-19, 60 Mirage)
    15 fighter/reconnaissance aircraft (Mirage)
  230 other aircraft
    35 transports (C-47, C-130, Falcon 20)
   150 trainers (Saab, MFI-17, T-37, T-33, Beech U-8, T-41)
    45 helicopters (Alouette III, H-13, H-19, H-43, Mi-8, S-61)

*Missiles:*
 MiG-19s carry Sidewinder AAM
 Mirages carry R530 AAM and AS30 ASM

*Air Bases:* Peshawar, Kohat, Mauripur, Samundri, Deigh Road, Risalpur, Sargodha, Gilgit, Chitral, Malir, and Miramshah

*Reserves:* About 9,000 trained reservists

## PARAMILITARY

The Frontier Corps numbers 30,000 hill tribesmen of the northwest frontier and guards the borders with Iran and Afghanistan.

# PANAMA

## Republic of Panama

## POWER POTENTIAL STATISTICS

Area: 28,753 square miles
Population: 1,837,000
Total Active Regular Armed Forces: 2,000 (0.11% population)

Gross National Product: $2.2 billion ($1,250 per capita)
Annual Military Expenditures: $32.6 million (1.48% GNP)
Fuel Production:
 Refined Petroleum Products: 2.9 million metric tons
 Manufactured Gas: 12 million cubic meters
Electric Power Output: 2.5 billion kwh
Merchant Fleet (ships 1,000 tons and over): 2,041 ships; 18.9 million gross tons (most are foreign owned, with convenience registries)*
Civil Air Fleet: 19 major transport aircraft

## POLITICO-MILITARY POLICIES AND POSTURE

Constitutional government in Panama was overthrown in 1968 and the recently elected president replaced by a military junta. A new constitution was adopted in 1972, creating a constitutional dictatorship with a titular presidency and all executive, legislative, and judicial power actually vested in the commander in chief of the National Guard, Brig. Gen. Omar Torrijos Herrera.

Panama became independent by secession from Colombia in 1903, followed by immediate recognition and protection by the United States. This intervention had the primary purpose of permitting construction of the

*A large portion of Panamanian shipping is becoming effectively part of the U.S. merchant marine as the United States shifts its convenience registries from Liberia to Panama.

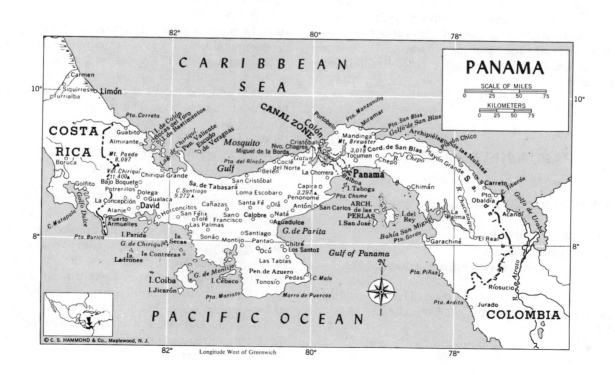

trans-isthmian canal, which had been blocked by what Americans considered Colombian intransigence.

Treaties signed in September 1977 and ratified by Panama and by the United States Senate in March and April 1978 will turn over control of the canal from the United States to Panama by the end of 1999. Permanent neutrality is guaranteed. The United States retains the right of intervention if the canal is closed or its operations interfered with.

Panama is a member of the OAS.

The Canal Zone is headquarters for the U.S. Southern Command (SOUTHCOM) which oversees United States defense interests in Latin America, including the administration of military assistance programs. About 10,000 troops of all services are stationed there, responsible for local and air defense, for four military training schools for Latin Americans, and for jungle and counterinsurgency warfare courses for U.S. and Latin American troops. SOUTHCOM supports missions with a total of 800 U.S. military personnel in most Latin American nations.

In 1977 the United States provided military assistance valued at $497,000, making a total of $7.96 million since 1950. A total of 4,623 students have been trained under the MAP.

Panama has a National Guard of 8,000, of whom 6,500 are primarily engaged in police activities. The remaining 1,500 are organized into seven light infantry companies. These forces have sixteen light armored cars. There is a 200-man air force with thirty aircraft, most of them helicopters, and a 300-man coast guard with one patrol ship (PGF), ten patrol boats (PB) and three mechanized landing craft (LCM). Air bases are Albrook AFB, France Field, and Tocumen (Panama City). Fields for light planes and landing strips are found in all provinces. There is a trend toward somewhat larger, more centralized, more mobile forces.

# PAPUA NEW GUINEA

## POWER POTENTIAL STATISTICS

Area: 183,540 square miles
Population: 3,024,000
Total Active Regular Armed Forces: 3,500 (0.12% population)
Gross National Product: $1.5 billion ($510 per capita)
Annual Military Expenditures: $24.8 million (1.65% GNP)
Electric Power Output: 700 million kwh
Civil Air Fleet: 15 major transport aircraft

## POLITICO-MILITARY POLICIES AND POSTURE

Papua New Guinea (PNG), a member of the Commonwealth, is a constitutional monarchy with the British sovereign as head of state. It is represented by a governor general who is a PNG citizen. Formerly administered as several trust territories by Australia, PNG became independent in 1975. It has a unified PNG Defence Force under a PNG Department of Defence.

PNG occupies the eastern half of the large island of New Guinea, which lies on the Sahul shelf, an undersea extension of the Australian land mass. It also includes the Bismarck Archipelago, of which New Britain, New Ireland, and Manus are the largest islands; Bougainville and Buka Islands in the western Solomons; and the Trobriand, Woodlark, D'Entrecasteaux, and Louisiade Island groups.

Papua New Guinea's strategic importance lies largely in its geographic position as a bridge between Australia and Indonesia. The distance across the Torres Strait to Australia's Cape York Peninsula is only 100 miles. The western half of the island of New Guinea, West Irian, has been part of Indonesia since 1963, and is officially called Irian Barat.

During World War II, the Japanese took Rabaul on New Britain early in 1942, and threatened the major Australian base of Port Moresby, now Papua New Guinea's capital. The Allies chose to defend Australia on New Guinea, and turned back the Japanese in a grueling campaign in Papua's rugged mountains and tropical rain forests. They then slowly took the rest of New Guinea and used it as a base for the island-hopping approach to Japan.

Papua New Guinea's mountains run generally east-west, rising in places to almost 15,000 feet, with sharp ridges and precipitous slopes. There are extensive swamps in addition to the jungle areas. The rivers are generally not navigable, except by small boats for limited distances. There is no railroad, and the road net is very limited, with no road traversing the country. The people belong to numerous ethnic groups, speaking 750 different languages, and literacy is low.

Australia provides about 42.5 percent of the PNG budget. In 1976 it agreed to give PNG $1.17 billion in aid over the following five years.

Since independence there has been a secessionist attempt by Bougainville, whose rich copper deposits provide PNG's main source of revenue. A compromise was negotiated in 1976, giving considerable autonomy to a newly created province of the North Solomons, including Bougainville and Buka. There has been disagreement with Australia over the international border that crosses the Torres Strait and its seabed resources, but this has been resolved.

The PNG Defence Force has a personnel strength of 3,500, organized as two infantry battalions of the Pacific Islands Regiment, plus naval and air arms. Australia

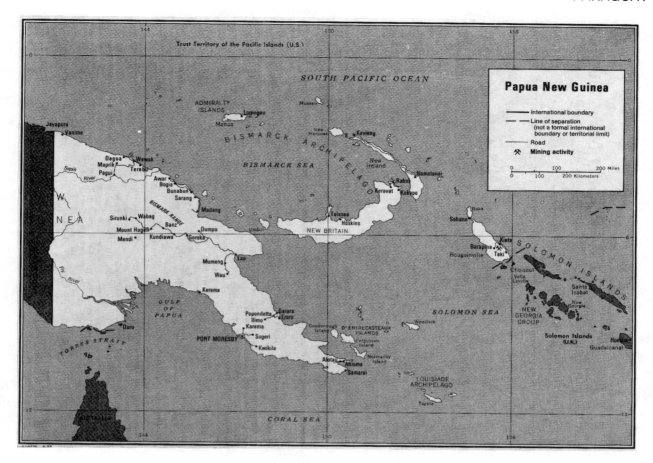

financed the establishment of the PNGDF, provided training, and continues to provide advanced training. New Zealand has also provided military aid, including army and air force instructors. There is a PNG Joint Services College at Lae, and a flying school is planned. In 1975 Australia provided four C-47 transports as the nucleus of the PNG air arm, which is being expanded by the addition of STOL transports and support aircraft, including GAF Nomads and helicopters. There are air bases at Port Moresby, Lae, Madang, Rabaul, and Wewak. The navy operates five patrol craft (PB and two mechanical landing craft (LCM).

# PARAGUAY

## Republic of Paraguay

### POWER POTENTIAL STATISTICS

Area: 157,047 square miles
Population: 3,143,000

Total Active Regular Armed Forces: 15,000 (0.48% population)
Gross National Product: $2.1 billion ($750 per capita)
Annual Military Expenditures: $41.2 million (1.96% GNP)
Fuel Production: Refined Petroleum Products: 278,000 metric tons
Electric Power Output: 550 million kwh
Civil Air Fleet: 4 major transport aircraft

### DEFENSE STRUCTURE

The president is commander in chief of the armed forces, with an army general as minister of national defense.

### POLITICO-MILITARY POLICY

In 1954, after more than twenty years of foreign war, civil war, and political instability, Gen. Alfredo Stroessner took power in Paraguay and has since run the country as a nominal elective democracy but in practice as a military dictatorship. Complete presidential control of the government continues, although increasing participation by parties other than that of the government is permitted.

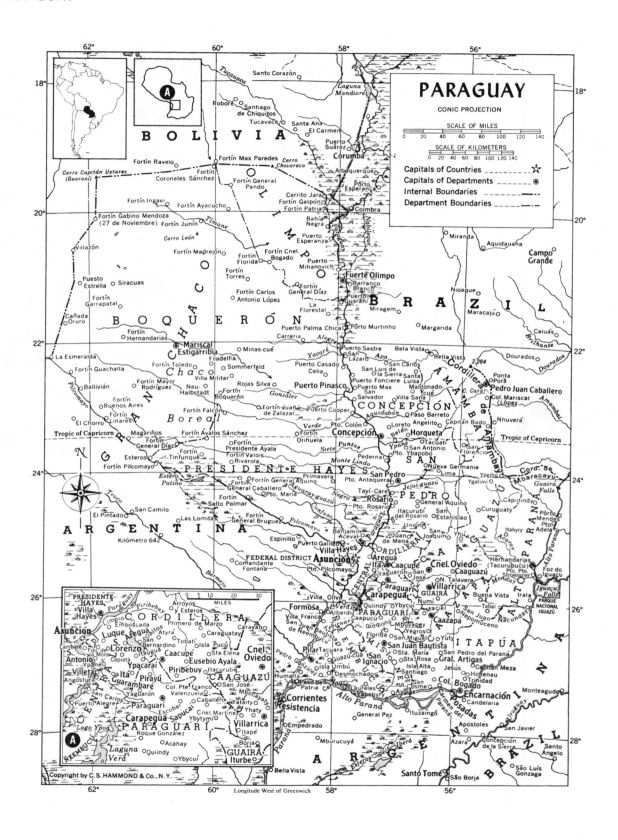

PARAGUAY

CONIC PROJECTION

SCALE OF MILES
0   20   40   60   80   100   120   140

SCALE OF KILOMETERS
0   20   40   60   80   100   120   140

Capitals of Countries ........ ☆
Capitals of Departments ........ ◉
Internal Boundaries ........
Department Boundaries ........

Longitude West of Greenwich

With a negligible external threat, the primary mission of the armed forces is internal security. The Paraguayans have a proud military tradition, having fought to the verge of national extinction against overwhelming odds in the War of the Triple Alliance (1864–70) and having decisively defeated Bolivia in the Chaco War (1932–35).

Military service is compulsory, at age eighteen. This involves two years of service in the active army, followed by nine years in the Army Reserve, ten years in the National Guard, and at least six years—to age forty-five—in the Territorial Guard.

## STRATEGIC PROBLEMS

Bounded by Argentina, Bolivia, and Brazil, Paraguay has access to the sea only by the Parana-Paraguay river system, which is controlled by Argentina. Argentina, Brazil, and Uruguay, which opposed Paraguay in the disastrous War of the Triple Alliance in 1864–1870, all have large colonies of Paraguayan exiles hostile to the present regime. Since Argentina and Brazil historically have had border disputes with Paraguay, the presence of these dissidents increases the threat. However, there is little chance that either nation would provoke a war in Paraguay, or that Paraguay would provoke conflict because of counterclaims on Brazilian territory.

Although there is little chance of insurgency because of strict military controls, there are guerrilla groups within the country, and the possibility of invasion by anti-Stroessner exiles does exist. Such groups invaded Paraguay in 1959 and six times in 1960; all seven efforts were quickly crushed.

In 1973 agreement was reached with Brazil to build the world's largest hydroelectric project at Itaipu on the Parana River.

## MILITARY ASSISTANCE

In fiscal year 1977 Paraguay received $757,000 in military assistance from the United States, making a total of $14.9 million since 1950. Under the MAP, 1,874 students have been trained.

The United States has both a military and an air mission in Paraguay. Argentina has a military and naval mission and Brazil has a military mission.

Paraguay sent a contingent of 200 troops to the Dominican Republic during the crisis of 1965, to serve with the OAS Inter-American Peace Force.

## ALLIANCES

Paraguay is a member of the OAS.

## ARMY

*Personnel:* 11,000 (8,000 are conscripts)

*Organization:*
     1 cavalry brigade
     3 infantry brigades
     3 artillery battalions
     6 engineer battalions

*Major Equipment Inventory:*
     9 M-4 medium tanks
     6 M-3 light tanks
    24 APCs (M-2 half-tracks)
       light artillery pieces (48 M-101, 105mm howitzers)
       4.2-inch mortars
     6 Piper L-4 liaison aircraft
     2 Bell OH-13 helicopters

*Reserve Forces:* There are about 60,000 men in the Army Reserve, the principal mobilization force. There are about 100,000 more in the National Guard and Territorial Guard.

## NAVY

*Personnel:* 1,900 (includes marines and coast guard)

*Major Units:*
     2 patrol escorts (Humaita class; PG; 4.7-inch guns)
     3 patrol ships (Bouchard class; PGF)
     1 patrol craft (PC)
     8 patrol boats (PB)
     1 medium landing ship (LSM)
     2 utility landing craft (LCU; used for cargo now)
    10 service craft (tenders, tugs, etc.)
     1 marine battalion
    10 aircraft trainers and helicopters

## AIR FORCE

*Personnel:* 2,100

*Major Aircraft Types:*
    11 combat aircraft (armed T-6)
    70 noncombat aircraft
       13 transports (C-47, DC-6, MS-760, Twin Otter)
        4 PBY amphibians
       36 trainers (T-23, T-6, Fokker S-11, U-17)
       17 helicopters (H-13, UH-12)

*Air Base:* Campo Grande (Asuncion)

## PARAMILITARY

Civil police forces in Paraguay number 8,500 with a responsibility for internal security as well as normal police functions.

# PERU

## Republic of Peru

## POWER POTENTIAL STATISTICS

Area: 496,222 square miles
Population: 17,053,000
Total Active Regular Armed Forces: 69,000 (0.40% population)
Gross National Product: $12.1 billion ($730 per capita)
Annual Military Expenditures: $254 million (2.10% GNP)
Crude Steel Production: 443,000 metric tons
Iron Ore Production: 5.1 million metric tons
Fuel Production:
    Coal: 85,000 metric tons
    Crude Oil: 3.7 million metric tons
    Refined Petroleum Products: 5.6 million metric tons
    Natural Gas: 550 million cubic meters
Electric Power Output: 8.0 billion kwh
Merchant Fleet (ships 1,000 tons and over): 39 ships; 374,000 gross tons
Civil Air Fleet: 29 major transport aircraft

## DEFENSE STRUCTURE

The president is the commander in chief of the armed forces, which are administered by independent ministries of war, air and navy. Control of the government has been in the hands of a military junta since the October 1968 coup d'etat.

## POLITICO-MILITARY POLICY

The revolutionary government of the armed forces, which seized power in 1968, continues in power, although the original president, Gen. Juan Velasco Alvarado, was deposed in 1975 by military leaders and replaced by Gen. Francisco Morales Bermudez. The new leaders have continued much the same leftist military government. The chief political party, the American Revolutionary Popular Alliance (APRA), supports many of the government's actions. A return to elected, civilian government has been promised for 1980. The first step, election of a constituent assembly to draft a new constitution, was taken in June 1978, with APRA gaining the largest percentage of votes.

Peru seems to be endeavoring to maintain the most modern air forces in Pacific South America. The armed forces are also contributing to the nation-building effort through a number of military civic action programs.

Two years' active military service is obligatory, although only a small number of men between twenty and twenty-five are actually drafted. Following active duty, five years are required in the reserve, and twenty more in the National Guard.

## STRATEGIC PROBLEMS

Peruvian history is replete with boundary disputes, losses, and gains. One long-standing dispute with Ecuador still persists, although the disputed region is firmly under Peruvian control. Peru remains unreconciled to the loss of territory to Chile following the War of the Pacific. Ideological differences also strain relations between the two nations.

Peru's claim to sovereignty over waters 200 miles from the coastline has created friction with U.S. tuna fishermen. After several incidents in which Peru seized eighteen U.S. tuna boats in these waters, military sales to Peru were suspended briefly in 1969.

Socioeconomic problems have created great discontent among Peruvian citizens, and were a major cause of the military takeover. Although the economic growth rate of the country continues to climb, so does the population. While development of petroleum and mineral resources has improved Peru's economy, a change in the pattern of ocean currents off the coast in 1972 resulted in the temporary disappearance of the anchovies that were one of the principal export resources of Peru. Loss of the fish meal in world markets had serious economic results in the nations which imported it, of which the United States, China, Cuba, and West Germany were the largest buyers. The anchovies reappeared in 1974, again causing economic problems in areas which had developed substitute products. In 1977 the anchovies were once more in small supply.

Guerrilla activity in the eastern mountain-jungle areas of Peru has been troublesome but is currently under control. Economic conditions periodically produce strikes, including a police strike in Lima in 1975.

## MILITARY ASSISTANCE

In 1977 Peru received $869,000 in U.S. military aid, making a total of $93.1 million since 1950. Under the MAP, 7,865 students have been trained.

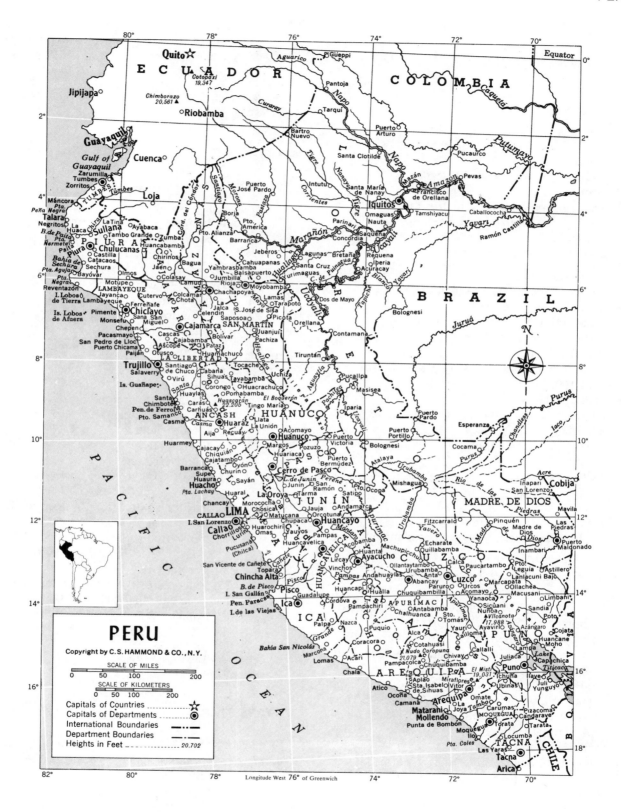

## PERU

Copyright by C.S. HAMMOND & CO., N.Y.

SCALE OF MILES
0    50   100        200

SCALE OF KILOMETERS
0    50   100        200

Capitals of Countries .............. ☆
Capitals of Departments ......... ◉
International Boundaries _____
Department Boundaries _._._._
Heights in Feet _ _ _ _ _ _ 20,702

## ALLIANCES

Peru is a member of the OAS, LAFTA, and the Andean Pact.

## ARMY

*Personnel:* 45,000

*Organization:*
  8 infantry and mechanized brigades
  1 armored brigade
  3 armed reconnaissance squadrons
  1 jungle unit (paratroop, commando, and mountain brigades)
    cavalry, artillery, and engineer battalions

*Major Equipment Inventory:*
260 medium tanks (M-4 Sherman, T-55)
100 light tanks (AMX-13)
120 APC (M-113)
150 armored cars (M-3, M-8, Commando, M-2 half-tracks)
170 105mm and 155mm artillery pieces (M-101, M-109, M-114 howitzers)
 40 76mm ZSU-23/4
    antiaircraft guns (40mm, 76mm, ZSU-23/4)
    SA-3 SAMs
  2 GAF Nomad light transport aircraft
  4 U-10 STOL aircraft
  8 Bell 47 helicopters

## NAVY

*Personnel:* 14,000 (including naval air arm and marines)

*Major Units:*
  8 diesel submarines (2 Type 209, 2 Guppy class, 4 Abtao class; SS)
  4 light cruisers (2 De Ruyter class, one with Exocet short-range SSMs; 2 Ceylon class; CL)
  5 destroyers (1 Holland class, substandard 4.7-inch guns; 2 Fletcher class; 2 Daring class, substandard 4.5-inch guns; DD)
  1 guided missile patrol combatant (modified Lupo class; PGG; Otomat SSMs; Albatross SAMs)
  2 patrol escorts (Cannon class; PG; 3-inch guns)
  2 tank landing ships (LST)
  2 medium landing ships (LSM)
 16 river patrol boats (PBR; 5 heavily armed)
 12 auxiliary ships (oilers, transports, etc.)
 15 service craft
 28 helicopters (Bell 47, UH-1, Jet Ranger, Alouette III)

 11 transport aircraft (2 Queen Air, 7C-47, 2 F-27)
  1 marine battalion (1,000 men) with amphibious vehicles, armored cars, and 81mm rocket launchers

*Naval Bases:* Callao, La Punta, Iquitos, San Lorenzo, Talara

## AIR FORCE

*Personnel:* 10,000

*Organization:*
  2 light bomber squadrons (Canberra)
  4 fighter squadrons (1 Mirage, 1 Su-22/MiG-21, 1 F-86, 1 Hunter)
  2 COIN squadrons (A-37)
  1 ASW patrol squadron (HU-16)
  1 maritime patrol squadron (PV-2)
  1 transportation group
  1 helicopter group

*Major Aircraft Types:*
147 combat aircraft
  27 Canberra light bombers
  12 Su-22 fighter-bombers
  12 MiG-21 fighters
  14 Mirage fighters
  14 F-86 fighters
  12 Hunter fighters
  27 A-37 COIN ground attack
   5 ASW patrol (Hu-16)
  24 maritime patrol (PV-2) (operated for navy)
343 other aircraft
  91 transports (C-130, Buffalo, C-46, C-54, DC-6, An-26, Queen Air, C-47, Beaver, Twin Otter, F-28)
 125 helicopters (Alouette III, Mi-8/6, UH-1, Bell 47, Bell 205, OH-58)
 127 trainers (T-6, T-33, T-34, T-37, T-41, T-42, U-17, PC-6)

*Air Bases:* Lima, Trujillo, Talara, Chiclayo, Pisco, Ancon, Arequipa, Cusco

## PARAMILITARY

There are about 18,000 men in the *Guardia Civil* and the *Guardia Republicana,* which are under the direction of the Ministry of Interior and Police.

The coast guard operates two patrol ships (PGF), four patrol craft (PC), six fast patrol craft (PCF), and several patrol boats (PB).

# PHILIPPINES

## Republic of the Philippines

### POWER POTENTIAL STATISTICS

Area: 115,707 square miles
Population: 46,388,000
Total Active Regular Armed Forces: 82,000 (0.18%
population)
Gross National Product: $20.5 billion ($460 per capita)
Annual Military Expenditures: $753.4 million (3.67%
GNP)
Iron Ore Production: 839,000 metric tons
Fuel Production:
Refined Petroleum Products: 8.7 million metric tons
Coal: 149,000 metric tons
Electric Power Output: 4.2 billion kwh
Merchant Fleet (ships 1,000 tons and over): 160 ships;
1 million gross tons
Civil Air Fleet: 70 major transport aircraft

### DEFENSE STRUCTURE

The prime minister of the Republic of the Philippines is the commander in chief of the Armed Forces of the Philippines (AFP) and as such has the sole power of employing them. He exercises this responsibility through the secretary of national defense. Within the department, the senior military officer is the chief of staff of the armed forces, exercising military command functions over the major services.

### POLITICO-MILITARY POLICIES

Since its independence in 1946 the Philippines has relied almost exclusively upon the United States for external security, and has used its armed forces essentially for internal security purposes. Recently the Philippines has attempted to establish itself as an independent, nonaligned nation. It continues to rely on its long-standing relationship with the United States, but also emphasizes its ties with Japan and its fellow ASEAN nations (Indonesia, Malaysia, Singapore, and Thailand; see South and Southeast Asia Regional Survey). Since 1972 it has established diplomatic relations with twelve Communist countries, including the Soviet Union and China. The Philippines has also worked for friendly relations with the Arab nations.

The strength of the armed forces is maintained by conscription, which is extremely selective, with only a small percentage of the available manpower drafted each year. Currently drafts are larger because of the situation in the south.

### STRATEGIC PROBLEMS

Between 1946 and 1950 the Communist-inspired Hukbalahap insurgency came close to destroying the republic. Thus between 1952 and 1954, under the leadership of Secretary of National Defense Ramon Magsaysay, the insurgency was almost eliminated by a combination of force and clemency. In recent years, however, the insurgency has revived. It centers in the north of the Philippines, on Luzon. Martial law was imposed in 1972 to deal with the problem, and the estimated number of insurgents dropped from 3,000 to 1,000. In 1977 it reportedly rose again to about 2,000. Recently government forces have successfully contained the rebels, now led by the so-called New People's Army. Martial law continues in effect, apparently to ensure the continued power of the president and prime minister, Ferdinand Marcos.

A more serious internal security problem than that posed by the Communists is the separatist Moslem rebellion in the southern Philippines, on Mindanao and in the Sulu Archipelago. The insurrection broke out in 1968 and intensified in 1972. More than 20,000 people have been killed since the latter year, and as many as 50,000 AFP troops have been committed there in a year (1977). The rebels have obtained arms from Libya, which has also been a leader in mediation efforts. A ceasefire was arranged in December 1976, but collapsed a year later. Both negotiations have recently been hampered by conflict within the rebel Moro National Liberation Front (MNLF).

Externally, the Philippine Republic has a latent dispute with neighboring Malaysia over the ownership of the state of Sabah, in northeastern Borneo. (It is through Sabah that arms from Libya have been funneled to the MNLF.) Malaysia now exercises sovereignty over Sabah, having inherited the 29,000-square-mile region from Great Britain. The Philippines claims that Britain never legally owned Sabah, which was the territory of the sultan of Sulu, whose island domain is now part of the Philippines. Neither side is likely to go to war over the dispute, and diplomatic relations, once severed, were resumed in December 1969 with agreement that the Sabah question be held in abeyance for the time being. The dispute could, nevertheless, be exploited by powers seeking to disrupt Southeast Asia and Australia.

### MILITARY ASSISTANCE

Since 1946 the United States has provided about $512.7 million in military assistance to its former dependency. In fiscal year 1977 U.S. aid totaled $7.6 million. In addition, the United States has given substantial economic aid and some $700 million in war rehabilitation grants and war damage claims. A U.S. Military Advisory Group has provided extensive advice and assistance. This was particu-

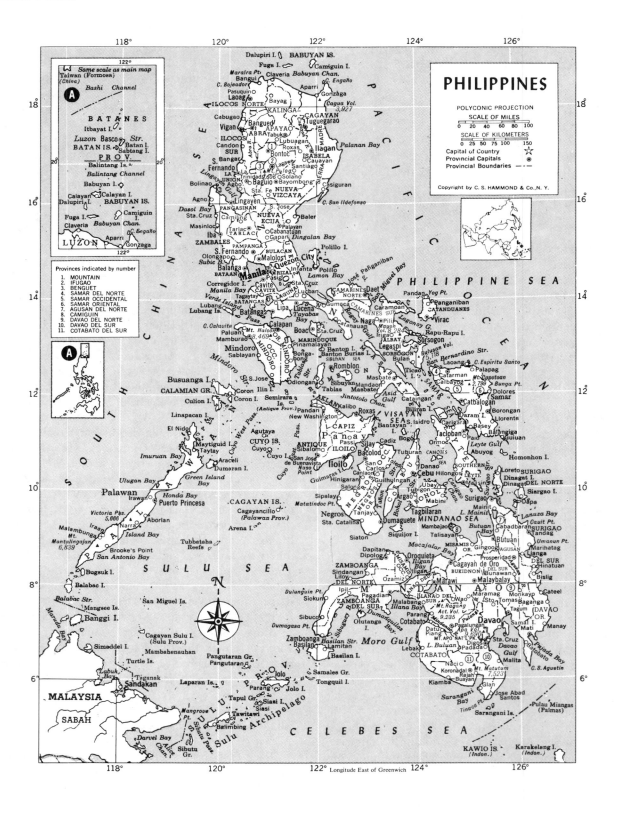

PHILIPPINES

POLYCONIC PROJECTION

SCALE OF MILES
0   20   40   60   80   100

SCALE OF KILOMETERS
0  25  50  75  100    150

★ Capital of Country
● Provincial Capitals
Provincial Boundaries -----

Copyright by C. S. HAMMOND & Co., N.Y.

Provinces indicated by number
1. MOUNTAIN
2. IFUGAO
3. BENGUET
4. SAMAR DEL NORTE
5. SAMAR OCCIDENTAL
6. SAMAR ORIENTAL
7. AGUSAN DEL NORTE
8. CAMIGUIN
9. DAVAO DEL NORTE
10. DAVAO DEL SUR
11. COTABATO DEL SUR

larly useful during the Hukbalahap insurgency. To bolster the defense of the Philippines, three military agreements were entered into with the United States: (1) the Military Bases Agreement, which gave the United States a ninety-nine year lease over certain military, air, and naval bases in the Philippines; (2) the Military Assistance Agreement, wherein the United States pledged to provide military assistance to the Philippines; and (3) the Mutual Defense Treaty, in which the Republic of the Philippines and the United States pledged to assist each other in case of an armed attack against either or both of them by a foreign aggressor. By a memorandun signed October 12, 1959, however, the ninety-nine-year lease has been shortened to twenty-five years.

Under the terms awarding Philippine independence, the United States retained a number of military bases in the archipelago, the most important at Clark Field and Subic Bay and scattered facilities in the southern islands. With some modifications, these terms were confirmed by a mutual defense treaty with the United States in 1952. However, the existence of these bases has aroused considerable resentment, despite the fact that sovereignty is recognized as joint, and continues to be a major political issue in the republic. Negotiations continue on the terms for continued U.S. use of Clark Field and Subic Bay.

## ALLIANCES

The Philippines was an active member of the now-disbanded Southeast Asia Treaty Organization, was strongly opposed to the extension of Communist influence in Southeast Asia and Australasia, supported the U.S. presence in South Vietnam, and contributed a noncombat civil action group of 2,000 men to community development efforts there. Since the end of the Vietnam War, while maintaining its alliance with the United States, the Philippines has sought recognition as a third world country, and has established friendly ties with Communist and Arab countries. It is a member of the Association of Southeast Asian Nations (ASEAN).

## ARMY

*Personnel:* 48,000

*Organization:*
 3 infantry divisions
 5 infantry brigades (separate)
 1 artillery group
 13 engineer construction battalions
  combat service support forces

*Major Equipment Inventory:*
 35 medium tanks (M-4)
 100 light tanks (M-24, M-41)

 35 scout cars (M-3)
 350 APCs (M-113)
 20 armored cars (Commando)
 65 light and medium artillery pieces (5 155mm, 60 105mm)
 20 light aircraft (BN-2A)
 1 SAM battalion (Hawk)

*Reserves:* There is an organized and trained reserve force of approximately one million. The existence of training division cadres greatly facilitates mobilization capability.

## NAVY

*Personnel:* 17,000 (including 5,500 marines, 2,000 coast guard)

*Major Units:*
 3 frigates (3 Cannon class; 1 Savage class; FF)
 13 Patrol ships (4 Casco class, PGF; 8 827 class, PCE; 1 Admirable class)
 2 patrol escorts (Auk class; PCE; 3-inch guns)
 20 patrol craft (PC)
 55 patrol boats (PB)
 2 coastal minesweepers (MSC)
 2 command ships
 5 motor gunboats (PGM)
 90 patrol boats (PB; coast guard)
 4 hydrofoil patrol craft (PCH)
 27 tank landing ships (LST)
 4 medium landing ships, (LSM)
 4 landing ships infantry (LSIL)
 3 utility landing craft (LCU)
 60 mechanized landing craft (LCM)
 10 auxiliary ships
 25 service craft
 3 helicopters
 1 marine brigade (5,500 men)

*Major Naval Base:* Sangley Point

## AIR FORCE

*Personnel:* 17,000

*Organization:*
 1 fighter wing
  2 fighter squadrons (F-86)
  2 fighter-bomber squadrons (F-5)
  1 COIN strike wing (4 squadrons—T-28, SF-160, C-47 gunships, UH-1 heli gunships)
 2 airlift wings
  6 troop carrier squadrons (C-130, C-47, Nomad, C-123, F-27, YS-11)

1 liaison squadron (BN-2A)
1 air rescue squadron (HU-16, H-13, H-19, H-34)
2 aviation engineer squadrons support forces

*Major Aircraft Types:*
139 combat aircraft
   35 F-86 day fighters
   30 F-5 fighter bombers
   74 COIN (26 T-28, 18 SF-260, 12 C-47, 18 UH-1)
216 other aircraft
   55 transports (8 C-130, 16 C-123, 18 C-47, 8 F-27, 54 S-11)
 121 training, rescue, and utility (T-28, T-34, T-33, T-41, HU-K, SF-260, BN-2A, Nomad)
   40 helicopters (FH-1110, UH-1, H-34, H-13, H-19, S-62, Hughes 500)
   25 F-8H

*Major Air Bases:* Clark AFB (U.S.), Angeles, Pampanga; Basa AB, Florida Blanca; Fernando AB, Lipa, Batangas; Sangley Pt., Cavite; Mactan AB, Lapu City; Edwin Andrew AB, Zamboanga City; Nichols AB, Manila.

## PARAMILITARY

The Philippine Constabulary, approximately 34,000 strong, is an efficient internal security organization. It is organized in sixty-eight provincial commands and eight combat battalions, with combat and service support units.

Other paramilitary forces include 57,000 Civilian Home Defense Forces, and 37,000 Armed Security Forces.

# POLAND

## Polish People's Republic

## POWER POTENTIAL STATISTICS

Area: 120,359 square miles
Population: 35,210,000
Total Active Regular Armed Forces: 272,500 (0.77% population)
Gross National Product: $95.2 billion ($2,740 per capita)
Annual Military Expenditures: $5.45 billion (5.72% GNP)
Crude Steel Production: 17.8 million metric tons
Iron Ore Production: 376,000 metric tons

Fuel Production:
  Coal: 179.3 million metric tons
  Lignite: 39.3 million metric tons
  Crude Oil: 460,000 metric tons
  Refined Petroleum Products: 577,000 metric tons
  Natural Gas: 6.0 billion cubic meters
  Manufactured Gas: 7.3 billion cubic meters
Electric Power Output: 109.4 billion kwh
Merchant Fleet (ships 1,000 tons and over): 297 ships; 3.0 million gross tons
Civil Air Fleet: 7 jet, 23 turboprop, and 5 piston transports

## DEFENSE STRUCTURE

The governmental structure is similar to that of the USSR, with the government controlled by the (Communist) Polish United Workers' Party. The minister of defense is the commander in chief of the armed forces, which he controls through the Ministry of Defense and the General Staff. He is responsible to the National Defense Council and the prime minister. Ultimate authority over the forces resides in the Politburo, which determines broader policies and fundamental strategy. The armed forces consist of the ground forces, air force, air defense force, navy, and internal defense and border troops.

Vice ministers of defense are usually the chiefs of the General Staff, Main Political Directorate, Main Inspectorate of Training, and Main Inspectorate of Territorial Defense. Commanders of the ground forces, navy, air force, air defense force, internal security forces, and frontier troops are directly under the minister of defense. Ground forces are predominant among the three integrated services. There are three military districts: the Warsaw Military District with headquarters in Warsaw, the Pomeranian Military District with headquarters in Bydogoszcz, and the Silesian Military District with headquarters in Wroclaw. The divisions located in the western military districts are maintained at a higher state of combat readiness than those in the eastern district.

Party influence is evident at all echelons of the armed forces. Political officers are in all units. Approximately 15 percent of all military personnel (80 percent of officers and 35 percent of noncommissioned officers) are party members.

## POLITICO-MILITARY POLICY

Poland emerged from World War II as an independent state but with different boundaries, and in a different political situation, from prewar Poland. The eastern half of the nation (about 70,000 square miles) had been lost to the Soviet Union. Poland was compensated for the loss of its eastern provinces by obtaining most of East Prussia and

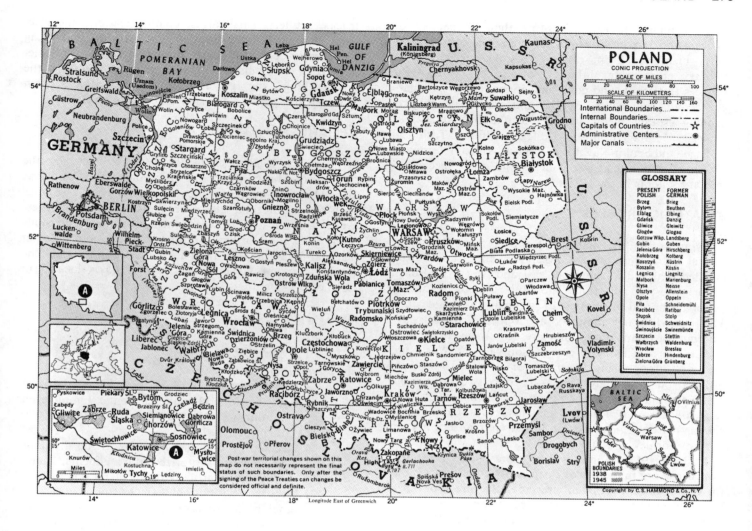

### POLAND
CONIC PROJECTION

SCALE OF MILES
0  20  40  60  80  100

SCALE OF KILOMETERS
0  20  40  60  80  100  120  140  160

International Boundaries......._ _ _ _
Internal Boundaries.............._ _ _ _ _ _
Capitals of Countries...........☆
Administrative Centers..........◉
Major Canals

### GLOSSARY

| PRESENT POLISH | FORMER GERMAN |
|---|---|
| Brzeg | Brieg |
| Bytom | Beuthen |
| Elblag | Elbing |
| Gdansk | Danzig |
| Gliwice | Gleiwitz |
| Głogów | Glogau |
| Gorzow Wlkp. | Landsberg |
| Gubin | Guben |
| Jelenia Góra | Hirschberg |
| Kolobrzeg | Kolberg |
| Kostrzyn | Küstrin |
| Koszalin | Köslin |
| Legnica | Liegnitz |
| Malbork | Marienburg |
| Nysa | Neisse |
| Olsztyn | Allenstein |
| Opole | Oppeln |
| Piła | Schneidemühl |
| Racibórz | Ratibor |
| Słupsk | Stolp |
| Swidnica | Schweidnitz |
| Swinoujscie | Swinemünde |
| Szczecin | Stettin |
| Wałbrzych | Waldenburg |
| Wrocław | Breslau |
| Zabrze | Hindenburg |
| Zielona Góra | Grünberg |

Post-war territorial changes shown on this map do not necessarily represent the final status of such boundaries. Only after the signing of the Peace Treaties can changes be considered official and definite.

POLISH BOUNDARIES 1938 1945

Copyright by C.S. HAMMOND & Co., N.Y.

all other German provinces east of the Oder-Neisse line (a total of about 40,000 square miles). Most of the German population of these provinces, some six million, had fled west at the approach of the Soviet army, and the remainder (about 2,000,000) were deported to Germany after World War II in accordance with the Allied Potsdam agreement of 1945. These new territories were resettled by Poles from overpopulated central Poland and from the eastern provinces lost to Soviet Russia. The Poles consider the territory east of the Oder-Neisse line as "recovered land," historically the cradle of the Polish state but gradually lost and Germanized during a millenium of conflict between Germans and Poles. Poland is one of the countries of the Mutual and Balanced Force Reduction "reduction area," and is a direct participant in the talks in Vienna toward reduction of forces in central Europe (see Western Europe Regional Survey).

All men between nineteen and fifty years of age are liable for military service: eighteen months in the army, two years in the air force, navy and special services, internal security troops, and frontier forces. This obligation after the age of twenty-seven is ordinarily fulfilled by service in the reserves. About 100,000 men are conscripted annually, less than 30 percent of the group that reaches draft age and around 35 percent of the portion of the group that is considered physically suitable and eligible for military service.

Efforts have been made to improve the quality of the officers corps, by making the service more attractive, with better educational qualifications and improved professionalism and promotion opportunities. Regulations enacted in the middle 1960s were designed to assure that the entire officers corps would have university degrees. By 1971, according to a Soviet publication, one out of four officers had "a higher education." More than 70 percent of officers and 35 percent of noncommissioned officers were party members. From officers' schools specializing in military engineering, infantry, armor, air force, rear services (logistics), and communications, cadets graduate as second lieutenants. Senior and midcareer officers training establishments include the General Staff War College, Military-Political College, Military-Technical College, and Senior Naval War College. In addition many Polish officers attend war colleges and other specialized military schools in the USSR.

## STRATEGIC PROBLEMS

Lying across the main land routes from Russia to central and western Europe, Poland has for centuries been invaded repeatedly from both east and west. The Polish people present an ethnic monolith united by strong nationalism and memories of a great historical past. The overwhelming majority are opposed to Russian-Communist domination. They are acutely aware of their low standard of living in comparison with the West, and they are strongly anti-Russian because of past injuries inflicted on Poland by Russia—partitions, deportations, the Katyn mass murder of prisoners of war, and Stalin's reign of terror. (They also tend to be anti-German for similar reasons, including the brutal German occupation during World War II.)

In June 1956, serious worker "bread and freedom" riots broke out in the city of Poznan. By quick concessions the Communist government prevented the spread of rebellion and saved the regime, but traces of unrest remain.

Numerous disorders broke out in Gdansk, Szczecin, Katowice, and elsewhere in December 1970 as workers protested substantial increases in food prices. First Secretary W. Gomulka and other key members of the Politburo resigned, and his successor, Gierek, promised reform. There was apparently no intervention by the Soviet Union. In June 1976 new riots, strikes, and violent demonstrations broke out over sharp price increases. The disturbances forced the cancellation of the increases. Both the Polish Communist leadership and the opposition groups realize that any attempt to overthrow the regime would bring a Soviet invasion like those of Hungary in 1956 and Czechoslovakia in 1968.

## MILITARY ASSISTANCE

Poland is dependent upon the Soviet Union for certain spare parts and replacements and for sophisticated electronic equipment. However, Poland produces much military equipment and is endeavoring to update materiel by a long-range research and development program. Polish industry produces tanks, armored personnel carriers, trucks, artillery, small arms, communications and electronic equipment, and miscellaneous items of engineering and chemical equipment. All combat aircraft are of Soviet design. The more modern aircraft are manufactured in the Soviet Union, the rest in Poland. There is a Russian advisory group at the Ministry of Defense level.

## ALLIANCES

Poland is a member of the Warsaw Pact and the Council of Mutual Economic Assistance (CEMA). It has signed bilateral treaties of friendship and mutual assistance with the USSR and all other Warsaw Pact countries. Under a status-of-forces agreement, two Soviet divisions comprising the Northern Group of Forces, and a Soviet Tactical Air Army (the 37th) are stationed in Poland. The headquarters of Soviet Forces in Poland is located in Legnica.

## ARMY

*Personnel:* 230,000

*Organization:*
  3 military districts (Warsaw, Wroclaw, Bydgoszcz)
  5 tank divisions (3 tank regiments, 1 motorized infantry regiment, 1 artillery regiment; 9,000 men each)
  8 mechanized infantry (motorized rifle) divisions (each with 3 motorized rifle regiments, 1 tank regiment, 1 artillery regiment, 11,000 men)
  1 airborne division (light-weight equipment)
  1 amphibious division (sea-land; smaller than motorized rifle divisions with additional amphibious transport vehicles)
  numerous regiments and separate battalions of the Internal Security Forces (WOW) and the Territorial Defense Forces (OT)

*Major Equipment Inventory:*
  3,400 medium tanks (T-34 and T-54; Polish-built T-55)
  150 light tanks (Pt-76)
  1,500 APCs (BTR-152, BTR-50P, OT-62, OT-64, BRDM, BMP)
        armored cars (FUG-A)
        scout cars (BTR-40P)
        ASU-57, SU-100, JSU-122, JSU-152 self-propelled guns
  700 light artillery pieces
  250 medium artillery pieces
  100 heavy artillery pieces
        ZSU-23/4 and ZSU-57/2 self-propelled anti-aircraft guns
        SSMs (FROG and Scud)

Snapper, Swatter, and Sagger antitank guided missiles

*Reserves:* There are approximately 800,000 trained reservists.

## NAVY

*Personnel:* 22,500

*Major Units:*
- 4 diesel submarines (Whiskey class; SS)
- 1 guided missile destroyer (Kotlin class; SS-N-1 SAM; DDG)
- 13 missile attack boats (Osa class; SS-N-2/Styx; PTG)
- 25 patrol craft (PC; most are frontier guard units)
- 15 motor torpedo boats (PT)
- 24 fleet minesweepers (T-43 and Krogulec classes; MSF)
- 25 minesweeping boats (miscellaneous classes; MSB)
- 23 medium landing ships (Polnocny class; LSM)
- 15 personnel landing craft (LCP)
- 6 auxiliary ships (training, tankers, etc.)
- 80 service craft
- 90 naval aircraft (10 Il-28 reconnaissance bombers, 50 MiG-17 fighters, 25 helicopters, 5 miscellaneous)
- 3 marine (naval infantry) regiments
  SSMs for coast defense (Samlet)

*Naval Bases:* Swinoujscie, Gdansk, Hel

## AIR FORCE (includes air defense forces)

*Personnel:* 60,000

*Organization:*
- 1 bomber squadron (Il-28)
- 36 interceptor squadrons (MiG-19/21)
- 18 fighter-bomber squadrons (MiG-17, Su-7, S-20)
- 3 fighter/reconnaissance squadrons (MiG-17)
- 4 transport squadrons (An-2/12/24, Il-14/18)
- 4 helicopter squadrons (Mi-2/4/8)
- 4 training squadrons (Wilga, Iskra, MiG-15)
- 30 SAM battalions (SA-23)
- 200 SAM launchers

*Major Aircraft Types:*
- 888 combat aircraft
  - 12 Il-28 light bombers
  - 480 MiG-21 interceptors
  - 96 MiG-19 interceptors
  - 108 MiG-17 fighter-bomber/reconnaissance
  - 96 Su-20 fighter-bombers
  - 96 Su-7 fighter-bombers
- 444 other aircraft
  - 90 transports (An-2/12/24, Il-14/18)
  - 54 helicopters (Mi-2/4/8)
  - 300 trainer/support aircraft

*Air Bases:* There are more than fifty, some joint Soviet-Polish, others solely for Soviet use.

*Reserves:* There are about 110,000 reservists.

### PARAMILITARY

There are 25,000 border troops (Frontier Guard) organized into mechanized brigades. On the Baltic coast, they have some small patrol boats. In addition organized paramilitary training is conducted by the National Defense League at about 100 training centers. There is also a paramilitary volunteer reserve of citizens' militia some half a million strong.

# PORTUGAL

## Portuguese Republic

### POWER POTENTIAL STATISTICS

Area: 35,340 square miles (including the Azores and Madeira)
Population: 9,833,000
Total Active Regular Armed Forces: 59,500 (0.60% population)
Gross National Product: $14.8 billion ($1,510 per capita)
Annual Military Expenditures: $575.8 million (3.9% GNP)
Crude Steel Production: 460,000 metric tons
Iron Ore Production: 48,000 metric tons
Fuel Production:
  Coal: 193,000 metric tons
  Refined Petroleum Products: 5.9 million metric tons
  Manufactured Gas: 134 million cubic meters
Electric Power Output: 13.9 billion kwh
Merchant Fleet (ships 1,000 tons and over): 86 ships; 1.1 million gross tons
Civil Air Fleet: 31 major transport aircraft

### DEFENSE STRUCTURE

In April 1974, after forty-eight years of civilian dictatorship, a group of military officers organized as the Armed Forces Movement took power in Portugal in a coup triggered by dissatisfaction with the long, bloody African colonial wars.

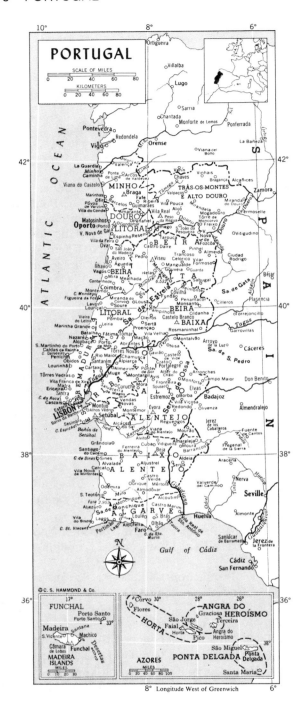

## POLITICO-MILITARY POLICY

Portugal has traditionally relied upon its remoteness from the center of Europe, as well as its long-standing alliance with Great Britain (since 1381; now largely nominal) for external security. It has in the past also been greatly influenced by events in Spain, its larger neighbor. Thus, the conservative, highly centralized regime of former Prime Minister Salazar (ideologically pro-Franco) remained neutral in World War II, but with some pressures from Britain and the United States provided air base rights to the Allies. After World War II the strongly anti-Communist Salazar regime brought Portugal into NATO as a charter member. Both Spain and Portugal are currently democratic, non-Communist, and NATO-oriented.

The armed forces are maintained by conscription. Before the 1974 coup many young men emigrated to escape conscription. The new regime's grant of independence to the rebellious African territories has greatly decreased the need for troops. The total number of armed forces has dropped from 217,000 in 1974 to 63,500 in 1978.

## STRATEGIC PROBLEMS

During the two years following the 1974 coup, Portugal suffered weak, frequently changing, and in some cases, strongly Communist-influenced governments, plus severe economic problems that were exacerbated by hastily imposed and sometimes inequitable land reforms. From mid-1976 to mid-1978 the prime minister was Mario Soares, a respected Socialist. His stabilizing policies, together with a heavy influx of financial assistance from the Western democracies, kept Portugal relatively free of turmoil and achieved modest economic gains while maintaining a relatively high degree of political freedom and individual rights. Granting independence to the African possessions (Guinea-Bissau in 1974 and Angola, Cape Verde, and Mozambique in 1975) removed a serious strategic problem for Portugal, although it has made it necessary for the home country to absorb sizable numbers of returning colonials.

In Portuguese Timor, the eastern half of an island in the easternmost portion of Indonesia, civil strife broke out between two opposing liberation factions in 1975. Portugal, internally shaky at that time, lost control of the Timor situation in mid-1975, and Indonesia moved in. In 1976, East Timor became an Indonesian province, ending 400 years of Portuguese rule.

During the period of unstable and far-leftist rule, the leaders of the conservative Azores Islands population made moves toward separating from Portugal, a matter of international importance because of the U.S. base in the Azores. This issue is now quiet, although the independence movement still exists.

Under the 1976 Socialist Constitution, the elected president is head of state and commander in chief of the armed forces. He appoints a prime minister, who is head of government. The president has the constitutional right to declare a state of emergency and to govern by decree.

In 1978 the high Portuguese inflation rate (27 percent annual rate for the first three months), high unemployment, and huge balance-of-payments deficit ($1.2 billion at the end of 1977) remained cause for concern. The Soares government fell in July, and President Antonio Eanes had difficulty forming a stable new government. Coup attempts by dissatisfied military factions remained a possibility.

## MILITARY ASSISTANCE

Portugal has received $327.5 million in military aid from the United States since 1950, and 3,421 students have been trained under the MAP. The present U.S. Military Advisory Group in Portugal numbers about twenty. Aid in fiscal year 1977 totaled $2.5 million.

## ALLIANCES

Portugal is a member of the NATO alliance. It also has bilateral treaties with the United Kingdom, the United States, and Spain. The treaty with the United States provides base rights in the Azores. Portugal has been admitted to membership in the Council of Europe and has applied for and been approved for EEC membership. Negotiations on the terms of EEC membership were slated for fall 1978.

## ARMY

*Personnel:* 40,000

*Organization:*
  6 regional commands
  1 infantry brigade
 16 infantry regiments
  4 independent infantry battalions
  3 artillery regiments
  2 artillery groups
  1 coast artillery regiment
  2 independent antiaircraft battalions
  2 cavalry regiments
  1 MP regiment
  1 tank regiment
  2 engineer regiments
  1 signal regiment

*Major Equipment Inventory:*
 100 medium tanks (M-47, M-4)
 250 light tanks (M-24, M-41)
  40 half-track APCs (M-16)
     armored cars and scout cars

  26 M-7 SP 105mm howitzers
     .50-caliber quad. antiaircraft guns
     40mm antiaircraft guns
     M-1 Long Tom 155mm howitzers towed
     M-1 105mm howitzers towed
     M-114 155mm howitzers towed

## NAVY

*Personnel:* 10,000 (including marines)

*Major Units:*
  3 submarines (Daphne class; SS)
 13 frigates (3 Almirante Pereira Da Silva class, 6 Joao Coutinho class; 4 Comandante Joao Belo class; FF)
 10 patrol craft (Cacine class; PC)
  8 patrol boats (PB)
  4 coastal minesweepers (MSC)
  1 utility landing craft (LCU)
 13 mechanized landing craft (LCM)
 10 auxiliary ships and service craft

*Major Naval Base:* Lisbon

## AIR FORCE

*Personnel:* 9,500

*Organization:*
  1 fighter-bomber squadron (G-91)
  1 transport squadron (C-130)
  1 transport squadron (C-212)
  2 helicopter squadrons (Alouette III and Puma)
  1 transport squadron (Cessna O-2)
  3 paratroop battalions

*Major Aircraft Types:*
  18 combat aircraft
    18 C-91 fighter-bombers
 125 other aircraft
    40 helicopters (30 Alouette III, 10 Puma)
    51 transports (24 Aviocar Casa C-212, 2 C-130, 25 Cessna O-2)
    34 trainers (18 T-37, 10 T-33, 6 T-38)

*Major Air Bases:* Montijo, Tancos, Sintra, Ota

## PARAMILITARY

There are 9,500 active duty personnel in the National Republic Guard for internal security.

# ROMANIA

## Socialist Republic of Romania

### POWER POTENTIAL STATISTICS

Area: 91,699 square miles
Population: 21,964,000
Total Active Regular Armed Forces: 165,500 (0.75%
   population)
Gross National Product: $57.0 billion ($2,630 per capita)
Annual Military Expenditures: $2.33 billion (4.09%
   GNP)
Crude Steel Production: 11.5 million metric tons
Iron Ore Production: 779,000 metric tons

Fuel Production:
   Coal: 7.3 million metric tons
   Lignite: 19.8 million metric tons
   Crude Oil: 14.6 million metric tons
   Refined Petroleum Products: 10 million metric tons
   Natural Gas: 32 billion cubic meters
   Manufactured Gas: 950 million cubic meters
Electric Power Output: 59.8 billion kwh
Merchant Fleet (ships 1,000 tons and over): 134 ships;
   1.25 million gross tons
Civil Air Fleet: 5 jet, 12 turboprop, and 2 piston
   transports

### DEFENSE STRUCTURE

As in the other Eastern European Communist states, the

armed forces of Romania are controlled by the Communist party. The military establishment consists of ground, naval, air defense (including military aviation), and frontier forces. It is administered by the minister of armed forces, who is responsible to the Defense Council and the head of state. The minister, who assumes the highest military rank, has several deputies, including the chiefs of the Main Political Directorate, General Staff, Directorate of Training, and Rear Services (logistics). Commanders of operational commands report directly to the minister. The highest level of tactical organization includes the commands of navy, air force, ground forces, frontier forces, and military districts.

Political indoctrination of the armed forces is the responsibility of the Main Political Directorate. Party and Communist youth organizations are at all levels of the forces. Almost all senior officers and the majority of junior officers are Communist party members.

## POLITICO-MILITARY POLICY

Although Romania still follows the Soviet pattern in its internal affairs, it is the least compliant of the Soviet allies. In June 1958, a status of forces agreement with the USSR, which had allowed the stationing of Soviet forces in Romania, lapsed when Soviet forces left the country. Beginning cautiously that same year Romania adopted a form of nationalistic communism. Since 1963 Romania has asserted virtual independence of the USSR in its foreign policy, and its membership in the Warsaw Pact is only nominal. In some matters Romania has taken stands in opposition to Soviet policy, as in its continuing friendly relations with Communist China and Israel. Romania's good relations with both Israel and Egypt made it possible for leaders of those countries to make initial contacts for peace negotiations through Romania.

The absence of Romanian troops from the Warsaw Pact forces that invaded Czechoslovakia in August 1968 was significant. The Romanians were presumably not considered sufficiently trustworthy allies to be kept informed of the invasion plans. Also, there was considerable speculation throughout the world (not least in Romania) that the Warsaw forces would next invade Romania. It is noteworthy that the Bucharest government, while continuing to assert its independence, and even making some ostentatious plans for resistance, also strongly reaffirmed its loyalty to Marxism-Leninism.

Military service is universal. Length of service is sixteen months in the ground forces and border troops and certain elements of the air force, and two years in the navy and the rest of the air force. Of the nearly 200,000 young men who reach the draft age annually, about 80 percent are physically and otherwise fit to serve. Men released from active duty remain in the reserve and subject to recall. Only those recently discharged are considered trained reserves and could be quickly mobilized and go into action without extensive retraining. There is insufficient emphasis on periodic reserve training to keep the older men up to date on new weapons and tactics.

## STRATEGIC PROBLEMS

There are long-standing territorial frictions with three of Romania's four neighbors. In 1940, even before either country was involved in World War II, the USSR annexed Bessarabia and northern Bukovina from Romania; these annexations were confirmed by the postwar peace treaty. The majority of the population of these regions is Romanian.

After the breakup of the Austro-Hungarian Empire, under the World War I peace treaties Romania received Transylvania, with a majority population of Romanians. This region, however, had been traditionally Hungarian, and has been a source of trouble and conflict between the two nations ever since.

Less serious is the Dobruja question with Bulgaria. The southern portion of the Dobruja (the region between the lower Danube and the Black Sea) has a slight Bulgarian majority in its population, but was awarded to Romania after the second Balkan War in 1913. Bulgaria still aspires to regain this territory (as it did briefly in World War II), but it is not likely to become a source of conflict.

## MILITARY ASSISTANCE

All major weapons and heavy equipment are of Soviet design, but because of Romania's independent policies, Romanian armed forces are not the first to receive newer equipment. Romania is attempting to reduce its dependence on the USSR and other Warsaw Pact countries by producing more military materiel within the country. There are no Soviet advisers with the Romanian armed forces, and no Soviet troops are stationed in Romania.

## ALLIANCES

Romania is a member of the Warsaw Pact, but is the least active participant in the alliance. The Romanian role in the Council for Mutual Economic Assistance (CEMA) has been relatively inactive. It has consistently avoided agreeing to any multilateral measure which would limit its control over its own economy. Romania has signed bilateral treaties of friendship and mutual assistance with the USSR, all other Warsaw Pact states, the People's Republic of China, and Mongolia.

## ARMY

*Personnel:* 135,000

*Organization:*
- 2 military districts, 3 divisions each, with headquarters at Iasi and Cluj
- 1 independent garrison (Bucharest)
- 2 tank divisions (3 tank regiments, 1 motorized rifle regiment, 1 artillery regiment each)
- 7 motorized rifle divisions (3 motorized rifle regiments, 1 tank regiment, 1 artillery regiment each)
- 1 mountain brigade
- 1 airborne regiment
- 1 artillery division

*Major Equipment Inventory:*
- 1,700 medium tanks (T-34, T-54, T-55, T-62)
- 900 APCs (BTR-152, BTR-50P)
- Snapper, Swatter and Sagger antitank guided missiles
- heavy assault guns (JSU-152)
- light artillery pieces
- medium artillery pieces
- SU-100 and JSU-122 self-propelled guns
- 200 antiaircraft guns
- SAMs (SA-2 Guideline)
- 75 FROG SSMs

*Reserves:* There are approximately 900,000 reserves

## NAVY

*Personnel:* 10,500

*Major Units:*
- 3 patrol ships (Poti class; PGF)
- 3 submarine chasers (Kronstadt class; PCS)
- 5 missile attack boats (Osa class; SS-N-2/Styx SSM; PTG)
- 18 fast patrol craft (Shanghai class; PCF)
- 13 motor torpedo boats (P-4 class; PT)
- 6 hydrofoil motor torpedo boats (Huchwan class; hydrofoil; PTH)
- 4 fleet minesweepers (MSF)
- 10 inshore minesweepers (T-301 class; MSI)
- 16 minesweeping boats (MSB)
- 26 river patrol craft (PBR)
- 4 auxiliary ships
- 25 service craft

*Naval Bases:* Constanta, Mamaia, Braila, Mangalia

*Reserves:* 25,000 to 30,000 reserves

## AIR FORCE (AIR DEFENSE FORCE, including military aviation)

*Personnel:* 25,000

*Organization:*
- 12 interceptor squadrons (MiG-19/21)
- 6 fighter-bomber squadrons (MiG-17)
- 1 reconnaissance/bomber squadron (Il-28)
- 3 transport squadrons (An-2/24/26, Li-2, Il-12/14)
- 2 helicopter squadrons (Mi-2/4/8, Alouette III)

*Major Aircraft Types:*
- 347 combat aircraft
  - 200 MiG-21 fighter-interceptors
  - 36 MiG-19 fighter-interceptors
  - 96 MiG-17 fighter-bombers
  - 15 Il-28 light bomber/reconnaissance aircraft
- 235 other aircraft
  - 75 transports (An-2/24/26, Li-2, Il-12/14)
  - 60 helicopters (Mi-2/4/8, Alouette III)
  - 100 trainer and support aircraft (MiG-15, L-29, etc.)
  - SAMs (SA-2)

*Air Bases:* Baneasa, Otopeni, and Popesti-Leordeni (Bucharest area), Tirgusor, Buzau, Zilistea, Galati, Tecuci, Iasi, Bacau, Satu Mare, Oradea, Arad, Timisoara, Brasov, Cluj, Calarasi, Craiova, Constanta, Mamaia.

*Reserves:* 45,000 to 50,000 trained reservists

## PARAMILITARY

There are approximately 40,000 men in border and internal security units plus a volunteer militia and armed workers' organizations numbering up to 500,000 members.

# RWANDA

## Republic of Rwanda

## POWER POTENTIAL STATISTICS

Area: 10,169 square miles
Population: 4,508,000

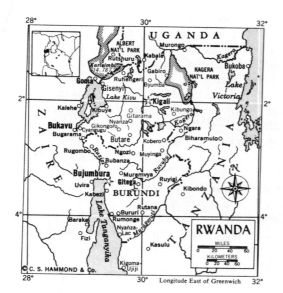

Total Active Regular Armed Forces: 4,000 (0.09%
    population)
Gross National Product: $603 million ($140 per capita)
Annual Military Expenditures: $12.4 million (2.06%
    GNP)
Electric Power Output: 142 million kwh
Civil Air Fleet: 1 major transport aircraft

## POLITICO-MILITARY POLICIES AND POSTURE

The president, Maj. Gen. Juvenal Habiyarimana, assumed power after a bloodless coup in 1973. As national defence minister, he heads the armed forces. All elements of the Rwandan government have been integrated into the National Revolutionary Movement for Development (MRND), founded in 1975. The MRND hierarchy extends from the presidency to local cells of several dozen families. MRND goals include elimination of regionalism, intertribal strife, and local corruption—all sources of potential instability.

Rwanda's internal and external strategic problems revolve around a major ethnic division, exacerbated by its central location among neighbors with similar internal security problems. The population is 13 percent Hamitic Tutsi (Watusi) and 86 percent Bantu Hutu. The exceptionally tall Tutsi were a dominant feudal cast ruling their Hutu serfs until the UN-supervised elections of 1961, which the Hutu won. This resulted in violence, and over

160,000 Tutsi fled to neighboring countries. In 1963, 3,000 Tutsi—supported by Chinese agents in Uganda—invaded Rwanda, but were defeated by the National Guard and police in a series of skirmishes. The attempt was repeated in late 1966 by some 2,000 Tutsi armed and trained by Chinese Communist agents in Burundi, with the same result. Burundi then broke relations with Communist China, and a security agreement was entered into by Zaire, Burundi, and Rwanda to prevent subversive activities.

Tensions between Rwanda and Burundi increased during extremely violent outbreaks of Hutu-Tutsi conflict in Burundi in 1972 and 1973. By 1976, however, relations had improved to the extent that Rwanda joined with Burundi and Zaire to form the Economic Community of the Great Lakes in reaffirmation of their 1966 security agreement. A few months later a new government came to power in Burundi and announced its intention to eliminate discrimination against the Hutu majority, further improving relations. Tanzania and Rwanda have also become friendlier. Rwanda's internal problems are exacerbated by a high population density and high birthrate, combined with a nonviable economy.

With its own dissident ethnic refugees living and plotting in neighboring countries, and with similar refugees from these surrounding countries seeking sanctuary in Rwanda, cooperation and understanding among all of these countries is essential. Rwanda apparently cooperates to some extent with Burundi on mutual security matters growing out of this ethnic dissidence, and with bordering Zaire, Uganda, and Tanzania on matters of refugees, insurgents, and mercenaries. Rwanda is a member of the OCAM and the OAU.

Belgian troops withdrew shortly after Rwanda's independence in July 1962, although Belgian military equipment and instructor-advisers have remained. Belgian military assistance has continued. Diplomatic relations with China were reestablished in November 1971, and China provided technical assistance for a highway and several agricultural projects.

Most foreign aid ($75 million in 1975) comes from Belgium, France, the EDF, and World Bank, although countries as diverse as North Korea, Libya, the United States, Canada, and Kuwait have bilateral projects. Uganda cut off oil shipments to Rwanda briefly in 1976, but they have resumed since August of that year.

The army numbers some 3,750, organized into a reconnaissance squadron, eight infantry companies, and a commando company. They are equipped with twelve armored cars, six light guns, and eight light mortars. The air force of 250 members has nine aircraft, four of which are transports (two C-47s and two Do-27s); the others are three AM3C COIN light trainers and two Alouette helicopters.

# SAUDI ARABIA

## The Kingdom of Saudi Arabia

## POWER POTENTIAL STATISTICS

Area: 873,972 square miles
Population: 7,984,000
Total Active Regular Armed Forces: 52,000 (0.65%
    population)
Gross National Product: $58 billion ($9,210 per capita)
Annual Military Expenditures: $12.9 billion (22.24%
    GNP)
Fuel Production:
    Crude Oil: 424 million metric tons
    Refined Petroleum Products: 33.6 million metric tons
    Natural Gas: 3.3 billion cubic meters
Electric Power Output: 8 billion kwh
Merchant Fleet (ships 1,000 tons and over): 47 ships;
    881,000 gross tons
Civil Air Fleet: 73 major transport aircraft

## DEFENSE STRUCTURE

In this slowly liberalizing absolute monarchy, the king
is commander in chief of the regular armed forces, one of
his most trusted brothers is the minister of defense and
aviation, and another brother is commander of the National
Guard, or White Army.

Long-continued use of U.S. materiel and U.S. assistance
in training have influenced the thinking of Saudi Arabian
military planners. Organization and tactical doctrine are
patterned after U.S. models.

## POLITICO-MILITARY POLICY

Saudi Arabia's fabulous oil wealth, with proven reserves
that could support the present massive production of crude
oil for at least ninety years, has placed the nation in a
position to influence international alignments and developments particularly in those highly industrialized nations
of Western Europe that are dependent upon the oil of the
Middle East.

The armed forces and the nation's tremendous oil-based
wealth are the primary instruments for maintaining Saudi
Arabia's position of predominance in the Arabian
Peninsula.

The National Guard (White Army) plays a special role
in Saudi Arabia. Its members are recruited by tribe, and

they have an especially intense loyalty to the royal family.
While the regular armed forces are concentrated in the
larger cities, the White Army is stationed throughout the
country. The White Army's modernization program has
lagged somewhat, and although these forces are now
becoming mechanized and have artillery, they will probably never have a full complement of modern weaponry.
The White Army could have significance as a counter-
balance to the regular ground forces if there should be
destabilizing events in Saudi Arabia, or divisions within
the royal family.

All armed forces service is voluntary, and recruits enlist
for a three-year term. Recruiting for the regular forces is
done on a nationwide basis, while the White Army is
recruited on a tribal or area basis, and units stationed at
various posts are recruited from tribes in those areas.
There are many royal princes serving in important leadership positions in both armies.

Most younger military officers are graduates of the
Royal Military College (Academy) in Riyadh, which offers
a three-year course in academic and military subjects;
graduates of technical schools may also obtain
commissions. The Army School Command directs a
system of service schools, including a Command and
General Staff College. Saudi Arabia sends many officers
to war colleges in the United States and Great Britain for
advanced training.

## STRATEGIC PROBLEMS

Rivalry with Egypt led Saudi Arabia to the brink of
war in Yemen during the period 1962–67. Saudi Arabia
supported the deposed Imam of Yemen in civil war against
the newly established Republic of Yemen, now Yemen
(San'a), which was in turn supported by Egypt. Under
financial pressure from Saudi Arabia, Egypt withdrew its
support of the Republic of Yemen after the disastrous war
with Israel in June 1967. In June 1970, Saudi Arabia
recognized the Republic of Yemen, thereby ending an
estrangement between the two countries that had lasted for
eight years.

The Marxist-oriented People's Democratic Republic of
Yemen (South Yemen) is generally hostile to Saudi Arabia,
while Oman maintains a unique independent posture,
carrying on friendly relations but refusing to acknowledge
Saudi dominance in the southeast portion of the Arabian
Peninsula.

A projected pipeline, planned for completion in 1980,
will stretch across Saudi Arabia from the Persian Gulf oil
fields to the Red Sea, and will make Saudi Arabia (and
Western Europe) less dependent on political conditions in
Iran and Afghanistan.

## SAUDI ARABIA

CONIC PROJECTION

SCALE OF MILES

0 50 100 200 300 400

SCALE OF KILOMETERS

0 100 200 300 400

Capitals of Countries ─────── ☆

International Boundaries ─ ─ ─ ─

Certain frontiers of Saudi Arabia, Qatar, Yemen Arab Republic, Oman, the Union of Arab Emirates and the People's Democratic Republic of Yemen are either in dispute or are not definitely delimited. On this map no attempt has been made to show these frontiers by means of the international boundary symbol; the dotted boundaries merely indicate the approximate extent of administrative control or influence, and should not be considered definitive.

Copyright by C.S HAMMOND & CO., N.Y.

Longitude East of Greenwich

## MILITARY ASSISTANCE

Saudi Arabia renders large-scale financial assistance to Syria, Jordan, North Yemen, and the PLO. Saudi Arabia announced the end of its considerable financial aid to Egypt after signing of the Egyptian-Israeli peace treaty in 1979. After Somalia turned out the Soviets in 1977, Somalia became a major recipient of Saudi assistance.

The U.S. Corps of Engineers has a multimillion dollar contract with Saudi Arabia to build several military facilities and some defense-related industries in the kingdom. Equipment and material to modernize the army, air force, navy, and National Guard are being procured on a large scale to insure a more effective means of defending the petroleum resources of this vast, underpopulated country.

## ALLIANCES

Saudi Arabia is a member of the Arab League.

## ARMY

*Personnel:* 40,000

*Organization:*
    4 infantry brigades
    2 armored brigades
    6 artillery battalions (3 of these are antiaircraft)
  16 SAM batteries (Hawk; see below)

*Major Equipment Inventory:*
  475 medium tanks
      200 AMX-30
      200 M-60
       75 M-47
  142 light tanks (M-41, M-24, AMX-13)
1,000 APCs (M-113)
  300 armored cars (AML-60, AML-90, M-6, M-8)
  350 howitzers (105mm, 155mm), antitank recoilless rifles (75mm), antitank rocket launchers (LAW), and artillery missiles (Vigilant)
   40 antiaircraft guns (Vulcan 20mm)

*Missiles:*
4,000 SSM antitank (Dragon; 600 trackers)
1,000 TOW (62 launchers)
      SAMS: 780 Hawk (16 batteries); Crotale

*Equipment on Order:*
  40 AH-1 helicopters

## NAVY

*Personnel:* 2,000

*Major Units:*
   1 patrol craft (PC)
   3 motor torpedo boats (Jaguar class; PT)
 20 fast patrol craft (PCF)
 65 patrol boats (PB)
 30 roadstead patrol boats (PBR)
   8 hovercraft (SRN-6; armed; can be used for patrol duties)
   4 coastal minesweepers (MSC)
   4 utility landing craft (LCU)
   5 service craft

*Naval Bases:* Jidda, Dammam

## AIR FORCE

*Personnel:* 10,000 (There are about 2,000 contract personnel who are training maintenance personnel and doing contract maintenance on the aircraft and technical equipment of the Saudi air force.)

*Organization:*
  6 fighter squadrons (2 Lightning, 4 F-5)
  2 operational training squadrons (F-5; combat-capable)
  2 basic training and COIN squadrons (Strikemaster; combat-capable)
  1 primary training squadron (T-41, T-34)
  2 transport squadrons (C-130, C-123, C-140, Boeing 707, Cessna 310)
  2 helicopter squadrons (AB-205, AB-206, Alouette III)
*Note:* The Strikemaster has a combat capability for ground attack.

*Major Aircraft Types:*
 152 combat aircraft
    72 F-5 fighters
    48 Lightning fighters
    32 Strikemaster trainer/ground attack
 134 other aircraft
    59 transports (39 C-130, 5 C-123, 2 C-140, 1 Boeing 707, 12 Cessna 310)
    32 trainers (18 T-34, 14 T-41)
    43 helicopters (2 Alouette III, 25 AB-205, 16 AB-206)

*Missiles:*
AAM Sidewinder
ASM Maverick

*Equipment on Order:*
120 fighters (F-5)
 20 Sea King and Commando helicopters
     Sale of F-15 fighters approved for 1980

*Air Bases:* Dhahran, Riyadh, Jidda Taif, Medina, Tabuk, Yanbu

## PARAMILITARY

The National Guard, or White Army, consists of approximately 30,000 tribal levies. Its mission is internal security. It is equipped with a number of armored cars and antitank weapons. Senior commanders are chosen from among trusted members of the royal family.

# SENEGAL

## Republic of Senegal

## POWER POTENTIAL STATISTICS

Area: 76,124 square miles

Population: 5,450,000

Total Active Regular Armed Forces: 6,000 (0.11% population)

Gross National Product: $1.9 billion ($353 per capita)

Annual Military Expenditures: $62 million (3.41% GNP)

Fuel Production: Refined Petroleum Products: 1.97 million metric tons

Electric Power Output: 603 million kwh

Merchant Fleet (ships 1,000 tons and over): 4 ships; 8,000 gross tons

Civil Air Fleet: 4 major transport aircraft

## POLITICO-MILITARY POLICIES AND POSTURE

The elected president determines and directs national policy, appoints the cabinet and senior military officials, and is commander in chief of the armed forces. He controls the military through a minister of armed forces. The chief of staff of the army is also commander of the gendarmerie.

Senegal professes a policy of nonalignment in international affairs. Relations with Guinea-Bissau are strained, however, because of sharp differences in political outlook and Guinean charges that Senegal supports plots against the Guinean government. Independence of Guinea-Bissau and repatriation of refugees have relieved a major security problem in the south. Close ties are continued with France, and also are maintained with the Gambia, an enclave within Senegal, with agreements for cooperation in defense and foreign affairs. Senegal supports regional federation and cooperation and is active in the UN, OAU, OCAM, and a number of other regional economic entities. Senegal contributed a contingent of forces to the UN peacekeeping forces in Lebanon in 1978.

Senegal has remained fairly stable internally since independence in 1960 and the split with Mali a few months later. Disturbances in 1962, 1967, and 1968 were put down effectively by the armed forces and the police. However, there are considerable internal economic difficulties, increased by the high population growth rate. There is a multiplicity of tribes, but ethnic conflicts appear minor; the fact that 80 percent of the population is Moslem is a stabilizing influence. In 1976 President Senghor created a three-party political system, reserving the centrist consensus role for his own socialist party. In elections in 1978 he and his party won convincingly.

Shortly after independence mutual defense and military assistance agreements were signed with France. These included an internal security agreement, base rights, transit and overflight privileges, and military training and equipment grants. Dakar remained headquarters for French *Zone d'Outre-Mer I,* and a French garrison, now 2,000 men, remains there. In addition to providing a ready unit for deployment anywhere in Africa, this force guards the airfield and certain key installations. It would also be available to assist the government in maintaining internal security under existing agreements. French forces consist of the following: army (1,200), 1 mixed regiment; navy (500), 2 coastal escorts; air force (300), 6 Noratlas transports.

Since the initial outfitting with French arms and equipment, Senegal's armed forces have received military assistance from the United States in the amount of $2.9 million from 1961 through 1977, and nineteen students have been trained under MAP. Between 1967 and 1976 France supplied $5 million in arms, and Canada supplied $1,000,000.

The armed forces are maintained by selective compulsory service of twenty-four months. There is a National Gendarmerie of 1,600 men.

## ARMY

*Personnel:* 5,500

*Organization:*
    3 infantry battalions (5 companies each)
    1 engineer battalion
    1 field artillery battery
    1 light antiaircraft battery
    1 mobile force (1 armored car co., 2 paratroop cos., 2 commando cos., 1 motor transport co., 1 signal co.) serves as general reserve

*Major Equipment Inventory:*
    8 armored cars (M-8)
      armored cars (AML, French)
      75mm Pack howitzers
    6 105mm howitzers
    8 81mm mortars
      30mm, 40mm antiaircraft guns

## NAVY

*Personnel:* 300

*Major Units:*
    3 patrol craft (PC)
   15 patrol boats (PB)
    5 roadstead patrol boats (PBR)
    3 landing craft (1 LCU; 2 LCM)
    1 service craft

*Naval Base:* Dakar

## AIR FORCE

*Personnel:* 200

*Major Aircraft Types:*
    4 O-2 aircraft (COIN capable)
    4 C-47 transports
    4 Broussard liaison aircraft
    2 Bell 47 helicopters

*Air Bases:* Yoff (Dakar), St. Louis, Tambacounda, Ziguinchor, Thies, and Kedougou

# SEYCHELLES

## POWER POTENTIAL STATISTICS

Area: 156 square miles

Population: 64,000
Gross National Product: $43.1 million ($710 per capita)
Electric Power Output: 25 million kwh
Merchant Fleet (ships 1,000 tons and over): 5 ships; 54,000 gross tons

## POLITICO-MILITARY POLICIES AND POSTURE

Seychelles became an independent republic within the Commonwealth on June 28, 1976. Its first president, James Mancham, had been chief minister under the British colonial government and was leader of the majority party; the first prime minister, Albert Rene, was leader of the opposition party. Their coalition government ended in 1977, when Rene deposed Mancham while the latter was out of the country to attend a Commonwealth conference. The coup was bloodless, although, in preparation for it, arms had been brought into the country, previously peaceful and without military weapons. In April 1978, twenty-one persons were arrested for allegedly plotting to depose Rene and place Mancham back in power. The Rene regime charged that Kenyan government officials had aided the plot.

Citizens of Seychelles are a fairly homogeneous population, mostly Creole descendants of French settlers and the Africans they brought to the islands as slaves. Seychelles attends the annual Franco-African summit conferences.

There is a United States Air Force space tracking station on Mahe, the largest island. Relations between U.S. personnel and the Seychelles people and government have been good.

The United Kingdom contributed $10 million, or 15 percent of the annual budget in 1971, plus loans and grants to cover virtually all capital expenditures. Since independence, it has continued to contribute significant amounts.

# SIERRA LEONE

## Republic of Sierra Leone

### POWER POTENTIAL STATISTICS

Area: 27,925 square miles
Population: 3,293,000
Total Active Regular Armed Forces: 2,000 (0.06%
population)
Gross National Product: $657 million ($230 per capita)
Annual Military Expenditures: $11.4 million (1.73%
GNP)
Iron Ore Production: 916,000 metric tons
Fuel Production: Refined Petroleum Products: 185,000
metric tons
Electric Power Output: 264 million kwh
Merchant Fleet (ships 1,000 tons and over): 3 ships;
5,000 gross tons
Civil Air Fleet: 2 piston transports and 1 jet operated by
British United Airways for Sierra Leone Airways

### POLITICO-MILITARY POLICIES AND POSTURE

Sierra Leone was granted independence by Great Britain in 1961, and became a sovereign republic within the Commonwealth in April 1971. The Sierra Leone Parliament, called the House of Representatives, is a unicameral body. The majority party leader is the president, who is both head of state and head of government; he is also minister of defence. In 1961 the Sierra Leone Battalion of the Royal West African Frontier Force became the nucleus of the Royal Sierra Leone Military Forces (RSLMF). In 1971 the RSLMF was renamed the Republic of Sierra Leone Military Forces.

Sierra Leone's policy is characterized by nonalignment. Sierra Leone condemns *apartheid* in South Africa and advocates the use of force by Britain to depose the white regime in Rhodesia. Implicitly, for defense against possible external aggression, the nation depends upon collective security and protection by Britain and the United States. Sierra Leone is a member of the Commonwealth, the OAU, and the Economic Community of West African States.

Sierra Leone is strategically significant for its excellent harbor in the West African bulge and its mineral wealth. The natural harbor at Freetown is one of the finest in West Africa, with anchorage for more than 200 ships of unrestricted draft. Diamonds are a major export, although production has dropped sharply in the last several years. Sierra Leone also exports sizable quantities of iron ore, bauxite, and titanium oxide.

Modest military and police forces are maintained to insure internal security and prevent infiltrations. Serious internal security problems stem from political and ethnic disputes. The two principal tribes, the Temne in the north and the Mende in the south, are generally opposed politically in the two major parties. The Creoles, descendants of freed African slaves from the British West Indies who founded the colony, allied with the Temne in a new government which in 1968 overthrew the existing military government with the assistance of army and police NCOs. The military government had assumed power in March of 1967 after an election deadlock and charges of corruption in the civilian government. In March 1971 a military coup led by the army commander in chief failed; the coup leaders were tried and executed. Immediately after the coup, Prime Minister Stevens asked Guinea for assistance (under terms of an agreement reached in 1970) in restoring stability to Sierra Leone. Guinea responded by sending airborne units and three MiG fighters. The ruling All People's Congress party has called for establishment of a one-party state. However, it faces not only tribal opposition but discontent because of corruption and poor economic performance.

Upon independence in 1961, British military equipment was turned over to the RSLMF, and British officers continued for several years to occupy key command and staff positions. With complete Africanization of the RSLMF only a small British training mission remains. Britain continues to be the source of military equipment, and RSLMF personnel are trained in Britain and Nigeria. Israel has also conducted military training and in 1966 assisted in the establishment of a military academy for officer cadets and youth movement leaders.

The RSLMF is 1,850 strong, organized in an infantry battalion, an armored car squadron, a signal squadron, supporting services, and a harbor and coastal patrol unit. The latter unit of about 150 men operates three fast patrol craft (PCF). There is a combined army/police organization (AM/POL) for land and coastal patrol.

The regular police force of about 2,000 includes a special constabulary of 600. There is a special police in industrial areas of about 300, and each chiefdom has its small police force. Sierra Leone has two Saab MF1-15 light trainer aircraft.

# SINGAPORE

## Republic of Singapore

### POWER POTENTIAL STATISTICS

Area: 225 square miles
Population: 2,354,000
Total Active Regular Armed Forces: 23,000 (0.98% population)
Gross National Product: $6.65 billion ($2,830 per capita)
Annual Military Expenditures: $411.2 million (6.18% GNP)
Fuel Production: Refined Petroleum Products: 23.7 million metric tons
Electric Power Output: 5 billion kwh
Merchant Fleet (ships 1,000 tons and over): 575 ships; 7.1 million gross tons
Civil Air Fleet: 25 major transport aircraft

### DEFENSE STRUCTURE

The president is commander in chief of the Singapore armed forces, but his role is largely ceremonial. Substantive issues are dealt with by the minister of defence, who is responsible to the cabinet and parliament. The services have separate structures and chiefs of staff, but the Ministry of Defence and developing joint services staff exercise close control. All males above the age of nineteen are subject to two or three years' service before passing into the reserve, and there has been discussion of some form of conscription of females if the anticipated shortage of available males occurs in the late 1970s and early 1980s.

### POLITICO-MILITARY POLICY

At independence in August 1965, Singapore had virtually no defense forces. The Singapore Regiment had more

foreigners on its rolls than Singaporeans. The government has taken energetic steps to build up the armed forces and replace expatriates with native Singaporeans. This process is nearing completion. It is deliberate policy to use the services as a means of integrating the diverse ethnic strains of the population.

Under the Five-Power Defence Pact, a New Zealand Army battalion (less one company) and a Royal Australian Air Force flight are maintained on station in Singapore. Units of the Australian and New Zealand navies call at Singapore from time to time, and they, along with forces stationed in the republic, carry out combined maneuvers.

It is difficult to consider the defense of Singapore separate from the defense of Malaysia. However, the circumstances surrounding Singapore's secession from Malaysia and other factors have limited cooperation between the armed services of the two states. Singapore has pursued defense policies designed to demonstrate the credibility of going it alone, while, at the same time, it maintains a close watch on security matters in West Malaysia.

Limited training areas have hampered the armed services, especially the army. At one time, army units were deployed to Taiwan for battalion training, but that program was halted. Conversations have been held on the feasibility of using training space in the Philippines without substantive result.

### ALLIANCES

Singapore is a member of the Five-Power Defence Pact that includes Australia, Malaysia, New Zealand, and the United Kingdom. Singapore also belongs to ASEAN. It is likely that Singapore would be willing to enter a future regional security arrangement if this should prove feasible.

### ARMY

*Personnel:* 16,000

*Organization:*
    3 brigades, composed of
        8 infantry battalions
        1 armored regiment
        3 artillery battalions
        1 engineer battalion
        1 signal battalion

*Major Equipment Inventory:*
   60 AMX-13 light tanks
  250 V-200 Command, M-113, APCs
      25-pounder guns
      120mm mortars
      106mm recoilless rifles

*Reserves:* about 10,000 men

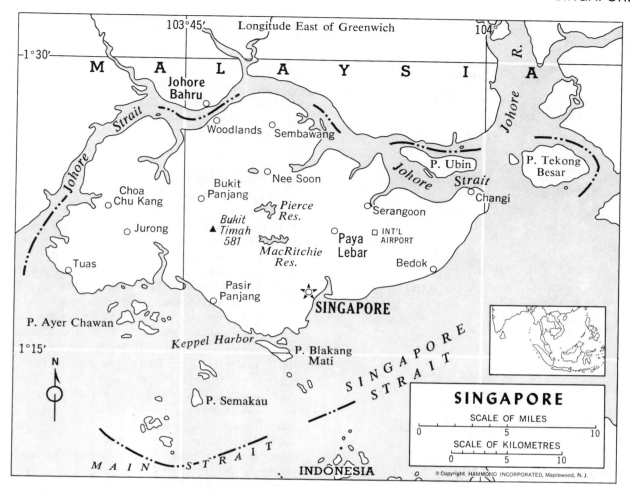

# NAVY

**Personnel:** 3,000

**Major Units:**
- 6 missile attack boats (Gabriel SSMs; TNC 48 class; PTG)
- 2 patrol craft (PC)
- 6 fast patrol craft (PCF)
- 2 coastal minesweepers (MSC)
- 4 patrol boats (PB; police subordinated)
- 6 tank landing ships (LST)
- 6 mechanized landing craft (LCN)

# AIR FORCE

**Personnel:** 4,000

**Organization:**
- 2 fighter squadrons (Hunter)
- 2 fighter-bomber squadrons (A-4)
- 1 training squadron (Strikemaster)

(Note: this training squadron has a ground attack capability)
- 1 training squadron (SF-260)
- 1 communications and rescue squadron (Alouette III, Bell Iroquois)
- 1 transportation and rescue squadron (Skyvan)
- 1 SAM squadron (Bloodhound)

**Major Aircraft Types:**
- 98 combat aircraft
  - 42 Hunter fighters
  - 40 A-4 fighter-bombers
  - 16 Strikemaster armed trainers
- 47 other aircraft
  - 14 SF-260 trainers
  - 7 Alouette III helicopters
  - 10 Bell 212 Iroquois
  - 6 Skyvan transports (3 have an SAR capability)

**Missiles:** SAM Bloodhound

**Major Air Bases:** Tengah, Changi, Seletar

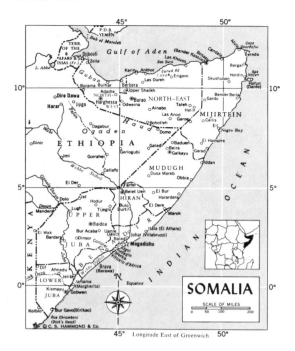

# SOMALIA

## Somali Democratic Republic

### POWER POTENTIAL STATISTICS

Area: 246,155 square miles
Population: 3,428,000
Total Active Regular Armed Forces: 32,750 (0.96%
population)
Gross National Product: $340 million ($110 per capita)
Annual Military Expenditures: $34.65 million (10.19%
GNP)
Electric Power Output: 45 million kwh
Merchant Fleet (ships 1,000 tons and over): 14 ships,
64,000 gross tons
Civil Air Fleet: 6 major transport aircraft

### POLITICO-MILITARY POLICIES AND POSTURE

In October 1969, following the assassination of the president, the army and police seized power. A Supreme Revolutionary Council (SRC) was established, the National Assembly and cabinet were dissolved, political parties were abolished, and the Constitution was suspended. The Somali Revolutionary Socialist party (SRSP) succeeded the Supreme Revolutionary Council in 1976, but the change was more cosmetic than substantive, as most former SRC officers assumed posts in the SRSP government. Maj.

Gen. Siad Barre, president since 1969, chairs the five-man Political Bureau.

The regime has supported liberation movements in countries under colonial rule, as well as those in illegally occupied territory. This particularly refers to about 1,000,000 Somalis living in Ethiopia, Kenya, and Djibouti. Although Somalia proclaimed a policy of nonalignment in foreign relations, its foreign policy was consistently anti-Western and pro-Communist until 1977.

The Somali people are made up of separate clan-families that are an important focus of loyalty. The Issas of Djibouti, for example, are such a Somali clan-family. The Darod clan-family is the largest, and most Somalis living in Kenya and Ethiopia belong to this group; Darods within Somalia have especially advocated unification of all Somalis in one nation-state. The fact that the Somalis are a nomadic people, and that many of them live in Somalia and also in Kenya or Ethiopia during the same year, further complicates the matter of Somalian nationality.

Somali irredentism and the Barre regime's ideological leanings turned the country toward a close alliance with the Soviet Union, a policy that began shortly after independence in 1960, before Barre took power. The USSR was willing to provide the military supplies and training Somalia sought in building a liberation army. In 1967 and 1968, following frequent border conflicts, Somalia renounced its claims against Kenya and Ethiopia. Soviet aid increased, however, after the 1969 coup, and by 1977 Somalia had a heavily armored 30,000 + -man military establishment.

The USSR, which had begun major improvements of its naval base at Berbera in 1975, fell out with the Somalis in 1977 over Soviet aid to the Marxist regime in Ethiopia. Somalia seized the opportunity of Ethiopia's internal disorder to support an invasion of Ethiopia's Ogaden region by the Western Somali Liberation Front (WSLF) in May 1977. In July regular Somali forces joined the conflict. November saw the expulsion of all Soviet and Cuban advisers from Somalia and the beginning of a massive Soviet-Cuban buildup in Ethiopia. The combined Soviet-Cuban-Ethiopian counteroffensive routed the Somalis, and in March and April 1978 Somalia withdrew all its forces from the Ogaden. The WSLF vowed to continue guerrilla raids in the region. The United States and USSR reached an informal understanding in early 1978 that no Ethiopian or Cuban forces would cross the Somali border.

This series of events and its disastrous climax in the Ogaden have created turmoil in Somalia's foreign policy and have undermined the stability of the regime. Somalia may turn to the West for arms, despite French, British, and American refusal to supply weapons until Somalia abandons its Ogaden aims. The Arab League (which Somalia joined in 1974) pledged defensive support for Somalia. Saudi Arabia is believed to have offered several hundred million dollars for military purchases in 1977 on condition that Somalia break with the USSR.

Reported intrusions by Somali forces into Kenya in 1976 and 1977 and the Ogaden war caused a severe strain on Somali-Kenyan relations. Although Kenya gave some logistical aid to Ethiopia, it does not pose a serious military threat to Somalia. Sudanese-Somali relations have warmed because of the two countries' common enmity toward Ethiopia. Somalia's main sources of development aid are China, EEC countries, and the Arab world.

Despite the Ogaden defeat, Somali nationalism remains strong. Somalia will continue to support the WSLF and other liberation groups fighting Ethiopia. Somalia retains a key interest in newly independent Djibouti, where the Somali Issa tribe composes half the population.

Military service is voluntary; but all students over eighteen years of age are required to undergo military training.

Somalia is a member of the Arab League.

## ARMY

*Personnel:* 30,000

*Organization:*
9 mechanized infantry battalions (700 men each)
7 tank battalions
2 commando battalions
10 field artillery battalions
2 heavy antiaircraft battalions
3 light antiaircraft battalions

*Major Equipment Inventory:*
250 medium tanks (T-34, T-54/55)
300 APCs (BTR-40, BTR-50, BTR-152)
200 guns and howitzers (76mm guns, 122mm howitzers, 100mm radar-controlled antiaircraft guns, 37mm antiaircraft guns, 14.5mm automatic antiaircraft cannon)

## NAVY

*Personnel:* 350

*Major Units:*
3 missile attack boats (Osa class; PTG; SS-N-2/ Styx SSMs)
6 patrol craft (PC)
4 fast patrol craft (Mol class; PCF)
4 motor torpedo boats (P-6 class; PT)
1 medium landing ship (Polnocny class; LSM)
4 mechanized landing craft (LCM)

*Major Naval Bases:* Berbera, Mogadishu, Kismayu

## AIR FORCE

*Personnel:* 2,500

*Organization:*
2 fighter squadrons (MiG-15, MiG-17, MiG-21)
1 light bomber squadron (Il-28)
1 transport squadron (An-24, An-26)
1 helicopter unit (Mi-4, Mi-8, AB-205)

*Major Aircraft Types:*
48 combat aircraft
12 fighters (MiG-21)
12 fighters (MiG-17)
12 fighters (MiG-15)
12 light bombers (Il-28)
72 other aircraft
19 transports (3 An-2, 12 An-24/An-26, 4 C-47)
18 helicopters (Mi-4, Mi-8, AB-205)
35 trainers (Piaggio P-148, Yak-11, MiG-15)

*Major Air Bases:* Hargesia, Mogadishu

## PARAMILITARY

Paramilitary forces are significant. There are about 7,000 police composed of 4,000 National Police, 500 Finance guards or customs police who are under control of the armed forces probably for port security duties, and 2,500 rural police or *Illaloes,* a constabulary. To 1964 the United States had supplied $1.57 million worth of training, facilities, radios, vehicles, and patrol boats for these security forces, and in 1968 West Germany supplied $750,000 worth of vehicles and facilities. A Home Guard was established at the time of the 1967 crisis and 3,000 men were called up for six months of duty and training. Upon completion of this tour another 3,000 were called up while those discharged went into a reserve pool. If continued, the reserve pool should now number 12,000 with another 3,000 on active duty.

# SOUTH AFRICA

## Republic of South Africa

## POWER POTENTIAL STATISTICS

Area: 471,819 square miles
Population: 27,754,000 (4,500,000 whites; total population figure includes population of "independent" black homelands)

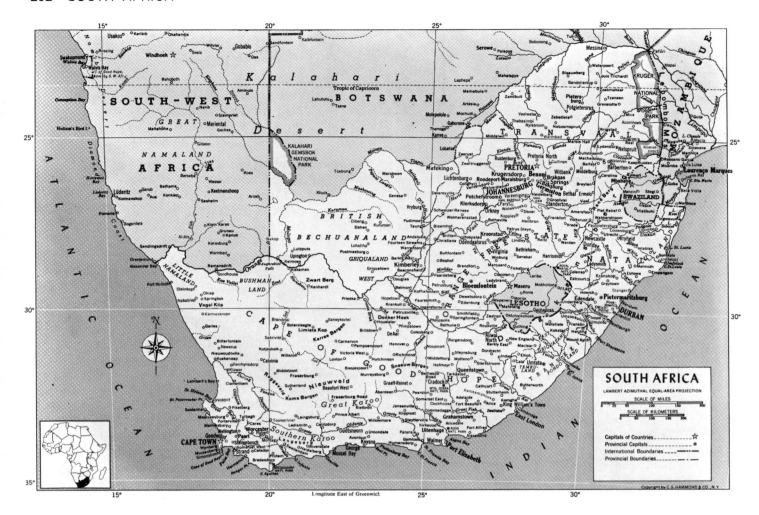

Total Active Regular Armed Forces: 54,300 (0.19%
  population)
Gross National Product: $38.9 billion ($1,450 per capita)
Annual Military Expenditures: $1.95 billion (5.01%
  GNP)
Crude Steel Production: 7.15 million metric tons
Iron Ore Production: 15.7 million metric tons
Fuel Production:
  Coal: 75.7 million metric tons
  Refined Petroleum Products: 14.4 million metric tons
  Manufactured Gas: 1.9 billion cubic meters
Electric Power Output: 87 billion kwh
Merchant Fleet (ships 1,000 tons and over): 42 ships;
  445,000 gross tons
Civil Air Fleet: 78 major transport aircraft

## DEFENSE STRUCTURE

Under a combined presidential-parliamentary system
the president, elected by a bicameral Parliament, is chief
of state and nominally commander in chief of the South
African Defence Force (Suid-Afrikaanse Weermag;
SADF). Actual power is vested in the prime minister, head
of the majority party in Parliament, who controls the
Defence Force through a minister of defence. Because of
South Africa's internal security situation, a Ministry of
Police (since combined into a Ministry of Justice, Police,
and Prisons) was established in 1966.

The Defence Force consists of the Permanent Force of
professionals, the Citizen Force of part-time soldiers, and
the Kommando Force, of a home guard nature. The
Permanent Force and the Citizen Force have ground, sea,
and air components, while the Kommandos have ground
and air units. The Defence Force has an integrated organization under a commandant general. Under him are chiefs
of staff of the army, navy, and air force, and an adjutant
general, a quartermaster general, and a surgeon general
whose functions are essentially administrative. For
operations, service components are integrated under a
commander, Joint Combat Forces, who reports to the
commandant general.

## POLITICO-MILITARY POLICY

South Africa's basic social policy of *apartheid* (separation of white and black races in most activities and stringent restriction of the civil rights of blacks) has caused most of the nation's strategic problems. These in turn have necessitated a series of responsive policies.

The threat of foreign-based black liberation movements, the potential for revolt among the black two-thirds of the population, the UN arms embargo endorsed by most nations, international pressure for majority rule in Rhodesia, and action in the UN and the International Court of Justice to remove South-West Africa (Namibia) from South Africa's authority, have all resulted in both policy statements and action.

To deter external attack and internal revolt, provisions for defense have been strengthened and a state of siege proclaimed. Defense capability is based upon a rapid mobilization of the highly trained Citizen Force to augment the small Permanent Force. Emphasis has been placed upon mobility and striking power for all permanent and mobilized units. Kommando units have been increased, given more intensive training, and provided with modern weapons. Physical security of key installations has been increased with fences, guard towers, lighting, and the like. Internal security matters are the subject of top-level coordination between SADF and the police. The share of GNP devoted to defense has doubled since 1973.

In November 1977 the UN Security Council voted unanimously for a worldwide embargo on arms sales to South Africa. This unprecedented action promises to carry more weight than previous embargo efforts. Nevertheless, the effects of the arms embargo have been attenuated by the development of a domestic armaments industry, and circumvented by obtaining certain sophisticated armaments such as high performance aircraft from France and Italy. This industry is being vigorously developed. South Africa has all of the essential skills, technology, and raw materials for complete self-sufficiency in production of armaments of the largest and most sophisticated variety. This potentiality is becoming reality, with the production of submarines and other warships, missiles, land combat vehicles, aircraft, and air defense systems. A two-year supply of oil has been stockpiled, oil exploration accelerated, and a tanker fleet acquired.

South Africa is third, behind the United States and Canada, in the production of uranium oxide. It has constructed a pilot uranium enrichment plant using a new, relatively inexpensive process. South Africa has both the technology and the resources to produce a nuclear explosion and could develop nuclear weapons in the near future, although the government's announced policy is to use uranium only for peaceful purposes. The United States has exerted strong pressures on South Africa not to proliferate.

The withdrawal of Portugal from its former colonies of Angola and Mozambique in 1975 brought about a major shift in South African policy toward the Smith regime in Rhodesia. Under prodding from the United States and the United Kingdom, South Africa began quietly pressing the Rhodesian government to move toward majority rule. South Africa supported the internal settlement reached in early 1978 between Smith and three black Rhodesian groups.

Portuguese withdrawal also brought change to South Africa's policy on Namibia (South-West Africa), administered by Pretoria under a 1919 League of Nations mandate. The UN terminated the mandate in 1966, and the International Court of Justice in 1971 ruled South Africa's continued control illegal. Responding to UN pressures, South Africa announced in 1976 that Namibia would be granted independence by the end of 1978. Subsequently, racial laws were greatly relaxed there. South Africa rejected the final UN plan for Namibia's independence in September 1978, and moved toward establishing an elected Namibian national assembly with law-making and budgetary powers but without sovereignty. The assembly met in May 1979. A key problem in the prolonged negotiations for Namibia's independence has been control of Walvis Bay, Namibia's only deep-water port. Walvis Bay was under British control in the late nineteenth century, while the rest of Namibia was a German colony, and has been administered separately by South Africa.

Only whites have the franchise in South Africa, and among them the Afrikaaners have predominated politically through the National Party, in power since 1948. (The National Party won 134 of 165 seats in the 1977 elections to the House of Assembly.) The nation's domestic policy centers on separate racial development. Through its homelands policy, eventually all blacks are to become citizens of one of eight independent states. Additionally, separate parliaments within South Africa will be constituted for whites, "coloreds," and Asians.

Citizens from seventeen to sixty-five years of age are liable for military service on call, and those seventeen to twenty-five are liable for up to four years' service. At present, active service, other than for those who volunteer for the Permanent Force, is for nine or twelve months, depending upon the arm of specialty, followed by service for the rest of the four years in the Citizen Force or Kommandos. Call-up is by selective draft with about 80 percent of eligible whites called, between 25,000 and 33,000 annually. Most members of the Defence Force are white. The police is 50 percent European (white), 45 percent Bantu (black), and the remainder colored (mixed) or Asiatic (East Indian).

## STRATEGIC PROBLEMS

The threat to white political hegemony posed by the

twenty million blacks, repressed under *apartheid* and increasingly agitated by the foreign-based liberation movements, is the gravest and most immediate strategic problem for South Africa.

Black frustration boiled over in the June 1976 "Soweto" riots. At least 176 died in that month alone in protests over language policy in black urban schools. A year later, continuing unrest in black townships, the death in prison of the popular black leader, Steve Biko, and government banning of a number of newspapers, individuals, and organizations, reflected the growing internal crisis for the Nationalist party government. Blacks have become steadily more active in political organizations. Several student, trade union, social, and religious groups are loosely affiliated in the Black Consciousness movement.

Meanwhile, three principal liberation groups operate outside South Africa. By far the most important is the African National Congress (ANC). It has transferred its headquarters to Mozambique and has secured the strong backing of the USSR. The ANC has established training bases near the South African border. The Pan-Africanist Congress (PAC) poses only a very weak challenge to ANC leadership of exiles. The South African Communist Party, declared illegal in 1950, is closely aligned with the ANC.

South Africa has poor or no diplomatic relations with nearly all OAU members and Communist nations. However, probably half the African states have commercial relations with South Africa. Mozambique, for example, despite being a front-line state is economically dependent on jobs for its migrant workers and the transit of South African goods to its ports. No longer able to rely on the West, Pretoria sought in 1975 to exploit its economic connections and seek political detente with several African nations. However, South Africa's brief intervention in Angola's civil war (1975), its homelands policy, and the racial strife of 1976 widened the breach between it and the rest of Africa. South African forces have continued battling SWAPO forces along the Caprivi strip of Namibia and have conducted raids into Angola and Zambia to strike at SWAPO bases.

South Africa's socioeconomic viability, geographic position, and constant and efficient attention to security matters enhance its ability to resist liberation movements from outside its borders. However, as blacks gain more education and economic strength, the almost inevitable relaxation of restrictions, combined with international pressure, may cause the government to seek an accommodation with its black citizenry or risk serious, and probably disastrous, insurgency.

## MILITARY ASSISTANCE

Until the arms embargo in 1963, some ground force weapons, ships, and most aircraft were purchased from Britain, with some aircraft from the United States. United

States equipment included M-41 light tanks, M-47 medium tanks, M-113 APC and M-2 half-tracks, M-3 scout cars, and Commando armored cars. Since the embargo, France has sold over $100 million in arms to South Africa, including Mirage III jet fighters with air-to-surface missiles, helicopters, transport, AMX tanks, AML armored cars, and three Daphne class coastal submarines. Italy has sold MB-326 armed jet trainers and components and tools with which to build 300 more. West German scientists and firms are reported to be helping to build nuclear reactors and to develop guided missiles. Under an agreement concluded in June 1971, French-designed Mirage III and F-1 jet fighters are built under license in South Africa.

Advice and cooperation in security matters has been extended to the Portuguese territories, Malawi, Botswana, Lesotho, and Swaziland, as well as to Rhodesia. Historically South Africa has been aligned with the West, fighting as a member of the Commonwealth with the allies in World Wars I and II, participating in the Berlin Airlift in 1948, and sending a fighter-bomber squadron to the UN Command in the Korean War from September 1950 until the armistice in 1953.

## ALLIANCES

South Africa keeps its membership in the UN, although it has withdrawn or has been expelled from some of the specialized agencies, and its delegates were expelled from the General Assembly when they attempted to attend a debate on Namibia in May 1979. When it became a republic in 1961 South Africa withdrew from the Commonwealth.

South Africa has no openly formal alliances with Rhodesia, stating that these are not necessary between good neighbors. However, the South African prime minister has expressed a willingness to send troops whenever and wherever they are requested. In 1967 the South African and Portuguese defense ministers met in Lisbon and proclaimed a common objective to pursue resolutely the defense of their positions in Africa.

The United States under a joint agreement maintains three space tracking stations in the vicinity of Pretoria. One is operated by the Department of Defense, the other two by NASA.

Under the Simonstown Naval Base Agreements of 1955 and 1961, the South African Navy cooperated with the Royal Navy and provided base facilities in return for assistance in arms procurement. Under a revised agreement, Britain has withdrawn Royal Navy units stationed at the base, and the two countries will jointly command the base. The British government under terms of the Simonstown Agreement supplied the South African government with a number of Westland Wasp helicopters to equip three frigates supplied earlier, as well as spare parts to keep the ships operational.

## ARMY

*Personnel:* 41,000 (including 34,000 conscripts)

*Organization:*
  2 divisions made up with mobilization of
    1 armored brigade
    1 mechanized brigade
    4 motorized brigades
    2 parachute battalions
    8 field and 2 medium artillery regiments
    9 light antiaircraft regiments
    9 engineer battalions
    5 signal regiments

*Major Equipment Inventory:*
  240 medium tanks (Centurion Mk.5, M-47, and
      Comet)
     light tanks (AMX-13, M-41)
1,500 armored cars (Staghound, AML-60/90)
  350 scout cars (Ferret, M3A1, Commando)
  350 APCs (Saracen, M-113)
     light and medium artillery, SP and towed
     105mm howitzers, 155 howitzers, 25-pounder
      guns
     antiaircraft artillery, 90mm 17-pounder
     SS-11, Entac ATGM
     Crotale, Tigercat, SAM

*Reserves:* About 205,000, including 23,000 in organized Citizen Force units, and 75,000 *Kommandos*

## NAVY

*Personnel:* 4,800 (3,400 permanent force, 1,400 national service in training)

*Major Units:*
  3 submarines (Daphne class; SS)
  4 frigates (1 Whiskey class, actually underarmed
    destroyer; 3 President class; FF)
  6 missile attack boats (PTG; with Gabriel SSMs;
    2–3 possibly not yet complete)
  5 patrol craft (PB)
10 coastal minesweepers (MSC)
  2 patrol boats (PB)
  2 auxiliary ships
10 service craft

*Naval Bases:* Simonstown, Capetown, East London, Port Elizabeth, Durban, Walvis Bay

*Reserves:* 4,750 trained reserves in Citizen Force

## AIR FORCE

*Personnel:* 8,500 (5,500 Regular, 3,000 Active Citizen Force)

*Organization:*
  Strike Command
    3 fighter/fighter reconnaissance squadrons
      Sabre, Mirage III, Mirage F1)
    2 light bomber squadrons (Canberra,
      Buccaneer)
  Maritime Command
    2 maritime patrol squadrons (Shackleton,
      Diaggio P-166)
    1 ASW flight (Wasp helicopters on destroyers
      and frigates)
  Transport Command
    4 transport squadrons (C-130, C-160, C-47,
      DC-4, Viscount, HS-125)
  Light Aircraft Command
    4 helicopter squadrons (Alouette III, Puma,
      Super Frelon)
    *6 refresher training squadrons (MB-326
      Impala, T-6, AM-3C)
    *2 forward air controller squadrons (Cessna
      185)
    *12 air commando squadrons, civil auxiliary
      (light civil aircraft; AM-3C, Kudu)
  Training Group
    Primary, basic, advanced weapons training, multi-
    engine, helicopter schools (T-6, Impala, C-47,
    Alouette II/III, Vampire)
  Maintenance Group
    Sabre, Mirage III

*Major Aircraft Types:*
  159 combat aircraft
    48 Mirage F1 fighters
    30 Mirage III fighter/fighter reconnaissance
    20 Sabre fighters
    24 light bombers (9 Canberra, 15 Buccaneer)
    26 maritime patrol (8 Shackleton, 18 P-166)
    11 Wasp ASW helicopters
  572 other aircraft
    67 transports (7 C-130, 6 Merlin IV, 9 C-160,
      30 C-47, 5 DC-4, 1 Viscount, 4 HS-125,
      5 Do-27)
    82 army support (FAC) (Cessna 185, AM-3C,
      Kudu)
    80 helicopters (40 Alouette III, 25 Puma, 15
      Super Frelon)
    343 training aircraft, primary, basic, multi-
      engine, advanced weapons, helicopter
      (T-6, Impala, Vampire, C-47, Sabre,
      Mirage III)

*Missiles:* Matra R-530, Aerospatiale AS-30, ASM, Cactus all-weather SAM, Sidewinder, AIM

*Active Citizen Force (ACF) squadrons.

*Air Bases:* Swartkop (Pretoria), Waterkloof, Lange-baanweg Cape, Rooikop, Dunnottar, Lyttleton, Ysterplatt, Bloemspruit, Bloemfontein, Pretoria, Durban, Capetown, Germiston, Port Elizabeth, Pietersburg, Potchefstroom

*Reserves:* The Citizen Air Force is organized into six squadrons operating Impala, AM-3C, and T-6 armed trainers and C-47 transports.

## PARAMILITARY

The National Police numbers about 32,700 (one-half white) and has a reserve of 12,000 (all white). An anti-terrorist police force of 3,000 is equipped with 430 riot trucks, 80 Saracen APCs, and heavy infantry weapons.

The Kommandos, or militia with an essentially home guard function, number about 75,000 and are organized into infantry, armored car, and air units.

# SPAIN

## Spanish State

## POWER POTENTIAL STATISTICS

Area: 194,883 square miles
Population: 37,774,000
Total Active Regular Armed Forces: 308,900 (0.82% population)
Gross National Product: $116 billion ($3,190 per capita)
Annual Military Expenditures: $4.2 billion (3.62% GNP)
Crude Steel Production: 10.9 million metric tons
Iron Ore Production: 7.6 million metric tons
Fuel Production:
    Coal: 10.5 million metric tons
    Lignite: 4.4 million metric tons
    Crude Oil*: 2.0 million metric tons
    Refined Petroleum Products*: 51.6 million metric tons
    Manufactured Gas: 2.65 billion cubic meters
Electric Power Output: 93.7 billion kwh
Nuclear Power Production: 8,700 megawatts
Merchant Fleet (Ships 1,000 tons and over): 479 ships; 6.9 million gross tons
Civil Air Fleet: 174 major transport aircraft

*Includes Canary Islands

## DEFENSE STRUCTURE

Spain was ruled for thirty-five years following the Spanish civil war (1936–39) by Gen. Francisco Franco. Before his death in November 1975, Franco had picked Prince Juan Carlos, grandson of Spain's last monarch, as his successor, and the prince was acting chief of state for Franco during the latter's lengthy last illness. As Juan Carlos I, he is chief of state and commander in chief of the armed forces. Spain is now a constitutional monarchy, with a representative, parliamentary government. The armed forces are administered through three separate, independent ministries: army, navy, and air. The principal planning and supervisory agency for all the armed forces is the High General Staff of the Army; the army is the predominant service.

## POLITICO-MILITARY POLICY

King Juan Carlos and his prime minister, Adolfo Suarez Gonzalez, are reform-minded conservatives who are working to liberalize Spanish government and society while maintaining order and stability. Changes since the king's accession include amnesty for many political prisoners, legalization of most political parties, free elections (1977), greater freedom of assembly, and the destruction of the dossiers kept by Franco's secret police on political opponents. The king appears to be warmly supported by the majority of the population.

Spain has relinquished Spanish Sahara, but wishes to maintain control of the nearby Canary Islands. The country is now oriented toward NATO and is expected to seek NATO membership. Spain is a member of most major world organizations and some Western regional ones as well. In 1970 Spain and the European Economic Community (EEC) concluded a preferential trade agreement, and Spain contributes to Western defense through bilateral military cooperation with the United States.

Relations with Eastern Europe also have been strengthened. In 1972 a commercial agreement with the USSR was signed; in 1973 diplomatic relations with the German Democratic Republic (as well as the People's Republic of China) were established. Spain has commercial and consular agreements with most Eastern European countries. It has consistently supported the Arabs in their dispute with Israel, and it maintains generally cordial relations with the countries of Africa, toward which it is drawn by geographic proximity, history, economics, and security considerations.

The armed forces are maintained by conscription; for all branches, the term of service is eighteen months.

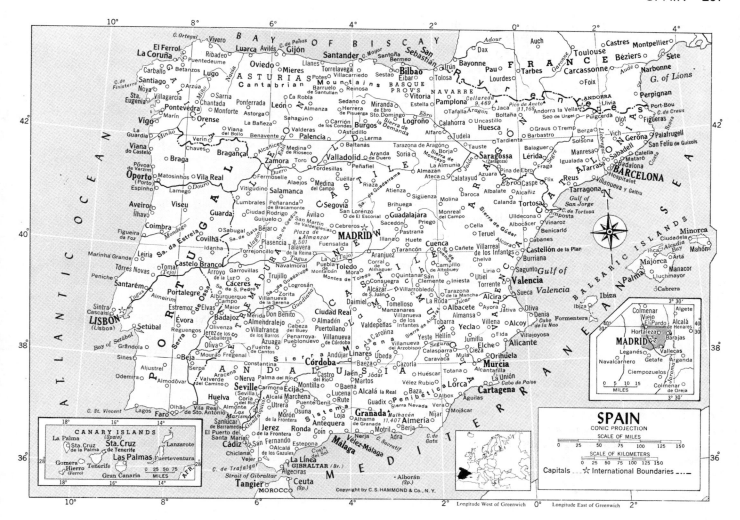

## STRATEGIC PROBLEMS

The combination of remoteness from European centers of conflict and the Pyrenees mountain barrier make the Iberian Peninsula the most self-contained and most easily defensible region in Europe. Thus there have been few foreign invasions, and none of them has been completely successful since the Moslem conquest of 711 A.D. The frontier with Portugal offers the only route for potential invasion by land.

For centuries Spain has shared with Britain's Gibraltar control of the north side of the western entrance to the Mediterranean Sea, and has maintained controlling footholds at Ceuta and Melilla in Morocco on the African shore of the straits. Britain's presence on the tip of the peninsula is of considerable psychological and political significance to Spain, which has long wished to gain control of this commanding position.

Spain's greatest strategic weaknesses today, as for several centuries, lie in internal divisions. Most of Spain's

600,000 Basques want autonomy within the Spanish state. The radical Basque National Freedom group (ETA) wants separation and uses violence. The region, three provinces in the Pyrenees, is highly industrialized and has a higher per capita income than Spain as a whole. Another distinct national group, with its own language and a strong movement for autonomy, is the Catalans. The Spanish government promised greater autonomy in 1977 for Catalonia. There have been a number of terrorist incidents in Catalonia, including the bombing murder of a former mayor of Barcelona in January 1978, but generally these are not connected with the autonomy movement. They are the work of small extreme leftist groups, whose activities throughout Spain have caused concern. Two of the most active groups are known as GRAPO and FRAP. Some of the leftist terrorist groups appear to have support from North Africa, specifically from Libya and Algeria. The Spanish Communist party (PCE) is moderate and supports the government on many issues. Old-line Franco supporters fear and oppose Juan Carlos's reforms, and there are some very small extremist groups on the right that have resorted to violence.

There is a separatist movement in the Canary Islands, and terrorists there have resorted to bombings. One Canary separatist group, MPAIAC, is based in Algeria. In February 1978, the Organization of African Unity Liberation Committee voted to urge the OAU to support the Canary separatists more vigorously.

## MILITARY ASSISTANCE

The United States has provided Spain with $648.1 million (through 1977) in military assistance; $3.7 million in 1977; 10,427 students have been trained under the MAP. The U.S. Military Advisory Group in Spain numbers about sixty. In addition the United States has made large expenditures in building and maintaining the major air and naval bases which Spain has provided to U.S. forces under the agreement.

## ALLIANCES

The 1970 bilateral Agreement of Friendship and Cooperation with the United States, which replaced the 1953 defense cooperation accord, was renewed in 1976 for a five-year period. It is not a formal treaty requiring United States Senate ratification. It authorizes U.S. military assistance to Spain in return for the use of certain facilities at the naval base at Rota (near Cadiz), and at air bases at Moron de la Frontera (near Seville), Torrejon (near Madrid), and Zaragoza. Rota is connected by fuel pipelines to the three bomber bases. About 9,000 U.S. military personnel are stationed permanently at these bases. The United States will pay $1.2 billion in loans and aid over the five-year period in return for use of the facilities. Under terms of the agreement, the United States may not store nuclear material on Spanish soil.

United States-Spanish defense relations are overseen by a joint committee, co-chaired by the Spanish foreign minister and the U.S. ambassador to Spain. The U.S. National Aeronautics and Space Administration (NASA) and the Spanish National Institute of Aerospace (INTA) jointly operate tracking stations in the Madrid area and the Canary Islands, under an agreement in force until 1984.

Spain also has a Treaty of Friendship and Cooperation with Portugal, which replaces the old Joint Iberian Defense Alliance of the Franco-Salazar period. The current treaty does not include military commitments.

## ARMY

*Personnel:* 220,000

*Organization:*
- 10 military regions (headquarters: Madrid, Seville, Valencia, Barcelona, Zaragoza, Burgos, Valladolid, La Coruna, Ceuta, Melilla) each accounting for one corps
- 1 armored division (cadre form)
- 2 mechanized/motorized infantry divisions (cadre form)
- 2 mountain divisions (cadre form)
- 12 independent infantry brigades
- 1 armored cavalry brigade
- 1 high mountain brigade
- 1 air transportable brigade
- 1 parachute brigade
- 2 artillery brigades
- 2 SAM battalions (Hawk, Nike-Hercules)
  various island and colonial garrisons: 8,000 in Canary Islands, 6,000 in Balearic Islands

*Major Equipment Inventory:*
- 700 medium tanks (M-47, M-48, M-60, M-4, AMX-30)
- 225 light tanks (M-24, M-41)
- 280 scout and armored cars (M-2, M-3, M-8, AML-60/90)
- 400 APCs (M-113)
- 160 guns/howitzers (105mm, 155mm, 175mm, 203mm SP)
- 320 howitzers (105mm, 155mm, 203mm)
- 16 self-propelled antitank guns (90mm)
  antitank guns (106mm recoilless rifle)
  antitank rocket launchers (66mm LAW, 3.5-inch)
  mortars (4.2-inch, 81mm)
  antitank guided missiles (SS-11, TOW, Milan)
- 12 SAM batteries (Hawk, Nike-Hercules)
- 250 antiaircraft guns (.50-cal. quad, 40mm, 90mm)
- 110 helicopters (AB-47, UH-1, AB-206, OH-58, CH-47, AH-1, Puma, Alouette III)

*Reserves:* There are about 600,000 trained reservists in a so-called Home Army, for which weapons and equipment are believed to be incomplete. The total mobilization capability could man about forty divisions.

## NAVY

*Personnel:* 55,400 (including 10,600 marines)

*Major Units:*
- 8 submarines (4 Daphne, 3 Guppy, 1 Balao class; SS)
- 1 light aircraft carrier (Independence class; CVL)
- 13 destroyers (2 Roger DeLauria, 5 Gearing, 5

Fletcher class; 1 Oquendo class substandard 4.7-inch guns; DD)

9 guided missile frigates (4 F30 class, Seasparrow SAMs; 5 Baleares class, Tartar/Standard SAMs; FFG)

9 frigates (1 Audaz, 2 Alava, 2 Pizarro class; 4 Atrevida class, light frigates, officially typed corvette; FF)

12 fast patrol craft (with provision for torpedo tubes; PCF)

4 patrol craft (PC)

5 patrol boats (PB)

15 roadstead patrol boats (PBR)

8 fleet minesweepers (MSF)

12 coastal minesweepers (MSC)

2 amphibious transports (1 Haskell, 1 Andromeda class; LPA; each carries 2 LCP)

1 dock landing ship (Cabildo class; LSD: carries 2 LCUs and 18 LCMs)

3 tank landing ships (Terrebonne Parish class; LST; each carries 4 LCP)

8 utility landing craft (LCU)

86 landing craft (2 LCU, 18 LCM, 66 LCP; assigned to LSD, LST, APA, AKA)

20 auxiliary ships

120 service craft

49 helicopters (10 Hughes 500, 4 Huey Cobra, 6 SH-3, 9 SH-19, 4 AB-204, 16 AB-47; 4 squadrons)

20 light aircraft (Piper)

*Major Naval Bases:* Cadiz, San Fernando, Cartagena, El Ferrol del Caudillo

*Reserves:* About 190,000 trained reservists, including marines; no reserve fleet

## AIR FORCE

*Personnel:* 33,500

*Organization:*

5 interceptor squadrons (1 Mirage F-1, 2 F-4, 2 F-5)

3 fighter-bomber squadrons (2 Mirage III/Saeta)

1 fighter/reconnaissance squadron (RF-4, RF-5)

1 ASW squadron (HU-16, P-3)

2 transport wings (C/KC-130, C-207, C-212, U-11, Navajo, Caribou)

*Major Aircraft Types:*

234 combat aircraft

124 fighters (21 Mirage F-1, 55 F-4, 48 F-5)

72 fighter bombers (48 Mirage III, 24 Saeta)

24 fighter reconnaissance (12 RF-4, 12 RF-5)

14 ASW aircraft (10 HU-16, 4 P-3)

339 other aircraft

187 trainer/utility (24 F-33, 15 T-42, 8 C-90, 8 O-1, 2 T-29, 30 T-6, 30 T-33, 25 Do-27, 45 Saeta)

60 helicopters (AB-206, OH-58, UH-1, AB-212, AB-205, Alouette III)

*Missiles:* Sidewinder, Sparrow AAM

*Equipment on Order:* Mirage F-1, AV-8, F-4, F-27, C-212, Cayuse

92 transports (12 C/KC-130, 20 C-207, 32 C-212, 8 U-11, 8 Navajo, 12 Caribou)

*Major Air Bases:* Torrejon (Madrid), San Pablo y Moron (Seville), Valencia, Talavera la Real, Sanjurjo (Zaragoza), Valladolid, Tetuan, Palma, Las Palmas de Gran Canaria, Getafe

*Reserves:* 80,000 reservists

## PARAMILITARY

There are 65,000 in the *Guardia Civil,* a highly trained, extremely efficient national gendarmerie; this is a volunteer force with officers assigned from the army.

The reserve Home Army noted above performs home guard functions.

# SRI LANKA

## Republic of Sri Lanka (Ceylon)

## POWER POTENTIAL STATISTICS

Area: 25,322 square miles

Population: 14,393,000

Total Active Regular Armed Forces: 9,000 (0.06% population)

Gross National Product: $3.2 billion ($220 per capita)

Annual Military Expenditures: $24.7 million (0.77% GNP)

Fuel Production: Refined Petroleum Products: 1.4 million metric tons

Electric Power Output: 1.4 billion kwh

Merchant Fleet (ships 1,000 tons and over): 9 ships; 71,000 gross tons

Civil Air Fleet: 8 major transport aircraft

## POLITICO-MILITARY POLICIES AND POSTURE

Prior to 1971, Sri Lanka relied almost exclusively on the United Kingdom for external security. There was a modest buildup in the armed services in the wake of an ultraleftist rebellion in April 1971, but no action has been taken to

## AIR FORCE

*Personnel:* 1,600

*Major Aircraft Types:*
   5 MiG-17 fighters
   9 Jet Provost trainers
   5 Dove, 4 Heron (transports and patrol)
   9 Chipmunk trainers
  12 helicopters, AB-206, Ka-26

compensate for the United Kingdom's withdrawal from the Indian Ocean, which also took place in 1971.

The armed forces of Sri Lanka, thus, are capable of little more than backing up the civil authorities in the event of internal disorder and of conducting limited patrol activity in the air and at sea. The United Kingdom provides some training assistance for officers, and the USSR has provided some pilot training for the air force. The United States supplied $3.3 million in MAP from 1968 through 1974 and trained thirty-nine students.

## ARMY

*Personnel:* 5,000

*Organization:*
  1 brigade, which includes supporting artillery, engineers, and signals
    Equipment includes APCs (Soviet BTR-152), armored cars, and scout cars, and light artillery

## NAVY

*Personnel:* 2,400

*Major Units:*
   1 patrol ship (River class; PGF; 4-inch gun; no ASW capability)
   6 fast patrol craft (PCF)
   5 patrol boats (PB)
  25 roadstead patrol boats (PBR)
   4 service craft

# SUDAN

## Democratic Republic of the Sudan

## POWER POTENTIAL STATISTICS

Area: 967,491 square miles
Population: 17,912,000
Total Active Regular Armed Forces: 37,100 (0.21% population)
Gross National Product: $4.3 billion ($230 per capita)
Annual Military Expenditures: $244 million (5.67% GNP)
Fuel Production: Refined Petroleum Products: 1.07 million metric tons
Electric Power Output: 672 million kwh
Merchant Fleet (ships 1,000 tons and over): 7 ships; 42,000 gross tons
Civil Air Fleet: 2 jet, 8 turboprop, and 1 piston transport

## DEFENSE STRUCTURE

The current Sudanese leadership came to power in a military coup in 1969. The military have been the prime supporters of the president, General Numayri, ever since. Numayri is commander in chief of the armed forces, as well as being his own prime minister and head of the Sudanese Socialist Union (SSU), the only legal party in Sudan. Under the Defense Ministry is the headquarters of the armed forces, which controls six regional commands —Northern, Eastern, Central, Western, and Southern Commands, and the Khartoum Garrison.

## POLITICO-MILITARY POLICY

Sudan officially pursues a policy of nonalignment in world affairs. It has been active as a member of the Arab League. Its staunch anti-Israel stance following the 1967 Middle East war has moderated to the point that Sudan has supported the Sadat peace initiative of 1977. Sudan has consistently opposed white-dominated regimes in southern Africa.

President Numayri has steered a careful course between East and West. Relations with the United States have been strained in the past over U.S. support for Israel and the release by Sudan of Palestinian terrorists who killed the American ambassador in Khartoum in 1973. However, since Numayri's visit to the United States in 1976, the two countries have vastly expanded contacts. Relations with the USSR, on the other hand, have deteriorated sharply since an abortive coup by Communist elements in Sudan in 1971. Sudan expelled the last Soviet military advisers in 1977, and the Soviet ambassador was recalled by Moscow for one year.

Enlistment in Sudan's military is voluntary. Most of the armed forces have been recruited from northern nomadic tribesmen. Following settlement in 1972 of the fourteen-year civil war, Sudan began a program of integrating southern guerrilla units into the national army.

## STRATEGIC PROBLEMS

Sudan has long been considered a natural bridge between the Arab world and black Africa. It is divided ethnically and religiously between some twelve million

Arabic-speaking Moslems in the northern twelve provinces and about five million Negro animist and Christian peoples in the southern three provinces. For generations the poorer southerners have felt oppressed by the more developed and politically dominant northerners. From 1958 until early 1972 most of the south was in armed revolt, seeking autonomy. The revolt resulted in at least a half million deaths and a quarter million refugees in the five countries bordering the south. The revolt was ended by an agreement of March 1972, creating South Sudan as an autonomous region.

Although the sources of the Nile River, which gives life to Egypt, lie in Ethiopia and Uganda, most of its course passes through Sudan. Increasing amounts are being diverted for various irrigation schemes, and potentially Sudan could control it totally and reduce the flow to Egypt to a trickle. For this reason Egypt, or powers occupying Egypt, have historically sought to dominate the Sudan. Since 1974 Sudan and Egypt have cooperated closely. They signed a defense pact (pointed against Libya) in 1976 and held a joint congress of their national assemblies in 1977, with a stated goal of political and economic integration.

The Numayri regime has experienced frequent coup attempts with varying degrees of foreign involvement. The most serious occurred in July 1976, when members of the opposition National Front seized parts of Khartoum and Omdurman. Most of the rebels had infiltrated from bases in Ethiopia and had Libyan support. Eritrean and other Ethiopian liberation movements then began to receive Sudanese assistance. However, in July 1977 Numayri and the National Front leader, Sadiq al-Mahdi, had an apparent reconciliation. In this resolution of the latest in a series of Mahdi-led revolts that stretches far back in Sudanese history, the SSU is expanded to serve as an umbrella organization incorporating the National Front movements. Modern elements of the military, urban sectors, and the generally non-Moslem South oppose the traditional Islamic nature of the National Front.

Sudan restored relations with Libya in 1978 when assured that Sudanese guerrilla bases in Libya were being closed. Sudan also reached an understanding with Ethiopia to cease the support of each other's opposition. Sudan's strongest ties, however, remain with the conservative Arab regimes, especially Saudi Arabia.

## MILITARY ASSISTANCE

In 1956 Britain left sufficient weapons and equipment to outfit the small armed forces then planned. Small British army and air training missions continued in Sudan through 1966. Naval training has been conducted in Britain and Yugoslavia. Air training has been conducted in Egypt, Britain, Ethiopia, Yugoslavia, and West Germany. Aircraft have been obtained from Britain, the Netherlands, Switzerland, and Egypt. Military training has been provided by Britain, the United States, Ethiopia, Pakistan, and India. Small arms, artillery, and vehicles have been purchased from West Germany and armored cars from Britain and the United States. From 1956 through 1977 the United States has provided $821,000 worth of military aid and trained 151 students under the MAP.

Following the 1967 change of policy toward the West, Sudan accepted large quantities of military aid from the Soviet Union, Czechoslovakia, and Yugoslavia. The Soviet program alone has amounted to about $150 million. Soviet and Czech contributions include tanks, armored personnel carriers, artillery, and jet aircraft, as well as training missions. This was the Soviet Union's first significant military assistance effort in sub-Saharan Africa. Since 1971, Communist China has made large loans for development purposes and has offered to supply Sudan with arms and with spares for Soviet weapons. In 1972 an agreement was reportedly signed under which the Chinese would provide training for the Sudanese army.

Sudan has provided training for Somalian staff officers, officer cadets, and signal and engineer NCOs. It is also alleged to have given sanctuary and training to Chadian and Eritrean dissidents, and to have allowed arms shipments to the Eritreans and to rebels against the Zaire government.

## ALLIANCES

Sudan is a member of the OAU and the Arab League.

## ARMY

*Personnel:* 35,000

*Organization:*
    6 infantry brigades
    1 independent infantry battalion
    1 armored brigade
    3 artillery regiments
    1 parachute regiment
    5 antiaircraft battalions
    1 engineer regiment

*Major Equipment Inventory:*
    100 T-54/55 medium tanks (50 each)
    20 T-34 medium tanks
    20 T-62 light tanks
    95 armored cars (Saladin and M-706 Commando)
    200 APCs (BTR-40, BTR-152, and Saracen)
    60 scout cars (Ferret)
    55 25-pounder guns
    40 105mm howitzers
       122mm guns and howitzers
    20 120mm mortars

80+ 40mm (Bofors) and 37mm and 85mm (Soviet) antiaircraft guns
SAMs (SA-2 Guideline)

## NAVY

*Personnel:* 600

*Major Units:*
2 patrol craft (PC)
6 fast patrol craft (PCF)
7 patrol boats (PB)
3 utility landing craft (LCU)
3 service craft

*Naval Bases:* Port Sudan, Khartoum

## AIR FORCE

*Personnel:* 1,500

*Major Aircraft Types:*
46 combat aircraft
16 MiG-21 fighters
15 MiG-17 fighter-bombers
15 Jet Provost ground attack aircraft
74 other aircraft
1 C-130 transport
4 F-27M troopship transports
5 An-24 transports
6 An-12 transports
2 C-47 transports
3 Pembroke light transports
8 PC-6A light transports
5 Mi-4 helicopters
10 Mi-8 helicopters
30 trainers (Provost and others)

*Equipment on Order:* 10 Mirage fighters, 10 SA-330 Puma helicopters, 5 C-130 transports.

*Air Bases:* Khartoum, Malakal, Juba, Atbara, Geneina, El Obeid, El Fashir, Wad Medani, Dongola, Merowe, Waw, and Port Sudan

## PARAMILITARY

There are 2,000 Frontier Police and 1,000 Civil Police.

# SURINAM

## POWER POTENTIAL STATISTICS

Area: 63,251 square miles
Population: 388,000
Total Active Armed Forces: 1,000 (0.26% population)
Gross National Product: $529 million ($1,240 per capita)
Electric Power Output: 1 billion kwh

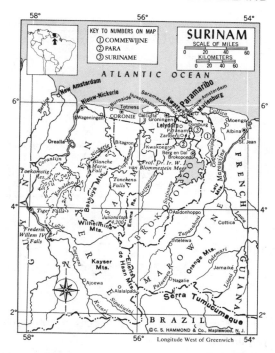

Merchant Fleet (ships 1,000 tons and over): 2 ships; 4,000 gross tons
Civil Air Fleet: 1 turboprop transport

## POLITICO-MILITARY POLICIES AND POSTURE

Formerly Dutch Guiana, then an autonomous member of the Kingdom of the Netherlands, Surinam became independent on November 25, 1975. The president is commander in chief of the small army. There is no air force but a small navy operates ten patrol boats.

The population is a mixture of descendants of Hindustanis, Creoles, Javanese, Bush Negroes, and Amerindians. The ethnic mixture causes some tensions, but a more serious problem is the underproduction of food. Surinam's major export, bauxite and related products, provides over 90 percent of the national income. There are border disputes with two neighbors. Guyana claims 6,000 square miles of bauxite-rich land, and French Guiana claims 780 square miles of jungle, where there is thought to be gold.

Surinam is a member of the OAS.

# SWAZILAND

## Kingdom of Swaziland

## POWER POTENTIAL STATISTICS

Area: 6,705 square miles
Population: 533,000

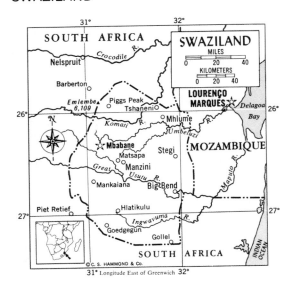

Total Active Regular Armed Forces: 1,500 (0.09%
   population)
Gross National Product: $224 million ($470 per capita)
Annual Military Expenditures: $2 million (0.89% GNP)
Iron Ore Production: 1.4 million metric tons
Fuel Production: Coal: 127,000 metric tons
Electric Power Output: 130 million kwh
Civil Air Fleet: 2 major transport aircraft

## POLITICO-MILITARY POLICIES AND POSTURE

Officially a constitutional monarch, Swaziland's head
of state, King Sobhuza II, has in reality ruled the country
since its independence from Britain in 1968. The traditional Royalist Imbokodvo movement has been the sole
legal political organization since 1973, when the king
banned all opposition parties, repealed the Constitution,
and suspended Parliament. In 1977 the king announced
that Swaziland would abandon attempts to form a
Western-style government and would instead rely on traditional local councils.

Swaziland depends economically on its relations with
both South Africa and Mozambique. It is a member of the
South African Customs Union. Some 29,000 Swazis work
in South Africa, and 90 percent of its imports arrive
through South Africa. The two countries have not
exchanged diplomatic representatives, and Swaziland has
criticized *apartheid*. Nevertheless, they maintain quietly
cooperative relations.

Some 80 percent of Swaziland's exports (mainly sugar,
iron, asbestos, timber, and meat) must pass along the
single railroad through Mozambique. Swaziland was initially concerned over the threat to this lifeline posed by
disturbances in newly independent Mozambique, but relations between the two have become increasingly close since
1976.

Internally, the government faces two key problems.
Although its economy has been expanding rapidly, most
of the growth is concentrated in the small European and
Eur-African population, which continues to hold privately
about 40 percent of the land. Meanwhile, most of the
Swazi subsistence farmers and herders experience over-
crowding of rural land. The second problem is that urban
youth, influenced by the militancy of South African
blacks, have shown increasing signs of disaffection with
traditional Swazi values.

Swaziland, a Commonwealth member, is active in
the OAU and adopts a generally nonaligned position in
external affairs. It exports to and receives aid from a
diverse group of nations.

In addition to a police force of 600 men, and the
new 500-man army, the king has a force of 4,000 Swazi
warrior-retainers. However, they probably do not possess
modern weapons and would have limited use as a paramilitary force until armed and trained.

# SWEDEN
## Kingdom of Sweden

## POWER POTENTIAL STATISTICS

Area: 173,665 square miles
Population: 8,285,000
Total Active Regular Armed Forces: 83,250 (1.0%
   population)
Gross National Product: $78.5 billion ($9,530 per capita)
Annual Military Expenditures: $2.99 billion (3.8%
   GNP)
Crude Steel Production: 5.2 million metric tons
Iron Ore Production: 30.5 million metric tons
Refined Petroleum Products: 14.3 million metric tons
Electric Power Output: 91.0 billion kwh
Nuclear Power Production: 7,400 megawatts
Merchant Fleet (ships 1,000 tons and over): 286 ships;
   6.9 million gross tons
Civil Air Fleet: 63 major transport aircraft

## DEFENSE STRUCTURE

The king is the supreme military authority of Sweden,
but in a limited constitutional monarchy he exercises the
responsibility through the minister of defense, who is
politically responsible to the prime minister. In recent
years administrative changes have strengthened centralized
operational and logistical control and surveillance by the

minister of defense over the three loosely integrated military services (each of which has its own commander in chief). Overall military planning and coordination are performed by an integrated Defense Staff under a supreme commander who is responsible to the king through the minister of defense.

## POLITICO-MILITARY POLICY

Since 1814, Sweden has avoided war through a policy of armed neutrality. Although unequivocally aligned with the Western powers in the bipolar world of post–World War II, Sweden nonetheless adheres unswervingly to its policy of neutrality. It has refused to join NATO or any other form of military alliance. However, it has economic ties through membership in the European Free Trade Association (EFTA) and a trade agreement with the European Economic Community (EEC). Sweden (unlike Switzerland) came to the conclusion that membership in the United Nations would not compromise its policy of neutrality. Sweden has strongly supported the international police activities of the United Nations, and has contributed individuals and units to most of the UN observer teams or peace-preservation forces; Swedish diplomats and soldiers have played leading roles in many of these activities. Sweden was critical of U.S. policy in Southeast Asia; in 1969 it recognized the North Vietnamese government and since 1972 has sent an ambassador to Hanoi.

Sweden relies upon a policy of deterrence as well as neutrality for preservation of its national security. As a result, for many years the Swedish armed forces have been more powerful, more modern, and better prepared than those of any other secondary power. To give credibility to its avowed determination to resist any aggression as effectively as possible, Sweden has been one of the world leaders in all aspects of military research, development, and production—with the notable exception of offensive nuclear weaponry. Sweden's armament industry is among the largest and most sophisticated of those of all the secondary powers, producing heavy artillery, tanks, warships, high performance jet aircraft, and all the lesser weapons of war.

Typical of Sweden's defensive and deterrent posture has been the development of nuclear bombproof facilities for the military, industry, civil administration, and civil defense. If this display of determination does not deter an aggressor, Sweden is probably capable of surviving all but a major nuclear assault, and of launching effective counterblows. There is an operational underground war headquarters, and vast quantities of weapons and materiel are stored underground. Even the largest warships can take refuge in deep harbors dug thousands of feet into coastal mountainsides, and there are similar air facilities cut into inland mountainsides. A number of highways are especially designed for use as runways. Sweden's defense expenditure per capita is by far the highest in Western Europe (exceeded in the world only by the United States and the USSR).

Additional evidence of national defense determination is the policy of universal compulsory service in the armed forces. Every physically fit male citizen between the ages of eighteen and fifty-seven is required to serve in the armed forces. After a period of ten months' training most of the conscripts are placed on indefinite leave. Thus, while theoretically full-fledged members of the armed forces, they are virtually reservists required to undergo periodic refresher training on an elaborate schedule. Administration is on a local, decentralized basis, and the total armed forces of Sweden—approximately 700,000 strong—can be mobilized into combat-ready units within two to three days.

## STRATEGIC PROBLEMS

Sweden's long Baltic coastline makes it particularly vulnerable to amphibious assault or devastating bombardment by the forces of any nation controlling the Baltic. At present the only possibly hostile Baltic nation is the USSR. Because of this vulnerability, Sweden has strongly fortified the island of Gotland, which dominates the Baltic and is an important base for air and naval strike forces. It has a strong coastal defense system.

Thinly populated northern Sweden, with its long frontier with Finland, is also vulnerable to possible Soviet overland attack across the intervening Finnish territory. Sweden's concern regarding these two vulnerabilities is reflected in its opposition to fortification and defense of Finland's Aland Islands, which dominate the northern Baltic and Gulf of Bothnia, and which are disturbingly close to Stockholm and Sweden's heartland. Presumably Sweden is prepared to seize these islands rapidly in the event of war.

## MILITARY ASSISTANCE

Sweden has been active in supporting UN peacekeeping operations, furnishing battalion-size units for the UN Emergency Force (UNEF) in Sinai and the Gaza Strip from 1956 to 1967, for the UN Operation in the Congo (UNOC) from 1960 to 1964, and for UN Forces in Cyprus (UNFICYP) from 1964 to the present. Truce observers have served in Palestine beginning in 1948, in Kashmir since 1951, in Greece from 1952 to 1954, in Egypt from 1956 to 1967, in Lebanon in 1958, in New Guinea in 1962, and in Yemen (1963–64).

While military assistance is not given on a grant basis, training missions have been dispatched to developing nations, notably Ethiopia. Swedish artillery and aircraft are sold widely throughout the world, and technical and training personnel are often provided to purchasers. Sweden favors delivery of foreign aid through multilateral agencies, especially the UN, but also provides bilateral aid to less developed countries.

## ALLIANCES

Sweden is a member of the UN, but is involved in no alliances.

# ARMY

*Personnel:*

12,500 regulars (officers and noncommissioned officers)
36,500 conscript trainees

*Organization:*

6 military regions, each able to operate independently with integrated forces of all services
16 infantry brigades (cadre only; 5,000–6,000 men each when mobilized)
8 Norrland brigades (trained and equipped for arctic warfare)
6 armored brigades (cadre only; 5,000–6,000 men each when mobilized)
7 artillery brigades (cadre)
1 parachute training group (cadre)
6 antiaircraft regiments (cadre)
1 SAM battalion (Hawk)
engineer, signal, and corps service units
Upon mobilization, these units would form some 100 battalions and a number of independent units (approximately 15 combat divisions). Territorial and local defense forces provide 100 more battalions and 400 to 500 more independent companies.
1 battalion in Cyprus (UN Forces)

*Major Equipment Inventory:*

80 medium tanks (Centurion)
light tanks (Strv-74; IKV-91)
SS-11 and Bantam antitank missiles, Carl Gustav and Mini-man antitank weapons
APCs (Pbv301/302)
90mm recoilless guns (jeep-mounted)
Redeye troop-portable lightweight SAM
105mm and 155mm guns; 155mm self-propelled guns
105mm and 155mm self-propelled howitzers
90 light aircraft (Bulldog, Do-27 and L-21)
50 helicopters (AB-204, AB-206)
antiaircraft guns (20mm and 40mm guns; 57mm self-propelled)
antiaircraft missiles (RB-70)
Hawk SAM (1 battalion)

*Reserves:* There are about 600,000 in an inactive status. High priority personnel are mobilizable within forty-eight hours; most of the balance, within two to three days. There are always approximately 100,000 reserves on active duty for fourteen to forty days.

# NAVY

*Personnel:* 22,100 (including coast artillery)

4,500 naval regulars (mostly officers and petty officers)
2,900 reservists on active duty
7,700 national servicemen
7,000 conscripts

*Major Units:*

20 diesel-powered submarines (3 Naecken class; 5 Sjoeormen class; 6 Draken class; 6 Hajen class; SS)
6 destroyers (4 Soedermanland class, fitted with short-range Seacat SAMs; 2 Halland class, to be retrofitted with RB O8A SSMs; DD)
26 frigates (Oeland class; FF)
4 light frigates (Visby class; FFL)
3 missile attack boats (Jaegaren class; PTG; Penguin SSMs; 12 more scheduled)
32 motor torpedo boats (PT)
30 patrol boats (PB)
24 fire support patrol craft (PCFS; high-speed, for support of amphibious operations)
3 minelayers (MM)
10 coastal minelayers (MMC; assigned to coast artillery)
36 inshore minelayers (MMI)
18 coastal minesweepers (MSC)
18 inshore minesweepers (MSI)
9 utility landing craft (LCU)
85 mechanized landing craft (LCM)
30 amphibious fire support craft (LCA)
7 auxiliary ships
45 service craft
20 mobile coastal batteries
45 fixed coastal batteries
25 helicopters

*Naval Bases:* Stockholm, Karlskrona, Goeteborg

# AIR FORCE

*Personnel:* 2,600 regulars, 5,700 conscripts for one year. (There are 5,000 full-time civilian employees in addition to the military.)

*Organization:* Five commands (Attack Command, Military Command of South Sweden, Military Command of East Sweden, Military Command of South Norrland, Military Command of North Norrland)

Twelve wings (2 to 3 squadrons each, 7 fighter, 3 attack, 1 reconnaissance, 1 composite of fighter, attack/reconnaissance)
17 fighter squadrons (Draken)
5 attack squadrons (3 Viggen, 2 Lansen)
1 light attack squadron (SK 60)
4 reconnaissance squadrons (2 Draken, 1 Viggen, 1 Lansen)

1 operational conversion unit (Viggen)
2 transport squadrons (C-130, C-47 Caravelle)
1 TOW target squadron (Lansen, SK 60)
flight training school (SK 60, Bulldog)
staff liaison flight (SK 60, Safir)
Air Force Academy (SK 60)
2 missile squadrons (Bloodhound II)

*Major Aircraft Types:*
500 combat aircraft
    350 Draken fighters/reconnaissance
    75 Viggen attack/reconnaissance
    55 Lansen attack/reconnaissance
    20 SK 60 light attack
305 other aircraft
    20 transports (C-130, C-47 Caravelle)
    250 trainer, support, communications (SK 60, bulldog, Safir)
    35 helicopters (AB-204, KV-107)
    (There are aircraft such as Lansen and Draken in storage.)

*Reserves:* There are 50,000 reserves mobilizable within forty-eight hours.

*Major Air Bases:* Ostersund, Ljunghyed, Karlsborg, Satenas, Angelholm, Nykoping, Kalmar, Norrkoping, Soderham, Uppsala, Kallinge, Tullinge, Lulea, Halmstad, Malmslatt, Vasteras.

*Air Defense Control System:* Sophisticated computerized control and air surveillance system, Stril 60 (comparable to American SAGE)

## PARAMILITARY

There are about 900,000 men, most of them over fifty-seven, and 90,000 women in local defense organizations. Civil defense service—general defense and factory defense—is compulsory for men and women not serving in the armed forces.

# SWITZERLAND
## Swiss Confederation

## POWER POTENTIAL STATISTICS

Area: 15,941 square miles
Population: 6,286,000
Total Active Regular Armed Forces: 31,400 (0.50% population; 620,000 more immediately mobilizable)
Gross National Product: $63.37 billion ($9,870 per capita)

Annual Military Expenditures: $1.6 billion (2.52% GNP)
Fuel Production:
    Refined Petroleum Products: 5.05 million metric tons
    Manufactured Gas: 122 million cubic meters
Electric Power Output: 44.7 billion kwh
Nuclear Power Production: 3,800 megawatts
Merchant Fleet (ships 1,000 tons and over): 25 ships; 251,000 gross tons
Civil Air Fleet: 80 major transport aircraft

## DEFENSE STRUCTURE

One of the seven members of Switzerland's Federal Council—the executive department of the republic's government—is the minister, or chief, of the Federal Department of Defense. He is assisted by a very small military planning staff. Administration is shared by the federation and the cantons. There is no overall military commander of the Swiss armed forces in peacetime; in time of war or national emergency the two houses of the Federal Assembly (the bicameral parliament) meet to elect a commander of the armed forces, who then becomes the nation's only general officer.

## POLITICO-MILITARY POLICY

Since the emergence of the Swiss state in the thirteenth century, the nation has traditionally been neutral, although prior to the early sixteenth century this was a bellicose independence, maintained and supported by the most renowned mercenary soldiery of Europe. Subsequently, and particularly since the early nineteenth century, Switzerland has been the most determined and consistently impartial neutral nation in the world.

To support this foreign policy of neutrality Switzerland has in modern times relied upon a completely defensive military policy that eschews a standing military force. The security of the nation is entrusted to a national militia, in which service is universal and compulsory for all physically fit male citizens between the ages of twenty and fifty, with officers serving up to age fifty-five. Each class of men reaching age twenty serves four months in a basic training program, followed by regular refresher training.

There are three classes of military service, according to age: *Auszug* (Elite), ages twenty to thirty-two, *Landwehr,* ages thirty-three to forty-two; and *Landsturm,* ages forty-three to fifty. Men of the *Auszug* are required to serve three weeks per year for refresher training, but after age twenty-eight this is generally excused for all men below the rank of sergeant. The *Landwehr* are called up for two weeks' training every two years; a period of two weeks' refresher training is required for noncommissioned officers of the *Landsturm* soon after they reach the age of forty-three. Officers and pilots receive more extensive training.

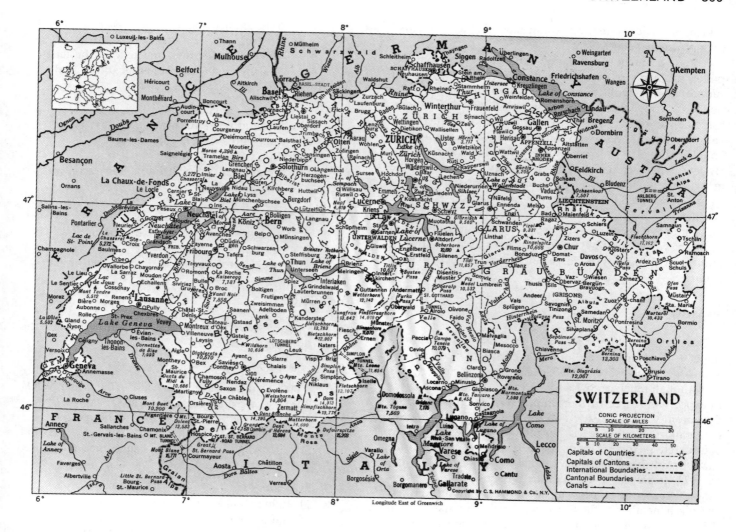

Swiss defensive strategy is based essentially on the concept of deterrence through demonstrated readiness. The entire national militia can be mobilized and ready for battle in mobile operational units and carefully prepared defensive positions within forty-eight hours. All of the approaches into Switzerland are prepared for demolition, and demolitions are prepositioned to destroy vital industrial plants and to block all major defiles within the country. An intensely fortified national redoubt has been prepared in the Alpine interior region of the country, its base areas the regions of Sargans in the northeast, St. Gothard Pass in the center, and St. Maurice in the southwest. Thus any potential aggressor is on notice that the conquest of Switzerland will be extremely costly, and that the potential prizes and wealth of the country will be destroyed before they can be seized.

The defensive policy and strategy have been sufficiently convincing and formidable to deter all potential aggressors since the time of the French Revolution, and were particularly successful in World Wars I and II.

## STRATEGIC PROBLEMS

Two of Switzerland's major strategic problems are complementry: lack of space, and the consequent vulnerability of the economic resources of the nation, which are concentrated in the lowlands of northern and western Switzerland. Swiss national military policy and defensive strategy are well designed to offset these disadvantages by capitalizing on the nation's strengths: the ability to mobilize the entire trained military manpower of the nation rapidly; the preplanned and prepositioned demolitions; and the apparent determination to withdraw from successive strong defensive positions into the nation's mountain redoubt as a last solution. It is likely that these evidences of determination would have a deterrent effect on any would-be aggressor.

The government is stable, untroubled by major domestic policy problems or significant disaffected elements, and supported by a politically sophisticated electorate in the policy of armed neutrality. However, Switzerland shows some concern about its nearly one million foreigners, the vast majority laborers, who come not only from contiguous countries but also from nearly every Mediterranean nation. By law, whatever their origin, they may not serve in the army. In any emergency serious enough for mobilization to be considered, they could face expulsion from the country.

There have been some terrorist incidents in Switzerland in recent years, and Switzerland has been used as a transit point and refuge by terrorists operating in neighboring countries.

## ALLIANCES

Switzerland belongs to no alliances, and has not joined the UN, but it maintains an observer at UN headquarters and it has joined several UN specialized agencies.

Although much of Swiss foreign trade (about two-fifths of exports and three-fifths of imports) is with the European Common Market (EEC), and although Swiss trade with Communist countries is negligible, Switzerland has considered membership in the EEC to be incompatible with its traditional neutrality (and its agricultural interests). In 1973, however, it did sign an agreement which establishes a free trade relationship with the Common Market, and it is a member of the European Free Trade Association (EFTA). It is also a member of the Organization for Economic Cooperation and Development (OECD). The Swiss have a policy they term solidarity, which involves acceptance of a moral obligation to contribute, as a neutral state, to world peace and prosperity by undertaking economic and humanitarian activities such as assistance to developing countries, support for the extension of international law and for the UN specialized agencies Switzerland has joined, and the extension of good offices.

## ARMY

*Personnel:*
   1,400 training force (instructor officers and NCOs)
  25,000 conscript trainees (average)
 578,000 total mobilizable within 24 hours

*Organization:*
   4 corps (1 for Alps, 3 for the plateau region)
   3 mountain divisions (all in the Alpine corps)
   3 mechanized divisions (1 per corps in plateau region)

   6 infantry divisions (2 per corps in plateau region)
   frontier, fortress, and redoubt brigades
   army engineer, communications, and logistics units

*Major Equipment Inventory:*
   630 medium tanks (Centurion, Pz-61, Pz-68)
   200 light tanks (AMX-13)
 1,250 APCs (M-113)
   140 155mm self-propelled gun/howitzers (M-109)
   150mm artillery pieces
   105mm artillery pieces
   81mm and 120mm mortars
   antiaircraft guns (Oerlikon 20mm and twin 35mm)
    10 river patrol boats (PBR; operated on lakes)

## AIR FORCE

The air force is an integral part of the army, as are the aircraft units included below.

*Personnel:*
   2,000 training force (instructor officers and NCOs)
   3,000 conscript trainees (average)
  42,000 total mobilizable within 48 hours (maintenance performed by civilian employees during peacetime, militarized in emergencies)

*Organization:*
  11 fighter-bomber squadrons (Venom)
   5 fighter-bomber squadrons (Hunter)
   2 fighter-interceptor squadrons (Mirage III)
   1 fighter/reconnaissance squadron (Mirage III-R)
   5 support squadrons (helicopter, transport, trainer, liaison; Alouette II/III, Ju-52, Do-27, Vampire)
  40 antiaircraft artillery batteries
   2 SAM battalions (Bloodhound II)

*Major Aircraft Types:*
 374 combat aircraft
   100 Hunter fighter-bombers
    36 Mirage III-S fighter-interceptors
    18 Mirage III-RS fighter/reconnaissance aircraft
   220 Venom fighter-bombers
 372 other aircraft
    26 transports (Ju-52, Do-27)
   250 miscellaneous trainer/support aircraft
    96 helicopters (including 86 Alouette II/III)
    30 Hunters on order

*Major Air Training Bases:* Dubendorf, Bayerne, Emmen, Magadino, Sion

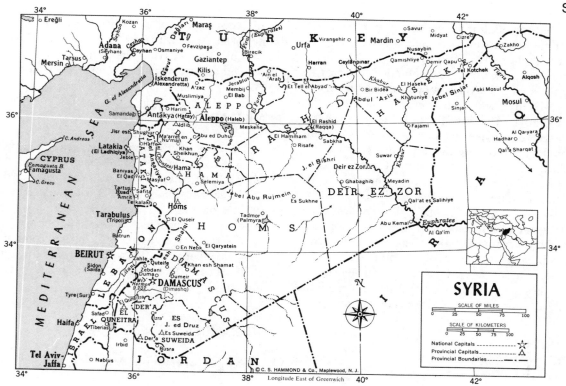

# SYRIA

## Syrian Arab Republic

### POWER POTENTIAL STATISTICS

Area: 71,498 square miles
Population: 8,260,000
Total Active Regular Armed Forces: 172,500 (2.09%
   population)
Gross National Product: $5.9 billion ($780 per capita)
Annual Military Expenditures: $873 million (14.8%
   GNP)
Fuel Production:
   Crude Oil: 10 million metric tons
   Refined Petroleum Products: 3.04 million metric tons
Electric Power Output: 2.5 billion kwh
Merchant Fleet (ships 1,000 tons and over): 4 ships;
   8,000 gross tons
Civil Air Fleet: 10 major transport aircraft

### DEFENSE STRUCTURE

The present government of Syria is dominated by a
relatively conservative nationalist faction of the Baath
Party, which replaced a more leftist wing of the party by

bloodless coup in November 1970. (A more militant wing
of the Baath party rules Iraq.) The General Staff organization is patterned after that of the Soviets.

### POLITICO-MILITARY POLICY

Syria is a hard-line Arab state in its policy toward Israel.
The Arab conflict with Israel, and the issue of recovering
sovereignty over the Golan Heights, are of greatest concern
to the regime of President Hafiz al Assad. Syrian support
for a Palestinian homeland is firm. Syria supports the PLO
and the militant Saiqa Palestinian faction. However, it
does not permit them to operate from Syrian territory.
Syria (with Jordan) also supports a non-PLO Palestine
Liberation Army that is based in Syria (about one brigade)
and Jordan (one battalion).

The regime of President Assad has demonstrated
unprecedented staying power; most of the many previous
governments were deposed by coups d'etat. This endurance
apparently results from Assad's complete control over the
Syrian branch of the Baath Party, the Syrian army, and the
security services. Assad and many of Syria's current political and military leaders are members of a minority Syrian
sect of Islam, the Alawites.

Syria has maintained a close relationship with the USSR
since 1954, and has received substantial Soviet economic
and military aid, especially since the 1973 war. Syria has

strongly opposed Egyptian rapprochement with Israel. As a result, Syria has denounced its former treaty with Egypt, and has broken diplomatic relations.

Military service is compulsory. Upon completion of his tour of duty the soldier becomes a member of the reserve for eighteen years, after which he reverts to inactive reserve status. The manpower for recruitment of about 15,000 to 20,000 men each year is selected from some 60,000 youth who reach military age during the induction year.

Most of the officers receive their training in one of three military schools: the Military Academy in Homs, the Naval Academy in Latakia, and the Air Force Academy located at Nayrab air base in Aleppo. All three academies conduct a two-year course leading to a commission. For advanced military training Syrian officers are sent to war colleges abroad, mostly to the USSR and other Communist countries. Selection for service academies as well as for war colleges abroad is made from those who pass the required entrance examination, and are staunch supporters of the Baath Party and the regime.

## STRATEGIC PROBLEMS

During the opening hours of the 1973 October war Syrian forces made significant gains into the Golan region, which had been occupied by Israeli troops since 1967. They could not reach the Hula Valley (Jordan Valley), however, and could not hold their gains against Israel's counter-offensive. They suffered considerable losses. One of the Syrian weaknesses appeared to be a command structure that lacks flexibility.

In 1970 and 1971 relations between Syria and Jordan were severely strained by Jordan's crackdown on Palestinian commandos. A Syrian military force intervened in Jordan in late 1970, but was defeated and driven out. Syria's relations with Jordan have improved significantly since the 1973 war. President Assad appears to value the military relationship with King Hussein's forces, whose support he would welcome in another war.

In mid-1976 Syria intervened in strife-torn Lebanon, and brought a temporary, relative peace. Subsequently the Arab League authorized the use of Syrian forces as the principal element in an Arab Deterrent Force in Lebanon (see Lebanon), and Syria continues to be heavily involved there.

Syria has been steadily improving all its forces. Many units have gained operational experience in Lebanon. However, that commitment has made it necessary to weaken the defense force between the Golan Heights and Damascus.

Two major pipelines to the Mediterranean coast cross Syria, one from Iraq and one from Saudi Arabia. This puts Syria in a position to exert some control over fuel oil for Western Europe. The pipelines have been out of order or shut down periodically during the past decade and have not been used for the past several years. Turkey has built a new pipeline to avoid the Syrian route, and supertankers have in any case made pipelines less significant.

## MILITARY ASSISTANCE

The bulk of the modern and heavy equipment of all of the Syrian armed forces has been provided by the USSR. Most of the equipment lost in the brief hostilities against the Israelis in 1967 and 1973 was replaced. On the eve of the October 1973 war, there were over 3,000 Soviet military and technical advisers in Syria. Soviet officers have served as advisers with Syrian combat units. They may have been present with the force invading Jordan in 1970. Since 1967 Soviet military aid has exceeded $2 billion.

## ALLIANCES

Syria belongs to the Arab League.

## ARMY

*Personnel:* 150,000

*Organization:*
   2 armored divisions
   3 mechanized divisions
   3 infantry brigades
   3 armored brigades
   4 parachute battalions
   5 commando battalions
   7 artillery regiments (including 6 antiaircraft artillery companies)
  20 SAM battalions (SA-2, SA-3, SA-6, SA-7)

*Major Equipment Inventory:*
   900 T-62 medium tanks
 1,600 medium tanks (T-54/55, T-34)
   100 PT-76 light tanks
 1,500 APC (BTR-50, BTR-152, BTR-40, BMP)
 1,200 artillery pieces (122mm, 130mm, 152mm, 180mm guns/howitzers)
   100 self-propelled guns (JSU-122/152, SU-100)
   165 antiaircraft guns (37mm, 57mm, 85mm, 100mm, ZSU-57/2, ZSU-2, ZSU-23/4)
   200 SAM launchers (SA-2 Guideline, SA-3 Goa, SA-6 Gainful, SA-7 Grail)
       57mm, 85mm, 100mm antitank guns
       RPG-7 antitank weapons
       Sagger antitank guided missiles
    60 SSM (Scud and FROG)

## NAVY

*Personnel:* 2,500

*Major Units:*
 2 light frigates (Soviet Petya class; FFL)
 4 minesweepers (2 T-43 class, MSF; 2 Vanya class, MSC)
 3 patrol craft (PC; 2 probably not operational)
12 missile attack boats (6 Osa class, 6 Komar class, with SS-N-2/Styx SSMs; PTG)
 8 motor torpedo boats (P-4 class; PT)
6–10 Ka25/Hormone helicopters

*Naval Bases:* Latakia, Baniyas, Tartus

## AIR FORCE

*Personnel:* 20,000

*Organization:*
12 fighter squadrons (9 MiG-21, 3 MiG-23)
 9 fighter-bomber squadrons (3 Su-7, 1 Su-20, 3 MiG-27, 2 MiG-17)
 2 transport squadrons (Il-14, An-12, An-24, Il-18, C-47)
 3 training/support squadrons (L-29, PA-31, Flamingo)
 3 helicopter squadrons (Mi-4, Mi-8, Ka-25, Super Frelon, SH-3, CH-47, AB-212)

*Major Aircraft Types:*
423 combat aircraft
　260 fighters (200 MiG-21, 60 MiG-23)
　163 fighter-bombers (54 Su-7, 35 MiG-17, 54 MiG-27, 20 Su-20)
215 other aircraft
　38 transports (7 C-47, 12 Il-14, 5 Il-18, 10 An-12, 4 An-24/26)
　77 trainer/support (L-29, PA-31, Flamingo)
　100 helicopters (10 Mi-4, 30 Mi-8, 9 Ka-25, 15 Super Frelon, 18 AB-212, 12 SH-3, 6 CH-47)

*Air Bases:* Damascus, Hamah, Dumayr, Palmyra, Sahles, Sahra, Rasafa, Aleppo, Sayqat, Blay, Khalk-halah, Masiriyah

*Reserves:* about 8,000 trained reservists

## PARAMILITARY

Organized, standing internal security forces are: gendarmerie, 5,000; Internal Security Camel Corps, 1,500; Civil Police, 1,800. A People's Army, reportedly about 150,000 men, is a home guard militia organization.

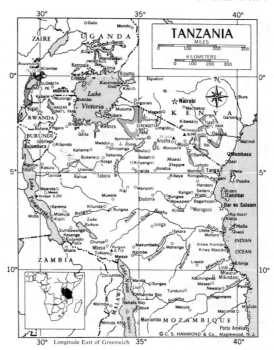

# TANZANIA

## United Republic of Tanzania

### POWER POTENTIAL STATISTICS

Area: 362,820
Population: 17,098,000
Total Active Regular Armed Forces: 17,000 (0.10% population)
Gross National Product: $2.835 billion ($166 per capita)
Annual Military Expenditures: $148.2 million (5.23% GNP)
Fuel Production: Refined Petroleum Products: 940,000 metric tons
Electric Power Output: 1.3 billion kwh
Merchant Fleet (ships 1,000 tons and over): 4 ships; 28,000 gross tons
Civil Air Fleet: 10 major transport aircraft

### DEFENSE STRUCTURE

The Tanzanian armed forces differ greatly from the defense establishments in other formerly British nations, largely as a result of the extensive remodeling of the army undertaken by President Nyerere following a mutiny in January 1964. Civilian control is exercised directly by the president, although nominally all defense matters are under the jurisdiction of the office of the second vice president. The first vice president of Tanzania (who by the terms of the 1977 Constitution is also the president of Zanzibar) is in addition the nominal head of the Zanzibar portions of the armed forces. The chief of staff theoretically commands the entire military establishment, which has been named the Tanzanian People's Defence Forces (TPDF). In practice, the senior officer on Zanzibar commands the island portion of the TPDF.

The size of the armed forces has grown by about 50 percent in the past five years; however, with the large supply of available manpower, no conscription is necessary. Enlistments are for a two-year term. Tanzania also has a nonmilitary National Service Corps, which is obligatory for all male high school and college graduates from the ages of eighteen to thirty-five. After the disbanding of the mutinous Tanganyika rifles in 1964, the bulk of the recruits for the TPDF were obtained from the National Service Corps. In order to involve the citizenry more actively in national building, Tanzania has organized a 35,000-man Citizen's Militia.

## POLITICO-MILITARY POLICY

Tanzania's foreign policy is nonaligned in international affairs, seeking friendly relations with all reciprocating countries. The notable exception is Tanzania's insistence on majority rule by the Africans of southern Africa and disapproval of any African country which is unduly influenced by the white southern African regimes or by outside powers. Dar es Salaam serves as the headquarters of the OAU's Liberation Committee. President Nyerere is one of the most vocal advocates of decolonization and majority rule for southern Africa. Tanzania, one of the five front-line states, has allowed various exiles and liberation movements to establish training bases and receive arms shipments within its territory.

Tanzania has rejected the internal settlement in Rhodesia, reiterating its support of the Patriotic Front. The government reportedly has allowed Cuban and Soviet supplies and advisers to the Patriotic Front to use the Tan-Zam Railway. Nyerere has expressed approval of Cuban aid to Ethiopia in defeating Somalia's incursion into the Ogaden (1977–78). On the other hand, Nyerere publicly reiterated Tanzania's nonalignment policy and its impatience with the lack of aid to the Third World from the USSR during Soviet President Podgorny's visit in 1977.

Because of Tanzania's strong support for FRELIMO's independence struggle, Mozambique and Tanzania have developed extremely close relations. Two battalions of Tanzanian troops were dispatched in late 1976 to Mozambique to bolster the Machel regime and aid in defense against Rhodesia. Tanzania has assisted Mozambique in controlling the borderland Makonde tribe. Relations with

Rwanda and Burundi have improved considerably since reduction of tribal strife in those two countries. Meanwhile, 1977 witnessed the bitter, total dissolution of the East African Community (created in 1967 to administer joint air, rail, postal, and harbor services and to establish common currency and marketing arrangements). Nyerere refused to associate with Ugandan President Amin after he came to power in 1971 and has allowed ex-President Obote to live in Tanzania. Uganda accused Tanzania of plotting invasions or assassinations of Amin, and there have been minor border incidents. The Kenyan-Tanzanian border has been closed pending resolution of complex economic claims by both nations.

## STRATEGIC PROBLEMS

There are few dangerous ethnic, political, or economic divisions among the Tanzanian people. A plethora of over 120 tribes, none large or powerful enough to constitute an independent political threat to the federal government, has actually served to minimize ethnic differences among the African population. The Arab, Asian, and European populations are too small to constitute a threat to established order. The religious divisions among Moslems, Christian, and native religionists are more significant, but at present show no signs of leading to disorders.

Tanzania adopted a permanent Constitution in April 1977 which united the mainland TANU party and Zanzibar's Afro-Shirazi party into the Chama Cha Mapinduzi (Revolutionary party). Despite party unification, Zanzibar continues to have a distinctly autonomous set of governing institutions.

The presence of 20,000 Chinese paramilitary railroad workers from 1970 to 1976 apparently caused no interference in Tanzanian affairs, nor have any of the local training centers for liberation movements.

## MILITARY ASSISTANCE

Tanzania's neutral policy, and its need for development and military assistance, have caused it to seek aid from all quarters. The Chinese completed construction of the 1,860-kilometer Tan-Zam Railway in 1976 at a cost of $460 million, and have initiated several other economic aid projects. Scandinavian countries, West Germany, the IBRD, and the UN furnish other major development aid. Tanzania's domestic development strategy of self-reliance and village socialism, while moderately successful politically, has resulted in short-term declines in agricultural productivity. Government nationalization programs have discouraged foreign investment.

Arms and training are received from a number of foreign countries, thus avoiding overdependence on any foreign power. Israel, China, West Germany, and Canada have helped train the air force and have furnished aircraft.

The Netherlands, Indonesia, and West Germany have provided naval training; West and East Germany and Communist China have provided patrol boats. China has trained and equipped the police, and Israel has trained police paratroops. The initial provision of arms was British, but this ceased when Tanzania temporarily broke diplomatic relations in 1965 over Rhodesia. Since then China and the Soviet Union have provided most military equipment. China has sent equipment for the TPDF, including two squadrons of MiG-17s (twenty-four aircraft), twenty-eight light and medium tanks, thirty-two guns and howitzers, an undisclosed number of antiaircraft guns, and light arms. In 1971 the Chinese built a naval base at Dar es Salaam and a military airfield near Morogoro. Tanzanian sailors and officers as well as pilots and technicians are receiving training in China.

Although Tanzania is sympathetic to the various southern African liberation movements, it is not known whether or not it provides direct military assistance. It does provide sanctuary and training, and allows rebels to base and train and receive arms from China in Tanzania. Also, its monetary contributions to the OAU's Liberation Coordinating Committee help support these movements.

## ALLIANCES

Tanzania is a member of the Commonwealth, the OAU, and the East African Community.

## ARMY

*Personnel:* 15,000

*Organization:*
   10 infantry battalions
    2 artillery battalions
    1 tank battalion

*Major Equipment Inventory:*
   14 light tanks (T-62)
   16 medium tanks (T-59)
   15 APCs (BTR-152/40)
   20 25-pounder guns
      76mm Soviet artillery pieces (light)
      Chinese mortars
      122mm howitzers (Chinese)
      14.5mm, 37mm antiaircraft guns

## NAVY

*Personnel:* 1,000

*Major Units:*
   10 fast patrol craft (7 Shanghai class; 3 P-6 class; PCF)
    4 hydrofoil motor torpedo boats (Huchwan class; PTH)

    4 motor torpedo boats (P-4 class; PT)
   10 patrol boats (PB)
    2 utility landing craft (LCU)

*Naval Base:* Dar Es Salaam

## AIR FORCE

*Personnel:* 1,000

*Major Aircraft Types:*
   35 combat aircraft
      35 MiG-17/19/21 fighters (acquired from China; to equip two squadrons)
   60 other aircraft
      19 transports (1 An-2, 5 DHC-3, 12 DHC-4, 1 HS-748)
      12 trainers (7 P-149, 5 PA-28-140)
       4 helicopters (Bell 47G, AB-206)
      25 utility/liaison

*Air Bases:* Dar es Salaam, Morogoro, Tabora, Zanzibar

## PARAMILITARY

Members of the National Service, Prison Service, Tanzanian Youth League, police, and other uniformed government employees receive military training and are considered available for paramilitary duties or to expand the army. The police, under the minister for home affairs and with a strength of 8,000, includes a 120-man paratroop company and a marine police unit with four patrol boats (YP). Ports patrolled by the Marine Police are Dar es Salaam, Zanzibar and Mtwara.

# THAILAND

## Kingdom of Thailand

## POWER POTENTIAL STATISTICS

Area: 198,455 square miles
Population: 46,443,000
Total Active Regular Armed Forces: 185,000 (0.40% population)
Gross National Product: $18.1 billion ($410 per capita)
Annual Military Expenditures: $950 million (5.25% GNP)
Fuel Production:
   Crude Oil: 7,450 metric tons
   Refined Petroleum Products: 7.3 million metric tons
Electric Power Output: 11.3 billion kwh

THAILAND

SCALE OF MILES

0    50    100    150    200

SCALE OF KILOMETERS

0    50    100    150    200

Capitals of Countries .................... ☆
International Boundaries ....... ▬ ▬ ▬ ▬

© C. S. HAMMOND & Co., Maplewood, N. J.

Longitude East of Greenwich

Merchant Fleet (ships 1,000 tons and over): 44 ships; 303,000 gross tons

Civil Air Fleet: 10 jet, 9 turboprop, 6 piston transports

## DEFENSE STRUCTURE

The king is nominal commander in chief of the armed forces. The prime minister, when military, usually is supreme commander of the armed forces, exercising control through the Ministry of Defense and Supreme Command Headquarters. However, the service commanders in chief exercise considerable independence in their own spheres.

## POLITICO-MILITARY POLICY

Thailand's politico-military policy always has been directed toward maintaining an independent position and maximizing its freedom of action.

Since 1950, Thailand has been committed to a policy of opposing communism in Southeast Asia, and that policy led it to join the Southeast Asia Treaty Organization and to support U.S. involvement in the Vietnam War. Thailand deployed irregulars to fight on the side of the Royal Lao government prior to 1975, permitted the United States to deploy substantial air power to Thai bases for operations throughout Indochina, and dispatched modest army and air force units to South Vietnam.

Since 1975, Thailand has been adjusting to the new realities of Southeast Asia and has sought to establish correct, though hardly cordial, relations with the Communist governments of the Indochina states. Relations with the United States have cooled, but the armed forces retain close relations with their U.S. counterparts and rely heavily on U.S.-procured equipment. Thailand also is believed to be interested in forming a regional security grouping parallel to, though not necessarily identical with, ASEAN.

The armed forces are maintained by conscription. All men between the ages of twenty-one and thirty are subject to two years of military service; about 20 percent actually serve.

## STRATEGIC PROBLEMS

Thailand faces a number of stragetic problems that pose serious challenges to the traditional Thai qualities of adroitness, compromise, and determination—qualities that helped keep Thailand independent during the colonial era in Southeast Asia.

The present governments of Cambodia, Laos, and Vietnam are controlled by those who were Thailand's enemies during the Vietnam War. Furthermore, for years all three have been supporting insurgency in Thailand. The long frontiers between Thailand and Cambodia and Laos can be infiltrated at almost any point by forces hostile to the Thai government. The Lao, with substantial Vietnamese support, have been engaged chiefly in attempting to subdue their own country, but there have been a number of bloody incidents along the border. Cambodian forces have launched a number of raids into Thailand and permanently occupied small enclaves generally considered to be on the Thai side of the border. Thai governments since 1975 have attempted to establish correct relationships with Thailand's neighbors without relaxing their own security measures. There is strong sentiment in the armed forces for more severe retaliatory measures, especially against Cambodia.

Thailand has maintained friendly relations with Burma, in contrast to the long hostility between the two in earlier centuries. Smuggling across the long border and occasional Thai tolerance and support of Burmese dissidents have complicated relations. Generally, however, the Thai have not felt compelled to deploy strong forces near the border with Burma except in isolated areas of insurgent activity.

In the far south, Malaysian-Thai relations have been complicated by the presence of Malaysian Communist terrorists who occupy base areas in Thailand, where they recruit among the ethnic Malay and Chinese populations. Thailand has been reluctant to commit major forces against these terrorists because they have not been a serious threat to Thai security outside the immediate vicinity of their jungle refuges. Combined operations in the far south in 1977–78 have disturbed the terrorists but not dislodged them. Thailand also is suspicious of Malaysian intentions toward the Pattani autonomy movement, which aims at restoration of the old sultanate, ceded to Thailand by the United Kingdom in 1909.

Elsewhere, Thai armed forces and police have to devote considerable effort and attention to a Communist-led insurgent movement that has been carrying out overt terrorist activity since 1965. This activity first appeared in the northeast, but there were subsequent outbreaks in the north, west-central, and mid-south (peninsular) regions. In the north, where there is a substantial non-Thai hill population, the insurgents have exploited anti-Thai sentiments, and elsewhere they have appealed to anti-Bangkok attitudes.

The Thai insurgents are led by members of the Communist party of Thailand, most of whose membership is recruited from the large Sino-Thai minority. A great deal of the external support for the Thai insurgents has come directly from China. Cambodia, Laos, and Vietnam also have made substantial contributions. Since 1975, Thailand has attempted to develop friendly relations with China in the hope of reducing direct support and possibly of influencing China to attempt to restrain Hanoi, Phnom Penh, and Vientiane. The Chinese response has been to emphasize friendly relations at the government-to-government level while continuing party-to-party support of Thai insurgents.

Although the organization of SEATO has been disbanded, Thailand continues to look to the United States for security support, both through continued association with the Southeast Asia Collective Defense Agreement, (the so-called Manila Pact, which established SEATO) and through a bilateral assistance agreement.

## MILITARY ASSISTANCE

Thailand has received substantial assistance from the United States—$1.2 billion since the first agreements were concluded in 1950. A much reduced U.S. Military Assistance Advisory Group remains in Thailand. Under the MAP 17,600 have received military training. However, Thailand increasingly has turned to overseas purchase and indigenous production to satisfy the material requirements of the armed forces.

## ALLIANCES

Thailand's alliance relationship with the United States is discussed in the preceding paragraphs. Thailand also is a member of ASEAN and has been an advocate of greater mutual cooperation in security matters with other ASEAN states, on both bilateral and multilateral bases.

## ARMY

*Personnel:* 130,000

*Organization:*
  6 infantry divisions
  3 regimental combat teams
 11 artillery battalions
  4 tank battalions
  3 antiaircraft battalions (1 with Hawk SAMs)
  1 signal battalion
  4 engineer battalions
  1 transport battalion

*Major Equipment Inventory:*
 195 light tanks (M-24 and M-41)
 260 light artillery pieces (105mm howitzers)
  24 medium artillery pieces (recoilless rifles, 106mm, 75mm, 57mm, 155mm howitzers)
     40mm antiaircraft guns
  40 SAM launchers (Hawk; 1 battalion)
 120 armored half-tracks (M-2 and M-16)
  16 armored cars (M-8)
 200 APCs (M-113)
 230 LVT amphibious assault vehicles
  20 V-150 Commando V-200
  60 light aircraft (Beech 99, O-1, L-18)
  65 helicopters (FH-1100, Jet Ranger, UH-1, CH-47, H-23)

*Reserves:* Approximately 350,000 trained reservists

## NAVY

*Personnel:* 20,000 (13,000 navy, 7,000 marines)

*Major Units:*
  4 frigates (1 Yarrow class with Seacat short-range SAMs; 1 Cannon class; 2 Takoma class; FF)
  2 light frigates (PF-103 class; FFL)
  4 patrol escorts (Trad class; PG; 3-inch guns)
 12 submarine chasers (PCS)
 17 patrol craft (PC)
  3 missile attack boats (PTG; with Gabriel SSMs; more building)
 20 patrol boats (PB)
  2 coastal minelayers (MMC)
  1 mine countermeasures support ship (MCS)
  4 coastal minesweepers (MSC)
 10 minesweeping boats (MSB)
  5 tank landing ships (LST)
  3 medium landing ships (LSM)
  8 utility landing craft (LCU; one not operational)
 26 mechanized landing craft (LCM)
 10 personnel landing craft (LCP)
  5 coast guard patrol vessels (CGC)
  5 auxiliary ships and support craft (tankers, training ships, etc.)
 15 service craft
    maritime reconnaissance aircraft (S-2 and HU-16)

*Major Naval Bases:* Bangkok, Paknam, Sattahip, Songkhla

*Reserves:* 30,000 trained naval reservists; 16,000 to 18,000 marine reservists

## AIR FORCE

*Personnel:* 35,000

*Organization:*
  6 combat wings (1 to 3 squadrons each)
    3 fighter squadrons (F-5)
    9 COIN ground attack squadrons (T-28, A/T-37, T-6, OV-10, AU-23)
    3 transport squadrons (Merlin, C-45, C-47, C-54, C-123, HS-748, Caribou)
    1 reconnaissance squadron (RT-33)
    1 helicopter wing (UH-1, H-34, H-13, CH-47, H-43)
    1 training and support wing (Chipmunk, CT-4, PL-2, SF-260, T-6, A/T-37, T-33, T-41)
  4 battalions of airfield defense troops

*Major Aircraft Types:*
 216 combat aircraft
  54 fighters (F-5)

157 COIN ground attack aircraft (32 OV-10, 45 T-28, 30 T-6, 20 AU-23, 30 A/T-37)
5 reconnaissance aircraft (RT-33)
286 other aircraft
46 transports (2 Merlin, 5 C-45, 20 C-47, 2 C-54, 13 C-123, 2 HS-748, 2 Caribou)
124 helicopters (4 CH-47, 50 UH-1, 10 H-43, 20 H-13, 40 H-34)
116 trainer/support aircraft (see types listed above)

*Major Air Bases:* Bangkok, Udon Thani, Don Muang, Khorat, Takhli, Ubon, Nongkai, Prachuab, Koke-kathion, Utapao, Nakhon Phanom

## PARAMILITARY

The Provincial Police has a strength of 28,000. The Thai Border Patrol Police has a strength of 8,000 men, and is equipped with forty-six aircraft, including ten Bell 204B, eleven Bell 205, and thirteen FH-1100 helicopters, and three Skyvan STOL transports. These, and all municipal highway and investigation police, are under Thai National Police Department, which is part of the Ministry of the Interior.

The Volunteer Defense Corps, with 10,000 men, is available for home guard type missions in times of emergency.

# TOGO

## Republic of Togo

## POWER POTENTIAL STATISTICS

Area: 21,853 square miles
Population: 2,493,000
Total Active Regular Armed Forces: 1,300 (0.05% population)
Gross National Product: $780 million ($300 per capita)
Annual Military Expenditures: $19.9 million (2.55% GNP)
Electric Power Output: 110 million kwh
Civil Air Fleet: 2 piston transports

## POLITICO-MILITARY POLICIES AND POSTURE

The president, as both chief of state and head of the government, is also commander in chief of the armed forces and minister of defense. The current military ruler, General Eyadema, has consolidated these positions with those he held formerly: chief of staff of the Togolese Armed Forces and commander First Battalion Togolese Infantry.

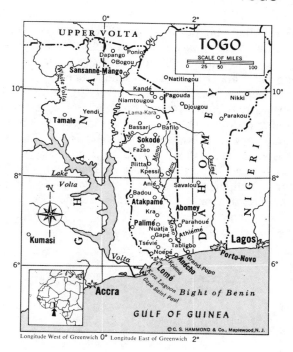

Since independence from French rule in 1960, Togo has maintained close relations with France, including a defense agreement, the details of which remain unpublished, as well as agreements for staging, transit, and overflight privileges, and military assistance. Togo is a member of OCAM and Conseil de l'Entente. Togo maintains a policy of nonalignment, and is a member and strong supporter of the UN. With Nigeria, Togo played a leading role in the creation of the Economic Community of West African States in 1975 and also hosted the Lome Convention (for economic cooperation) signings that year. The only significant foreign policy problem is the long-standing agitation by the Ewe, Togo's largest tribe, for reunification of the French and British Togolands. This has caused some tension with Ghana, to which British Togoland was annexed in 1957.

Since a military coup in 1967, rule is by decree and ordinance, although a new constitution is being drafted, and a return to civilian government is promised.

Potential ethnic conflict exists between the culturally dominant coastal tribes, particularly the Ewes, and the poor but more warlike northern tribes—mainly the Cabrais, who provide the best soldiers for the army. The economy, formerly agricultural, has become largely dependent upon export of a 70-million-ton phosphate deposit. A 550-million-ton deposit of high-grade iron ore and large deposits of limestone and bauxite are also economically important.

United States MAP totaled $18,000 through 1977, and four students were trained.

The 1,000-man army is organized into one infantry battalion, a reconnaissance unit with armored cars, an engineer unit, a band, and supporting elements. Weapons, equipment, and training are French. The navy, with 200 men, operates two fast patrol craft (PCF) and possibly other craft. Augmented by French air force personnel on temporary duty, the air force has about 100 men and operates one C-47 transport, two DHC-5 Buffaloes, five Magister trainers, three MB-326 trainers, two Broussard liaison aircraft, and two Alouette helicopters. There is an international airport at Lome, and there are four airstrips in the interior. Paramilitary forces include a gendarmerie of 1,000 men.

# TRINIDAD AND TOBAGO

## POWER POTENTIAL STATISTICS

Area: 1,980 square miles (Trinidad: 1,864; Tobago: 116)
Population: 1,129,000
Total Active Regular Armed Forces: 1,000 (0.09% population)
Gross National Product: $3.2 billion ($2,186 per capita)
Annual Military Expenditures: $48.4 million (1.51% GNP)
Fuel Production:
  Crude Oil: 11.1 million metric tons
  Refined Petroleum Products: 16.8 million metric tons
  Natural Gas: 1.3 billion cubic meters
Electric Power Output: 1.6 billion kwh
Merchant Fleet (ships 1,000 tons and over): 2 ships; 5,000 gross tons
Civil Air Fleet: 12 major transport aircraft

## POLITICO-MILITARY POLICIES AND POSTURE

As an independent member of the Commonwealth, Trinidad and Tobago maintain a link with Britain through a governor general appointed by the sovereign. The prime minister, appointed by the governor general from a bicameral legislature, directly commands the army, while the Coast Guard and police come under the minister of home affairs.

Trinidad and Tobago is a member of the OAS. It takes an independent stand on many international issues but because of its small size relies on Britain, and on mutual security provided through membership in international organizations, to prevent foreign economic or military domination.

The favorable per capita GNP results from substantial petroleum production. However, declining production, high population density and growth rate, unemployment, and other economic problems have produced tensions threatening to internal stability. In April 1970 severe riots took place; they were fomented by black power agitators and affected a part of the army. More disorders in 1971 resulted in declaration of a state of emergency, and the problem continued into 1972.

In 1941 the United States and Britain signed a lend-lease agreement which included the granting to the United States of base rights on Trinidad for ninety-nine years. In response to a request by Trinidad and Tobago, the United States relinquished the last of these, the naval base at Chaguaramas, in 1967.

Britain has provided arms and training for Trinidad and Tobago's armed forces. The army has a strength of about 800, organized as one infantry battalion and supporting headquarters and services. There is a 1,000-man reserve which includes a second infantry battalion. A 200-man Coast Guard operates four patrol craft (PC), three patrol boats (PB), and one training craft. They are based at Staubles Bay. Airfields include Piarco on Trinidad and Crown Point on Tobago, plus twelve small strips on Trinidad. There is no air force.

# TUNISIA

## Republic of Tunisia

## POWER POTENTIAL STATISTICS

Area: 63,378 square miles
Population: 6,327,000
Total Active Regular Armed Forces: 15,800 (0.25% population)
Gross National Product: $5.7 billion ($930 per capita)

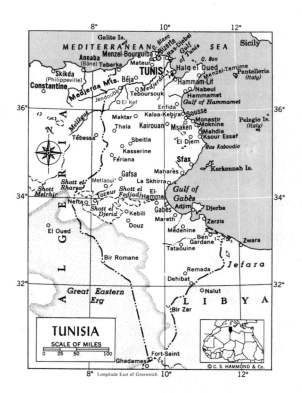

TUNISIA
SCALE OF MILES
0  25  50  100

Annual Military Expenditures: $153 million (2.68%
  GNP)
Iron Ore Production: 494,000 metric tons
Fuel Production:
  Crude Oil: 3.7 million metric tons
  Refined Petroleum Products: 1.17 million metric tons
  Natural Gas: 214 million cubic meters
Electric Power Output: 1.7 billion kwh
Merchant Fleet (ships 1,000 tons and over): 19 ships;
  95,000 gross tons
Civil Air Fleet: 16 major transport aircraft

## DEFENSE STRUCTURE

A strong president of a one-party political system is
chief of state, head of government, and commander in
chief of the armed forces. He appoints his cabinet, including the minister of defense, through whom he administers
the armed forces. The Tunisian National Army (TNA) was
formed upon independence in 1956 with key positions
going to reliable party and resistance movement *(fallagha)*
members, although most of the troops were Tunisian
veterans of the French army. The naval and air arms are
small adjuncts of the TNA and subordinated to it.

## POLITICO-MILITARY POLICY

Tunisia has consistently supported policies of moderation in international affairs and collective security through

international organizations, particularly the UN. To this
end, in 1960 a brigade was sent to the UN operation in the
Congo.

In its attempt to bring reason and moderation to the
Arab side in the dispute with Israel, Tunisia has become
the target of ideological and subversive attacks from the
radical Arab states. These external threats, given greater
emphasis by the buildup of Soviet-supplied arms in
neighboring Algeria and Libya, have provided an incentive
for strengthening Tunisia's defenses, modifying the past
policy of channeling scanty resources into social services
and national development.

Absolute defense against such strongly armed neighbors
as Algeria and Libya is beyond Tunisia's capabilities.
Therefore, the stated defense objective is a small army of
well-trained professionals to provide deterrence, to deal
with minor incursions, and to delay any major attack so
that an international organization or friendly powers
would have time to come to Tunisia's aid. To this end
increased military assistance has been sought from the
United States. In return, Tunisia has continued to urge
moderation in the Arab-Israeli conflict (while affirming
solidarity with the Arab nations), did not join in
condemnation of America's role in Vietnam, has voiced
concern over the increased Soviet military presence in the
Mediterranean, and has not joined the radical Arab
opposition to Sadat's peace initiative. Tunisia also
maintains close relations with France.

Military service is compulsory, although selective.
Conscription is at age twenty, followed by one year of
active service, nine years in the first reserve, and fifteen
years in the second reserve.

## STRATEGIC PROBLEMS

Tunisia's strategic problems include the possibility of an
attack by radical neighbors, and internal dissent sparked
by external subversive efforts as well as its own faltering
economy. The naval base at Bizerte, and the port of Tunis,
permitting control of the narrow waters between Tunisia
and Sicily, make Tunisia's location as strategically important today as it was in World War II. Tunisia's proven oil
reserve of sixty million tons is significant.

The Destourian Socialist party dominates all political
and socioeconomic organizations. The country has been
free of domestic strife except for periodic university
unrest. This changed in late 1977 as labor unrest
developed, prompting a government crackdown on labor
leaders. Serious rioting and a number of cabinet resigna-
tions occurred during a general strike in January 1978.

Tunisia is uncomfortably positioned between two
radical Arab states. Its modern stand on the Middle East
has antagonized Algeria despite a 1971 treaty of friendship
and cooperation between the two. More recently Tunisia
has supported the division of former Spanish Sahara
between Morocco and Mauritania. In 1974 Tunisia

withdrew from a plan to unite with Libya. Relations thereafter deteriorated even further over an alleged Libyan attempt to assassinate Tunisia's president and an offshore oil drilling dispute. These external pressures and growing signs of internal unrest cast a high degree of uncertainty over Tunisia's future when the aging President Bourguiba departs the scene.

## MILITARY ASSISTANCE

France has provided training and equipment. Sweden provided training aircraft and pilot instruction in 1960–61 on a sales basis, as did Italy in 1965–66. Britain also has sold some arms to Tunisia. A 1961 military assistance treaty with Egypt was apparently never implemented.

From 1960 onward the United States has been the major supplier of arms, all on a grant aid basis. Between 1960 and 1972, $31.4 million in arms was furnished. In this same period about $2.0 million of excess military stocks was provided and 455 persons were trained under the MAP. In 1968 a formal Military Assistance and Advisory Group was established in Tunis. Aid has included training with U.S. forces in West Germany and the United States, modernizing the infantry weapons of the army, and the beginning of an air defense system.

## ALLIANCES

Tunisia is a member of the OAU. Although a member of the Arab League, Tunisia has frequently boycotted its meetings because of differences with league polities which preclude the possibility of peace with Israel. Tunisia is also a member of the moribund Maghreb Consultative Committee and has tried to advance cooperation among the four Northwest African states, but with little success.

## ARMY

*Personnel:* 12,000

*Organization:*
    6 combined-arms battalions
    1 Sahara patrol group (regiment)
    1 artillery group
    1 commando battalion

*Major Equipment Inventory:*
    50 light tanks (M-41 and AMX-13)
    30 armored cars (Saladin and M-8)
    10 105mm self-propelled howitzers
    10 155mm howitzers
       40mm antiaircraft guns (Bofors)

*Reserves:* About 25,000 trained reservists

## NAVY

*Personnel:* 2,600

*Major Units:*
    1 frigate (Savage class; FF)
    1 patrol ship (Le Fougeux class; PGF)
    2 fast patrol craft (PCF)
    2 coastal minesweepers (MSC)
    3 patrol craft (P-48 class; PC; fitted with SS-12 short-range SSMs)
    10 patrol boats (PB)
    3 tugs

*Naval Bases:* Tunis, Bizerte

*Reserves:* about 3,000

## AIR FORCE

*Personnel:* 1,200

*Major Aircraft Types:*
    22 combat aircraft
    12 F-86 fighters
    10 MB-326 armed trainers/ground attack aircraft
    40 other aircraft
        3 Flamant light transports
       12 T-6 trainers
       12 SF-260 trainers
        1 SA-330 Puma
       12 Alouette II/III helicopters

*Air Bases:* Tunis (El Aouina), Monastir, Bizerte, Gabes, Sfax, Djerba

*Reserves:* about 2,500 trained reservists

## PARAMILITARY

A gendarmerie of six battalions totals 5,000. There is a National Guard of 5,000.

# TURKEY
## Republic of Turkey

## POWER POTENTIAL STATISTICS

Area: 301,380 square miles
Population: 43,767,000
Total Active Regular Armed Forces: 495,000 (1.13% population)
Gross National Product: $45 billion ($1,070 per capita)
Annual Military Expenditures: $2.3 billion (5.11% GNP)
Crude Steel Production: 1.46 million metric tons
Iron Ore Production: 3.35 million metric tons

Fuel Production:

    Coal: 4.6 million metric tons

    Lignite: 6 million metric tons

    Crude Oil: 2.6 million metric tons

    Refined Petroleum Products: 13.6 million metric tons

Electric Power Output: 22 billion kwh

Merchant Fleet (ships 1,000 tons and over): 145 ships;
    1.7 million gross tons

Civil Air Fleet: 16 jet, 7 turboprop transports

## DEFENSE STRUCTURE

The president of the Republic of Turkey constitutionally exercises power as a strong executive; he is the actual as well as nominal commander in chief of the armed forces. This responsibility is exercised through the prime minister and the minister of national defense. The army is the predominant element of the partially integrated armed forces. The chief of the general staff is also commander in chief of the armed forces.

## POLITICO-MILITARY POLICIES

For several centuries Russia has been the principal traditional enemy of Turkey. After World War I, Turkey followed an essentially neutral policy, in which an important element was rapprochement with Soviet Russia. Soviet domination of the Balkans after World War II brought renewed Russian pressure to obtain control over the Turkish Straits. Despite occasional gestures of friendship on both sides, security from the Soviet Union has been the principal element of Turkish foreign and military policy since 1945. Turkish appeals for support in opposing Soviet threats stimulated the enunciation of the Truman Doctrine in 1947, and the beginning of a bilateral alliance with the United States. This same Turkish policy caused Turkey to contribute a highly effective brigade to the UN Forces during the Korean conflict and to join the NATO alliance in 1952 and the Baghdad Pact (later the CENTO alliance) in 1955. CENTO has its headquarters at Ankara. More recently Turkey has taken steps to normalize its relations with the Soviet Union, without weakening its membership in NATO. In 1973, during the Arab-Israeli confrontation, Turkey made clear both that NATO bases might not be used to ship war materiel to Israel, and that any Soviet airlift to Arab nations might not traverse Turkish air space.

In 1971, Turkey established diplomatic relations with the People's Republic of China.

Since the United States Congress put an embargo on U.S. military aid to Turkey during the Cyprus crisis in 1974, Turkey has received large amounts of economic assistance from Communist countries—$1.4 billion between 1954 and 1976—$1.2 billion of it from the Soviet Union. At the end of 1977, Turkey was the recipient of the fourth largest amount of Soviet aid. Libya has promised (1977) extensive aid in the construction of new industrial projects. Turkey, Iran, and Pakistan signed a treaty in 1977 with a view toward establishing a free trade area.

The Turkish armed forces are raised by conscription. The term of service is twenty months for all services. The quality of the armed forces is greatly enhanced by a proud national military tradition, and by the toughness, frugality, courage, loyalty, and self-reliance of the Turkish peasants, who make up the bulk of the rank and file. Since World War II, about 30 percent of the annual budget has been for defense.

## STRATEGIC PROBLEMS

Turkey's location between the Mediterranean and Black seas, and between Europe and Asia, is one of the most significant in the world, militarily and strategically. Turkey has been the principal obstacle to imperial and Soviet Russian expansion into the Mediterranean and also to Soviet movement into the oil-rich Middle East. By its participation in the NATO and CENTO alliances, and because of the effectiveness and reliability of the Turkish armed forces, Turkey has become one of the key elements of the chain of mutual security alliances that has resisted Communist expansionism since 1947. The recent expansion of the Soviet navy, and increased Soviet naval activity in the eastern Mediterranean have reemphasized the importance of Turkey's role on NATO's southeastern flank.

The security of the Straits (Bosporus, Sea of Marmara, and Dardanelles) is perhaps the greatest Turkish strategic problem. For 200 years the right of foreign warships to go through them has been the subject of controversy—and of agreements. The Montreux Convention of 1936 allowed Turkey to fortify the Straits, and provided for free passage in peacetime of warships under a certain size, and for closing the Straits in wartime to belligerents as long as Turkey should remain neutral. A related problem is the defense of the small and isolated region in Europe north and west of the Straits. The defense of Turkey's eastern frontiers with the USSR and Iran is facilitated by extremely rugged mountains. A security weakness in this area, however, is the presence of two ethnic minorities: the Kurds and the Armenians.

Largely because of frustrations with the frequently closed oil pipeline across Syria, Turkey in 1977 opened a new pipeline from the Kirkuk oilfields of Iraq across Turkey to the Mediterranean. It carries a relatively high volume of oil and is one of the most efficient pipelines in the Middle East, but it has already been closed at least once, as a result of disagreement with Iraq over price.

Turkey's interest in preventing the absorption of Cyprus by Greece, while basically motivated by support of the Turkish Cypriot minority, is also influenced by the strategic location of the island off Turkey's southern shore, and by the long history of Greek-Turkish enmity. When an estimated 40,000 Turkish troops were landed on Cyprus in 1974, a sizable section of U.S. public opinion, and especially that of Greek-Americans, was outraged by the use of U.S.-supplied arms against Greeks. The United States Congress voted to cut off aid to Turkey, imposing an embargo on all arms, even those for which payment had already been made. (See Cyprus and Greece.) The embargo went into effect in February 1975, and in July of that year Turkey took over some of the U.S. bases that provided crucial NATO intelligence through electronic surveillance of the Soviet Union. In addition Turkey declared invalid the U.S.-Turkish Defense Cooperation Agreement of 1969, the basis for the U.S. military presence in Turkey. In August 1978, the United States Congress finally responded to presidential pleas and voted an end to the arms embargo, paving the way for the reopening of the U.S. bases.

Except for the small Armenian and Kurdish minorities, and an equally insignificant Greek minority in western Anatolia and European Turkey, the population is homogeneous. Communism has had little impact upon the predominantly Moslem people and is unlikely to have more, despite the low standard of living of most Turks. Leftist disaffection is apparent among university students and intellectuals, however, and has resulted in many riots, bombings, kidnappings, and murders. This unrest, partly directed against the presence of American NATO personnel, has at times created some governmental instability. There are also some extremist, violent, right-wing student groups.

## MILITARY ASSISTANCE

Largely because of Turkey's strategic location, and its military reliability, the United States has provided it with more than $3.2 billion in military assistance since 1950. There have been 19,150 students trained under MAP. There has also been military assistance from West Germany.

## ALLIANCES

Turkey is a member of the UN and both NATO and CENTO. It is a member, along with Pakistan and Iran, of the Regional Cooperation for Development, established in 1964. It also has extensive bilateral arrangements with the United States.

Izmir is a major NATO base and headquarters area, and the main location of a number of U.S. installations in Turkey. Although the number of U.S. military personnel in Turkey is being drastically reduced, partly because the presence of these affluent soldiers and their dependents has caused considerable unrest, there are still about 4,700 U.S. military personnel stationed in Turkey. There are extensive U.S. and NATO radar and other surveillance installations. At least 200 U.S. military aircraft and some Greek combat air units, part of NATO's Sixth Allied Tactical Air Force, are based in Turkey. Izmir is also a major base for the U.S. Sixth Fleet. There is a major U.S. air base at Incirlik, near Adana.

## ARMY

(Except for some fortress and territorial formations, all units are assigned to NATO.)

*Personnel:* 400,000

*Organization:* 3 armies: one in European Turkey, protecting the northern approach to the Straits; one in western Anatolia, concentrated near the Asiatic side of the Straits; and one in eastern Anatolia, concentrated near the Soviet frontier.

```
  6 army corps; two for each army
  1 armored division (M-48 tanks)
  1 mechanized infantry division
 12 infantry divisions
  4 armored cavalry brigades
  4 armored brigades (M-48 tanks)
  3 mechanized infantry brigades
  2 parachute battalions
  2 SSM battalions (Honest John)
```

*Major Equipment Inventory:*
```
1,500  medium tanks (M-47 and M-48)
       light tanks (M-24 and M-41)
       tank destroyers (M-36)
       armored cars (M-8)
 500+  APCs (M-113 and M-59)
       105mm and 155mm self-propelled guns
       105mm, 155mm, and 203mm howitzers
       40mm, 75mm, and 90mm antiaircraft
         artillery pieces
       SS-11 ATGW
       SSM Honest John launchers
   40  light aircraft (Do-27, Do-28, Beaver)
```

```
   20  helicopters (AB-206, Bell 47, CH-47)
```

*Reserves:* There are over 800,000 trained reservists.

## NAVY

*Personnel:* 45,000 (including 3 battalions of marines)

*Major Units:*
```
 12  diesel submarines (9 Guppy class, 3 Type 209;
       SS)
 12  destroyers (5 Gearing, 1 Sumner, 1 Smith,
       5 Fletcher class; DD)
  2  frigates (Berk class; FF)
  6  patrol ships (PC 1638 class; PGF)
  8  missile attack boats (4 Luerssen class; 4 Kartal
       class; PTG; Harpoon SSMs)
 13  motor torpedo boats (PT)
 36  patrol craft (PC)
  4  patrol boats (PB)
 21  coastal minesweepers (MSC)
  4  inshore minesweepers (MSI)
  6  minelayers (MM)
  1  coastal minelayer (MMC)
  9  minesweeping boats (MSB)
  4  tank landing ships (LST)
 33  utility landing craft (LCU)
 20  mechanized landing craft (LCM)
 20  auxiliary ships
 30  service craft
  3  helicopters (AB-205; ASW)
 16  S2E ASW aircraft
```

*Reserves:* 70,000 trained reservists

*Major Naval Bases:* Goelcuek, Istanbul, Izmir

## AIR FORCE

(All formations are assigned to NATO's Sixth Allied Tactical Air Force)

*Personnel:* 50,000

*Organization:*
```
  2 tactical air forces
    2 fighter-interceptor squadrons AW (F-102)
    2 fighter-interceptor squadrons (F-5)
    5 fighter-bomber squadrons (F-100)
    2 fighter-bomber squadrons (F-104)
    2 fighter-bomber squadrons (F-5)
    3 fighter/reconnaissance squadrons (RF-84F,
        RF-5)
    4 transport squadrons (C-45, C-47, C-54,
        C-130, Viscount, Transall)
    1 helicopter squadron (UH-1, H-19)
    2 SAM battalions (Nike-Hercules; 6 batteries)
```

*Major Aircraft Types:*
- 349 combat aircraft
  - 130 F-5 interceptor/fighter-bombers
  - 38 F-104 fighter-bombers
  - 100 F-100 fighter-bombers
  - 36 F-102 AW fighter-interceptors
  - 30 RF-84 fighter/reconnaissance aircraft
  - 15 RF-5 fighter/reconnaissance aircraft
- 224 other aircraft
  - 12 C-47 transports
  - 6 C-45 transports
  - 3 C-54 transports
  - 10 C-130 transports
  - 20 Transall transports
  - 23 helicopters (UH-1, H-19)
  - 150 trainer/support aircraft (including T-33, TF-102, TF-104, T-37, T-41, T-42, T-34, T-11, F-100F, and F-5)

*Equipment on Order:* 40 F-4, 42 F-5 Tiger II

*Major Air Bases:* Izmir, Adana, Bandirma, Diyarbakir, Esluboga, Sivas, Etimesgut, Eskisehir, Yesilkoy, Merzifon, Balikesir.

*Reserves:* There are 80,000 trained reservists.

## PARAMILITARY

75,000 National Gendarmerie (3 mobile brigades)
20,000 National Guard

# UGANDA

## Republic of Uganda

## POWER POTENTIAL STATISTICS

Area: 91,134 square miles
Population: 13,002,000
Total Active Regular Armed Forces: 21,000 (0.16% population)
Gross National Product: $886 million ($70 per capita)
Annual Military Expenditures: $71 million (8.01% GNP)

Electric Power Output: 1.0 billion kwh
Merchant Fleet (ships 1,000 tons and over): 1 ship; 6,000 gross tons
Civil Air Fleet: 5 piston transports

## POLITICO-MILITARY POLICIES AND POSTURE

In early 1979 the brutal and erratic dictatorship of Idi Amin Dada was overthrown by the combined efforts of Tanzanian military forces and Ugandan exiles based in Tanzania. The new government, which included representatives from a wide range of tribal groups and political positions, immediately received offers of extensive economic assistance from western nations and international organizations as it moved to restore the nation's economy, morale, and armed forces. The army and air force had been all but destroyed by the 1979 war and Amin's earlier bloody purges.

Amin had taken power in January 1971, seizing it through a military coup from the former president, Milton Obote. Obote took refuge in Tanzania and received support from President Nyerere. There were repeated border clashes thereafter, and Amin's invasion of Tanzanian territory in October 1978 precipitated the Tanzanian invasion that brought his downfall.

The Ugandan army traces its origins to the British colonial King's African Rifles. Africanization of the officer corps, pay raises, and increasing political influence followed a 1964 mutiny of Ugandan soldiers. Under Amin, the army was recruited from all tribal groups, except the

Acholi and Langi tribes. These tribes were the target of widespread massacres in 1977, and all of their members in the army reportedly were killed. There was an inner corps of elite Nubians and Kakwa (Amin's small tribal group). These composed the notorious Public Safety Unit, State Research Bureau, and other internal security units. Several hundred Palestinians reportedly formed Amin's personal bodyguard.

Amin's regime was one of the most brutally repressive in Africa. Some 40,000 Asians were expelled from Uganda in 1972. Meanwhile tens of thousands of Ugandans were killed in the aftermath of the 1971 coup and during the 1972 defeat of an invasion by Obote supporters. Amin survived several coup and assassination attempts from various quarters. Each incident was followed by mass executions.

Central control of events disintegrated in 1976–77 as corruption and lawlessness permeated the military. Amin narrowly escaped assassination in mid-1976 and responded with numerous executions to the humiliation of the July Entebbe rescue by Israel of hijacked air passengers. In the ensuing economic blockade by Kenya, Amin faced uprisings from within the army and among university students. In early 1977 these elements were systematically eliminated in a wave of terror against them and the Christian elites, most notably Archbishop Luwum. By early 1978 Amin felt secure enough in his control over the Ugandan military to convene a long-promised National Consultative Forum.

With the collapse of the East African Community and the frequent Ugandan charges that its one-time partners were plotting Amin's overthrow, relations with Tanzania and Kenya were hostile. Following Entebbe in 1976, Kenya and Uganda massed troops on their border. These tensions cooled somewhat in early 1978. During Amin's last year there, Uganda received little foreign aid from the West. The United Kingdom broke relations in 1976, the first such action initiated by Britain against a Commonwealth member. Uganda completely reversed its policy toward the USSR after its 1975 denunciations of Soviet African policy. The Russians became a prime source of aid and replaced the fighter aircraft destroyed by Israeli commandos in 1976. Amin's erratic foreign policy pronouncements and his reputation for barbarity drew condemnation from a broad variety of international forums and nations.

Initially training and equipment for the armed forces were supplied by the British. In recent years Israeli military assistance has been extensive; however, early in 1972 the Israeli military mission was expelled. In 1973, 300 Ugandan soldiers received training in Libya. Aircraft have been received from Israel, the Soviet Union, and Czechoslovakia. Light weapons may have been furnished by the Soviet Union, Czechoslovakia, and Communist China.

The General Service Units (GSU) of the police number 800 men, trained for riot control. Under the Ministry of Interior they have remained a genuinely multitribal force, still conditioned by the apolitical standards of the British civil service. The police air wing operates three helicopters, a Twin Otter, and several other aircraft.

## ARMY*

*Personnel:* 20,000

*Organization:*
   2 brigades of 4 infantry battalions each
   2 border guard battalions
   1 mechanized battalion
   1 parachute/commando battalion
   1 artillery regiment

*Major Equipment Inventory:*
   25 medium tanks
      20 T-34, T-54/55
      5 M-4
   16 Ferret scout cars
   250 APCs, BRDM, BTR-40/152, OT-64,
      122mm guns, mortars, Sagger ATGM, antiaircraft guns

## AIR FORCE*

*Personnel:* 1,000

*Organization:*
   1 fighter squadron (MiG-21)
   1 fighter squadron (MiG-17)
   1 transport squadron (C-47)

*Major Aircraft Types:*
   24 combat aircraft
      24 fighters (10 MiG-21, 12 MiG-17, 2 MiG-15)
   48 other aircraft
      7 transports (1 Caribou, 6 C-47)
      24 trainers (12 L-29 Delfin, 8 Magister, 4 P-149)
      17 helicopters (6 AB-205, 2 AB-206, 2 Wasp, 7 Mi-4)
      There have been reports of offers of Mirage fighters from Libya but these have not been confirmed.

*Major Air Bases:* Gulu, Kampala, Entebbe

---

*All figures are for the period before the 1979 Tanzanian invasion and civil war.

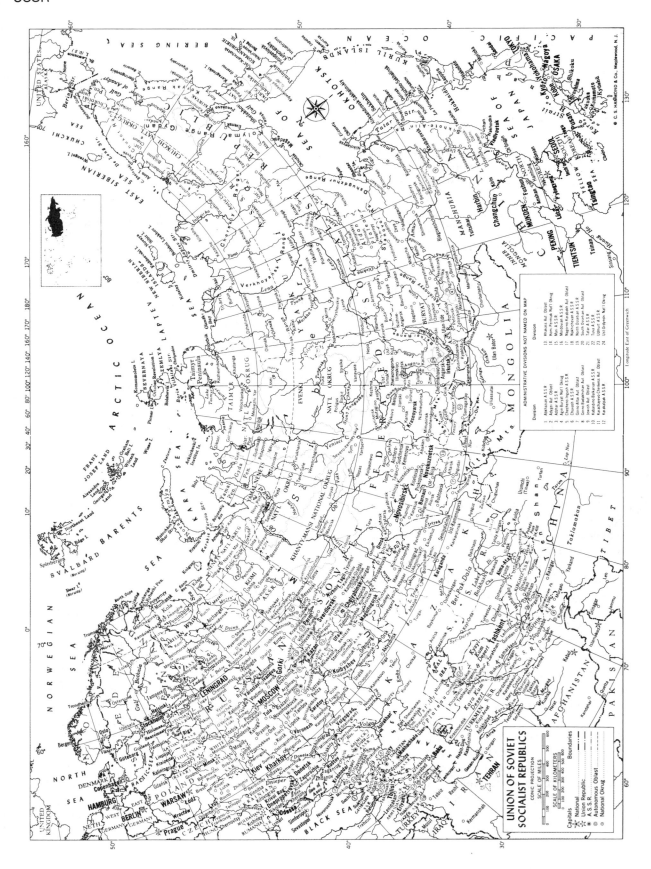

**UNION OF SOVIET
SOCIALIST REPUBLICS**

CONIC PROJECTION

SCALE OF MILES

SCALE OF KILOMETERS

Capitals
National
Union Republic
A.S.S.R.
Autonomous Oblast
National Okrug

Boundaries
National
Union Republic
A.S.S.R.
Autonomous Oblast
National Okrug

ADMINISTRATIVE DIVISIONS NOT NAMED ON MAP

| Division | Division |
|---|---|
| 1  Abkhazian A.S.S.R. | 13  Khakass Aut. Oblast |
| 2  Adygei Aut. Oblast | 14  Kom. Permak Nat'l Okrug |
| 3  Ajarin A.S.S.R. | 15  Mari A.S.S.R. |
| 4  Agin-Buryat Nat'l Okrug | 16  Mordovian A.S.S.R. |
| 5  Chechen-Ingush A.S.S.R. | 17  Nakhichevan A.S.S.R. |
| 6  Chuvash A.S.S.R. | 18  North Ossetian A.S.S.R. |
| 7  Gorno-Altai  Oblast | 19  South Ossetian Aut. Oblast |
| 8  Gorno Badakhshan Aut. Oblast | 20  Tatar A.S.S.R. |
| 9  Jewish Aut. Oblast | 21  Tuva A.S.S.R. |
| 10  Kabardino-Balkarian A.S.S.R. | 22  Udmurt A.S.S.R. |
| 11  Karachayevo-Cherkess Aut. Oblast | 23  Ust-Ordynsk Nat'l Okrug |
| 12  Karakalpak A.S.S.R. | 24 |

© C. S. HAMMOND & Co., Maplewood, N. J.

# UNION OF SOVIET SOCIALIST REPUBLICS

## POWER POTENTIAL STATISTICS

Area: 8,649,490 square miles

Population: 262,586,000

Total Active Regular Armed Forces: 3,780,000 (1.44% population)

Gross National Product: $1,034.3 billion ($3,990 per capita)

Annual Military Expenditures: $127 billion (12.6% GNP)

Crude Steel Production: 145 million metric tons

Iron Ore Production: 238 million metric tons

Fuel Production:

Crude Oil: 520 million metric tons

Refined Petroleum Products: 479 million metric tons

Natural Gas: 289 billion cubic meters

Manufactured Gas: 36 billion cubic meters

Coal: 712 million metric tons (includes lignite)

Electric Power Output: 1,152 billion kwh

Nuclear Power Production: 19,816 megawatts

Merchant Fleet (ships 1,000 tons and over): 2,456 ships; 15.6 million gross tons

Civil Air Fleet: at least 350 jet, 800 turboprop, and 200 piston transports.

## DEFENSE STRUCTURE

The Union of Soviet Socialist Republics is a Communist federative state comprising fifteen Union republics with control highly centralized in the government in Moscow. The elective Supreme Soviet is theoretically the supreme body of state authority. The thirty-three-member Presidium, elected by the Supreme Soviet, includes prominent members of the Communist party and rules between brief, occasional sessions of the Supreme Soviet; it appoints members of the Council of Ministers, appoints and dismisses the high command of the armed forces, and has authority to decree mobilization.

De facto, the ultimate power in the Soviet system is exercised by the leaders of the Communist party of the Soviet Union (CPSU). The party imposes its will through the government apparatus. The most powerful policy-making organ in the Communist party is the politburo. The secretariat of the party's Central Committee provides day-to-day executive and administrative direction for the entire party machine. Together, the politburo and the secretariat constitute the real seat of power of the USSR.

The three top military bodies in the Soviet Union are the Council of Defense, the Main Military Council, and the General Staff. Chairman of the Council of Defense is Leonid Brezhnev, general secretary of the Communist party and since May 1976 a marshal of the Soviet Union. The council is responsible for all defense preparations and has the power to make any changes in military bodies, including the whole structure of the Soviet armed forces. The Main Military Council, a deliberative body in time of peace, is concerned with problems of strategy and leadership. It is now chaired by the minister of defense, Marshall Ustinov, and Brezhnev is probably a member. Its World War II equivalent was the Stavka (headquarters of the Supreme High Command), and in case of war it would be replaced by a new Stavka. The General Staff is immediately under the Main Military Council. It resembles the traditional German general staff; many of the early Bolshevik military leaders were trained in the general staff concept by German officers in the first years of the USSR.

There are five major components of the Soviet armed forces: strategic rocket forces, air defense forces, ground forces (army), navy, and air force. The Main Political Directorate of the Soviet army and navy is responsible for political indoctrination of the armed forces. Its chief is also a first deputy minister of defense and has a direct channel to the Central Committee of the party.

## POLITICO-MILITARY POLICY

The modern Communist government of the USSR apparently is generally following the expansionist policy that was pursued by Russian governments during the four preceding centuries, although the slogans and rationale are very different from those of Czarist imperialism. Expansion of the USSR in the past thirty-five years has taken the form of establishing vast spheres of influence and a determination to create buffer states that are not only friendly but, when possible, subservient to the Soviet Union.

The major European question that has come close to precipitating conflict between the USSR and its World War II allies has been the problem of Germany and European security. The USSR would not agree to the Western proposal for the unification of Germany on the basis of free elections, and objected to the remilitarization of West Germany. In response to the admission of West Germany to NATO as a sovereign state in 1955, the Soviet government announced the conclusion of a twenty-year defense alliance (the Warsaw Treaty Organization) between the USSR and its seven European satellites: Albania, Bulgaria, Czechoslovakia, East Germany, Hungary, Poland, and Romania. (Albania has since withdrawn.) The German problem has now been effectively defused by the acceptance by all parties of the current situation as the status quo indefinitely. In 1970 the Federal Republic of Germany (West Germany) accepted the Oder-Neisse line as the German-Polish border. In 1975, at Helsinki, the nations of Europe, and also the United States, recognized the borders of all European countries, including the boundary between the Germanies. The enclave of West Berlin within the boundaries of the Democratic Republic of Germany (East Germany) remains a potential source of friction.

Early Soviet scientific successes in space exploration and missile development did much to restore Soviet international prestige, severely damaged by brutal suppression of the Hungarian rebellion. This prestige was further enhanced by Soviet accomplishments during the late 1950s in the improvement and stockpiling of nuclear weapons, modernization of the armed forces, and upgrading of the Soviet air defense system against possible strategic nuclear attack.

The Soviet and Warsaw Pact invasion of Czechoslovakia in 1968 may be seen as marking the beginning of a revised Soviet approach to foreign and military matters. Several trends are now apparent in Soviet politico-military policy in the decade since that invasion, a decade roughly coinciding with the era of Leonid Brezhnev's leadership.

The Brezhnev regime followed the Czechoslovakian invasion with efforts to bring the Warsaw Pact countries more firmly under its control. It also attempted to increase the buildup of Soviet forces in those countries, and to modernize and increase the WTO countries' own forces. A doctrine of "proletarian internationalism" that justified Soviet (nominally Warsaw Pact) intervention in Czechoslovakia, and any similar instances in the future, was developed; this is generally known in the West as the "Brezhnev Doctrine." At the same time, Brezhnev began moves toward detente with the United States, moves that were accepted by President Nixon in 1972. The Soviets agreed to participate in the MBFR talks, beginning in 1973 (see Western Europe Regional Survey), reached some agreement with the United States in the SALT talks, participated in the talks preceding the Conference on Security and Cooperation in Europe at Helsinki, and signed the final act of that conference (1975; see Eastern Europe Regional Survey). When President Carter, as well as some Soviet citizens, pushed for Soviet honoring of the human rights provisions of the Helsinki act, detente cooled considerably on the Soviet side.

During 1978 and 1979 the Soviet Union became more and more involved in events in Afghanistan, where pro-Soviet regimes were having increasing difficulty in maintaining control over the rural regions of the country, which were dominated by anti-Communist guerrillas opposed to Afghan ties with the USSR. On December 25 Soviet troops initiated a massive invasion of Afghanistan for the apparent dual purposes of (a) once-and-for-all suppressing the growing insurgency, and (b) establishing a position of military strength from which it could influence affairs in Iran and Pakistan.

During this same period the Soviet Union supported North Vietnam in its war with South Vietnam, partly as a counter to Chinese aid and influence. Presumably partly as a result of U.S. failure in the Vietnam War, and the subsequent reluctance of the American public to support foreign interventions, the Soviet Union has markedly expanded its activities in Africa in the past several years. In late 1975, the Soviet Union gave assistance to the MPLA faction in Angola, and Soviet and more massive Cuban aid was largely responsible for MPLA success in the Angolan civil war. The strong Soviet acitivty in Africa may be considered in part an attempt at a strategic end run around the Middle East confrontation states in the direction of Middle East oil and sea lanes. Egypt, where the Soviet Union had a large adviser force and to which it had served as major arms supplier, asked the Soviets to leave in 1972, and then fought its most successful war against Israel (1973) without Soviet advice or personnel.

The devotion of resources to building up strategic nuclear weapons that had begun before Khrushchev's fall (October 1964) and increased greatly during the subsequent period of collective leadership, culminated in the achievement of rough parity about 1969. During the past decade, emphasis has shifted to conventional weapons development and buildup. Although realistic comparisons between the United States and the USSR are difficult to make, most authorities agree that the Soviet Union is greatly outspending the United States (by about 80 percent in overall military expenditures according to U.S. Department of Defense estimates), and that it not only greatly outnumbers the United States in manpower but outnumbers it in most conventional weapons categories as well. At the same time, the rough strategic nuclear equivalence that has been achieved could make it possible for the Soviet Union to threaten, or even to carry out, local or theater war without any certainty of the United States resorting to strategic nuclear war.

In land-based missiles, the Soviets now outnumber the United States, having deployed about 1,400. The fourth generation of Soviet ICBMs is now being deployed, replacing older missiles at the rate of 100 to 150 each year, and a fifth generation is being developed and nearing the flight-testing stage. All the new missiles now being deployed (SS-17, SS-18, and SS-19) can carry several MIRV warheads. The SS-17 and SS-19 are substantially larger than the U.S. Minuteman, and the SS-19 has especially high accuracy and nuclear yield. The SS-18 has attracted attention in the Western press because of its large size and throw weight (warhead). The Soviets have about 950 SALT-accountable SLBMs, most with single warheads. However, the MIRVed SS-N-18 is now being deployed in the new Delta III class. Like the SS-N-8, deployed in earlier Delta versions, it is a very long-range missile, capable of hitting U.S. targets from the Arctic and North Pacific. In strategic bombers, the United States outnumbers the USSR by more than 100 percent. Some Soviet bombers have cruise missiles, but the Soviets have nothing as sophisticated as the U.S. ALCMs (air-launched cruise missiles). The new Soviet bomber called Backfire by NATO is between a heavy and a medium bomber in its characteristics and capabilities. Whether or not it is to be treated as a heavy bomber for purposes of arms limitations has been a SALT stumbling block.

In USSR–U.S. disarmament negotiations, the crucial problem has always been Soviet insistence that there be no inspection, which meant no verification, of arms control compliance, versus U.S. insistence that there must be no disarmament without verification. Technology has eased this problem, with satellites and highly sophisticated cameras to make verification feasible without on-site inspection. Agreements ending antiballistic missile deployment and freezing for five years the number of fixed ICBM and SLBM launchers were signed in 1972. In SALT II negotiations, disagreement on whether to limit cruise missiles—important to U.S. strategy—and whether to consider the Soviet Backfire bomber a heavy bomber and thus subject to limitation, delayed the drafting of a treaty. The revelation (1978) that the Soviet Union has satellite ''killers'' that can shoot down observation satellites was disquieting, since it makes verification less sure. (See also disarmament discussion under United States.)

The Soviet law on military service promulgated in 1967 reduced the length of conscripted service, which is universal, to two years for the Strategic Rocket Forces, ground forces, air forces, air defense forces, and border defense units, and three for naval and border-defense-afloat personnel. Those called up who have advanced education have a one and a half-year obligation (two years for the navy). The call-up age is eighteen years, with inductions in May–June and November–December. Compulsory premilitary training is carried out in schools, factories, and collective farms by reservists, either officers or men, providing many older officers with jobs and giving the potential conscript some rudimentary military training. After active duty, servicemen are transferred to the reserves, where they remain until the age of fifty.

In an effort to prevent competent young officers from moving prematurely into the reserves, the law sets precise age limits on service by age, rank, and length of service. Marshals, four-star generals, and admirals never have to retire, but colonel generals must retire at sixty, lieutenant generals and major generals at fifty-five, colonels at fifty, lieutenant colonels and majors at forty-five, and captains and senior lieutenants at forty. Extensions of five and ten years are permitted under some circumstances. In the reserves, general officers continue to serve to age sixty-five, lieutenant colonels and colonels to sixty, and majors and below to fifty-five.

Educational requirements for Soviet officers are increasing steadily. More than 50 percent of the officer corps are technicians and engineers. There are more than 135 specialized military schools and 18 war colleges, with courses lasting from two to five years.

Soviet reinforcement planning allows for rapid mobilization of both reservists and active personnel in training

units to bring the understrength divisions (about half the total) to full complement. These units would have to be moved from the interior by rail or road and in many cases it would take some time for them to become operational. Nevertheless the fact that the Soviet Union maintains so many formations, if only as skeletons, and that it has some sixty divisions in Europe alone, means that it can deploy a very large number of combat strength divisions in central Europe within weeks of mobilization.

The Soviet army insists on the primacy of offensive action, involving rapid movement by mobile forces to bring a heavy concentration of armor into the enemy rear. This doctrine calls for army units to attack from the line of march and to cover up to 70 miles in twenty-four hours, operating along independent axes. A Soviet field army holding a sector of 70 to 80 miles would attack on a front of about 30 miles, with divisional attack frontages of about 7 miles each.

The overriding impression from a study of Soviet military literature is that the Soviet command is placing increasing reliance on airborne forces which it considers capable of performing strategic missions independently, both in direct relation to the Soviet Union and possibly to protect its interests in more distant areas. In the last fifteen years a great amount of money and time have been spent on developing transport aircraft, assault guns, multiple rocket launchers, and other equipment for use by airborne troops. Transport capacity appears to be adequate to move from two to three fully equipped divisions 1,000 miles in one lift.

The importance of the Soviet navy in the Soviet military establishment has been increased by new technological developments, and the extension of Soviet power and interests beyond the land perimeters of the USSR. The navy's prime missions are strategic strike and countering the strategic threat posed by the maritime strike capability of the western nations, particularly that of the United States. In fulfilling its missions, the Soviet navy must move out of the confines of its four fleet areas (Northern, Baltic, Black Sea, and Pacific) to the high seas. At the same time it must maintain the capability of cooperating with the Soviet army in coastal areas.

Although the organization of the Soviet navy has not changed much since the end of World War II, the strategic concept for its use is quite different. The cautious stationing of ships along the coast has given way to emphasis on global deployment. Soviet ships range over vast areas of the Atlantic and Pacific oceans. The task force in the Mediterranean is showing the Soviet flag and tying up the U.S. Sixth Fleet. There is also intensified Soviet naval activity in the Caribbean, south Atlantic Ocean, Indian Ocean, Persian Gulf, and Red Sea. The reopening of the Suez Canal has made it easier for the Soviets to maintain their naval presence in the waters of the Middle and Far East. The significance of this, both strategically and economically, in a world highly dependent upon the flow of oil from these areas, is enormous and will have great impact on U.S. as well as USSR military planning.

## STRATEGIC PROBLEMS

The USSR has long and difficult borders. Its western frontier in Europe is crossed by two major natural invasion routes from the west with little or no truly defensive terrain. Maintaining the integrity of the long border across Asia presents overwhelming military and logistic problems.

The geopolitical situation poses threats to the USSR from potential enemies on two fronts, Germany in the west and China in the east. Viewed through Soviet eyes and the perspective of history, the danger of attack from the west cannot be ignored merely because Germany today is different from the nation which twice attacked Russia during this century. Although China currently is militarily weak, its potential is enormous, and there is abundant historic and ideological hostility toward the USSR. Possible future collaboration between Japan and China would pose a potential threat to the Soviet Union, and the 1978 treaty of friendship and cooperation between those countries must be disturbing to Soviet strategists.

The mutual distrust and potentially explosive relationship between the USSR and the People's Republic of China has become an important element in the global balance of power. With the Chinese acquiring operational nuclear weapons, the Soviet strategic problem becomes more significant. Almost all cities and military and industrial complexes in the Soviet Far East and Central Asia are vulnerable to a surprise Chinese attack that could inflict heavy damage. Once the Chinese begin to deploy the new 3,500-mile-range missiles that they are already producing, they will be capable of hitting major targets in metropolitan Russia.

Although Sino-Soviet war may not be imminent, there is good evidence of preparation for it on both sides of the 4,000-mile frontier. The Soviets have expanded their forces in the frontier area from fifteen divisions to possibly as many as fifty motorized and tank divisions. This ground force of well over 800,000 men is supported by 75,000 border ground troops, more than 1,000 combat aircraft, and naval craft on the Amur River. Backing up these conventional forces are a substantial number of missiles with nuclear warheads.

The USSR, like the Tsarist regimes before it, has long been interested in Afghanistan. It is possible that increasing unrest in Afghanistan in the late 1970s, combined with growing Moslem fundamentalism such as that involved in the 1978–79 revolution in Iran, is seen as a threat to the southern SSRs with predominantly Moslem populations. Further, Afghanistan has been seen for more than a century as a possible way-station toward the old Russian dream of a warm-water outlet on the Indian Ocean. These considerations undoubtedly influenced the Soviet decision to invade Afghanistan in December 1979.

## MILITARY ASSISTANCE

It is estimated that the total value of military assistance provided by the USSR to thirty-five countries in Eastern Europe, Asia, the Near East, Africa, and Latin America since 1966 is $14.26 billion. Of this total, $6.3 billion has gone to the Near East, with Egypt ($2.47 billion) and Syria ($1.76 billion) the largest recipients. Asia received $3.71 billion, of which the largest sum, $2.99 billion, went to Vietnam. India and Iraq received $1.38 billion and $1.34 billion respectively.

## ALLIANCES

In addition to being a member of the UN and the leading member of the Warsaw Pact alliance, the USSR has bilateral treaties of friendship and mutual assistance with all other Communist nations (including the People's Republic of China), with the exception of Albania.

## STRATEGIC ROCKET FORCES

*Personnel:* 350,000

*Missile Inventory:*
Approximately 1,600 intercontinental ballistic missiles (ICBMs) with ranges of up to 7,500 miles
238 SS-9
830 SS-11
109 SS-7/8
 60 SS-13
 40 SS-17
 50 SS-18
150 SS-19

There are 91 silos under construction. Most missiles are liquid-fueled, resulting in a delayed reaction time. Some solid-fueled missiles are apparently now being deployed. Protection of launch sites is achieved by "hardening" in massive underground silos and by dispersion. Warhead yields range up to 25 megatons; some missiles have multiple warheads, and some models of the SS-9/17/18/19 are believed to be independently targeted.

Approximately 700 medium-range ballistic missiles (MRBMs) and intermediate-range ballistic missiles (IRBMs)
100 SS-5
 20 SS-20
500 SS-4

MRBMs have ranges up to 1,200 miles; IRBM ranges are up to 4,000 miles. These are deployed near Soviet land frontiers, and threaten Western Europe, Japan, and China. Most of these are also fixed-emplacement, liquid-fueled missiles in hardened sites. These earlier systems will be supplemented, and eventually replaced, by mobile, solid-fueled missiles, such as the SS-14.

## AIR DEFENSE COMMAND

*Personnel:* 550,000; about half in ground units (PVO-Voysk) and half in air operational units (PVO-Strany); ground units are supported by the army; air units by the air force.

*Antiaircraft Artillery Equipment:*
light artillery pieces: 23 mm and 57mm; for close-in defense 1,000 feet and below. Many of these are self-propelled, on tracked chassis, including the twin-barrelled ZSU-57/2, and the quadruple-barrelled ZSU-23/4.
medium artillery pieces: 85mm, 100mm, and 130mm; almost completely replaced by surface-to-air missiles.

*Surface-to-air missiles (SAMs):*
5,000 SA-2
4,500 other SAMs
  Fixed:
    SA-1 Guild*: roughly comparable to the U.S. Nike-Ajax; still deployed around Moscow
    SA-2 Guideline: a two-stage missile, with a slant range of 27 miles and intercept capability at altitudes from 1,000 to 80,000 feet. At least four versions exist (one for naval use), and the latest version is believed to have nuclear capability. The SA-2 has been used with ground forces.
    SA-3 Goa: a two-stage missile, intended primarily for low-altitude air defense. Three versions known to exist—one for naval use. Some SA-3 units may be assigned to ground forces air defense; range about 15 miles.
    SA-5 Griffon: a long-range SAM, also called Tallinn system, thought by some to have a limited ABM capability
  Mobile:
    SA-4 Ganef: twin-mounted on a tracked carrier, for use with ground forces, comparable in capabilities to Guideline but much more mobile

*This and all other code names are assigned by NATO.

    SA-6 Gainful: triple-mounted on a tracked carrier, intended as a low-altitude complement to Ganef with the ground forces
    SA-7
    SA-8
    SA-9

*Antiballistic Missile (ABM):*
  Galosh: a multistage missile deployed around Moscow; 64 launchers have missiles installed. It is presumed to have a range of several hundred miles with a warhead yield of more than one megaton. There are some indications that a more advanced version exists and will eventually replace some or all Galosh presently deployed.

*Fighter Aircraft:*
  2,700 defensive interceptor and all-weather fighters (MiG-17/19/21/25, Su-9/11/15, Yak-25/28, and Tu-28; most equipped with air-to-air missiles, Acrid, Alkali, Anab, Ash, Atoll, Awl)

*Airborne Warning and Control System (AWACS):*
  10 modified Tu-126 Moss turboprop transports carry airborne detection radars to detect and track enemy aircraft while vectoring interceptors toward these targets.

## ARMY (Ground Forces)

The Soviet army is prepared for both nuclear and conventional war. It is trained to advance on a broad front at high speed. Infantry is provided with covered armored personnel carriers to facilitate advance across radioactive terrain. All major Soviet units are equipped with tactical nuclear missiles, and are also well equipped for offensive and defensive chemical warfare. The conventional firepower of a Soviet division is comparable to that of a NATO division. Logistics, which was always the weakest point in the Soviet military system, is evidently being improved and adapted to the requirements of high-speed advance and the extended range of operations. Soviet organizational doctrine provides for limited numbers of support troops in the divisions, which therefore are dependent on higher echelons for support.

Soviet divisions have three degrees of combat readiness. Category I, 35 to 50 percent of the total, are divisions at, or near, full strength. These include the Soviet divisions in Eastern Europe and most of those stationed on the Chinese border. Category II, about one-quarter of the total, are divisions at more than half strength. Category III, the remaining one-quarter, are divisions at less than half strength. All divisions have full equipment, but much of it in categories II and III is in storage. In case of war, the Soviet army will probably return to the World War II front (army group) organization, with each front incorporating several combined arms armies, one or more tank armies, a tactical air army, missile and artillery units, airborne troops, and special forces.

Major components of a motorized rifle division are three motorized rifle regiments, one medium tank regiment, one artillery regiment, one each rocket artillery, FROG (surface-to-surface missile), engineer, antiaircraft, and signal battalion, a reconnaissance, helicopter, and chemical warfare company, and rear services units. All motorized rifle regiments have been upgraded in firepower and mobility. In addition, within the next few years most, if not all, Soviet divisions will be equipped with the T-62 main battle tank. Total strength is 10,485 men (1,094 officers, 9,391 enlisted), 188 tanks, 308 APCs, 48 howitzers, and 1,350 trucks.

The Soviet tank division consists of three medium tank regiments, one motorized rifle regiment, one each rocket launcher, FROG, antiaircraft, engineer, reconnaissance, and signal battalion, a helicopter company, and chemical warfare and rear services units. Total strength is 8,415 men, 316 tanks, c. 190 APCs, c. 1,300 trucks, and 10 to 15 helicopters.

Each airborne division has three airborne regiments, one artillery regiment, and one each engineer, multiple rocket launcher, signal, antiaircraft, medical, supply and transport, and maintenance battalion. There are also indications that a tactical nuclear missile (FROG) battalion recently became an organic part of the airborne division.

The trend in the Soviet army seems to be toward further improvement of the mobile striking forces and airborne forces. Operational and logistical exploitation of the helicopter, refinement of command and control, and management of the nuclear and conventional battle, including the concept of the automated battlefield, will increasingly occupy the attention of the Soviet command. There will be qualitative advances in conventional weapons and in the variety of nuclear missiles. Greater attention will be paid to officer training, especially in the technical fields.

*Personnel:* 1,750,000

*Organization:*
   17 military and special military districts
   102 motorized rifle divisions
   51 tank divisions
   7 airborne divisions
      Numerous artillery, engineering, signal, antiaircraft, chemical and missile units

*Deployment:*
   Eastern Europe
      31 divisions: 20 in Germany (Group of Soviet Forces, Germany) including 10 tank divisions; 4 in Hungary (Southern Group of Forces) including 2 tank divisions; 2 in

ing a tank division; 5 in Czechoslovakia (Central Group of Forces); all or most are in category I, or full readiness status.
   European USSR (west of Urals, north of Caucasus):
      60 divisions: includes 22 tank divisions: about 28 divisions in category II, and 14 in category III.
   Central USSR (Siberia, between the Urals and Lake Baikal):
      5 divisions: includes 2 tank divisions; all or most are category III, below half strength
   Southern USSR (Trans-Caucasus, Turkestan):
      28 divisions: includes 4 tank divisions; 2 divisions in category I; 4 in category II, and 5 in category III.
   Soviet Far East (east of Lake Baikal):
      51 divisions: about 21, including 10 tank divisions, are in category I; 21 are in category II; 2 of the 33 Far East divisions are in Mongolia (Soviet Forces, Mongolia).

*Major Equipment Inventory:*
   1,500+ heavy tanks (T-10, modification of JS-2/3, with 122mm gun)
   45,000+ medium tanks (T-62, with 122mm gun; T-54/55, both with 100mm gun; new T-64 and T-72)
   1,500+ light reconnaissance tanks (PT-76, amphibious, with 76mm gun)
   45,000 APCs (BMP, BRDM, BTR-60/50/40/152)
   3,000 heavy artillery pieces (152mm, 180mm, and nuclear-capable 203mm; many self-propelled)
   10,000 medium artillery pieces (122mm and 130mm; many self-propelled)
   6,000 light artillery pieces (82mm and 100mm; many self-propelled)
   10,000 antitank guns (57mm; some self-propelled ASU-57 85mm, 76mm, 100mm)
   2,000 truck-mounted rocket launchers, multibarrelled (240mm, 122mm, 140mm, 200mm, 250mm, 280mm)
   8,000 light antiaircraft pieces (14.5mm, 23mm, 57mm, 100mm towed, ZSU-52/2 and ZSU-23/4 self-propelled)
      mobile tactical missiles (Scud, FROG, and Scaleboard; ranges of 15 to 500 miles)
      Sagger antitank missiles

*Reserves:* At least nine million trained reserves are available for mobilization; of these about 500,000 are probably earmarked to bring Category II and III divisions, and supporting units, up to strength. The remainder are available as replacements and to create new units. Training is reported to be haphazard and inadequate.

## NAVY

With over 2,500 ships and about 1,300 aircraft, the Soviet navy ranks as the second largest in the world. The buildup in both scope and strength became obvious in the 1960s when new Soviet naval units started roaming all oceans. The Soviet navy is strong in surface ships, submarines, and a naval air force. It has the largest submarine force and the longest-range submarine missile in the world—a genuinely intercontinental ballistic missile and a range of at least 4,000 miles.

The commander in chief of the Soviet navy is directly under the minister of defense. The line of direct command goes from the commander in chief to the fleets and flotilla.

The Soviet navy has reorganized its naval infantry (a marine-type force) to increase its capability for intervention and amphibious landings. It is well equipped, trained, and led. The basic organizational structure of the naval infantry is the regiment. Naval infantry regiments are organized into several battalions. Elements include infantry, tanks, artillery, engineers, and frogmen. Each fleet has at least one regiment, the Pacific Fleet somewhat more.

*Personnel:* 400,000+ (includes naval air force of 50,000, and 12,000 naval infantry). About 175,000 are serving afloat.

*Organization:*
  Four fleets: Baltic Sea, Black Sea, Northern (Barents Sea), and Pacific Ocean.
  One flotilla: Caspian Sea

*Major units:*
Ballistic missile submarines:
  6 Delta III class (SSBN): nuclear powered; 16 SS-N-18 long-range (5,000 nautical miles) MIRVed missiles
  8 Delta II class (SSBN): nuclear powered; 16 SS-N-8 long-range (4,200 nautical miles) missiles
  15 Delta I class (SSBN): nuclear powered; 12 SS-N-8 missiles
  34 Yankee class (SSBN): nuclear powered; 16 SS-N-6/Sawfly medium-range (1,300 nautical miles) missiles (1 modified to fire the new long-range [2,500 nautical miles] SS-NX-17)
  1 Hotel III class (SSBN): nuclear powered; 3 SS-N-8 missiles
  7 Hotel II class (SSBN): nuclear powered; 3 SS-N-5/Serb theater (700 nautical miles) missiles (missiles not SALT accountable)
  13 Golf II class (SSB) long range; 3 SS-N-5/Serb missiles (not SALT accountable)
  9 Golf I class (SSB) long range; 3

SS-N-4/Sark theater (350 nautical miles) missiles (not SALT accountable); some may be in reserve
Cruise missile submarines:
  14 Charlie class (SSGN): nuclear powered; 8 SS-N-7 antiship missiles (30 nautical miles)
  1 Papa class (SSGN): nuclear powered; 10 possible SS-N-7 antiship missiles
  29 Echo II class (SSGN): nuclear powered; 8 SS-N-3/Shaddock (250 nautical miles) or new SS-N-12 (300 nautical miles) antiship missiles
  16 Juliett class (SSG): long range; 4 SS-N-3 antiship missiles
  8 Whiskey class (SSG): medium range; 2 or 4 SS-N-3 antiship missiles; one or more in reserve
Attack submarines:
  21 Victor class (SSN): nuclear powered
  13 November class (SSN): nuclear powered
  1 Alpha class (SSN): nuclear powered
  5 Echo class (SSN): nuclear powered
  7 Tango class (SS): medium-range; SS-N-15 SUBROC ASW weapon (25 nautical miles)
  4 Bravo class (SS): short-range
  59 Foxtrot class (SS): long-range
  15 Zulu class (SS): long-range; another 5 in reserve
  10 Romeo class (SS): medium-range
  54 Whiskey class (SS): medium-range; another 100 in reserve
  5 Quebec class (SS): short-range; another 15 in reserve
Aircraft carriers:
  2 Kiev class (CVH): 35 Forger VTOL fighters/Hormone helicopters; 8 SS-N-12 antiship missiles (300 nautical miles); SUW-N-1 ASW weapon; SA-N-3/Goblet and SA-N-4 (point defense) SAMs
Cruisers:
  2 Moskva class (CHG): 18 Hormone ASW helicopters; SUW-N-1 ASW weapon; SA-N-3 SAMs
  6 Kara class (CG): gas turbine propulsion; SS-N-14 ASW weapon, SA-N-3 and SA-N-4 SAMs
  10 Kresta II class (CG): SS-N-14 ASW weapon; SA-N-3 SAMs
  4 Kresta I class (CG): 4 SS-N-3 antiship missiles; SA-N-1/Goa SAMs
  4 Kynda class (CG); 8 SS-N-3 antiship missile launchers plus reloads on board; SA-N-1 SAMs
  10 Sverdlov class (CG/CL): 6-inch guns main armament; the one CG has SA-N-2/Guide-

line SAMs; the two command-type ships have SA-N-4 SAMs; the others have no missile systems.

1 Chapayev class (CL): 6-inch guns; no missiles

Destroyers:

19 Kashin class (DDG): gas turbine; SA-N-1 SAMs; several retrofitted with modified SS-N-2/Styx antiship missiles (25 nautical miles)

8 Kanin class (DDG): SA-N-1 SAMs

3 Mod.-Kildin class (DDG): modified SS-N-2 antiship missiles; one more in reserve

8 Kotlin class (DDG): 5.1-inch guns; SA-N-1 SAMs

18 Kotlin class (DD): 5.1-inch guns

14 Skoryy class (DD): 5.1-inch guns; another 25 in reserve

Frigates:

20 Krivak class (FF): gas turbine; SS-N-14 ASW weapon; SA-N-4 SAMs

1 Koni class (FF): gas turbine; SA-N-4 SAMs

37 Riga class (FF)

3 Kola class (FF): obsolete class used only in Caspian Sea

49 Petya class (FFL): combined diesel/gas turbine propulsion

20 Mirka class (FFL): combined diesel/gas turbine propulsion

Patrol combatants:

14 Nanuchka class (PGG): 6 SS-N-9 antiship missiles (60 nautical miles); SA-N-4 SAMs

1 Sarancha class (PGGH): 4 SS-N-9; SA-N-4 SAMs; hydrofoils fitted

## AIR FORCE

Tactical aviation with its ground attack and fighter-interceptor aircraft, light bombers and reconnaissance planes makes up the bulk of the air force. It is organized in 12 air armies. Long range aviation with nine air divisions is organized in three air armies, two of which are deployed in Europe and one in the Far East.

The Air Transport Command has over 2,000 transport planes. The largest aircraft in service is the Antonov AN-22 with a maximum range of nearly 6,000 nautical miles (nm), or over 2,500 nm with maximum load of 176,000 lb. The Soviet transport force is made up of 48 An-22, 800 An-12 (range 1,800 nm), 20 Il-76 (range 2,600 nm), and some Il-18s (range 2,000 nm). Military transport can readily be augmented by nearly 400 Aeroflot (Soviet airline) aircraft, Tu-104s, Tu-114s, Tu-124s, and Tu-134s.

There has been no let-up in the pace of modernization in the Soviet air force. About fifteen new types of Soviet aircraft have appeared in the past ten years.

*Personnel:* 255,000 (not including Air Defense units)

*Organization:*

Long-range Air Force
Intercontinental Bomber Force
  75 Mya-4
  75 Tu-20
Medium Bomber Force
  150 Tu-16
  300 Tu-22
  50 Backfire
Tactical Air Force (A tactical air army is based in each of these countries: East Germany, Poland, Czechoslovakia, and Hungary.)
Air Transport Command

*Major Aircraft Types* (not including Air Defense units):

9,650 combat aircraft
  150 strategic bombers
    75 Mya-4 Bison* long-range bombers
    75 Tu-20 Bear* long-range turboprop bombers (armed with Kangaroo ASM)
  500 medium bombers
    300 Tu-22 Blinder supersonic bombers (about half with Kitchen ASM)
    150 Tu-16 Badger bombers armed with Kelt ASM
    50 Backfire
6,000 fighter/fighter bombers
    MiG-17 Fresco
    MiG-19 Farmer
    MiG-21 Fishbed
    MiG-23 Flogger
    MiG-25 Foxbat
    MiG-27 Flogger D
    Su-7 Fitter
    Su-17 Fitter C
    Su-19 Fencer
    Yak-25 Flashlight
    Yak-28P Firebar
3,000 tactical attack light bombers
    Il-28 Beagle light bomber
    Yak-28 Brewer supersonic light bomber
9,565 other aircraft
    50 long-range tankers (converted Mya-4 and Tu-20 bombers)
2,000 short-, medium-, and long-range transports (Il-14 Crate, An-24 Coke, An-12 Cub, An-14 Clod, Il-18 Coot, and Il-76 Candid)
    15 heavy transports (An-22 Cock)

*One-sylllable NATO code names are for propeller (piston- or turbine-powered) aircraft; two-syllable names are for pure jet.

2,500 helicopters (Mi-1 Hare, Mi-4 Hound, Mi-6 Hook, Mi-8 Hip, Mi-10 Harke, Mi-12, Mi-24 Hind)

4,950 miscellaneous trainer/support aircraft which include trainer versions of operational aircraft

50 tactical reconnaissance aircraft (Yak-26 Mangrove)

*Reserves:* There is a highly trained air reserve totalling about 600,000 men. Most of the Aeroflot medium- and long-range civil airliners are convertible to military use.

*Air Bases:* There are about 500 air bases. Of these over 90 are in the Arctic or sub-Arctic regions. About two-thirds of the operational bases are in Europe.

## PARAMILITARY

There are approximately 300,000 MVD—internal security (125,000) and border troops (175,000); in addition, the Soviet DOSAAF (Volunteer Organization for Support of the Army, Air Force, and Navy) trains the population in basic military skills.

# UNITED KINGDOM OF GREAT BRITAIN AND NORTHERN IRELAND

## POWER POTENTIAL STATISTICS

Area: 94,214 square miles
Population: 55,846,000
Total Active Regular Armed Forces: 338,200 (0.60% population)
Gross National Product: $243.9 billion ($4,360 per capita)
Annual Military Expenditures: $12.8 billion (5.25% GNP)
Crude Steel Production: 22.3 million metric tons
Iron Ore Production: 4.6 million metric tons
Fuel Production:
 Coal: 123.8 million metric tons
 Crude Oil: 12 million metric tons

Refined Petroleum Products: 99.3 million metric tons
Natural Gas: 37.3 billion cubic meters
Manufactured Gas: 10.3 billion cubic meters
Electric Power Output: 283.5 billion kwh
Nuclear Power Production: 11,100 megawatts
Merchant Fleet (ships 1,000 tons and over): 1,377 ships; 30.5 million gross tons
Civil Air Fleet: 506 major transport aircraft

## DEFENSE STRUCTURE

The sovereign is the nominal commander in chief of all the armed forces. Actual control is exercised by the prime minister and the Cabinet, through the secretary of state for defence. Within the Cabinet all defense matters are considered by the Defence and Overseas Policy Committee, which includes the prime minister, the secretary of state for defence, the foreign secretary, the home secretary, the chancellor of the exchequer, and such others as are appointed by the prime minister; the secretary of state for defence is responsible to Parliament for carrying out the decisions of this committee and for administering the Ministry of Defence. His principal assistant in carrying out these tasks is a civil servant, the permanent under-secretary of state for defence.

Within the Ministry of Defence are the three service departments, each headed by an under-secretary of state (one each for navy, army, and air force), although each department retains its individual identity (Admiralty Board, Army Board, and Air Force Board). Directly under the secretary of state for defence, and next to him in rank within the Ministry, are two defence ministers, one for administration, the other for equipment. There is a Military Defence Staff, coordinating planning and operations for all of the services; each of the services retains its traditional General Staff (or equivalent); overall defense military planning is directed by the Chiefs of Staff Committee, under the chairmanship of the chief of the Defence Staff, and with the three service staff chiefs as members. Under the secretary of state is a Defence Council (of which he is chairman), responsible for exercising the powers of command and administrative control over the largely integrated services. Members of this council are: secretary of state, the two defence ministers, the three service parliamentary under-secretaries of state, the chief of the Defence Staff, the chiefs of the three service staffs, the chief scientist, and the permanent under-secretary of state for defence.

A substantial degree of military integration has been achieved through centralized operational directives to overseas commands, and through assignment of multi-service logistical responsibilities to various agencies of the three services; for instance, the navy is responsible for procurement of petrol, oil, and lubricants (POL).

## UNITED KINGDOM

BONNE PROJECTION

Copyright by C.S. Hammond & Co., N.Y.

SCALE OF MILES

0   20   40   60   80

KILOMETERS

0 10 20  40  60  80

Capitals of Countries ☆

Canals

## POLITICO-MILITARY POLICY

In the years since World War II it has been necessary for Britain to make a painful transition to relate policies to the facts of diminished power and wealth, and thus of reduced influence in world affairs. Nevertheless, residual reservoirs of power are substantial, including Britain's position as leader of the Commonwealth.

Traditionally the most important of Britain's politico-military objectives were to command the seas surrounding the British Isles; to maintain the European balance of power; to keep open the shipping lanes to Britain to provide food for the people and raw materials for industry; to protect overseas possessions and to encourage them (since 1783) to become self-governing and economically and militarily self-reliant within a worldwide British system (formerly called an empire, and more recently a commonwealth).

Among the most important traditional military policies supporting these objectives were the following: to undertake whatever military operations were necessary to prevent any major European power from controlling the Low Countries; to maintain a fleet at least as large and as powerful as the combined naval forces of the next two most powerful European maritime nations; to dominate the Mediterranean and the Middle East littoral; to avoid major land force involvement in a European war, but rather to encourage Continental allies to bear the brunt of land operations while Britain bore the major burden of naval and amphibious operations; to maintain major forces overseas, particularly in Asia and the Indian Ocean; to secure and protect overseas possessions and all sources of valuable materials.

It is probable that all of the cited objectives are still valid, within a more limited frame of reference. However, none of the major traditional policies listed above is fully applicable today. Thus Britain's need to protect itself through seapower requires emphasis on retaining a formal or informal alliance with the United States; its reduced ability to influence continental affairs, on the other hand, requires more direct involvement on the Continent and provision to Continental allies of substantial evidence of willingness to participate militarily, politically, and economically as an equal partner.

Slowly but inexorably the policies for dominating the Mediterranean, the Middle East, the Indian Ocean, and the rimlands of Southern Asia have been abandoned in the years since World War II. The last vestiges of these policies were the retention of control of the Persian Gulf, maintenance of major military forces at the principal exits from the Indian Ocean (Aden and Singapore), and the retention of other bases in the Indian Ocean. By 1974 even these vestiges of far-flung power east of Suez had been abandoned.

The British withdrawal from Aden was complete in 1968, and the Headquarters Far East Command at Singapore was closed November 1, 1971. It was succeeded by Headquarters ANZUK Force (Australian, New Zealand, United Kingdom). Malaysian and Singapore forces fill out this five-power command. The U.K. furnishes an infantry battalion group on station at Singapore, as well as Nimrod maritime patrol bombers and ASW helicopters. Patrolling the Indian Ocean and Mozambique Channel and the South China Sea are Royal Navy frigates. The RAF maintains staging posts at Masirah and Gan, and the navy has a base at Hong Kong. The army has five infantry battalions (three of them Gurkhas) and an artillery regiment there.

Britain relies upon voluntary enlistment to maintain its armed forces. To gain flexibility and attract recruits, volunteers are offered options of early release, on eighteen months' notice, provided they serve at least three years, though long-term service is still encouraged.

## STRATEGIC PROBLEMS

Britain's greatest strategic problem is its lack of sufficient raw materials to feed its population and its vital industries. It can obtain these raw materials only by sea, and thus is vulnerable to any hostile force capable of interfering with its overseas lanes of trade. It is this potential vulnerability that has been the principal determinant of British objectives and British policies since the end of the sixteenth century. Next in importance among Britain's strategic problems is its proximity to the continent of Europe, and its vulnerability to attack across the narrow waters of the English Channel and North Sea, and the even narrower waters of the Strait of Dover (22 miles across). This has been the basis of traditional British sensitivity to the possibility that a hostile power could establish dangerous bases in the Low Countries.

Another strategic vulnerability is the concentration of a large population, and of an extensive industrial complex, in a limited area. This vulnerability, which was serious in World War II, has become critical in the era of nuclear-armed missiles. This has convinced the British government and people—despite the changing political complexion of the leadership—that Britain must maintain an effective and convincing deterrent to possible aggression.

Within the past decade strong nationalist groups in Scotland and Wales have become significant. Their demands for autonomy or independence have brought about (1978) the passage by Parliament of the Devolution Bill, which provides for the establishment of Scottish and Welsh legislative assemblies with considerable powers for local autonomy. However, in referenda held in the two regions in 1979, devolution was not approved by the required 40 percent of the registered voters.

In Northern Ireland, approximately one-third of the population of about 1.5 million are Irish Catholics, with strong religious, cultural, and emotional ties with the people of the Republic of Ireland. More than half of the remainder are Scotch-Irish in origin and strongly Protestant, anti-Irish, and anti-Catholic in attitude. Feelings run high between these two groups, and are exacerbated by the activities of a group of terrorists claiming to be members of the outlawed Irish Republican Army. The terrorists, disavowed by the government of Ireland, are seeking to bring about the union of Northern Ireland with Ireland by employing urban guerrilla tactics of murder, arson, and bombing. In an effort to control the situation, Britain has employed at times as many as seventeen major units of all services on internal security duty in Northern Ireland. In early 1978, there were 14,000 U.K. troops in Northern Ireland, and naval units patrolling offshore to intercept arms runners. The height of the violence was reached in 1972, when 482 people were killed; by 1977 the number had dropped to 111. Violence continued at this level, however, and the Provisional IRA—the "Provos," a more violent wing of the group—promised a ten-year guerrilla war against the British.

As Britain developed sizable black and Asian populations in the 1960s and 1970s, from its former overseas possessions, racial antagonisms developed, erupting in violence. The National Front, right-wing and racist, aimed its appeals at working-class white Britons. Scores of demonstrators and policemen were injured in riots in London and Birmingham in 1977. Although there was no immediate threat to internal security, the violent attacks on Britain's traditionally unarmed policemen were destructive of public confidence in order and safety, especially since they followed a period of bloody IRS terrorist bombings in England that had peaked in 1974 and 1975 and then tapered off.

One strategic security problem is the preservation of control over certain overseas territories where British rights or sovereignty are challenged. Most important among these is Gibraltar, which Spain seeks to regain, demanding that Britain renounce the rights gained by the Treaty of Utrecht in 1713. Of less significance are Belize, where British rights are disputed by neighboring Guatemala, and the Falkland Islands, claimed by Argentina.

In 1973 Britain and Iceland became involved in a "Cod War" over fishing rights off Iceland's coasts. After numerous incidents between fishing trawlers and Icelandic gunboats, the British government sent three frigates to the area. Temporary agreement was finally reached in October, limiting catches, numbers of boats, and areas in which they might fish. The issue is not resolved, however, since Iceland apparently intends to defy a ruling in favor of Britain by the International Court of Justice.

## MILITARY ASSISTANCE

In the sense that it relies to a considerable degree upon the United States for the production of all or parts of many of the most expensive weapons systems, Britain has been the recipient of U.S. military assistance. For the most part, however, American aid has taken the form of making available weapons and equipment for purchase by Britain. A small military advisory group (currently one civilian employee) is stationed in Britain.

Over the years since World War II Britain has provided to other nations far more military aid than it received from the United States. Most of this assistance has been given to other Commonwealth nations, and mainly to those that have received their independence since 1945.

## ALLIANCES

The United Kingdom, a UN member with a permanent seat on the Security Council, is a participant in seven major alliances, and a number of lesser or subsidiary bilateral alliances.

First, Britain is the leading member of the Commonwealth of Nations. The sovereign of Great Britain is accepted by all members of this free association of independent states as the head of the Commonwealth. There is no other tangible link, and the objectives of the members are rarely in full accord with each other. The purposes of the alliance are vague, but generally are economic in practical effect. Nevertheless, there are implied political and military commitments, more demanding upon Britain and the other English-speaking members, perhaps, than on the others. The members of the Commonwealth are: United Kingdom, Canada, Australia, New Zealand, India, Sri Lanka, Ghana, Nigeria, Cyprus, Sierra Leone, Jamaica, Trinidad and Tobago, Uganda, Kenya, Malaysia, Tanzania, Malawi, Malta, Zambia, Gambia, Singapore, Guyana, Botswana, Lesotho, Barbados, Mauritius, Bahamas, Bangladesh, Swaziland, Tonga, Western Samoa, and Fiji. The United Kingdom has separate defense agreements or understandings with most of these, and provides most with various forms of military assistance.

The United Kingdom is also a member of the two remaining major regional alliances established between 1950 and 1954 to deter threatened Communist aggression in Europe and Asia: NATO and SEATO. Related to NATO is the earlier Western European Union (WEU) which was established by the Brussels Treaty between Britain, France and the Benelux countries in 1948, and has been enlarged by the addition of Italy and West Germany.

Britain in 1971 joined with Malaysia, Singapore, Australia, and New Zealand in the so-called Five-Power

Pact for the defense of British Commonwealth interests in Southeast Asia (see Malaysia).

Britain's principal alliance is that with the United States. A special relationship between these two nations has existed since Prime Minister Winston Churchill and President Franklin D. Roosevelt met aboard warships in Argentia Bay, off Newfoundland, in August 1941. Rarely, if ever, have two major powers established so close and cordial a wartime alliance as that which existed between them in World War II. The peacetime relationship that followed is equally unprecedented. America's ties with Canada are perhaps closer than those with the United Kingdom, but the Canadian alliance is one for the defense of the homelands of the participants, one being a major partner and the other a relatively minor one. In the continuing Anglo-American alliance the United Kingdom is, perforce, now a junior partner, but nonetheless still a major power with worldwide interests, influence, and commitments. This alliance between the two major English-speaking nations is perhaps the most powerful force for peace in the world today.

The United Kingdom joined the European Common Market on January 1, 1973, without relinquishing its membership in the European Free Trade Association (EFTA), a step which followed the trend of its foreign trade and was widely considered to augur further changes in foreign policy.

## ARMY

*Personnel:* 178,700

*Organization:*
- 1 corps headquarters
- 4 division headquarters
- Armor
  - 11 armored regiments
  - 8 armored reconnaissance regiments
- Artillery
  - 13 field regiments
  - 1 missile regiment
  - 1 heavy regiment
  - 1 commando regiment
  - 3 air defense regiments
  - 1 guided weapons regiment
  - 1 locating regiment
- Engineers
  - 9 regiments
  - 1 amphibious regiment
- Infantry
  - 50 battalions
  - 5 Gurkha battalions
- Special Air Service
  - 1 regiment

*Deployment:*
- In Great Britain
  - U.K. Land Forces including
    - U.K. element of SACEUR's (Supreme Allied Command Europe) Strategic Reserve (Land)
    - U.K. element of ACE (Allied Command Europe) Mobile Force (Land)
    - Forces for reinforcing BAOR (British Army of the Rhine) and forces for the defense of the U.K. Base
    - SAS (Special Air Service) Regiment
    - 1 Gurkha infantry battalion
- In Northern Ireland
  - Headquarters Northern Ireland
    - 3 brigade headquarters
    - 1 armored reconnaissance regiment
    - 3 armored reconnaissance squadrons
    - 3 field engineer squadrons
    - 13 units in infantry role
    - 1 SAS squadron
    - 2 army air corps squadrons
    - 11 Ulster Defense Regiment (UDR) battalions
- In West Germany
  - British Army of the Rhine (BAOR)
    - 1 corps headquarters
    - 1 armored division
    - 2 division headquarters
    - 4 armored brigades
    - 1 field force
    - 2 artillery brigades
- In Berlin
  - 1 infantry brigade
- In Cyprus
  - 1 armored reconnaissance squadron
  - 1 engineer squadron
  - 1 infantry battalion
  - 2 infantry companies
  - 1 detachment army air corps
- At Gibraltar
  - 1 engineer squadron
  - 1 infantry battalion
- At Malta
  - 1 commando artillery battery (including a commando engineer troop)
- In Belize
  - 1 armored reconnaissance troop
  - 1 artillery battery
  - 1 engineer troop
  - 1 infantry battalion
  - 1 detachment army air corps
- In Brunei
  - 1 Gurkha infantry battalion

In Canada
   British army training unit
In Hong Kong
   1 Gurkha engineer squadron
   1 U.K. infantry battalion
   3 Gurkha infantry battalions
   1 squadron army air corps
In Oman
   British army training team
   1/2 engineer squadron

*Major Equipment Types:*
1,000 Chieftain heavy tanks
  175 Scorpion armored reconnaissance vehicles
   50 Scimitar armored reconnaissance vehicles
   75 Saladin armored scout cars
  500 Ferret armored scout cars
   40 Fox armored scout cars
  350 Saracen armored personnel carriers
  500 Trojan armored personnel carriers
  100 Spartan armored personnel carriers
   75 Abbot 105mm SP howitzers
   35 M-109 155mm SP howitzers
   20 M-107 175mm SP howitzers
   10 M-110 203mm SP howitzers
      mortars (51mm, 81mm)
      recoilless antitank guns (84mm, 120mm)
      antitank rocket launchers (LAW M-72)
      Vigilant Swingfire ATGM
      Honest John, Lance SSM
      40mm antiaircraft guns
      Rapier, Thunderbird, Blowpipe SAM
  200 helicopters (Scout, Sioux, Lynx, Gazelle)
      light aircraft (Beaver)

*Reserves:* The Army Regular Reserves numbers 110,000.
The Territorial Army and Voluntary Reserve numbers
60,100. The Ulster Defence Regiment numbers 7,600.

# NAVY

*Personnel:* 71,500

*Organization:*
Commander in Chief, Fleet (headquarters, Northwood)
Polaris Force
Royal Marines (four 800-man commandos with a
   brigade headquarters, the balance of the force
   serving on various duties afloat and ashore)

*Major Units:*
Operational Fleet
   4 ballistic missile nuclear-powered submarines
      (Resolution class; Polaris SLBMs; SSBN)

   9 nuclear-powered submarines (3 Swiftsure, 5
      Valiant, 1 Dreadnought class; SSN)
  17 diesel-powered submarines (13 Oberon, 5
      Porpoise class; SS)
   1 aircraft carrier (Ark Royal class; CV; 39 air-
      craft)
   2 V/STOL-helicopter aircraft carriers (1
      Hermes class, 1 Bulwark class; CVH)
   2 helicopter cruisers (Tiger class; short-range
      Seacat SAMs; CH; 4 helicopters)
   8 guided missile cruisers (1 Type 82 class, Sea
      Dart SSMs/SAMs; 7 County class, Seaslug
      SAMs, Seacat SAMs, Exocet SSMs; CG)
   6 guided missile destroyers (Sheffield class; Sea
      Dart SAMs/SSMs; DDG)
  54 frigates (FF)
      8 Amazon class (Seacat SAMs and Exocet
         SSMs, both short-range)
     25 Leander class (Seacat SAMs and Exocet
         SSMs, both short-range)
      7 Tribal class (Seacat short-range SAMs)
      9 Rothesay class (Seacat short-range
         SAMs)
      5 miscellaneous classes (1 with Seacat
         short-range SAMs)
  10 patrol ships (PGF)
   6 patrol craft (PC)
   4 fast patrol craft (PCF)
   2 amphibious assault transport docks (Seacat
      short-range SAMs; LPD)
   7 tank landing ships (LST)
   2 medium landing craft (LSM)
   3 utility landing craft (army-operated; LCU)
  25 mechanized landing craft (8 assigned to
      LPDs; LCM)
   3 special warfare support craft (LCW)
  30 personnel landing craft (8 assigned to LPDs)
   1 minelayer (MM)
  16 coastal minehunters (MSHC)
  18 coastal minesweepers (MSC)
   5 inshore minesweepers (MSI)
   4 hovercraft (patrol and amphibious warfare)
  70 auxiliary ships
 150 service craft

Reserve Fleet, refit or conversion, standby
   1 ASW carrier (CVS)
   7 submarines
      1 Polaris (SSBN)
      3 fleet submarines (SSN)
      3 Oberon class submarines (SS)
   1 assault ship (LPD)
   2 guided missile destroyers (DLG)
   8 general purpose frigates (DEG)
   2 antiaircraft frigates (DER)

2 aircraft directional frigates (DER)
1 antisubmarine frigate (DE)
4 coastal minesweepers/minehunters (MSC)
4 maintenance, support, auxiliaries

Fleet Air Arm
1 squadron Buccaneer (Strike) on CV
1 flight Gannet (AEW) on CV
1 squadron Phantom fighter on CV
1 squadron Gannet (AEW) at RAF station
5 squadrons Sea King helicopters (ASW)
   1 on CV
   1 on CVH
   2 on CG
   1 at Prestwick, Scotland
1 squadron Sea King helicopters (training) at shore station
40 flights Wasp helicopters (ASW) on FF and DDG
1 squadron Wasp helicopters (training) at shore station
7 flights Wessex helicopters (ASW) on DDG
2 squadrons Wessex helicopters (training) at shore stations
2 squadrons Wessex helicopters (Commando assault) on CVH
1 squadron Wessex helicopters (fleet requirements) at shore station

*Deployment:*
In Great Britain
  Commander in Chief Fleet
  Polaris Force
  other ships of the fleet, including those assigned to EASTLANT
  brigade headquarters, Royal Marines
  Royal Marine Commandos
In Northern Ireland
  1–2 CMS patrols
  1–2 fleet tenders
In North Sea
  frigates
  destroyer (STANAVFORLANT)
  submarines
  MCMV (STANFORCHAN)
  survey vessels
In North Norway
  Royal Marine Commando group (including 1 commando artillery battery and 1 commando engineer troop)
At Gibraltar
  1 frigate
At Malta
  Royal Marine Commandos
In the Mediterranean
  1 CVS
  destroyers

  frigates
  submarines
  1 frigate (NAVOCFORMED)
  1 survey ship
In Antarctica
  1 ice patrol ship
In the Caribbean
  1 group on deployment (includes submarine)
  1 LPD (training cruise)
  1 frigate
In the Falkland Islands
  Royal Marine detachment
In Hong Kong
  patrol craft

*Reserves:* The Royal Navy and Marine Regular Reserves number 30,600. The Volunteer Reserves and Auxiliary Forces number 6,700.

*Major Naval Bases:* Portsmouth, Devonport, Chatham, Rosyth, Portland, Gibraltar, Hong Kong

## AIR FORCE

*Personnel:* 88,000

*Organization and Deployment:*
In Great Britain
  RAF Strike Command
    Strike/Attack
      6 bomber squadrons (Vulcan)
      2 attack squadrons (Buccaneer)
    Air Defense
      2 fighter-interceptor squadrons (Lightning)
      5 fighter squadrons (Phantom)
    Reconnaissance
      1 photo reconnaissance squadron (Canberra)
      1 strategic reconnaissance squadron (Vulcan)
      1 tactical reconnaissance squadron (Jaguar)
    Offensive Force
      1 fighter-bomber squadron (Harrier; VTOL)
      2 squadrons Jaguar
    Airborne Early Warning
      1 squadron Shackleton
    Maritime Patrol
      4 patrol squadrons (Nimrod)
    Strategic Transport
      1 squadron VC-10
    Tactical Transport
      4 squadrons Hercules

Helicopter Support
    1 squadron Wessex
    2 squadrons Puma
Tanker
    2 tanker squadrons (Victor)
Search and Rescue
    ½ squadron Wessex
    1½ squadrons Whirlwind
Surface-to-air Missiles (SAM)
    1 squadron Bloodhound
    1 squadron Rapier
RAF Support Command
  light transports
  helicopters
  trainers
  miscellaneous support
  air elements of UKMF (United Kingdom Mobile
    Force) and ACE
  RAF regiment squadrons
In Northern Ireland
  helicopters (Puma, Wessex)
  1 RAF regiment squadron
In North Sea
  Victor tanker
  Nimrod patrol
  Vulcan maritime reconnaissance
In West Germany
  RAF Germany
    Strike/Attack
      2 attack squadrons (Buccaneer)
      4 fighter-bomber squadrons (Jaguar)
    Air Defense
      2 fighter squadrons (Phantom)
    Reconnaissance
      1 photo reconnaissance squadron
        (Canberra)
      1 strategic reconnaissance squadron
        (Vulcan)
      1 tactical reconnaissance squadron
        (Jaguar)
    Offensive Support
      2 fighter-bomber squadrons (Harrier;
        VTOL)
    Helicopter Support
      1 squadron Wessex
    Surface-to-air missiles (SAM)
      1 squadron Bloodhound
      4 squadrons Rapier
    RAF regiment squadrons
In Cyprus
  1 helicopter squadron (Whirlwind)
  1 RAF regiment squadron
At Gibraltar
  1 fighter-bomber squadron (Hunter)

At Malta
  Canberra reconnaissance
  Nimrod patrol
In Belize
  Puma helicopters
  RAF regiment detachment
  radar detachment
At Hong Hong
  1 helicopter squadron (Wessex)
In Oman
  RAF detachments Salalah, Masirah

*Major Aircraft Types:*
548 combat aircraft
  60 Vulcan bombers
  40 Buccaneer attack aircraft
140 Jaguar fighter-bomber/reconnaissance
  10 Hunter fighter-bombers
  40 Lightning fighter-interceptors
126 Phantom fighters
  18 Canberra reconnaissance
  10 Vulcan reconnaissance
  54 Harrier fighter-bombers
  12 Shackleton AEW
  38 Nimrod patrol
905 other aircraft
    8 VC-10 transports
  48 Hercules transports
  50 Wessex helicopters
  25 Puma helicopters
    8 Whirlwind helicopters
  16 Victor tankers
  50 light transports (HS-125, Basset Pembroke)
700 trainers/miscellaneous support (Chipmunk,
    Jet Provost, Jetstream, Bulldog, Gnat,
    Hawk)

*Major Air Bases:* Stanmore, Wattisham, Conningsby, Oldham, Brampton, Linton-on-Ouse, White Waltham, Waterbeach, Bassingbourne, Binbrook, Coltishall, Chivenor, Finningley, Gaydon, Stradishall, Syerston, Leeming, Oakington, Aclington, Waddington, Cottesmore, Scampton, St. Mawgan, Wyton, Marham, Wittering, Kinloss, Ballykelly, Lindholm, Church Fenton, Lynham, Odiham, Bawtry, Topcliffe, St. Anthan, Benson, Mancy, Shawbury, Boscombe, High Wycombe, Upavon, Brize Norton, Abingdon, Fairford, Pitreavie

*Reserves:* The Royal Air Force Regular Reserves number 33,300. The Volunteer Reserves and Auxiliary Forces number 300.

# UNITED STATES OF AMERICA

## POWER POTENTIAL STATISTICS

Area: 3,628,150 square miles (50 states, including interior waterways and bodies of water)

Population: 219,334,000

Total Active Regular Armed Forces: 2,989,000 (1.36% population)

Gross National Product: $1,890 billion ($7,890 per capita)

Annual Military Expenditures: $113 billion (5.98% GNP); FY 1980 budget: $135.5 billion

Crude Steel Production: 116.3 million metric tons

Iron Ore Production: 80.5 million metric tons

Fuel Production:

  Coal: 609.5 million metric tons

  Lignite: 22.8 million metric tons

  Crude Oil: 401.6 million metric tons

  Refined Products: 700.6 million metric tons

  Natural Gas: 559 billion cubic meters

  Manufactured Gas: 25.8 billion cubic meters

Electric Power Output: 2 trillion kwh

Nuclear Power Production: 82,200 megawatts

Merchant Fleet (ships 1,000 tons and over): 600 ships; 14.7 million gross tons

Civil Air Fleet: 2,716 major transport aircraft

## DEFENSE STRUCTURE

Under the U.S. Constitution, responsibility and authority for national defense are divided between the executive and legislative branches of government. The president is commander in chief of the armed forces in peace and war; he is responsible for the formulation and execution of defense policy and for the administration of the defense establishment. His administrative defense responsibilities are carried out by the Department of Defense, whose top officials he appoints; these officials also assist him in policy making. In addition, the National Security Council advises the president on all matters related to national security—whether foreign, domestic, or military. Its staff is headed by the president's assistant for national security affairs. In the past few administrations, when this official was McGeorge Bundy (Kennedy and Johnson), Walt W. Rostow (Johnson), Henry Kissinger (Nixon), or Zbigniew Brzezinski (Carter), he has exerted major influence on strategic issues.

The Constitution gives Congress the authority to "raise and support" the armed forces; these general military powers are largely exercised through the making or withholding of appropriations. Congress also has the sole constitutional power to declare war. Although the president has in the past, as commander in chief, ordered military action short of declared war, the 1973 War Powers Act now requires that any emergency military action by a president must cease after thirty days if it has not been approved by Congress.

During and after World War II, there was a considerable increase in the practical powers of the executive branch over military policy and posture, with a corresponding decrease in congressional power. In recent years, two developments have led Congress to make vigorous, and to some extent successful, efforts to regain its eroded prerogatives: (1) the long and frustrating Vietnam War, initiated and conducted by successive presidents and their Defense Department officials; (2) the fears engendered by the Watergate affair of a strong and irresponsible presidency, and the opportunity thus offered congressmen to place pressure on the president. In addition to passing the 1973 War Powers Act, Congress has placed specific restrictions on the foreign military assistance the executive branch may give, including prohibition of aid or sales to Chile, and restrictions on sales to countries that include Argentina, Uruguay, and Turkey, as well as all factions in Angola.

One manifestation of congressional resurgence in national security affairs is its much more active role in setting priorities for defense spending. Formerly, Congress merely pruned executive budget requests, and occasionally increased funds, but now some defense policy is actually made in Congress by shifting of sizable blocks of funds from one military service or weapons system to another. An example is Congress's push for a stronger role for the navy than that which the Defense Department wanted in fiscal year (FY) 1979. This approach is in part made possible by congressional aides who have special knowledge and experience in a variety of defense areas; these men constitute a newly powerful force in the making of military policy.

Under the 1947 National Security Act, as amended, the Department of Defense (DOD) is a unified instrument for policy and action under the direction of the secretary of defense. The three autonomous military departments (Army, Navy, and Air Force, with the Marine Corps within the Navy Department), and their civilian secretaries, are subject to the centralized authority of the secretary of defense. For instance, supply purchases for all services are made by one Defense Supply Agency; the Readiness Command is a mission-centered headquarters made up of both army and air force elements; and weapons development for all services is coordinated by the DOD director of research and engineering.

Recent changes (1976, 1977) in U.S. strategic intelligence organizations are designed to improve their coordination, restrict their activities, and bring them under firmer

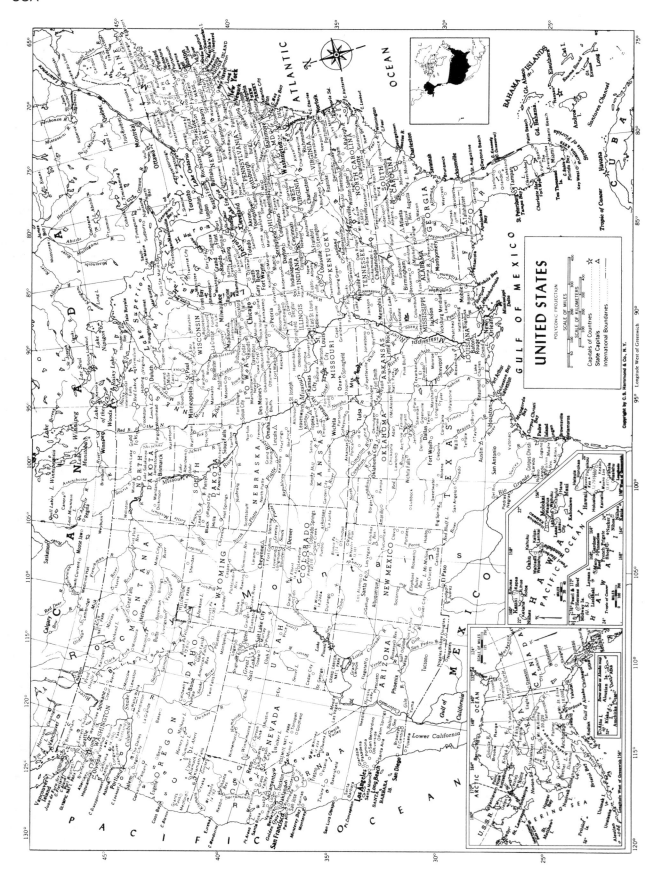

UNITED STATES

POLYCONIC PROJECTION

SCALE OF MILES

SCALE OF KILOMETERS

Capitals of Countries ☆
State Capitals ☆
International Boundaries

Copyright by C. S. Hammond & Co., N.Y.

control of constitutional authorities. Central Intelligence Agency appropriations are now subject to detailed congressional review. The director of the CIA controls funds for all intelligence agencies and also has been designated head of a proposed National Intelligence Tasking Center (December 1977). At the same time, a 20 percent cutback in the CIA operations division indicates a curtailment of covert operations, all of which the president must now approve. Formerly the intelligence agencies of the army, navy, and air force were under the Defense Intelligence Agency (DIA); the new organization places them—and also the DIA—operationally directly under the CIA.

## POLITICO-MILITARY POLICY

Nuclear explosives and the great military power of the hostile Soviet Union have been the major determinants of U.S. military policy since World War II. The United States found itself in the early 1950s in the position of world leader against continued Communist-Soviet encroachment. The strategic policy adopted was containment of communism; the method adopted was building U.S. military strength, plus collective security through a system of mutual assistance treaties and military and economic aid to friendly and neutral countries. With the growing power of the (Communist) People's Republic of China, containment of China was implicitly added to U.S. policy.

Overall U.S. foreign and defense policy now appears to be in a period of transition, and the new policy that will emerge is not yet certain. Some landmarks stand clearer than ever: protection of U.S. freedom and sovereignty through unsurpassed military strength; unquestioned commitment to defend the NATO allies and to help build up their defenses; determination to remain a strong Pacific power; and willingness to use force and risk war if vital U.S. interests are involved. However, the firm, undergirding, consensus-supported policy of containment of communism that was the guide for all decisions for twenty-five years is no longer solid. Establishment of full diplomatic relations with Communist China (1979) suggested a possible move toward supporting that country as a counter-weight to the Soviet Union. The Vietnam experience has strongly impressed the American people with the cost of war and the complexity of the issues involved (the absence of "good guys" and "bad guys"), and has left them and their elected representatives severely shaken in their previous confidence in the ability of military technology and U.S. military effort to achieve policy goals. Yet nothing has thus far taken the place of containment as a cohesive, coordinating, overall policy to which all major decisions can be referred.

In the post-Vietnam era, Congress gives and withholds military aid funds on a country-by-country basis that pays little heed to restricting the spread of Soviet- or China-backed regimes. Detente with the Soviet Union and diplomatic contact with Communist China, both begun in 1972, have given a new, more constructive tone to relations with those countries, but they have not replaced, and realistically cannot replace, containment as an overall guiding policy. The Soviet Union remains a powerful state with a political value system antithetical to that of the United States, a dangerous potential enemy with devastating power, and a formidable and aggressive world economic rival.

The need to ensure supplies of oil from the Arab states has contributed to a new degree of military assistance and diplomatic support for these states. At the same time, the U.S. commitment to Israel's independence remains firm. The Carter administration expressed and implemented these two policy positions in 1978 by narrowly wrenching through Congress an arms sales package that will send U.S. jet fighters to Saudi Arabia and Egypt, as well as to Israel.

Since the beginning of the nuclear era, the United States has moved, in nuclear weapons strength relative to the Soviet Union, from holding a monopoly on nuclear weapons, to having a preponderance of nuclear strength, to the current position of rough equivalence. Rough equivalence is now U.S. policy.

Quantities of weapons are only the beginning of nuclear strategy, however. The problem of national defense in the era of weapons too destructive to use has been formidable. The U.S. approach on strategic nuclear weapons, fairly consistently pursued, has been toward ample power to wreak unacceptable destruction, deployed in such a way as not to provoke attack, accompanied by efforts to limit mutually the quantity, destructiveness, and provocativeness of the weapons deployed.

Production of long-range nuclear-warhead missiles, emphasized in the late Eisenhower administration to close the hypothetical missile gap with the Soviet Union, gave the United States a preponderance of nuclear offensive power. In the early 1960s efforts were concentrated on protecting (hardening) and dispersing the missile launching sites, thus resulting in relative invulnerability of missiles to enemy attack, without making them more provocative. The same purpose was served by the development of nuclear-powered submarines, with the ability to cruise under water at great speed, for long periods, and armed with long-range Polaris nuclear-warhead missiles.

During the early 1960s mutual nuclear deterrence of the United States and USSR became fairly stable, with each nation having enough striking power to retain the capability to inflict "unacceptable" damage on its adversary after receiving a first nuclear strike. U.S. policy was that this condition was better than the instability, uncertainty, and consequent danger of nuclear war that might result from deployment of new weapons systems.

In 1974 Defense Secretary James R. Schlesinger proposed that the U.S. targeting strategy of ensuring survivability for a second-strike force that was targeted on Soviet cities be changed to a new, more flexible policy. Citing USSR missile projects with the "potential net throw weight [i.e., the potential total nuclear yield] for a major counterforce capability," he urged that the United States must not fall behind but must also develop the capacity to strike at Soviet missile forces, that is, to deliver counterforce strikes. Approved by NATO and Congress that year, the counterforce capability remains basic U.S. deterrence strategy.

U.S. policy, in fulfillment of this strategy, calls for a triad of strategic bombing weapons systems—ICBMs, SLBMs (submarine-launched missiles), and lower-level penetration bombers—on the assumption that this diversity will ensure that some missile deliveries will survive to reach their targets. So far as theater war is concerned—war other than general nuclear war—U.S. strategic planning calls for the capability to fight one and a half wars simultaneously—that is, a major war in Europe, plus a smaller war elsewhere.

During the past few years there has been increased concern in the Defense Department and the military service about U.S.-NATO capability to meet a Soviet–Warsaw Pact conventional warfare attack in Europe. With nuclear deterrence at least temporarily stable, the relative danger of such a conventional attack has increased, and Soviet bloc forces outnumber U.S.-NATO forces in Europe in manpower and, especially, in tanks and other conventional weapons. Fearful that Warsaw Pact strength might prevail in such a conventional struggle "below the nuclear threshold," defense officials had, by mid-1976, been successful in convincing Congress of the urgency of upgrading the U.S. conventional warfare capability.

During 1977, the number of U.S. servicemen and servicewomen stationed overseas increased by 27,000, to 490,000, reversing a downward trend that had continued since 1968. The number in West Germany increased by 15,800, the largest jump, bringing the total there to 224,300.

In 1977, President Carter announced plans for a five-year U.S. troop withdrawal from Korea, with 6,000 to be withdrawn by the end of 1978. With Japan's concern, and strong opposition from Congress, revisions were made wherein only 800 combat troops and 2,600 support personnel were to be withdrawn by the end of 1978. Also added were assurances of increased U.S. military aid and the continued protection of the U.S. nuclear "umbrella." Following reports in 1979 of large increases in North Korean forces, withdrawal of the remaining 32,000 troops was postponed until at least 1981.

By 1978 it was clear that the Soviet Union was engaged in a rapid buildup of its armaments, and was surpassing the United States in many new categories, including naval vessels (principal surface combatants) and tactical aircraft.

Opposition to defense spending, which had been strong in Congress and among the U.S. public following the Vietnam War, had bottomed out two years earlier. Although President Carter's campaign statements appeared to call for cuts in defense spending, and Secretary of Defense Harold Brown has stressed defense economy, the president's proposed defense budget for fiscal year 1980 is $135.5 billion, up from $126 billion in fiscal 1979. Inflation accounts for most of the increase, but another indication of somewhat increased administration commitment to defense spending is the percentage it represents of total federal budget outlays: 30.2 percent in 1973, down to 22.8 percent in 1978, slightly up to at least 23 percent in 1979, with administration projections placing it at 25 percent for 1983.

The Defense Appropriations Act for fiscal 1977 included, for the first time, the Culver-Nunn Amendment, which provided for measures to standardize U.S. military equipment and weapons with those of other NATO countries; new weapons were to be interoperable, and the United States would buy some weapons manufactured by its NATO allies. The trend toward increased support for NATO has continued, is evident in the Defense Department's fiscal 1979 fund requests for buildup of NATO land forces, and has been stressed in statements by Secretary Brown. Talk about possible withdrawal of U.S. troops from Europe, common in the press and by government officials several years ago, has ceased. (However, the increased emphasis on support for NATO, without a sharply increased budget, has forced sharp cutbacks in funds for training and maintenance, which many military men consider worrisome and unwise.)

The proposed fiscal 1979 budget showed sharp cuts in navy shipbuilding, reflecting Defense Department concern over serious past cost overruns and doubts as to the relative importance of the navy's mission. However, strong navy supporters in Congress succeeded in restoring much navy funding. Their efforts were made easier by the strong increase in the Soviet navy and the large number of Soviet ships in the Atlantic. Also absent from the 1979 budget were funds for the proposed B-1 manned penetration bomber. The president and Congress in effect agreed to rely for the time being on the old B-52G bomber, modified to carry the air-launched cruise missile, plus other B-52s and FB-111s, for the penetration bombing role in the triad strategy.

The president also deferred production of the neutron "bomb," a high-radiation, tactical nuclear warhead for artillery shells or surface-to-surface missiles. In summary, current defense funding stresses upgrading U.S. conventional forces, buildup of NATO land forces, somewhat less emphasis on strategic nuclear weapons, and less funding for those elements of the navy not included in the triad.

U.S. arms-control policy has basically the same primary aim as U.S. strategic defense policy—the prevention of nuclear war while maintaining the sovereignty and independence of the United States. From the beginning of the nuclear era, the United States has held that control and disarmament of nuclear weapons must be predicated on reliable inspection procedures, while the Soviet position has been that weapons should simply be destroyed, and that inspection to verify such destruction would be an intolerable security threat to the Soviet Union. In 1963 the little common ground between these positions yielded the Treaty for a Partial Nuclear Test Ban and the Hot Line agreement, which provides for a direct communications link between the leaders of the two superpowers. The Hot Line has since been used in crises to assure mutual understanding of intentions, and has been made technologically more secure. Recent agreements (1974, 1976) have brought underground testing, which was not covered by the 1963 treaty, down to a yield of no more than 150 kilotons, and negotiations appear to presage an agreement for a comprehensive test ban.

Special negotiations on limiting long-range nuclear missiles have been going on since 1969 between the United States and the Soviet Union—the Strategic Arms Limitation Talks (SALT). Agreements reached in 1972 (1) virtually ended antiballistic missile (ABM) deployment, limiting each power to two ABM installations, and (2) froze the deployment of ICBM and SLBM rocket launchers for five years. The development of MIRVs (multiple independently targeted reentry vehicles [warheads] delivered by a single launcher) was a destabilizing force that made limitation of warheads almost impossible to verify, and limitation of launchers seemed the only feasible approach. In 1974 in Vladivostok, SALT guidelines were issued that called for the United States and the USSR to have a maximum of 2,400 offensive strategic vehicles each—including ICBMs, SLBMs, and long-range strategic bombers; 1,300 of these could be equipped with MIRVs.

The SALT II agreements, signed June 18, 1979, basically call for putting the Vladivostok guidelines into effect and making them binding through 1985. The 2,400 limit on delivery systems is retained, and this number is to be reduced to 2,250 by 1981. Of these, 1,320 can be launchers of MIRVed missiles, including 1,200 land- and sea-based MIRVed missile launchers (820 land-based) and 120 bombers with cruise missiles. Only one new type of missile is to be developed by each side.

SALT II also includes a protocol, to be in force until 1981, banning the deployment of mobile-launched ICBMs (the U.S. MX missile), and of ground- and sea-launched cruise missiles with ranges above 360 miles (600 km).

The SALT II treaty encountered serious opposition in Senate hearings. In many cases, even witnesses who supported ratification urged that more U.S. defense spending was necessary to compensate for the growing U.S. strategic inferiority they said was recognized and codified by the treaty. Following the Soviet invasion of Afghanistan (December 1979), the Senate suspended consideration of the treaty.

SALT and test-ban agreements of recent years have been made possible because new technical developments, including observation satellites, have made verification of arms control compliance possible without the on-site inspection to which the Soviets have always objected. However, MIRVs pose special problems for verification, as has the loss to the United States of monitoring stations in Iran. The USSR's new capability for destroying satellites has also caused some concern.

A Nuclear Nonproliferation Treaty, forbidding the transfer of nuclear weapons to countries that do not have them, was ratified by the United States Senate in 1969. The proliferation of highly destructive conventional weapons systems throughout the world has increased greatly in recent years and may be a serious destabilizing factor. President Carter has made efforts (not always consistent, some critics assert) to lower U.S. sales of conventional weapons to other countries.

Manpower for U.S. armed forces is now obtained through voluntary service, with conscription legislation remaining in force on a "standby" basis, should there not be enough volunteers to reach force level requirements. To implement the all-volunteer policy, determined efforts are being made to make military service attractive to young people. A major problem has been to maintain without conscription adequate reserve forces composed of trained men.

## STRAGETIC PROBLEMS

In the era of long-range nuclear bombing and nuclear-armed ICBMs, the nation's major strategic problem is possible attack by a hostile nuclear power. At present, only the USSR is a potential attacker, although China may achieve a limited ICBM capability by the early 1980s. Nuclear deterrence and its corollary and prerequisite, the capability of delivering retaliatory nuclear missile strikes, constitute the strategy for meeting the threat of nuclear attack. This strategy is complemented by an air defense capability for meeting bomber attacks.

Air and aerospace defense of North America is the responsibility of the joint U.S.–Canadian North American Air Defense Command (NORAD). The U.S. component, the air force's Aerospace Defense Command (ADCOM), represents more than 70 percent of NORAD's resources. NORAD operational headquarters is under Cheyenne Mountain, near Colorado Springs, Colorado. When NORAD was established in 1958, the greatest danger was still from nuclear-armed bombers, and the NORAD force was composed largely of interceptor aircraft, plus some Bomarc and Nike missiles. A Distant Early Warning (DEW) line was established, stretching from the Aleutians to Greenland, with a radar, computer, and communications network that would immediately mobilize air defense to meet any threat from the north. Since the chief current threat is from missiles (although the DEW line is maintained), NORAD's antibomber fighter and radar strengths have been reduced. NORAD's fighter-interceptor force is now composed of six air force fighter-interceptor squadrons, ten U.S. National Guard fighter-interceptor squadrons, and three Canadian squadrons.

A Ballistic Missile Early Warning System (BMEWS) was established in 1960, with stations in Alaska, the United Kingdom, and Greenland. NORAD now also has Spacetrack, a system of phased-array radar and powerful telescopic cameras for tracking all orbiting objects. There is a phased-array radar in Florida and one in North Dakota (formerly part of the aborted antiballistic missile system), plus Over-the-Horizon Forwardscatter early warning satellites. This global air and space surveillance is intended to ensure that no attack on the United States can be a surprise, and that appropriate responsive action can be taken.

A relatively new and potentially serious strategic problem is the sharp increase in the strength of the Soviet navy (see Union of Soviet Socialist Republics). To some observers, the ability of the U.S. Navy to keep open the sea lanes to NATO and to sources of strategic material in case of war appeared seriously threatened in the late 1970s.

The presence of Cuba, a Communist country closely allied with the Soviet Union, only ninety miles from the mainland United States, poses a significant strategic problem. Short-range ballistic missiles could be fired from there against the United States; none are now deployed there. Cuba could also be used as a staging base or recovery base for Soviet bombers. U.S. action in the 1962 Cuban missile crisis made clear that the United States will take strong action to prevent the use of Cuba as a base against it.

With a two-ocean navy and the availability of massive air transport, the Panama Canal has a less pivotal role in U.S. national security than formerly, although it has great strategic and economic importance. Negotiations for new treaty arrangements with Panama began in 1964, following anti-American riots in the Canal Zone. Two treaties were signed in 1977, one providing for Panamanian control of the canal by the year 2000, and the other guaranteeing the zone's permanent neutrality and giving the United States the right to help defend that neutrality. Panama gets control of the Canal Zone (but not the canal) immediately. Both treaties were narrowly ratified by the Senate in 1978 after vigorous lobbying efforts by supporters and opponents. A U.S. garrison in the Canal Zone, the U.S. base at Guantanamo, Cuba, and close surveillance of Caribbean regimes are measures designed to protect the canal and its approaches.

With increased world needs for oil from the Persian Gulf, and British withdrawal of forces from "East of Suez" areas, the United States began in 1971 to expand the former British base of Diego Garcia in the Indian Ocean. By 1977 the base, with a deep-water anchorage suitable for the largest aircraft carriers, included satellite and radio communications systems and an 8,000-foot runway, which was being extended.

There is at present no serious threat to U.S. national, state, or local government from internal subversion, although scattered outbreaks of civil disorder and isolated terrorist acts may be expected.

## ALLIANCES

North Atlantic Treaty Organization (NATO). NATO members are pledged to consider an attack on one as an attack on all (see Western Europe, Regional Survey).

Organization of American States (OAS). The United States is a signatory of the Inter-American Treaty of Reciprocal Assistance, approved for signature at Rio de Janeiro, September 2, 1947. Under the treaty the OAS Council can call a meeting of the foreign ministers of member nations to make decisions in crises (see Central America and West Indies Regional Survey).

ANZUS Pact. Security treaty signed at San Francisco, September 1, 1951. Australia, New Zealand, and the United States are parties (see South and Southwest Pacific, Regional Survey).

Southeast Asia Collective Defense Treaty. Signed at Manila, September 8, 1954. Australia, France, New Zealand, Pakistan, the Philippines, Thailand, and the United Kingdom are also parties. Although the SEATO organization has been disbanded, the treaty remains in force (see South and Southeast Asia, Regional Survey).

The Pacific Charter. Signed at Manila, September 8, 1954. Australia, France, New Zealand, Pakistan, the Philippines, Thailand, and the United Kingdom are also parties.

The U.S. has bilateral defense agreements with Turkey, Iran, and Pakistan, signed on March 5, 1959, in Ankara, pledging aid against aggression aimed at any of these countries. The treaty with Iran was declared ineffective by the Khomeini regime but could be reactivated in the event of a serious threat.

The United States has bilateral alliances with the following nations: Japan, Republic of Korea (South Korea), and Spain. A 1954 mutual defense treaty with the Republic of China (Taiwan) was terminated by the United States at the end of 1979, as part of the normalization of relations with mainland China agreed on in late 1978.

The United States has bilateral alliances or agreements, including military assistance agreements, with most of the other participants in the regional alliances listed above.

## MILITARY ASSISTANCE

The table on p. 351 lists the nations which have received U.S. military assistance under the Mutual Defense Act of 1949 and the Foreign Assistance Act of 1961.

# VALUE OF MILITARY AID (Military Assistance Program)
## (Dollars in thousands)*

| Country | FY 1977 | FY 1950–1977 | Country | FY 1977 | FY 1950–1977 |
|---|---|---|---|---|---|
| **East Asia** | | | Netherlands | — | 1,217,156 |
| Burma | — | 76,387 | Norway | — | 893,829 |
| Cambodia | — | 1,192,816 | Portugal | 2,482 | 327,466 |
| China (Taiwan) | 8,801 | 2,650,331 | Spain | 3,669 | 648,139 |
| Indochina | — | 709,575 | | | |
| Indonesia | 10,354 | 164,605 | Turkey | — | 3,168,200 |
| Japan | — | 854,865 | United Kingdom | — | 1,034,479 |
| Korea | 18,042 | 4,914,551 | Yugoslavia | — | 693,856 |
| Laos | — | 1,502,932 | **Europe Total** | 7,274 | 18,883,301 |
| Malaysia | 284 | 2,630 | **Africa** | | |
| Philippines | 7,601 | 512,700 | Benin | — | 82 |
| Thailand | 12,014 | 1,182,414 | Cameroon | — | 277 |
| Vietnam | — | 15,083,975 | Ethiopia | 3,790 | 204,064 |
| **East Asia Total** | 57,096 | 28,847,781 | Ghana | 81 | 606 |
| | | | Guinea | — | 899 |
| **Near East and South Asia** | | | Ivory Coast | — | 158 |
| Afghanistan | 195 | 5,367 | Kenya | 195 | 1,180 |
| Bangladesh | 49 | 49 | Liberia | 131 | 8,753 |
| India | 256 | 95,393 | Libya | — | 15,419 |
| Iran | 4 | 834,179 | Mali | — | 2,847 |
| Iraq | — | 46,695 | Morocco | 789 | 41,956 |
| Jordan | 10,409 | 236,934 | Niger | — | 63 |
| Lebanon | 42 | 15,155 | Nigeria | — | 1,507 |
| Nepal | 31 | 2,033 | Senegal | 49 | 2,930 |
| Pakistan | 326 | 673,857 | Sudan | 103 | 821 |
| Saudi Arabia | 1 | 36,325 | Tunisia | 386 | 10,715 |
| Sri Lanka | 6 | 3,339 | Upper Volta | — | 90 |
| Syria | — | 56 | Zaire | 2,435 | 29,946 |
| Yemen | 357 | 541 | **African Total** | 7,959 | 322,313 |
| **NESA Total** | 11,676 | 1,949,923 | | | |
| | | | **American Republics** | | |
| **Europe** | | | Argentina | 737 | 46,880 |
| Austria | 24 | 97,625 | Bolivia | 1,649 | 38,553 |
| Belgium | — | 1,237,673 | Brazil | 33 | 223,576 |
| Denmark | — | 617,725 | Chile | — | 97,373 |
| Finland | 16 | 179 | Colombia | 658 | 96,838 |
| France | — | 4,153,053 | Costa Rica | — | 1,830 |
| Germany | — | 900,947 | Cuba | — | 10,575 |
| Greece | 1,072 | 1,594,408 | Dominican Republic | 724 | 30,800 |
| Iceland | 11 | 11 | Ecuador | 403 | 43,436 |
| Italy | — | 2,290,308 | El Salvador | 647 | 10,304 |
| Luxembourg | — | 8,247 | Guatemala | 595 | 23,608 |
| | | | Haiti | 97 | 3,391 |
| | | | Honduras | 826 | 12,767 |
| | | | Jamaica | — | 1,066 |
| | | | Mexico | 128 | 2,410 |

*Department of Defense, Security Assistance Agency, *Military Assistance and Foreign Military Sales Facts,* December 1977.

| Country | FY 1977 | FY 1950–1977 |
|---|---|---|
| Nicaragua | 649 | 18,243 |
| Panama | 497 | 7,962 |
| Paraguay | 757 | 14,891 |
| Peru | 869 | 93,140 |
| Uruguay | 288 | 46,838 |
| Venezuela | 42 | 13,890 |
| American Republics Total | 9,599 | 838,371 |
| General, Regional, and Other costs | 65,245 | 3,476,709 |
| Grand Total | 158,849 | 54,318,398 |

## ARMY

*Personnel:* 785,447

*Organization:*

  3 commands in continental United States: Forces Command, Training and Doctrine Command, and Materiel Development and Readiness Command
  3 overseas armies: U.S. Army Europe, U.S. Army Japan, and Eighth Army, Korea
  3 armored divisions
  2 airborne divisions
  7 infantry divisions
  3 mechanized infantry divisions
  1 cavalry division
  3 independent infantry brigades
  1 independent air cavalry combat brigade
  1 artillery brigade
  1 independent armored brigade
  2 air defense artillery brigades
  1 air defense artillery group
  3 independent armored cavalry regiments

*Deployment:*

  Continental U.S.: 3 armies, 1 corps, 1 airborne corps, 3 mechanized infantry divisions (less 1 brigade), 1 cavalry division, 1 armored division (less 1 brigade), 4 infantry divisions, 2 airborne divisions
  South Korea: 1 field army headquarters, 1 infantry division, 1 air defense artillery brigade
  Germany: 1 field army of 2 corps, 2 infantry divisions, 2 armored divisions, 1 brigade mechanized infantry division, 1 brigade armored division, 1 brigade (Berlin), 1 air defense command

*Major Equipment Inventory:*

  M-60 medium tanks (M-60A1 with 105mm gun, M-60A1E2 with 152mm Shillelagh MGM-51A guided missile system)
  M-48 medium tanks (90mm gun)
  M-551 Sheridan assault vehicle (Shillelagh)
  M-113 and M-114 armored personnel carriers

  MGM-31 Pershing SSM Ia and II
  MGM-29A Sergeant SSM
  Lacrosse SSM
  MGR-1A/B Honest John SSM
  MGR-3A Little John SSM
  MGM-52C Lance SSM (replacing Honest John and Little John)
  MIM-23A Hawk SAM
  MIM-14A Nike-Hercules SAM (plus 36 National Guard batteries)
  Chaparral/Vulcan low-altitude air defense system
  Redeye man-portable SAM
  heavy artillery pieces (mostly M-107, M-109, and M-110 self-propelled guns and howitzers)
  medium artillery pieces
  light artillery pieces
  Dragon, TOW antitank weapons
  8,000 helicopters (including AH-1, UH-1, and YUH-60 Blackhawk)
  1,000 fixed-wing aircraft

*Reserves:* The United States Army has two separate and independent reserve components. The Army National Guard has approximately 400,000 members, and the Army Reserve has about 260,000 members.

The Army National Guard is organized in eight combat divisions (five infantry, one mechanized infantry, two armored) and eleven infantry, six mechanized infantry, three armored, one air defense artillery, four engineer brigades, plus combat and combat service support units. The Army Reserve is organized in nineteen Army Reserve commands, twelve training divisions, two maneuver area commands, and thirteen brigades (including two infantry and one mechanized infantry), plus combat and combat service support units. National Guard and Army Reserve units are to be ready for action five weeks after mobilization is ordered. Reserve units, in any number and combination, are mobilized by order of the president. Call up of individual reservists requires presidential declaration of a national emergency or congressional action. These provisions apply to all services.

## NAVY

*Personnel:* 539,650 (not including Marine Corps)

*Organization:* The Chief of Naval Operations (CNO) commands the operating forces of the navy. The commandant of the Marine Corps (see below) is responsible to the Chief of Naval Operations for the readiness and performance of Marine Corps elements assigned to the operating forces of the navy. Under the CNO are the two major fleets (the Atlantic Fleet and the Pacific Fleet); the Naval Forces, Europe; the Military Sea

Transportation Services (MSTS); and, in time of war, the Coast Guard. There are four numbered fleets, Second, Third, Sixth, and Seventh. The two principal operational fleets are the Sixth Fleet in the Mediterranean, which is under the operational control of CINCNAVEUR, but which is administratively supported by CINCLANTFLT, and the Seventh Fleet, in the Western Pacific and South China Sea, under operational and administrative command of CINCPACFLT. MSTS provides sea transportation for military cargo and personnel of all services.

*Major Units:*
- 41 ballistic missile nuclear-powered submarines (with 656 Poseidon and Polaris SLBMs; SSBN)
- 68 nuclear-powered attack submarines (SSN)
- 10 diesel submarines (SS)
- 3 nuclear-powered aircraft carriers (CVN)
- 10 aircraft carriers (CV)
- 7 nuclear-powered guided missile cruisers (CGN)
- 20 guided missile cruisers (CG)
- 39 guided missile destroyers (DDG)
- 54 destroyers (DD)
- 7 guided missile frigates (FFG)
- 58 frigates (FF)
- 2 patrol escorts (PG)
- 1 missile attack boat (PTG)
- 1 hydrofoil fast patrol craft (PCH)
- 4 fast patrol craft (PCF)
- 20 patrol boats (PB)
- 40 river patrol boats (PBR)
- 2 amphibious command ships (LCC)
- 2 amphibious assault ships (LHA)
- 14 amphibious assault transport docks (LPD)
- 7 amphibious assault helicopter ships (LPH)
- 13 dock landing ships (LSD)
- 28 other amphibious ships (2 LPA, 6 LKA, 20 LST)
- 25 fleet minesweepers (MSP)
- 105 auxiliary ships
- 1,100 service craft

*Naval Air Organization:*
- 65 fighter/attack squadrons
- 10 reconnaissance squadrons
- 4 helicopter support squadrons
- 17 helicopter ASW squadrons
- 12 airborne early-warning AEW squadrons
- 24 patrol squadrons
- 20 ASW squadrons (fixed-wing and helicopter)
- 41 other squadrons (training, etc.)

*Naval Aircraft:*
- 2,580 combat aircraft
  - 732 fighter (F-4, F-14)
  - 1,228 attack (A-6, A-7)
  - 133 antisubmarine (S-2, S-3, SH-3)
  - 376 patrol and reconnaissance (P-3, RA-5, RF-8)
  - 111 warning (E-1, E-2)
- 2,730 other aircraft
  - 43 refueler
  - 52 observation
  - 1,113 training
  - 338 transport and utility
  - 1,166 other helicopters
  - 18 drone control

*Missiles:*
- 656 SSM Polaris and Poseidon long-range ballistic missiles, Harpoon short-range SSM
- ASROC antisubmarine
- SUBROC submarine-launched antisubmarine

*Reserves:* There are approximately 100,000 members of the naval reserve. In addition there are hundreds of reserve warships—mostly submarines, aircraft carriers, battleships, and cruisers—in the so-called mothball fleet. The major operational naval reserve units are naval aviation: thirty-two squadrons of fixed-wing aircraft and five squadrons of helicopters.

## AIR FORCE

*Personnel:* 573,064

*Organization:*
Strategic Air Command (SAC: commander in chief, SAC, is responsible directly to the president, through the secretary of defense and the Joint Chiefs of Staff)
- 2 air forces, with 10 air divisions and 1 strategic aerospace division, made up of:
  - 17 bomb wings (B-52/KC-135)
  - 2 bomb wings (FB-111/KC-135)
  - 3 strategic missile wings (Titan II)
  - 6 strategic missile wings (Minuteman)
  - 1 strategic reconnaissance wing (SR-71, U-2)
  - 1 strategic reconnaissance wing (RC/EC-135)
  - 4 air refueling wings (KC-135)
  - 2 air refueling groups (KC-135)

Tactical Air Command (TAC: commander TAC is also air commander of the Joint U.S. Readiness Command)
- 2 air forces, made up of:
  - 15 tactical fighter wings (6 F-4, 2 F-111, 1 A-7, 1 F-15, 1 F-4/F-105, 1 F-4/UH-1, 2 A-10/A-7, 1 F-15/EC-135/UH-1)
  - 2 tactical reconnaissance wings (RF-4)

1 special operations wing (CH-3, UH-1, MC/AC-130)

1 tactical training wing (F-4, F-5, F-15, F-111, A-10, UH-1)

2 tactical air control wings (O-2, OV-10, CH-3)

1 airborne warning and control wing (E-3A, EC-130, EC-135)

Aerospace Defense Command (ADC: the U.S. element of North American Defense Command, NORAD, joint U.S.–Canadian defense command)

6 air divisions

16 fighter-interceptor squadrons, including 10 squadrons Air National Guard (3 F-101, 1 F-4, 6 F-106) and 6 squadrons Regular Air Force (F-106)

Pacific Air Forces (PACAF)

2 air forces (1 each in Philippines and Japan) made up of:

1 air base division (O-2)

3 tactical fighter wings (F-4, RF-4, F-5, MC-130, T-33, T-38, T-39)

1 tactical composite wing (F-4, OV-10)

2 air base wings (1 Air National Guard; EC-135, T-33, F-4, T-39, UH-1)

U.S. Air Forces in Europe (USAFE)

3 air forces (1 each in England, Spain, and West Germany), with:

8 tactical fighter wings (5 F-4, 2 F-111, 1 F-15)

2 tactical reconnaissance wings (RF-4, RF-5, F-5)

2 tactical airlift wings rotational (C-130, KC-135, C-9, C-5, C-141)

Alaskan Air Command (AAC)

Military Airlift Command (MAC)

2 air forces, with:

5 tactical airlift wings (C-130)

8 military airlift wings (C-141, C-5)

1 aeromedical airlift wing (C-9)

3 VC-137 and VC-140 squadrons

Air Training Command

Air Force Systems Command

Air Force Logistics Command
(supporting services and special centers)

*Major Equipment Inventory:*

Missiles:

Surface-to-surface ICBMs (SAC)

54 Titan II (3 wings)

450 Minuteman II (3 wings)

550 Minuteman III (with MIRV warhead) (3 wings)

Air-to-air

AIR-2 Genie rocket (F-101, F-106)

AIM-4 Falcon (5 configurations) (F-4, F-101, F-106)

AIM-7 Sparrow (2 configurations) (F-4, F-15)

AIM-9 Sidewinder (8 configurations) (F-4, F-15)

Air-to-surface

AGM-28 Hound Dog (B-52)

AGM-45 Shrike (F-4, F-105)

AGM-65 Maverick (A-7, A-10, F-4, F-16)

AGM-69A SRAM (B-52, FB-111)

AGM-78A Standard ARM (F-105)

GBU-8, GBU-15 (F-4)

ALCM to be carried by B-52 bombers

3,577 combat aircraft

486 bombers (B-52, FB-111)

2,676 fighter/interceptor/attack (A-7, A-10, F-4, F-5, F-15, F-105, F-106, F-111)

415 reconnaissance/electronic warfare (RF-4, SR-71, EC/RC-135, DC/WC-130, E-4, U-2)

3,632 other aircraft

526 tankers (KC-135)

854 cargo/transport (C-5, C-9, C-130, C-141, VC-137, VC-140)

37 search and rescue (fixed-wing) (HC-130)

249 helicopter (includes rescue) (UH-1, HH-3, HH-53)

1,750 trainer (T-29, T-33, T-37, T-38, T-39, T-41, T-43)

216 utility observation

*Reserves:* The Air National Guard has 92,000 personnel, organized in 88 squadrons, with 1,556 aircraft. They are committed as follows:

Tactical Air Command and Pacific Air Forces

28 fighter-bomber squadrons (12 F-100, 4 F-105, 1 F-4, 11 A-7)

8 tactical reconnaissance squadrons (2 RF-101, 6 RF-4)

2 light ground attack squadrons (A-37)

6 tactical air support squadrons (O-2)

1 tactical electronic warfare squadron (EC-130)

Aerospace Defense Command

8 interceptor squadrons (3 F-101, 5 F-106)

2 electronic warfare squadrons (EB-57)

Military Airlift Command

18 tactical airlift squadrons (C-130)

1 tactical airlift squadron (C-7)

2 aerospace rescue and recovery squadrons (HC-130/HH-3)

Strategic Air Command

12 air refueling squadrons (KC-135)

The Air Reserve has 48,000 people, organized in 37 squadrons with 427 aircraft. They are capable of immediate active service.

17 transport squadrons (2 C-7, 4 C-123, 11 C-130)
3 fighter-bomber squadrons (F-105)
5 light ground attack squadrons (A-37)
4 aerospace rescue squadrons (2 HC-130, 2 HH-1/3)
1 airborne early warning squadron (EC-121)
1 weather reconnaissance squadron (WC-130)
1 special operations squadron (CH-3)
2 heavy air refueling squadrons (KC-135)

Personnel of an additional 18 squadrons fly in association with MAC in C-5, C-141, C-9 MAC squadrons.

## MARINE CORPS

*Personnel:* 196,000

*Organization:*

3 marine divisions (1st in California, 2d in North Carolina [elements in Mediterranean and Caribbean], 3d in Okinawa)
3 tank battalions (each associated with a division)
3 SAM battalions (24 missiles each; each associated with a division)
3 marine aircraft wings (1st in Japan, 2d in North Carolina, 3d in California)
25 fighter-attack squadrons (F-4, A-4, A-6, AV-8)
3 composite reconnaissance squadrons (RF-4 and EA 6)
24 helicopter squadrons (CH-46, CH-53, UH-1, AH-1)
8 other squadrons (KC-130, OV-10)

*Major Equipment Inventory:*

M-48 and M-60 medium tanks
LVTP-5 amphibious APCs
M-113 APCs
Hawk SAMs
105mm, 155mm, 203mm howitzers
175mm guns
385 combat aircraft, including helicopters
100 other aircraft

*Reserves:* There are approximately 34,000 Marine Corps reservists, mostly in the 4th Marine Division and 4th Marine Aircraft Wing.

## COAST GUARD

*Personnel:* 36,730

*Organization:* Under Department of Transportation. In time of war or by presidential declaration, the Coast Guard is under the Navy Department.

*Major Units:*

40 high endurance cutters (WHEC)
16 medium endurance cutters (WMEC)
75 patrol craft (WPB)
2 training ships
7 icebreakers (WAGB)
89 buoy tenders
2 lightships
29 tugs
2 oceanographic cutters
10 construction tenders
2,061 operational boats
51 fixed-wing aircraft
111 helicopters

## PARAMILITARY

There is no national police force or constabulary, nor is there any central law enforcement authority; this power is divided among the federal, state, and local governments.

The Civil Air Patrol is an official auxiliary of the U.S. Air Force. It numbers 64,000 volunteers, of which 19,000 are teen-age cadets, and operates 2,600 privately owned and 600 CAP-owned aircraft in more than 1,800 individual units, in eight regions. There is a wing in each state, the District of Columbia, and the Commonwealth of Puerto Rico. Missions include search and rescue, civil defense augmentation, disaster relief, and communications in support of emergency and civil defense activities and internal operations. More than 155,000 sorties have been flown, assisting over 16,000 people threatened by disaster and saving more than 1,250 lives.

The Office of Civil Defense under the secretary of the army directs the nation's civilian response to a nuclear attack. There are 10,000 civilian employees and about 20,000 part-time volunteers. The national organization is decentralized under state and local government. The program includes development of a nationwide fallout shelter system through dual-purpose use of available buildings, marking these shelters, stocking with food, water, medical supplies, and radiological monitoring instruments. The program also includes some 3,000 protected Emergency Operating Centers (EOCs) for use by key state and local officials in directing emergency operations; the Emergency Broadcast System employing stations of the civilian broadcasting industry; a Broadcast Station Protection Program of fallout protection, emergency power, and radio links to the EOCs for over 600 radio stations; a warning system linking over 1,500 warning points to the North American Air Defense Command Center in Colorado; and a radiological monitoring system of more than 65,000 monitoring locations and communications, linked with U.S. military communications, to tie all of these elements together.

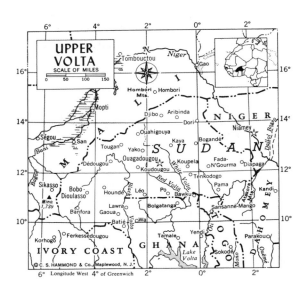

# UPPER VOLTA
## Republic of Upper Volta

### POWER POTENTIAL STATISTICS

Area: 105,869 square miles
Population: 6,582,000
Total Active Regular Armed Forces: 2,600 (0.04%
  population)
Gross National Product: $684 million ($110 per capita)
Annual Military Expenditures: $23.3 million (3.4%
  GNP)
Electric Power Output: 57 million kwh
Civil Air Fleet: 3 piston transports

### POLITICO-MILITARY POLICIES AND POSTURE

The current president, General Lamizana, achieved his
position by a military coup in January 1966. Political
parties were banned in 1974, as the military reneged on its
promise of transition to civilian rule, but democratic
processes were resumed in 1977, and a referendum was
held favoring return to civilian rule. General Lamizana
was then elected president. He has the support of a
six-party coalition in the National Assembly. The armed
forces of Upper Volta are administered through the
minister of defense.

Upper Volta has maintained close relations with France
since independence in 1960, although it did not join the
French Community. Staging, transit, and overflight
privileges were accorded France and there is a military
assistance agreement for arms, equipment, and training.

For defense Upper Volta relies essentially on whatever
collective security can be provided by its memberships in
the UN, OAU, OCAM, Conseil de l'Entente, and the
Economic Community of West African States. After a
period of violence in 1974–75, Upper Volta and Mali
settled a border dispute. A half million citizens work in
Ivory Coast, with which Upper Volta has good relations.

In 1966 and 1967 the army easily suppressed abortive
countercoup attempts by supporters of the ousted
politicians. Ethnic divisions do not threaten stability.
The dominant Voltaic Mossi comprise about one-half the
population. The Mandingo tribes are next in importance,
with smaller proportions of Fulani, Haussa, and Tuareg
tribesmen. Islam has made little penetration, and most of
the people retain their animist beliefs or have been
converted to Christianity.

Upper Volta's stability is threatened by its faltering
agricultural economy and its growing population. There
are important mineral deposits—manganese, copper, tin,
limestone, bauxite, and graphite—but these are not being
exploited because of the high cost of a 712-mile trip to the
coast.

Prior to and just after independence, during the period
1957–61, France furnished military instructors and $18
million in equipment. Another $25 million was provided
for administration of veterans' affairs and military
pensions for the 200,000 Voltaic veterans of French service.
These veterans represent a pool of trained manpower as
well as a potential pressure group. Shortly after independence the United States provided $90,000 for military
equipment and trained sixteen students under the MAP.
Israel has also furnished some police training and police
advisers.

Military service for two years is compulsory by law,
but the armed forces are kept up to strength by volunteers.
The army numbers 2,500 and is organized as two infantry
battalions, an armored car reconnaissance squadron with
M-8 armored cars, a paratroop company, and an engineer
company. The air force is 100 strong and operates three
C-47 transports, one Aero Commander 500B light
transport, and two Broussard liaison aircraft. Major bases
are Ouagadougou and Bobo-Dioulasso. There is a National Guard, or gendarmerie, of 1,500.

# URUGUAY
## Republic of Uruguay

### POWER POTENTIAL STATISTICS

Area: 68,548 square miles
Population: 2,902,000

URUGUAY

CONIC PROJECTION

SCALE OF MILES

0    20    40    60

SCALE OF KILOMETERS

0    20    40    60

Capitals of Countries - - - - - - - - ☆

Department Capitals - - - - - - - - ◉

International Boundaries _ _ _ ▪ _ ▪ _

Department Boundaries _ _ _ _ _ _ _

Copyright by C.S. Hammond & Co., N.Y.

Longitude West 56° of Greenwich

Total Active Regular Armed Forces: 29,500 (1.02%
population)
Gross National Product: $3.1 billion ($1,110 per capita)
Annual Military Expenditures: $79.9 million (2.58%
GNP)
Crude Steel Production: 34,841 metric tons
Fuel Production: Refined Petroleum Products: 1.8
million metric tons
Electric Power Output: 3.0 billion kwh
Merchant Fleet (ships 1,000 tons and over): 13 ships;
81,000 gross tons
Civil Air Fleet: 6 major transport aircraft

## DEFENSE STRUCTURE

Following a week-long rebellion by the armed services in
February 1973, agreement was reached with the elected
president, Juan M. Bordaberry, which established military
control of the government within the Constitution. In June
1973 Bordaberry closed the legislature and assumed dictatorial powers. The military commanders on June 12, 1976,
deposed Bordaberry and in September appointed Aparicio
Mendez president for a five-year term. A military-civilian
National Security Council appointed by the military
commanders runs the government. The minister of defense
in the president's cabinet is a civilian.

## POLITICO-MILITARY POLICY

In the period from 1968 to 1972 Uruguay, suffering
severe economic distress and runaway inflation, was
plagued by strikes and by the terrorist activity of the urban
guerrilla group known as Tupamaros. President Jorge
Pacheco declared a state of siege in 1971 but was unable
to control the Tupamaros. His successor, Bordaberry,
declared a state of internal war in April 1972, suspending
some individual rights and giving the army powers of
search and arrest. The Tupamaros were arrested in large
numbers and the movement liquidated. Many members
fled to other Latin American countries.

Success in this area led the military to move against
corruption in business and politics and finally resulted in
early 1973 in the confrontation with Bordaberry, and
creation of the National Security Council. An appointed
Council of State of prominent leaders replaces the legislature for some functions, but the real power lies in the
military members of the National Security Council.

The civilian, military-controlled government has
attempted to eliminate all Communist influences and other
political opposition. Labor unions have been abolished
and dissidence is harshly discouraged. The government has

announced plans for a new constitution in 1980 and
election of a single candidate for president in 1981.

Uruguay strongly advocates nonintervention in the
affairs of other nations, and in 1965 voted in the OAS
against intervention in the Dominican Republic. However,
the secretary general of the OAS at the time was a
Uruguayan who personally went to the Dominican Republic to mediate the internal dispute and the intervention.

## STRATEGIC PROBLEMS

With the suppression of the Tupamaros and subsequent
outlawing of the Communist party in Uruguay, threats to
internal security from dissident groups under a military-
controlled government are minimal.

The limits of territorial claims in the broad waters of the
River Plate were the source of a dispute with Argentina
that flared into near-confrontation in 1973 and was settled
with agreement on a treaty late in the year.

## MILITARY ASSISTANCE

The United States keeps a small Military Assistance
Advisory Group in Uruguay and provided $288,000 worth
of military assistance in 1977, making a total of $46.8
million since 1950. After the United States refused to give
more aid because of alleged human rights violations, the
Uruguayan government renounced all further aid. Under
the MAP, 2,807 students have been trained.

## ALLIANCES

Uruguay is a member of the OAS.

## ARMY

*Personnel:* 20,000

*Organization:*
    4 infantry regiments
    3 armored regiments
    9 cavalry squadrons
    4 artillery batteries
    6 engineer battalions

*Major Equipment Inventory:*
    35 light tanks (17 M-24, 18 M-3)
    24 light artillery pieces (105mm, M-101A1 howitzer)
    25 APCs (M-113, M-2 half-tracks)

*Reserves:* 100,000 are available to expand all army units
to the next larger unit upon mobilization. These are men

who have completed voluntary service, and citizens who have received part-time training.

## NAVY

*Personnel:* 3,500 (including naval infantry)

*Major Units:*
3 frigates (1 Dealey class; 1 Cannon class; FF)
2 patrol ships (1 Auk class; 1 Aggressive class; PGF)
1 patrol craft (PC)
6 patrol boats (PB)
2 mechanized landing craft (LCM)
3 auxiliary ships
5 service craft
3 S-2 ASW aircraft
7 trainers (T-6/7/34)
2 L-21A liaison aircraft
7 helicopters (Bell 47, H-13/34)

*Naval Base:* Montevideo

*Naval Air Bases:* Carrasco, Laguna del Sauce, Laguna Negra

## AIR FORCE

*Personnel:* 3,000

*Organization:*
1 fighter-bomber squadron (F-80, T-33)
1 COIN squadron (A-37, T-6)
1 reconnaissance squadron (U-8/17, T-11)
2 transport squadrons (C-47, C-46, C-95, F-27, F-227, Beaver, Queen Air)

*Major Aircraft Types:*
56 combat aircraft
  12 fighter bombers (F-80, T-33)
  20 COIN (A-37, T-6)
  24 reconnaissance (U-8/17, T-11)
57 other aircraft
  32 transports (13 C-47, 5 C-46, 2 F-27, 2 F-227, 3 Beaver, 5 C-95, and 2 Queen Air)
  20 trainers (T-6/33)
  5 helicopters (Bell 47, UH-1, H-23)

*Air Bases:* Carrasco, Isla de la Libertad, Laguna del Sauce, Punta del Este, Melilla, Laguna Negra

## PARAMILITARY

Police forces number 22,000, of whom about 1,000 are specially trained to cope with urban guerrilla warfare.

# VENEZUELA

## Republic of Venezuela

## POWER POTENTIAL STATISTICS

Area: 352,143 square miles
Population: 14,541,000
Total Active Regular Armed Forces: 43,450 (0.30% population)
Gross National Product: $33 billion ($2,590 per capita)
Annual Military Expenditures: $708.4 million (2.15% GNP)
Crude Steel Production: 750,000 metric tons
Iron Ore Production: 15.4 million metric tons
Fuel Production:
  Crude Oil: 119.8 million metric tons
  Refined Petroleum Products: 51.4 million metric tons
  Natural Gas: 10.9 billion cubic meters
Electric Power Output: 28 billion kwh
Merchant Fleet (ships 1,000 tons and over): 58 ships; 540,000 gross tons
Civil Air Fleet: 70 major transport aircraft

## DEFENSE STRUCTURE

The president of the republic is commander in chief of the National Armed Forces, which consist of four independent services: army, navy, air force, and national guard. The president administers the armed forces through the minister of defense (who is usually chief of the Joint Staff). In his defense responsibilities the president is advised by a Supreme Council of National Defense, consisting of the Council of Ministers, the chief of the Joint Staff, the commanders of the four services, and any other officials or experts whom the president wishes to include.

## POLITICO-MILITARY POLICY

Since the overthrow of dictator Marcos Perez Jimenez through joint civilian and military efforts in 1958, the country has been controlled by civilian democratic forces, with regular elections.

Since 1917, when the exploitation of oil began, Venezuela's economy has progressed from an agrarian base to one that is highly industrialized. Venezuela is fifth among the world's oil producers. The large revenue from oil, and the resultant economic prosperity, have been major factors in relative governmental stability. Decreasing oil production and the world oil crisis of late 1973 stimulated the government to nationalize the petroleum industry.

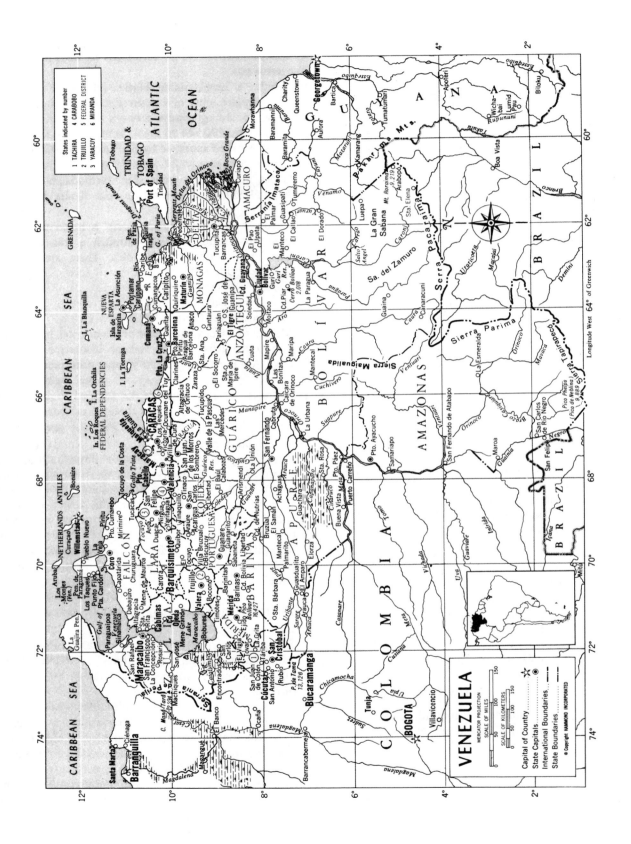

Recent governments, attempting to ensure stability in the face of guerrilla warfare threats, and to ensure their own power in a nation whose history is replete with military coups, have conscientiously shown their interest in the well-being of the military.

Under a long-standing border dispute, Venezuela claims 58,000 square miles of Guyanese territory, about three-fifths of Guyana. An agreement was made between representatives of the two countries in 1970 not to press claims for the ensuing twelve years. Venezuela has supported independence for Belize against the claims of Guatemala. The government has contributed funds to other Latin American governments for development programs.

The bulk of the armed forces is made up of two-year conscripts, who are selected through a state lottery system from all able-bodied eighteen-year-olds. There are no organized reserves.

## STRATEGIC PROBLEMS

Venezuela's major strategic problem arose from the avowed aim of Cuba's Castro to foment revolution in Venezuela. Violence and guerrilla activity were widespread in the early 1960s, the principal agency of unrest the *Fuerzas Armadas de Liberacion Nacional* (Armed Forces of National Liberation). The most serious threats were two uprisings by pro-Castro naval officers in 1962, and guerrilla efforts to influence the 1968 elections.

In 1963 the government, largely through the influence of the military, and led by the interior minister, Carlos Andres Perez (elected president ten years later), took strong action against terrorism and ordered mass arrests of all known Communists and sympathizers. Terrorism continued at a somewhat decreased rate until the pre-election guerrilla activity of mid-1968, when pro-Castro guerrillas were able briefly to take over some towns and villages. They continued this activity after the elections, taking advantage of the confusion of a governmental changeover. While terrorists are still sporadically active, the threat to governmental security is not great.

## MILITARY ASSISTANCE

From 1950 to 1977 Venezuela obtained $13.9 million in U.S. military assistance. Under the MAP, 5,511 students have been trained. Each U.S. service has a resident mission in Venezuela. In July 1972 Venezuela purchased $60 million in arms from France.

## ALLIANCES

Venezuela is a member of the OAS.

## ARMY

*Personnel:* 27,950

*Organization:*
- 1 armored brigade (medium, light)
- 1 cavalry regiment (horse)
- 12 infantry battalions (mechanized)
- 2 tank squadrons (medium, light)
- 6 artillery groups (18 battalions)
- 5 engineer and antiaircraft battalions supply groups

*Major Equipment Inventory:*
- 140 medium tanks (AMX-30)
- 50 light tanks (AMX-13, M-3 Stuart)
- 50 APC (M-113)
- 95 armored cars (M-8, M-2 half-tracks)
- 14 tank destroyers (M-50)
- 10 155mm howitzers, self-propelled (AMX-155)
- 135 light artillery pieces (105mm, M-101)
- 20 antitank guns (76mm, self-propelled)
- 40mm antiaircraft guns

## NAVY

*Personnel:* 7,500 (including 4,000 marines)

*Major Units:*
- 4 diesel submarines (2 Type 209; 2 Guppy class; SS)
- 4 destroyers (DD)
  - 2 Aragua class (1 with Seacat short range SAMs; 4.5-inch guns)
  - 2 Sumner class
- 5 frigates (FF)
  - 1 Lupo class (Otomat SSMs, Albatross SAMs, both short range)
  - 4 Almirante Clemente class
- 3 fast patrol craft (121-foot; 76mm gun; PCF)
- 3 missile attack boats (121-foot; Otomat SSMs; PTG)
- 21 patrol boats (PB)
- 5 landing ships (4 LSM and 1 LST)
- 12 personnel landing craft (LCP)
- 5 auxiliary ships
- 15 service craft
- 2 helicopters (Bell 47)
- 6 ASW aircraft (S-2A)
- 4 search and rescue SAF (HU-16)
- 8 liaison (O-2)
- 3 transports (C-47)

*Naval Base:* Puerto Cabello

## AIR FORCE

*Personnel:* 8,000

*Organization:* 3 commands: Combat Command (combat-transport); Instruction Command (training); Logistics Command (supply)

1 fighter squadron AW (F-86K)
1 fighter-bomber squadron (Mirage, F-86)
1 fighter squadron (F-5)
1 bomber squadron (Canberra)
1 COIN squadron (OV-10)
1 training group (T-2, T-6, T-33, T-34, Queen Air, Jet Provost)
1 transport and liaison group (U-8, C-130, C-123, C-54, C-47, 1 Cessna 500, Cessna Skywagons)
1 helicopter group (Jet Ranger, UH-1, UH-19)

*Major Aircraft Types:*
106 combat aircraft
    40 F-86 fighter/fighter-bombers
    24 F-5 fighters
    18 Mirage fighter-bombers
    24 Canberra bombers
    18 OV-10 counterinsurgency (COIN)
250 other aircraft
    112 trainers (T-2, T-6, T-33, T-34, Queen Air, Jet Provost)
    86 transport/liaison (C-47, C-123, C-130, Queen Air, U-17)
    52 helicopters (Alouette III, Jet Ranger, UH-1, U-19)

*Air Bases:* Caracas, Maracay, Maiquetia, La Carlota, Maturin, Maracaibo, Barcelona, Barquisimeto, Palo Negro

## PARAMILITARY

The *Fuerzas Armadas de Cooperacion,* popularly known as the National Guard, is composed of about 10,000 men, and is used for internal security, customs, and forestry. The National Guard operates its own military academy, officers' school of application, and staff college. The guard operates sixteen patrol boats.

# VIETNAM

## Socialist Republic of Vietnam

## POWER POTENTIAL STATISTICS

Area: 126,436 square miles
Population: 51,883,000
Total Active Regular Armed Forces: 515,000 (1.42% population)
Gross National Product: $7.3 billion ($157 per capita)

Annual Military Expenditures: $307 million (4.2% GNP)
Fuel Production: Coal: 4.25 million metric tons
Electric Power Output: 3.4 billion kwh
Merchant Fleet (ships 1,000 tons and over): 23 ships; 107,000 gross tons

## DEFENSE STRUCTURE

The president is the constitutional commander of the armed forces. There is a National Defense Council composed of the president, premier, defense minister, and other high civil and military officials. The defense minister, since 1946 Vo Nguyen Giap, exercises direct control over the armed services, largely through the General Staff and directorates for political affairs, training, and logistics. Informal control is exercised through the Communist party of Vietnam, to which large numbers of military personnel belong.

## POLITICO-MILITARY POLICY

In the wake of the collapse of South Vietnam in 1975, the armed forces assumed responsibility for garrisoning the south, rooting out the remaining resistance forces, and providing cadres to assist in administering the newly won territory and its population. At the same time, they had to provide continued support for their Communist allies in Laos. Rather than demobilize, the armed forces were compelled to continue conscription at fairly high levels. Available evidence indicates slightly higher force levels than during the war.

The new Five-Year Plan, published in 1976, obviously envisioned a shift in priorities for the armed forces toward a major role in postwar reconstruction, including support of very ambitious plans to open up new areas for agriculture and industry, as well as for long-term massive internal shifts of population. At the same time, the armed forces had to carry out all of their more traditional security missions.

As relations with Cambodia and China became strained, additional requirements were placed on the armed forces to defend Vietnam's territory. After several years of border incidents between the Cambodians and the Vietnamese the government sent troops into Cambodia in December 1978. Assisted by Cambodian anti-Khmer Rouge forces, and with some use of staging areas in Laos, they rapidly gained control of virtually all of Cambodia and deposed the Pol Pot government. China reacted by invading Vietnam in mid-February 1979. Chinese troops made significant gains, but before the strongly resisting Vietnamese could mobilize on a major scale to throw back the invaders, Peking ordered its troops to withdraw. Thus at mid-1979 Vietnam had friendly neighbors in Cambodia and Laos and a stable condition on the border with China.

100° 104° 108° 112°

24°

C  H  I  N  A

Chengkiang  Silung  Lingyün  Ishan  Pinglo  Wuchow
Nonpan Kiang  Kwangnan  Poseh  Liuchow  Mengshan
Kaiyüan  Kienshui  Yü Kiang  Tienpao  Tuyang Shan  Tropic of Cancer  Kweiping  Si Kiang
Kokiu  Wenshan  Nanning  Henghsien  Watlam  Loting
Manhao  Yen Minh  Trung Khanh Phu  Tsungshan  Hoppo  Mowming
Fan-si-pan  Bao Lac  Ha Giang  Cao Bang  That Khe  Lungtsin  Weichow Tao
10,306  Muong Khuong  Luc An Chau  Bac Cang  Pingsiang  Shinwanta Shan
Lao Cai  Chapa  Bao Ha  Lang Son  Pakhoi  Ye Bao  Luichow  Tsamkong
9,570  Red R.  Tuyen Quang  Thai Nguyen  Tien Yen  Mon Cai  Van Hoa  Hoihong
Phong Saly  Nghia Lo  Yen Bai  Bac Ninh  Hon Gay  Yen  Yingk Bay
Son La  Phu Tho  Vinh Yen  Dao Cat Ba  GULF
Dien Bien Phu  Son Tay  Hanoi  Haiphong  OF
Hoa Binh  Thai Binh
BURMA  Nam Dinh  Dao Bach Long Vi  Kiungchow Str.  Hoihow
Phu Loi  Ninh Binh  (Nightingale I.)  Kiungchow
7,405  Bai Thuong  TONKIN
Sam Neua  Thanh Hoa  Tahsien
Luang  Plateau du Tran Ninh  Phu Tinh Gia  NORTH  HAINAN
Prabang  Plain of  Nong Het  Cua Rao  Aihsien  Yülin  Lingshui
Tha-deua  Jars  Con Cuong  Phu Qui  VIETNAM  C. Bastion
Vinh
THAILAND  Vientiane  Phuc Loi  Ha Tinh  C. Mui Duong
Ron
Huong Khe  Ba Don
Thakhek  Quang Khe  Robert I.
Dong Hoi  Money I.
Loc Lieu  Paracel Is.
Lang Mo  and Reefs
I. du Tigre  Triton I.  (China)
SOUTH CHINA SEA  Quang Tri  Baie de Chon May
Hue  Da Nang
(Tourane)
Quang Nam  Hoi An
Tam Ky
Quang Ngai
Mo Duc
Bong Son
Kontum  Phu My
Pleiku  Binh Dinh
Qui Nhon
Plateau du  Song Cau
Kontum  SOUTH
Thuy Hoa
Ban Me Thuot  VIETNAM
Nha Trang  Baie de Bên Gòi
Lang Bian  Cam
Mts.  Ranh
Da Lat  Cam Ranh Bay
Phan Rang
Phan Thiet
Mui Dinh
BANGKOK  CAMBODIA
(Krung Thep)  Battambang
Siem Reap  Saigon
Phnom Penh  Vung Tau (Cap St. Jacques)
Kompong Som  Long
Xuyen  Can Tho  Mouths of the Mekong
Rach Gia  Tra Vinh (Phu Vinh)
Dao Phu Quoc
Vinh Loi (Bac Lieu)
Con Son
MALAY  GULF OF SIAM
Nakhon Si Thammarat
Pak Phanang  Pte. de Ca Mau  Les Deux Frères
(Pt. Bai Bung)
PENINSULA  Hon Khoai
Hat Yai  Songkhla

100° 104° Longitude East of Greenwich 108° 112°

VIETNAM
SCALE OF MILES
0  50  100  150  200
KILOMETERS
0  50  100  150  200
International Boundaries
Capitals of Countries  ☆

© C. S. HAMMOND & Co., Maplewood, N.J.

There has been speculation that Vietnam intends to construct some sort of Indochina federation, in which Vietnam would play a major role, with Cambodia and Laos in subordinate positions. Obviously the armed forces would have important tasks to carry out if this federation should become reality.

## STRATEGIC PROBLEMS

The increasing acerbity of Sino-Vietnamese relations, resulting in cessation of all assistance from China and the cutting of land communications from the USSR across China, compels Vietnam to rely more than ever on waterborne support from Eastern Europe and the USSR. However, port facilities in Vietnam are limited. These facts may result in efforts to restore and improve U.S.-constructed ports in South Vietnam, especially at Cam Ranh Bay. If Vietnam is compelled to offer the Red Navy basing rights at Cam Ranh in return for Soviet assistance, there is some risk of further alienating China, already apprehensive about the Red Navy's presence in Southeast Asian waters. China also could attempt to exploit ethnic differences in the rugged mountains adjacent to the common border.

As Vietnam's relations with both Cambodia and China worsened, Vietnamese diplomatic activity among the ASEAN states indicated Hanoi's sense of isolation. Thailand, omitted from the early Vietnamese moves as a demonstration of residual Vietnamese resentment of the Thai role in the Indochina war, was included with its ASEAN partners as time wore on.

## MILITARY ASSISTANCE

Vietnam relied on and received heavy and continuing military support from both the USSR and the PRC prior to 1975. Even with the elimination of Chinese support, Vietnam can draw on large stocks of U.S. materiel, some captured, some inherited from the Saigon government. To maintain its Soviet-equipped forces, however, Vietnam must rely on the USSR.

## ALLIANCES

Vietnam is allied most closely with the USSR and Laos.

## ARMY

*Personnel:* 500,000

*Organization:*
  14 divisions (10,000–12,000 per division) plus support regiments
  10 independent artillery regiments
   3 independent armored regiments
  20 independent infantry regiments

  45–50 SAM battalions (SA-2 Guideline, 2 to 6 launchers per battalion)
  24 antiaircraft regiments

*Major Equipment Inventory:*
   175 medium tanks (65 T-34, 110 T-54)
   300 light tanks (PT-76)
       107mm, 122mm, and 140mm rocket launchers
       APCs (BTR-40, M-2, K-61)
       SU-76 and JSU-122 self-propelled guns
       various caliber guns and howitzers (75mm, 105mm, 122mm, 130mm, and 152mm)
 6,000 antiaircraft artillery pieces (100mm, 85mm, 57mm, 37mm—half are radar-directed; several thousand antiaircraft machine guns; ZSU-23/4 and ZSU-57/2 self-propelled antiaircraft guns)
       SAMs (SA-2 Guideline, SA-3, SA-7)
Captured by North Vietnam from South Vietnam. Numbers are approximate.
 1,080 medium tanks (M-47, M-48, 160 M-60)
   260 light tanks (M-24, M-41, AMX-13)
 1,700 APCs (M-113)
   165 half-tracks
   445 armored cars (M-8 and V-150 Commando)
       artillery, antiaircraft, and antitank guns

*Reserves:* unknown

## NAVY

*Personnel:* 5,000

*Major Units:*
     3 patrol ships (1 Barnegat class; 2 Admirable class; PGF)
     3 submarine chasers (SO-1 class; PCS)
    19 patrol craft (59/71 classes; PGM; PC)
    22 fast patrol craft (PCF)
    18 motor torpedo boats (PT)
     2 missile attack boats (Komar class with SSN-2/Styx; PTG)
    50 patrol boats (PB)
   800 river patrol boats (miscellaneous classes; PBR)
     3 tank landing ships (LST)
     6 medium landing ships (miscellaneous classes; LSM)
     5 medium landing ships (US LSM-1 class; LSM)
    19 miscellaneous landing craft
  100+ armed junks
    14 auxiliaries
    45 service craft

*Major Naval Bases:* Haiphong, Vinh, Hue, Chu Lai, Qui Nhon, Cam Rahn Bay, Can Tho

## AIR FORCE

*Personnel:* 10,000

*Organization:*

1 light bomber squadron (Il-28)

6 interceptor squadrons (2 MiG-19, 4 MiG-21)

7 fighter/fighter-bomber squadrons (MiG-15/17, Su-7)

*Major Aircraft Types:*

185 combat aircraft

100 MiG-15/17, Su-7 fighter-bombers (20 MiG-15, 70 MiG-17, 10 Su-7)

40 MiG-21 interceptors (armed with Atoll AAMs)

35 MiG-19 interceptors

10 Il-28 light bombers

156 other aircraft

89 transports (40 Il-14, 6 Il-12, 20 Li-2, 20 An-2, 3 An-24)

25 trainer/support aircraft

30 helicopters (Mi-1, Mi-4)

12 heavy helicopters (Mi-6)

Captured by North Vietnam from South Vietnam:

1,000 aircraft abandoned by South Vietnam (including 87 F-5, 76 A-37, 26 A-1, 35 C-47, 23 C-130, 45 C-119, 32 Caribou, 111 O-1, 29 CH-47, 400 UH-1) (Note: C-47s and C-119s included many gunships.)

*Major Air Bases:* Gia Lam, Dien Bien Phu, Dong Hoi, Vinh, Hoa Lae, Saigon (Tan Son Nhut), Nhatrang, Bien, Bienhoa, Binh Thuy, Dalat, Da Nang, Phan Rang, Pleiku, Cana

## PARAMILITARY

The People's Armed Security Forces and the frontier and coastal security troops total an estimated 20,000.

An armed militia of some 425,000 for home defense is organized by regions.

# YEMEN (ADEN)
# People's Democratic Republic of Yemen

## POWER POTENTIAL STATISTICS

Area: 111,000 square miles
Population: 1,765,000

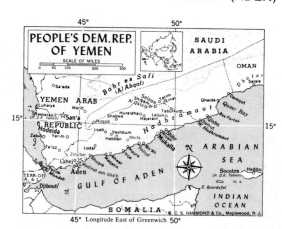

Total Active Regular Armed Forces: 16,450 (0.92% population)
Gross National Product: $490 million ($290 per capita)
Annual Military Expenditures: $55 million (11.2% GNP)
Fuel Production: Refined Petroleum Products: 1.8 million metric tons
Electric Power Output: 300 million kwh
Civil Air Fleet: 6 piston transports

## POLITICO-MILITARY POLICIES AND POSTURE

South Yemen is small in size, has a weak economy (only one percent of its land is arable), and has a Communist government. The capital and port of Aden is strategically located near the southern entrance to the Red Sea, and the South Yemeni island of Perim in the Bab el Mandeb Strait could control that entrance.

British efforts to prepare the combined colonial regions of Aden and the South Arabian Protectorate for an orderly transition to independence in 1968 were frustrated by a combination of anticolonial nationalism and internal dissension among the various segments of the population. Terrorism and counterterrorism against each other and against the British by the Egyptian-backed Front for the Liberation of Occupied South Yemen (FLOSY) and the indigenous National Liberation Front (NLF) caused the British to withdraw earlier than they had originally intended. With the National Liberation Front generally successful in the internal disorders, Britain recognized this group as the basis for an independent government and granted independence on November 30, 1967. The president is head of state and supreme commander of the armed forces.

Throughout 1968 government troops fought with FLOSY adherents and remaining dissidents in the former sheikhdoms north and northeast of Aden, in a generally successful campaign to establish government authority over the entire country. Defensive operations were also conducted against alleged Saudi Arabian incursions across the ill-defined border. In October 1971 army and air force units attacked targets in North Yemen (now officially Yemen Arab Republic), and relations between the two nations continued strained, to the point that in October 1972 open warfare erupted. The conflict ended the same month with a ceasefire arranged by the Arab League. Both sides agreed to a union of the two Yemens, to be formed within eighteen months. The proposed merger fell through. In May 1973 border clashes between the two countries erupted again. In renewed hostilities along the border in February 1979, South Yemen forces occupied border towns in North Yemen. After the United States promised prompt shipments of equipment and advisors to the North and the Soviet Union rushed 3,000 Soviet and Cuban troops and advisors to the South, a truce under Arab League supervision was reached in March. In April an agreement on union was announced.

A mutiny in June 1978 resulted in the assassination of South Yemen's titular head, President Salim Rubayir Ali. For several years Ali, a pragmatic nationalist, had been contesting the Marxist revolutionary views of Abdul Fatah Ismail, the chairman of South Yemen's single party (the National Front), and seeking increased ties and cooperation with peninsular states and a less devoted Communist ideological approach. Two days before the mutiny, North Yemen's President Ghashmi had been assassinated, allegedly by South Yemeni intrigue. The success of Chairman Ismail in the revolt suggests that South Yemen will strengthen its already close ties with the Soviets.

An arms agreement with the Soviet Union was signed in 1968, and substantial amounts of Soviet equipment are on hand, including 12 MiG-17 fighters and possibly some MiG-21 fighters. There are Soviet and Cuban military technicians and instructors in South Yemen. Early in 1971 Communist China established a military mission in Aden staffed by several dozen officers. China's $55 million aid program centered largely on construction of a military road from Aden to Mukalla. The island of Socotra, off the Horn of Africa, is a Soviet naval anchorage, and Aden is regularly visited by Soviet naval ships and aircraft.

The army was developed upon independence from the former Federal Regular Army (Aden Protectorate Levies), the Eastern Protectorate's Hadhrami Bedouin Legion, and the Mukalla Regular Army; all British- and Royalist-oriented personnel were removed and replaced by politically reliable National Front members.

South Yemen is a member of the Arab League.

## ARMY

*Personnel:* 15,000

*Organization:*
  10 infantry brigades

  2 armored car battalions
  artillery batteries
  T-34, T-54/55 medium tanks
  armored cars and scout cars
  light and medium artillery
  antiaircraft guns (ZSU-23/4)
  SAM SA-7

## NAVY

*Personnel:* 450

*Major Units:*
  2 submarine chasers (Soviet SO-1 class; PCS)
  3 inshore minesweepers (MSI)
  2 fast patrol craft (PCF)
  7 patrol boats (PB)
  5 mechanized landing craft (LCM)

## AIR FORCE

*Personnel:* 1,000

*Organization:*
  1 fighter squadron (MiG-21)
  1 fighter-bomber squadron (MiG-17)
  1 transport squadron (Il-14, An-24)
  1 helicopter squadron (Mi-4, Mi-8)
  1 training flight (MiG-15)

*Major Aircraft Types:*
  36 combat aircraft
    12 MiG-21
    24 MiG-17
  25 other aircraft
    10 transports (3 Il-14, 3 An-24, 4 C-47)
    10 helicopters (4 Mi-4, 6 Mi-8)
    5 trainers (MiG-15)

## PARAMILITARY

Paramilitary units include the National Security Police and the National Front Militia of unknown strength and composition.

# YEMEN (SAN'A)
## The Yemen Arab Republic

### POWER POTENTIAL STATISTICS

Area: 75,290 square miles
Population: 5,078,000

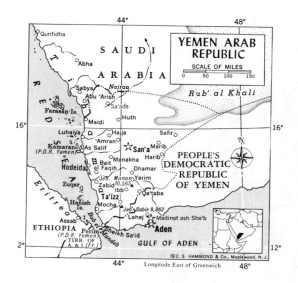

YEMEN ARAB REPUBLIC

San'a and the Soviet Union in support of Aden. Following a truce under Arab League supervision, a new agreement on union of the two countries was announced in March.

In the fall of 1977 President Ibrahim Hamdi was assassinated, apparently by unknown North Yemeni assailants. He was succeeded by another military commander, Lt. Col. Ghashmi, who was himself assassinated in June 1978, apparently by pro-Communist South Yemeni agents. The fundamental policy of both presidents was to establish the dominance of the central government over powerful tribal elements.

Saudi Arabia seeks to maintain a dominant influence in the affairs of North Yemen and plays a major role in training, supporting, and equipping its armed forces. The Saudis would prefer that San'a dismiss the few Soviet advisers who remain from earlier USSR military assistance programs.

The army, which includes the air force and navy, numbers about 15,000 men; some of the officers have been trained in Egypt and the USSR. Equipment is Soviet. It includes at least 30 T-34 medium tanks, 50 SU-100 assault guns, 70 BTR-40 armored personnel carriers, 50 76mm guns, 100 antiaircraft guns of various calibers, 10 F-5 and 12 MiG-17 fighters, 8 Il-28 light bombers, some Il-14 and C-47 transports and AB-204 and Mi-4 helicopters. A small 300-man naval force operates eight patrol boats (PB) at the main port of Al Hudaydah. Some 20,000 tribal levies may be considered a potential reserve.

Military assistance from the United States totaled $357,000 in 1977, and thirty-eight students received training in 1976 and 1977 under the MAP. Total MAP aid to Yemen through 1977 equaled $541,000.

North Yemen is a member of the Arab League.

Total Active Regular Armed Forces: 15,000 (0.29% population)
Gross National Product: $1.63 billion ($300 per capita)
Annual Military Expenditures: $50.4 million (3.09% GNP)
Electric Power Output: 100 million kwh
Civil Air Fleet: 9 major transport aircraft

## POLITICO-MILITARY POLICIES AND POSTURE

The strategic significance of North Yemen derives from the fact that its border with South Yemen runs just inside the entrance to the Red Sea. North Yemen has some of the most arable lands of the Arabian Peninsula along its coast and on the seaward mountain slopes, and is relatively populous.

Under a 1971 constitution there is a Consultative Assembly, partly elected and partly appointed by the president of the council. The assembly elects the three-to-five-member Presidential Council, which in turn elects one of its members president. The revolution that began as a military revolt against Imam Muhammad al-Badr in 1962 ended in 1969, after withdrawal of Egyptian and Saudi Arabian troops. In March 1970 an agreement was reached with Saudi Arabia, calling for reconciliation of all tribes and factions, and the return of all exiles (except the imam and his family). Saudi Arabia recognized the Yemen Arab Republic and promised economic aid. Since then there have been recurring efforts toward union with the Marxist regime in Aden. There have also been intervals of intense animosity between the two countries, during which tribal and paramilitary units have made cross-border forays in an attempt to destabilize conditions in the ill-defined border areas. Most recently, in February 1979 serious hostilities caused responses from the United States in support of

# YUGOSLAVIA
## Socialist Federal Republic of Yugoslavia

### POWER POTENTIAL STATISTICS

Area: 98,766 square miles
Population: 22,074,000
Total Active Regular Armed Forces: 244,000 (1.10% population)
Gross National Product: $48.0 billion ($2,210 per capita)
Annual Military Expenditures: $2.34 billion (4.87% GNP)
Crude Steel Production: 3.2 million metric tons
Iron Ore Production: 4.3 million metric tons
Fuel Production:
Crude Oil: 3.9 million metric tons
Refined Petroleum Products: 10.8 million metric tons

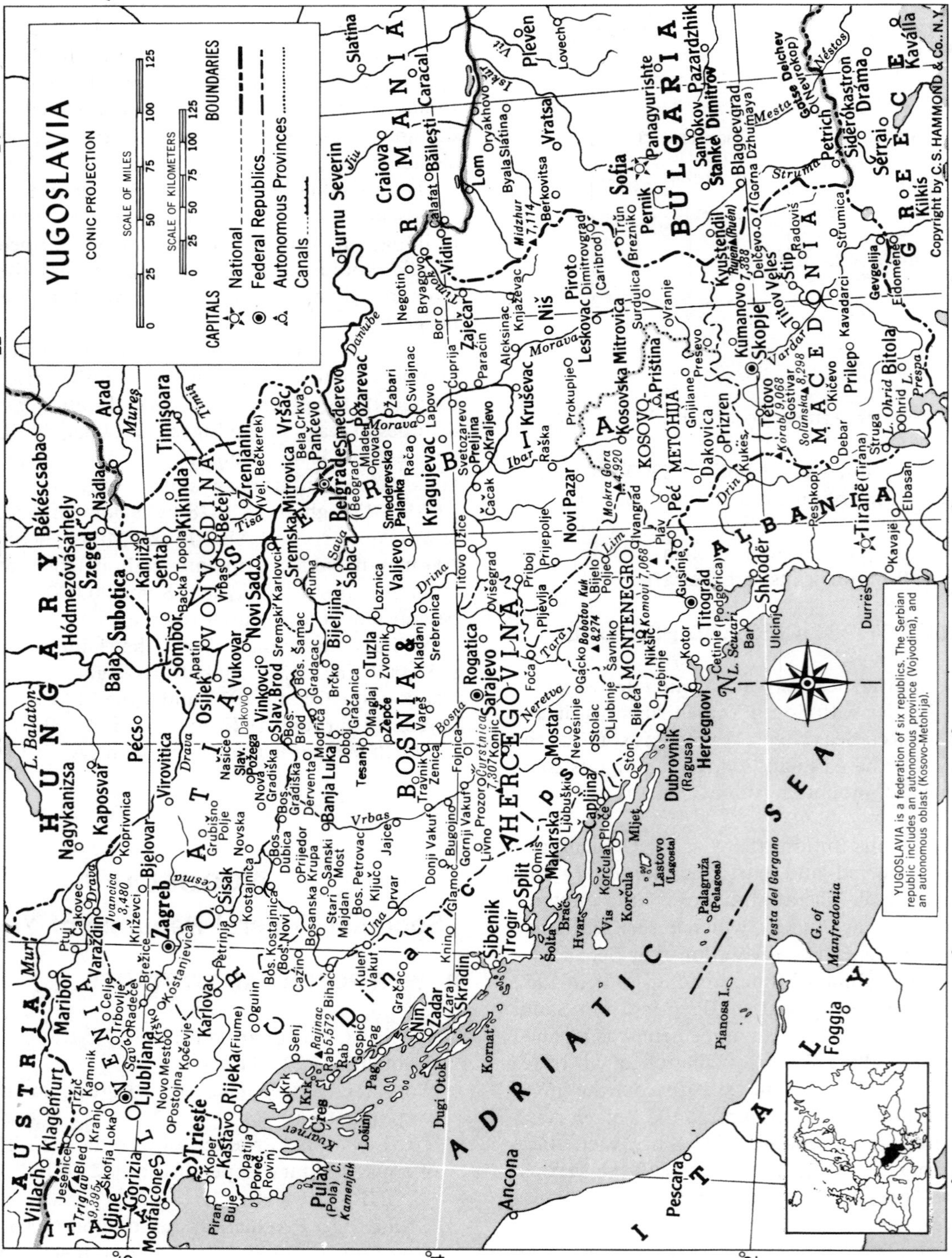

## YUGOSLAVIA

CONIC PROJECTION

SCALE OF MILES

0 25 50 75 100 125

SCALE OF KILOMETERS

0 25 50 75 100 125

CAPITALS

☆ National

⊙ Federal Republics

△ Autonomous Provinces

BOUNDARIES

National ━━━━

Federal Republics ━ ━ ━

Autonomous Provinces ·········

Canals

YUGOSLAVIA is a federation of six republics. The Serbian
republic includes an autonomous province (Vojvodina), and
an autonomous oblast (Kosovo-Metohija).

Copyright by C. S. HAMMOND & Co., N. Y.

Longitude East of Greenwich

*AUSTRIA*

*HUNGARY*

*ROMANIA*

*BULGARIA*

*GREECE*

*ALBANIA*

*ITALY*

*CROATIA*

*SLOVENIA*

*VOJVODINA*

*BOSNIA & HERCEGOVINA*

*SERBIA*

*MONTENEGRO*

*MACEDONIA*

*KOSOVO*

*METOHIJA*

*ADRIATIC SEA*

*Dinaric Alps*

Lignite: 35.7 million metric tons
Coal: 587,000 metric tons
Natural Gas: 1.7 billion cubic meters
Manufactured Gas: 150 million cubic meters
Electric Power Output: 48.6 billion kwh
Nuclear Power Production: 632 megawatts
Merchant Fleet (ships 1,000 tons and over): 244 ships; 2.2 million gross tons
Civil Air Fleet: 28 jet and 20 piston transports

## DEFENSE STRUCTURE

The Yugoslav League of Communists (Communist party) controls the government, including all elements of the military establishment, its leaders occupying key positions. The president, Marshal Tito, who heads the Communist party, is the commander in chief of the armed forces and the chairman of the Council of National Defense.

The Department of National Defense and the federal secretary for national defense are responsible for preparing defense plans, organizing and training the armed forces, and organizing and mobilizing human and material resources (including the formation of a guerrilla resistance in the event of invasion). The department includes an integrated General Staff of the Armed Forces for the army, navy, and air force.

## POLITICO-MILITARY POLICY

Yugoslavia's foreign policy is based on the principle of independence and neutrality. Yugoslavia declares itself a socialist country, but not part of the Communist bloc. It maintains close ties with nonaligned nations and strives to assume leadership of nations outside the Western and Soviet alliance systems.

Since 1948, Yugoslavia's relations with the USSR have followed a fluctuating pattern of tensions and improvements. They worsened after the Soviet invasion of Czechoslovakia, which Tito criticized, and improved after the 1971 visit by Soviet Communist party leader Brezhnev to Belgrade. They have since remained stable, with Tito attempting to make them more cordial.

At present Yugoslavia maintains friendly relations with most of its neighbors. Relations with Albania have improved since 1971, when Albania and Yugoslavia announced their intention to exchange ambassadors. The Yugoslavs have continued their attempts to cultivate Albania since the deterioration of the latter's relations with China. The long dispute with Italy over Trieste was resolved in the 1976 Osimo agreements. Bulgaria's irredentist claims to Yugoslav Macedonia have strained relations between the two countries in the past.

Military service is universal. All male citizens between the ages of nineteen and twenty-seven are liable for military service. The length of service is eighteen months in the army, air force, and navy. There is compulsory reserve service, for officers up to sixty years of age, and for others up to age fifty-five. Women between nineteen and forty years of age can serve in reserve noncombat activities. Full mobilization could bring the strength of the armed forces to over 1,300,000 men.

## STRATEGIC PROBLEMS

In the north and east, Yugoslavia borders on neutral Austria and three members of the Warsaw Pact: Hungary, Romania, and Bulgaria. For the most part, this long border has few obstacles, and is open to an enveloping invasion in the event of a Soviet-Yugoslav conflict. The Pannonian Plain that spans the Hungarian-Yugoslav border makes the capital, Belgrade, about 100 miles south, extremely vulnerable. The border with Bulgaria, however, is mountainous, the Adriatic coast is rugged, and most of Yugoslavia is well protected by its extensive mountain core.

In order to resist a Warsaw Pact invasion, Yugoslavia probably would need extensive help from the outside. Since it must be assumed that the invaders would use the Ljubljana Gap to seize the port of Rijeka (Fiume) and to sever Yugoslavia's land communication with Italy, communications with the outside world could be maintained only through the remaining Dalmatian ports and through Greece. In view of the presence of strong Soviet naval forces in the Mediterranean, these communications could be kept open only in cooperation with the U.S. Mediterranean Fleet. However, in order to avoid exacerbating relations with Moscow after its invasion of Czechoslovakia, Tito stated publicly that Yugoslavia does not ask for any protection from NATO.

The multinational and multireligious population of Yugoslavia is divided by many old ethnic and religious antagonisms. The independence movement in Croatia is particularly strong and active. Bulgaria's claims to Macedonia, although not currently being pressed, are a possible future source of trouble. Many of the 1,000,000 Albanians in Yugoslavia, most of them in the autonomous province of Kosovo, would like to see union of that province with Albania, and there is reported to be an underground Albanian National Liberation Movement advocating this goal. The existence of a sizable Hungarian minority in the autonomous province of Voyvodina, bordering Hungary, could conceivably furnish an excuse for outside intervention. The present regime has successfully handled the problem of Yugoslavia's heterogeneity by two approaches—firm suppression of separatist activists, plus the creation of a federal system that gives the individual republics considerable real independence and self-determination. These federal reforms were carried out in 1971 and 1974.

It is reasonable to assume that, if threatened with foreign invasion, the people will unite for the defense of their country under the leadership of the present government. Mindful of Czechoslovakia's quick subjugation, and of its own historical development of guerrilla combat, Yugoslavia's 1969 national defense law stresses the doctrine of the people in arms and the ignominy of surrender. In conformity with this principle, the Territorial Defense Force is continuously in being, and plans are closely coordinated with the regular forces for instant action in a national emergency.

Much speculation centers on whether Yugoslavia will be able to remain unified and pursue its independent course between East and West after the death of the octogenarian Tito. It is probable that the federal system is solid enough to keep the loyalties of the various nationalities, and it is doubtful that the Soviet Union will invade without the excuse of nationalist uprisings or other disturbances. However, even a small group of pro-Soviet activists or nationalist extremists could cause enough trouble to serve as a pretext for Soviet intervention.

The constitutional provisions for Tito's successor are also not reassuring. After his death, the chairman of the presidency will rotate among the remaining eight members, changing each year. Without strong permanent leadership, the federal system may falter.

## MILITARY ASSISTANCE

Because of its vulnerable position between NATO and Soviet-bloc nations, and its determination to maintain an independent Third World position, Yugoslavia has sought to avoid complete dependence on either group for armaments. This has necessitated a buildup of defense industries which now are able to supply Yugoslavia's needs except for the heaviest and most sophisticated equipment. Light aircraft, tanks, submarines, most artillery weapons, trucks, and small arms are made locally.

After Tito's break with Stalin in 1948, Yugoslavia developed ties with the United States and other Western countries and received extensive American military and economic assistance, given to help Tito preserve independence from the USSR. United States military assistance to Yugoslavia from 1950 to 1965 amounted to $703 million. There has been no American military aid since then.

After relations improved with the USSR, Yugoslavia bought Soviet military equipment totalling over $200 million in surplus ruble funds.

In its attempt at leadership among Third World developing and nonaligned nations, Yugoslavia gains additional leverage by its ability to supply arms from its significant armaments industry to countries that may not wish to depend for armaments on the Soviet Union, Communist China, or Western countries. Arms are sold, without grant-aid.

Yugoslavia has consistently supported the peacekeeping efforts of the United Nations. A reinforced battalion was furnished the United Nations Emergency Force in the Gaza strip of Palestine from 1957 until its withdrawal in May 1967. A small detachment was sent to the United Nations Operations in the Congo.

## ALLIANCES

In 1953, before Yugoslavia had built up its defenses with self-help and U.S. military aid, and before NATO and U.S. aid had strengthened the defenses of Greece and Turkey, these three countries signed the Balkan Defense Pact at Ankara, Turkey. This was a five-year treaty of friendship and collaboration which provided for common defensive measures. It was strengthened and extended for twenty years in 1954, but for reasons that include NATO and the Cyprus troubles, the treaty has since lost its value for the signatories.

## ARMY

*Personnel:* 200,000

*Organization:* Four army commands with headquarters at Belgrade (First), Skoplje (Third), Zagreb (Fifth), and Sarajevo (Seventh).
   8 army corps
         1 armored division (including artillery and antitank regiments)
         9 infantry divisions (including artillery and antitank regiments)
        30 independent infantry brigades
        12 independent tank brigades
         1 airborne brigade
         1 marine brigade
        12 antiaircraft regiments

*Major Equipment Inventory:*
   2,000 medium tanks (M-4/47/60, T-34/54/55)
         light tanks (PT-76 and AMX-13)
         APCs (M-2 halftrack, M-3, BTR-50P/60P/152)
         tank destroyer/assault guns (SU-100)
         57mm airborne self-propelled guns (ASU-57)
         57mm self-propelled antiaircraft guns (ZSU-57/2)
         37mm antiaircraft guns
         40mm antiaircraft guns

Sagger and Snapper antitank missiles
TOW antitank missiles
armored cars (M-8)
76.2mm mountain guns
75mm mountain howitzers
76mm antitank guns
90mm self-propelled antitank guns
88mm coast defense guns
105mm self-propelled howitzers
105mm and 155mm howitzers
155mm guns
120mm heavy mortars
81mm and 60mm mortars
57mm, 75mm, 82mm, 106mm recoilless
   rifles

*Reserves:* There are 1,200,000 reservists available for mobilization, some to bring units up to strength, others to expand the thirty-three brigades to divisions.

## NAVY

*Personnel:* 14,000

*Major Units:*
   5 submarines (3 Heroj class; 2 Sutjeska class; SS)
   1 destroyer (Split class; DD)
   10 missile attack boats (Osa class; SS-N-2/Styx SSM; PTG)
   2 missile attack boats (Type 211/Rade Koncar class; PTG)
   14 submarine chasers (Kraljevica class; PCS)
   3 submarine chasers (miscellaneous classes; PCS)
   14 motor torpedo boats (Shershen class; PT)
   23 patrol craft (miscellaneous classes; PC)
   4 coastal minesweepers (Smeli class; MSC)
   10 inshore minesweepers (6 M-117 class; 4 Ham class; MSI)
   13 river minesweepers (miscellaneous classes; MSM)
   26 utility landing vessels (most DTM class; LCU)
   25 auxiliary ships
      helicopters (Mi-8, Ka-25)

*Major Naval Bases:* Zadar, Sibenik, Split, Dubrovnik, Kotor, Pula

## AIR FORCE

*Personnel:* 30,000

*Organization:*
   2 air corps headquartered at Zagreb and Zemun
   2 interceptor divisions (5 squadrons of MiG-21, 1 squadron of MiG-19, and 4 squadrons of F-86D)
   3 fighter-bomber divisions (3 squadrons of F-84 G; 3 squadrons of Jastreb light attack; 3 squadrons of Kraguj close support aircraft)
   2 reconnaissance squadrons, one for each air corps (RT-33A and RF-86F)
   8 SAM battalions (SA-2 Guideline)

*Major Aircraft Types:*
   455 combat aircraft
      150 MiG-21 interceptors
      15 MiG-19 interceptors
      50 F-86D interceptors
      20 F-84G fighter-bombers
      30 RT-33 reconnaissance/fighter aircraft
      150 Jastreb/Galeb light attack aircraft
      40 Kraguj close support aircraft
   447 other aircraft
      15 C-47 transports
      4 DC-6 transports
      15 Il-14 transports
      18 Mi-4 helicopters
      20 Mi-8 helicopters
      10 Il-18 transports
      40 Whirlwind helicopters
      35 SA-341 Gazelle helicopters
      300 trainer/support aircraft (including UTVA-60/66)

*Air Bases:* Zemun, Ljubljana, Zagreb, Kotor, Titograd, Batajnica, Nis, Sombor, Sarajevo, Pleso, Pula, Nickoic, Mostar, Skoplje, Vrsac, Cerklje, Salusani.

## PARAMILITARY

Yugoslavia has a force of 19,000 Frontier Guards under the Ministry of National Defense and a National Police or *Milija* of 163,000. Territorial Defense units, incorporating armed workers and partisan organizations closely affiliated with the armed forces, probably include virtually every able-bodied adult citizen (accounting for a total strength of up to 3,000,000 men and women by the end of 1972). At the time of the 1968 invasion of Czechoslovakia arms were issued to many of these partisans, and bases in the mountains were stocked with arms and other supplies.

# ZAIRE
# Republic of Zaire

## POWER POTENTIAL STATISTICS

Area: 905,063 square miles
Population: 27,474,000

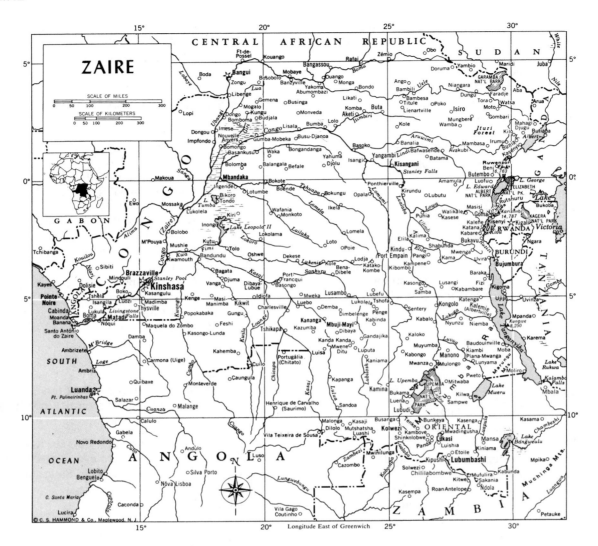

Total Active Regular Armed Forces: 36,200 (0.13%
  population)
Gross National Product: $3.59 billion ($140 per capita)
Annual Military Expenditures: $147 million (4.09%
  GNP)
Fuel Production:
  Coal: 90,000 metric tons
  Crude Oil: 1.26 million metric tons
  Refined Petroleum Products: 379,000 metric tons
Electric Power Output: 5.1 billion kwh
Merchant Fleet (ships 1,000 tons and over): 10 ships,
  95,000 gross tons
Civil Air Fleet: 49 major transport aircraft

## DEFENSE STRUCTURE

President Joseph Mobutu, former army commander in
chief, who seized control of a government torn by internal
dissension in November 1965, is also state commissioner
for defense. He controls the armed forces directly as
commander in chief. The armed forces are maintained
through voluntary enlistment.

## POLITICO-MILITARY POLICY

Policies have centered on building a competent and
loyal military force with help from the Western powers,
securing the borders against the infiltration of arms and
agents by Communists and other dissidents, preventing
secession, and extending government control throughout
the land.

Despite past attempts of radical African states at
subversion in Zaire, it joins them in supporting the
southern African liberation movements and actively
supports the Angolan nationalist groups by according
recognition and allowing their bases to be located in Zaire.
However, Zaire continues to maintain extensive trade with
South Africa and Zimbabwe Rhodesia.

## STRATEGIC PROBLEMS

Dominating central Africa, and rich in copper, cobalt, uranium, and other minerals, the Congo—as Zaire was called in the colonial era—was a prize that fell to Belgium in the late nineteenth century. Since independence (1960) it has been a target for Communist subversion. The secession of mineral-rich Katanga was an attempt by the Katangans (apparently with Belgian encouragement) to salvage the mining area from the chaos which for several years engulfed the rest of the country. The Katanga secession and a serious army revolt were put down by a four-year occupation of much of the country by a UN peacekeeping force of 15,000–20,000 troops. Concurrently a massive UN and Western training and technical assistance program sought to prepare the Congo for self-government and self-defense.

After the UN forces withdrew in 1964, the northeast Congo erupted in Communist-led tribal warfare. Russian and Chinese arms were delivered via Sudan; an insurgent cadre was trained in the radical African states and Communist countries, and foreign Communist agents (including Cubans) were active in the rebel leadership. With the help of white mercenary commandos, who were supported by a mercenary air force (reportedly U.S.-sponsored), the rebellion was suppressed by 1965. Subsequent brief revolts in 1966 and 1967 were suppressed. Scattered instances of tribal and religious violence were promptly brought under control during the next ten years.

Mobutu's regime has become highly personalized and riddled with corruption. Its stability reached a high point in 1973 during the peak in world copper prices, on which Zaire's economy largely depends. (Two-thirds of its export income is from copper.) Mobutu capped a "Zaireani-zation" campaign with a combination of nationalizations and private Zairean takeovers of numerous foreign businesses in 1973 and 1974. By 1978, incompetence, corruption, and the sharp fall in copper prices had bankrupted the economy to such a degree that Mobutu had to reverse the nationalization program and effectively turn over administration of the economy to the IMF and Western technicians. They faced an uphill battle to overcome a $3 billion foreign debt, a 75 percent inflation rate, and a severely disrupted commercial infrastructure.

Domestic unrest intensified in the mid-1970s. Of several resurgent opposition movements, by far the most serious challenge came from remnants of the Katanga gendarmes. The Katangans had reorganized in Angola into the National Front for the Liberation of the Congo (FNLC). They assisted the MPLA in winning the 1975–76 Angolan civil war. (Zaire had supported the rival FNLA and still provides it bases in Zaire.) FNLC forces invaded Shaba Province in the spring of 1977 and again in May of 1978. Both attacks were turned back, with Moroccan troops in 1977 and French and Belgian troops in 1978. The 1978 attack, however, severely disrupted mining operations in Kolwezi, further clouding the country's economic prospects.

Zaire's relations with Angola are hostile; each nation's support of the other's rebel movements remains a serious mutual threat. Zaire restored diplomatic ties to the Congo (Brazzaville) in 1970, but the two countries are not friendly. Zaire has satisfactory to excellent relations with its other neighbors, none of which constitutes a serious security problem.

## MILITARY ASSISTANCE

After the UN had put down the army revolt and the Katanga secession, the government invited six nations, through the UN, to assist in rebuilding the armed forces as an effective force for internal security and defense of the borders. Belgium trained the ground forces, Italy the air force, Norway the naval element, Israel the paratroop-commandos, Canada the communications and transport units, while the United States provided supply and administrative support. The United States, which had paid half the $500 million cost of the UN intervention, contributed $299 million in military assistance from 1964 through 1977. Under the MAP 789 persons have been trained. Italy's initial contribution was about $5 million. Belgian aid has been slightly over $1 million a year, and some 500 Belgian adviser-instructors work with the army. Nigeria has assisted in police training. An organization known as WIGMO (Western International Ground Maintenance Organization, alleged to be a U.S. instrument) has kept the government's aircraft in operation and provided the pilots, mostly Cuban exiles. During the 1967 revolt Ghana helped ease the pilot shortage by sending pilots to fly armed trainers.

## ALLIANCES

Zaire has no alliances other than the military aid agreements. It is a member of the OAU. It withdrew from OCAM in 1972.

## ARMY

*Personnel:* 33,000

*Organization:*
    12 infantry battalions
    6 paratroop battalions
    1 tank battalion
    4 commando battalions
    1 heavy weapons battalion
      support units

*Major Equipment Inventory:*
    30 light tanks
    20 APCs (M-113)

scout cars (Ferret and M-3)
40 half-tracks (M-2)
80 armored cars (AML-60/90)
light and medium artillery pieces (75mm,
122mm)
130mm guns and howitzers
antitank guns, Snapper ATGM, antiaircraft guns

## NAVY

*Personnel:* 200

*Major Units:*
3 motor torpedo boats (PT)
20 patrol boats (PB)

## AIR FORCE

*Personnel:* 3,000

*Organization:*
2 air groups
1 fighter squadron (Mirage 5)
3 light ground attack squadrons (T-6/28D,
MB326GB)
1 light reconnaissance squadron (Pembroke)
3 transport squadrons (C-54, C-47, Caribou,
Buffalo)
1 light transport squadron (Cessna 310)
2 helicopter squadrons (Alouette II/III,
UH-1, AB-205, Bell 47, SA-330 Puma)
2 training squadrons (SF-260M, T-6)
2 logistic support squadrons (C-46, Caribou,
C-130)
1 liaison squadron (Do-27/28, Auster)

*Major Aircraft Types:*
64 combat aircraft
17 Mirage 5 fighters
20 T-28D armed trainers
10 T-6G armed trainers
17 Aermacchi MB326GB light ground attack
aircraft
157 other aircraft
4 Pembroke reconnaissance aircraft
4 C-54 transports
1 DC-6 transport
6 C-130 transports
10 C-47 transports
4 Caribou transports
15 Buffalo transports
25 Cessna 310 light transports
12 SIAI-Marchetti SF-260M trainers
20 T-6 trainers
15 Cessna 150 trainers
45 helicopters (Alouette II/III, Bell 47, UH-1,
AB-205, and Puma)

*Major Air Bases:* Kinshasa, Kisingani, Lubumbashi,
Luluabourg, Mbandaka, Kamina, Likasi, and Kolweze

## PARAMILITARY

There is a civil police force of 21,000, about half of
whom are trained for internal security. The police operate
a small water patrol force in three locations: in the Zaire
estuary from Matadi to the sea, on the Zaire River where it
forms the border with Congo (Brazzaville), and on Lake
Tanganyika.

There are six National Guard and seven gendarmerie
battalions of unknown strength.

# ZAMBIA
# Republic of Zambia

## POWER POTENTIAL STATISTICS

Area: 290,724 square miles
Population: 5,559,000
Total Active Regular Armed Forces: 6,500 (0.12%
population)
Gross National Product: $2.5 billion ($480 per capita)
Annual Military Expenditures: $79 million (3.16% GNP)
Fuel Production:
Coal: 789,000 metric tons
Refined Petroleum Products: 896,000 metric tons
Electric Power Output: 7.2 billion kwh
Merchant Fleet (ships 1,000 tons and over): 1 ship;
6,000 gross tons
Civil Air Fleet: 10 major transport aircraft

## POLITICO-MILITARY POLICIES AND POSTURE

President Kenneth Kaunda has ruled Zambia since
independence in October 1964. In 1972 Kaunda banned the
opposition United Progressive Party and established a
one-party state. He chairs the Central Committee of the
United National Independence Party (UNIP), which
directs the work of his cabinet. Kaunda also serves as
defense minister. In June 1976 the armed forces were
unified into the Zambia National Defence Forces.

Zambia is a member of the OAU and the Commonwealth. It adheres closely to its proclaimed nonaligned
position in world affairs. The central pillar of Zambian
foreign policy is the liberation of the African peoples of
southern Africa. Zambia is one of the five front-line states
opposing white minority rule in Rhodesia, South Africa,
and Namibia.

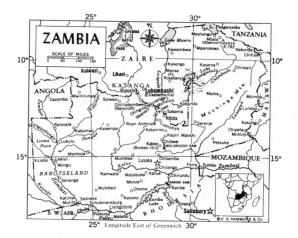

Zambia's central position, small police force, and size have made it—somewhat involuntarily—a base for various liberation groups operating in southern Africa. Officially it forbade use of its territory by these movements in the 1960s, but gradually shifted to welcoming them. Support for FRELIMO forces operating in Mozambique prior to its independence in 1975 earned Kaunda the lasting friendship of Mozambique's leadership.

The major shift in Zambian policy came in 1973 when Rhodesia temporarily closed its border with Zambia to all but copper exports, in order to force Kaunda to control Rhodesian guerrillas. In spite of grave economic consequences, President Kaunda declared the border permanently closed and set about redirecting Zambian trade through Tanzania, Zaire, and Angola. Subsequently, Zambia became the primary base for the Zimbabwe African People's Union (ZAPU) headed by Joshua Nkomo.

The cost of Zambia's sanctions against Rhodesia has been high, in dollar terms more than $500 million to 1978. Alternate trade routes are much longer and often congested. One of the routes—the Benguela Railway—has been closed since mid-1975 because of the Angolan civil war. The Chinese completed construction of the Tan-Zam Railway at about the same time, and it absorbed much of the Benguela line traffic. However, the Tan-Zam has found a bottleneck at Dar es Salaam's underdeveloped port. Foreign aid has compensated only a small portion of the cost of sanctions. The IMF has loaned Zambia $400 million.

Zambia has taken a position in opposition to Rhodesia's 1978 "internal settlement" and has condemned the three black Rhodesians who formed an interim government with whites. Kaunda has allowed ZAPU forces to step up their incursions into Rhodesia. Consequently, Rhodesian security forces have launched several preemptive and retaliatory strikes inside Zambia, which Zambian forces have been too weak to counter. Kaunda has warned the West since 1976 that Zambian insecurity or unsatisfactory progress toward majority rule in Rhodesia could force him to call on Soviet and Cuban assistance. About seventy-five Cuban advisers were working with ZAPU forces in 1978. Zambia has also served as a base for SWAPO guerrillas operating against South African forces in Namibia. South African units have made limited raids into Zambia in pursuit of SWAPO insurgents.

Zambia has improved relations with Neto's MPLA regime in Angola. Kaunda had supported the UNITA rebels during the independence struggle with Portugal. During the 1975–76 Angolan civil war Kaunda urged coalition government among the competing Angolan movements. Zambia was one of the last African states to establish relations with the Marxist MPLA regime, which won the civil war with Cuban help. In late 1976, Zambia expelled UNITA leaders and welcomed the new Angolan government to membership in the group of front-line states. On Zambia's northern border, economic arrangements and periodic security discussions characterize proper but not close relations with Zaire. Tanzania's President Nyerere, on the other hand, is a close friend of Kaunda. Zambia and Malawi are discussing a possible rail link.

The current government is in more danger from internal discontent than from an invasion. Rhodesian incursions remain a threat but are mainly directed at refugee and ZAPU camps. Zambian police have become involved in quelling internal disputes within the Zambia-based liberation movements. Of greater concern is the economic crisis precipitated by the decline of world copper prices (over 90 percent of Zambian export earnings come from copper), the rise in oil import costs, and the boycott of Rhodesia. The resulting unemployment has generated a rapid increase in crime and strong sentiment for ending the boycott. Kaunda, whose UNIP has enjoyed intertribal support, handily won affirmation in the 1973 one-party elections, but he faced considerable domestic dissatisfaction as the 1978 elections approached.

Upon independence British military equipment in Zambia was turned over to the Defence Force, and additional equipment has since been granted or sold by Britain. For some time after independence, the recruiting of white officers and NCOs was permitted by Britain, which made up deficiencies by secondment from the British army and Royal Air Force. Training of Zambian personnel, including officer cadets, has been conducted in Britain, Canada, and Ireland. However, Zambianization of the Defence Force has become a matter of national policy. In 1970, the British commander of the Zambian army was replaced by a Zambian. In 1971 fifteen British officers in the Zambian Defence Force were dismissed and ordered to leave the country. Their positions were taken over by Zambians.

The police forces total at least 6,250 and have taken on increasingly paramilitary characteristics. Among such units are the 1st and 2d Mobile Police Battalions of 750 men each and four Police Strike Force companies of 150 men each.

## ARMY

*Personnel:* 5,500

*Organization:*
    1 brigade (3 infantry battalions, 1 reconnaissance squadron)
    1 artillery battery
    1 engineer company
    1 signal company

*Major Equipment Inventory:*
    30 Ferret scout cars
    16 105mm howitzers
    Rapier SAM

## AIR FORCE

*Personnel:* 1,000
    2 ground attack squadrons (MB326, Jastreb, SF260)
    2 transport squadrons (C-47, Caribou, Buffalo)

*Major Aircraft Types:*
    30 combat aircraft
        30 light ground attack/trainer (18 MB326, 4 Jastreb, 8 SF-260)
    77 other aircraft
        16 transports (5 C-47, 4 Caribou, 7 Buffalo)
         8 Commando liaison (6 Beaver, 2 Pembroke)
        36 trainers (2 Galeb, 6 Chipmunk, 20 Saab MF1-15, 8 T-6)
        17 helicopters (10 AB-205, 7 Bell 47)

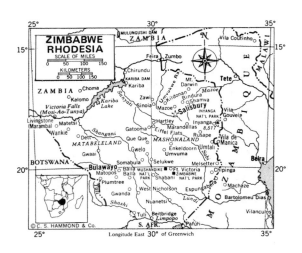

# ZIMBABWE RHODESIA

## POWER POTENTIAL STATISTICS

Area: 150,333 square miles
Population: 7,431,000
Total Active Regular Armed Forces: 4,600 (0.06% population)
Gross National Product: $3.50 billion ($520 per capita)
Annual Military Expenditures: $166 million (4.74% GNP)

Iron Ore Production: 384,000 metric tons
Fuel Production: Coal: 3.5 million metric tons
Electric Power Output: 7.5 billion kwh
Civil Air Fleet: 11 major transport aircraft

## GOVERNMENT AND DEFENSE STRUCTURE

The British colony of Southern Rhodesia unilaterally declared its independence in November 1965. Although internationally considered an illegal government, Rhodesia proclaimed itself a republic in 1970. Until 1976 Prime Minister Ian Smith headed a government whose basic principle was continued white minority rule. In a major turnabout, Smith announced in September 1976 that Rhodesia would move to majority African rule in two years. Following the breakdown of international efforts to precipitate an accord between the Smith regime and externally based "liberation" movements, Smith reached an internal agreement with three African leaders for a transition government, which was sworn in on March 21, 1978. Smith and the three black leaders—Bishop Abel Muzorewa, Reverend Ndabaningi Sithole and Senator Chief Jeremiah Chirau—constituted an Executive Council whose main tasks were to draft a new constitution, make all executive decisions, and review legislation of Parliament and the Ministerial Council. This latter body was to function as a cabinet with each ministerial post occupied by both a white and a black. The country was renamed Zimbabwe Rhodesia.

In June 1979 Bishop Abel Muzorewa's United African National Union became the first government of Zimbabwe Rhodesia under its new constitution. The constitution provided for majority rule but reserved some seats in the legislature for the minority whites and gave them the power to block constitutional change. The new government faced problems of maintaining its territory, sovereignty, and internal order against guerrilla forces of the Patriot Front—supported by neighboring black nations—and of winning much-needed recognition of its legitimacy from the United Kingdom and the United States.

In December 1979, after weeks of negotiation in London, the leaders of the three major black groups—Muzorewa, Robert Mugabe of the Zimbabwe African National Union (ZANU), and Joshua Nkomo of the Zimbabwe African People's Union—reached agreement on a truce and transition to a new constitution and government. In the interim, Rhodesia (so named) became a British colony, with a Commonwealth peacekeeping force to oversee the assembly of the guerrilla forces within the country and maintain order during election of a new government.

## POLITICO-MILITARY POLICY

A rapidly deteriorating strategic position since 1974 induced Smith's Rhodesian National Front Party to accept the previously unthinkable prospect of majority rule. Portugal's withdrawal from Mozambique, Guinea-Bissau, and Angola, and the subsequent establishment of the FRELIMO government there, left Rhodesia surrounded on three sides by hostile regimes. These soon became united under Tanzanian chairmanship as the five "front-line" states whose goal was to force majority rule in Zimbabwe (Rhodesia), Namibia, and South Africa. The sudden Portuguese withdrawal caused a redirection of South African policy. The South African government reached the conclusion that the best chance for security lay in an early peaceful transition to majority rule in Rhodesia. In 1975 South Africa therefore recalled its police forces, which had assisted in anti-guerrilla operations since 1967.

Following the breakdown of talks between Smith and insurgent leaders in early 1976, the front-line states declared a policy of armed struggle, Mozambique closed its border to Rhodesian commerce, guerrilla action intensified, white emigration from Rhodesia increased sharply, and joint United States–South African diplomacy made clear to Prime Minister Smith that the white minority would stand alone if it failed to establish majority rule.

No agreement was reached between the Rhodesian government and African leaders at the conference held under British auspices at Geneva in late 1976. In early 1977 Smith decided to negotiate an internal settlement with non-warring African parties. The accord reached a year later excludes the two externally based liberation movements, the Zimbabwe African National Union (ZANU) and the Zimbabwe African People's Union (ZAPU), although the ban on the two parties was removed

and amnesty offered to guerrillas who laid down their arms.

Smith's strategy was to secure a government for Rhodesia that satisfied Western insistence on majority rule, attracted enough support among black Rhodesians to defuse the insurgent groups, yet maintained the substantial socio-economic advantages of the white population. The domestic corollary of this policy involved easing of race discrimination. In a step which caused a split within the National Front, Rhodesia modified its Land Tenure Act in 1977, opening much land previously reserved for whites to future black ownership. Considerable resistance to social change permeated the white community.

Rhodesia responded to the ever increasing ZANU and ZAPU terrorist attacks by conducting periodic raids into their respective sanctuaries in Mozambique and Zambia. Since 1973, some 250,000 Rhodesian blacks in war zones have been relocated into "protected villages," primarily to curtail rebel recruitment.

The three moderate black leaders who allied with the Rhodesian Front apparently have a considerable following in the country. Senator Chirau heads only the small Zimbabwe United People's Organization (ZUPO). Bishop Muzorewa heads the United African National Council (UANC) and is the most popular leader in the Shona tribal group which constitutes 80 percent of Rhodesia's African population. Reverend Sithole runs the ANC-Sithole party, a splinter group from ZANO, which Sithole used to head (and still claims). The three leaders were undoubtedly motivated to the accord with Smith when the front-line states in late 1976 decided to back only the newly created Patriotic Front of ZANU/ZAPU forces.

## THE STRATEGIC SITUATION

In mid-1979 several thousand guerrillas were operating inside Rhodesia, with thousands more training in Zambia, Angola, Tanzania and Mozambique. In addition to inflicting numerous civilian and military casualties, the Patriotic Front offensive was extracting severe economic costs. Overall domestic production dropped by over 6 percent a year in 1976 and 1977. The tourist trade declined sharply, while emigration and the demands of the military for manpower created industrial and agricultural labor shortages. The sole external commercial link through South Africa was plagued by bottlenecks.

The internal solution failed to win immediate international support. The OAU condemned it, and the UN Security Council rejected it. The United States and United Kingdom reiterated their position that the Patriotic Front must be included for any agreement to be viable. As the new government took office, however, the new Conservative government in the U.K. moved toward recognition. South Africa expressed only cautious support. The chief objections to the settlement concern its provision for a de facto white veto over constitutional change for ten years and retention of the white dominated police, military, and judicial structures.

Though increasingly effective in disrupting Rhodesia, the Patriotic Front suffered internal conflict. Robert Mugabe of ZANU and Joshua Nkomo of ZAPU deeply mistrust one another. To some extent this schism reflects tribal differences. More important, the two have different supporters and employed different strategies. Nkomo has solid Soviet backing and the close support of Angola and Zambia. Mugabe's bases in Mozambique are supplied largely by China. Nkomo has committed far fewer troops to combat, prompting Mugabe's charge that he planned to seize power with fresh forces after Mugabe won the war. Mugabe's ZANU has experienced considerable factionalism among its rather independent-minded military leaders.

## ARMY

*Personnel:* 3,400

*Organization:*
   3 brigade headquarters (see Reserves)
      2 infantry battalions (one with Ferret scout and Staghound armored cars)
      1 artillery battery
      1 Special Air Service squadron (parachute commandos)

*Major Equipment Inventory:*
  100 Staghound armored cars
   20 scout cars (Ferret)
      light artillery (25-pounder, 105mm howitzers, M-101 A)
      105mm recoilless rifles

*Reserves:* There are 3 brigade establishments or headquarters, two of which are based on the regular infantry battalions cited above. The Territorial Forces referred to below would be used to bring these brigades up to strength:
  8,400 Territorial Force
      4 infantry battalions (subordinated to the 3 brigade headquarters)
  25,000 Reserve Force
      command headquarters and supporting units

      8 infantry battalions
      1 artillery battery

## AIR FORCE

*Personnel:* 1,200

*Organization:*
   2 fighter-bomber squadrons (Hunter and Vampire)
   1 light bomber squadron (Canberra)
   2 armed reconnaissance/training squadrons (AM-3C, Provost, T-28)
   1 transport squadron (C-47, AL-60)
   1 helicopter squadron (Alouette III)

*Major Aircraft Types:*
  57 combat aircraft
    12 Hunter fighter-bombers
    12 Vampire fighter-bombers
    10 Canberra light bombers
     6 AM-3C armed trainers
    12 Provost armed trainer/reconnaissance aircraft
     5 T-28 armed trainers
  25 other aircraft
     4 Vampire trainers
     3 Canberra trainers
     4 C-47 transports, 6 AL-60 light transports
     8 Alouette III helicopters

*Air Bases:* New Sarum (Salisbury), Thornhill (Gwelo), Cranbourne, Bulawayo, Umtali

*Reserves:* Territorial and reserve personnel are assigned; numbers not known.

## PARAMILITARY

The active police force is some 6,400 strong and has Staghound armored cars. It is trained and organized for counterinsurgency. The police reserve numbers 28,500. Army auxiliaries, or "private armies," estimated at from 7,500 to 9,000, are irregular bands, some of whose members were fighters for Patriotic Front forces before the "internal settlement" of March 1978. Poorly paid and briefly trained, they have been used by the government against guerrillas with varying success, and by the black moderate parties in electioneering.

# GLOSSARY

A-1, Skyraider (formerly AD). US, Douglas; single-engine piston attack aircraft; first in service 1945; over 3,200 built; 10,000 pounds external armament; maximum speed 365 mph; maximum range 3,000 miles.

A-3, Skywarrior (formerly A3D), USAF designation B-66 (Destroyer). US, Douglas; carrier-based twin-engine jet reconnaissance and light bomber; operational from 1956; 12,000 pounds of armament; maximum speed 610 mph; ceiling 41,000 feet; tactical radius 1,000 miles.

A-4, Skyhawk (formerly A4D). US, McDonnell-Douglas; originally designed as a carrier-based single-engine single-seat light-weight jet attack bomber; operational from 1956; still in production (over 2,500 built); maximum speed 676 mph; range with external tanks over 2,000 miles; 10,000 pounds of conventional or nuclear weapons carried on one center and four underwing attachment points; in service with US Navy and Marines, Argentina, Australia, Israel, and New Zealand.

A-5, Vigilante (formerly A3J). US, North American-Rockwell; carrier-based twin-engine jet reconnaissance/attack bomber; maximum speed Mach 2.1; ceiling 70,000 feet; range 2,650 miles; can carry a combination of conventional and nuclear weapons on external attachment points; operational from 1960. RA-5C is multi-sensor reconnaissance version.

A-6, Intruder (formerly A2F). US, Grumman; carrier-based twin-engine low-level jet attack bomber; all-weather capability; operational from 1963; maximum speed 685 mph; ceiling 41,000 feet; maximum range 2,800 miles; 18,000 pounds of conventional or nuclear weapons carried on five attachment points. EA-6B is an electronic intelligence and countermeasures version which retains some strike capability. KA-6 is a tanker version.

A-7, Corsair II. U.S. Ling-Temco-Vought; carrier-based single-engine jet light attack bomber; operational from 1966; maximum speed 700 mph; combat radius 700 miles; 15,000 pounds of conventional or nuclear weapons can be carried on six attachment points. A-7A/B/E are Navy versions; A-7D is Air Force version.

A-10, Thunderbolt II. US, Republic Fairchild; single-seat twin-jet close-support aircraft; maximum speed 450 mph; combat radius 288 miles; armament one 30mm GAU-8 Gatling-type multibarrel cannon. Also carries up to 16,000 pounds external ordnance on 11 pylons.

A-32, Lansen. Sweden, Saab; single-seat single-engine jet; attack version of Lansen (Lance) fighter-interceptor.

A-37. See T-37.

A-60 Saab 105). Sweden, Saab; two-place twin-engine jet trainer/utility aircraft; operational from 1965; can carry 1,500 pounds of armament; maximum speed 450 mph; ceiling 40,000 feet; range 850–1,000 miles.

A-106. Italy, Agusta; single-seat single-engine helicopter designed for ASW operations; carries two torpedoes and equipment for contact identification; maximum speed, 110 mph; maximum range (with external tanks), 460 miles.

A-109, Hirundo. Italy, Agusta; twin-engine eight-seat high performance general purpose (turboshaft engine) helicopter; maximum speed 172 mph; service ceiling 17,400 feet; one engine 8,850 feet; maximum range, sea level: 388 miles; 6,560 feet: 457 miles.

AAA. Antiaircraft artillery (20mm to 130mm guns).

AAM. Air-to-air missile; guided or self-homing rocket-propelled missile fired from one aircraft against another.

AB-47. Italy, Agusta-Bell; license-built version of Bell 47 (q.v.)

379

AB-204. Italy, Agusta-Bell; license-built version of UH-1 (q.v.)

AB-205. Italy, Agusta-Bell; license-built version of UH-1D/UH-1H; see UH-1.

AB-206. See Jet Ranger.

AB-212. See UH-1N.

Abbot (FV433). Britain, Vickers; operational from 1965; self-propelled 105mm gun, one howitzer, with full-traversing turret; also carries one 7.62mm machine gun; crew of four; weight 19 tons; maximum speed (road) 30 mph; range (road) 300 miles.

ABM. Antiballistic missile.

AC-47. Gunship version of C-47.

AC-119. US, Fairchild-Hiller, armed gunship conversion of C-119 (q.v.); equipped with Vulcan cannon and 7.62mm mini-guns and various lights, infrared sensors, and light-intensifying equipment for night attacks; powered by two piston and two jet engines.

AC-130. US, Lockheed; armed gunship conversion of C-130 (q.v.); equipped approximately the same as AC-119 (above), but with larger overall number of guns.

AD: US designation for destroyer tender.

ADCOM/NORAD. Air Defense Command/North American Air Defense (Command).

AEC. Mk 3 armored car.

Aero Commander (also designated L-26 or U-4). US; twin-engine piston light transport; 230 mph cruising speed.

AGM. Air-to-ground missile. See ASM.

AGM-12. See Bullpup.

AGM-22. See SS-11.

AGM-45. See Shrike.

AGM-53. See Condor.

AGM-65. See Maverick.

AGM-69. See SRAM.

AGM-78. See Standard ARM.

AGM-84. See Harpoon.

AGS. US designation for a hydrographic survey ship.

AH-1, Huey Cobra. US, modification as gunship; pilot sits back of gunner in tandem; maximum speed 219 mph; various combinations of armament; 40mm grenade launcher; 7.62 mini-gun in nose; rocket and machine gun pods on stub wings.

AIM. Air-intercept missile. See AAM.

AIM-4. See Falcon.

AIM-7. See Sparrow.

AIM-9. See Sidewinder.

AIM-17. See Quail.

AIM-47A. US, Hughes; AAM; 12 feet long; range 40 nautical miles; speed Mach 5; 800 were ordered for F-12A, which never entered series production; advanced infrared and pulsed radar homing.

Airtourer. New Zealand, Aero Engine Services Limited; two-seat single-engine piston light trainer; maximum speed 164 mph; service ceiling 18,000 feet; range 670 miles.

AJ-37. See Viggen.

Ajax. See Nike.

AKA. US designation for attack cargo ship.

AKL. US designation for a light naval cargo ship.

AL-60, Conestoga. Italy/Mexico, Lockheed Associates; single-engine six-seat piston light utility transport; maximum speed 156 mph; range 645 miles.

Albatross (HU-16). US, Grumman; twin-engine piston utility amphibian; operational from 1949, over 450 built; crew of five, 10 to 22 passengers; maximum speed 235 mph; ceiling 21,000 feet; range 2,800 miles.

Alize (Br 1050). France, Breguet; carrier-based, three-place, single-engine turboprop ASW aircraft;

operational from 1959; 87 built; 2,000 total pounds of armament carried internally and externally; maximum speed 285 mph; ceiling 26,000 feet; range 1,500 miles.

Alkali (NATO codename). Soviet Union; radar-guided, passive homing, solid-fuel rocket-motor AAM, carried on MiG-17, MiG-19, and Su-9.

Alouette. France, Aerospatiale; light helicopter; II model, nearly 1,300 sold from 1955; four passengers; 530-shp turbine; maximum speed 115 mph; ceiling 7,000 feet; maximum range 330 miles. III model; built from 1959 through present; six passengers; may be armed with combination of light and heavy machine guns and rockets; 870-shp turbine; maximum speed 131 mph; ceiling 19,650 feet; range (with 6 passengers) 190 miles; see also SA-315.

AM-3C. Italy, Aeritalia/Aermacchi; single-engine, three-seat, piston light armed trainer aircraft; maximum speed 173 mph; range 615 miles; armament two 7.62mm machine gun pods.

AML-60. France; armored car for reconnaissance, convoy protection, and counterinsurgency operations; crew of three; five tons; 55 mph; range 400 miles; 60mm mortar and 7.5mm machine guns.

AML-90. France; armored car; same as four-wheeled AML-60, but with 90mm gun.

AMX-13. France; light tank; 14.8 tons; 75mm gun; crew of three; latest models also carry four SS-11 anti-tank guided missiles; operational since 1952.

AMX-30. France; medium tank; 32.5 tons; 105mm gun; deep fording capability; 800 hp; 250-mile range; co-axial 7.62mm machine gun; 12.7mm antiaircraft machine gun; 40 mph.

AMX-105. France; self-propelled 105mm howitzer; two versions—one with howitzer mounted in fully traversing turret; both versions mounted on AMX-13 chassis; 16 to 16.5 tons; howitzer range 15,000 to 16,000 yards.

AMX-155. France; self-propelled 155mm howitzer mounted on modified AMX-13 chassis; howitzer range over 20,000 meters.

AMX-VTT. France; armored personnel carrier; 12 troops and crew of two; 14 tons; AMX-13 chassis.

AN. US designation for a net tender.

An-2 (NATO codename Colt). Soviet Union, Antonov; single-engine piston utility biplane; operational from 1947; over 5,000 built; maximum speed 160 mph; ceiling 16,000 feet; range 560 miles; 10–14 passengers.

An-12 (NATO codename Cub). Soviet Union, Antonov; heavy cargo plane; four-engine 4,000 hp turbo-props; 44,000-pound payload; maximum cruising speed 370 mph; range with half payload 2,000 miles; 100 passengers; operational from 1959.

An-14 (NATO codename Clod). Soviet Union; twin-engine six-seat piston light transport; maximum cruising speed 118 mph; range 290 miles. A later 15-passenger turboprop model, An-14M, appeared in 1972.

An-22 (NATO codename Cock). Soviet Union, Antonov; ultra-heavy cargo plane; four-engine 15,000-hp turboprops; maximum payload 221,443 pounds; maximum speed 460 mph; maximum range 6,800 miles; 300–350 passengers; operational from mid-1967.

An-24/An-26 (NATO codename Coke). Soviet Union, Antonov; twin-engine turboprop transport; 44–50 passengers; 300 mph speed; ceiling 27,000 feet; range (depending on load) 325–1,500 miles; operational from 1962.

Anab (NATO codename). Soviet Union: AAM with infrared and semiactive homing versions; carried by Yak-28P (Firebar), Su-9 (Fishpot), and Su-11 (Flagon-A).

Andover (HS-748). Britain, Hawker-Siddeley; twin-engine turboprop rear-loading transport; 58 troops or 40 paratroops; 15,000-pound payload; civilian version carries up to 62 passengers; operational from 1961; maximum cruising speed 290 mph; ceiling 25,000 feet; range with maximum payload 700 miles.

AO. US designation for oiler.

AOE. US designation for fast combat support ship; provides the fleet with both fuel and ammunition through underway replenishment.

AOR. US designation for a replenishment oiler; provides both fuel and supplies to fleet through underway replenishment.

APA. US designation for an attack transport; usually carries a reinforced infantry battalion and the landing craft with which to land it.

APD. US designation for a high-speed transport; usually converted from a destroyer or destroyer escort.

AR. US designation for a repair ship.

Argosy. Britain, Hawker-Siddeley; four-engine turboprop medium-range transport; operational from 1962; 69 troops or 54 paratroops; maximum payload 29,000 pounds; cruising speed 270 mph; ceiling 21,000 feet; maximum range 2,500 miles.

Argus. See CL-28.

AS. US designation for a submarine tender.

AS-11. See SS-11 (France, Nord).

AS-12. France, Nord; SS-12 wire-guided antitank missile converted to use automatic telecommand guidance from an aircraft; weight 167 pounds; range approximately four miles; 63-pound warhead.

AS-20. France, Nord; radio-controlled air-to-surface missile; 315 pounds; range 3.75 nautical miles; 9.5 feet long.

AS-30. Improved version of AS-20; range up to 6.5 nautical miles; weight 1,150 pounds; 507-pound warhead.

AS-33. Similar to AS-30, but with inertial guidance; operational from 1966; range 6.2 nautical miles; weight 1,150 pounds.

ASEAN. Association of Southeast Asian Nations.

Ash (NATO codename). Soviet Union; AAM with infrared and radar-homing versions; carried by Tu-28 (Fiddler).

ASM. Air-to-surface missile; guided or self-homing; rocket-propelled or free-fall projectile launched from an aircraft against ground or sea target.

ASPAC. Asian and Pacific Council.

ASROC (RUR-5A; Anti-Submarine Rocket). US, Honeywell; rocket-assisted antisubmarine ballistic weapon; operational from 1961; equips destroyers, escort vessels, and cruisers in US Navy and others

(e.g., Japan); weapon has its own eight-missile launcher, but can also be fired from Terrier launchers (q.v.); is essentially a ballistic rocket carrying acoustic homing torpedoes or a nuclear depth charge; range one to six miles; firing weight 1,000 pounds.

ASU-57. Soviet Union, self-propelled 57mm gun on tracked chassis; designed for airborne operations; crew of two; weight 3.5 tons.

ASW. Antisubmarine warfare.

AT. Antitank.

AT-26, Xavante. See MB-326B.

ATGM. Antitank guided missile.

Atlantique (BR-1150). France, Breguet; maritime patrol aircraft; twin-engine turboprop, two 6105-shp RR Tyne engines; maximum speed 409 mph; service ceiling 32,800 feet; cruise speed 345 mph; maximum range 5,590 miles; standard bombs; HVAR (high-velocity air rocket), depth charges, homing torpedoes, ASM nuclear warheads, MAD sonobuoys.

Atoll (NATO codename). Soviet Union; AAM with infrared, heat-seeking guidance; similar to US Sidewinder.

AU-23A. See PC-6.

AU-24A, Stallion. US Helio Aircraft Co.; single-engine turboprop STOL aircraft; 8- to 11-seat utility aircraft. Can be armed for COIN operations; maximum speed 216 mph; range 1,090 miles.

Auster (Beagle) AOP 6. Britain, Auster/Beagle; single-engine piston light liaison aircraft; operational from 1945; maximum speed 125 mph; ceiling 14,000 feet; range 315 miles.

AVP. US designation for a small seaplane tender.

AWL (NATO codename). Soviet Union; little-known radar or infrared guidance AAM carried by interceptors. (Similar in configuration to US AAM Sparrow.)

AWX. All weather (aircraft).

B-1. US, North American–Rockwell; four-engine jet; proposed supersonic strategic bomber for USAF; cancelled 1978.

B-25, Mitchell. US, North American; World War II twin-engine piston light bomber; over 4,300 built; 4,000 pounds of armament; maximum speed 275 mph; ceiling 24,000 feet; range 1,350 miles.

B-26, Counter Invader. US, twin-engine piston; modification and modernization of Douglas B-26 Invader for counterinsurgency operations; armed with eight .50 caliber machine guns in nose and up to 11,000 pounds of bombs; maximum speed 395 mph; ceiling 30,000 feet, range 1,500 miles; over 40 converted from 1963.

B-52, Stratofortress. US, Boeing; eight-engine long-range jet, heavy bomber; operational from 1955; 744 built; 35-ton payload; maximum speed over 650 mph; ceiling over 50,000 feet; maximum range 12,500 miles.

B-57. US, Martin; license-built version of British Canberra (q.v.) twin-engine jet light bomber.

BA-64. Albania; APC.

BAC 167, Strikemaster. Britain, BAC; light single-engine jet ground attack aircraft based on Jet Provost BAC-145 trainer.

Bandeirante. See C-95 and EMB-110, -111.

Bantam. Sweden; antitank guided missile; range 2,000 meters; speed 190 mph; weight 13 pounds; wire-guided, optically tracked.

Barak. Israeli version of Mirage (q.v.).

Battalion. Usually a unit of 500 to 1,000 men of one arm. Two or more battalions combine to form a brigade or regiment (q.v.). Battalion-sized units of artillery and armor in British, Commonwealth, and some other armies are known as regiments. Battalion-sized units of US cavalry are known as squadrons. Soviet SAM battalions consist of only 80 to 150 men.

Battery. The basic firing unit of artillery, usually four to eight guns, depending upon the army. Three batteries usually constitute an artillery battalion (US practice) or regiment (British practice).

Be-12 (NATO codename Mail). Soviet Union, Beriev; twin-turboprop maritime-reconnaissance amphibian; operational from 1965.

Beagle 206, Basset. Britain, Beagle; twin-engine piston light transport carrying five to eight people; maximum speed 220 mph; maximum range 1,645 miles.

Beagle Pup. Britain, Beagle; two-seat single-engine piston light aircraft; used as primary trainer; maximum speed (estimated) 125 mph; range (estimated) 300 miles.

Beaver (U-6A, US; DHC-2, Canada). Canada, DeHavilland; single-engine piston STOL utility transport; maximum speed over 160 mph; ceiling 18,000 feet; range with maximum payload 480 miles; seven passengers; over 1,600 built since 1948.

Beech 99. US, Beechcraft; twin-engine turboprop 17-seat aircraft; operational from mid-1968; maximum cruising speed (depending on version) 254 to 284 mph; range (with maximum fuel and 1,800 pounds payload) 1,100 miles; ceiling (depending on version), 24,000 to 26,000 feet.

Beech F33C, Bonanza. US, Beechcraft; four- or five-seat single-engine piston trainer; advanced version of commercial Beech Bonanza to be used in training and liaison; maximum speed 204 mph; service ceiling 18,300 feet; range 890 miles.

Beech King Air (C-90). US, Beechcraft; light twin-engine turboprop multiengine trainer or VIP transport; maximum speed 240 mph, range 1,265 miles; seats ten.

Beech Queen Air (U-8F), Seminole. US, Beechcraft; light twin-engine piston transport; maximum speed 214 mph; ceiling 31,000 feet; range 1,600 miles; over 400 built since 1959.

Belfast. Britain, Short Brothers; four-engine turboprop military transport; 200 men or 78,000 pounds of cargo; maximum speed 310 mph; ceiling 30,000 feet; range with maximum payload 1,000 miles; operational from 1964; only ten built.

Bell 47 (OH-13), Sioux. US, Bell; three-place utility helicopter; maximum speed 105 mph; ceiling 18,500 feet; maximum range 250 miles; operational from 1960.

Bell 204. See UH-1.

Bell 205. See UH-1.

Bell 206. See Jet Ranger.

Bell 214. See UH-1.

Ben Gurion. Israel; an Israeli modification of early-model Centurion medium tanks made by conversion to 105mm gun and other improvements.

Bloodhound. Britain, BAC; surface-to-air missile; semi-active homing guidance; effective against aircraft under 1,000-foot altitude and up to over 50,000-foot altitude; maximum range 50 miles or more; operational since 1958.

Blue Steel. Britain, Hawker-Siddeley; air-to-surface missile; a liquid-rocket stand-off bomb for "V-bomber" force; 200-mile range; thermo-nuclear warhead.

BMP. Soviet Union; fully tracked armored infantry combat vehicle (AICV); carries 8–10 troops; armed with 73mm smooth-bore gun and wire-guided Sagger antitank missile; has amphibious capabilities; operational from 1967.

BN2A. Islander, Defender. Britain, Britten-Norman; land-based twin-engine multi-seat piston light transport (also light attack, search and rescue [SAR], reconnaissance) aircraft; cruising speed 160 mph; maximum range with tip tanks 1,040 miles; proposed armament, fixed guns, gun or rocket pods.

BO-5. Germany, Messerschmidt-Bolkow-Blohm; five-seat turboshaft high-speed helicopter; gross weight 5,600 pounds, maximum speed 231 mph.

Boeing 707, 720 (USAF designation VC-137). US, Boeing; four-engine jet long-range transport; initial flight July 1954; many stages of development since then; four jet engines (turbojet and turbofan), each 17,500 pounds thrust; maximum speed Mach 0.95; service ceiling 42,000 feet; range 7,600 miles; can carry as many as 215 passengers; tanker model built for USAF KC-135 (Stratotanker).

Bomarc (MIM-10). US, Boeing; long-range surface-to-air missile; built with various modifications from 1952; speed Mach 2.8; range 440 miles; intercept capability from low-level to 100,000 feet; nuclear warhead.

BRDM. Soviet Union, 1959; four-wheeled amphibious armored reconnaissance vehicle; crew of three; later models equipped with antitank missiles.

Breguet 765. See Sahara.

Breguet 1150. See Atlantique.

Brigade. A formation of from 3,000 to 6,000 men, usually of several battalions of the same arm. In the US Army a brigade is essentially the equivalent of the former three-battalion regiment.

Brigade Group. Britain; an infantry brigade reinforced by artillery, tanks, and other supporting units.

Britannia. Britain, Bristol; four-engine turboprop medium transport; operational from 1957; 82 built; up to 133 passengers; maximum cruising speed 402 mph; range 4,160 miles.

Bronco. See OV-10.

Broussard. France, Max Holste; utility aircraft; six passengers; operational from 1953; 335 built; maximum speed 160 mph; ceiling 17,000 feet; range 745 miles.

BTR-40. Soviet Union, 1950s; four-wheeled armored personnel carrier and scout car; 5.3 tons; 50 mph; range 175 miles; driver plus nine troops.

BTR-50P. Soviet Union; tracked amphibious armored personnel carrier; suspension and power train similar to PT-76 light tank; 16 tons; 27 mph; driver plus 14 troops.

BTR-60P. Soviet Union; eight-wheeled amphibious armored personnel carrier; 12.7mm machine gun.

BTR-152. Soviet Union; 1950s; six-wheeled armored personnel carrier; 9.2 tons; 34 mph; crew of three plus 12 troops.

Buccaneer. Britain, Hawker-Siddeley; twin-engine two-seat jet strike aircraft; operational from 1962; speed Mach 0.9.

Buffalo (CV-7A or C-8A, US; DHC-5 or CC-115, Canada). Canada, DeHavilland; twin-engine turboprop STOL tactical transport; Canadian Forces version (CC-115) has more powerful engines; operational from 1965; crew of three, 41 troops, 35 para-troops, or 24 stretchers and six seats; maximum payload 13,843 pounds; maximum speed 271 mph; ceiling, 30,000 feet; range with maximum payload 507 miles; aircraft is basically a developed version of the Caribou (q.v.) with an enlarged fuselage and two turboprop engines.

Bulldog. Britain, Scottish Aviation; single-engine two-seat, piston primary trainer; maximum speed 150 mph; range 621 miles.

Bullpup (AGM-12). US, Maxson Corp.; air-to-surface missile; radio command guidance. AGM-12B, Bullpup A; 10.5 feet long; range six nautical miles; 250-pound high-explosive warhead; overall weight 571 pounds; used by Navy and Air Force. AGM-12C, Bullpup B; 12.75 feet long; range 8.5 nautical miles; 1,000-pound high-explosive warhead; over-all weight 1,785 pounds; Navy only. AGM-12D; nuclear warhead. AGM-12E; high-fragmentation warhead.

BV-202. Norway, armored personnel carrier (APC) in the Norwegian Army.

C-4M. Kuda modification of AM-3C built in South Africe for the light aircraft command.

C-5, Galaxy. US, Lockheed; four-engine long-range jet heavy transport; maximum payload 265,000 pounds; maximum speed 571 mph; maximum range 6,500 miles; operational from late 1969; ceiling 34,000 feet.

C-9, Nightingale. US, McDonnell-Douglas; twin-engine jet; military version of DC-9 commercial jet liner; used exclusively for medical evacuation purposes by Military Airlift Command.

C-42, Regente. Brazil, Neiva; four-seat utility, liaison, and observation, single-engine piston aircraft; maximum speed 137 mph; service ceiling 11,800 feet; maximum range 576 miles.

C-45. US, Beechcraft; twin-engine piston light transport; four passengers; T-7 navigational training version; T-11 bombing training version.

C-46, Commando. US, Curtiss-Wright; World War II twin-engine piston transport; 36 passengers; 3,180 built.

C-47, Dakota or Skytrain (DC-3). US, Douglas; twin-engine transport; 21 passengers; over 10,000 built.

C-54, Skymaster (DC-4). US, Douglas; World War II four-engine piston transport; 44 passengers; over 1,000 built.

C-82, Packet. See C-119.

C-95, Bandeirante. Brazil, Embraer; 12-passenger, twin-turboprop, light transport/utility aircraft; two 550-shp engines; maximum cruising speed 267 mph; service ceiling 25,000 feet; maximum range 1,240 miles.

C-118, Liftmaster (DC-6). US, Douglas; four-engine piston transport; 64–92 passengers; 27,000 pounds of cargo; maximum speed 360 mph; range 4,900 miles.

C-119, Flying Boxcar. US, Fairchild-Hiller, twin-engine piston transport; 62 paratroops; 30,000 pounds cargo; maximum speed 295 mph; range 3,480 miles; developed from C-82 Packet. Latest version, AC-119K Shadow, is an attack gunship carrying 20mm Vulcan cannon and 7.62mm Mini-gun machine guns (each firing 6,000 rounds per minute) plus advanced detection equipment.

C-121, Constellation and Super Constellation. US, Lockheed; four-engine piston transport; operational from 1951; 63–99 passengers; 40,000 pounds cargo; maximum speed 375 mph; range 2,100 miles.

C-123, Provider. US, Fairchild-Hiller; twin-engine piston tactical transport; maximum speed 253 mph; payload 19,000 pounds; range with maximum payload 1,340 miles; first built in 1954; C-123K was converted from C-123B in 1966–67 with addition of two 2,850-pound thrust turbojets to improve performance.

C-124, Globemaster. US, Douglas; four-engine piston transport; 200 troops; 74,000 pounds of cargo; maximum speed 300 mph; maximum range 6,820 miles.

C-130, Hercules. US, Lockheed; four-engine turboprop transport; over 1,000 built since 1956 in various versions; payload 35,000 to 45,000 pounds; maximum speed 380 mph; ceiling 40,000 feet; range 1,800 to 4,700 miles depending on model.

C-131, Samaritan. US, Convair; twin-engine piston transport; 48 passengers; maximum speed 313 mph; range 1,600 miles; military version of Convair 240/440 series commercial airliners.

C-133, Cargomaster. US, Douglas; four-engine turboprop heavy transport; operational from 1957; over 200 troops; 80,000- to 100,000-pound payload; maximum speed 359 mph; ceiling 24,000 feet; range 2,200 to 4,300 miles.

C-135, Stratofreighter. US, Boeing; long-range four-engine jet transport; operational from 1961; 126 troops; maximum payload 50,000 pounds; maximum speed 640 mph; range 4,500 miles; military version of Boeing 707-series commercial jet liner. See KC-135 and Boeing Model 707, 720.

C-140, Jet Star. US, Lockheed; four-engine jet light transport; used for VIP transport, liaison duties, and similar functions.

C-141, Starlifter. US, Lockheed; four-engine turbofan long-range cargo and troop transport; operational from 1965; 154 troops or 123 paratroops; maximum payload 71,000 pounds; maximum speed 570 mph; ceiling 41,000 feet; range with maximum payload 4,000 miles.

C-207, Azor. Spain, CASA; two-engine piston transport; maximum speed 283 mph; range 1,620 miles; 30 passengers or freight; crew of four.

C-212, Aviocar. Spain, CASA; 15-seat twin-engine turbo-prop paratroop or aeromedical transport aircraft; maximum speed 249 mph at 12,000 feet; service ceiling 24,606 feet; range with maximum fuel 1,198 miles.

CA. US designation for a heavy cruiser, armed with 8-inch guns.

CA-27. See CF-86.

Cactus. France, surface-to-air missile; Mach 1.2.

Canberra. Britain, BAC; twin-jet light bomber; operational from 1951; 1,329 built, including 403 in US as B-57; 6,000 pounds of armament; maximum speed 600 mph; ceiling 48,000 feet; maximum range over 2,300 miles.

Caribou (C-7A or CV-2A, US; DHC-4, Canada). Canada, DeHavilland; twin-engine piston STOL transport; 159 built for US from 1959; total of 248 built; 32 passengers or 26 paratroops; maximum payload 8,700 pounds; maximum speed 215 mph; ceiling 27,000 feet; range with maximum payload 240 miles.

Carl Gustav. Sweden; a recoilless 84mm antitank weapon.

CASA 223, Flamingo. Spain, CASA; light two-seat utility/trainer; fully acrobatic piston aircraft; maximum speed 155 mph; gross weight 1810 lbs.

CASA 3524. Spain, CASA; light twin-engine turboprop transport.

CC-106, Yukon. Canada, Canadair; license-built piston version of Britannia (q.v.)

CC-109. See Cosmopolitan.

CC-115. See Buffalo.

CC-138. See Twin Otter.

Centurion. Britain; medium tank in production from post-World War II to 1960s; Mk. III to VIII armed with 20-pounder (83.4mm) gun; IX and X with 105mm gun; 51 tons; 21.5 mph; road range 115 miles; cross-country range 75 miles; crew of four.

Cessna 180. US, Cessna; single-engine piston utility aircraft; six passengers; maximum speed 170 mph; ceiling 19,000 feet; range 900 miles; over 5,000 built.

Cessna 185 (Skywagon). See U-17A.

Cessna 310 (U-3). US, Cessna; twin-engine six-passenger aircraft; over 2,700 built from 1953; maximum speed 242 mph; ceiling 21,300 feet; range 1,340 miles.

Cessna 402. Eight-passenger version of Cessna 310.

Cessna 500, Citation. US, Cessna; twin-engine light jet transport; cruising speed 404 mph; ceiling 41,000; range (with six passengers) 1,535 miles.

Cessna FR-172. France, Reims Aviation; four-seat single-engine piston light aircraft; license-built Cessna 172; equipped to carry Matra rocket launchers in COIN role; maximum speed 153 mph; service ceiling 17,000 feet; range 740 miles.

CF-5. Canadian-built version of F-5 jet fighter.

CF-86 (CA-27), Sabre. Canadian Forces version of F-86 jet fighter; built in Australia.

CF-100, Canuck. Canada, Avro; twin-engine jet two-seat interceptor in service from 1951; maximum speed 650 mph; range 2,000 miles; carries fifty-two 2-3/4 inch air-to-air rockets in each of two wing-tip pods or eight .50 cal. machine guns in a belly-pack; over 500 built; one version served with Belgian Air Force.

CF-101, Voodoo. Canadian-built version of F-101 jet interceptor.

CF-104, Starfighter. Canadian-built version of F-104.

CG. US designation for guided missile cruiser. Missile armament now takes precedence over other weapons.

CH-46, Sea Knight. US, Boeing-Vertol; twin-rotor medium helicopter; operational from 1962; over 500 built; 17–25 troops; maximum speed 166 mph; ceiling 14,000 feet; range with maximum fuel 750 miles.

CH-47, Chinook. US, Boeing-Vertol; twin-rotor medium helicopter; operational from 1962; 33–44 troops or 23,450-pound maximum payload; maximum speed 190 mph; 9,500-foot ceiling; combat radius 115 miles.

CH-53 (S-65), Sea Stallion. US, Sikorsky; heavy assault helicopter; operational from 1966; over 100 built; 38 troops or 28,000-pound payload; maximum speed 195 mph; ceiling 21,000 feet; range 255 miles (up to 540 with external tanks).

CH-54 (S-64), Sky Crane. US, Sikorsky; crane helicopter for lifting external loads or pods of up to 22,890 pounds; maximum speed 127 mph; ceiling 13,000 feet; range with maximum fuel 253 miles.

CH-113, Labrador. Canada; version of US Boeing-Vertol CH-46 built in US for Canadian Armed Forces.

Chaparral/Vulcan. US; a low-altitude air defense system comprising Sidewinder AAMs (q.v.) modified for use as SAMs and mounted on a tracked vehicle, combined with a radar-directed Vulcan 20mm cannon mounted on a modified M-113 APC.

Charioteer. Britain; World War II medium tank; a Cromwell tank rearmed with a 20-pounder (83.4mm) gun; 28.5 tons; crew of three to four.

Chieftain. Britain; main battle tank; 120mm gun; 50 tons; maximum speed 25 mph; range 250 miles; crew of four.

Chipmunk. Britain, Hawker-Siddeley; single-engine piston primary trainer; maximum speed 138 mph; range 280 miles.

Civic Action. Employment of military units in building up the economic infrastructure of a developing nation or in providing various social services to civilians in remote areas.

CL. US designation for a light cruiser, armed with 6-inch guns.

CL-13, Sabre. Canada, Canadair; license-built version of F-86 Sabre.

CL-28, Argus. Canada, Canadair; long-range maritime reconnaissance version of Britannia (q.v.); 8,000 pounds internal and 7,600 pounds external armament; ASW equipment; maximum speed 288 mph; range 4,000 miles.

CL-41, Tutor. Canada, Canadair; two-seat single-engine jet trainer; 200 produced from 1961; G model can be armed with 4,000 pounds of gun pods, bombs, or rockets; maximum speed 480 mph; ceiling 44,500 feet.

CL-215. Canada, Canadair; twin-engine piston amphibious utility aircraft; water bomber, transport, air evacuation; cruising speed 181 mph; range 1,405 miles; can carry 36 troops or 18 stretchers.

CLAA. US designation for an antiaircraft cruiser armed predominantly with antiaircraft guns.

CLG. Old US designation for a guided-missile light cruiser; armament includes surface-to-air missiles. Now replaced by CG (q.v.).

Cobra. Germany, Bolkow; wire-guided antitank missile; 30.7 inches long; 20.2 pounds; 190 mph; range 400–1,600 meters; not to be confused with AH-1G Huey Cobra helicopter gunship (see UH-1).

COH-58. Canada; version of US Bell OH-58 (q.v.).

COIN. US acronym for counterinsurgency.

Comet. Britain; medium tank from late World War II period; 17-pounder (77mm) gun; 33.5 tons; crew of five.

Comet. Britain, DeHavilland; four-engine jet transport; operational from 1958; range 2,590 miles; service ceiling 39,000 feet; cruising speed 542 mph.

Commando (XM706). US, Cadillac-Gage; 4-wheeled amphibious armored car/armored personnel carrier; 65 mph; range 300 miles; some carry turret-mounted 20mm cannon; crew of 4 (plus 7 troops in APC version).

Condor (AGM-53A). US, North American–Rockwell; air-to-surface missile; TV guidance; 40 nautical mile range; for use from A-6A and A-7 aircraft.

Convair 440. See C-131.

Corps. A type of unit common throughout an army, as Ordnance Corps; more commonly a large formation of two or more divisions plus supporting combat and logistical units.

Corvette. Designation, principally British, of a class of ASW convoy escort ships, about 180-foot, with 3-inch gun and ASW weapons; often converted from another type such as minesweeper; US designation is PCE (q.v.).

Cosmopolitan CC-109. US, General Dynamics (Convair); twin-engine turboprop Canadian-built version of C-131 (q.v.); powered by Allison 501D-13 turboprops; maximum speed 309 mph; service ceiling 24,000 feet; range 1,230 miles; used by Canadian Armed Forces as medium-range transport.

Crotale. France, Thomson-CSF; land-mobile, automatic, all-weather surface-to-air guided missile; propulsion single-stage solid propellant, infrared and radar guidance.

CUH-1N. Canada; Iroquois (q.v.) helicopter for Canadian Armed Forces.

CVA. US designation for an attack aircraft carrier; fleet carrier of the largest type, carrying up to 100 aircraft.

CVAN. Nuclear-powered CVA.

CVL. US designation for a light aircraft carrier; smaller than CVA and carrying fewer planes; many converted from other hulls.

CVS. US designation for a support aircraft carrier; usually carry ASW aircraft.

D-18. See C-45.

DAF-YP-408. Netherlands; eight-wheeled armored personnel carrier; 12 tons, 50 mph; range 310 miles; crew of two plus ten troops.

Daphne. France; class of diesel attack submarines; 850 tons; 190 feet; 12 21-inch torpedo tubes; speed 16 knots surfaced or submerged.

DC-3. See C-47.

DC-4. See C-54.

DC-6. See C-118.

DD. US designation for a destroyer; must be a multipurpose ship armed with 5-inch guns or the missile equivalent.

DDG. US designation for a guided-missile destroyer; must be armed with surface-to-air missiles or surface-to-surface missiles.

DDR. US designation for radar picket destroyer.

DE. Old US designation for a destroyer escort.

DEG. Old US designation for a guided-missile destroyer escort.

Delfin (Dolphin). See L-29.

Devon. Military version of Dove (q.v.).

DHC-2. See Beaver.

DHC-3. See Otter.

DHC-4. See Caribou.

DHC-5. See Buffalo.

DHC-6. See Twin Otter.

Division. A formation of combined arms, that is, infantry, armor, artillery, etc.; usually from about 10,000 to 15,000 men; infantry may be mechanized or motorized (infantry in armored personnel carriers and strong in tanks), airborne (parachute-landed), air mobile (helicopter-borne), or Marine (specially structured and equipped for landing across a defended beach). In the US Air Force, a division consists of two or more wings.

Djinn (SA-1221). France, Sub-Aviation; two-seat light helicopter; 178 made from 1956; maximum speed 81 mph; maximum range 200 miles; ceiling 5,900 feet.

DL. Old US designation for a ship larger than destroyer (e.g., destroyer leader). All ships reclassified as light cruisers or destroyers.

DLG. Old US designation (see DL explanation above).

DLGN. Old US designation (see DL explanation above).

Do-27, Skyservant. West German, Dornier; single-engine piston utility aircraft carrying up to six passengers; 680 built from 1956; maximum speed 174 mph; ceiling 10,000 feet; range 492 miles.

Do-28, Skyservant. West Germany, Dornier; twin-engine piston version of Do-27; maximum speed 184 mph; ceiling 20,500 feet; range 745 miles.

Dove. Britain, Hawker-Siddeley; twin-engine piston light transport seating up to 11 passengers; 540 built; maximum speed 230 mph; ceiling 21,000 feet; range 880 miles.

Dragon, M-47. US, McDonnell-Douglas, Raytheon; anti-tank missile; man portable, rocket powered; weight 27 lbs., range 3,280 feet.

Dragonfly. See T-37.

Draken (Dragon J-35, S-35). Sweden, Saab; single-seat, double-delta-wing, supersonic, single-engine jet fighter; entered service in 1960; still in production; maximum speed Mach 2.2; ceiling 65,000 feet; armed with two 30mm cannon, air-to-air missiles, bombs or rockets; "J" is fighter version, "S" and "RF" reconnaissance version, "F" fighter-bomber version.

EA-6b, Intruder. US, Grumman; enlarged-fuselage version of A-6 (q.v.) with crew of four; the two additional crewmen operate electronic devices to suppress enemy electronic activity and obtain tactical electronic intelligence data.

EBR-75. France, Panhard; eight-wheeled armored car with 75mm gun; there are two versions differing only in turret design and weighing 13.5 to 15.2 tons; crew of four; another version of the basic design mounts a 90mm gun.

EBR-ETT. France, Panhard; eight-wheeled armored personnel carrier based on EBR armored car chassis; 13.5 tons; 65 mph; driver plus 14 troops.

ECM. Electronic countermeasures.

EFTA. European Free Trade Association.

EMB-110. See C-95. EMB-111 is a maritime patrol modification of the EMB-110.

EMB326G Xavante. See MB-326G.

Entac (US, MGM-32A). France, Nord; wire-guided anti-tank missile; in service from 1957; weight 27 pounds; speed 190 mph; range 2,000 meters.

Etendard IV. France, Dassault; single-engine carrier-based transsonic jet attack aircraft; operational from 1962; two 30mm cannon and 3,000 pounds of external armament; maximum speed Mach 1.08; ceiling 49,000 feet; combat radius 460 miles (1,000 miles with external fuel).

EV-1, Mohawk. US, Grumman; two-seat observation aircraft; twin-engine turboprop; gross weight 18,000 pounds; maximum speed 308 mph; range 1,010 miles with external tanks; armament six wing strongpoints for bombs or rockets; has STOL capability. The EV-1 is the basic Mohawk (OV-1) modified by the addition of radar target locator pods on the center line with wing tips.

Exocet. France, Aerospatiale (Nord); SSM designed for use by warships against other surface ships; length 16 feet, 9-1/2 inches; range about 20 miles; launching weight 1,587 pounds; designed to fly six to ten feet above the water and operate efficiently in an ECM environment; terminal guidance is by active homing head.

F-4 (formerly Navy F4H, Air Force F-110), Phantom II. US, McDonnell-Douglas; twin-engine two-seat long-range jet attack fighter; operational from 1959; various models for US services and foreign countries; carries 16,000 pounds of armament; maximum speed Mach 2.4; ceiling 71,000 feet; combat radius 1,000 miles.

F4U, Corsair. US, Chance-Vought; World War II single-engine piston fighter; featured unusual inverted-gull wing; last model built in 1953; served with US Navy and Marine Corps, French Navy, and other air forces; four 20mm cannon; maximum speed 470 mph; range 1,120 miles; ceiling 40,000 feet; over 12,000 built.

F-5, Tiger II, formerly Freedom Fighter. US, Northrup; light twin-jet tactical fighter; maximum speed Mach 1.38; operational from 1963; ceiling over 50,000 feet; range with maximum fuel 1,750 miles, with maximum payload 380 miles; carries up to 6,200 pounds of armament including two 20mm cannon plus rockets, bombs, and Sidewinder AAMs.

F6F, Hellcat. US, Grumman; World War II single-engine piston, single-seat fighter.

F-8, Crusader. US, Ling-Temco-Vought; single-engine jet carrier-based fighter; operational from 1956; maximum speed Mach 1.97; four 20mm cannon and two to four Sidewinder AAMs.

F-9. People's Republic of China, Shen Yang Aircraft Production Complex; single-engine single-seat jet strike fighter; maximum speed Mach 2.0; combat radius 300 to 500 miles; loaded weight 22,000 pounds; possibly a Chinese copy of MiG-21; production rate of about 10 per month.

F9F-2, Panther. US, Grumman; single-engine single-seat jet naval fighter; operational from 1948; four 20mm cannon; maximum speed 640 mph; range 1,500 miles; ceiling 50,000 feet; swept-wing development became F9F-6, Cougar (q.v.).

F9F-6, Cougar. US, Grumman; carrier-based transsonic fighter; operational from 1950s.

F-27, Friendship. Netherlands, Fokker (US, Fairchild-Hiller, FH-227); twin-engine turboprop transport; operational from 1958; 40–52 passengers; cruising speed at 20,000 feet 265 to 290 mph, depending on model; ceiling 28,000 feet; range: with maximum fuel, 1,200 miles; with maximum payload, 430–670 miles.

F-27M, Troopship. Netherlands, Fokker; military version of F-27; 45 troops or 13,800 pounds of cargo; large cargo and parachute-drop doors on each side of fuselage.

F-28, Fellowship. Netherlands, Fokker MK 1000; 79-passenger, twin-engine jet transport; gross weight 65,000 pounds; maximum cruising speed 528 mph; maximum cruising altitude 30,000 feet; range 1,266 miles.

F-47, Thunderbolt. US, Republic; World War II single-engine piston fighter; WWII designation P-47;

eight .50 cal. machine guns; a total of 15,329 built; maximum speed 426 mph; range with wing tanks 2,700 miles; ceiling 43,000 feet.

F-51, Mustang. US, North American; World War II single-engine piston fighter; maximum speed 437 mph; ceiling 40,000 feet; six .50 caliber machine guns; over 15,000 built.

F-80, Shooting Star. US, Lockheed; single-engine jet fighter-bomber; operational from late 1945; over 1,600 built; six .50 caliber machine guns in nose; two 1000-pound bombs; maximum speed 590 mph; range 1,300 miles.

F-84, Thunderjet. US, Republic; single-engine jet fighter-bomber; operational from 1946; 4,457 built; six .50 caliber guns (four in nose, two in wing roots) and 4,000 pounds of bombs; maximum speed 620 mph; ceiling 40,000 feet; range with maximum fuel 2,000 miles; F-84F, Thunderstreak, is the swept-wing version of the straight-wing F-84G; six .50 caliber guns and 6,000 pounds of bombs; maximum speed 695 mph; 2,711 built; maximum range 1,600 miles.

F-86, Sabre. US, North American; single-engine jet fighter; operational from 1948; 4,500 built; maximum speed 707mph; ceiling 50,000 feet; range 900 miles; F-86D and K are all-weather versions.

F-100, Super Sabre. US, North American; single-engine jet operational from 1954; 2,300 built; four 20mm cannon and 7,500 pounds of bombs and rockets; maximum speed Mach 1.3; range 1,500 miles.

F-101, Voodoo. US, McDonnell; supersonic twin-engine jet fighter-interceptor; operational from 1957; over 800 built; four 20mm cannon, three Falcon AAMs, or two Genie nuclear-armed rockets; maximum speed Mach 1.85; ceiling 52,000 feet; maximum range with external tanks 2,980 miles.

F-102, Delta Dagger. US, Convair; single-engine jet all-weather interceptor; operational from 1956; 875 built; six Falcon AAMs and twenty-four 2 3/4-inch rockets; maximum speed Mach 1.25; ceiling 54,000 feet; combat radius 550 miles.

F-104, Starfighter. US, Lockheed (also built in Canada, Belgium, Japan, Germany, Netherlands, and Italy); single-engine jet multimission fighter; operational from 1958; maximum speed Mach 2.2; ceiling 58,000 feet; combat radius 750 miles; 4,800 pounds of armament (one 20mm Vulcan cannon plus various combinations of rockets, bombs, and Sidewinder AAMs).

F-105, Thunderchief. US, Republic; single-engine jet all-weather fighter-bomber; operational from 1958; maximum speed Mach 2.15; ceiling 60,000 feet; range with maximum fuel 2,000 miles; 12,000 pounds of armament (20mm Vulcan cannon, three 3,000-pound bombs, sixteen 750-pound bombs, rocket pods, etc.).

F-106, Delta Dart. US, Convair; single-engine jet all-weather interceptor; operational from 1959; 320 built; two Genie nuclear-armed rockets plus six Falcon AAMs; maximum speed Mach 2.31; ceiling 57,000 feet; range 1,500 miles.

F-111. US, Convair; two-seat twin-engine jet tactical fighter-bomber with variable-geometry wings; operational from 1967; maximum speed Mach 2.5; ceiling over 60,000 feet; range with maximum fuel over 3,800 miles.

Falcon (Mystere 20). France, Dassault; light twin-engine jet executive transport; operational from 1963; 14 passengers; maximum speed Mach 0.85; ceiling 42,000 feet; maximum range 1,900 miles.

Falcon (AIM-4A/C/D; Super Falcon AIM-4E/G; Nuclear Falcon AIM-26A). US, Hughes; air-to-air missile; 6.5 feet long; 120 pounds; speed Mach 2 plus; range five nautical miles. Super Falcon is 8.25 feet long; range of five nautical miles; speed Mach 2.5. Nuclear Falcon is 6.75 feet long with a nuclear warhead; range five nautical miles; speed Mach 2.

FB-111. US, General Dynamics; strategic bomber version of F-111; slightly longer wingspan; improved range.

Ferret. Britain, Daimler; four-wheeled armored scout car; four to five tons; 58 mph; range 190 miles; crew of two.

FF. US designation for frigate which, unlike the destroyer, is armed primarily for a single role rather than multipurpose operations.

FFG. US designation for a frigate armed with surface-to-surface or surface-to-air guided missiles.

FH-1100. US, Fairchild-Hiller; light observation helicopter.

Firestreak. Britain, Hawker-Siddeley; air-to-air missile; length 10.5 feet; 300 pounds; speed Mach 2 plus; range 4.3 nautical miles; infrared guidance.

Flamant (M.D.315). France, Dassault; light twin-engine prop transport; operational from 1949; ten passengers; maximum speed 236 mph; ceiling 26,240 feet; range 755 miles.

FN4RM/62FAB. Belgium; lightweight four-wheeled armored reconnaissance vehicle; eight to nine tons; 130 hp; 65 mph; range 350 miles; one version armed with 90mm cannon, the other with a 60mm mortar and two machine guns; both carry crew of three.

Fokker S-11 Instructor. Netherlands, manufactured in Brazil; land-based single-engine two-seat piston primary trainer; maximum speed 400 mph; range 400 miles.

4K4F. Austria; armored personnel carrier; capacity ten fully equipped men; 12.5 tons; 220-hp engine; carries 12.7mm machine guns or 20mm cannon. A variant, the JPz-4K, has the APC's hull, tracks and suspension, but is armed with a 105mm gun in a French AMX-13 turret; crew of 3; 16.8 tons; 300-hp engine; maximum speed 40 mph.

FROG (Free Rocket Over Ground). Soviet Union; NATO designation for unguided tactical surface-to-surface rockets with conventional, chemical, or nuclear warheads. FROG-1 mounted on a JS-3 tank chassis; operational from 1957; estimated range of 15 miles. FROGs 2–5 in slightly different forms; mounted on modified PT-76 tank chassis; estimated ranges up to 30 miles. FROG-7, first seen in 1967, is mounted on large eight-wheeled vehicles.

FUG-1966, FUG-A. Hungary; license-built versions of Soviet BRDM/BTR-40–type armored vehicles.

FV-432, Trojan. Britain; tracked armored personnel carrier; 14 tons; 32 mph; range 400 to 500 miles; crew of two plus ten troops; similar to US M-113.

FV-1609. Armored personnel carrier.

G-91. Italy, Fiat; single-engine jet light fighter-bomber; later version is twin-engine jet; operational from

1959; 1,500 pounds of armament on four attachment points and four .50 caliber machine guns; maximum speed 675 mph; ceiling 40,000 feet.

G-122. Italy, Aeritalia; twin-engine turboprop medium transport; maximum speed 329 mph; range 2,020 miles; crew of three and 44 troops, or 36 stretchers and eight attendants or seated casualties.

GAF Nomad. Australia, Government Aircraft Factories; two-engine turboprop STOL utility transport; operational since 1972; maximum cruising speed 199 mph; range 760 miles; gross weight 8,000 pounds; two pilots and up to 12 passengers.

Gainful. Soviet Union; NATO codename for SA-6 (US designation); first seen in 1967; mobile surface-to-air missile; probably now operational with Soviet ground forces; three missiles (exact propulsion system unknown) mounted on fully tracked chassis similar to that of ZSU-23/4 (q.v.); apparently designed as a low-altitude complement to the SA-4 Ganef (q.v.).

Galeb (Soko G2-A, Seagull). Yugoslavia. Soko; two-seat single-engine jet basic trainer; maximum speed 500 mph; maximum range 770 miles; can be armed with two .50 caliber machine guns, bombs, and rockets.

Ganef. Soviet Union; NATO codename for SA-4 (US designation); mobile surface-to-air missile; deployed for use of Soviet ground forces (including some believed deployed with Soviet forces in Egypt); two ramjet-powered missiles (each with four strap-on, solid-fuel boosters) mounted on a fully tracked chassis; range comparable to SA-2; altitude capability thought to be lower than SA-2 (because of less high-altitude threat in tactical situations).

Gannet. Britain, Westland; three-seat single-engine double-turboprop airborne early warning aircraft; maximum speed 250 mph; range 800 miles; carries two radar operators in the midships cabin.

Gaskin. Soviet Union; NATO codename for SA-9 (US designation); mobile short-range low-altitude surface-to-air missile; development of SA-7 Grail with larger warhead and greater range; infrared homing and radar direction; solid propulsion; effective altitude 15,000 feet; mounted on modified BRDM-2.

Gecko. Soviet Union; NATO codename for SA-8 (US designation); mobile short-range, all-weather, all-terrain, dual-thrust, solid-propellant, surface-to-air missile; radar guidance; high explosive warhead; effective altitude 150 to 19,700 feet.

Genie (Air-2A). US, Douglas; unguided air-to-air rocket with nuclear warhead; length 9-1/2 feet; weight 820 pounds; speed Mach 3; range six miles; carried by F-101 and F-106.

Gilois. France; tank-mounted scissors bridge for spanning canals, antitank ditches, and small watercourses impeding an armored advance. The smaller model, mounted on an AMX-13 tank chassis, spans 38 feet with a 35-ton capacity; the larger model, on an AMX-30 tank chassis, has a greater capacity.

Gnat. Britain, Folland (also built in India by Hindustani); single-seat, single-engine jet light-weight fighter; maximum speed Mach 0.98; ceiling 40,000 feet; combat radius 250 miles; two 30mm cannon and 2,000 pounds of external armament.

Goa. Soviet Union; NATO codename for SA-3 (US designation); surface-to-air missile about 20 feet long; range 13 miles to an altitude of 45,000 feet; intended for low-altitude air defense; Goa's fire-control radar is codenamed Low Blow; acquisition radar is codenamed Flat Face; naval version is SA-N-1 with Peel Group guidance radar.

Gomhouria. Egypt; single-engine piston primary trainer; 130 mph; ceiling 15,000 feet; range 600 miles.

Grail. Soviet Union. NATO code name for SA-7; small warhead optically sighted infrared heat-seeking shoulder-fired surface-to-air missile; can also be mounted in batteries of four or eight on scout cars or trucks.

Griffon. Soviet Union; NATO codename that has been applied to SA-5 surface-to-air ABM-type, long-range air defense missile; radar homing, 2–3 stage solid propellant; length 54 feet; diameter-booster 3-1/4 feet, second stage 2-2/3 feet; launch weight 22,000 pounds; range 155 miles.

Group. A unit consisting of two or more aircraft squadrons, although in some air forces squadron-sized units are referred to as groups. In Britain's RAF and other air forces patterned on it, a group consists of two or more wings (each of two or more squadrons). In armies, usually applied to a temporary composite formation of like or different combat units.

Guarani II. See IA-50.

Guideline. Soviet Union; NATO codename for SA-2 (US designation); surface-to-air missile; Soviet designator is VK750 or V750VK; operational from 1957; solid-fuel booster, liquid-fuel sustainer; length with booster 35 feet; weight with booster is 4,875 pounds; naval version is SA-N-2; 288-pound HE warhead; command guidance; speed Mach 3.6; ceiling over 80,000 feet; fire-control radar is codenamed Fan Song and acquisition radar is Spoon Rest.

GY-80, Horizon. France, SOCATA; four-seat single-engine piston light monoplane; estimated maximum speed 150 mph; estimated range 800 miles.

H-6. See OH-6.

H-13. See OH-13.

H-19, Chickasaw (also referred to as UH-19). US, Sikorsky; transport helicopter; operational from 1950; over 1,200 built; up to ten passengers; maximum speed 115 mph; range 400 miles; nonmilitary version is Sikorsky S-55.

H-23, Raven. US, Hiller; three-place utility helicopter; operational with US Army from 1957; over 1,200 built; maximum speed 100 mph; ceiling 15,000 feet; range 500 miles.

H-34, Choctaw. US, Sikorsky; piston-engine utility helicopter used for troop transport (CH-34) and ASW (SH-34 Seabat); up to 16 passengers; maximum speed 134 mph; ceiling 9,500 feet; range with maximum fuel 250 miles; over 1,000 built; later models are turbine-powered; nonmilitary version is Sikorsky S-58.

H-37, Mojave. US, Sikorsky; twin-engine heavy helicopter; operational from 1956; 26 troops; maximum speed 130 mph; range 220 miles; ceiling 8,700 feet; also referred to as CH-37 and Sikorsky S-56.

H-43, Huskie. US, Kaman; turbine-powered, twin-rotor, utility helicopter; rescue version is HH-43; maximum payload 3,800 pounds; maximum speed 120 mph; ceiling 25,000 feet; range 275 to 500 miles.

H-53. See CH-53.

HA-200. See Saeta.

HA-220. Spain, Hispano; single-seat ground-attack version of HA-200 (above.).

Harpoon (AGM-84A). US, McDonnell-Douglas, Texas Instruments; long-range ship-to-ship (SSM), air-to-ship (ASM), and subsurface-to-surface (SSM) missile; powered by turbojet; speed Mach .94; range 90 miles; inertial guidance; radar homing; weight 1,000–1,400 pounds.

Harrier. Britain, Hawker-Siddeley; the western world's only operational fixed-wing V/STOL fighter; operational from 1968; in service with Royal Air Force and US Marine Corps; maximum speed 737 mph; ceiling over 50,000 feet; range (ferry) 2,300 miles; armed with various combinations of rockets, bombs, missiles, and guns—all carried externally; powered by single vectored-thrust turbofan jet engine.

Harvard. See T-6.

HAWK (MIM-23A). US, Raytheon/Northrup (also built by a 5-nation NATO consortium); small transportable surface-to-air missile; acronym stands for Homing All-Way Killer; homes on radar reflections from ground-based radar (semiactive); effective from low-level to normal tactical aircraft altitudes; 16-1/2 feet long; 1,295 pounds; speed Mach 2.5; slant range 22 miles; three missiles on each launcher.

HC-54, US, Douglas; a variant of C-54 (q.v.) equipped for search/rescue missions.

HE-111. Germany, Heinkel; twin-engine piston World War II bomber; now obsolete but still in service with Spanish Air Force.

Herald. Britain, Handley-Page; twin-turboprop medium transport; operational from 1959; 50 passengers or maximum payload of 11,700 pounds; maximum speed 350 mph; ceiling 28,000 feet; range with maximum fuel 1,750 miles.

Hercules. See C-130.

Heron. Britain, Hawker-Siddeley; four-engine piston light transport; up to 17 passengers; cruise speed 180 mph; range 1,500 miles.

HH-52. US, Sikorsky; 12-passenger helicopter; turboshaft engine; single rotor and tail rotor; maximum speed 109 mph; maximum range 474 miles.

HH-53. See CH-53 Sea Stallion.

HJT-16, Kiran. India, HAL; two-seat single-engine jet basic trainer; maximum speed 432 mph; endurance one hour forty-five minutes on internal fuel.

Honest John (MGR-1A/B). US, McDonnell-Douglas/Emerson; unguided tactical surface-to-surface rocket in service in 1950s and 1960s; still in service with some armies; conventional, chemical, and nuclear warheads; 26 feet long; 4,700 pounds; speed Mach 1.5; range 12 miles; launched from a rail mounted on a five-ton truck.

Hornet. See Super Frelon.

HOT (High subsonic, Optically guided, Tube launched). France, Nord; and West Germany, Bolkow; wire-controlled antitank missile; operational from 1968; length 4-1/4 feet; weight (missile and launcher container) 55 pounds; maximum speed 625 mph; range 75 to 4,000 meters.

Hound Dog (AGM-28B). US, North American–Rockwell; air-to-surface stand-off missile; thermo-nuclear warhead; two carried by B-52G/H bombers; speed Mach 2; range over 600 miles; operational from 1960; 400 in service.

HS-30. West Germany; armored personnel carrier; 14 tons; 40 mph; range 180 miles; driver plus seven troops; one of a family of armored vehicles including a reconnaissance vehicle with 20mm gun, a mortar carrier, a command vehicle, and an antitank missile carrier.

HS-125, Dominie. Britain, Hawker-Siddeley; originally the De Havilland 125; twin-engine light jet transport; both civilian and military versions; maximum cruising speed 510 mph at 31,000 feet; ceiling 41,000 feet; range (maximum fuel and payload) 1,940 miles; over 200 built since 1964.

HS-748. See Andover.

HSS-1, Seabat. US, Sikorsky; old designation for SH-34; see H-34.

HT-2. India, HAL; two-seat, single-engine piston trainer; operational from 1953; maximum speed 130 mph; ceiling 16,500 feet; range 350 miles.

HU-16. See Albatross.

Hu Chwan. People's Republic of China; US designation for a class of hydrofoil patrol boat; two 21-inch torpedo tubes, two twin 14.5mm machine guns; name means Little Tiger.

Huey Cobra. See AH-1.

Hughes 269. Brazil (US designation H-55 Osage); two- to three-seat light helicopter trainer; piston powered; maximum speed 86 mph; range 204 miles.

Hughes 500. See OH-6 Cayuse.

Humber MK. IV. Britain, Humber; armored car; World War II; crew of three; one 37mm gun, one 7.92mm machine gun; maximum speed 45 mph; range 250 miles; weight 7.1 tons.

Hunter. Britain, Hawker; single-engine jet fighter-bomber; operational from 1954; 1,985 built; four 30mm cannon in nose plus 7,000 pounds of external armament; maximum speed 715 mph; ceiling 50,000 feet; maximum range 1,800 miles.

Huskie. See H-43.

IA-35, Huanquero. Argentina, FMA; multirole eight-seat twin-engine (750 hp. each) piston aircraft; used for advanced training and instrument and weapon training and as ambulance aircraft; maximum speed 225 mph; service ceiling estimated at 20,000 feet; range 975 miles; weapon trainer version can carry two .50 caliber machine guns plus underwing bombs or rockets; weight 440 pounds.

IA-50, Guarani II. Argentina, FMA; twin-engine turbo-prop, light transport; operational from 1967; up to 15 passengers or maximum payload of 3,300 pounds; maximum speed 310 mph; ceiling 41,000 feet; range with maximum fuel 1,600 miles (with maximum payload 1,250 miles).

IA-58, Pucara (A-X2). Argentina, FMA; twin-engine turboprop COIN combat aircraft; maximum speed 308 mph; ceiling 29,000 feet; range with maximum fuel 2,235 miles; armament two 20mm Hispano cannon and four 7.62FN machine guns.

IAI-201, Arava. Israel, Israel Aircraft Industries; twin engine turboprop STOL light transport; maximum speed 217 mph; service ceiling 28,550 feet, one engine 11,150 feet; range, maximum fuel, 867 miles, maximum payload 301 miles.

IAPF. Inter-American Peace Force.

IBRD. International Bank for Reconstruction and Development.

ICBM. Intercontinental ballistic missile; 4,000- to 8,000-mile range; thermonuclear warhead.

IKV-91. Sweden, Hagglund and Soner; tank destroyer with 90mm gun in fully traversing turret; two machine guns; maximum speed (road) 42 mph; (water) five mph; weight 16.5 tons; range 375 miles.

Il-12 (NATO codename Coach). Soviet Union, Ilyushin; twin-engine piston transport; operational from 1946; over 3,000 built; carries 27–32 passengers; maximum speed 252 mph; range 1,240 miles.

Il-14 (NATO codename Crate). Soviet Union, Ilyushin; twin-engine piston transport; operational from 1953; 32 passengers; maximum speed 258 mph; ceiling 22,000 feet; range over 900 miles.

Il-18, Moskva (NATO codename Coot). Soviet Union, Ilyushin; four-engine turboprop medium transport; operational from 1957; up to 110 passengers or maximum payload of 30,000 pounds; maximum cruising speed 400 mph; range with maximum fuel 4,000 miles (with maximum payload 2,300 miles); resembles Lockheed Electra.

Il-28 (NATO codename Beagle). Soviet Union, Ilyushin; twin-engine jet light bomber; operational from 1950; 4,500 pounds of internal armament; maximum speed 580 mph; ceiling 41,000 feet; range 1,500 miles.

Il-38 (NATO codename May). Soviet Union, Ilyushin; a modification of Il-18 Coot for ASW; changes include MAD (magnetic anomaly detection) boom in tail and an internal weapons bay in center fuselage; conversion is similar to that of Lockheed Electra into P-3 Orion ASW aircraft.

IMF. International Monetary Fund.

Impala. South Africa, Atlas (Aermacchi MB-326 being built under license); light single-engine jet trainer/counterinsurgency aircraft; operational since 1966; maximum speed 525 mph; ceiling 39,000 feet; combat radius 75 miles; 3,000 pounds of armament.

IRBM. Intermediate range ballistic missile; range 500 to 3,000 miles; thermonuclear warhead.

Iroquois. See UH-1.

Iskra. See TS-11.

Isku. Finland; a class of guided missile patrol boat (PTG); first built in 1970; first non-Soviet design to fire Styx SSM; length 86.5 feet; displacement 115 tons; maximum speed 25 knots; four Styx, one twin 30mm gun.

J-32, Lansen (Lance). Sweden, Saab; a single-engine jet all-weather interceptor; operational since 1950s.

J-35. See Draken.

J-37. See Viggen.

Jastreb (Hawk). Yugoslavia, Soko; light ground-attack version of Galeb jet trainer; operational from 1967; maximum speed 500 mph; three .50 caliber machine guns plus bombs and rockets.

Javelin. Britain, Gloster; delta-wing all-weather single-engine jet fighter; operational from 1956; four 30mm cannon or two cannon and four Firestreak AAMs; maximum speed 695 mph.

Jet Provost (BAC 145). UK; single-engine two-seat jet primary and basic trainer; maximum speed 440 mph; service ceiling 36,750 feet; maximum range 900 miles; can carry two 7.62mm machine guns and up to 3,000 pounds of bombs; later modification is BAC 167 Strikemaster (q.v.).

Jet Ranger (TH-57A Sea Ranger, US Navy; OH-58A, Kiowa, US Army; also Bell 206A). US, Bell; five-seat turbine powered helicopter; see also OH-58.

JPz4-5. West Germany; tank destroyer with hull-mounted 90mm gun; 49 mph; range 240 miles; 23 tons; one of family of tracked amored vehicles designed to operate with Leopard medium tank as a team; also includes APC, 120mm mortar carrier, and SS-11 antitank missile carrier.

JS-2. Soviet Union; World War II heavy tank; 122mm gun; 45 tons; maximum speed 23 mph; crew of four.

JS-3. Soviet Union; post-World War II heavy tank; 122mm gun; 46 tons; maximum speed 23 mph; crew of four.

JSU-122. See SU-122.

JSU-152. See SU-152/JSU-152.

Ju-52. Germany, Junkers; pre-World War II three-engine piston transport; produced in civil and military versions; total of 3,234 built; maximum speed 165 mph; range 800 miles.

K-61. Soviet Union; amphibious assault vehicle.

Ka-25 (NATO codename Hormone). Soviet Union, Kamov; twin-engine turboshaft armed ASW helicopter assigned to Soviet ASW ships; gross weight 16,100 pounds; maximum speed 137 mph; crew of three; 12 passengers in transport version; internal weapons bay for antisubmarine stores, including torpedoes.

Ka-26 (NATO codename Hoodlum). Soviet Union, Kamov; general-purpose twin-engine piston helicopter; gross weight 7,165 pounds; maximum speed 105 mph; normal range 248 miles.

Kangaroo (NATO codename). Soviet Union; air-to-surface missile carried by Tu-20 Bear heavy bomber; turbojet powered; 50 feet long; 30-foot span; range 300 miles plus.

KC-130, Hercules. US, Lockheed; tanker version of C-130 (q.v.).

KC-135, Stratotanker. US, Boeing; jet tanker. See C-135. 820 C-135/KC-135 delivered.

Kelt (NATO codename). Soviet Union; air-to-surface missile carried by Tu-16 Badger medium bomber; 31 feet long; 15-foot span; range over 100 miles.

Kennel (NATO codename). Soviet Union; air-to-surface antishipping missile carried under the wings of Tu-16 medium bombers. These missiles are swept-wing and resemble a small jet fighter; turbojet-powered; 26 feet long; 14-foot span; range 50 miles plus. As a surface-to-surface missile launched by rocket booster it is used for coast defense by Poland and Cuba and bears the NATO codename Samlet.

KH-4. Japan, Kawasaki; four-seat, piston light general-purpose helicopter developed by Kawasaki from the Bell 47 (q.v.); see also OH-13.

Kiowa. See OH-58.

Kipper (NATO codename). Soviet Union; air-to-surface missile carried by Tu-16; 31 feet long; 16-foot span; range over 120 miles.

Kitchen (NATO codename). Soviet Union; air-to-surface missile carried by Tu-22 Blinder supersonic medium bombers; 36 feet long; eight-foot span; range over 200 miles.

KM, KM-2. See LM-1, LM-2.

Kraguj. Yugoslavia; single-seat light piston counterinsurgency aircraft; operational from 1967; two 7.9mm machine guns; light bombs, two 12-round rocket pods.

Krishak (HAOP-27). India, HAL; single-engine liaison and utility piston aircraft; operational from 1964; maximum speed 130 mph; ceiling 19,000 feet; range 290 miles.

Kurir. Yugoslavia; three-place, single-engine piston liaison/utility aircraft; maximum speed 115 mph; ceiling 10,000 feet; range 470 miles.

KV-107. Japan, Kawasaki; Boeing-Vertol CH-46, Sea Knight (q.v.), built in Japan.

L-4. US, Piper; two-seat, single-engine piston light aircraft; utility version of the Piper Cub.

L-19. See O-1.

L-21. US, Piper; a version of the Piper Cub (see L-4) with a more powerful engine.

L-29, Delfin (NATO codename Maya). Czechoslovakia, Aero Vod; one- or two-seat, single-engine jet; basic and advanced trainer; counterinsurgency version; nose camera; underwing stores can include two 1,100-pound bombs, eight AG rockets, or two 7.62mm machine guns; maximum speed, 16,400 feet, 407 mph; service ceiling 36,000 feet; maximum range 397 miles, external tanks, 555 miles.

L-39. Czechoslovakia, Aero Vod; single-engine two-seat jet advanced trainer; maximum speed 454 mph, Mach 0.83; average ceiling 37,225 feet; maximum range: tip tanks empty, 680 miles; tip tanks full, 930 miles.

L-42, Regente. Brazil, Neiva; four-seat single-engine piston liaison and observation aircraft (a later development of the C-42); maximum speed 149 mph; service ceiling 12,000 feet; maximum range 590 miles.

L-188, Electra. US, Lockheed; four-engine turboprop transport.

Labrador. See CH-113.

Lacrosse (MGM-18A). US; field artillery surface-to-surface missile; operational from 1958; radar-command terminal guidance; 19 feet long; 2,360 pounds; range 20 miles; nuclear or conventional warheads.

LAFTA. Latin American Free Trade Association.

Lama. See SA-315.

Lance (MGM-52A). US, Ling-Temco-Vought; tactical surface-to-surface missile; replacement for Little John (q.v.) and Honest John (q.v.); 20 feet long; 3,200 pounds; launched from tracked transporter or lightweight, wheeled launcher; ranges from 30 to 75 miles; operational from 1969; nuclear or conventional warhead.

Lansen. See J-32.

LCG. Britain; landing craft, gun; a landing craft like an LCU, armored and armed with a three-inch or larger gun and rockets for close-in support of a landing; US designation, LSSL (landing ship, support, large).

LCI. US and Britain; World War II landing craft, infantry; 158 feet long; 15 knots; capable of beaching and debarking 60–100 troops over ramps.

LCM. US; landing craft, mechanized; 50 to 75 feet long; ten knots; carries one tank or its equivalent weight (30 to 60 tons) in other mechanized equipment, which is landed over a bow ramp when beached; transported deck-loaded on APA and AKA, well-loaded in LSD and LPD.

LCU. US; landing craft, utility; 105 to 135 feet long; ten knots; carries three to five tanks or their equivalent (175 tons) in other mechanized equipment, which are landed over bow ramp when craft is beached.

LCVP. US; landing craft, vehicle-personnel; 36 feet long; ten knots; carries 30 troops or a small vehicle, which are landed over a bow ramp when beached; transported deck- or davit-loaded on APA and AKA.

Leander Class. Britain; class of general-purpose frigates in service with Royal Navy and others; operational from 1964; displacement 2,450 tons (standard); 2,860 tons (full load); one Wasp (q.v.) ASW helicopter, quadruple Seacat (q.v.) SAM launcher, two sextuple 3-inch Mk4 launchers, two twin 4.5-inch dual purpose guns, two single 40mm guns (or two single 20mm guns on Seacat-equipped versions), depth charges; overall length 372 feet; speed 30 knots.

Lear 23. US, Lear; twin-engine jet light transport; operational from 1964; up to six passengers or 2,300 pounds; maximum speed 560; ceiling 45,000 feet; maximum range 1,000 to 1,800 miles depending on load.

Leopard. West Germany, Krauss-Maffei; medium tank; 105mm gun; 39 tons; 43 mph; range 350 miles; crew of four.

Li-2 (NATO codename Cab). Soviet Union, Lisunov; World War II (and after) license-built version of US C-47 twin-engine piston transport.

Lightning. Britain, BAC; supersonic, twin-engine jet, all-weather interceptor, or multirole, ground attack fighter; operational from 1958; maximum speed Mach 2.1; ceiling 60,000 feet.

Little John (MGR-3). US, Emerson; lightweight, transportable surface-to-surface tactical rocket; rocket and launcher together weigh less than 3,000 pounds (rocket alone weighs 780 pounds); nuclear or conventional warheads; range over ten miles.

LM-1, LM-2, Nikko. Japan, Fuji Heavy Industries; four-seat single engine piston trainer; modification of the T-34 (q.v.).

LPD. US designation for landing platform, dock; an amphibious ship developed from the LSD; has a floodable well deck which carries LCU, LCM, or LVT; well is covered by a flight deck for six transport helicopters; 500 to 570 feet long; 20 knots; eight 3-inch automatic antiaircraft guns; 840 to 930 troops.

LPH. US designation for landing platform, helicopter; an amphibious ship with the appearance of an aircraft carrier (may be converted from a CVS or CVL);

600 feet long; 20 knots; carries 30 transport helicopters and 2,000 troops.

LSD. US designation for landing ship, dock; World War II and later; amphibious ship with floodable well deck for carrying LCU, LCM, and LVT; 450–550 feet long; 15 to 24 knots; 400 to 600 troops; other decks carry vehicles; some are fitted with helicopter platforms.

LSIL. US designation for landing ship, infantry, large; World War II; 160 feet long; 14 knots; capable of beaching and debarking 60 to 100 troops over a bow ramp.

LSM. US designation for landing ship, medium; World War II; 200 feet long; 12.5 knots; ocean-going; carries three to five tanks or equivalent mechanized equipment which it lands over a bow ramp when beached.

LSSL. US designation for landing ship, support, large; World War II; an LSM converted with one 5-inch gun and multiple barrage-rocket launchers for close support of landings.

LST. US designation for landing ship, tank; World War II and later amphibious ship for landing tanks and mechanized equipment, which it lands over a bow ramp when beached; 300–525 feet long; 10 to 20 knots; 150–430 troops; 15,000 to 20,000 square feet of space for vehicles; up to 2,000 tons cargo.

Luz-1. Israel, Rafael; air-to-surface missile; carried by fighter-bomber versions of Kfir and F-4 Phantom; used against antiaircraft weapons; has a 440-pound conventional warhead, television-guided, cannot be jammed; range 50 miles.

LVTP5. US; landing vehicle, tracked, personnel; used by marine corps in 1950s–60s; 40 tons; crew of three plus up to 34 troops; land speed 30 mph; water six to eight mph, land range 190 miles, water 57 miles.

M-2/M-3. US, White; half-tracked armored personnel carrier or scout car; World War II; over 41,000 built; still in extensive use by Israel.

M3A1/M5, Stuart I-IV. US; World War II light tank; 37mm gun; 13.5–16.5 tons; 35–40 mph; crew of three or four.

M-4, Sherman. US; World War II medium tank; the few still in use are probably the later M4A3E8 with high-velocity 76mm gun; either US or Canadian-made; 36 tons; 30 mph; crew of five; 50,000 produced.

M-6. US; armored car.

M-8, Greyhound. US; World War II six-wheeled armored car; 7.4 tons; 37mm gun; 56 mph; over 8,500 built; unarmed version is M-20.

M-16. US; APC based on M-3 half-track (see M2/M3).

M-18, Hellcat. US; 76mm gun on tracked chassis in a full-traversing turret; operational from World War II; crew of five; weight 18.5 tons; also carries one .50 caliber machine gun; maximum speed (road) 55 mph; range over 200 miles.

M-20. See M-8.

M-24, Chaffee. US; World War II and later; light tank; 75mm gun; crew of five; 34 mph; 19 tons.

M-36, Slugger. US; World War II; tank destroyer; 90mm gun turret-mounted on M-4 tank chassis; 30 tons; crew of five; 28 mph.

M-41, Walker Bulldog. US; 1950s; light tank; 76mm gun; 23 tons; 41 mph; crew of four.

M-42, Duster. US; twin 40mm antiaircraft gun mounted on M-41 tank chassis.

M-44. US; self-propelled 155mm howitzer; operational from 1956; weight 28.4 tons; crew of five; maximum speed (road) 35 mph.

M-47, Patton. US; 1950s; medium tank; 90mm gun; 48 tons; 37 mph; crew of five.

M-48, Patton. US; 1950s/60s; medium tank; 90mm gun; 49.5 tons; 32 mph; crew of four; range 160 miles (except diesel M-48A3, 300 miles).

M-59. US; APC on tracked chassis; crew of two and ten troops; weight 18 tons; operational from 1953; maximum speed (road) 33 mph.

M-60, Patton. US; 1960s; main battle tank; 105mm gun; 51 tons; range 310 miles; 30 mph; crew of four.

M-60A1E2. US; main battle tank; 152mm gun launcher; weight 57 tons; range about 280 miles.

M-103. US; 1950s/60s; heavy tank; 120mm gun; 54.4 tons; 21 mph; range 100 miles; crew of five.

M-106. US; APC.

M-107. US; self-propelled 175mm gun on a tracked chassis; gun's range is 18.8 miles; crew of six; weight 25 tons; maximum speed 34 mph; cruising range 450 miles.

M-109. US; self-propelled 155mm howitzer on a tracked chassis; gun's range 18,000 yards; weight 26 tons; range 440 miles.

M-110. US; self-propelled 8-inch howitzer on a tracked chassis; gun's range 10.2 miles; rest of characteristics same as M-107 (q.v.).

M-113. US; 1960s; amphibious armored personnel carrier; 11.5 tons; 42 mph; crew of two plus 11 infantrymen.

M-114. US; tracked APC; improved version of M-113 (q.v.)

M-577. US; APC on tracked chassis; crew of two plus 12 troops.

M-706. US; armored car.

MAC-1. US, Chrysler; four-wheeled armored car used by Mexico; 6.7 tons; 65 mph; range 300 miles; 20mm gun; crew of four.

Magister (CM170). France, Fouga; light twin-engine jet trainer; operational from 1956; about 900 built in France and abroad under license; maximum speed 443 mph; ceiling 40,000 feet; range 575 miles; two .50 caliber machine guns plus two rocket pods, two 110-pound bombs, or two AS-11 missiles.

Malafon. France, Latecoere; surface-to-surface or surface-to-underwater winged naval missile; solid-fuel rocket boosters; 21-inch, acoustic-homing torpedo weighing 1,150 pounds; launch weight 2,865 pounds; range 11 miles; operational from 1965.

Mandrake. Soviet Union, Yakovlev; NATO codename for a single-seat long-range twin-engine very high altitude jet strategic reconnaissance aircraft; operational since 1963; exact YAK designation unknown, but it is thought to be a development of the YAK-25 with a new straight-wing extended span, much like the US U-2 and RB-57F Canberra.

MAP. US Military Assistance Program.

Marder. West Germany; full-tracked APC; carries ten (including crew); maximum speed 45 mph; one 20mm cannon.

MARTEL, AS-37 (Missile, Anti-Radar and Television). France and Britain, Matra and Hawker-Siddeley; television-guided or radar-homing air-to-surface missile; operational from 1967; range "tens of miles"; length 12 feet.

Marut, HF-24. India, HAL; supersonic single-seat twin-engine jet fighter; operational from 1964; maximum speed Mach 1.02; range 400 miles; four 30mm cannon; retractable pack of 48 air-to-air rockets or four 1,000-pound bombs.

Masurca, Mk.2. France; naval surface-to-air missile; length 28 feet; launch weight 4,387 pounds; range over 25 miles.

Matra R-511. France, Matra; air-to-air guided missile; operational from about 1960; length ten feet; weight 400 pounds; maximum speed Mach 1.8; range four nautical miles; semiactive homing.

Matra R-530. France, Matra; air-to-air guided missile; operational from 1967; interchangeable semiactive radar and infrared homing heads; 60-pound proximity-fuse HE warhead; weight 430 pounds; speed Mach 2.7; range 11 miles.

Maverick (AGM-65). US, Hughes; medium-range air-to-surface missile; solid propellant; television guidance speed Mach 1.2; range 33 miles.

MB-326B. Italy, Aermacchi; light single-engine jet trainer/ground-attack aircraft; operational from 1961; maximum speed 509 mph; ceiling 41,000 feet; range 690 miles; two .50 caliber machine-gun pods; four air-to-air rocket pods or six 260-pound bombs; South African version, Impala; Brazilian version, Xavante.

MB-326G. Higher-powered version of MB-326B; up to 4,000 pounds of armament on six underwing attachment points; maximum speed 539 mph; ceiling 47,000 feet; combat radius, armed, 800 miles.

MBFR. Mutual and balanced force reductions (in Europe).

Mentor. See T-34.

Merlin. US, Swearingen; 8- to 11-seat twin-turboprop light transport; maximum speed 325 mph; ceiling 27,000 feet.

Meteor. Britain, Gloster; twin-engine jet fighter; operational from 1946; maximum speed 592 mph; range 710 miles; ceiling 44,000 feet; carries four 20mm cannon, 2,000 pounds of bombs and rockets.

MGM-18. See Lacrosse.

MGM-29. See Sergeant.

MGM-31. See Pershing.

MGM-52. See Lance.

MGM-71. See TOW.

MGR-1. See Honest John.

MGR-3. See Little John.

Mi-1 (NATO codename Hare). Soviet Union, Mil; utility helicopter; up to three passengers; maximum speed 125 mph; range 200 miles.

Mi-2 (NATO codename Hoplite). Soviet Union, Mil; a variant of the Mi-1 (q.v.) equipped with two turboshaft engines in place of the Mi-1's single piston engine; now produced solely in Poland; carries six to eight passengers; maximum speed 130 mph; maximum payload 1,765 pounds; ceiling 13,755 feet; range (with maximum fuel) 360 miles.

Mi-4 (NATO codename Hound). Soviet Union, Mil; utility helicopter; 8–11 passengers or up to 14 troops; operational from 1952; maximum payload 3,800 pounds; maximum speed 130 mph; ceiling 18,000 feet; range 150–250 miles; several thousand built; one 1,700-hp piston engine.

Mi-6 (NATO codename Hook). Soviet Union, Mil; heavy utility helicopter; operational from 1957; two 5,500-shp turbines; 65 passengers; maximum payload 26,000 pounds; maximum speed 185 mph; ceiling 14,750 feet; range with 17,000-pound payload, 385 miles.

Mi-8 (NATO codename Hip). Soviet Union, Mil; general-purpose two-turboshaft transport helicopter; crew of two or three and 28 passengers; can carry 12 stretchers; internal freight 8,820 pounds; externally carried freight, 6,614 pounds; maximum speed 155 mph; range 233 miles.

Mi-10 (NATO codename Harke). Soviet Union, Mil; a flying crane development of Mi-6 using same engines; first seen in 1961; maximum payload 33,070 pounds.

Mi-12 (NATO codename Homer). Soviet Union, Mil; world's largest and heaviest helicopter; maximum payload 88,636 pounds; crew of six; four 6,500-shp turbines; fuselage is 121 feet long; span over rotor tips is 220 feet.

MiG-15 (NATO codename Fagot). Soviet Union, Mikoyan-Gurevich; swept-wing single-engine jet fighter; operational from 1948; two 23mm and one 37mm cannon; two 550-pound bombs; maximum speed 668 mph; ceiling 48,000 feet; range 560 miles; two-seat trainer version is MiG-15 UTI (NATO codename Midget).

MiG-17 (NATO codename Fresco). Soviet Union, Mikoyan-Gurevich; swept-wing single-engine jet fighter; operational from 1953; three 23mm cannon; ceiling 55,000 feet; range 600 miles; "D" and "E" models have limited all-weather capability and are armed with both cannon and AAMs.

MiG-19 (NATO codename Farmer). Soviet Union, Mikoyan-Gurevich; swept-wing twin-engine, jet fighter; "A" model is day fighter; "B" model limited all-weather interceptor; operational from 1955; three 30mm cannon and AAMs; maximum speed 900 mph; ceiling 58,000 feet; range with external tanks 1,370 miles.

MiG-21 (NATO codename Fishbed). Soviet Union Mikoyan-Gurevich; short-range delta-wing single-engine jet supersonic fighter; operational since 1956; maximum speed Mach 2.1 above 36,000 feet, Mach 1.06 at low level; combat radius varies with altitude, external stores, and mission but averages approximately 350 miles; in the fighter role it carries Atoll AAM or two pods, each containing 16 55mm rockets, or a gun pod with a twin-barrel 23mm cannon; in the fighter-bomber role, four 240mm ASM, two 1,100-pound and two 550-pound bombs; in the reconnaissance role, a camera pod or infrared or other sensors. Later models have a limited all-weather capability with airborne intercept radar; the two-seat trainer version has the NATO codename Mongol.

MiG-23 (NATO codename Flogger). Soviet Union, Mikoyan-Gurevich; single-seat single-engine variable-geometry jet fighter interceptor; maximum speed Mach 2.5; range with ferry tanks 1,550 miles; combat radius 597 miles; 23mm cannon plus air-to-air missiles. See MiG-27.

MiG-25 (NATO codename Foxbat). Soviet Union, Mikoyan-Gurevich; high-altitude twin-engine all-weather jet interceptor; operational from 1969; maximum speed Mach 2.8 to 3.2; ceiling over 70,000 feet; was reportedly based in Egypt with Soviet forces; also equips Soviet units in USSR and Eastern Europe.

MiG-27 (NATO codename Flogger D). Soviet Union, Mikoyan-Gurevich; single-seat single-engine variable-sweep jet fighter-bomber; maximum speed Mach 2.3; range with ferry tanks 1,550 miles; combat radius 597 miles; 23mm Gatling-type cannon plus 8,000 pounds of bombs, including nuclear weapons.

Milan. France and West Germany, Nord-Bolkow; wire-guided antitank missile; 2.5 feet long; 24 pounds; 400 mph; range 25–2,000 meters.

Minuteman I/II/III (LGM-30A/B/F/G). US, Boeing; three-stage solid-fuel ICBM; one-megaton thermonuclear warhead; 800 Minuteman I were operational by 1965; 200 Minuteman II became operational in 1966–67; Minuteman III is now replacing some of the earlier models and is equipped with a MIRV (multiple independently targetable re-entry vehicle) containing three warheads; launch weight 65,000–70,000 pounds; speed Mach 22; range 6,000 to 7,000 miles.

Mirage III. France, Dassault; single-engine supersonic all-weather delta-wing jet interceptor and ground-support aircraft; operational from 1960; about 1,000 built; maximum speed Mach 2.17; ceiling 54,000 feet; ground-attack combat radius 560 miles; high-altitude subsonic combat radius 745 miles; III B is two-seat trainer retaining full combat capability; III C is all-weather interceptor and day ground-attack fighter; III D is two-seat version of III O, the Australian license-built version of the III E; III E is the long-range, fighter-bomber/intruder version; III R is a reconnaissance version of III E; III S is the Swiss-built version of III E with improved radar and Falcon AAMs.

Mirage IV. France, Dassault; two-seat twin-engine supersonic delta-wing jet atomic bomber operational from 1964; 62 built; operational radius of over 1,000 miles at Mach 1.7 at high altitude; maximum speed Mach 2.2; ceiling 65,000 feet.

Mirage 5. France, Dassault: single-engine jet fighter-bomber; operational late 1971; essentially a simplified version of III E.

Mirage F-1. France, Dassault; single-engine single-seat swept-wing all-weather multipurpose jet fighter; maximum speed Mach 2.2 at 40,000 feet, Mach 1.2 at low altitude; endurance three hours 45 minutes; armament two 30mm DEFA cannon in fuselage; one strongpoint under fuselage and two under each wing for maximum external load of 8,820 pounds; provision for Sidewinder antiaircraft missile on each wing tip.

MIRV. Multiple independently targetable re-entry vehicle warhead for ICBMs.

MMC. US designation for coastal minelayer; usually a small, short-range ship carrying a limited number of moored contact or controlled mines to be laid off friendly coasts.

MMF. US designation for fleet minelayer; an ocean-going ship which can operate with the high-seas fleet; defend itself from air and surface attack, and lay mines offensively. US MMFs carry up to 1,000 mines.

Model 61. Japan; operational 1962; medium tank; 90mm gun; 35 tons; crew of four.

Moss (NATO codename). Soviet Union, Tupolev; four-engine turboprop AWACS (Airborne Warning and Control System) aircraft version of Tu-114 transport (q.v.).

MRBM. Medium-range ballistic missile; range up to 1,000 or 1,500 miles; thermonuclear warhead.

MRV. Multiple re-entry vehicle; multiple warhead for ICBMs; not independently targeted.

MS-760 (Paris III). France, Potez; twin-engine jet light transport; five passengers; maximum speed 415 mph; ceiling 39,000 feet; range 970 miles.

MSBS M-1. France; SLBM with range of 1,380 miles; carries a 500-kiloton warhead; from 1976 forward M-1 is to be replaced by M-2 with a thermonuclear warhead of one megaton yield and a range of 1,864 miles.

MSC. US designation for coastal minesweeper; small, under 140 feet long.

MSF. US designation for fleet minesweeper; large ocean-going mechanical sweeper to accompany fleet.

MSI. US designation for inshore minesweeper; small, about 110 feet, and shallow draft for mechanical and influence sweeps in inshore waters in advance of landings or in harbor approaches.

MSO. US designation for ocean minesweeper; large, ocean-going, nonmagnetic ship capable of mechanical and influence sweeping with the fleet; a more modern type than the MSF.

Musketeer. US, Beechcraft; two-seat single-engine piston light trainer; in production since 1962; maximum speed 140 mph; range 880 miles.

Mya-4 (NATO codename Bison). Soviet, Myasishchev; four-engine jet heavy bomber; now used primarily in tanker and maritime-reconnaissance roles; operational from 1958.

Mystere IV. France, Dassault; single-engine swept-wing jet fighter; operational from 1954; over 400 built; two 30mm cannon; maximum speed Mach 0.94; ceiling 45,000 feet; range 575 miles.

Neptune. See P-2.

NF-5. Canada, Canadair; version of F-5 aircraft (q.v.) built for the Netherlands.

Nike-Ajax (MIM-3A). US, Douglas; surface-to-air missile; operational from 1953; 15,000 built; length 34 feet; 2,455 pounds; speed Mach 2.25; range 25 miles; ceiling 63,000 feet.

Nike-Hercules (MIM-14A). US, Douglas; surface-to-air missile; operational from 1958; 15,000 built; nuclear or high-explosive warhead; length 41.5 feet; 10,400 pounds; speed Mach 3.65, range 80 miles; ceiling 153,000 feet.

Nimrod. Britain, Hawker-Siddeley; highly modified version of Comet four-engine jet transport; used for maritime reconnaissance and ASW; 41 in service.

Noratlas. France, Norad; twin-engine piston transport; operational from 1952; up to 45 passengers; maximum speed 270 mph; ceiling 24,000 feet.

Nuoli. Finland; class of fast patrol boat (PTF); production started 1961; length 72 feet; displacement 46.5 tons; maximum speed over 40 knots; one 40mm and one 20mm gun; mines and depth charges.

O-1, Bird Dog (L-19). US, Cessna; two-place single-engine piston liaison aircraft; operational from 1950; about 5,500 built; maximum speed 115 mph; ceiling 8,000 feet; range 530 miles.

O-2. US, Cessna; military version of 337 Super Skymaster; twin-engine piston liaison/utility aircraft; four passengers or equivalent cargo or armament; four armament attachment points under wings; maximum speed 200 mph; ceiling 20,000 feet; range 750 miles; operational in 1968; 200 built.

OAS. Organization of American States.

OAU. Organization for African Unity.

Oberon class. Britain; class of diesel submarines in service with Royal Navy and other navies; overall length, 295 feet; displacement, 1,610 tons (standard), 2,030 (surface), 2,410 (submerged); eight 21-inch torpedo tubes; speed, 12 knots (surface), 17 knots (submerged); operational from mid-1960s.

OH-6, Cayuse. US, Hughes; light observation helicopter; operational from 1966; 317-shp turbine; four troops or various machine gun and rocket pod combinations; maximum speed 140 mph; ceiling 15,000 feet; range 410 miles.

OH-13, Sioux (Model 47). US, Bell (built under license in Italy, Japan, and Britain); three passengers or 1,000 pounds of cargo; 280-hp engine; maximum speed 105 mph; ceiling 20,000 feet; range 300 miles.

OH-23, Raven. See H-23.

OH-58, Kiowa. US, Bell; four-seat, turbine-powered helicopter; civil version is called Jet Ranger

OT-62, OT-64, OT-66. Czechoslovakia; license-built versions of Soviet BTR-50 and -60 series APCs.

Otter (US designation, U-1A; Canadian, DHC-3). Canada, DeHavilland; single-engine piston STOL utility aircraft; operational from 1953; over 500 built; nine to ten passengers; maximum speed 160 mph; ceiling 18,000 feet; range 960 miles; can also operate on skis or floats.

Ouragan (Hurricane). France, Dassault; single-engine jet fighter.

OV-10, Bronco. US, North American–Rockwell; two-seat twin-turboprop COIN aircraft; operational from 1967; used by US Air Force, Marines, and Navy as forward air control aircraft, helicopter escort, light attack aircraft, etc.; also in service with Thai Air Force and West German Luftwaffe; can carry various combinations of guns, bombs, and missiles up to a maximum payload of 3,600 pounds; maximum speed 288 mph; maximum range 1,428 miles; combat radius 228 miles.

P-2, Neptune (formerly P2V). US, Lockheed; twin-engine piston maritime reconnaissance and ASW aircraft; operational from 1945; over 1,000 built; two turbojets added later to improve performance; 8,000 pounds of armament; ASW detection gear; maximum speed over 300 mph; ceiling 22,000 feet; range 3,850 miles.

P2J. Japan, Kawasaki; Lockheed SP-2H Neptune with fuselage stretched, electronics added, and piston engines replaced by two 2,850-shp turboprops, two 3,085-pound-thrust turbojets; normal cruising speed 253 mph; long-range cruising speed 196 mph; cruising range 2,765 miles; began entering service in 1970.

P-3, Orion (formerly P3V). US, Lockheed; maritime patrol and ASW aircraft; operational from 1961; based on Electra four-engine turboprop airliner; maximum speed 475 mph; ceiling 28,000 feet; maximum radius 2,500 miles; maximum radius with three hours on station 1,900 miles; 20,000 pounds of mines, depth charges, torpedoes, sonobuoys, flares, and markers can be carried internally and on six underwing points.

P-4 (NATO class designator, Komsomolets). Soviet Union; motor torpedo boat; entered service in 1951; aluminum hull; maximum speed over 50 knots; length 63 feet; displacement 21 tons; two 18-inch torpedo tubes; one twin 14.5mm machine gun mount; depth charges; in addition to USSR is in service in Albania, Bulgaria, China, Cuba, Cyprus, North Korea, Romania, North Vietnam, and Yemen (Aden).

P-5M, Marlin (also P-5B). US, Martin; maritime reconnaissance flying boat; 12,000 pounds of armament; ASW detection gear; two piston engines supplemented by tailmounted jet engine; maximum speed 250 mph; range 2,000 miles.

P-6. Soviet Union; motor torpedo boat; entered production in 1954; wooden hull; length 85 feet; displacement 65 tons; maximum speed about 45 knots; range at 30-knot cruising speed about 450 nautical miles; two 21-inch torpedo tubes, two twin 25mm power-operated cannon, depth charges (two sizes) and mines; Pot Head radar; in service in USSR, Cuba, Algeria, Egypt, East Germany, Indonesia, Iraq, Poland, North Vietnam, Guinea; China has constructed about 80 duplicates, some of which may have been given to North Korea; total of about 600 built if Komar and MO-VI (q.v.) variants are included.

P-149. Italy, Piaggio; single-engine piston trainer developed from the similar P-148; up to five seats; 190 mph; ceiling 19,000 feet; range 680 miles.

P-166M (Albatross). Italy, Piaggio; twin-engine two-seat piston coastal patrol aircraft; maximum speed 222 mph; range 1,200 miles.

PA-28-140, Cherokee. US, Piper; single-engine two- or four-seat piston light trainer/utility aircraft; maximum speed 142 mph; maximum range 839 miles.

PA-31, Turbo-Navajo. US, Piper; twin-engine six- to nine-seat piston light transport; maximum speed 261 mph; maximum range 1,730 miles.

PBM, Mariner. US, Martin; twin-engine piston flying boat, patrol bomber; operational from late World War II.

PBR. US designation for river patrol boat; 30 to 50 feet long; shallow draft, fast; often hydrojet propelled; armored and armed with a combination of machine guns, mortars, and recoilless weapons.

Pbv 301. Sweden, Hagglund; APC on tracked chassis; driver plus nine troops; weight 11.7 tons; maximum speed 28 mph; one 20mm cannon; operational from 1962.

Pbv 302. Sweden; tracked amphibious armored personnel carrier; 13 tons; 40 mph; range 190 miles; 20mm gun; crew of two plus ten troops.

PBY, Catalina. US, Consolidated-Vultee; World War II; twin-engine piston maritime reconnaissance/patrol bomber flying boat; over 2,000 built; maximum speed 195 mph; range 2,500 miles.

PC. Old US designation for coastal submarine chasers. New designation is PCS.

PC-6, Porter. Switzerland, Pilatus, and US, Fairchild (AU-23A); land-based, eight- or ten-seat single-engine piston, STOL light transport; maximum speed 161 mph; maximum range 1,006 miles; later version PC-6A (q.v.) is turboprop powered.

PC-6A, Turbo-Porter. US/Switzerland, Fairchild/Pilatus; single-engine eight- to ten-seat turboprop powered light transport; maximum cruising speed 161 mph; maximum range 1,006 miles; armament 20mm cannon and guns or rocket pods.

PCE. Old US designation for coastal escort ships. Now lumped into PCS designation.

PCF. US designation for a class of fast patrol craft for inshore interdiction and control of fishing and coastal craft; 24 knots.

PCH. US designation for coastal submarine chasers equipped with hydrofoils.

PCS. US designation for coastal submarine chaser; 136 feet long; armed with 40mm guns and ASW weapons; equivalent of British seaward defense craft.

PD-808. Italy, Piaggio; six- to nine-seat twin-engine jet VIP transport, ECM, or navigation trainer aircraft; maximum speed 529 mph; range 1,322 miles.

Pembroke. Britain, Hunting; twin-engine piston transport; operational from 1952; ten passengers; maximum speed 224 mph; ceiling 22,000 feet; range 1,100 miles.

Penguin. Norway; Norwegian-designed and built SSM; entered service in 1970; length nine feet, seven inches; weight 740 pounds (including 264-pound warhead); inertial guidance and passive infrared homing; range of 10 to 15 miles.

Pershing (MGM-31A). US, Martin; two-stage, selective-range, surface-to-surface missile; highly mobile; nuclear warhead; simplified support equipment; air transportable in CH-47, C-123, or C-130; operational from 1962; originally designed with launcher and support equipment in wheeled or tracked versions; four vehicles—erector-launcher with missile (less warhead), test and power vehicle, communications vehicle, and warhead transporter; launch weight 10,000 pounds; range 115–460 miles.

PF. Old US designation for a patrol frigate. Replaced by designation PGF.

PG. US designation for a patrol escort armed with 76mm guns or greater. Normally more modern than a PGF. Capable of operating in the marginal seas.

PGF. US designation for gun-armed ship capable of operating in the marginal seas but used primarily for patrol or picket duty. Normally an obsolescent ship not suited to sophisticated missions.

PGG. US designation for a guided missile patrol combatant. Must be equipped with anti-ship missile system. Capable of operating in the marginal seas.

PGM. US designation for coastal motor gunboat.

Phoenix (AIM-5A). US, Hughes; air-to-air missile; 1,400 pounds; 13 feet long; range 40 nautical miles; for fleet defense by F-14 Tomcat (originally designed for use with F-111B); radar homing by prime source.

PL-1, PL-2, Chienshou. Republic of China (Taiwan); two-seat single-engine piston primary trainer built in Taiwan at the Aeronautical Research Laboratory, Taichung; also built in Vietnam, Thailand, and South Korea; maximum speed 150 mph; maximum range 405 miles.

Plejad. Sweden; a class of fast patrol boat (PTF) constructed in West Germany between 1955 and 1960; length 157.5 feet; displacement 170 tons; maximum speed 37.5 knots; range at 30-knot cruising speed 600nm; six 21-inch torpedo tubes, two 40mm guns, mines.

PO-2 (NATO codename Mule). Soviet Union, Polikarpov; operational from 1928; two-seat single-engine piston biplane trainer; maximum speed 97 mph; ceiling 13,000 feet.

PO-2. Soviet Union; class of minesweeping boat employed for use in harbor, coastal, inshore, and estuarial areas and for general-purpose duties.

Polaris/Poseidon. US, Lockheed; ballistic missiles designed to be launched from submerged submarines; Polaris versions have ranges of from 1,500 to 2,500 miles. Poseidon has range of almost 3,000 miles and can carry MIRV warhead.

Provost. Britain, Hunting; single engine, two-seat piston-powered; armed trainer/reconnaissance aircraft; maximum speed 200 mph; armament, two .30 caliber machine guns; 500 pounds bombs; or 60 pounds rockets.

PT. US designation for motor torpedo boats.

PT-13, 17. US, Stearman design, Boeing; (Kaydet); World War II (and earlier); two-seat single-engine piston biplane primary trainer; over 10,000 built when production ceased in 1945; maximum speed 105 mph; range 385 miles; ceiling 13,000 feet.

PT-19. US, Fairchild; World War II; single-engine two-seat piston monoplane primary trainer; maximum speed 125 mph; range 430 miles; ceiling 13,000 feet.

PT-76. Soviet Union; amphibious light tank; 1950/60s; 76mm gun; 15.5 tons; 31 mph on land, 7 mph on water.

PTF. Old US designation for fast patrol craft employed for various special missions. Replaced by PT boats.

PTG. US designation for coastal missile attack boat.

Puma. France/Britain, Aerospatiale/Westland; twin-turbine single-rotor medium transport helicopter; operational from 1970; maximum speed 174 mph; maximum range 390 miles (with extra tanks, 865 miles); ceiling 15,750 feet; crew of two plus 20 troops (or over 2.5 tons of cargo).

PV-2, Harpoon. US, Lockheed; World War II maritime reconnaissance bomber; two piston engines; carries 4,000 pounds of bombs internally and an additional 2,000 pounds externally; 0.50-inch machine guns; maximum speed 265 mph; maximum range about 2,000 miles; over 500 built.

PX-S. Japan, Shin-Meiwa; STOL maritime reconnaissance flying boat; four 2,850-shp turboprop engines; maximum speed 340 mph; range 3,000 miles; ceiling 29,000 feet.

Pz-61. Switzerland; medium tank; 105mm gun; 35 tons; 30 mph; range 190 miles.

Pz-68. Switzerland; improved version of Pz-61 tank.

PZL-104. See Wilga.

Quail (AIM-20). US, McDonnell-Douglas; decoy missile carried internally by B-52s; launched to confuse enemy radars because its radar profile is very similar to a B-52.

Rapier. Britain, BAC; surface-to-air missile; operational in 1970; for low-altitude defense.

Rb08. Sweden, Saab; SSM for ship-to-ship or surface-to-surface use; evolved from a French-designed target drone; operational from 1970; also called Aerospatiale M.20; operated from coastal defense batteries and two destroyers; terminal homing; launch weight 1,985 pounds.

Redeye. US, General Dynamics; portable, tube-launched SAM; carried and fired by one man; uses infrared homing; version proposed for air-launch from helicopters, called MRAM (Multi-Mission Redeye Air-Launched Missile); two each in pods on each side of helicopter; for air-to-ground use against such targets as tanks; Redeye is operational with US Army and Marine Corps.

Red Top. Britain, Hawker-Siddeley; air-to-air missile; 11.5 feet long; speed Mach 3; range six nautical miles; infrared homing; carried as standard armament on later marks of the Lightning and Sea Vixen.

Regiment. US Marine Corps: an infantry regiment consists of three infantry battalions, and an artillery regiment consists of three light and one medium artillery battalions. Britain: an infantry regiment is a traditional and administrative unit parent to a number of separate infantry battalions which may be deployed with different infantry brigades; artillery and armored regiments of 24 guns or 35 to 50 armored vehicles, respectively, are the equivalent of US artillery or armored battalions. The artillery regiments comprise two batteries of two troops each; the armored regiments are composed of squadrons (US equivalents being company or troop) which consist of troops (US equivalent being platoons). US Army: The British infantry regiment example has been followed for all of the combat arms.

Regimental landing team. US; a Marine infantry regiment reinforced with the necessary supporting arms and services to enable it to conduct an amphibious operation.

RF-4, RF-5, RF-80, RF-84, RF-86, RF-101, RF-104, RT-33, etc. US; reconnaissance versions of the basic aircraft; usually stripped of guns and armor for greater speed and mounting a variety of cameras and other sensors.

RIM-66. See Standard RIM-66.

Roland. France/West Germany, Nord-Bolkow; light surface-to-air missile for use against low-flying aircraft; launched from a light armored vehicle; eight feet long; launch weight 140 pounds; speed Mach 2; range 1,600 to 19,700 feet.

Ruissalo. Finland; a class of motor gunboat (PGM); convertible to minesweeper; built from 1959; length 114 feet; displacement 130 tons; maximum speed 20 knots; one 40mm and one 20mm gun, one Squid ASW mortar, mines and sweep gear; versions sold to Colombia are used as customs launches and carry only a single 20mm gun.

S-2 (S-2D, S-2F), Tracker. US, Grumman; twin-engine piston carrier-based antisubmarine search-and-attack aircraft; operational from 1954; over 1,000 built; maximum speed 265 mph; ceiling 21,000 feet; range 970 miles or patrol endurance of nine hours; ASW detection gear; homing torpedoes; depth charges, bombs, rockets, and sonobuoys. The C-1A Trader is a utility transport version for carrier onboard delivery (COD) of passengers and high-priority cargo. The E-1B Trader is an airborne early-warning and fighter direction version.

S-32. Sweden, Saab; reconnaissance version of A-32 (q.v.).

S-35. Sweden, Saab; reconnaissance version of Draken (q.v.).

S-37. Sweden, Saab; reconnaissance version of Viggen (q.v.).

S-51. US, Sikorsky; four-seat single-rotor helicopter; opertional from 1947; over 300 built in both civil and military versions; maximum speed 95 mph; ceiling, 13,200 feet; maximum range 300 mph.

S-55. See H-19.

S-58. See H-34.

S-65-OE. US, Sikorsky; a variant of the CH-53 (q.v.).

SA-2. See Guideline.

SA-3. See Goa.

SA-4. See Ganef.

SA-5. See Griffon.

SA-6. See Gainful.

SA-7. See Grail.

SA-8. See Gecko.

SA-9. See Gaskin.

SA-315, Lama. France, Aerospatiale; helicopter; Alouette III engine on Alouette II airframe; Indian version built by HAL called Cheetah.

SA-330. See Puma.

SA-341, Gazelle. Brazil, Aerospatiale (France origin), built under license by Embraer in Brazil; five-seat light observation helicopter; single engine turbo-shaft powered, maximum speed 165 mph; hovering ceiling 10,170 feet, maximum range 403 miles.

Saab 105. See A-60.

Saab MF1-15. Sweden; single engine two- to three-seat piston-powered light trainers; maximum speed 160 mph; endurance 4 hours 45 minutes.

Saab MF1-17. Military version of MF1-15.

Sabra. Israel; main battle tank; built by Israel Army Ordnance; 40 tons; mounts 105mm gun (British); 1,000 hp diesel engine (American); entered service 1972.

Sabre 27. Australian license-built version of the F-86 (q.v.).

Sabre 32. Later version of Sabre 27.

Saeta (E-14). Spain, Hispano; also referred to as HA-200; twin-engine jet armed trainer; operational from 1960; over 100 built in Spain; 90 built in Egypt under license as Al-Kahira; maximum speed 435 mph; ceiling 40,000 feet; range 1,050 miles; two underwing attachment points for armament.

Safir (Saab 91-D). Sweden, Saab; single-engine four-seat piston training and utility aircraft; over 300 built;

maximum speed 165 mph; ceiling 16,000; range 650 miles; can be armed with two light machine guns.

SAGE. Semiautomatic ground environment; air-defense system built about an electronic digital computer that reports and acts on a developing situation; operational in US Aerospace Defense Command.

Sagger (NATO codename). Soviet Union; wire-guided anti-tank missile; improved version of Snapper (q.v.).

Sahara. France, Breguet; four-engine piston heavy transport; operational from 1958; 145 troops or 34,000 pounds of cargo; maximum speed 230 mph; range 2,900 miles.

Saladin. Britain, Alvis; post-World War II; six-wheeled armored car; 11 tons; speed 45 mph; 76mm gun; range 250 miles; crew of three.

Salish. Soviet Union; NATO codename; SSM similar to Samlet.

SAM. Surface-to-air missile.

Samlet. See Kennel.

Saracen. Britain, Alvis; six-wheeled armored personnel carrier; ten tons; 43 mph; range 240 miles; crew of two plus ten troops.

SC. Old US designation for coastal submarine chaser; replaced by PCS.

Scorpion (M-56). US; self-propelled antitank gun (SPAT); 90mm; 7.5 tons; crew of four; 27 mph; air droppable.

Scorpion. Britain, Alvis; tracked light reconnaissance vehicle; weight 7.5 tons; range 400 miles; maximum speed (road) 45 mph; light-weight 76mm gun; aluminum; zinc-magnesium alloy armor.

Scout. See Wasp.

Scud. Soviet Union; NATO designation for mobile tactical surface-to-surface missile; various versions are mounted on tracked or wheeled launchers; ranges of 50 to 100 miles; nuclear capability.

Seacat. Britain, Short Brothers and Harland; short-range naval surface-to-air missile.

Sea Hawk. Britain, Armstrong-Whitworth; carrier-based twin-engine jet fighter-bomber; four 20mm cannon; 1,000 pounds of external armament; maximum speed 600 mph; combat radius 230 miles.

Seakiller. Britain; short-range surface-to-surface missile.

Sea King. US, Sikorsky; twin-turbine single-rotor helicopter; used as transport (26 troops), for ASW duties, air/sea rescue, astronaut recovery, etc.; used by US, Danish, Canadian, Malaysian, Brazilian, Japanese, Italian, British, and German armed forces; license-built in Canada, Britain, Japan, and Italy.

Sea Venom. Britain, DeHavilland; carrier-based single-engine single-seat jet fighter; four 20mm cannon; 500 pounds of external armament; maximum speed 560 mph; ceiling 37,000 feet; operational from early 1950s.

Sea Vixen. Britain, DeHavilland; carrier-based single-engine single-seat all-weather jet fighter; operational from 1959; 2,000 pounds of external armament.

Sergeant (MGM-29A). US, Sperry; medium-range tactical surface-to-surface missile; operational from 1962; launch weight 10,000 pounds; range 28 to 85 miles.

SF-5. Spain, CASA; a version of the F-5 (q.v.) being produced in Spain with cooperation of Construcciones Aeronauticas SA (CASA).

SF-260 MX. Italy, SIAI Marchetti; light three-seat single-engine piston armed trainer; maximum speed 211 mph; service ceiling 21,370 feet; maximum range 894 miles; can be armed with wing pylons carrying bombs and rockets.

SH-3. See Sea King.

SH-34. See H-34.

Shackleton (MR Mk.3). Britain, Hawker-Siddeley; maritime reconnaissance aircraft; operational from 1960; four turboprops plus two auxiliary turbojets.

Shaddock (NATO codename). Soviet Union; surface-to-surface cruise missile; comes in shipborne or vehicle-launched versions; about 40 feet long; range somewhere between 200 and 400 miles.

Shafrir. Israel; air-to-air missile; very much like the US Sidewinder heat-seeking missile carried on Mirage and Israeli version of Mirage, the Barak.

Sheridan (M-551). US; lightweight assault vehicle; air-droppable; aluminum hull; mounts 152mm gun/launcher in fully-traversing turret.

Sherman. See M-4.

Shrike (AGM-45). US, Texas Instruments; air-to-surface antiradar missile; ten feet long; 390 pounds; range 8.5 nautical miles; S-band passive homing.

Sidewinder (AIM-9B/C/D). US, Philco, Raytheon, and Motorola; air-to-air missile; operational from 1954; "C" version uses semiactive radar homing; "B" and "D" versions use infrared homing; launch weight 185 pounds; warhead weight 25 pounds; range from 2 to 11 miles depending on version; modified missiles serve as basis for Chaparral SAM system (q.v.); Sidewinder also produced in Europe for NATO.

SK-37. See Viggen.

SK-60. Sweden, Saab; light attack version of A-60 (q.v.).

Skyvan. Britain, Short; operational from 1963; light twin-turboprop transport; maximum payload 4,600 to 5,000 pounds; maximum cruising speed 201 mph; maximum range 660 miles; ceiling 22,500 feet.

SLBM. Submarine-launched ballistic missile.

SM-1. Poland; license-built version of Mi-1 (q.v.).

SM-2. Poland; development of the SM-1.

SM-4. Poland; three-seat single-engine piston light helicopter; cruising speed 72 mph; ceiling 10,800 feet; range (with maximum fuel) 185 miles.

SM-1019. Italy, SIAI-Marchetti; two-seat single-engine turboprop version of the 0-1 produced in Italy; powered by a 317shp Allison 250-B15G turboprop; maximum cruising speed 155 mph; can carry up to 500 pounds of rockets, bombs, or camera packs on two underwing racks.

Snapper (NATO codename). Soviet Union; wire-guided antitank missile; 50 pounds; 3.7 feet long; speed 200 mph; range 500 to 2,300 meters; can penetrate over 12 inches of armor; usually carried in multiple launchers on BRDM armored car.

SP-2. See P-2.

Sparrow IIIB (AIM-7E). US, McDonnell-Douglas; air-to-air missile; launch weight 400 pounds; warhead weight 60 pounds; speed Mach 2.5; range 12 nautical miles; semiactive homing.

Spica. Sweden; a class of fast patrol boats (PTF) built in Sweden between 1966 and 1968; length 141 feet; displacement 200 tons; maximum speed over 40 knots; six 21-inch torpedo tubes, one 57mm gun, mines; Spica II on order for Sweden and Denmark is two feet longer and eight tons heavier.

Squadron. A unit of from 9 to 25 aircraft depending on the air force and the size of the aircraft; a battalion-sized unit of US cavalry; a unit of British, Commonwealth, or other armies, cavalry or armor of 100 to 200 men or 10 to 15 tanks.

SR-71, Blackbird. US, Lockheed; two-seat twin-jet strategic reconnaissance aircraft; maximum speed more than Mach 3; range 2,982 miles at Mach 3 at 78,750 feet.

SRAM (AGM-69). US, Boeing; acronym for "short-range attack missile", air-to-surface missile; 14 feet long; 2,200 pounds; inertial guidance; range 120 nautical miles; for B-52G/H, FB-111A, and B-1A.

SRN-6. Britain, British Hovercraft Corporation; a class of hovercraft.

SS. US designation for diesel-powered submarine; SSN denotes nuclear-powered submarine; SSBN stands for nuclear-powered ballistic missile submarine; SSC is a small coastal submarine; SSB denotes a diesel-powered missile submarine.

SS-4 (NATO codename Sandal). Soviet Union; single-stage liquid-fuel MRBM; range 900 to 1,100 miles; type based in Cuba in 1962.

SS-5 (NATO codename Skean). Soviet Union; single-stage, storable-liquid-fuel IRBM; range about 2,000 miles.

SS-6 (NATO codename Sapwood). Soviet Union; liquid-fuel ICBM; first Soviet ICBM; basic missile plus various upper stages is launch vehicle for Vostok and Soyuz manned spacecraft.

SS-7 (NATO codename Saddler). Soviet Union; storable-liquid-fuel ICBM.

SS-8 (NATO codename Sasin). Soviet Union; two-stage storable-liquid-fuel ICBM; range about 6,200 miles.

SS-9 (NATO codename Scarp). Soviet Union; ICBM; range over 9,000 miles; can carry one 25-megaton, three 4- to 5-megaton, six 1- to 2-megaton or 18 200-kiloton warheads (MRVs); FOBS (Fractional Orbit Bombardment System) launcher; has depressed trajectory capabilities for sending warheads in below early-warning radar coverage.

SS-10 (NATO codename Scrag). Soviet Union; three-stage storable-liquid-fuel ICBM; length 121 feet; diameter of first stage base approximately nine feet; range estimated at 4,950 miles.

SS-11 (US, AGM-22A). France, Nord; wire-guided anti-tank missile; operational from 1962; over 120,000 built; four feet long; launch weight 66 pounds; speed 360 mph; range 500 to 3,000 meters; air-launched version called AS-11.

SS-11. Soviet Union; storable-liquid-fuel ICBM; performance is comparable to US Minuteman (a solid-fuel ICBM).

SS-12. France, Nord; more powerful development of SS-11; launch weight 167 pounds; range 6,000 meters; air-launched version called AS-12.

SS-13 (NATO codename Savage). Soviet Union; three-stage solid-fuel ICBM; similar to US Minuteman; range 5,000 to 6,000 miles.

SS-14 (NATO codename Scapegoat). Soviet Union; two-stage solid-fuel IRBM; range 2,500 miles.

SSBS. S-2. France; IRBM with range of 1,864 miles carries 150-kiloton warhead; fired from underground silos.

SSM. Surface-to-surface missile.

Staghound (T-17E1). US-built, used by British; World War II four-wheeled armored car; 12 tons; 37mm turret-mounted gun.

Standard ARM (AGM-78A). US, General Dynamics; air-to-surface antiradar missile; 14 feet long; 1,300 pounds; HE warhead; passive radar homing; carried by A-6A and F-105D.

Standard RIM-66. US, General Dynamics; ship-launched medium-range surface-to-air missile; speed Mach 2.8; range 30 miles; solid propellant.

Stenka. Soviet Union; NATO designation for antisubmarine version of Osa PTFG; two twin 30mm guns; four fixed 16-inch ASW torpedo tubes and two depth-charge racks in place of SSMs; operated in peacetime by KGB Border Guards; about 30 built, none exported.

STOL. Short Take-Off and Landing; applied to aircraft with capability of operating from fields of less than 1,000 feet in length through use of special flaps, slots, and wing designs (cf. V/STOL and VTOL).

Storm. Norway; a class of motor gunboat (PGM) built from 1965; length 118 feet; displacement 125 tons; maximum speed 35 knots; one 76mm dual-purpose gun (Swedish boats have a 57mm gun), one 40mm gun, six Penguin SSMs; in service in Norway, Sweden, and Venezuela.

Strikemaster. See BAC 167.

Strv-74. Sweden; operational from 1958; light tank with 75mm gun and one or two machine guns; weight 26 tons; two 170 hp engines.

Strv-S. Sweden, Bofors; medium tank; 105mm gun and two machine guns mounted rigidly in hull and aimed by steering tank or lowering and elevating suspension; a third machine gun is mounted on top of the hull for antiaircraft defense; 37 tons; crew of three.

Styx (NATO codename). Soviet Union; naval SS-N-2 surface-to-surface missile; solid-fuel rocket booster; rocket sustainer; radar homing guidance; 20 feet long; nine-foot wingspan; range over 15 miles; carried by Komar and Osa class PTG.

Su-7 (NATO codename Fitter). Soviet Union, Sukhoi; single-seat single-engine jet ground-attack fighter; operational from 1960; maximum speed about Mach 1.6; two 30mm cannon plus two wing and two fuselage attachment points for bombs or other stores.

Su-9 (NATO codename Fishpot). Soviet Union, Sukhoi; single-seat single-engine jet all-weather fighter; probably operational 1958–59; can carry four Alkali or two Anab AAMs (in latter configuration, one is radar-homing-head version, the other Anab is equipped with an infrared homing head); maximum speed Mach 1.8; only about 200 produced for service with Air Defense Command.

Su-11 (NATO codename Flagon-A). Soviet Union, Sukhoi; single-seat twin-engine delta-wing jet fighter; probably operational from 1969; normally carries two Anab AAMs (one radar-homing version, one with infrared homing head); maximum speed Mach 2.5.

Su-17 (NATO codename Fitter C). Soviet Union, Sukhoi; single-seat single-engine jet ground-attack fighter; variable-geometry wing; maximum speed Mach 2.17; maximum range 900 miles; two wing-root 30mm cannon; bombs and rockets; gross weight 29,750 lbs.

Su-20. Export version of Su-17.

SU-76. Soviet Union; World War II assault gun; 76mm gun mounted on a lengthened T-70 light tank chassis; 12.5 tons; 25 mph; crew of four; also used in Korean War.

SU-85. Soviet Union; World War II assault gun; 85mm gun hull-mounted on T-34 medium tank chassis; 29 tons; 24 mph; crew of five.

SU-100. Soviet Union; World War II and after; assault gun; 100mm gun hull-mounted on T-34 chassis; 32 tons; 32 mph; crew of four.

SU-122. Soviet Union; World War II and and after; assault gun; 122mm gun/howitzer hull-mounted; 32 tons; 34 mph; crew of four. JSU-122 featured same gun hull-mounted on heavy tank chassis; 46 tons; crew of five.

SU-152/JSU-152. Soviet Union; 152mm gun/howitzer on heavy tank chassis.

SUBROC (UUM-44A; SUBmarine ROCket). US, Goodyear; advanced tactical missile for use by submarines against other submarines; operational in late 1965; carries a nuclear depth charge; launching weight 4,000 pounds; range 22–26 miles; fired from the submarine's torpedo tubes.

Subroto. India; license-built version of Andover transport aircraft (q.v.).

Superconstellation. See C-121.

Super Frelon. France, Sud; heavy transport and anti-submarine helicopter; three 1,500-shp turbines; operational from 1966; 30 troops; maximum speed 149 mph; ceiling 10,000 feet; range 585 miles.

Super Mystere. France, Dassault; supersonic single-engine jet interceptor and fighter-bomber; two 30mm cannon; 2,200 pounds external armament; maximum speed Mach 1.125; ceiling 55,000 feet.

Super Sherman or Isherman. Israel; a US World War II M4 Sherman medium tank modernized with a diesel engine, wider tracks for desert use, and a French 105mm gun.

Swatter (NATO codename). Soviet Union; radio-guided antitank missile; improved version of Snapper (q.v.).

Swingfire. Britain, BAC; ground- or air-launched wire-guided antitank missile; 3.5 feet long; range 150 to 3,000 meters; operational from 1967.

Sycamore. Britain, Bristol; operational from 1949; four-seat single-rotor helicopter; maximum speed 127 mph; ceiling 15,500 feet; maximum range 324 miles.

T-2 Buckeye. US, North–American Rockwell; land- or carrier-based two-seat general-purpose trainer; maximum speed 540 mph; service ceiling 42,000 feet; range 1,047 miles; armament can be installed (guns, practice bombs, rockets); early version, single-engine jet; later, twin.

T-6, Harvard or Texan (formerly AT-6, SNJ). US, North American; single-engine two-seat piston training aircraft operational from 1938; over 10,000 built; T-6G is armed version; maximum speed 210 mph; ceiling 24,000 feet; range 870 miles.

T-7. See C-45.

T-10. Soviet Union; 1957; heavy tank; 122mm gun; 50.5 tons; 25 mph; range 160 miles; crew of four.

T-11. See C-45.

T-23. Uirapuru. Brazil, Aerotec; two-seat single-engine piston primary trainer; side-by-side seating; maximum speed 140 mph; maximum range 495 miles; service ceiling 14,760 feet.

T-25, Universal. Brazil, Neiva; two-seat single-engine piston basic trainer; side-by-side seating; maximum speed 201 mph; maximum range 620 miles, service ceiling 26,250 feet.

T-28, Trojan. US, North American; single-engine two-seat piston trainer; operational from 1950; almost

2,000 built; T-28D armed COIN version; maximum speed 346 mph; ceiling 37,000 feet.

T-29. See C-131.

T-33, Shooting Star (also formerly, Navy, TV-2). US, Lockheed; single-engine two-seat jet; trainer version of F-80 jet fighter; operational from 1949; over 5,700 built; armed and reconnaissance versions in service; maximum speed 600 mph; ceiling 47,000 feet; range 1,345 miles. Armed version carries machine guns, bombs, rockets; reconnaissance version carries cameras.

T-34. Soviet Union; World War II and after; medium tank; 85mm gun; 32 tons; 32 mph; crew of five.

T-34, Mentor. US, Beechcraft; single-engine two-seat piston trainer; operational from 1950; 1,000 built; maximum speed 185 mph; ceiling 18,000; range 735 miles.

T-37, Dragonfly. US, Cessna; twin-engine jet trainer; operational from 1954; over 1,000 built; "B" and "C" models have provision for light armament; maximum speed 425 mph; ceiling 38,000 feet; range 930 miles. AT-37D or A-37B is more powerful and heavily armed COIN version; internally mounted 7.62mm GE Minigun (six barrels; 6,000 rounds per minute) and 4,700 pounds of external armament; maximum speed 507 mph; ceiling 41,765 feet; range 1,012 miles.

T-38, Talon. Two-seat trainer version of F-5 (q.v.).

T-39, Sabreliner. US, North American; twin-engine jet combat-readiness trainer and utility transport; maximum speed 595 mph; Mach 0.8; service ceiling 45,000 feet.

T-41, Mescalero (Cessna 172). US, Cessna; four-place single-engine piston training/utility aircraft; operational from 1966; used by US Air Force and Army and many foreign countries; over 400 built (over 11,000 commercial versions previously built); maximum speed 150 mph; ceiling 17,000 feet; range 800 miles.

T-42, Cochise. US, Beechcraft; four- or six-seat twin-engine piston light transport; maximum speed 236 mph; range 1,225 miles.

T-43. US, Boeing; military version of the civil air liner Boeing Model 737-200 twin-engine jet; navigational trainer and transport; crew of two, twelve navigator trainees, four navigation proficiency positions, and three navigation instructors; maximum speed 586 mph, service ceiling 42,000 feet (estimated); range 3200 miles (estimated).

T-54. Soviet Union. 1953; medium tank; 100mm gun; 36 tons; 32 mph; crew of four.

T-55. Soviet Union, early 1960s; medium tank; 100mm gun; 36 tons; 32 mph; crew of four.

T-59. Communist China; medium tank; a Chinese-built version of T-54B which includes a smoke discharger, but no infrared equipment.

T-62. Soviet Union; late 1960s; medium tank; 115mm smooth-bore gun; 37 tons; crew of three.

T-62. Chinese light tank.

T-64. Soviet Union; medium tank; weight 45 tons; 120mm gun/launcher; crew of four; speed 25 mph.

T-72. Soviet Union; new medium tank; weight 38.5 tons; 115mm gun with 40 rounds of ammunition stored in an automatic loader; coaxial 7.62mm machine gun with 3,500 rounds and a 12.7mm antiaircraft machine gun; speed 37 mph; crew of three; driver, commander, and gunner are provided with night-vision devices.

T-301. Soviet Union; class of MSC; 100 feet long; ten knots; one twin-37mm gun; one twin-25mm gun; over 70 built from 1946 to 1956.

Talos (RIM-8). US, Bendix; long-range naval surface-to-air missile; solid-fuel booster; ramjet sustainer; range over 65 miles.

Tartar (RIM-24). US, General Dynamics; naval surface-to-air missile for use against both low- and medium-altitude targets; operational from 1961; launch weight 1,200 pounds; speed Mach 2.5; range over ten miles; effective from 1,000 to 40,000 feet.

Tebuan (Wasp). Malaysian Air Force designation for the CL-41 ground attack/trainer aircraft. See CL-41 Tutor.

Terrier. US, General Dynamics; two-stage naval SAM; one variant designed for land use by US Marine Corps; length 27 feet; launch weight 3,300 pounds; range over ten miles.

TF-26, Xavante. See MB-326G.

TH-55. See Hughes 300, Hughes 269.

Thunderbird. Britain, BAC; mobile surface-to-air missile; operational from 1958; solid-fuel rocket boosters and sustainer; semiactive radar homing; 21 feet long; range 15 miles.

TI-67. Israel. Israeli designation for captured T-54/55 tanks fitted with a 105mm gun and otherwise modified.

Tigercat. Britain, Short Brothers and Harland; mobile land-based version of Seacat surface-to-air missile.

Titan II. US, Martin; two-stage, storable-liquid-fuel ICBM; operational from 1961; launch weight 329,000 pounds; range over 9,000 miles; 54 in service; carries over a 5-megaton warhead.

TOW (MGM-71A; Tube launched, Optically tracked, Wire guided). US, Hughes; high-performance antitank missile; fired from tripod, vehicles, or helicopters; range over one mile; to replace 106mm recoilless rifle and the Entac and SS-11 missiles with US forces; also ordered by other countries.

Tracker. See S-2.

Transall (C-160). French–West German consortium; twin-turboprop military transport; operational from 1968; 93 troops or 60 to 80 paratroops; maximum payload 35,000 pounds; maximum speed 330 mph; ceiling 28,000 feet; range with maximum payload 730 miles.

Trojan. See FV-432, T-28.

Troop. In the British, Commonwealth, and some other armies a small unit of cavalry or armor equivalent to the platoon in US practice, or one-half (four guns) a battery of artillery. In US cavalry or armor a company-sized unit, 100 to 200 men or 15–17 armored vehicles.

Troopship. See F-27M.

TS-11. Iskra (Spark). Poland; single-engine jet, two-seat advanced trainer; maximum speed 447 mph; gross weight 8,377 pounds; range 907 miles; armament 23mm gun and four racks for bombs or rockets.

Tu-4. Soviet Union, Tupolev; Soviet-built version of the Boeing B-29 Superfortress four-engine piston bomber; classed as very long range bomber in World War II, later reclassified as medium bomber; maximum speed 261 mph (sea level); maximum speed 354 mph (at 32,808 feet); range at 9,845 feet 3,107 miles; 11,000-pound bombload.

Tu-16 (NATO codename Badger). Soviet Union, Tupolev; twin-engine jet medium bomber; operational from 1954; about 2,000 built; maximum speed 620 mph; range 4,250 miles; carries conventional or nuclear bombs internally, antishipping missiles or stand-off ASMs externally; three twin-23mm cannon for defense.

Tu-20 (NATO codename Bear). Soviet Union, Tupolev; four-engine long-range turboprop, heavy bomber and reconnaissance aircraft; carries Kangaroo ASM in addition to 23mm cannon in turrets; also known as Tu-95.

Tu-22 (NATO codename Blinder). Soviet Union, Tupolev; twin-engine medium-range jet bomber; maximum speed Mach 1.5; ceiling 60,000 feet; range 1,250 miles; some carry Kitchen ASM; also in service with Soviet Navy.

Tu-28 (NATO codename Fiddler). Soviet Union, Tupolev; twin-engine long-range jet interceptor; maximum speed Mach 1.75.

Tu-104 (NATO codename Camel). Soviet Union, Tupolev; twin-engine medium-range jet transport; up to 100 passengers; maximum payload 19,000 to 26,000 pounds; maximum speed 614 mph; ceiling 37,000 feet; range 1,860 miles; operational from 1956.

Tu-114 (NATO codename Cleat). Soviet Union, Tupolev; four-engine long-range turboprop transport based on Tu-20 Bear; a modified Tu-114 serves as the basis for the Moss AWACS aircraft.

Tu-124 (NATO codename Cookpot). Soviet Union, Tupolev; twin-engine jet transport; 22 to 56 passengers; maximum payload 13,228 pounds; maximum speed 603 mph; ceiling over 33,000 feet; maximum range 1,305 miles; operational from 1961.

Tu-154 (NATO codename Careless). Soviet Union, Tupolev; three-engine jet transport; maximum speed 594 mph; range 2,600 miles; service ceiling 40,000 feet; crew of three, 164 passengers.

Tutor. See CL-41.

Twin Otter (DHC-6). Canada, DeHavilland; twin-engine turboprop STOL light transport; operational from 1967; 13–20 passengers or maximum payload of 5,100 pounds; maximum cruising speed 210 mph; ceiling 26,700 feet; range: with maximum payload, 100 miles; with maximum fuel, 945 miles.

U-2. US, Lockheed; single-engine single-seat high-altitude long-range reconnaissance aircraft; maximum speed 520 mph above 36,000 feet; ceiling over 60,000 feet.

U-4. See Aero Commander.

U-6. See Beaver.

U-8, Seminole. US, Beechcraft; military version of commercial Queen Air 65; four- to six-seat twin-engine piston-powered light transport; maximum speed 239 mph; range 1,220 miles.

U-10, Helio H-295 Super Courier. US, Helio; single-engine six-seat piston STOL utility monoplane; maximum speed 165 mph; service ceiling 20,500 feet; range 660 miles.

U-11, Aztec. US, Piper; five-seat twin-engine piston light transport; maximum speed 253 mph; range 1,310 miles.

U-17 (Cessna 185E Skywagon). US, Cessna; six-place single engine piston utility aircraft; operational from 1965 (over 1,200 commercial versions built from 1961); maximum speed 175 mph; ceiling 17,000 feet; range 885 miles.

U-22, Bonanza. US, Beechcraft; two-seat single engine piston trainer; maximum speed 204 mph; range 880 miles.

UH-1, Iroquois (Bell 204B). US, Bell; turbine-powered military helicopter; operational from 1960; over 6,000 built; "B" models converted to "gunships" with combination of machine guns, rocket pods, and 40mm grenade launchers; "E" model is a 10-place troop transport; maximum speed 140 mph; ceiling 12,000 feet; range 350 miles; nickname Huey.

UH-1N (212 Bell). US, Bell; a twin engine version of the UH-1 which has a Twin Pac Pratt and Whitney PT6T turboshaft; maximum speed, 121 mph; service ceiling, 11,500 feet; maximum range, 296 miles; can carry 14 passengers; has 220 cubic feet internal cargo space or 4,000 pounds externally.

UH-12. US, Hiller; a variant of the H-23 (q.v.).

UH-19. See H-19.

UH-23. See H-23.

UH-60. See YUH-60, Blackhawk.

UTVA-60/66. Yugoslavia, Fabrica Aviona; four-seat single-engine piston utility monoplane; maximum speed 155 mph; maximum range 466 miles; gross weight 4,000 pounds; can be fitted with guns under wings.

V750VK (or VK750). Soviet designation for SA-2 Guideline (q.v.).

Vampire. Britain, DeHavilland; single-engine jet fighter-bomber; operational from 1946; four 20mm cannon; 2,000 pounds external armament; maximum speed 570 mph.

Vautour. France, Sud; twin-engine jet attack bomber and interceptor; operational from 1956; 30 built; four 30mm cannon; 3,000 pounds internal and 2,000 pounds external armament; maximum speed Mach 0.9; range 2,400 miles.

VC-10. Britain, BAC; four-engine long-range jet transport; operational from 1964; up to 174 passengers; maximum speed Mach 0.86; ceiling 42,000 feet; range with maximum payload 5,000 miles.

Venom. Britain, DeHavilland; a development of the Vampire (q.v.); single-engine jet fighter; operational from 1950; maximum speed 585 mph; ceiling over 40,000 feet; range over 800 miles; carries four 20mm cannons and up to 2,000 pounds of bombs and rockets.

Victor. Britain, Handley-Page; four-engine jet medium bomber; operational from 1958; cruising speed Mach 0.92; cruise ceiling 55,000 feet; combat radius high-low 1,700 miles, high 2,300 miles; carries nuclear weapons, stand-off ASMs, or 35 1,000-pound bombs.

Viggen (Thunderbolt; AJ-37, JA-37, S-37, SK-37). Sweden; an advanced multimission combat aircraft; AJ-37 is single-seat single-engine delta-canard-configuration all-weather jet attack fighter with secondary interceptor capability, designed to replace A-32 (q.v.); JA-37 is single-seat interceptor version, with secondary attack capability, designed to replace J-35 Draken (q.v.); S-37 is single-seat reconnaissance version to replace S-32 (q.v.); SK-37 is two-seat trainer version to enter service simultaneously with AJ-37; maximum speed Mach 2.0; maximum range (with external armament) over 1,000 miles; carries various combinations of guns, bombs, rockets, missiles, and mines.

VIGILANT (Visually Guided Infantry Light Anti Tank). Britain, BAC; wire-guided antitank missile; operational from 1963; launch weight 31 pounds; warhead 13 pounds; speed 350 mph; range 230 to 1,600 meters.

Vigilante. See A-5.

Vijayanta. India, Avadi; 105mm gun; 37 tons; crew of four; resembles British Chieftain tank with Centurion turret; initially made with British help and components; now totally Indian built.

Viscount. Britain, Vickers; four-engine turboprop medium transport; operational from 1953; 444 built; up to 72 passengers; maximum payload 14,500 pounds; maximum cruising speed 355 mph; ceiling 28,500 feet; range 1,700 miles.

VTOL. Vertical Take-Off and Landing; applies to aircraft which, by means of tiltable propellers, directed fans, jets, or a combination of these means, can rise vertically and change from vertical to horizontal flight. V/STOL applies to aircraft combining features of both STOL and VTOL, but using a vertical approach only when necessary.

Vulcan. Britain, Hawker-Siddeley; four-engine jet medium bomber; operational from 1956; maximum speed Mach 0.94; cruising ceiling 55,000 feet; combat radius high-low 1,700 miles, high 2,300 miles; carries nuclear weapons, stand-off ASMs or 21 1,000-pound bombs.

Vulcan. US, GE; a six-barrel 20mm cannon; maximum rate of fire is 6,000 rounds per minute; used in both aircraft role (e.g., F-4E, F-104, F-105, AC-119, AC-130, etc.) and as land-based weapon as part of the Chaparral/Vulcan system (q.v.).

Walleye. US, Martin/Hughes; a television-guided glide bomb; 1,100 pounds; 11 feet long.

Wasp/Scout. Britain, Westland; naval ASW helicopter is named Wasp; army version is named Scout; four passengers or two ASW homing torpedoes; maximum speed 120–130 mph; ceiling 12,000 feet; range 270–315 miles.

Wellington. Britain, British Hovercraft Corporation; a class of hovercraft.

Wessex. Britain, Westland; turbine-powered version of the Sikorsky S-58/H-34 utility helicopter (q.v.); operational from 1961; up to 16 passengers; maximum speed 130 mph; ceiling 14,000 feet; range 300 to 600 miles depending on amount of fuel.

Whirlwind. Britain, Westland; Series 3, Mk 9/10 military helicopter; turbine-powered conversion of earlier piston version which, in turn, was a British model of the US Sikorsky S-55/H-19; operational from 1962; ten passengers; maximum speed 105 mph; ceiling 16,000 feet; range 300 miles.

Wilga/Gelatik (PZL-104). Poland/Indonesia; four-seat piston light training/utility/liaison monoplane; built in Poland as the Wilga (Thrush) and in Indonesia as the Gelatik (Rice Bird); maximum speed 127 mph; range 435 miles.

Wing. In US Air Force practice, a combat group plus the logistical and control units which render it self-supporting. In US Marine practice, a large unit of several combat groups and specialized squadrons plus logistical and control organizations to render it self-sufficient. In RAF practice, two or more squadrons.

Winjeel, CA-25, Australia; two-seat Australian-built piston primary trainer.

WPB. US; designation for US Coast Guard patrol boats; lengths vary from 82 to 95 feet; displacement varies from 65 to 106 tons; speed about 20 knots; lightly armed with 20mm or 40mm cannon, 81mm mortar, etc.

Xavante. See MB-326B.

Yak-11 (NATO codename Moose). Soviet Union, Yakovlev; two-seat single-engine piston trainer; operational from 1946; maximum speed 286 mph; ceiling 23,000 feet; range 800 miles.

Yak-12. USSR, Yakovlev; two-seat single-engine light piston primary trainer.

Yak-18 (NATO codename Max). Soviet Union, Yakovlev; two-seat single-engine piston trainer; operational from 1946; maximum speed 185 mph; range 400 miles; there is a four-passenger version.

Yak-25 (NATO codename Flashlight). Soviet Union, Yakovlev; two-seat, twin-jet, all-weather inter-ceptor/fighter; operational since 1955; swept wing (45°); maximum speed Mach 0.95 at 36,000 feet; armament, one 30mm cannon plus bombs.

Yak-26 (NATO codename Mangrove). Soviet Union, Yakovlev; two-seat twin-jet tactical reconnais-sance aircraft; a development of the Yak-25 Flashlight fighter with extended wing tips, reduced armament (one 30mm cannon), and a transparent nose section for an observer.

Yak-28 (NATO codename Brewer); Soviet Union, Yako-vlev; two-seat multipurpose tactical bomber version of the Yak-28P Firebar; performance that of Yak-28P but armament includes internal weapon bay and two 30mm cannon in fuselage.

Yak-28P (NATO codename Firebar). Soviet Union, Yako-vlev; two-seat twin-jet all-weather inter-ceptor/fighter; first seen in 1961; a development of the Yak-25; swept wing (45°); maximum speed Mach 1.1 at 36,000 feet; range 1,200–1,600 miles at 570 mph; armed with two Anab AAM; a light bomber version is called Brewer.

YDT. US Navy designation for a diving tender.

YNG. US Navy designation for a gate vessel; i.e., a ship that tends antisubmarine nets.

YP. Old US designation for a harbor patrol craft; now usually used to refer only to an armed craft used for training.

YS-11. Japan, NAMC; twin-engine turboprop medium-range transport; operational from 1964; over 180 built; up to 60 passengers; maximum payload 12,000 to 16,000 pounds; maximum cruising speed 300 mph; range 700 to 1,300 miles depending on payload and fuel.

YUH-60A, Blackhawk. US, Sikorsky; twin-engine turbo-engine tactical transport helicopter; 11 troops, crew of three; gross weight 22,000 pounds; cruising speed 184 mph; to replace the UH-1.

Zlin 326. Czechoslovakia, Moravan; two-seat, single engine piston trainer; maximum speed 143 mph; service ceiling 18,050; range 403 miles.

ZSU-23/4. Soviet Union; 1967; self-propelled antiaircraft gun; quadruple 23mm cannon mounted in turret with integral gun-laying radar (NATO codename Gun Dish); 800–1,000 rounds per minute per gun; tracked chassis apparently same as that used for SA-6 Gainful (q.v.).

ZSU-57/2. Soviet Union; 1957; self-propelled twin 57mm antiaircraft guns mounted in open turret on a T-54 tank chassis.

# SOURCES

Published sources used in the preparation of this book include the following:

## Books

Fahey, James C., ed. *Ships and Aircraft of the U.S. Fleet,* 8th ed. Annapolis: U.S. Naval Institute, 1965.

Gervasi, Tom. *Arsenal of Democracy.* New York: Grove Press, 1977.

Green, William, and Gordon Swanborough. *The Observer's Basic Military Aircraft Directory.* London: Frederick Warne, 1975.

———. *The Observer's Soviet Aircraft Directory.* London: Frederick Warne, 1975.

Munson, Kenneth. *Civil Airliners Since 1946.* New York: Macmillan, 1967.

Taylor, John W. R., and Gordon Swanborough. *Military Aircraft of the World.* New York: Charles Scribner's Sons, 1975.

## Public Documents

Canada, Department of National Defence. *Defence/Defense.* Ottawa: Information Canada, 1976.

Canada, Minister of National Defence. *White Paper on Defence.* Ottawa: Information Canada, 1977.

International Bank for Reconstruction and Development. *World Bank Atlas: Population, Per Capita Product and Growth Rates.* Washington, 1977.

Taiwan (Republic of China), Economic Planning Council, Executive Yuan. *Taiwan Statistical Data Book.* 1976.

United Kingdom. *Statement on the Defence Estimates, 1977.* Presented to Parliament by the Secretary of State for Defence, February 1977. London: Her Majesty's Stationery Office, 1977.

U.S., Arms Control and Disarmament Agency, Bureau of Economic Affairs. *World Military Expenditures and Arms Transfers, 1967-76.* December 1977.

U.S., Central Intelligence Agency. *National Basic Intelligence Fact Book.* Washington: Government Printing Office, January 1979.

U.S., Congress, House of Representatives, Defense Appropriations Subcommittee of the House Committee on Appropriations, Statement by Gen. George S. Brown, USAF, Chairman, Joint Chiefs of Staff, on *United States Military Posture for Fiscal Year 1979.*

U.S., Defense Intelligence Agency. *Handbook on the Chinese Armed Forces.* July 1976.

U.S., Department of the Army. *FM-40, Handbook on Soviet Ground Forces.* June 30, 1975.

U.S., Department of Commerce, Maritime Administration. *Merchant Fleets of the World.* Washington: Government Printing Office, August 1976.

U.S., Department of Energy, Energy Information Administration. *International Petroleum Annual, 1976.* June 1978.

U.S., Department of State. *Background Notes.* Washington: Government Printing Office, 1976, 1978, 1979.

———. *Geographic Bulletin: Status of the World's Nations.* Washington: Government Printing Office, January 1978.

## Periodic Publications

*Air Force Magazine*
*Air International*
*Air Force Policy Letter for Commanders.* (U.S. Air Force) 1977, 1978.
*Air Progress*
*Air University Review*
*The Americana Annual.* 1975–79.
*Army*
*Asia Yearbook, 1973.* (Hong Kong: Far Eastern Review) 1973.
*Aviation Week and Space Technology*
*Britannica, Book of the Year*
*Facts on File*
*International Defense Review*
*Jane's All the World's Aircraft, 1977–78.* (London: Janes) 1977.
*Jane's Fighting Ships, 1976–77,* (London: Janes) 1976.
*Jane's Weapon Systems, 1977–78.* (London: Janes) 1977.
*Keesing's Contemporary Archives*
*Marine Corps Gazette*
*Military Balance 1978–79.* (London: The International Institute for Strategic Studies) 1978.

*Military Review*

*National Defense*

*NATO's Fifteen Nations*

*Naval War College Review*

*New York Times*

*Newsweek*

*Proceedings, (United States Naval Institute.)*

*Strategic Review.* (Washington: United States Strategic Institute) 1977–78.

*Strategic Survey 1978.* (London: The International Institute for Strategic Studies) 1978.

*Survival* (London: The International Institute for Strategic Studies) 1975, 1976, 1977.

*Time*

*Times of the Americas*

*U.S. News and World Report*

*Wall Street Journal*

*Washington Post*

*Weyer's Warships of the World, 1973.* (Annapolis, Md.: Naval Institute Press) 1973.

*World Aviation Directory, Summer 1977.* (Washington: Ziff-Davis Publishing Co.) 1977.

DISCARD

ARCTIC OCEAN

N

Komsomolets I.
SEVERNAYA ZEMLYA
(NORTH LAND)
October Revolution I.
Bolshevik I.
C. Chelyuskin
TAIMYR PEN.
L. Taimyr
Nordvik
Khatanga

NEW SIBERIAN IS.
DeLong Is.

EAST SIBERIAN SEA

LAPTEV SEA

Borden I.
SVERD
QUEEN EL ISLA
Pt. Patrick I.
Lands End
Melville I.
MAG. POLE
Parry
Banks I.
Victoria I.

Bear Is.
Wrangel I.
Barrow
Pt. Barrow
BEAUFORT SEA
Amundsen Gulf
M'Clure Str.

Verkhoyansk
Srednekolymsk
Arctic Circle
Pt. Hope
Bering Str.
Nome
Ft. Yukon
UNITED STATES

UNION OF SOVIET
Oimyakon
Gizhiga
St. Lawrence I.
Anadyr
Fairbanks
ALASKA
Anchorage
Dawson
Whitehorse

Vilyuysk
Yakutsk
Olekminsk
Okhotsk
Magadan
KAMCHATKA PEN.

SOCIALIST REPUBLICS

Krasnoyarsk
L. Baikal
Irkutsk
Chita
Shilka
Ulan-Ude
Ulan Bator
Kerulen

Nikolaevsk
Komsomolsk
Khabarovsk
Sakhalin
Cape Lopatka
KURIL IS.

SEA OF OKHOTSK
Petropavlovsk
Kamchatski
Komandorskie Is.
Attu
ALEUTIAN ISLANDS

BERING SEA
Pribilof Is.

Gulf of Alaska
Kodiak I.
Sitka
Juneau
Pr. of Wales I.
Prince Rupert
QUEEN CHARLOTTE IS.
Edmonton
Saskatoon
Calgary
Regina

Great Bear Lake
Great Slave Lake
Athabasca
Peace
Churc.
N O R
C A N
A M E R

MONGOLIA
GOBI (Desert)
Paotow
Peking (Peiping)
Tientsin
Tsinan
Harbin
Changchun
Mukden
Vladivostok
Hokkaidō
N. KOREA
Seoul
S. KOREA

Lanchow
CHINA
Nanking
Wuhan
Chengtu
Changsha
Chungking
Hwang Ho
Yangtze Kiang
Kunming
Foochow
Canton
Shanghai
EAST CHINA SEA
SEA OF JAPAN
Honshū
JAPAN
Tokyo
Yokohama
Nagoya
Osaka
Shikoku
Kyūshū
Ryukyu Is.

Hanoi
MACAO (Port.)
HONG KONG (Br.)
Taipei
Taiwan (Formosa)
Hainan
Luzon
Manila
PHILIPPINES
Mindanao

Bonin Is. (Jap.)

Vancouver I.
Vancouver
Seattle
Portland
Boise
C. Mendocino
San Francisco
Los Angeles
Salt Lake City
Denver
UNITED
Minnea
Platte
Salt
Kansas
Arkansas
Colorado
El Paso
Mont
MEXICO

MARIANA IS.
Guam
CAROLINE IS.

Wake I. (U.S.)
MARSHALL IS.
Johnston Atoll (U.S.)

Midway Is. (U.S.)
UNITED STATES
HAWAII
Honolulu
Hawaii
Tropic of Cancer

Guadalupe (Mex.)
C. San Lucas
Guadalajara
Mexico City
Revillagigedo Is. (Mex.)
Clipperton I. (Fr.)

NORTH PACIFIC OCEAN

INDIA
BURMA
Rangoon
Bangkok
THAILAND
S. VIETNAM
Saigon
CAMB.
G. of Siam
MALAYSIA
SINGAPORE
SARAWAK
SABAH
BRUNEI (Br.)
SOUTH CHINA SEA
VIETNAM
Sumatra
Borneo
Celebes
Palau

TERRITORY OF THE PACIFIC ISLANDS (U.S. Trust Terr.)
NAURU
New Guinea
GILBERT IS. (Br.)
Howland I. (U.S.)
Baker I. (U.S.)
Canton I. (U.S.)
PHOENIX IS. (U.S.& Br.)

Palmyra I. (U.S.)
Washington I. (Br.)
Fanning I.
Christmas I. (U.S.& Br.)
Jarvis I. (U.S.)
Malden I. (U.S.& Br.)
Starbuck I. (U.S.& Br.)

Equator
GALAPAG
C
A

Djakarta
Java
Christmas I. (Austr.)
Cocos Is. (Austr.)
INDONESIA
SUNDA ISLANDS
Timor
ARAFURA SEA
IRIAN BARAT
PAPUA NEW GUINEA (Austr. Adm.)
Darwin
C. York
BISMARCK ARCH. (Austr.)
SOLOMON IS.
Sta. Cruz Is. (Br.)
ELLICE IS. (Br.)
Rotuma I. (Br.)
W. SAMOA
Tutuila (U.S.)
MARQUESAS IS. (Fr.)

INDIAN OCEAN
Port Hedland
AUSTRALIA
Perth
Kalgoorlie
Fremantle
C. Leeuwin
Albany
Adelaide
Murray
Townsville
Rockhampton
Brisbane
Newcastle
Sydney
Canberra
Melbourne
CORAL SEA
NEW HEBRIDES (Br. & Fr.)
New Caledonia (Fr.)
Loyalty Is. (Fr.)
FIJI
TONGA
COOK IS. (N.Z.)
SOCIETY IS. (Fr.)
Tahiti
Papeete
TUAMOTU ARCH. (Fr.)
AUSTRAL IS. (Tubuai) (Fr.)
Tropic of Capricorn
Pitcairn I. (Br.)
Ducie I. (Br.)
Easter I. (Chile)
Sala y Go (Chile)

Norfolk I. (Austr.)
Lord Howe I. (Austr.)
Kermadec Is. (N.Z.)
North Cape
Auckland
North I.
NEW ZEALAND
Wellington
Christchurch
Chatham Is. (N.Z.)
Dunedin
South I.
Stewart I.
Bass Str.
Tasmania
Hobart
TASMAN SEA

SOUTH PACIFIC OCEAN

Auckland Is. (N.Z.)
Antipodes Is. (N.Z.)
Campbell I. (N.Z.)
Bounty Is. (N.Z.)
Macquarie I. (Austr.)

THE WORLD
MERCATOR PROJECTION
EQUATORIAL SCALES
MILES
0 500 1000 1500 2000 2500
KILOMETERS
0 500 1000 1500 2000 2500
Capitals of Countries ............ ●
© C.S. HAMMOND & Co., Maplewood, N.J.

ANTARCTICA
Balleny Is.
Scott I.
Antarctic Circle
Longitude East of Greenwich
Longitude West of Greenwich